07715
640768

ide

Published by

Camber Publishing Ltd

ISBN 1-874783-56-X

Distributed to the aviation trade by:

AFE Ltd
Unit 1a, Ringway Trading Estate,
Shadowmoss Road,
Manchester M22 5LH
Tel: 0161 499 0023 **Fax:** 0161 499 0298

Distributed to the book trade by:

Crécy Publishing Ltd
Unit 1a, Ringway Trading Estate,
Shadowmoss Road,
Manchester M22 5LH

Tel: 0161 499 0024 **Fax:** 0161 499 0298

www.airplan.u-net.com

The UK VFR Flight Guide

Compiled by Louise Southern

Designed by Rob Taylor

Contributors:

Jeremy M Pratt

Mike Rudkin

Mike Talbot

Effective information date 04.12.99

© Camber Publishing Ltd

Important

The UK VFR Flight Guide is a guide only and it is not intended to be taken as an authoritative document. In the interests of safety and good airmanship the AIP (including supplements, amendments and AIRACs), Pre-flight Information Bulletins, NOTAMS and AICs should be checked before flight as information can, and does, change frequently and often with little notice. Whilst every care has been taken in compiling this guide, relying where possible on official information sources, the publisher and editorial team will not be liable in any way for any errors or omissions whatsoever.

Regular amendments available at: **www.airplan.u-net.com**

Contents

Airmet/MetFAX

AIRMET

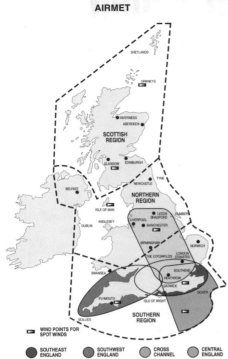

WIND POINTS FOR SPOT WINDS

● SOUTHEAST ENGLAND ● SOUTHWEST ENGLAND ● CROSS CHANNEL ● CENTRAL ENGLAND

Southern Region	09068 771340
Northern Region	09068 771341
Scottish Region	09068 771342
UK Sig Weather Forecast	09068 771343
UK Upper Winds Forecast	09068 771344
UK Update & Outlook Forecast	09068 771345
Southwest England Forecast	09068 771346
Southeast England Forecast	09068 771347
Cross-Channel Forecast	09068 771348
Central England Forecast	09068 771349

MetFAX Helpline: Tel: 08700 750075 Fax: 08700 750076

Fax Number	Product Description
09060 700 400	Main Index of all Fax Services
09060 700 501	Aviation Index page
09060 700 502	Surface Analysis chart
	Surface T+24 Forecast chart
09060 700 503	F215 UK Low Level Weather chart
	F214 UK Spot Wind chart
09060 700 504	Surface T+48, 72, 96 & 120 Forecast chart
	3 day planning text (S England, S Wales)
09060 700 544	Surface T+48, 72, 96 & 120 Forecast chart
	3 Day planning text (N England, N Wales)
09060 700 505	Explanatory notes for F215
09060 700 506	4 Tephigrams temp./height chart

Satellite Images	
09060 700 538	Guide to satellite Images
09060 700 537	Satellite Image (Visible & Infra-Red)
09060 700 539	Satellite Image (Infra-Red)

European	
09060 700 541	RAFC European FL100-450 Sig Wx.
	F614 European Med-high Spot Winds
09060 700 542	F415 European Low Level Weather
	F414 European Low Level Spot Winds

Airmet	
09060 700 510	Airmet Index Page
09060 700 507	Regional Airmet South Text
09060 700 508	Regional Airmet North Text
09060 700 509	Regional Airmet Scottish Text
09060 700 511	Airmet UK Weather Text
09060 700 512	Airmet UK Upper Winds Text
09060 700 513	Airmet UK Update and Outlook
09060 700 514	Airmet South West England Text
09060 700 515	Airmet South East England Text
09060 700 516	Airmet Central England Text
09060 700 517	Airmet Cross Channel Text

TAF and METAR Bulletins	
09060 700 520	TAF & METAR Index Page
09060 700 530	TAF - 18hr. Bulletin
09060 700 540	TAF & METAR Decode

Important note: 0336 calls are charged at 50p per minute at all times. Quoted durations are approximate and may vary depending on size of forecast.

The automated METAR and TAF service is accessed by telephoning:

0881 800 400

This is a premium rated number.
Once connected the service will require the 3 figure code number for the airfield who's weather you require.

Code No	Aerodrome	METAR	9hr TAF	18hr TAF
222	Aberdeen	•	•	•
224	Alderney	•	•	
228	Belfast/Aldergrove	•	•	
232	Belfast/City	•	•	
234	Benbecula	•	•	
236	Biggin Hill	•	•	
238	Birmingham	•	•	•
242	Blackpool	•	•	
244	Boscombe Down	•		•
246	Bournemouth	•	•	
248	—			
252	Bristol	•	•	
254	Brize Norton	•		•
256	Cambridge	•	•	
258	Cardiff	•	•	
262	Carlisle	•	•	
266	Coventry	•	•	
268	Cranfield	•	•	
272	Culdrose	•		•
274	East Midlands	•	•	•
276	Edinburgh	•	•	•
278	Exeter	•	•	
282	Farnborough	•		•
286	Glasgow	•	•	•
288	Gloucestershire	•	•	
292	Guernsey	•	•	
296	Humberside	•	•	
298	Inverness	•	•	
322	Isle of Man	•	•	
324	Jersey	•	•	
326	Kinloss	•		•
328	Kirkwall	•	•	
334	Leeds Bradford	•	•	
336	Leeming	•		•
338	Leuchars	•		•
342	Liverpool	•	•	•
344	London/City	•	•	
346	London/Gatwick	•	•	•
348	London/Heathrow	•	•	•
352	London/Stansted	•	•	•
354	Londonderry	•	•	
356	Lossiemouth	•		•
358	Luton	•	•	•
362	Lydd	•	•	
364	Lyneham	•		•
366	Campbeltown	•		•
368	Manchester	•	•	•
372	Manston	•		•
374	Marham	•		•
376	Newcastle	•	•	•
378	Norwich	•	•	
382	Odiham	•		•
384	Perth	•	•	
386	Plymouth	•	•	
388	Prestwick	•		•
392	St Mawgan	•	•	
394	Scatsa	•	•	
396	Scillies/St Mary's	•	•	
Code No	Aerodrome	METAR	9hr TAF	18hr TAF

Code No	Aerodrome	METAR	9hr TAF	18hr TAF
398	Shawbury	•		•
422	Shoreham	•	•	
424	Southampton	•	•	
426	Southend	•	•	
428	Stornoway	•	•	•
432	Sumburgh	•	•	
434	Swansea	•	•	
436	Teeside	•	•	
438	Tiree	•	•	
442	Unst	•	•	
444	Valley	•		•
446	Waddington	•		•
448	Wattisham	•		•
452	Wick	•	•	
454	Wittering	•		•
456	Yeovilton	•		•
522	Amsterdam	•	•	•
524	Beauvais	•	•	
526	Brest	•	•	
528	Brussels	•	•	
532	Caen	•	•	
534	Calais	•	•	
536	Cherbourg	•	•	
538	Cork	•	•	
542	Deauville	•	•	
542	Dinard	•	•	
546	Dublin	•	•	•
548	Le Mans	•	•	
552	Le Touquet	•	•	
554	Lille	•	•	•
556	Luxembourg	•	•	•
558	Morlaix	•	•	
562	Ostend	•	•	
564	Paris/Charles De Gaulle	•	•	•
566	Paris/Le Bourget	•	•	
568	Paris/Orly	•	•	•
572	Rennes	•	•	
574	Reims	•	•	
576	Rotterdam	•	•	•
578	Shannon	•	•	•
582	Toussus Le Noble	•	•	

Forecast Offices

The following offices are able to provide TAFs and METARs if you are unable to obtain them from another source:

Belfast/Aldergrove Airport	018494 23275
Birmingham	0121 717 0580
Bracknell Central Forecast Office*	01344 356267
Cardiff Weather Centre	01222 390492
Glasgow Weather Centre*	0141 221 6116
Isle of Man Airport	01624 821641
Jersey Airport	01534 492229
Jersey Airmet	0696 60033
Leeds Weather Centre	01132 457687
Manchester Weather Centre*	0161 429 0927

*These Forecast Offices can be consulted to clarify a forecast, for special forecasts and for route forecasts.

Met. codes used in METARs (Aviation Routine Weather Reports) and TAFs (Terminal Aerodrome Forecasts).

LOCATION INDICATOR
The ICAO Four Letter Code for the airfield

TIME
– METAR. The observation time in hours and minutes UTC, followed by Z (Zulu).
– TAF The period of forecast validity.
The number may be a six number group, the first two numbers being the date.

WIND
Wind direction is given in degrees true (three digits) rounded to the nearest 10°, followed by wind speed (two digits). Wind speed may be given in knots (KT), kilometres per hour (KMH) or metres per second (MPS).
G = Wind Gust
00000 = Wind Calm
VRB = Variable Wind Direction
V = Variation in wind direction of 60° or more

VISIBILITY
Minimum horizontal visibility is given in metres.
9999 = Visibility 10km or greater
0000 = Visibility less than 50 m
- METAR only. Where there is a marked difference in visibility depending on direction, more than one visibility may be reported, followed by direction in which that visibility exists e.g. S = south, NE = north east etc.

RUNWAY VISUAL RANGE - METAR Only
R = RVR, followed by runway designator and the touch down zone visibility in metres. If visibility is greater than the maximum RVR that can be assessed, or more than 1500 metres, it will be preceded by a P. M = RVR below the minimum that can be assessed.
At non-UK aerodromes the additional designator may be added after the RVR: U = Up; D = Down; N = No change. If there is a significant variability in RVR the letter V will be used in-between the minimum and maximum RVRs.

CLOUD
Cloud amount may be described as:
FEW (few) = 1-2 OKTAS
SCT (Scattered) = 3-4 OKTAS
BKN (Broken) = 5-7 OKTAS
OVC (Overcast) = 8 OKTAS
Note: 1 OKTA = 1/8 cloud cover

Cloud base is given in hundreds of feet above aerodrome level (aal).

Cloud type is not identified, except:
CB = Cumulo-nimbus
TCU = Towering Cumulus
SKC = Sky Clear
NSC = No Significant Cloud (TAF only)

If the sky is obscured the letters VV are inserted followed by the vertical visibility in hundreds of feet.
VV/// = Sky obscured, vertical visibility cannot be assessed.

CAVOK
(Pronounced KAV-O-KAY) will be used to replace the visibility, RVR, weather and cloud groups if the following conditions apply:
a Visibility: 10km or more
b Cloud: no cloud below 5000ft or below highest Minimum Sector Altitude, whichever is greater and no CB at any height
c No significant weather at or near the airfield

AIR TEMPERATURE/DEWPOINT
These are given in degrees Celsius
M = Minus

QNH
Rounded down to the next whole millibar and given as a four figure group in millibars/hectopascals, preceded by Q. If the value is less than 1000, the first number is 0.

SUPPLEMENTARY INFORMATION

METARs
RE = Recent weather
WS = Windshear
TREND. Certain major aerodromes will include a trend indicator for any forecast change in conditions during the two hours after the observation time.
BECMG = Becoming, TEMPO = Temporary; may be followed by time (in hours and minutes UTC) preceded by FM (from), TL (until) or AT (at).
NOSIG = No significant changes forecast during the trend period.
BECMG is an expected permanent change in conditions, expected to last less than one hour in each instance and not total more than half the forecast period.
TEMPO is a temporary fluctuation in conditions expected to last less than 1 hour at a time and not occur in total during more than half the forecast period.

TAFs
Probability:
PROB 30 = 30% probability
PROB 40 = 40% probability
The abbreviations FM, TEMPO and BECMG are followed by time(s) (UTC) to the nearest hour.

AMENDMENTS
AMD is inserted after TAF and before the ICAO four letter code. AMD is used when the orginal TAF is withdrawn and replaced for some reason.

RETARD
(R) used when the TAF is received late. Most often seen on METFAX.

WEATHER

Weather Phenomena			
Description	**Precipitation**	**Visibility Factor**	**Other**
MI Shallow	DZ Drizzle	BR Mist	PO Well developed dust/sand whirls
BC Patches			
PR Partial Covering	RA Rain	FG Fog	
DR Drifting	SN Snow	FU Smoke	SQ Squalls
BL Blowing	SG Snow Grains	VA Volcanic Ash	FC Funnel Cloud(s) (tornado or water-spout)
SH Shower(s)	IC Diamond Dust	DU Widespread Dust	SS Sandstorm
TS Thunderstorm	PE Ice-Pellets	SA Sand	DS Duststorm
FZ Super-Cooled	GR Hail	HZ Haze	
	GS Small Hail		

Intensity or Proximity Qualifier

- Light i.e. -SH
Moderate (no qualifier) i.e. SH
+ Heavy i.e. +SH

VC In the vicinity (within 8 km of the airfield, but not actually at the airfield)
NSW (TAF only) = No Significant Weather

Military Weather State Colour Codes
– MINIMUM weather conditions

Colour	Visibility	Base of lowest cloud: 3/8 (scattered) or more
Blue	8km	2500ft AGL
White	5km	1500ft AGL
Green	3700m	700ft AGL
Yellow	1600m	300ft AGL
Amber	800m	200ft AGL
Red	Less than 800m	Below 200ft AGL or sky obscured
Black	Airfield not usable for reasons other than cloud base or visibility. Black will precede actual colour code.	

ICAO UK airfield locators

EGAA	Belfast (Aldergrove)
EGAB	Enniskillen (St. Angelo)
EGAC	Belfast (City)
EGAD	Newtownards
EGAE	Londonderry (Eglington)
EGAL	Langford Lodge
EGBB	Birmingham
EGBD	Derby
EGBE	Coventry
EGBG	Leicester
EGBJ	Gloucestershire (Staverton)
EGBK	Northampton (Sywell)
EGBL	Long Marston
EGBM	Tatenhill
EGBN	Nottingham
EGBO	Halfpenny Green
EGBS	Shobdon
EGBT	Turweston
EGBW	Wellesbourne Mountford
EGCB	Manchester (Barton)
EGCC	Manchester
EGCD	Woodford
EGCE	Wrexham (Borras)
EGCF	Sandtoft
EGCG	Strubby
EGCJ	Sherburn-in-Elmet
EGCK	Caernarfon
EGCL	Fenland
EGCP	Thorne (Doncaster)
EGCS	Sturgate
EGCV	Sleap
EGCW	Welshpool (Montgomeryshire)
EGDC	Chivenor
EGDG	St. Mawgan
EGDL	Lyneham
EGDM	Boscombe Down
EGDN	Netheravon
EGDP	Portland (RN Helicopter Station)
EGDR	Culdrose
EGDT	Wroughton
EGDX	St. Athan
EGDY	Yeovilton
EGEC	Campbeltown
EGED	Eday
EGEF	Fair Isle
EGEG	Glasgow City (Heliport)
EGEH	Whalsay
EGEN	North Ronaldsay
EGEP	Papa Westray
EGER	Stronsay
EGES	Sanday
EGET	Lerwick (Tingwall)
EGEW	Westray
EGFC	Cardiff (Tremorfa Heliport)
EGFE	Haverfordwest
EGFF	Cardiff
EGFH	Swansea
EGFP	Pembrey
EGGD	Bristol Airport
EGGP	Liverpool
EGGW	Luton
EGHA	Compton Abbas
EGHB	Maypole
EGHC	Lands End (St. Just)
EGHD	Plymouth (City)
EGHE	Scilly Isles (St. Marys)
EGHF	Lee-on-Solent
EGHG	Yeovil
EGHH	Bournemouth
EGHI	Southampton (Eastleigh)
EGHJ	Bembridge
EGHK	Penzance (Heliport)
EGHL	Lasham
EGHN	Sandown (Isle of Wight)
EGHO	Thruxton
EGHP	Popham
EGHR	Chichester (Goodwood)
EGHS	Henstridge
EGHT	Tresco (Heliport)
EGHU	Eaglescott
EGHY	Truro
EGJA	Alderney
EGJB	Guernsey
EGJJ	Jersey
EGKA	Shoreham
EGKB	Biggin Hill
EGKE	Challock
EGKH	Lashenden (Headcorn)
EGKK	London (Gatwick)
EGKR	Redhill
EGLA	Bodmin
EGLB	Brooklands
EGLC	London/City
EGLD	Denham
EGLF	Farnborough
EGLG	Panshanger
EGLJ	Chalgrove
EGLK	Blackbushe
EGLL	London (Heathrow)
EGLM	White Whaltham
EGLS	Old Sarum
EGLW	Westland (London heliport)
EGMA	Fowlmere
EGMC	Southend
EGMD	Lydd
EGMF	Farthing Corner
EGMH	Manston (Civil)
EGMJ	Little Gransden
EGNA	Hucknall
EGNB	Brough
EGNC	Carlisle
EGND	Huddersfield (Crosland Moor)
EGNE	Retford /Gamston
EGNF	Netherthorpe
EGNH	Blackpool
EGNJ	Humberside
EGNL	Barrow (Walney island)
EGNM	Leeds Bradford
EGNO	Warton
EGNR	Hawarden
EGNS	Isle of Man
EGNT	Newcastle
EGNU	Full Sutton
EGNV	Teeside
EGNW	Wickenby
EGNX	East Midlands
EGNY	Beverley (Linley Hill)
EGOD	Llandbedr
EGOE	Ternhill
EGOS	Shawbury
EGOV	Valley
EGOW	Woodvale
EGOY	West Freugh
EGPA	Kirkwall
EGPB	Sumburgh
EGPC	Wick
EGPD	Aberdeen (Dyce)
EGPE	Inverness
EGPF	Glasgow
EGPG	Cumbernauld
EGPH	Edinburgh
EGPI	Islay
EGPJ	Fife (Glenrothes)
EGPK	Prestwick
EGPL	Benbecula
EGPM	Scatsta
EGPN	Dundee
EGPO	Stornoway
EGPR	Barra
EGPS	Peterhead (Longside)
EGPT	Perth (Scone)
EGPU	Tiree
EGPW	Unst
EGQB	Ballykelly
EGQK	Kinloss
EGQL	Leuchars
EGQS	Lossiemouth
EGSA	Shipdham
EGSB	Bedford (Castle Mill)
EGSC	Cambridge
EGSD	Great Yarmouth (North Denes)
EGSF	Peterborough (Conington)
EGSG	Stapleford
EGSH	Norwich
EGSJ	Seething
EGSK	Hethel
EGSL	Andrewsfield
EGSM	Beccles
EGSN	Bourn
EGSO	Crowfield
EGSP	Peterborough (Sibson)
EGSQ	Clacton
EGSR	Earls Colne
EGSS	London (Stansted)
EGST	Elmsett
EGSU	Duxford
EGSV	Old Buckenham
EGSW	Newmarket (Racecourse)
EGSX	North Weald
EGSY	Sheffield (City)
EGTA	Aylesbury (Thame)
EGTB	Wycombe Air Park (Booker)
EGTC	Cranfield
EGTD	Dunsfold
EGTE	Exeter
EGTF	Fairoaks
EGTG	Filton
EGTK	Oxford (Kidlington)
EGTO	Rochester
EGTP	Perranporth
EGTR	Elstree
EGTU	Dunkeswell
EGTW	Oaksey Park
EGUB	Benson
EGUC	Aberporth
EGUL	Lakenheath
EGUM	Manston (Military)
EGUN	Mildenhall
EGUO	Colerne
EGUW	Wattisham
EGUY	Wyton
EGVA	Fairford
EGVK	Old Sarum
EGVN	Brize Norton
EGVO	Odiham
EGVP	Middle Wallop
EGWC	Cosford
EGWN	Halton
EGWU	Northolt
EGXC	Coningsby
EGXD	Dishforth
EGXE	Leeming
EGXG	Church Fenton
EGXH	Honington
EGXJ	Cottesmore
EGXN	Newton
EGXT	Wittering
EGXU	Linton-on-Ouse
EGXV	Leconfield
EGXW	Waddington
EGXZ	Topcliffe
EGYC	Coltishall
EGYD	Cranwell
EGYE	Barkston Heath
EGYM	Marham

Use block capitals throughout, insert all clock times in 4 figures using UTC. Numbers below relate to item numbers on the flight plan form.

ITEM 7: **Aircraft Identification**. The aircraft's registration (when it is being used as the RT callsign, or if the aircraft in non-radio) or the flight identification, with a maximum of 7 characters.

ITEM 8: **Flight Rules/Type of Flight**

Flight Rules
I for IFR
V for VFR
Y for IFR first
Z for VFR first
If using Y or Z specify in ITEM 15 where flight rules will change.

Type of Flight
S Scheduled air service
N Non-scheduled air transport operation
G General aviation
M Military
X Other category

ITEM 9: **Number** & **Type of Aircraft**, **Wake Turbulence Category**.

Insert number of aircraft *only* if more than one.

Insert type of aircraft as ICAO aircraft type designator. If no such designator exists insert ZZZZ and specify at ITEM 18 preceded by TYP/.

Wake Turbulence Category
H - Heavy, MTOW of 136000kg or more
M - Medium MTOW 7001kg - 135999kg
L - Light MTOW 7000Kg or less

ITEM 10: **Equipment**,

N No comm/nav equipment
S Standard comm/nav equipment (VHF RTF, ADF, VOR, ILS)

or insert one or more of the following letters as appropriate;

A - Loran A
C - Loran C
D - DME
E - DECCA
F - ADF
H - HF RTF
I - Inertial Navigation
L - ILS
M - OMEGA
O - VOR
P - DOPPLER
R - RNAV Route Equipment
T - TACAN
U - UHF RTF
V - VHF RTF
Z - Other (specify at item 18, preceded by COM/ or NAV/)

SSR Equipment; after the slash (/)
N - None
A - Transponder Mode A
C - Transponder Mode C

ITEM 13: **Departure Aerodrome** and **Time**.

Insert ICAO four letter aerodrome designator. If no ICAO designator exists enter ZZZZ and specify in ITEM 18, preceded by DEP/.

Insert estimated off-block time (UTC).

ITEM 15: **Cruising Speed, Level** & **Route**.

Insert True Air Speed for cruising portion of route. Use four figures preceded by K (Kilometres) or N (Knots). For Mach number three numbers preceded by M.

Insert cruising level as Flight Level (F followed by three numbers); or Altitude (A followed by three figures showing hundreds of feet); or Standard Metric Level (S followed by tens of metres); or altitude in tens of metres (M followed by four figures) or VFR for VFR flight with no specific cruising level.

For route, designator of first ATS route (if appropriate), and each point of change of speed, level, ATS route or flight rules, followed by designator of next ATS route.

For flight outside designated ATS routes, use coded designator, or lat/long coordinates, or bearing and distance from a navigation aid. DCT (Direct) can be used to join successive points unless both points are defined as geographical co-ordinates or bearing and distance.

If the departure aerodrome is not on an ATS route, insert DCT before the first point.

ITEM 16: **Destination Aerodrome, Total Elapsed Time, Alternate Aerodrome** and **2nd Alternate Aerodrome**.

Insert ICAO four letter designator for destination aerodrome, if no designator exists enter ZZZZ, and specify name in ITEM 18 preceded by DEST/.

Insert Total Elapsed Time in hours/minutes.

Insert alternate aerodrome(s) as ICAO designator, or if no designator exists then ZZZZ and specify name in ITEM 18 preceded by ALTN/.

ITEM 18: **Other Information**.

0 if None

EET/ - signficant point(s) or FIR boundary designator(s) with estimated *elapsed* time(s).

REG/ - registration if different to aircraft identification in ITEM 7

OPR/ - name of operator if appropriate

STS/ - reason for special handling by ATC

TYP/ - types of aircraft, if ZZZZ specified at item 9

COM/ - comm equipment if Z specified in item 10

NAV/ - nav equipment if Z specified in item 10

DEP/ - Departure aerodrome name if ZZZZ inserted at item 13

DEST/ - Destination aerodrome name if ZZZZ inserted at item 16

ALTN/ - Alternate aerodrome name if ZZZZ inserted at item 16

RMK/ - any other plain language remarks as appropriate

ITEM 19: **Supplementary Information**.

Endurance:

E/ - fuel endurance in a four-figure group to express hours/minutes

Persons on Board:

P/ -

Emergency Radio:

R/(Radio) -

Cross out U if UHF 243MHz not available.

Cross out V if VHF 121.5MHz not available.

Cross out E if emergency locater beacon - aircraft (ELBA) not available.

Survival Equipment:

S/(Survival Equipment) -

Cross out all indicators if survival equipment not carried

Cross out P if polar survival equipment not carried

Cross out D if desert survival equipment not carried

Cross out M if maritime survival equipment not carried

Cross out J if jungle survival equipment not carried

Jackets:

J/(Jackets) -

Cross out all indicators if no life-jackets are carried

Cross out L if life-jackets are not equipped with lights

Cross out F if life-jackets are not equipped

with flourescein

Cross out U or V to indicate radio capability of life-jackets.

Dingies:

(Number) - Cross out indicators D and C if no dinghies are carried, or insert number

(Capacity) - Insert total capacity, in persons, of dinghies carried

(Cover) - Cross out C if dinghies are not covered

(Colour) - Insert colour of dinghies carried

Aircraft Colour and Markings:

A/(Aircraft colour and markings) - insert colour of aircraft and significant markings

Remarks:

N/(Remarks) - Cross out indicator N if no remarks, or indicate other survival equipment/remarks.

Pilot in Command:

C/(Pilot) - Insert name of pilot in command

Filing a flight plan

A VFR flight plan must be filed at least 60 minutes before clearance to start or taxi is requested. Normally the flight plan is filed at the departure airfield who will pass it on to the relevant Parent ATSU Flight Briefing Unit. If the departure airfield will not be able to file the flight plan, it should be telephoned or faxed directly to the appropriate Parent ATSU Flight Briefing Unit:

Flight Briefing Unit Telephone Number	Fax Number
Belfast 018494 22152	018494 22388
LONDON/Heathrow 0208 745 3111 0208 745 3163	0208 745 3491 0208 745 3492
Manchester 0161 499 5502	0161 499 5504
Scottish Acc 01292 479800 Ext.2636	01292 671048

The ATSU or FBU must be advised as soon as possible of any cancellations, delays that will exceed 30 minutes, or changes to flight plan details.

If the flight lands at a place other than the flight plan destination, the destination must be informed within 30 minutes of the planned ETA there.

Name/Model	ICAO
2/180 Gyroplane	HG18
47G2/Bell	KH2
47G2A/Bell	KH2A
47G3B-KH4/Bell	KH4
A109/109A/II	A109
AB 47 G/G-2/2A/2A1/	
3B1/4/4A	A47G
AB 47 J/J-2A/3/3B-1	A47J
Aero145	O145
Aero Commander 685	AC85
Aero Commander 695	AC95
Aero-Jodel D-11A	AE11
Aeronca Champion	AR58
Aeronca Chief/Super Chief	AR11
Aeronca Sedan	AR15
Aero Star	TS60
Aero Star 600/700	PA60
Aircoupe A2	FO2
Aircruiser	VT11
Air Cruiser	AC72
Airtourer	VT10
ARV ARV-1	ARV1
Autogyro (Ultralight/Microlight)	GYRO
Balloons	BALL
Beagle Pup B121	BT12
Beech Bonanza 33	BE33
Beech Bonanza 35	BE35
Beech Bonanza 36	BE36
Beech Baron 55	BE55
Beech Baron 58	BE58
Beech Beech F90	BE9T
Beech Beech Jet 400	BE40
Beech Duchess 76	BE76
Beech Duke 60	BE60
Beech King Air C90, E90	BE9L
Beech King Air 100	BE10
Beech Starship, Model 2000	BEST
Beech Sundowner 23/ Musketeer 23	BE23
Beech Super King Air 200	BE20
Beech Super King Air 300	BE30
Beech Super King Air 350	B350
Beech Twin Beech 18	BE18
Bell 412	NB12
Bell B/A 206B-1	CCB4
Bell Jet Ranger/ Long Sea Ranger	B06
BN-2A/B Islander/Defender	BN2P
BN-2A Mk111 Trislander	TRIS
BO 105	NB05
BO 105A/C/D/S	MBH5
BO 105LS A-1, A-3	MDH5
BO 209, S Monsun	MB09
Brave	PA36
Buccaneer/LA-4/200EP/EPR	LA4
Buecker BUE 131 Jungmann	BJ31
CAP 10/10B	CP10
CAP 20/20L	CP20
CAP 21	CP21
CAP 230	CP23
Cessna 120	C120
Cessna 140	C140
Cessna 150	C150
Cessna 152	C152
Cessna 170	C170
Cessna 172/Skyhawk/ HawkXPII/Cutlass	C172
Cessna 172RG	C72R
Cessna 177RG	C77R
Cessna 185/Skywagon	C185
Cessna 190	C190
Cessna 195	C195
Cessna 310/T310	C310
Cessna 337	C337
Cessna Pressurised 337	P337
Cessna 340/340A	C340
Cessna 401/402/4026	C402
Cessna 411	C411
Cessna Caravan 1	C208
Cessna Cardinal 177	C177
Cessna Centurion/ Turbo Centurion 210	C210
Cessna Chancellor 414A	C414
Cessna Citation Jet 522	C525
Cessna Citation	C500
Cessna Citation II/S2	C550
Cessna Citation III/VI/VII	C650
Cessna Citation V	C560
Cessna Conquest/ Conquest II	C441
Cessna Crusader T303	C303
Cessna Golden Eagle 421	C421
Cessna Pressurised Centurion	P210
Cessna Skylane 182/RG, Turbo Skylane/RG	C182
Cessna Skymaster	C336
Cessna Stationair/Turbo Stationair/6	C206
Cessna Stationair/ Turbo Stationair 7/8	C207
Cessna Titan	C404
CFM Shadow	SHAD
CH-47	CEM47
Champion	CL60
Champion Citabria	AR7
Champion Lancer 402	CH40
Chipmunk DHC-1	DH1
Christen Eagle II	SOCH
Commander 112/114	CM11
Commander 200	M200
Commander 500	AC50
Commander 520	AC52
Commander 560	AC56
Corsair	C425
Cougar GA-7	GA7
CP 301 Emeraude	CP30
Decathlon	BL8
Diamond 1/1A	MU30
Diplomate ST 10	S10
DO27	DO27
DR100,105,1050,1051	DR10
DR220,221	DR22
DR 250	DR250
DR 300	DR30
DR 360	DR36
DR 400	DR 40
Ecureuil AS350	S350
Ecureuil AS351	S351
Ecureuil AS355	S355
Europa	EUPA
Falco	F8L
Falcon 10	FA10
Falcon 20FJF/20C/ 20D/20E/20F	FA20
Falcon 20G/20GF,	FA20
Mystere Falcon 200	FA21
Falcon 50	FA50
Falcon 900	FA90
G109/109B	G109
G115/115A	G115
Gardan GY100	GY10
Gazelle Sa341/342	GAZL
Glassair II/III	GLAS
Glider/Sailplane	GLID
Grumman Cheetah, Tiger, Traveler	AA5
Grumman Yankee AA-1B	AA1
Gulfstream I	G159
Gulfstream II/III/IV	GULF
HN-300C	BI30
Horizon GY 80	S80
HR 100	HR10
HR 200	HR20
HS125	HS25
Jet Commander	JCOM
Jet Commander 840/980/1000	AC6T
Jetstream 31/32	JSTA
Jodel D112/D120	D11
Jodel D140	D140
Kachina 2150A	MOR2
Kitfox	FOX
L-4-200 Buccaneer	LA4
LA-250	LA25
Lancair 235/320/360	LNC2
Lancair IV	LNC3
Learjet 23	LJ23
Learjet 24	LJ24
Learjet 25	LJ25
Learjet 28	LJ28
Learjet 31	LJ31
Learjet 35	LJ35
Learjet 55	LJ55
Learjet 60	LJ60
Luscombe 11	L11
Maule M-4	M4
Maule M-5	M5
Maule M-6	M6
Maule M-7	M7
Mooney 20, 21, 22, 201, 231	M20
Meta-Sokol L40	O40
MU2	MU2
P64-Oscar	OSCR
Pilatus PC-12	PC12
Piper Apache	PA23
Piper Aztec	PA27
Piper Cherokee/Archer II/ Dakota/Warrior	PA28
Piper Cherokee Arrow	P28R
Piper Cherokee 6/Lance/ Saratoga	PA32
Piper Cheyenne I/II	P31T
Piper Cheyenne III/IV	PA42
Piper Chieftain/Navajo	PA31
Piper Clipper	PA16
Piper Commanche	PA24
Piper Cub Special	PA11
Piper Cub Trainer	J2
Piper Cub Trainer 3	J3
Piper Family Cruiser	PA14
Piper Malibu	PA46
Piper Pacer	PA20
Piper Seminole	PA44
Piper Seneca	PA34
Piper Super Cruiser	PA12
Piper Super Cub	PA18
Piper Tri-Pacer/Colt	PA22
Piper Twin Commanche	PA30
Piper Vagabond	PA17
Piper Vagabond Trainer	PA15
R 1180T, 1180TD	R100
R 2160, 2160D, 2100, 2100A, 2112	R200
R 3000/3100/3120/3140	R300
Rallye	RALL
RF3	RF3
RF4	RF4
RF5	RF5
RF6	RF6
RF6B	SPF6B
RF7	SPF7
RF9	RF9
Robinson R22	R22
Robinson R44	R44
SF260	F260
SF260TP	F26T
Stagger Wing 17	BE17
Stampe	SV4
Stearman	B75
Steen Skybolt	BOLT
Super Acro Sport	ASPO
Swift	GC1
T67M Firefly 160	RF6
Tampico TB-09	TAMP
TBM 706	TBM7
Texan	T6
Tiger Moth 82A	DH82
Tobago TB-10	TOBA
Tomahawk	PA38
Trinidad TB-20/21	TRIN
Turbo Commander 690C	AC6T
Turbo Viking	BL31
Turbulent	D31
Twin Otter DHC-6	DH6
Vari-Eze	KREZ
Vari EZE/Long EZ	LGEZ
Yak 50	YK50
Yak 52	YK52
Zlin 42	Z42
Zlin 43	Z43
Z-50L	Z50

As you may notice from this guide, the number of gliding airfields that will accept powered aircraft is increasing. There are a number of hazards and practices associated with such airfields which are unfamiliar to the powered pilot. The following points are designed as general guidance and pilots intending to visit a gliding airfield **are strongly advised to ensure they are properly briefed on the specific field they intend to visit.** All gliding airfields require telephone PPR so this is not another chore to remember. **There is nothing more likely to reverse the trend of gliding airfields accepting powered aircraft than demonstrations of poor airmanship or obstruction of their activities.** Having said the heavy bit, GO OUT AND ENJOY!

1.**MAINTAIN A VERY GOOD LOOKOUT.** Not only does steam give way to sail but remember, a glider cannot go around! Even the hottest competition model will continue to descend when committed to a landing. DO NOT OBSTRUCT THE LANDING AREA! Remember that Gliding fields are primarily for gliding, you are a guest and give preference at all times.

2.**FLYING IN THE LOCAL AREA WHEN JOINING OR LEAVING THE CIRCUIT?** Then there are two very relevant tips to remember. Firstly… **keep a very good lookout close to cloudbase…** On thermic days this is where the Gliders will be, an unstable day with developing, or developed Cumulus will see many gliders turning beneath them, if you are descending through cloud it makes sense to do this further from your destination than you might normally do. Secondly… By the very nature of their activities glider pilots are more used to flying in close proximity to other aircraft than we powered pilots. Sometimes this can be very disconcerting! (It certainly has worried me when I've gone gliding)! But remember, as they do it a lot they are very aware of aircraft in their proximity, keep a very good lookout and may even have heard you coming! The best reaction is to assume you have not been seen and apply the Rules of the Air.

3.**USE THE GLIDER COMMON FREQUENCIES.** All gliding fields require PPR, when you get it make sure you know which of the common gliding frequencies are used by the local club and make circuit reports on it. You are very unlikely to get an answer but at least someone **MAY** know you are there. Remember, not all local Gliders will be listening out on radio, traffic awareness is not its primary function so **remain vigilant at all times.**

4.**LOOK OUT FOR CABLES.** Do not carry out overhead joins, as this is where the winch will deposit any departing gliders, sometimes up to 3000ft agl! You may see the cable drogue parachute but you will **not** see the cable. If you hit it in flight it will kill you, which would really spoil your visit! Remember also that tug aircraft will be towing cables, don't get too close and **always give them priority,** they have a job to do and this is only courteous airmanship.

5.**LANDING (LOOK OUT FOR CABLES AGAIN)!** After landing, roll beyond the launch point. This is because most gliders will be planning their landing to arrive at the launch point so that it is only a short push, (or tow), to regain the end of the launch queue. They'll then have plenty of room to land behind and to the right of you, (remember the Rules of the Air). It's quite obvious where the launch point is as the launch control caravan will be here and so will the launch queue of gliders. Give them a wide berth and do not land if a launch is in progress. After landing turn **left** and wait. Have a good look up final approach and on the base legs. Nothing coming? Then taxy back down the strip keeping close to the edge. If a tug or Glider should appear on final then stop and wait until it has landed. Continue to taxy back and **pass behind the launch queue. Don't taxy in front of the queue, you will be crossing the cables, the danger of this is quite obvious.** Park by the Launch control caravan but not between it and the winch as you will be obstructing the winch drivers view of the control caravan's visual signals, (a bit like an Aldis light).

6.**BE AWARE OF YOUR PROPWASH.** When manoeuvring or parking be very aware of your propwash if you are using increased revs. The area around the launch point is generally very busy with people awaiting a launch, gliders being towed or manhandled, trailers, caravans, and vehicles. The possibilities for damage caused by loose stones or propwash is self-evident.

7.**DEPARTING.** The same rules apply. Don't take off until the launch cable is on the ground following a launch remember the drogue chute on the cable will make this easy to accertain. Continue to be extremely vigilant until well clear of the site. At sites, which have Aerotow facilities, it is quite likely that there will be noise abatement routes or procedures. Find out if there are and follow them!

IF YOU ARE IN ANY DOUBT ABOUT LOCAL PROCEDURES THEN ASK ONE OF THE RESIDENT INSTRUCTORS. THERE WILL ALMOST CERTAINLY BE ONE NEAR THE LAUNCH CONTROL CARAVAN.

8.**BAD GROUND.** Many gliding fields are exactly that, a large field with useable and, sometimes, very unusable areas. Ensure you know where the area suitable for powered aircraft use is. Currock Hill is a case to point where a very large grass area has a relatively small area suitable for powered aircraft use.

Gliding fields invariably have some form of catering and facilities for an overnight stay at very reasonable cost. They are not as forbidding as they may seem to power pilots but when you do visit them show them you are a good airman. This article is by no means comprehensive and I find I learn something new at each site I visit. By showing the Gliding fraternity that we are considerate of their operations, the more likely it is that they will be willing to allow powered aircraft the use of their sites, which opens up a whole new range of airfields to visit.

Aberdeen/Dyce	1		Lydd	1
Andrewsfield	3		Lyneham (RAF)	3
Barrow	3		Manchester	1
Belfast/Aldergrove	1		Manchester/Barton	3
Belfast/City	2		Manston	1
Bembridge	3		Mona (RAF)	3
Beverley	3		Netherthorpe	3
Biggin Hill	1		Newcastle	1
Birmingham	1		Newtownards	3
Blackbushe	3		Northampton/Sywell	3
Blackpool	1		Northolt (RAF)	3
Bodmin	3		Norwich	1
Bourn	3		Nottingham	3
Bournemouth	1		Old Sarum	3
Bristol	1		Oxford	3
Brize Norton (RAF)	3		Perranporth	3
Caernarfon	3		Perth	3
Cambridge	1		Peterborough/Conington	3
Cardiff	1		Peterborough/Sibson	3
Carlisle	2		Plymouth	1
Chalgrove	3		Prestwick	1
Chichester/Goodwood	3		Redhill	3
Clacton	3		Retford/Gamston	3
Compton Abbas	3		Rochester	3
Coventry	1		Sandown	3
Cranfield	3		Sandtoft	3
Crowfield	3		Scilly Isles	3
Cumbernauld	3		Seething	3
Denham	3		Sherburn in Elmet	3
Dundee	3		Shipdham	3
Dunkeswell	3		Shobdon	3
Dunsfold	3		Shoreham	1
Duxford	3		Sleap	3
Eaglescott	3		Southampton	1
Earls Colne	3		Southend	1
East Midlands	1		St Mawgan (RAF)	3
Edinburgh	1		Stapleford	3
Elstree	3		Sturgate	3
Enniskillen	2		Sumburgh	1
Exeter	1		Swansea	3
Fairoaks	2		Teesside	1
Farnborough	3		Thruxton	3
Fenland	3		Valley (RAF)	3
Filton	3		Warton	3
Glasgow	1		Wellesbourne	3
Gloucestershire	2		Welshpool	3
Halfpenny Green	3		White Waltham	3
Haverfordwest	3		Wycombe Air Park	3
Hawarden	3		Yeovil	3
Humberside	1			
Inverness	2			
Isle of Man	1			
Kirkwall	2			
Lands End	3			
Lasham	3			
Lashenden	3			
Leeds/Bradford	1			
Leicester	3			
Little Gransden	3			
Liverpool	1			
Llanbedr	3			
London/City	1			
London/Gatwick	1			
London/Heathrow	1			
London/Stansted	1			
London/Westland heliport	2			
Londonderry	2			
Luton	1			

1 = Designated Customs and Excise airports
2 = Certain limited Customs and Excise facilities available, contact the aerodrome manager *before* arranging a flight
3 = Non-Customs and Excise airports which have a concession for flight to and from EC and certain non-EC countries. Pilots must obtain details from the aerodrome manager before making arrangements.

It is a requirement of the Act that the commander of any aircraft flying between Great Britain and the Republic of Ireland, Northern Ireland, the Isle of Man or the Channel Islands or Inbound to Great Britain from those places , **must**, on exit or entry to Great Britain, **land at an airport designated in the act.** The same requirement exists for flights entering or leaving Northern Ireland when flying to, or from Great Britain, the Republic of Ireland, the Isle of Man or the Channel Islands.

To comply with the requirements of this legislation the captains of aircraft affected by the Act **must.**

1. Obtain clearance from the examining Police officer before take-off from and after landing at an airport designated in the act.

2. Must comply with the requirements of the examining officer in respect of any examination of the captain, passengers, or crew, if carried.

Designated Airports in Gt. Britain, Northern Ireland, Isle of Man, & Channel Islands

ABERDEEN • EAST MIDLANDS • LONDON HEATHROW • ALDERNEY • EDINBURGH • LONDON STANSTED • BELFAST ALDERGROVE • EXETER • LONDON LUTON • BELFAST CITY • GLASGOW • LYDD • BIGGIN HILL • GLOUCESTERSHIRE • MANCHESTER • BIRMINGHAM • GUERNSEY • MANSTON • BLACKPOOL • HUMBERSIDE • NEWCASTLE • BOURNEMOUTH • I.O.M. RONALDSWAY • NORWICH • BRISTOL LULSGATE • JERSEY • PLYMOUTH • CAMBRIDGE • LEEDS BRADFORD • PRESTWICK • CARDIFF • LIVERPOOL • SOUTHAMPTON • CARLISLE • LONDON CITY • SOUTHEND COVENTRY • LONDON GATWICK • TEESSIDE

BRISTOL FILTON is not an airport designated under the act but the same facility will be available if application is made at least 24hrs prior to the flight. Such application should be made during normal office hours to. **Tel:** 01272 699094

Flights from Non Designated Airports

If a pilot wishes to make a direct flight from a non-designated airport he/she **must** seek prior permission from the Chief Constable in whose area the non-designated airport is located. Permission should be sought **as far in advance as possible.**

Requirements for Civil Helicopters

Pilots of civil helicopters flying into Norther Ireland are required to notify the Royal Ulster Constabulary Force control and Information centre. **Tel: 01232 650222 Ext 22430**, of the point and time for crossing the Northern Ireland coast, **this is in addition to the normal requirements of the Act.** Any amendment to the crossing point and/or time must be advised to **Belfast Aldergrove Approach, (120.90)** who will notify the R.U.C. on the pilots behalf.

Police Force Contact Numbers

Avon and Somerset	01275 818181	London (Metropolitan)	0207 230 1212
Bedfordshire	01234 841212	London (City)	0207 601 2222
Cambridgeshire	01480 456111	Merseyside	0151 709 6010
Cheshire	01244 350000	Norfolk	01603 768769
Cleveland	01642 326326	Northampton	01604 700700
Cumbria	01768 891999	Northumbria	01661 872555
Derbyshire	01773 570100	North Wales	01492 517171
Devon and Cornwall	01392 52101	North Yorkshire	01609 783131
Dorset	01929 462727	Nottinghamshire	0115 9670999
Durham	0191 386 4929	South Wales	01656 55555
Dyfed-Powys	01267 236444	South Yorkshire	0114 2768522
Essex	01245 491491	Staffordshire	01785 57717
Gloucestershire	01242 521321	Suffolk	01473 613500
Greater Manchester	0161 872 5050	Surrey	01483 571212
Gwent	01633 838111	Sussex	01273 475432
Hampshire	01962 868133	Thames Valley	01865 846000
Hertfordshire	01707 331177	Warwickshire	01926 415000
Humberside	01482 326111	West Mercia	01905 723000
Kent	01622 690690	West Midlands	0121 626 5000
Lancashire	01772 614444	West Yorkshire	01924 375222
Leicestershire	0116 2530066	Wiltshire	01380 722341
Lincolnshire	01522 532222		

Scotland

Central Scotland	01786 456000	Lothian and Border	0131 311 3131
Dumfries and Galloway	01387 52112/5	Northern	01463 715555
Fife	01592 418888	Strathclyde	0141 532 2000
Grampian	01224 639111	Tayside	01382 223200

Northern Ireland

Royal Ulster Constabulary 01232 650222

Isle of Man & Channel Islands

Isle of Man	01624 631212	Jersey	01534 612612
Guernsey	01481 725111		

(Who also have responsibility for Alderney)

Pre-flight abbreviations Coverage:

A1	*Route and general information.*
A2	*Selected international airfields within the London FIR.*
A3	*Other selected airfields.*
A4	*Selected airfields in the Scottish FIR.*
A5	*Other (smaller) airfields and obstacles.*
A6	*Permanent NOTAMs (usually cross-referring to AIP amendments).*
A8	*Royal Flights and navigation warnings.*

For clarification or up-dated information regarding pre-flight information bulletins, call 0181 745 3464 / 3452

For clarification or up-dated information regarding NOTAMs, call 0181 745 3450 / 3451

°C	Degrees Compass
°M °m	Degrees Magnetic
°T	Degrees True
ACFT, *ACFT*	Aircraft
AD, *AD*	Aerodrome
A/G	Air/Ground Station
ABn	Aerodrome Beacon
ADF	Automatic Direction Finder
ADIZ	Air Defense Identification Zone (US)
ADR	Advisory Zone
AFIS	Aerodrome Flight Information Service
AGL, agl	Above Ground Level
AI	Attitude Indicator
AIAA	Area of Intense Aerial Activity
AIC	Aeronautical Information Circular
AIP	Aeronautical Information Publication
airex	*Air Exercise (usually by military aircraft)*
AIS	Aeronautical Information Service
alt	*alternate or alternative*
alt, Alt	altitude
ALTN	Alternate Destination
AM	Amplitude Modulation
amdt	*amendment*
AME	Authorised Medical Examiner
AMSL, amsl	Above Mean Sea Level
ANO	Air Navigation Order
AOPA	Aircraft Owners & Pilots Association
Ap	Approach lights
APAPI	Abbreviated Precision Approach Path Indicator
APP, *APP*	Approach
aprx	*approximately*
ARA	Advisory Radio Area
ARP	*Aerodrome Reference Point*
ARP	Aerodrome Reference Point
ARR, Arr	Arrival
ASR	Altimeter Setting Region
ATA	Actual Time of Arrival
ATC	Air Traffic Control
ATIS	Automatic Terminal Information Service
ATPL	Air Transport Pilot Licence (UK)
ATS	Air Traffic Services
ATSU	Air Traffic Service Unit
ATZ	Aerodrome Traffic Zone
authy	*authority*
AUW	All Up Weight
AVASIS	Abbreviated VASIS
avbl, Avl	Available
AVGAS	Aviation Gasoline
Awy, awy(s)	*airway(s)*
Az	Azimuth
BAA	British Airports Authority
bdry	*boundary*
blks	*blocks (usually referring to sections of apron or manoeuvring area)*

Bn	Beacon
Brg, *brg*	Bearing
btn	*between*
C of A	Certificate of Airworthiness
C of E	Certificate of Experience
C of G	Centre of Gravity
C of T	Certificate of Test
C	Centre (runway designator)
c/l	*centre line*
C/S, c/s	Callsign
CAA	Civil Aviation Authority
CAAFU	Civil Aviation Authority Flying Unit
CAP	Civil Air Publication
CAS	Calibrated Airspeed
cas	*controlled air space*
CDI	Course Deviation Indicator
CFI	Chief Flying Instructor
CHAPI	Compact Helicopter Approach Path Indicator
chg	*change*
chk	*check*
CIV, civ	Civilian
CLNC, clnc	Clearance
clsd	*closed*
CMATZ	Combined Military Aerodrome Traffic Zones
com, COM	Communication
CSU	Constant Speed Unit
CTA	Control Area
CTR	Control Zone
DA	Decision Altitude
DAAIS	Danger Area Activity Information Service
DACS	Danger Area Crossing Service
DEPT, dept	Departure/Depart
DEST	Destination
DF	Direction Finding
DH	Decision Height
DI	Direction Indicator
Dist, *dist*	Distance
Dly, *dly*	Daily
DME	Distance Measuring Equipment
DR	Dead Reckoning
EAS	Equivalent Air Speed
EEC	European Economic Community
EGT	Exhaust Gas Temperature
Elev, *elev*	Elevation
eqpt	*equipment*
est	*established*
ETA	Estimated Time of Arrival
ETD	Estimated Time of Departure
ETE	Estimated Time En route
Ex, *exc*	Except
Ext	Extension
	extending/retracting
Extv	Extensive
FAA	Federal Aviation Authority
FAF	Final Approach Fix
FAP	Final Approach Point
FAT	Final Approach Track
FBO	Fixed Base Operator
Fcst	Forecast
FIR	Flight Information Region
FIS	Flight Information Service
FL	Flight Level
FLT, *flt*	Flight
FM	Frequency Modulation
fm	*from*
FPL	Filed Flight Plan
FPM	Feet Per Minute

FREQ, *freq*	Frequency
FT, ft	Feet
G/S	Ground Speed
GA	General Aviation
GEN	General
Gn	Green
GND, *gnd*	Ground Control
GP	Glide Path
GPS	Global Positioning System
GPWS	Ground Proximity Warning System
Grad	Gradient
H24	Continuous Service (24 hours)
Hdg	Heading
HEL	*helicopter*
HF	High Frequency
Hgt, *hgt*	Height
HI	Heading Indicator
HIRTA	High Intensity Radio Transmission Area
HJ, *HJ*	Sunrise to Sunset
HN, *HN*	Sunset to Sunrise
HO	Service available to meet Operation requirements
Hol(s)	Holiday(s)
hPa	Hectopascal
Hrs, *Hrs*	Hour(s)
HSI	Horizontal Situation Indicator
HT	High Tension
HX	No specific working hours
IAF	Initial Approach Fix
IAP	Instrument Approach Procedure
IAS	Indicated Airspeed
IBn	Identification Beacon
ICAO	International Civil Aviation Organisation
Ident	Identification
IFR	Instrument Flight Rules
ILS	Instrument Landing System
IM	Inner Marker
IMC	Instrument Meteorological Conditions
In(s)	Inch(es)
Inbd	Inbound
Info	Information
Inop	Inoperative
intxn	*intersection*
IR	Instrument Rating
ISA	International Standard Atmosphere
Kg,kg	Kilograms
kHz	Kilohertz
Km	Kilometres
Kts	Knots
L	Left (runway designator)
LARS	Lower Airspace Radar Service
Lat	Latitude
lbs	Pounds
Lctr	Locater Beacon
LCZ	Localizer - Instrument Landing System
LDA	Landing Distance Available
ldg	*landing*
LFA	*Low Flying Area*
LFZ	*Local Flying Zone*
lgts	*lights*
LH	Left Hand
LHS	Left Hand Side
LITAS	Low Intensity Two-colour Approach Slope System
LLZ	Localizer - Instrument Landing System (ICAO)
LMT	Local Mean Time
LOC	Locater Beacon
LOM	Locater Outer Marker
Long	Longitude
LORAN	Long Range Aid to Navigation
Ltrs	Litres
M, *m*	Metres
Mag, *mag*	Magnetic
MAP	Missed Approach Point
MATZ	Military Aerodrome Traffic Zone
MAX, *max*	Maximum
Mb	Millibar
MDA	Minimum Descent Altitude
MDH	Minimum Descent Height
MEF	Maximum Elevation Figures
MET, *met*	Meteorological, Meteorology
METAR	Aviation routine weather report
MF	Medium Frequency
MHz	Megahertz
MIL, *mil*	Military
Min	Minute(s)
Min	Minimum
mkd	*marked*
Mkr	Marker
MM	Middle Marker
MOD	Ministry of Defence
Mod	Modified
MSA	Minimum Sector Altitude
MSD	Minimum Separation Distance
MSL	Mean Sea Level
MTA	Military Training Area
MTOW	Maximum Take Off Weight
MTWA	Maximum Total Weight Authorised
mvmt	*movement*
NATS	National Air Traffic Service
Nav aid	Navigation Aid
Nav	Navigation
NDB	Non-Directional Beacon
NM, nm	Nautical Miles
no	*number*
NOTAM	Notice To Airmen
O/H, *O/H*	Overhead
O/R, *o/r*	On Request
OBI	Omni Bearing Indicator
OBS	Omni Bearing Selector
Obst, *obst*	Obstruction
OCA	Obstacle Clearance Altitude
OCH	Obstacle Clearance Height
OCL	Obstacle Clearance Limit
OCNL	Occasionally
OM	Outer Marker
opr	*operating*
OPS, *ops*	Operations
OT	Other Times
PAPI	Precision Approach Path Indicators
PAR	Precision Approach Radar
Pax	Passenger(s)
perm	*permanently*
PFA	Popular Flying Association
PH, *ph*	Public Holidays
PJE	*Parachute Jumping Exercise*
PN	Prior Notice
PNR	Prior Notice Required
POB	Persons on Board
Posn	Position
PPL	Private Pilot's Licence
PPO	Prior Permission Only
PPR	Prior Permission Required
proc	*procedure*
Prop	Propellor
Psi	Pounds per Square Inch
psn	*position*
pt	*point*
pwr	*power*

QDM	Magnetic Bearing TO Station
QDR	Magnetic Bearing FROM Station
QFE	Atmospheric Pressure at aerodrome elevation (or runway threshold)
QNH	Altimeter sub-scale setting to obtain ALTITUDE amsl
QTE	True Bearing FROM Station
QUJ	True Bearing TO Station
R	Radial (° FROM a beacon/position)
R	Right (runway designator)
RAD	Radar
Rad, *rad*	Radius
RAMP	Ramp Control
RAS	Radar Advisory Service
RAS	Recitified Air Speed
RASA	Radar Advisory Service Area
RCC	Rescue Co-ordination Centre
rcl	*runway centre line*
rcvd	*received*
ref	*reference*
RFF	*Rescue and Fire Fighting (category)*
Rgn	Region
RH	Right Hand
RHS	Right Hand Side
RIS	Radar Information Service
RMI	Radio Magnetic Indicator
RMKs rmks	Remarks
RNAV	Area Navigation System
RPS	Regional Pressure Setting
RT, *rtf*	Radiotelephony
RVR	Runway Visual Range
Rwy, *rwy*	Runway
Rx	Receiver
SAR, SAR	Search and Rescue
Sched, *sched*	Schedule
sec	*sector*
sfc, SFC	Surface
shld	*should*
SID	Standard Instrument Departure
SL	Sea Level
SMOH	Since Major Overhaul
SR	Sunrise
SRA	Surveillance Radar Approach
SS	Sunset
SSA	Sector Safe Altitude
SSR, *ssr*	Secondary Surveillance Radar
STAR	Standard Instrument Arrival Route
stn, Stn	Station
STOL	Short Take Off and Landing
svce	*service*
SVFR	Special Visual Flight Rules
TA, *trans alt*	Transition Altitude
TACAN	Tactical Air Navigation Aid
TAF	Terminal Area Forecast
TAS	True Air Speed
tbn	*to be notified*
TBO	Time Between Overhauls
TCA	Terminal Control Area
TDZ	Touch Down Zone
Temp	Temperature
temp	*temporary*
tfc	*traffic*
Thr, *thr*	Threshold
til	*until*
tkof	*take-off*
TL, *trans lev*	Transition Level
TMA	See TCA
TODA	Take Off Distance Available
TORA	Take Off Run Available
trk	*track*
trng	*training*
TT	Total Time
TTSN	Total Time Since New
TVOR	Terminal VOR
TWR, *twr*	Tower
Twy, *twy*	Taxiway
tx	*transmission or transmit*
Tx	Transmitter
u/s	*unserviceable*
UFN	Until Further Notice
UHF	Ultra High Frequency
UIR	Upper Flight Information Region
Unltd, *unl*	Unlimited
Unsvc, *u/s*	Unserviceable
UTC	Co-ordinated Universal Time
Va	Design Manoeuvring Speed
VAR	Magnetic Variation
VASI	Visual Approach Slope Indicator
VDF	VHF Direction Finder
Vfe	Maximum speed with flaps extended
VFR	Visual Flight Rules
VHF	Very High Frequency
Vis	Visibility
Vle	Maximum speed with landing gear extended
VLF	Very Low Frequency
Vlo	Maximum speed with landing gear
VMC	Visual Meteorological Conditions
Vmca	Minimum control speed with critical
Vne	Never Exceed Speed
Vno	Maximum Normal Operating Speed
VOLMET	Spoken Meteorological Information for aircraft in flight
VOR	VHF Omni Range
VRP	Visual Reference Point
Vx	Speed for best angle of climb
Vy	Speed for best rate of climb
W/P	Waypoint
W/V	Wind Velocity
wdn	*withdrawn*
wef, *wef*	With Effect From
wfu, *wfu*	withdrawn from use
wi	*within*
WIE	With Immediate Effect
WIP	Work In Progress
Wx	Weather
XPDR	Transponder
Z	Zulu (UTC)

Take Off Distance Factors		
VARIATION	INCREASE IN TAKE-OFF DISTANCE (to 50')	FACTOR
10% increase in aircraft weight	20%	1.2
Increase of 1000' in runway altitude	10%	1.1
Increase in temperature of 10°C	10%	1.1
Dry Grass		
- Up to 8 inches	20%	1.2
Wet Grass		
- Up to 8 inches	30%	1.3
2% uphill slope	10%	1.1
Tailwind component of		
10% of lift off speed	20%	1.2
Soft ground or snow *	at least 25%	at least 1.25

Landing Distance Factors		
VARIATION	INCREASE IN LANDING DISTANCE (from 50')	FACTOR
10% increase in aircraft weight	10%	1.1
Increase of 1000' in runway altitude	5%	1.05
Increase in temperature of 10°C	5%	1.05
Dry Grass		
- Up to 8 inches	20%	1.2
Wet Grass		
- Up to 8 inches	40%	1.40
2% downhill slope	10%	1.1
Tailwind component of		
10% of landing speed	20%	1.2
snow *	at least 25%	at least 1.25

The Take Off Run Available (TORA)

The TORA is the length of the runway available for the take off ground run of the aircraft. This is usually the physical length of the runway.

The Emergency Distance (ED)

The ED is the length of the TORA plus the length of any stopway. A stopway is area at the end of the TORA prepared for an aircraft to stop on in the event of an abandoned take off. The ED is also known as the ACCELERATE - STOP DISTANCE AVAILABLE.

The Take Off Distance Available (TODA)

The TODA is the TORA plus the length of any clearway. A clearway is an area over which an aircraft may make its initial climb (to 50' in this instance). The TODA will not be more than 1.5 X TORA.

The Landing Distance Available (LDA)

The LDA is the length of the runway available for the ground run of an aircraft landing. In all cases the landing distance required should never be greater than the landing distance available.

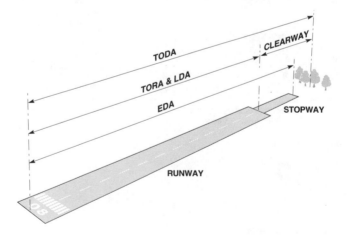

Temperature & Pressure

TEMPERATURE

°C scale: 50, 40, 30, 20, 10, 0, −10, −20, −30, −40, −50, −60
°F scale: 120, 110, 100, 90, 80, 70, 60, 50, 40, 30, 20, 10, 0, −10, −20, −30, −40, −50, −60, −70

PRESSURE

Kg/cm² : 7, 6, 5, 4, 3, 2, 1, 0
lbs/sq" : 100, 90, 80, 70, 60, 50, 40, 30, 20, 10, 0
Bars : 7, 6, 5, 4, 3, 2, 1, 0

Metric/Imperial Measurement

Metres	Feet	Feet	Metres
1	3.28	1	0.30
2	6.56	2	0.61
3	9.84	3	0.91
4	13.12	4	1.22
5	16.40	5	1.52
6	19.69	6	1.83
7	22.97	7	2.13
8	26.25	8	2.44
9	29.53	9	2.74
10	32.81	10	3.05
20	65.62	20	6.10
30	98.43	30	9.14
40	131.23	40	12.19
50	164.04	50	15.24
60	196.85	60	18.29
70	229.66	70	21.34
80	262.47	80	24.38
90	295.28	90	27.43
100	328.08	100	30.48
200	656.16	200	60.96
300	984.25	300	91.44
400	1,312.34	400	121.92
500	1,640.42	500	152.40
600	1,968.50	600	182.88
700	2,296.59	700	213.36
800	2,624.67	800	243.84
900	2,952.76	900	274.32
1000	3,280.84	1000	304.80
2000	6,561.70	2000	609.60
3000	9,842.50	3000	914.40
4000	13,123.40	4000	1,219.20
5000	16,404.20	5000	1,524.00
6000	19,685.00	6000	1,828.80
7000	22,965.90	7000	2,133.60
8000	26,246.70	8000	2,438.40
9000	29,527.60	9000	2,743.20
10000	32,808.40	10000	3,048.00

Km/Nautical Miles/Statute Miles

NM	Km	St	Km	NM	St
1	1.85	1.15	1	.54	.62
2	3.70	2.30	2	1.08	1.24
3	5.56	3.45	3	1.62	1.86
4	7.41	4.60	4	2.16	2.49
5	9.26	5.75	5	2.70	3.11
6	11.11	6.90	6	3.24	3.73
7	12.96	8.06	7	3.78	4.35
8	14.82	9.21	8	4.32	4.97
9	16.67	10.36	9	4.86	5.59
10	18.52	11.51	10	5.40	6.21
20	37.04	23.02	20	10.80	12.43
30	55.56	34.52	30	16.20	18.64
40	74.08	46.03	40	21.60	24.86
50	92.60	57.54	50	27.00	31.07
60	111.12	69.05	60	32.40	37.28
70	129.64	80.55	70	37.80	43.50
80	148.16	92.06	80	43.20	49.71
90	166.68	103.57	90	48.60	55.92
100	185.2	115.1	100	54.0	62.1
200	370.4	230.2	200	108.0	124.3
300	555.6	345.2	300	162.0	186.4
400	740.8	460.3	400	216.0	248.6
500	926.0	575.4	500	270.0	310.7
600	1111.2	690.5	600	324.0	372.8
700	1296.4	805.6	700	378.0	435.0
800	1481.6	920.6	800	432.0	497.1
900	1666.8	1035.7	900	486.0	559.2

Conversion Factors:

Centimetres to Inches x .3937
Inches to Centimetres x 2.54
Metres to Feet x 3.28084
Feet to Metres x 0.3048

Statute Miles to Nautical Miles x 0.868976
Statute Miles to Kilometres x 1.60934
Kilometres to Statute Miles x 0.62137
Kilometres to Nautical Miles x 0.539957
Nautical Miles to Statute Miles x 1.15078
Nautical Miles to Kilometres x 1.852

Conversions

Km/Nautical Miles/Statute Miles

ST	NM	Km
1	.87	1.61
2	1.74	3.22
3	2.61	4.83
4	3.48	6.44
5	4.34	8.05
6	5.21	9.66
7	6.08	11.27
8	6.95	12.87
9	7.82	14.48
10	8.69	16.09
20	17.38	32.19
30	26.07	48.28
40	34.76	64.37
50	43.45	80.47
60	52.14	96.56
70	60.83	112.65
80	69.52	128.75
90	78.21	144.84
100	86.9	161.0
200	173.8	321.9
300	260.7	482.8
400	347.6	643.7
500	434.5	804.7
600	521.4	965.6
700	608.3	1126.5
800	695.2	1287.5
900	782.1	1448.4

Conversion Factors:
lbs to Kilograms x 0.45359
Kilograms to lbs x 2.20462

Weight lbs/Kg

lbs	Kg		Kg	lbs
1	.45		1	2.20
2	.91		2	4.41
3	1.38		3	6.61
4	1.81		4	8.82
5	2.27		5	11.02
6	2.72		6	13.23
7	3.18		7	15.43
8	3.63		8	17.64
9	4.08		9	19.84
10	4.54		10	22.05
20	9.07		20	44.09
30	13.61		30	66.14
40	18.14		40	88.18
50	22.68		50	110.23
60	27.22		60	132.28
70	31.75		70	154.32
80	36.29		80	176.37
90	40.82		90	198.42
100	45.4		100	220.5
200	90.7		200	440.9
300	136.1		300	661.4
400	181.4		400	881.8
500	226.8		500	1102.3
600	272.2		600	1322.8
700	317.5		700	1543.2
800	362.9		800	1763.7
900	408.2		900	1984.2
1000	453.6		1000	2204.6
2000	907.2		2000	4409.2
3000	1360.8		3000	6613.9
4000	1814.4		4000	8818.5
5000	2268.0		5000	11023.1
6000	2721.5		6000	13227.7
7000	3175.1		7000	15432.3
8000	3628.7		8000	17637.0
9000	4082.3		9000	19841.6
10000	4535.9		10000	22046.2

Volume (Fluid)

Litres	Imp. Gall	U.S. Gall
1	0.22	0.26
2	0.44	0.53
3	0.66	0.79
4	0.88	1.06
5	1.10	1.32
6	1.32	1.59
7	1.54	1.85
8	1.76	2.11
9	1.98	2.38
10	2.20	2.64
20	4.40	5.28
30	6.60	7.93
40	8.80	10.57
50	11.00	13.21
60	13.20	15.85
70	15.40	18.49
80	17.60	21.14
90	19.80	23.78
100	22.00	26.42
200	44.00	52.84
300	66.00	79.26
400	88.00	105.68
500	110.00	132.10
600	132.00	158.52
700	154.00	184.94
800	176.00	211.36
900	198.00	237.78
1000	220.00	264.20

U.S. Gall	Imp. Gall	Litres
1	0.83	3.79
2	1.67	7.57
3	2.50	11.36
4	3.33	15.14
5	4.16	18.93
6	5.00	22.71
7	5.83	26.50
8	6.66	30.28
9	7.49	34.07
10	8.33	37.85
20	16.65	75.71
30	24.98	113.56
40	33.31	151.41
50	41.63	189.27
60	49.96	227.12
70	58.29	264.97
80	66.61	302.82
90	74.94	340.68
100	83.27	378.54

Imp. Gall	U.S. Gall	Litres
1	1.20	4.55
2	2.40	9.09
3	3.60	13.64
4	4.80	18.18
5	6.00	22.73
6	7.21	27.28
7	8.41	31.82
8	9.61	36.37
9	10.81	40.91
10	12.01	45.46
20	24.02	90.92
30	36.03	136.38
40	48.04	181.84
50	60.05	227.30
60	72.06	272.76
70	84.07	318.22
80	96.08	363.68
90	108.09	409.14
100	120.09	454.60

Conversion Factors:
Imperial Gallons to Litres x 4.54596
Litres to Imperial Gallons x 0.219975
U.S. Gallons to Litres x 3.78541
Litres to U.S. Gallons x 0.264179
Imperial Gallons to U.S. Gallons x 1.20095
U.S. Gallons to Imperial Gallons x 0.832674

Millibars/Inches

Mbs	ins	Mbs	ins	Mbs	ins	Mbs	ins	Mbs	ins
950	28.054	970	28.644	990	29.235	1010	29.825	1030	30.416
951	28.083	971	28.674	991	29.264	1011	29.855	1031	30.445
952	28.113	972	28.703	992	29.294	1012	29.884	1032	30.475
953	28.142	973	28.733	993	29.323	1013	29.914	1033	30.504
954	28.172	974	28.762	994	29.353	1014	29.943	1034	30.534
955	28.201	975	28.792	995	29.382	1015	29.973	1035	30.564
956	28.231	976	28.821	996	29.412	1016	30.002	1036	30.593
957	28.260	977	28.851	997	29.441	1017	30.032	1037	30.623
958	28.290	978	28.880	998	29.471	1018	30.062	1038	30.652
959	28.319	979	28.910	999	29.500	1019	30.091	1039	30.682
960	28.349	980	28.939	1000	29.530	1020	30.121	1040	30.711
961	28.378	981	28.969	1001	29.560	1021	30.150	1041	30.741
962	28.408	982	28.998	1002	29.589	1022	30.180	1042	30.770
963	28.437	983	29.028	1003	29.619	1023	30.209	1043	30.800
964	28.467	984	29.058	1004	29.648	1024	30.239	1044	30.829
965	28.496	985	29.087	1005	29.678	1025	30.268	1045	30.859
966	28.526	986	29.117	1006	29.707	1026	30.298	1046	30.888
967	28.556	987	29.146	1007	29.737	1027	30.327	1047	30.918
968	28.585	988	29.176	1008	29.766	1028	30.357	1048	30.947
969	28.615	989	29.205	1009	29.796	1029	30.386	1049	30.977

Mbs	ins
1050	31.007

To convert Inches into millibars multiply by 33.86
To convert millibars into Inches multiply by 0.0295

Note: DMEs associated with a specific runway normally read distance from the threshold of the runway in use.

Station	Navaid	Ident	Freq.	Range	Co-ordinates
Aberdeen (Dyce)	Lctr	ATF	348.0	25	N5704.65 W00206.34
	NDB	AQ	336.0	15	N5708.30 W00224.28
	VOR/DME	ADN	114.3		N5718.63 W00216.03
	DME 16	I-AX	109.90		N5712.07 W00212.04
	DME 34	I-ABD	109.90		N5712.07 W00212.04
Aberporth	NDB	AP	370.50	20	N5206.98 W00433.57
Alderney	Lctr	ALD	383.00	30	N4942.53 W00211.98
BallyKelly	TACAN	BKL	109.10		N5503.69 W00700.89
Barkway	VOR/DME	BKY	116.25		N5159.38 E00003.71
Barra	NDB	BRR	316.0	15	N5701.55 W00726.95
Barrow (Walney Island)	NDB	WL	385.0	15	N5407.87 W00315.81
	DME	WL	109.40		
Belfast (Aldergrove)	VOR/DME	BEL	117.20		N5439.66 W00613.79
	Lctr	OY	332.0	15	N5441.56 W00605.12
	DME 25	I-AG	109.90		N5439.63 W00612.02
	DME 17	I-FT	110.90		N5439.31 W00613.74
Belfast (City)	Lctr	HB	420.0	15	N5436.93 W00552.86
	DME 22	I-BFH	108.10		N5437.17 W00552.48
	DME 04	HBD	108.10		N5437.17 W00552.48
Bembridge	NDB	IW	426.0		N5040.82 W00106.30
Benbecula	VOR/DME	BEN	113.95		N5728.67 W00721.92
	DME	BCL	108.10		N5728.50 W00722.21
Berry Head	VOR/DME	BHD	112.05		N5023.91 W00329.61
Biggin Hill	DME 21	I-BGH	109.35		N5120.22 E00002.10
	VOR/DME	BIG	115.10		N5119.85 E00002.08
Birmingham	Lctr	BHX	406.0	25	N5227.27 W00145.14
	DME 15	I-BIR	110.10		N5227.42 W00144.79
	DME 33	I-BM	110.10		N5227.42 W00144.79
Blackbushe	NDB	BLK	328.0	15	N5119.40 W00050.69
	DME	BLC	116.20		N5119.40 W00050.69
Blackpool	Lctr	BPL	420.0	15	N5346.37 W00301.67
	DME 28	I-BPL	108.15		N5346.22 W00301.71
Boscombe Down	TACAN	BDN	108.20		N5108.93 W00145.15
Bourn	NDB	BOU	391.50	15	N5212.65 W00002.73
Bournemouth	Lctr	BIA	339.0	20	N5046.66 W00150.54
	Lczr 26	IBH	110.50		N5046.62 W00151.48
	DME 08	I-BMH	110.50		N5046.72 W00150.38
	DME 26	I-BH	110.50		N5046.72 W00150.38
Bovingdon	VOR/DME	BNN	113.75		N5143.56 W00032.98
Brecon	VOR/DME	BCN	117.45		N5143.53 W00315.78
Bristol	Lctr	BRI	380.0	25	N5122.81 W00243.03
	DME 09	I-BON	110.15		N5123.09 W00243.22
	DME 27	I-BTS	110.15		N5123.09 W00243.22
Brize Norton	TACAN	BZN	111.90		N5144.89 W00136.21
	Lctr	BZ	386.0	20	N5144.95 W00136.09
Brookmans Park	VOR/DME	BPK	117.50		N5144.98 W00006.40
Brough	NDB	BV	372.0	15	N5343.51 W00034.90
Burnham	NDB	BUR	421.0	15	N5131.13 W00040.61
Caernarfon	NDB	CAE	320.0	15	N5306.00 W00420.40
Cambridge	Lctr	CAM	332.50	15	N5212.65 E00010.96
	DME	I-CMG	111.30		N5212.42 E00010.88
Cardiff	Lctr	CDF	388.50	20	N5123.59 W00320.29
	DME 12	I-CDF	110.70		N5123.92 W00320.43
	DME 30	I-CWA	110.70		N5123.92 W00320.43
Carlisle	Lctr	CL	328.0	20	N5456.40 W00248.33
	DME	CO	110.70		N5456.40 W00248.31
Carnane	NDB	CAR	366.50	25	N5408.46 W00429.50
Chiltern	NDB	CHT	277.0	25	N5137.38 W00031.11
City of Derry	Lctr	EGT	328.50	25	N5502.73 W00709.30
	DME 26	I-EGT	108.3		N5527.51 W00709.56
Clacton	VOR/DME	CLN	114.55		N5150.91 E00108.85
Coltishall	TACAN	CSL	116.50		N5244.71 E00120.93
Compton	VOR/DME	CPT	114.35		N5129.50 W00113.18
Compton Abbas	NDB	COM	349.5	10	N5057.98 W00209.22
Coningsby	TACAN	CGY	111.10		N5305.46 W00010.13
Connell	NDB	CNL	404	15	N5627.81 W00523.70
Cottesmore	TACAN	CTM	112.30		N5244.12 W00039.04
Coventry	Lctr	CT	365.50	20	N5224.66 W00124.35
Cranfield	Lctr	CIT	850.0	15	N5207.78 W00033.42
	VOR	CFD	116.50		N5204.45 W00036.64

Cranwell	NDB	CWL	423.0	25	N5301.58 W00029.34
	TACAN	CWZ	117.40		N5301.71 W00029.12
Cumbernauld	NDB	CBN	374.0		N5558.53 W00358.49
	DME	CBN	117.55		N5558.53 W00358.47
Daventry	VOR/DME	DTY	116.40		N5210.81 W00106.83
Dean Cross	VOR/DME	DCS	115.20		N5443.31 W00320.43
Detling	VOR/DME	DET	117.30		N5118.23 E00035.83
Dover	VOR/DME	DVR	114.95		N5109.75 E00121.55
Dundee	Lctr	DND	394.0	25	N5627.31 W00306.9C
	DME 10	DDE	108.10		N5627.09 W00301.41
East Midlands	Lctr	EME	353.50	20	N5249.96 W00111.67
	Lctr	EMW	393.0	10	N5249.72 W00127.27
	DME 09	I-EMW	109.35		N5249.97 W00119.80
	DME 27	I-EME	109.35		N5249.97 W00119.80
Edinburgh	Lctr	EDN	341.0	35	N5558.70 W00317.12
	Lctr	UW	368.0	25	N5554.30 W00330.15
	DME 06	I-VG	108.90		N5557.10 W00322.37
	DME 24	I-TH	108.90		N5557.10 W00322.37
Enniskillen	NDB	EKN	357.50	15	N5423.65 W00738.65
	DME	ENN	116.75		N5423.92 W00739.21
Epsom	NDB	EPM	316.0	25	N5119.16 W00022.31
Exeter	Lctr	EX	337.0	15	N5045.13 W00317.70
	DME 08	I-ET	109.9		N5044.12 W00324.86
	DME 26	I-XR	109.9		N5044.12 W00324.86
Fairford	TACAN	FFA	113.40		N5140.89 W00147.86
Fairoaks	NDB	FOS	348.0	8	N5120.78 W00033.83
	DME	FRK	109.85		N5120.78 W00033.83
Farnborough	DME 25	I-FNB	111.5		N5116.84 W00046.45
Fenland	NDB	FNL	401.0	15	N5244.50 W00001.70
Fife	NDB	GO	402.0	15	N5610.95 W00313.20
Filton	Lctr	OF	325.0	25	N5131.31 W00235.41
	DME 09	I-BRF	110.55		N5131.25 W00235.48
	DME 27	I-FB	110.55		N5131.25 W00235.48
Flotta	NDB	IOF	357.0		N5849.80 W00308.60
Gamston	VOR/DME	GAM	112.80		N5316.88 W00056.83
Glasgow	VOR/DME	GOW	115.40		N5552.23 W00426.74
	Lctr	AC	325.0	25	N5548.85 W00432.56
	Lctr	GLG	350.0	15	N5555.46 W00420.16
	DME 05	I-UU	110.10		N5552.18 W00426.04
	DME 23	I-OO	110.10		N5552.18 W00426.04
Gloucestershire	Lctr	GST	331.0	25	N5153.51 W00210.07
	DME	GOS	115.55		N5153.53 W00210.08
Goodwood	VOR/DME	GWC	114.75		N5051.31 W00045.40
Great Yarmouth (North Denes)	Lctr	ND	417.00	10	N5238.15 E00143.62
Guernsey	Lctr	GRB	361.0	30	N4926.05 W00237.94
	VOR/DME	GUR	109.40		N4926.22 W00236.22
Halfpenny Green	NDB	HG	356.0	10	N5231.05 W00215.68
Haverfordwest	NDB	HAV	328.0	10	N5149.93 W00458.10
	DME	HDW	116.75		N5149.93 W00458.18
Hawarden	Lctr	HAW	340.0	25	N5310.75 W00258.77
	DME 23	I-HDN	110.35		N5310.73 W00258.73
Henton	NDB	HEN	433.50	30	N5145.58 W00047.41
Honiley	VOR/DME	HON	113.65		N5221.40 W00139.81
Humberside	Lctr	KIM	365.0	15	N5334.43 W00021.22
	DME 21	I-HS	108.75		N5334.43 W00021.20
Inverness	VOR/DME	INS	109.20		N5732.55 W00402.49
Islay	Lctr	LAY	395.0	20	N5540.97 W00614.96
	DME	ISY	109.95		N5540.97 W00614.96
Isle of Man	VOR/DME	IOM	112.20		N5404.01 W00445.81
	Lctr	RWY	359.00	20	N5405.17 W00436.51
	DME 26	I-RY	110.90		N5404.85 W00437.57
Jersey	Lctr	JW	329.0	25	N4912.35 W00213.20
	VOR/DME	JSY	112.20		N4913.26 W00202.76
	DME 09	I-JJ	110.90		N4912.50 W00212.12
	DME 27	I-DD	110.30		N4912.57 W00211.34
Kinloss	NDB	KS	370.0	20	N5739.02 W00335.22
	TACAN	KSS	109.80		N5739.55 W00332.10
Kirkwall	Lctr	KW	395.0	40	N5857.57 W00254.69
	VOR/DME	KWL	108.60		N5857.58 W00253.63
Lakenheath	TACAN	LKH	110.20		N5224.39 E00032.48
Lambourne	VOR/DME	LAM	115.60		N5138.76 E00009.10
Lands End	VOR/DME	LND	114.20		N5008.18 W00538.21
Lashenden	NDB	LSH	340.0	15	N5109.28 E00038.53

Location	Type	Ident	Frequency	Range	Coordinates
Leeds Bradford	Lctr	LBA	402.50	25	N5351.90 W00139.17
	DME 32	I-LF	110.90		N5351.88 W00139.75
	DME 14	I-LBF	110.90		N5351.88 W00139.75
Leicester	NDB	LE	383.50	10	N5236.38 W00102.10
Lerwick	NDB	TL	376.0	25	N6011.30 W00114.78
Leuchars	TACAN	LUK	110.50		N5622.36 W00251.82
Lichfield	NDB	LIC	545.0	50	N5244.80 W00143.16
Linton-On-Ouse	TACAN	LOO	109.0		N5403.02 W00114.94
Liverpool	NDB	LPL	349.50	25	N5320.37 W00243.50
	DME 09	LVR	111.75		N5319.95 W00250.95
	DME 27	I-LQ	111.75		N5319.95 W00250.95
London	VOR/DME	LON	113.60		N5129.23 W00028.00
London City	NDB	LCY	322.0	10	N5130.27 E00004.05
	DME 10	LST	111.15		N5130.35 E00003.27
	DME 28	LSR	111.15		N5130.35 E00003.27
London Gatwick	NDB	GE	338.0	15	N5109.86 W00004.14
	Lctr	GY	365.0	15	N5107.83 W00018.95
	DME 08R	I-GG	110.90		N5109.16 W00011.53
	DME 26L	I-WW	110.90		N5109.16 W00011.53
London Heathrow	DME 09R	I-BB	109.50		N5127.83 W00027.51
	DME 09L	I-AA	110.30		N5128.73 W00027.55
	DME 27R	I-RR	110.30		N5128.73 W00027.55
	DME 27L	I-LL	109.50		N5127.83 W00027.51
	DME 23	HTT	110.70		N5128.43 W00026.01
	Lctr	HRW		20	N5128.73 W00027.56
London Luton	Lctr	LUT	345.0	20	N5153.68 W00015.15
	DME 08	I-LTN	109.15		N5152.39 W00022.10
	DME 26	I-LJ	109.15		N5152.39 W00022.10
London Manston	DME	I-MSN	111.75		N5120.47 E00120.75
London Stanstead	NDB	SSD	429.0	20	N5153.68 E00014.70
	DME 05	I-SED	110.50		N5153.16 E00014.02
	DME 23	I-SX	110.50		N5153.16 E00014.02
Lydd	VOR/DME	LYD	114.05		N5059.98 E00052.71
	NDB	LYX	397.0	15	N5058.26 E00057.20
	DME	LDY	108.15		N5057.51 E00056.33
Lyneham	NDB	LA	282.0	40	N5130.50 W00200.35
	TACAN	LYE	109.8		N5130.44 W00159.53
Machrihanish	VOR/DME	MAC	116.0		N5525.80 W00539.02
Manchester	Lctr	MCH	428.0	15	N5321.19 W00216.38
	VOR/DME	MCT	113.55		N5321.42 W00215.73
	DME 06L	I-MM	109.50		N5321.19 W00216.38
	DME 24L	I-NN	109.50		N5321.19 W00216.38
Manchester Barton	NDB	BAE	325.0		N5328.14 W00223.23
Manchester Woodford	Lctr	WFD	380.0	15	N5320.26 W00209.50
	DME 25	I-WU	109.15		N5320.26 W00209.50
Mayfield	VOR/DME	MAY	117.90		N5101.03 E00006.96
Midhurst	VOR/DME	MID	114.0		N5103.23 W00037.50
Mildenhall	TACAN	MLD	115.90		N5221.80 E00029.29
Newcastle	VOR/DME	NEW	114.25		N5502.30 W00141.90
	Lctr	NEW	352.0	40	N5503.03 W00138.56
	Lctr	WZ	416.0	10	N5500.40 W00148.43
	DME 07	I-NC	111.50		N5502.22 W00141.35
	DME 25	I-NWC	111.50		N5502.22 W00141.35
New Galloway	NDB	NGY	399.0	35	N5510.65 W00410.11
Newton Point	TACAN	NTP	108.70		N5531.18 W00136.62
Northampton (Sywell)	NDB	NN	378.50	15	N5217.95 W00047.82
Northolt	DME 25	I-NHT	108.55		N5133.18 W00024.53
Norwich	Lctr	NH	371.50	20	N5240.58 E00123.08
	Lctr	NWI	342.50	20	N5240.65 E00117.49
	DME 27	I-NH	110.90		N5240.65 E00116.99
Nottingham	NDB	NOT	430.0	10	N5255.30 W00104.76
Ockham	VOR/DME	OCK	115.30		N5118.30 W00026.83
Odiham	TACAN	ODH	109.60		N5113.97 W00056.90
Ottringham	VOR/DME	OTR	113.90		N5341.90 W00006.21
Oxford	Lctr	OX	367.50	25	N5149.95 W00119.37
(Kidlington)	DME	OX	117.70		N5149.95 W00119.37
Pembrey	TACAN	PEM	116.60		N5143.90 W00421.50
Penzance (Heliport)	NDB	PH	333.0	15	N5007.70 W00531.00
Perth	VOR	PTH	110.40		N5626.55 W00322.11
Plymouth	Lctr	PY	396.50	20	N5025.40 W00406.73
	DME 31	I-PLY	109.50		N5025.40 W00406.71
Pole Hill	VOR/DME	POL	112.1		N5344.63 W00206.20
Prestwick	NDB	PIK	355.0	30	N5530.37 W00434.63
	Lctr	PW	426.0	15	N5532.66 W00440.89

Name	Type	Ident	Freq	Range	Coordinates
Redhill	NDB	RDL	343.0	10	N5112.97 W00008.33
Rochester	NDB	RCH	369.0	10	N5121.23 E00030.22
St Abbs	VOR/DME	SAB	112.50		N5554.45 W00212.38
St Athan	TACAN	SAT	114.80		N5124.38 W00326.09
St Mawgan	NDB	SM	356.50	20	N5026.88 W00459.67
	TACAN	SMG	112.60		N5026.06 W00501.81
Scatsta	Lctr	SS	315.50	25	N6027.58 W00112.90
Scilly Isles (St Mary's)	Lctr	STM	321.0	15	N4954.85 W00617.47
Scotstownhead	NDB	SHD	383.0	80	N5733.55 W00149.03
Seaford	VOR/DME	SFD	117.0		N5045.63 E00007.31
Shawbury	DME	SWB	116.80		N5247.88 W00239.75
Shefield City	Lctr	SMF	333.0	15	N5323.56 W00122.99
	DME 28	I-SFH	111.35		N5323.58 W00122.99
Sherburn-In-Elmet	NDB	SBL	323.0	10	N5347.37 W00112.50
Shobdon	NDB	SH	426.0	20	N5214.68 W00252.55
Shoreham	Lctr	SHM	332.0	10	N5050.13 W00017.73
	DME	SRH	109.95		N5050.17 W00017.60
Sleap	NDB	SLP	382.0	10	N5550.02 W00246.07
Southampton	Lctr	EAS	391.50	15	N5057.30 W00121.36
	VOR/DME	SAM	113.35		N5057.31 W00120.70
	DME 20	I-SN	110.75		N5057.31 W00121.36
Southend	Lctr	SND	362.50	20	N5134.58 E00042.01
	DME 24	I-ND	111.35		N5134.22 E00041.86
Stornoway	NDB	SAY	431.0		N5812.84 W00619.56
	DME	ISV	110.60		N5812.80 W00619.60
	VOR/DME	STN	115.1		N5812.41 W00610.98
Strumble	VOR/DME	STU	113.1		N5159.68 W00502.41
Sumburgh	Lctr	SBH	351.0	25	N5952.94 W00117.69
	VOR/DME	SUM	117.35		N5952.72 W00117.19
	DME 09	SUB	108.50		N5952.89 W00117.72
	DME 27	I-SG	108.50		N5952.89 W00117.72
Swansea	Lctr	SWN	320.50	15	N5136.13 W00403.95
	DME	SWZ	109.20		N5136.21 W00403.91
Talla	NDB	TLA	363.0	25	N5530.16 W00325.83
	VOR/DME	TLA	113.80		N5529.95 W00321.16
Tattenhill	NDB	TNL	327		N5248.88 W00145.93
Teeside	Lctr	TD	347.50	25	N5433.62 W00120.01
	DME 05	I-TSE	108.50		N5430.49 W00125.68
	DME 23	I-TD	108.50		N5430.49 W00125.68
Tiree	VOR/DME	TIR	117.70		N5629.59 W00652.53
Topcliffe	TACAN	TOP	113.70		N5412.34 W00122.70
Trent	VOR/DME	TNT	115.70		N5303.23 W00140.20
Turnberry	VOR/DME	TRN	117.50		N5518.80 W00447.03
Vallafield	TACAN	VFD	114.90		N6045.02 W00055.65
Valley	TACAN	VYL	108.40		N5315.44 W00432.64
Waddington	TACAN	WAD	117.10		N5309.92 W00031.61
Wallasey	VOR/DME	WAL	114.10		N5323.51 W00308.06
Warton	NDB	WTN	337.0	15	N5345.10 W00251.13
	TACAN	WTN	113.20		N5344.42 W00253.56
	DME 26	WQ	109.90		N5344.65 W00252.91
Wattisham	TACAN	WTM	109.30		N5207.31 E00056.42
Welshpool	NDB	WPL	323.0	10	N5237.80 W00309.23
	DME	WPL	115.95		N5237.78 W00309.23
Westcott	NDB	WCO	335.0	30	N5151.18 W00057.75
West Freugh	NDB	WFR	339.0	25	N5451.55 W00456.05
Whitegate	NDB	WHI	368.50	25	N5311.10 W00237.38
Wick	Lctr	WIK	344.0	30	N5826.80 W00303.78
	VOR/DME	WIK	113.60		N5827.53 W00306.02
Wittering	TACAN	WIT	117.60		N5236.48 W00029.92
Woodley	NDB	WOD	352.0	25	N5127.16 W00052.73
Yeovil	Lctr	YVL	343.0	20	N5056.48 W00239.87
	DME	YVL	109.05	25	N5056.45 W00239.20
Yeovilton	TACAN	VLN	111.0		N5100.30 W00238.32

Definitions: PROHIBITED Area (prefix P). Airspace within which the flight of aircraft is prohibited.
RESTRICTED area (prefix R). Airspace within the flight of aircraft is restricted in accordance with certain specified condition.

All prohibited and restricted areas extend upwards from the surface, unless otherwise noted.
# indicates an area where pilots are warned that entry (even if inadvertent) might make the aircraft liable to counter measures. The phrase 'subject to appropriate permission' should be taken to mean that prior written permission must be obtained from the authority listed in the RAC section of the AIP, and the flight must be carried out subject to any conditions contained within such permission.
ALWAYS CHECK PROHIBITED/RESTRICTED AREA INFORMATION BY THE LATEST AIP & NOTAM INFORMATION, AND IF IN DOUBT - STAY OUT!

Identification/ Name	Upper Vertical Limit (AMSL)	Type of restriction	Remarks
R002 Devonport	2000	Restricted	Flight permitted at not less than 1450ft AMSL if making an instrument approach to land on runway 06, or a departure from runway 24, at Plymouth airport. Flight also permitted if taking off or landing at HMS Drake Helicopter Landing Site subject to appropriate permission. Helicopters are permitted to take-off or land at a ship in the Devonport Dockyard subject to appropriate permission.
P047 Winfrith	1000	Prohibited	
R095 Sark	2374	Restricted	Flight not permitted without permission from States Board of Administration, Guernsey
R101 Aldermaston	2400	Restricted	Flight permitted if taking off or landing at the helicopter landing area at Aldermaston, subject to appropriate permission.
R104 Burghfield	2400	Restricted	Flight permitted if taking off or landing at the helicopter landing area at Burghfield, subject to appropriate permission.
R105 Highgrove House	2000	Restricted	Applies only to helicopters and microlight aircraft.
P106 Harwell	2500	Prohibited	
R107 Belmarsh	2000	Restricted	Applies only to helicopters. Flight by helicopter permitted if carrying out an IFR approach from the East to London City airport.
R151 High Down	1500	Restricted	Applies only to helicopters
R152 Bristol	1700	Restricted	Applies only to helicopters. Flight permited within Filton ATZ when under control of Filton ATC.
R204 Long Lartin	2200	Restricted	Applies only to helicopters
R212 Whitemoor	2000	Restricted	Applies only to helicopters
R214 Woodhill	2400	Restricted	Applies only to helicopters.
R311 Capenhurst	2200	Restricted	Flight permitted if taking off or landing at the helicopter landing area at Capenhurst, subject to appropriate permission.
R312 Springfields	2100	Restricted	Flight permitted at not less than 1670ft amsl for the purpose of landing at Blackpool airport. Flight permitted south of a line N5346.46 W00244.54 to N5345.18 W00250.44 for the purpose of landing or taking off at Warton airfield. Flight permitted if taking off or landing at the helicopter landing area at Springfields, subject to appropriate permission.
R313 Scampton	9500	Restricted	Active Mon-Fri 0830-1700 (winter), 0730-1600 (summer) and as notified by NOTAM when Red Arrows are training. Pre-flight information on 01400 261201 ext. 7281 and 01522 720271 ext. 7451/7452. Waddington Radar 127.35
R315 Full Sutton	2000	Restricted	Applies only to helicopters.
R318 Altcourse	1100	Restricted	Applies only to helicopters.
R319 Manchester	1700	Restricted	Applies only to helicopters.
R320 Doncaster	2100	Restricted	Applies only to helicopters.
R321 Wakefield	1600	Restricted	Applies only to helicopters.
R413 Sellafield	2200	Restricted	Flight permitted if taking off or landing at the helicopter landing area at Sellafield, subject to appropriate permission.
P414 Lisburn#	2000	Prohibited	
P417 Omagh#	2500	Prohibited	
P419 Strabane#	2500	Prohibited	
P420 Long Kesh#	2000	Prohibited	

Identification/ Name	Upper Vertical Limit (AMSL)	Type of restriction	Remarks
R421 Belfast#	2000	Restricted	Flight permitted for the purpose of landing or taking off at Belfast/City airfield if the aircraft is under the control of Belfast/City ATC.
P422 Londonderry#	2500	Prohibited	
P424 Armagh#	2500	Prohibited	
P425 Ballykinler#	2000	Prohibited	
R431 Maghaberry#	2000	Restricted	Flight permitted for the purpose of landing or taking off at Belfast/Aldergrove if the aircraft is under the control of Belfast/Aldergrove ATC.
R432 Frankland/Durham	2200	Restricted	Applies only to helicopters.
P433 Cookstown#	2500	Prohibited	
P434 Dungannon#	2500	Prohibited	
P435 Magherafelt#	2500	Prohibited	
P436 South Armagh#	2500	Prohibited	
P438 Enniskillen Town#	2000	Prohibited	
R501 Chapelcross	2400	Restricted	Flight permitted if taking off or landing at the helicopter landing area at Chapelcross, subject to appropriate permission.
P502 Magilligan Camp#	2000	Prohibited	
R503 Ballykelly#	2000	Restricted	Flight permitted if making an instrument approach to Rwy 26 or 08 at Londonderry/Eglinton A/F: or after departing Rwy 26 or 08 whilst maintaining Rwy heading provided that the aircraft is under control of Londonderry/Eglinton ATC.
R504 Shotts	2800	Restricted	Flight permitted by any helicopter operated by or on behalf of a Police Force for any area of the UK
R603 Rosyth	2000	Restricted	Flight permitted within 'Kelty Lane' if approaching to land at, or departing from, Edinburgh airport.
R610A The Highlands	5000	Restricted	Flight permitted outside the hours of the Highlands Restricted Area (HRA) and during Scottish public holidays. Areas *generally* active Mon-Thu 1500-2300 (winter), 1400-2200 (summer). When HRA is active, crossing permission may be possible from Tain Range on 122.75. Entry may also be possible subject to authorisation if requested from the Military Tactical Booking Cell (0800 515544) before the proposed flight.
R610B The Highlands	5000	Restricted	LOWER LIMIT 750ft AMSL. See notes for R610A.
R610C The Highlands	2000	Restricted	See notes for R610A.
R610D The Highlands	2000	Restricted	See notes for R610A.
P611 Coulport/Faslane	2200	Prohibited	
P813 Dounreay	2100	Prohibited	

Tempory Restricted Airspace, Red Arrows Displays, Emergency Restrictions of Flying and Royal Flights

The latest information regarding Temporary Restricted Airspace, Red Arrows displays, Emergency Restrictions of Flying and Royal flights is all available by dialling a specially provided Freephone number. The number is:

0500 354802

Danger areas

Definitions: DANGER area (D). Airspace within which activities dangerous to the flight of aircraft may exist or take place.

DACS (Danger Area Crossing Service).

DAAIS (Danger Area Activity Information Service).

The first frequency given is the primary frequency to be contacted during the hours of operation. Where a second frequency is given , this should be called if contact cannot be established on the first frequency. The second frequency is sometimes a FIR controller frequency. These frequencies often very busy, or even not manned, so you cannot always rely on establishing contact and obtaining a DACS/DAAIS on such a frequency.

All danger areas extend upwards from the surface, unless otherwise noted.

= hours of activity are one hour earlier during the summer period.

ALWAYS CHECK DANGER AREA INFORMATION BY THE LATEST AIP, PRE-FLIGHT INFORMATION BULLETIN & NOTAM INFORMATION. AND IF IN DOUBT - STAY OUT!

Identification/ Name	Upper Limit (AMSL)	Hours of Activity (UTC)	Remarks
D001 Trevose Head	1000	Mon-Thu 0800-2359, Fri 0800-1800#	DACS St. Mawgan App 126.50. DAAIS London Information 124.75
D003 Plymouth	ALT 55000 SFC*	Mon-Thu 0800-2359, Fri 0800-1600# & as notified	DACS Plymouth Radar 121.25, London Information 124.75. Pre-flight information 01752 557550
D004 Plymouth	ALT55000 SFC*	Mon-Thu 0800-2359, Fri 0800-1600# & as notified	DACS Plymouth Radar 121.25, London Information 124.75. Pre-flight information 01752 557550
D006 Falmouth Bay	1500	Mon-Thu 0800-2359, Fri 0800-1600# & as notified	DACS Culdrose App 134.05, or DAAIS London Information 124.75. Pre-flight information 01326 552201
D006A Falmouth Bay	22000	Mon-Thu 0800-2359, Fri 0800-1600# & as notified	DACS Plymouth Radar 121.25, London Information 124.75. Pre-flight information 01326 552201
D007 Fowey Inner	2000	Mon-Thu 0800-2359, Fri 0800-1600# & as notified	DACS Plymouth Radar 121.25 or London Information 124.75. Pre-flight information 01637 872201 ext. 2045/2046
D007A Fowey	22000	Mon-Thu 0800-2359, Fri 0800-1600# & as notified	DACS Plymouth Radar 121.25 or London Information 124.75. Pre-flight information 01752 557550
D007B Fowey	22000	Mon-Thu 0800-2359, Fri 0800-1600# & as notified	As for D007A
D008 Plymouth	ALT 55000	Mon-Thu 0800-2359, Fri 0800-1600# & as notified	As for D007A. Some activities suspended for Concorde on SL1/SL4
D008A Plymouth	ALT 22000	Mon-Thu 0800-2359, Fri 0800-1600 # & as notified	As for D007A
D008B Plymouth	ALT 55000 SFC*	Mon-Thu 0800-2359, Fri 0800-1600 # & as notified	As for D007A
D009 Wembury	22000	Mon-Thu 0800-2359, Fri 0800-1600 # & as notified	As for D007A
D009A Wembury	55000	Mon-Thu 0800-2359, Fri 0800-1600 # & as notified	As for D007A
D011 Dartmoor	10000 OCNL 20000	Mon-Fri 0800-2359# & as notified	SI 1979/1721, SI 1980/949, SI 1980/950
D012 Lyme Bay	18000 OCNL 25000	Mon-Thu 0800-2359#, Fri 0800-1600# & as notified	DACS Portland 124.15 or London Information 124.75. Pre-flight information 01752 557550
D013 Lyme Bay	60000	Mon-Thu 0800-2359#, Fri 0800-1600# & as notified	As D012
D015 Bovington	3600	When notified	DAAIS Bournemouth TWR 125.60
D017 Portland	ALT 22000 ONCL notification to ALT 55000	Mon-Thu 0800-2359#, Fri 0800-1600# & as notified	DACS Portland 124.15 or London Information 124.75. Pre-flight information 01752 557550
D021 Portland	15000	Mon-Thu 0800-2359#, Fri 0800-1600# & as notified	As D017

* Subject to co-ordination procedure above ALT 22000

Identification/ Name	Upper Limit (AMSL)	Hours of Activity (UTC)	Remarks
D023 Portland	ALT 22000 ONCL notification to ALT 55000	Mon-Thu 0800-2359#, Fri 0800-1600# & as notified	As D017
D026 Lulworth	15000	Mon-Fri 0800-2359# & as notified	DAAIS London Information 124.75. Pre-flight information 01752 557550
D031 Portland	15000	Mon-Thu 0800-2359#, Fri 0800-1600# & as notified	DACS Portland 124.15 or London Information 124.75. Pre-flight information 01752 557550
D036 Portland	ALT 19000 ONCL notification to ALT 55000	Mon-Thu 0800-1700#, Fri 0800-1400# & as notified	Pre-flight information 01752 557751
D037 Portland	ALT 55000	Mon-Fri 1000-1800# inclusive & as notified	As D036
D038 Portland	ALT 55000	Mon-Fri 0800-1800# inclusive & as notified	As D036
D039 Portland	ALT 55000	Mon-Fri 0800-1800# inclusive & as notified	As D036
D040 Portland	ALT 22000 ONCL notification to ALT 55000	Mon-Fri 0800-1800# inclusive & as notified	As D036
D044 Lydd Ranges	3200	0800-2359# & as notified	DAAIS Lydd App 120.70 or London Information 124.60
D060 Browndown	ALT 1500	When notified	DAAIS: Solent APP 120.225
D061 Woodbury Common	ALT 1500 SFC	When notified	DAAIS: Exeter App128.150 when open
D110A Braunton Burrows		1000	When notified DAAIS London Information 124.75
D110B Braunton Burrows		3300	When notified DAAIS London Information 124.75
D112 (N) Hartland (North)	10000 OCNL 20000		Mon- Fri 0800-1800# DACS London Information 124.75
D112 (S) Hartland (South)	10000 OCNL 20000		Mon- Fri 0800-1800# DACS London Information 124.75
D113 Castlemartin (W)	15150	Mon-Fri 0800-2359# & as notified	DAAIS London Information 124 75
D114 Castlemartin (E)	10000	When notified Mon-Fri	DAAIS London Information 124.75
D115A Manorbier	27000	Mon-Fri 0830-1700# & as notified	DAAIS London Information 124.75
D115B Manorbier	40000 OCNL 50000	Mon-Fri 0830-1700# & as notified	DAAIS London Information 124.75
D117 Pendine	27000	Mon-Fri 0800-1800# & as notified No firing during public holidays	DAAIS Pembrey Range 122.75 or London Information 124.75
D118 Pembrey	ALT 10000	Mon-Thu 0900-1700# Fri 0900-1400# & as notified	DAAIS Pembrey Range 122.75
	ALT 5000	SR-SS outside main activity ops hrs	DAAIS: not available
D119 Bridgewater Bay	5000	When notified	DAAIS Yeovilton App 127.35 or London Information 124.75
D121 St. Thomas' Head	600	H24	DAAIS Bristol App 128.55 or London Information 124.75
D123 Imber	50000	H24	DACS / DAAIS Salisbury Operaticns 122.75. Pre-flight information 01980 6747˚0 or 674730.
D124 Lavington	As notified up to unlimited	When notified	As D123
D125 Larkhill	50000	H24	As D123

Identification/ Name	Upper Limit (AMSL)	Hours of Activity (UTC)	Remarks
D126 Bulford	1400 OCNL 2500	H24	As D123
D127 Porton	ALT1200 ALT8000 ONCL notification to ALT 12000	0600-1800 daily 1800-0600 daily	DAAIS Boscombe Down Zone 126.70, or London Information 124.75
D128 Everleigh	1400 OCNL 50000	H24	As D123
D129 Weston-On-Green	FL120	H24	DAAIS Brize Radar 134.30
D130 Longmoor	ALT 1500 ALT 2300	H24 When notified Mon-Fri	DAAIS Dunsfold APP 135.175, Farnborough APP 125.25, London Information 124.60. Pre flight information 0204 745 3451
D131 Hankley Common	1400	When notified	DAAIS Farnborough App 125.25 or London Information 124.60
D132 Ash Ranges	As notified up to 2500	When notified	DAAIS: Farnborough APP 125.25 or London Information 124.60
D133 Pirbright	1400 OCNL 2200	0800-2359# & as notified	DAAIS Farnborough App 125.25 or London Information 124.60
D133A Pirbright	1200	0800-2359# & as notified	As D133
D136 Shoeburyness	10000	When notified Mon-Fri 0800-1800#	DAAIS Southend APP 128.95 or London Information 124.60
D138 Shoeburyness	35000 OCNL 60000	Mon-Fri 0600-1800 # & when notified	As D136
D138A Shoeburyness	35000 OCNL 60000	Mon-Fri 0600-1800# & when notified	As D136
D138B Shoeburyness	5000	When notified as D138, but not Sat & Sun	As D136
D139 Fingringhoe	1000 OCNL 2000	H24	
D141 Hythe Ranges	2000	0800-2359# & when notified	DAAIS Lydd Info 120.70 or London Information 124.60
D145 Hullavington	2000	When notified	DAAIS Lyneham Zone 123.40
D146 Yantlet	3000	When notified 0800-1700#	DAAIS Southend APP 128.95
D147 Pontrilas	10000	H24	
D201 Aberporth	Unlimited	Mon-Fri 0800-2300# & as notified	DACS Aberporth Control 133.50, Aberporth Information 122.15, London Military 135.15
D201A Aberporth	Unlimited	Mon-Fri 0800-2300# & as notified	As D201
D201B Aberporth	Unlimited	When notified	As D201
D202 Llanbedr	6000	Mon-Fri 0800-2300# & as notified	DACS Llanbedr Radar 122.50
D203 Sennybridge	23000 OCNL 50000	H24	
D206 Cardington	ALT 6000	Mon-Fri 0400-2259 & as notified	
D207 Holbeach	ALT 23000 ALT 5000	Mon-Thu 0900-1700, Fri 0900-1200#. Sept - April inc. Tue & Thur 1800-2200# & as notified SR-SS outside main activity ops hrs	DAAIS London Information 124.60 DAAIS: not available
D208 Stanford	2500 OCNL 7500	H24	DAAIS Lakenheath Zone 128.90
D211 Swynnerton	As notified up to 2400	When notified	
D213 Kineton	2400	When notified	DAAIS Coventry 119.25
D215 North Luffenham	2400	When notofied	DAAIS Cottesmore App. 130.20
D216 Credenhill	2300 OCNL 150	H24	
D303 Holcombe	2300	When notified	
D304 Upper Hulme	ALT 3500	When notified 0800-1800# occasionaly up to 2100 Oct-Mar inc.	DAAIS: Manchester App 119.40

Identification/ Name	Upper Limit (AMSL)	Hours of Activity (UTC)	Remarks
D305 Beckingham	1500	When notified	
D306 Cowden	ALT 5000	SR-SS	
D307 Donna Nook	ALT 10000	Mon-Thu 0900-1630#;	DAAIS: Donna Nook Range
	ONCL 2300	Fri 0900-1500# Sep-Apr inc.	Control 122.75
		Tue & Thu 1800-2200# & as notified	
	ALT 5000	SR-SS outside main activity ops hrs	DAAIS: not available
D308 Wainfleet	ALT 23000	Mon & Wed 1300-2300#;	DAAIS Wainfleet Range
		Tue & Thurs 0900-1700#;	Control 122.75
		Fri 0900-1500# & as notified Mon-Fri only	
	ALT 5000	SR-SS outside main activity ops hrs	DAAIS: not available
D314 Harpur Hill	2900	Mon-Fri 0800-1900#	DAAIS Manchester App 119.40
D316 Neatishead	ALT55000	Mon-Fri SR to SS & when notified	DACS London Radar
	ALT 5000		135.275. Pre-flight information RAF Neatishead 01692 630930 Ext.7442
D317 Neatishead	ALT 55000	Mon-Fri SR to SS & when notified	As D316
	ALT 5000		
D401 Ballykinier	3200	0800-2359# daily	
D402A Luce Bay (N)	3000 OCNL	Mon-Thurs 0800-2230#; Fri 0800-1630#	DACS West Freugh APP 130.05 or Scottish
	23000	& as notified	Mil via Scottish Information 119.875
D402B Luce Bay (N)	3000 OCNL	When notified	DACS at & below FL245 West Freugh APP
	23000		130.05 or Scottish Mil via Scottish Information 119.875
D402C Luce Bay (N)	4000	Mon-Fri 0730-1530#.	DACS West Freugh APP 130.05
D403 Luce Bay	35000	Mon-Thu 0900-2230#; Fri 0900-1630#	As D402B
		& as notified	
D403A Luce Bay	3000	H24	DACS West Freugh APP 130.05
D405 Kirkcudbright	15000 OCNL	Mon-Fri 0800-2359# & when notified	DACS West Freugh APP 130.05 or Kirkcudbright Range 122.10
	50000		
D405A Kirkcudbright	1000	Mon-Fri 0800-2359#	as for D405
D406 Eskmeals	50000 OCNL	Sep-Mar: Mon-Fri 0800-1700;	DAAIS London Information 125.475
	80000	Apr-Aug: Mon-Fri 0700-1900#	
		& as notified	
D406B Eskmeals	50000 OCNL	When notified	DAAIS London Information 125.475
	80000		
D406C Eskmeals	50000	When notified	DACS Eskmeals Range 122.75
D407 Warcop	10000 OCNL	0900-1700# daily	DAAIS Pennine Radar 128.675
	13500		
D407A Warcop	2500	Tue, Wed, Thurs & Sat 1800-0200#	DAAIS Pennine Radar 128.675
D408 Feldom	ALT 2500 notification to ALT 5600	Tue-Sun 0830-1630# & as notified	DAAIS Leeming APP 127.75 or London Information 125.475
D409 Catterick	ALT 3400	When notified	DAAIS Leeming APP 127.75 or London Information 125.475
D410 Strensall	1000	When notified 0800-1800#	
D411 Portpatrick Wigtownshire	1000	Mon-Fri 0800-1630# & as notified	DACS West Freugh APP 130.05 or DAAIS Scottish Information 119.875
D412 Staxton	10000	Mon-Fri 0830-1630# when notified	DAAIS London Information 125 475
D441 Ellington Banks	2400	When notified Mon-Sat 0900-1700	DAAIS Linton APP 129.15
D442 Bellerby	ALT 3000	H24	
D505 Magilligan	ALT 2000 notification to ALT 6500	0800-2359# daily	
D508 Ridsdale	4100	Mon-Fri 0800-1700# & as notified	DACS Newcastle APP 124.375. Pre-flight information Newcastle ATC 0191 286 0966 Ext. 3251

Identification/ Name	Upper Limit (AMSL)	Hours of Activity (UTC)	Remarks
D509 Campbeltown	As notified up to ALT 55000	When notified	DAAIS at & below FL245 West Freugh APP 130.05 or Scottish Information 119.875
D510 Spadeadam	ALT 5500 notification to ALT 18000	Mon-Thurs 0900-1700#, Fri 0900-1600# & as notified	DAAIS Newcastle APP 124.375 & Carlisle TWR 123.60. DACS Spadeadam 122.10
D512 Otterburn	20000 OCNL 25000	H24	DAAIS Scottish Information 119.875
D512A Otterburn	22000	When notified	As D512
D513 Druridge Bay	10000	When notified Mon-Fri 0830-1630#	As D512
D513A Druridge Bay	55000	When notified	as D512
D513B Drurudge Bay	55000	When notified	as D512
D601 Garelochhead	4000	0800-2359# daily & as notified	
D602 Cultybraggan (Tighnablair)	2500	When notified	
D604 Barry Buddon	1500 OCNL 9000	H24	DAAIS Leuchars APP 126.50
D607 Firth of Forth (Middle)	As notified to 55000	When notified	DAAIS Scottish Information 119.875
D608 Firth of Forth (Outer)	As notified to 55000	When notified	DAAIS Scottish Information 119.875
D609 St. Andrews	1000 OCNL 55000	H24	DAAIS Scottish Information 119.875
D701 Hebrides	30000	Mon-Fri 1000-1800# & as notified.	DAAIS Scottish Information 127.275. When D701A is activated, D701 becomes an integral part of it & is activated to the same altitude.
D701A Hebrides	AS notified up to unlimited	When notified	As D701
D701B Hebrides	AS notified up to unlimited	When notified	As D701
D701C Hebrides	10000 OCNL 15000	When notified	As D701
D701D Hebrides	AS notified up to unlimited	When notified	As D701
D701E Hebrides	10000	When notified Mon-Fri 1630-SS, Sat 1300-SS#	DAAIS Scottish Information 127.275. Activated after normal civilian aircraft movements at Benbecula have ceased.
D702 Fort George	2100	0800-1600# daily & as notified	DAAIS Inverness Tower 122.60 or Scottish Information 126.25
D703 Tain	ALT 15000	Mon & Thu 0900-1700#;	ACFT visiting Dornoch or Fearn AD during range opening Hrs Conatct TainRange 122.750 before entry
	Notification to 5000	Tue & Wed 0900-2359#; SR-SS outside main ops hours	DAAIS not avl.
D708 Rosehearty	11000 OCNL 22000	Mon-Fri 0900-1700# Tue & Wed 2100-2259 May-Aug & as notified	DAAIS Rosehearty Range 122.75
D710 Raasay	1500	When notified Mon-Sat SR-SS	DAAIS Scottish Information 127.275
D801 Cape Wrath (North West)	As notified up to ALT 55000	When notified	DAAIS Scottish Information 126.25
D802 Cape Wrath (South East)	As notified up to ALT 55000	When notified	As D801
D803 Garvie Island	As notified up to ALT 40000	When notified Mon-Fri 0800-1800#	As D801
D807 Moray Firth	1500	Mon-Fri 0700-2359# & as notified	DAAIS Lossiemouth 119.35
D809(N) Moray Firth (North)	As notified up to ALT 55000	When notified	DAAIS Scottish Information 126.50
D809(C) Moray Firth (Central)	As notified up to ALT55000	When notified	As D809(N)
D809(S) Moray Firth (South)	As notified up to ALT 55000	When notified	As D809(N)

All hours are Local

Culdrose
Vertical limits:	Surface to 5800ft ALT
Activity:	Considerable helicopter & fixed-wing activity. Night operations may take place with ACFT using reduced navigation/anti-collision lights.
Active Times:	Peak activity Mon-Thur 0830-1700, Fri 0830-1630
Contact Frequencies:	Culdrose LARS 134.05

Kinloss/Lossiemouth
Vertical limits:	Surface to FL150
Activity:	Intensive military activity
Active Times:	Peak activity Mon-Thur 0800-2359, Fri 0800-1800
Contact Frequencies:	Lossiemouth LARS 119.35

Lincolnshire
Vertical limits:	2500ft ALT to FL180
Activity:	Considerable military flight training
Active Times:	Peak activity Mon-Fri 0700-1600
Contact Frequencies:	Waddington LARS 127.35
	Cottesmore LARS 130.20
	Coningsby LARS 120.80

Oxford
Vertical limits:	Surface to 5000ft ALT
Activity:	Intensive military and civilian activity from the many aerodromes in this area, heavy jet, training, instrument etc.
Active Times:	Permanently active
Contact Frequencies:	Brize Radar LARS 134.30

Spadeadam
Vertical limits:	Surface to 4500ft ALT
Activity:	Military activity associated with electronic warfare training range D510
Active Times:	Peak activity Mon-Thur 0900-1700, Fri 0900-1600 and as notified
Contact Frequencies:	DACS: Spadeadam APP122.10 hrs as above
	DAAIS: Newcastle LARS 124.375 H24
	Carlisle APP 123.60

Shawbury
Vertical limits:	Surface to FL70
Activity:	Intensive instrument training, general handling and training by military helicopters and fixed-wing ACFT. Night operations may take place with ACFT using reduced navigation/anti-collision lights.
Active Times:	Permanently active Mon-Thu 0700-0130, Fri 0700-1700
Contact Frequencies:	Shawbury LARS 120.775

Vale of York
Vertical limits:	Surface to FL200
Activity:	Considerable military flight training
Active Times:	Peak activity Mon-Thur 0700-2359, Fri 0700-1600
Contact Frequencies:	Leeming LARS 127.75
	Linton LARS 129.15

Valley
Vertical limits:	2000ft to 6000ft AMSL
Activity:	Considerable flight training
Active Times:	Peak activity Mon-Thur 0800-1800, Fri 0800-1700
Contact Frequencies:	Valley LARS 134.35
	London Flight Info. 124.75

Wash
Vertical limits:	Surface to FL50
Activity:	Holding patterns associated with Danger Areas D207 & D308
Active Times:	Permanently active Monday - Friday
Contact Frequencies:	Waddington LARS 127.35 H24
	Cottesmore LARS 130.20
	Marham LARS 124.15

Yeovilton (N)
Vertical limits:	2000ft to 5000ft ALT
Activity:	Intense helicopter instrument flying training. Night operations may take place with ACFT using reduced navigation/anti-collision lights.
Active Times:	Peak activity Mon-Thur 0800-1730, Fri 0800-1600
Contact Frequencies:	Yeovilton LARS 127.35

Yeovilton (S)
Vertical limits	Surface to 6000ft ALT
Activity	Intense helicopter instrument flying training. Night operations may take place with ACFT using reduced navigation/anti-collision lights.
Active Times	Mon-Thu 0830-1700, Fri 0830-1600
Contact Frequencies	Yeovilton LAS 127.35
	Plymouth Military Radar 124.15

Warton Radar
	Advisory Service Area
Vertical limits:	5000ft regional QNH to FL195 not provided below 5000ft regional QNH
Availability:	Mon-Fri 0730-2000 (Winter) 0630-1900 (Summer)
Contact Frequencies	Warton Radar 129.525
	Note: Warton Radar is now the primary service provider, as Manchester no longer has the capacity to provide this service. Provision of the Warton LARS service is unaffected other than frequency change.

Northern Radar
	Advisory Service Area
Vertical limits:	FL100 to FL245
Availability:	Scottish Control 0730-2200 (winter); 0630-2100 (summer)
	Pennine Radar 0700-2100 (winter); 0600-2000 (summer)
Contact Frequencies	
	Scottish Control 124.50 (North of ADR W911D)
	Pennine Radar 128.675 (South of ADR W911D)

Boscombe Down
	Advisory Radio Area
Vertical limits:	FL50 to FL245, but excluding controlled airspace.
Activity:	Considerable test flight activity. Such flights often have limited manoeuvrability and may not be able to comply with the rules of the air.
Hours of operation:	
	Mon-Thu 0830-1700, Fri 0830-1600 (summer)
	Mon-Thu 0930-1830, Fri 1030-0930 (winter)
Contact Frequencies:	
	Boscombe LARS 126.70
	Bournemouth APP 119.625
	Bristol LARS 128.55
	Brize LARS 134.30
	Cardiff LARS 125.85
	Exeter LARS 128.15
	Farnborough LARS 125.25
	Filton LARS 122.725
	London Radar 135.15
	Lyneham APP 123.40
	Middle Wallop APP 118.275
	Plymouth LARS 121.25
	Portland LARS 124.15
	Southampton APP 128.85
	Yeovilton LARS 127.35

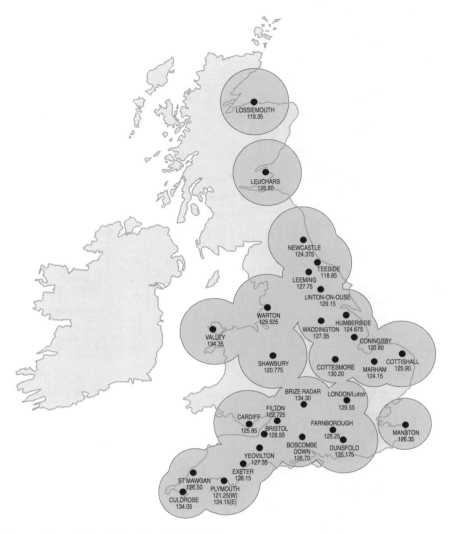

Lower Airspace Radar Service (LARS) Units

Even outside the published hours, pilots should attempt to contact the LARS unit in case it is open beyond normal hours. Some LARS units (mostly military ones) may close for up to a week during holiday periods - see Pre-flight Information Bulletins.

LARS	Contact Frequency	ATC Hours (Local)
Boscombe Down	Boscombe Zone 126.70	Mon-Thur 0830-1700; Fri 0830-1600
Bristol	Bristol APP 128.55	H24
Brize Norton	Brize 134.30	H24
Cardiff	Cardiff APP 125.85	H24
Coltishall	Coltishall 125.90	Mon-Thur 0830-1730, Fri 0830-1700
Coningsby	Coningsby 120.80	Mon-Fri 0800-1700
Cottesmore	Cottesmore 130.20	Mon-Fri 0800-1700

Culdrose	Culdrose 134.05	Mon-Thur 0830-1700 or SS, Fri 0830-1400 or SS
Dunfold	Dunsfold APP 135.175	Mon-Fri 0800-1830 other times may be arranged
Exeter	Exeter APP 128.15	Available during times of watch. See Airfield entry
Farnborough	Farnborough 125.25	Mon-Fri (not PH) 0700-2000 Summer 1hr earlier
Filton	Filton APP 122.725	Mon-Fri 0645-2030. Service north of River Avon
Humberside	Humberside APP 124.675	Mon-Fri 0630-2145, Sat 0630-1830, Sun 0630-1945 (Winter) Sun-Fri 0530-2045, Sat 0530-1900 (Summer)
Leeming	Leeming 127.75	Mon-Thur 0800-2359, Fri 0800-1800; Sat & Sun, PH 0900-1715
Leuchars	Leuchars 126.50	H24
Linton-On-Ouse	Linton 129.15	Mon-Thur 0745-1715; Fri 0745-1700
Lossiemouth	Lossiemouth 119.35	Mon-Thur 0800-1800; Fri 0800-1700
London Luton	Luton APP 129.55	H24
Manston	Manston 126.35	Mon-Fri 0800-1800, Sat-Sun 0900-1700
Marham	Marham 124.15	Mon-Thur 0800-2359; Fri 0800-1800
Newcastle	Newcastle APP 124.375	H24
Plymouth*	Plymouth MIL 121.25	Mon-Thu 0800-1700, Fri 0830-1400
St Mawgan	St Mawgan 126.50	Mon-Thur 0700-2359; Fri-Sun 0650-2200
Shawbury	Shawbury 120.775	Mon-Fri 0800-1700
Teeside	Teeside APP 118.85	Mon-Sat 0630-2200.Sun 0645-2200 (Winter) Mon-Sat 0530-2100 Sun 0545-2100 (Summer) And by arrangement
Valley	Valley 134.35	Mon-Thur 0800-2359, Fri 0800-1800
Waddington	Waddington 127.35	H24
Warton	Warton 1249.525	Mon-Fri 0800-1700
Yeovilton	Yeovilton 127.35	Mon-Thur 0830-1700, Fri 0830-1600

*ACFT operating E of western edge of Awy A25 call Plymouth Military 124.15.
ACFT operating W of western edge of Awy A25 call Plymouth military 121.25

Military Aerodrome Traffic Zone (MATZ) Units

If planning to enter or pass close to a MATZ, pilots are strongly advised to call on the appropiate frequency, even outside the notified hours of operation. Some MATZs may close for up to a week during holiday periods - see Pre-flight Information Bulletins.

ATZ	Contact Frequency	ATC Hours (local)
Barkston Heath	Cranwell 119.375	Mon-Fri 0730-1730, summer 1hr earlier
Benson	Benson 120.90	H24
Boscombe Down	Boscombe Zone 126.70	H24
Church Fenton	Fenton 126.50	Mon-Thu H24, Fri-Sun 0700-2359. summer 1hr earlier
Colitishall	Colitishall 125.90	H24
Coningsby	Coningsby 120.80	H24
Cottesmore	Cottesmore 130.20	H24
Cranwell	Cranwell 119.375	H24
Culdrose	Culdrose 134.05	H24
Dishforth	Leeming 127.75	H24
Fairford	Brize Radar 119.00	H24
Honington	Lakenheath 128.90	H24
Kinloss	Lossiemouth 119.35	H24
Lakenheath	Lakenheath 128.90	H24
Leeming	Leeming 127.75	H24
Leuchars	Leuchars 126.50	H24
Linton-On-Ouse	Linton 129.15	Mon-Thur H24, Fri-Sun 0700-2359. summer 1hr earlier
Lossiemouth	Lossiemouth 119.35	H24
Marham	Marham 124.15	H24
Merryfield	Merryfield Tower 122.10	Mon-Fri 0700-1700 summer 1hr earlier
Middle Wallop	Boscombe Zone 126.70	H24
Mildenhall	Lakenheath 128.90	H24
Mona	Valley 134.35	H24
Odiham	Farnborough 125.25	H24
Predannack	Culdrose 134.05	H24
St Mawgan	ATC 126.50, A/C landing 125.550	H24
Shawbury	Shawbury 120.775	H24
Ternhill	Shawbury 120.775	H24
Topcliffe	Leeming 127.75	H24
Valley	Valley 134.35	H24
Waddington	Waddington 127.35	H24
Wattisham	Wattisham 125.80	H24
West Freugh	West Freugh 130.05	H24
Wittering	Cottesmore 130.20	H24
Yeovilton	Yeovilton 127.35	H24

DATE	EGAA Belfast Aldergrove SR/SS	EGBB Birmingham SR/SS	EGPF Glasgow SR/SS	EGLL London Heathrow SR/SS	EGCC Manchester SR/SS	EGSH Norwich SR/SS	EGHD Plymouth SR/SS	EGPB Sumburgh SR/SS
Jan 3	0847/1611	0817/1605	0847/1556	0807/1605	0824/1603	0806/1552	0816/1625	0905/1513
Jan 15	0839/1629	0810/1622	0838/1615	0801/1621	0816/1620	0759/1609	0811/1640	0852/1537
Feb 1	0813/1704	0747/1654	0811/1652	0739/1652	0752/1653	0726/1641	0750/1710	0817/1621
Feb 15	0749/1729	0726/1717	0746/1718	0718/1714	0730/1717	0714/1704	0730/1731	0746/1653
Mar 1	0708/1806	0647/1750	0702/1757	0641/1746	0650/1751	0635/1738	0655/1802	0659/1739
Mar 15	0638/1829	0620/1812	0631/1822	0614/1807	0622/1814	0608/1800	0629/1822	0620/1808
Apr 1	0553/1904	0538/1843	0544/1858	0533/1837	0539/1847	0525/1832	0549/1851	0526/1852
Apr 15	0523/1927	0510/1904	0513/1923	0507/1857	0510/1908	0458/1853	0523/1910	0450/1321
May 1	0442/2001	0433/1935	0431/1959	0431/1927	0431/1941	0420/1924	0448/1938	0359/2006
May 15	0419/2023	0411/1955	0406/2022	0410/1946	0410/2001	0358/1944	0429/1956	0329/2035
June 1	0355/2051	0350/2020	0340/2052	0350/2010	0347/2027	0336/2009	0409/2019	0254/2112
June 15	0347/2102	0343/2030	0332/2104	0344/2019	0340/2038	0330/2019	0404/2028	0248/2127
July 1	0353/2104	0348/2032	0337/2105	0349/2021	0348/2039	0335/2021	0409/2030	0249/2128
July 15	0406/2054	0400/2024	0351/2054	0400/2014	0357/2031	0347/2013	0420/2023	0306/2113
Aug 1	0434/2026	0425/1959	0421/2025	0424/1940	0424/2005	0412/1948	0443/2001	0345/2035
Aug 15	0455/2002	0445/1937	0444/1959	0443/1929	0444/1942	0432/1925	0501/1940	0413/2004
Sept 1	0529/1905	0525/1844	0530/1900	0521/1838	0526/1847	0512/1832	0537/1851	0510/1854
Sept 15	0601/1835	0545/1816	0554/1828	0540/1810	0546/1818	0533/1804	0555/1824	0538/1818
Oct 1	0635/1749	0615/1733	0629/1741	0609/1729	0618/1735	0603/1721	0623/1744	0621/1724
Oct 15	0558/1720	0631/1711	0653/1711	0630/1703	0640/1707	0625/1654	0642/1719	0650/1649
Nov 1	0734/1641	0709/1631	0731/1630	0701/1628	0714/1630	0658/1618	0713/1646	0735/1600
Nov 15	0758/1620	0731/1612	0756/1607	0722/1610	0736/1610	0720/1559	U/33/1629	0806/1533
Dec 1	0829/1601	0759/1555	0829/1546	0749/1554	0806/1552	0748/1541	0759/1614	0845/1505
Dec 15	0842/1558	0812/1553	0843/1543	0802/1553	0819/1550	0801/1540	0811/1613	0902/1459

Airfields in BLOCK CAPITALS are in the main listing with an airfield diagram. Airfields in Lower Case are in the Private Airfields text listing.

ABERDEEN
ABERPORTH
Aboyne
ALDERNEY
Allensmore
ANDREWSFIELD
ASHCROFT FARM (Bryan's Landings)
AUDLEY END
AYLESBURY(Thame)
BADMINTON
BAGBY (Thirsk)
Ballykelly
Barkston Heath
BARRA
BARROW (Walney Island)
BATTLEFLAT
BAXTERELY
BECCLES
BEDFORD (Castle Mill)
BELFAST (Aldergrove)
BELFAST (City)
BELLARENA
BELLE VUE
BEMBRIDGE
BENBECULA
BENSON
BEVERLEY (Linley Hill)
BIDFORD
BIGGIN HILL
BIRMINGHAM
BLACKBUSHE
BLACKPOOL
BODMIN
Boones Farm (High Garrett)
BOSCOMBE DOWN
BOSTON
BOUGHTON
BOURN
BOURNEMOUTH (Hurn)
BREIGHTON
Bridgnorth (Ditton Priors)
BRIMPTON (Wasing lower farm)
BRISTOL
BRIZE NORTON
Bromsgrove (Stoney Farm)
Brooklands
BROUGH
BRUNTINGTHORPE
Buckingham (Thornborough Grounds)
BUTE
CAERNARFON
CAMBRIDGE
CAMPBELTOWN
Camphill
CARDIFF
CARK (Grange-over-Sands)
CARLISLE

Castletown
Challock
CHARTERHALL
CHATTERIS (Mt.Pleasant, Stonea, ASI airfield)
CHICHESTER (Goodwood)
CHILBOLTON (Stonefield Park)
Chiltern Park
CHIRK
CHURCH FENTON
CITY OF DERRY (Londonderry Eglinton)
CLACTON
CLENCH COMMON
Clipgate (Barham)
CLUTTON HILL FARM
COAL ASTON
COLERNE
Coll (Ballard)
COLONSAY (Machrins)
COLTISHALL
COMPTON ABBAS
CONINGSBY
COSFORD
COTTERED
Cottesmore
COVENTRY
CRANFIELD
CRANWELL
CROFT FARM (Defford)
CROMER (Northrepps)
CROWFIELD
CROWLAND (Spalding)
CULDROSE
CUMBERNAULD
CURROCK HILL
DAVIDSTOW MOOR
DEANLAND (Lewes)
DEENETHORPE
DENHAM
DERBY
DISHFORTH
Donemana
DORNOCH
Draycott (Swindon)
DRAYTON ST.LEONARDS
DUNDEE
DUNKESWELL
DUNNYVADEN
DUNSFOLD
Dunstable Downs
DUXFORD
EAGLESCOTT
EARLS COLNE
EAST FORTUNE
EAST MIDLANDS
East Winch
Eastbach Farm
Easton Maudit
EDAY
EDINBURGH
Eggesford
ELMSETT

ELSTREE
ENNISKILLEN (St Angelo)
ENSTONE
Errol
ESHOTT
EXETER
FADMOOR (Moors National Park)
FAIR ISLE
Fairford
FAIROAKS
Fakenham (Manor Farm)
FARNBOROUGH
FARTHING CORNER
FARWAY COMMON
Fearn
FELTHORPE
FENLAND
FESHIEBRIDGE (Aviemore)
FETLAR
FIFE (Glenrothes)
FILTON
FINMERE
FINNINGLEY VILLAGE (Ninescores Farm)
FISHBURN
Flotta
Folkestone (Lyminge)
FOULA
FOWLMERE
FULL SUTTON
GARSTON FARM
GERPINS FARM
GIGHA ISLAND
GLASGOW
GLENFORSA (Mull)
Glenormiston (Innerleithen)
GLOUCESTERSHIRE
GREAT MASSINGHAM
GREAT ORTON (Carlisle)
Green Farm
GREENLANDS (Emlyn's Field)
GUERNSEY
HALFPENNY GREEN
HALTON
HANLEY (Hanley William)
Hanworth (Gunton Park)
HARDWICK
HAVERFORDWEST
HAWARDEN
HAXEY
HAYDOCK PARK (Newton le Willows)
HENLOW
HENSTRIDGE
HERMITAGE
HINTON IN THE HEDGES
Hook
Hougham
HUCKNALL
HUDDERSFIELD (Crosland Moor)
Hull (Hill Farm)
HULL (Mt.Airy)
HUMBERSIDE

HUSBANDS BOSWORTH (Rugby)
INSCH
INVERNESS
ISLAY
ISLE OF MAN (Ronaldsway)
ISLE OF SKYE (Broadford)
ISLE OF WIGHT (Sandown)
JERSEY
KEMBLE
Kimbolton (Huntingdon)
(Stow Longa)
Kings Lynn (Tilney St. Lawrence)
KINGSMUIR
KINLOSS
KIRKBRIDE
KIRKBYMOORSIDE
Kirkcudbright (Plunton)
KIRKWALL
KNOCKIN (Oswestry)
LAINDON
Lakenheath
LAMB HOLM
LAMBLEY (Jericho Farm)
LANDS END (St Just)
Lane Farm (Hay-on-Wye)
LANGAR
Langham
LASHAM
LASHENDEN (Headcorn)
LEDBURY (Velcourt)
LEEDS BRADFORD
LEEMING
Lee-on-solent
LEICESTER
LERWICK (Tingwall)
LEUCHARS
LINTON-ON-OUSE
LITTLE GRANSDEN
LITTLE SNORING
LITTLE STAUGHTON
LIVERPOOL
LLANBEDR
LONDON (City)
LONDON (Gatwick)
LONDON (Heathrow)
LONDON (Luton)
LONDON (Stansted)
LONG ACRES FARM
LONG MARSTON
LONG STRATTON
LOSSIEMOUTH
LOUTH (Hall Farm)
LOUTH (Stewton)
LUDHAM
LUNDY ISLAND
LYDD
Lymm Dam
LYNEHAM
MANCHESTER
MANCHESTER (Barton)
MANCHESTER (Woodford)
MANSTON

MARHAM
MARSHLAND (Wisbech)
MAYPOLE
Melbourne (Melrose Farm)
Merryfield
MIDDLE WALLOP
Mildenhall
MILSON (Cleobury Mortimer)
MONA
MONEWDEN (Cherry Tree Farm)
Montrose
Moorlands
MOVENIS
MULLAGHMORE
NAYLAND
NETHERAVON
NETHERTHORPE
Newark (Beeches Farm)
NEWBURY (Racecourse)
NEWCASTLE
NEWMARKET HEATH
NEWNHAM (Nr. Baldock Herts)
NEWTON
Newton Peveril Farm
NEWTOWNARDS
NORTH COATES
NORTH RONALDSAY
NORTH WEALD
NORTHAMPTON (Sywell)
NORTHOLT
NORWICH
NOTTINGHAM
Nuthampstead (Royston)
Nympsfield (Stroud)
Oaklands Farm (Oxford)
OAKSEY PARK
OBAN (North Connel)
ODIHAM
OLD BUCKENHAM
OLD SARUM
OTHERTON
OUT SKERRIES
OXFORD
PANSHANGER
PAPA STOUR
PAPA WESTRAY
Park Farm (Eaton Bray)
PEMBREY
PERRANPORTH
PERTH (Scone)
PETERBOROUGH (Conington)
PETERBOROUGH (Sibson)
PETERLEE
PLOCKTON
PLYMOUTH (City)
POCKLINGTON
POPHAM
Portmoak (Kinross)
Predannack
PRESTWICK
RAYNE HALL FARM (Braintree)
REDHILL

Redlands (Swindon)
REDNAL (Shropshire)
RETFORD (Gamston)
RHEDYN COCH
(Emlyn's other field)
Rhigos
Rhos-Y-Gilwen Farm
ROCHESTER
RODDIGE
Rosemarket
ROSSENDALE (Lumb)
Rush Green (Hitchin)
Rushetts Farm
ST ATHAN
ST MAWGAN (Newquay)
St.MICHAELS
St.Neots (Honeydon)
SACKVILLE LODGE (Riseley)
SALTBY
SANDAY
Sandhill Farm
SANDTOFT
SCATSTA
SCILLY ISLES (St Mary's)
SEETHING
Seighford
SHAWBURY
SHEFFIELD (City)
Shennington (Edgehill)
Shepton Mallett
(Lower Withial Farm)
SHERBURN-IN-ELMET
SHOBDON
SHOREHAM
SHOTTESWELL (Banbury)
SHUTTLEWORTH (Old Warden)
SITTLES FARM
SKEGNESS (Water Leisure Park)
SLEAP
Sollas
SOUTH BURLINGHAM
SOUTHAMPTON (Eastleigh)
SOUTHEND
Spanhoe
STAPLEFORD
STOKE AIRFIELD
Stones Farm
STORNOWAY
STRATHALLAN
Strathaven
Stretton
STRONSAY
STRUBBY
STUBTON PARK
STURGATE
SUMBURGH
Sutton Bank (Thirsk)
SUTTON MEADOWS
SWANSEA
SWANTON MORLEY
TATENHILL
TEESSIDE
Ternhill

THORNE (Doncaster)
Thorpe-Le-Soken
THRUXTON
THURROCK (Orsett)
Tibbenham
TIBBENHAM (Priory Farm)
TILSTOCK
TIREE
TOP FARM
TOPCLIFFE
TRURO
TURWESTON
UNST
Upavon
Vallance-by-Ways
VALLEY
WADDINGTON
Wadswick Strip
Waits Farm (Sudbury)
WALTON WOOD
WARTON
WATTISHAM
WELLESBOURNE MOUNTFORD
WELSHPOOL
WEST FREUGH
WESTBURY-SUB-MENDIP
Weston Zoyland
Weston-on-the-Green
WESTRAY
WEYBOURNE (Muckleburgh)
WHALSAY
WHARF FARM
Whitby (Egton)
WHITERASHES
WHITE WALTHAM
WICK
WICKENBY (Lincoln)
Wigtown
Winfield (Berwick-on-Tweed)
Wing Farm (Warminster)
WITTERING
WOMBLETON (Pickering)
WOODVALE
Wroughton
WYCOMBE AIR PARK (Booker)
WYTON
YEARBY
YEOVIL (Westland)
YEOVILTON
YORK (Rufforth)

Foreign Airfields
CALAIS-DUNKIRK
DINARD (Pleurtuit-St Malo)
DUBLIN
LA ROCHELLE (Laleu)
LE TOUQUET (Paris-Plage)
OSTEND

For	See
Aldergrove	Belfast
Aviemore	Feshiebridge
Barton	Manchester
Bembridge	Isle of Wight
Bigglewade	Shuttleworth
Bristol Filton	Filton
Booker	Wycombe Air Park
Conington	Peterborough
Crosland Moor	Huddersfield
Eglinton	City of Derry
Gamston	Retford
Glenrothes	Fife
Goodwood	Chichester
Headcorn	Lashenden
Hurn	Bournemouth
Londonderry	City of Derry
Linley Hill	Beverley
Luton	London
Machrinhanish	Campbeltown
Mull	Glenforsa
Newquay	St Mawgan
Old Warden	Shuttleworth
Oswestry	Knockin
Ronaldsway	Isle of Man
Rufforth	York
Sandown	Isle of Wight
Sibson	Peterborough
Stansted	London
Staverton	Gloucestershire
Sywell	Northampton
Walney Island	Barrow
Woodford	Manchester

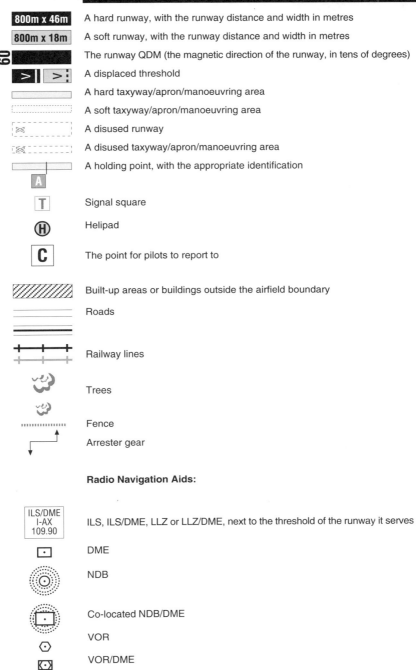

800m x 46m	A hard runway, with the runway distance and width in metres
800m x 18m	A soft runway, with the runway distance and width in metres
60	The runway QDM (the magnetic direction of the runway, in tens of degrees)
> | >	A displaced threshold
	A hard taxyway/apron/manoeuvring area
	A soft taxyway/apron/manoeuvring area
	A disused runway
	A disused taxyway/apron/manoeuvring area
A	A holding point, with the appropriate identification
T	Signal square
(H)	Helipad
C	The point for pilots to report to
	Built-up areas or buildings outside the airfield boundary
	Roads
	Railway lines
	Trees
	Fence
	Arrester gear

Radio Navigation Aids:

ILS/DME I-AX 109.90	ILS, ILS/DME, LLZ or LLZ/DME, next to the threshold of the runway it serves
	DME
	NDB
	Co-located NDB/DME
	VOR
	VOR/DME
	TACAN

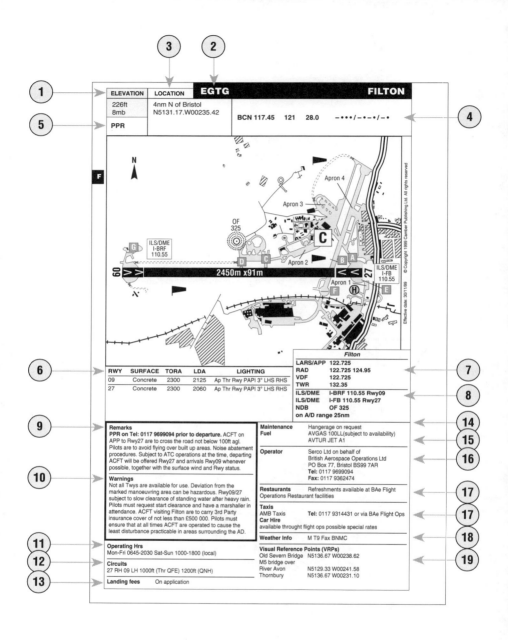

ELEVATION	**LOCATION**
226ft	4nm N of Bristol
8mb	N5131.17.W00235.42
PPR	

EGTG **FILTON**

BCN 117.45   121   28.0   — • • • / — • — • / — •

N

OF 325

ILS/DME
I-BRF
110.55

60

2450m x91m

27

ILS/DME
I-FB
110.55

Apron 4
Apron 3
Apron 2
Apron 1

Filton

LARS/APP	122.725
RAD	122.725 124.95
VDF	122.725
TWR	132.35
ILS/DME	I-BRF 110.55 Rwy09
ILS/DME	I-FB 110.55 Rwy27
NDB	OF 325
on A/D range 25nm	

RWY	SURFACE	TORA	LDA	LIGHTING
09	Concrete	2300	2125	Ap Thr Rwy PAPI 3° LHS RHS
27	Concrete	2300	2060	Ap Thr Rwy PAPI 3° LHS RHS

Remarks
PPR on Tel: 0117 9699094 prior to departure. ACFT on APP to Rwy27 are to cross the road not below 100ft agl. Pilots are to avoid flying over built up areas. Noise abatement procedures. Subject to ATC operations at the time, departing ACFT will be offered Rwy27 and arrivals Rwy09 whenever possible, together with the surface wind and Rwy status.

Warnings
Not all Twys are available for use. Deviation from the marked manoeuvring area can be hazardous. Rwy09/27 subject to slow clearance of standing water after heavy rain. Pilots must request start clearance and have a marshaller in attendance. ACFT visiting Filton are to carry 3rd Party insurance cover of not less than £500 000. Pilots must ensure that at all times ACFT are operated to cause the least disturbance practicable in areas surrounding the AD.

Operating Hrs
Mon-Fri 0645-2030 Sat-Sun 1000-1800 (local)

Circuits
27 RH 09 LH 1000ft (Thr QFE) 1200ft (QNH)

Landing fees   On application

Maintenance	Hangerage on request
Fuel	AVGAS 100LL(subject to availability)
	AVTUR JET A1
Operator	Serco Ltd on behalf of
	British Aerospace Operations Ltd
	PO Box 77, Bristol BS99 7AR
	Tel: 0117 9699094
	Fax: 0117 9362474
Restaurants	Refreshments available at BAe Flight
Operations Restaurant facilities	
Taxis	
AMB Taxis	**Tel:** 0117 9314431 or via BAe Flight Ops
Car Hire	
available throught flight ops possible special rates	
Weather Info	M T9 Fax BNMC

Visual Reference Points (VRPs)

Old Severn Bridge	N5136.67 W00238.62
M5 bridge over	
River Avon	N5129.33 W00241.58
Thornbury	N5136.67 W00231.10

1. The airfield elevation in feet Above Mean Sea Level (AMSL). The figure in mbs (hPas) indicates the *approximate* mbs/hPas difference between QNH & QFE. The figure is based on 1 mb/hPa = 30 feet. It is only an approximate guide and should only be used to cross-check the QFE as reported by the airfield.

2. The airfield ICAO code (where applicable) and airfield name.

3. Location geographically, and by Latitude & Longitude. Lat. and Long. are given to 2 decimals (*not* seconds) of a minute. Diversion AD – Diversion aerodrome, for use in emergency only, no PPR required and no landing fees.

4. Location as a radial (i.e. magnetic bearing from) and range (nautical miles) from suitable VOR/DMEs. Exceptionally, a VOR without DME may be listed.

5. PPR (Prior Permission Required). PPR should be taken to mean that a telephone call must be made before departure requesting permission to use the airfield. See also section 9 for other restrictions (e.g. non-radio aircraft not accepted etc.).

6. Details of the runway directions, surface, lengths and widths (in metres) and lighting are given. TORA = Take-off Run Available. LDA = Landing Distance Available.

7. Radio frequencies. The name in italics is the radio callsign of the airfield. The following callsigns should be used:

AbbreviationCallsign

- ZONE   Zone
- APP   Approach
- RAD   Radar
- VDF   Homer
- TWR   Tower
- GND   Ground
- AFIS   Information
- A/G   Radio
- FIS   'London/Scottish Information' as applicable
- FIRE This frequency (when shown) is available only when the airport fire service is attending an incident.

8. Radio navigation aids are shown by their type, ident and frequency. Where directions/distances are shown they are ° magnetic TO the airfield/runway listed, and nautical miles.

9. PPR conditions. Plain language remarks regarding the use of the airfield.

10. Plain language warnings relevant to users of the airfield and flight in the immediate vicinity.

11. Operating hours are as notified (UTC), they may vary with little or no prior notice.

12. Circuit directions and heights, where this information is known

13. Landing fees. This information is based on supplied data. Special rates or supplements may apply at certain times, airfield pages are not amended for a change of landing fee information only.

14. Maintenance availability where known

15. Fuel availability. Please note that at many airfields fuel is not available at all times when the airfield is open.

16. The postal address, telephone and fax numbers of the airfield operator.

17. Restaurants, Taxis, Car Hire. Basic detail where known. Inclusion of a company name or telephone number does not imply recommendation or endorsement by the airfield operator or the publisher.

18. Weather Information – weather reports & forecasts available for the airfield and where they can be obtained:

M = METAR (usually only available during the normal opening hours of the airfield).

M* = METAR not distributed. It will probably be necessary to contact the airfield direct for this report.

T9 = 9 hour TAF.

T18 = 18 hour TAF.

T = TAF of other duration (mostly military airfields).

Fax = METAR & TAF available via MetFAX service (see Met section of Flight Planning for full details).

123 = Three figure airfield code for use with automated METAR & TAF telephone service. (see Met section of Flight Planning for full details).

A = ATIS (see radio box for frequency).

VS = METAR included on VOLMET South broadcast.

VN = METAR included on VOLMET North broadcast.

VM = METAR included on VOLMET Main broadcast.

VSc = METAR included on VOLMET Scottish broadcast.

AirS = Airfield is within AIRMET Southern coverage *.

AirN = Airfield is within AIRMET Northern coverage *.

AirSc = Airfield is within AIRMET Scottish coverage *.

AirSE = Airfield is within AIRMET Southeast England coverage *.

AirCen= Airfield is within AIRMET Central England coverage *.

AirSW= Airfield is within AIRMET Southwest England coverage *.

* Used only if TAFs are not available. Where coverage overlaps the most localised forecast is given.

Forecast office. Where no forecast office is designated, that designated to other airfields in the area is given. Forecast office telephone numbers are given in the MET section of the Flight Planning pages. For military and government airfields the stated Forecast Office may be able to provide METARs and TAFs.

BEL = Belfast/Aldergrove Airport.

BCFO= Bracknell Central Forecast Office.

GWC = Glasgow Weather Centre.

IOM = Isle of Man Airport.

JER = Jersey Airport.

MWC = Manchester Weather Centre.

19.   Other information, such as controlled airspace regulations, special procedures, Visual Reference Points (VRP's) etc. may also be listed after the main airfield page.

Effective date: 30/11/99

A

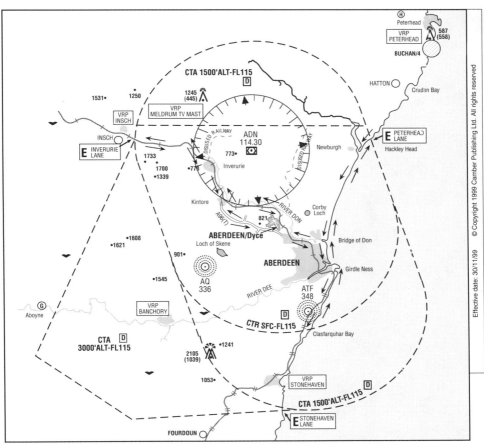

Effective date: 30/11/99

Visual Reference Points (VRPs)

VRP	VOR/NDB	VOR/DME
Banchory N5703.00 W00230.10	ADN R212°/ATF 268°M	ADN 212°/17nm
Insch N5720.57 W00236.85	ADN R286°/AQ 337°M	ADN 286°/11nm
Meldrum TV Mast N5723.20 W00224.00	ADN R322°/AQ 007°M	ADN 322°/6nm
Peterhead N5730.42 W00146.60	ADN R059°/SHD 163°M	ADN 059°/20nm
Stonehaven N5657.75 W00212.60	ADN R181°/ ATF 212°M	ADN 181°/21nm
Turiff N5732.32 W00227.60	ADN R341°/ SHD 273°M	ADN 341°/15nm

ELEVATION	LOCATION	EGPD			ABERDEEN
215ft 7mb	5nm NW of Aberdeen N5712.25 W00212.02	ADN 114.30	168	6.7	• – / – • • / – •
PPR					

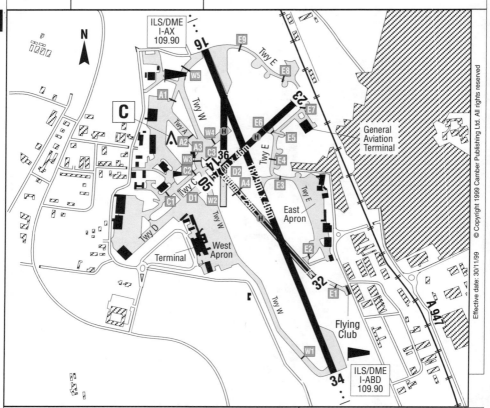

RWY	SURFACE	TORA	LDA	LIGHTING
16/34	Asphalt	1829	1829	App Thr Rwy PAPI3°LHS
36	Asphalt	Helistrip	260x23	
05/23	Asphalt	Helistrip	577x46	23-Thr Rwy CHAPI7°(210)
14/32	Asphalt	Helistrip	660x23	

	Aberdeen
ATIS	114.30 121.85
APP	120.40
RAD	128.30 120.40 121.25 134.10
VDF/Hmr	120.40 128.30 121.25 118.10
TWR	118.10
GND	121.70
FIRE	121.60
HANDLING	Caledonian 130.62 Servisair 130.60
ILS/DME	I-AX 109.90 Rwy16 I-ABD 109.90 Rwy34
VOR/DME	ADN 114.30
NDB	ATF 348 range 25nm
NDB	AQ 336 range 15nm

Remarks

PPR to non-radio ACFT. Helicopter operations outside published Hrs. ACFT less than 5700kgs to join final not less than 1000ft QFE. Handling: All arriving light ACFT will be directed to Caledonian Airborne General Aviation terminal unless another handling agent has been specified. Caledonian 01244 770222, Servisair 01224 723357, Execair 01244 723636.

Warnings

TV masts 1290ft amsl 12.5nm to NW, and 443ft aal (648ft amsl) 146°T/2.9nm. Loganair & Scottish Air Ambulance service flights may take place outside a/d Hrs. Light ACFT beware of large helicopter downwash/vortices. Intense helicopter activity adjacent to full length of E apron. Rwy16 PAPIs should not be used until on extended centreline.

Operating Hrs
Mon-Sat 0520-2050 Sun 0545-2050 2050-2130 (Summer)
Mon-Sat 0620-2150 Sun 0645-2150 2150-2230 (Winter)
and by arrangement

Landing Fee   On application

Maintenance   By arrangement
Fuel   AVGAS 100LL restricted Hrs
Tel: 0860 310313
AVTUR JET A1

Operator   Aberdeen Airport Ltd
Aberdeen Airport, Dyce, Grampian, Scotland AB2 0DU
Tel: 01224 722331 (BAA) 723714 (NATS)
Telex: 73120 (NATS)
Caledonian Airbourne Handling
Tel: 01224 770222
Fax: 01224 770012

Restaurants   Buffet and bar at airport

Car Hire
Avis   **Tel:** 01224 722282
Godfrey Davis   **Tel:** 01224 722486
Hertz   **Tel:** 01224 722373
Budget   **Tel:** 01224 771777
Taxis   Available at terminal

Weather Information   M T9 T18 Fax 222 A Vsc GWC

CTA/CTR-CLASS D AIRSPACE
Normal CTA/CTR-Class D Airspace rules apply
Transition altitude 5000ft

Entry/Exit Lanes
To facilitate the operation of ACFT to and from Aberdeen, the following entry/exit lanes have been established. They are all 3nm wide:
1) Peterhead lane
2) Stonehaven lane
3) Inverurie lane – for ACFT taking off from Rwy16 or landing on Rwy34 follow the A96 until Kintore.
Use of the lanes is subject to ATC clearance. ACFT in the lanes must remain clear of cloud, in sight of the surface, fly not above 2000ft QNH with a minimum visibility of 3 km.
ACFT using the lane shall keep the centre line on the left.
Pilots must maintain adequate clearance from the ground or other obstacles.

A

ELEVATION	LOCATION			
425ft 14mb	4nm ENE of Cardigan N5206.70 W00433.41 **Diversion AD**	STU 113.10 BCN 117.45	076 304	19.1 ••• / – / •• – 53.4 – ••• / – • – • / – •
PPR				

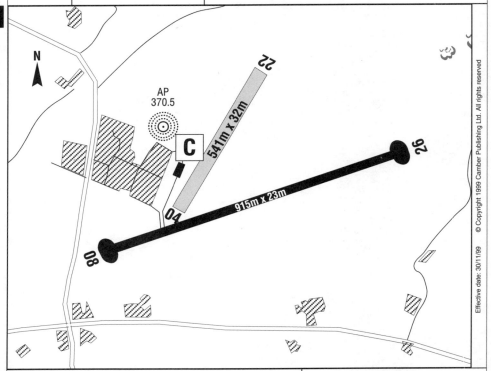

RWY	SURFACE	TORA	LDA	LIGHTING		Aberporth	
08/26	Asphalt	915	915	Portable electric	**AFIS**	122.15	
04/22	Grass	541	541	Winter only	**NDB**	AP 370.5*	
					*on A/D range 20nm		

Remarks
Make initial approach not below 3200ft QNH unless in visual contact with surface. Except for ACFT already in receipt of prior permission ATC Services may be withdrawn during published operation hours and three hours notice will be required to re-activate. Activity outside normal operation hours; Air Traffic Services not always provided. Visual aids to location: Ibn AP Red.

Warnings
Winch launch gliding takes place SR-SS Sat, Sun, PH and occasional weekdays. AD is located just inside the Southern boundary of Weapons Range Danger Area D201. DACS Aberporth 122.15/Aberporth Control 133.50/London Military 135.15. Turbulence may be experienced Thr26 during strong westerly winds.

Maintenance	Nil
Fuel	AVGAS 100LL, AVTUR JET A1 with FS11
Operator	MOD(PE) DERA Aberporth Cardigan Dyfed SA43 2BU **Tel:** 01239 813090 (ATC) **Tel:** 01239 813219 (If ATC unmanned)
Restaurants	Local restaurants available
Taxis/Car Hire	Arranged through ATC
Weather Info	M T Fax BNMC

Operating Hrs and by arrangement	Mon-Fri 0830-1600 (Local)
Circuits	04/08 RH 22/26 LH
Landing fee	£7.56 per 500kgs up to 3.5 MT + VAT & £8.50 insurance

ELEVATION	LOCATION	**EGJA**			**ALDERNEY**
291ft 10mb	1nm SW of St Annes N4942.37 W00212.88	**GUR 109.40**	049	22.1	– – • / • • – / • – •
PPR	**Diversion AD**	**JSY 112.20**	353	29.8	• – – – / • • • / – • – –

© Copyright 1999 Camber Publishing Ltd. All rights reserved

Effective date: 30/11/99

RWY	SURFACE	TORA	LDA	LIGHTING
03/21	Grass	497	497	Nil
14/32	Grass	732	732	Thr Rwy**
08/26†	Asphalt/Grass*	880	880	App Thr Rwy APAPI 3° LHS

* Asphalt strip 18m wide. ** Portable electric. † +50m extension

	Alderney
APP	**Guernsey 128.65**
TWR	**Alderney 125.35**
NDB	**ALD 383**
	Range 30nm
	(0.5nm E of Rwy26 Thr)

Remarks
Not available to non-radio ACFT. Channel Islands CTR regulations apply. ACFT must be able to maintain R/T communication with Jersey Zone, Guernsey Approach and Alderney TWR. Pilots will avoid over flying St Annes below 700ft aal. Third party insurance is required in the sum of £500,000. Duty free shop.

Warnings
Exercise caution because of turbulence caused by nearby cliffs. Rwy surfaces undulating. First 50m (grass) of Rwy08 liable to rutting. Rwy03/21 and 14/32 are marked by inset concrete blocks. The Rwys are classed as grass Rwys but along the centre of Rwy08/26 reinforcing with asphalt has been carried out. Animals grazing in fields on final approach to Rwy03 & 32; low boundary fence with orange/white markers short of Rwy03 & 32 Thr. ACFT using Rwy08/26 may see a white RVR light at upwind ends when Rwy lights are on. Due to costal location, birds are a hazard throughout most of the year, particularly in the migration season.

Operating Hrs
Mon-Sat 0740-1830, Sun 0855-1830 (Local)

Circuits — 700ft QFE 26 & 32 LH 08 & 14 RH
No circuits 03/21

Landing Fee — £8.30 per 1000kgs or part thereof (flights over 55nm), £6.75 per 1000kgs or parts thereof (flights under 55nm), £5.25 per 1000kgs or parts thereof (local flights), Fuel uplift or overnight stay discounts – single£6 twin £12

Maintenance — Nil
Fuel — AVGAS 100LL

Operator — States of Guernsey
States of Guernsey Airport Guernsey Channel Islands
Tel: Alderney 01481 822851 **Fax:** 01481 822352
Tel: Guernsey 01481 37766

Restaurants — Light refreshments available at AD

Taxis
Alderney Taxis — **Tel:** 01481 822611/822992
Cycle Hire
J.B. Cycle Hire — **Tel:** 01481 822294/322762

Weather Info — M T9 Fax 224 JER

A

CTR Class D Airspace
Normal CTA/CTR Class D Airspace rules apply
Alderney Control Zone Radius 5nm SFC/2000ft aal
1. Unless otherwise authorised by Guernsey ATC, an ACFT shall not fly at less than 2000ft above AD elevation and within 5nm of the AD.
2. If at any time the ACFT is less than 2000ft within 5nm of the AD, then a continuous watch is to be made with **Guernsey ATC**
3. Carriage of SSR transponders is mandatory within the Channel Isles CTR.
4. If R/T failure occurs, track 070° out of the zone from Alderney, from overhead the AD at 2000ft.
5. ACFT operating SVFR will normally be cleared Cap de la Hague to Alderney.

Channel Island Visual Reference Points (VRPs)

VRP	VOR/DME FIX
Alderney NDB N4942.53 W00211.98	JSY 353°/30nm, GUR 048°/23nm, SAM 209°/82nm
Cap de la Hague N4943.00 W00156.00	JSY 012°/30nm, GUR 061°/31nm, SAM 202°/78nm
Carteret Lighthouse N4922.00 W00148.00	JSY 052°/13nm, GUR 102°/32nm
Casquets Lighthouse N4943.00 W00222.00	JSY 341°/33nm, GUR 033°/19nm, SAM 213°/84nm
Cap de Flamanville N4931.00 W00153.00	JSY 024°/19nm, GUR 084°/28nm
Corbiere Lighthouse N4911.00 W00215.00	JSY 258°/8nm, GUR 142°/21nm, DIN 353°/36nm
East of Iles Chausey N4853.00 W00139.00	JSY 147°/26nm, GUR 136°/50nm, DIN 048°/25nm
Granville N4850.00 W00139.00	JSY 150°/28nm, GUR 138°/52nm, DIN 053°/22nm
Ile de Brehat N4851.00 W00300.00	JSY 244°/44nm, GUR 208°/39nm, DIN 292°/40nm
Miniquiers N4857.00 W00208.00	JSY 197°/17nm, GUR 153°/35nm DIN 358°/22nm
N East Point (of Guernsey) N4930.42 W00230.52	JSY 318°/25nm, GUR 045°/5.6nm
S East Corner (of Jersey) N4910.00 W00202.00	JSY 176°/3nm, GUR 130°/28nm, DIN 007°/35nm
St Germain N4914.00 W00138.00	JSY 091°/16nm, GUR 112°/40nm, DIN 028°/42nm
West of Minquiers N4857.00 W00218.00	JSY 216°/19nm, GUR 162°/32nm, DIN 343°/23nm

ELEVATION	LOCATION	**EGSL**				**ANDREWSFIELD**

ELEVATION	LOCATION			
286ft 10mb	4nm WNW of Braintree N5153.70 E00026.95 **Diversion AD**	CLN 114.55	281	26	– • – • / • – • • / – •
PPR		LAM 115.60	041	18.6	• – • • / • – / – –

Circuits

Red barn — Salings — Water Twr

A120

Gravel pits

Visiting A/C — **C**

60 ▷ 799m x 18m x 18m 27

Effective date: 30/11/99

RWY	SURFACE	TORA	LDA	LIGHTING
09(L/R)	Grass	799	720	Thr Rwy
27(L/R)	Grass	799	799	Thr Rwy APAPI 3° LHS

Operating as two parallel Rwys.

	Andrewsfield
APP	**Essex Rad 120.625**
A/G AFIS	**130.55**

Remarks
PPR by telephone only. Not available at night for public transport flights. Use at night by ACFT requiring a licensed AD is confined to operations by Andrewsfield Aviation Ltd using Rwy27. Rwy09 is not available for landings by night by ACFT required to use a licensed AD.

Warnings
Located on the E edge of Stansted CTR and under the Stansted CTA (base 2000'AMSL). All inbound traffic must call Essex Radar 120.625. Microlight circuits at 500ft agl inside the normal circuit pattern.

Operator	Andrewsfield Aviation Ltd Saling Airfield Great Stebbing Great Dunmow Essex CM6 3TH **Tel:** 01371 856744 **Fax:** 01371 856500
Restaurants	Hot and cold food available
Taxis Cabman Cars Eastern Taxis **Car Hire** M+M Car Hire	**Tel:** 01371 876363 **Tel:** 01371 873323 **Tel:** 01376 325078
Weather Info	AirCen BNMC

Operating Hrs	0830-2100 (Local) or by prior arrangement
Circuits	RH 700ft QFE
Landing Fee	Single £4.00 Twin £6.00 Helicopters £6.00 inc VAT
Maintenance	MK Aero support **Tel:** 01371 856796
Fuel	AVGAS 100LL

ELEVATION	LOCATION	ASHCROFT (Bryans Landings)		
150ft 5mb	2nm SW of Winsford Cheshire N5309.85 W00234.29	MCT 113.55	231	15.5	– – / – • – • / –
PPR	Diversion AD	WAL 114.10	129	24	• – – / • – / • – • •

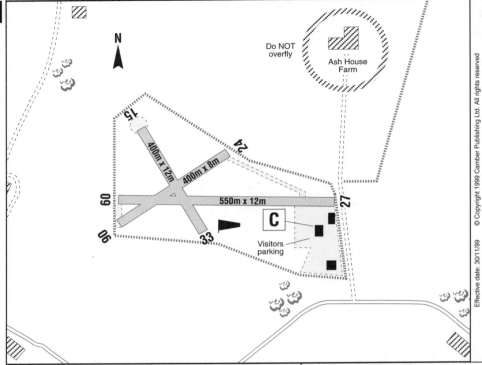

RWY	SURFACE	TORA	LDA	LIGHTING
09/27	Grass	550x12	U/L	Nil
15/33	Grass	400x12	U/L	Nil
06/24	Grass	400x8	U/L	Nil

	Ashcroft
A/G	122.525 Only manned by arrangement & for annual fly-in

Remarks
PPR essential. AD easily identified by white roofed hangar with 'Ashcroft' in black letters. There is also a white radio telescope dish 1nm ESE of the AD. Use mown strips only, there may be long grass either side of the Rwys. Overnight parking available by arrangement by owners risk. Please sign visitors book in control tower. *Bryan's fly-ins are famous for their atmosphere and catering*

Warnings
AD is often waterlogged after heavy rain, if unusable white crosses displayed at Rwy Thrs. DO NOT LAND WHEN WHITE CROSSES DISPLAYED. Wooden fences around the AD boundary 4ft 6ins high. Please do not overfly local farmhouses. AD is close to Whitegate NDB, (WHI), an entry-exit point for Liverpool CTR, visitors can contact Liverpool APP 119.85.

Maintenance	Nil
Fuel	Nil
Operator	Bryan Lockyear Ashcroft Farm Darnhall Winsford Cheshire CW7 4DQ **Tel:** 01270 528378
Restaurants	Boot & Slipper 2nm from AD
Taxis	Ace Cars **Tel:** 01606 862149
Weather Info	AirCen MWC

Operating Hrs	SR-SS
Circuits	To South 800ft QFE (May vary for annual fly-in)
Landing fee	Nil but donations gratefully received

Small charge for Annual fly-in donated to local charities

ELEVATION	LOCATION				
283ft 11mb	1nm SW of Saffron Walden	BPK 114.55	043	20	— • • • / • — — — • / — • —
	N5200.52 E00013.57	LAM 115.60	011	21.9	• — • • / • — / — —
PPR	**Diversion AD**	BKY 116.25	083	6.2	— • • • / — • — / — • — —

Effective date: 30/11/99

RWY	SURFACE	TORA	LDA	LIGHTING		
18/36	Grass	800x30	U/L	Nil		

Slight upslope Rwy18
Caution: Tall trees on APP36 reducing available LDA to 700m

	Audley
APP	Essex Radar 120.625
A/G	122.35*
	*by arrangement

Remarks
All circuits to avoid over flying Saffron Walden. AD situated on the edge of Stansted CTA. Inbound ACFT to contact Essex Radar on 120.625.

Warnings
Caution is necessary on approach to Rwy36 due to a line of trees across the extended centre-line 50m before the AD boundary. Visiting pilots must report to the control point at the green hangar to sign movements book.

Operator	Audley End Development Co Ltd Brunoketts Wendens Ambo Saffron Walden Essex CB11 4JL **Tel:** 01799 541354/541956 **Fax:** 01799 542134
Taxis Car Hire	Adtax **Tel:** 01799 521164 Practical Car Hire **Tel:** 01799 541456
Weather Info	AirCen BNMC

Operating Hrs	By arrangement SR-SS
Circuits	18 RH 36 LH Avoid over flying Saffron Walden (1nm NE of AD)
Landing Fee	Single £5.00 Twin £10 private Single/twin £10.00 commercial
Maintenance Fuel	Nil Nil

ELEVATION	LOCATION		
289ft 9mb	3nm NE of Thame N5146.52 W000546.40	BNN 113.75 287 15 CPT 114.35 036 20	– • • • / – • / – • – • – • / • – – • / –

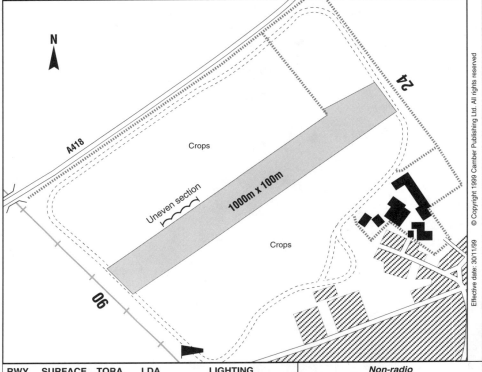

RWY	SURFACE	TORA	LDA	LIGHTING		Non-radio		
06/24	Grass	1000x100	U/L	Nil		APP	Luton	129.55

Remarks
No PPR required. Primarily a gliding site but light ACFT & microlights welcome at own risk. AD available at weekends only when PPR is not required. Please park adjacent to glider launch point at Thr of Rwy in use.

Warnings
No overhead joins due launch cables. AD may suffer from waterlogging after periods of heavy rain.
Noise: Avoid overflying village of Haddenham,1.5nm SE of the AD. The gliding club advise that although they are always happy to see powered visitors they have no facilities – not even a loo!

Operator	Upward Bound Trust Gliding Club Mr P Chamberlain 89 Leverstock Green Road Hemel Hempstead Herts HP3 8PR **Tel:** 01442 261747
Restaurants	Nil
Taxis/Car Hire	Nil
Weather Info	AirCen BNMC

Operating Hrs	Weekends only Sat-Sun in Summer; Sun only in Winter
Circuits	All circuits to be on N side at 1000ft QFE No overhead joins Keep a good lookout for gliders
Landing fee	Donations gratefully received
Maintenance Fuel	Nil Nil

ELEVATION	LOCATION		BADMINTON
495ft 17mb	3.5nm ENE of Chipping Sodbury N5132.98 W00217.92	BCN 117.45 111 37.3 − • • • / − • − • / − •	
PPR			

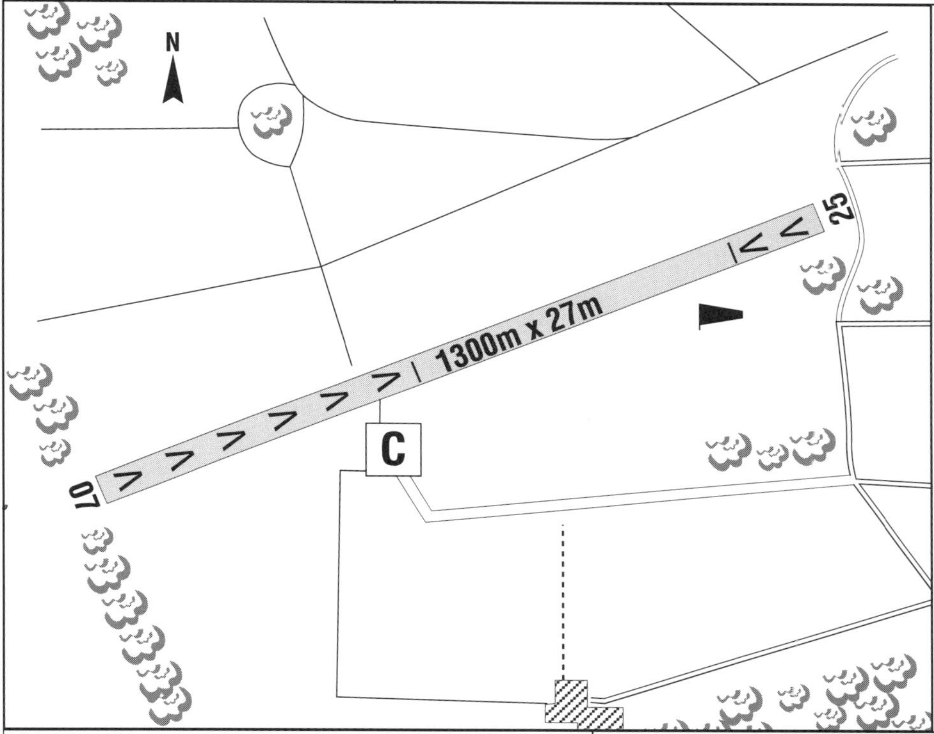

1300m x 27m

C

Effective date: 30/11/99

B

RWY	SURFACE	TORA	LDA	LIGHTING
07	Grass	850	800	Nil
25	Grass	800	1250	Nil

Non radio	
A/G	123.175
APP	Lyneham 123.40
APP	Filton 122.725

Remarks
PPR by telephone only. U/L AD. APP to Rwy25 should be high enough to cross the public road safely. Rwy07 Thr displaced 500m. Rwy25 Thr displaced 100m. Avoid over-flying hamlet of Little Badminton if possible.

Warnings
Care must be taken during August and March when Rwy may be fenced against stock. Horse trials in May.

Operator	The Duke of Beaufort Badminton Aerodrome Badminton South Glos GL9 1DD **Tel:** 01454 218838 (Hangar) **Tel:** 01454 218220 **Tel** 01249 721076 (Mr H Richardson evenings & w/ends) **Fax:** 01454 218159
Restaurants	
Taxis/Car Hire	
Weather Info	AirSW BNMC

Operating Hrs	By arrangement
Circuits	07 LH 25 RH
Landing Fee	On Application
Maintenance Fuel	Nil 100LL

BAGBY (Thirsk)

ELEVATION	LOCATION				
160ft 5mb	2nm SE of Thirsk N5412.62 Long.W00117.55 **Diversion AD**	OTR 113.9 POL 112.10 NEW 114.25	312 051 169	52 40.1 51.2	– – – / – / • – • • – – • / – – – / • – • • – • / • / • – –

Bagby

Crops

708m x 20m

Crops

24

06

N

(H)

RWY	SURFACE	TORA	LDA	LIGHTING
*06/24	Grass	708x20	U/L	Rwy Single PAPI 4°**

* 3% upslope on Rwy06
** Electric Rwy lighting available for a fee

	Bagby
APP	Topcliffe 125.00
A/G *	123.25
	* Not always manned

Remarks
Light ACFT including twins are welcome. During Topcliffe Hrs of operation Departing traffic from Rwy24 contact Topcliffe APP 125.00 **before** take-off advising flight intentions. ACFT Dep Rwy24 commence gentle left turn ASAP avoiding Topcliffe ATZ. Do not overfly Bagby village.

Warnings
For non radio ACFT telephone briefing recommended at weekends.

Operator	Mr JM Dundon Bagby Airfield Bagby Thirsk YO7 2PH **Tel:** 01845 597385 (AD) **E-mail** E: bagbyair@aol.com **Tel/Fax:** 01845 597747 (office) **Mobile:** 07774 680186
Accomodation	Hotels in Thirsk
Restaurants	Bar meals and club facilities at AD 1200-1400 & all day weekends
Taxis Prices **Car Hire** Moss Motors	**Tel:** 01845 522799 **Tel:** 01845 522042
Weather Info	AirN MWC

Operating Hrs   0800-SS (Local) & by arrangement
(Services available 0930-1900 local)

Circuits   24 LH 06 RH 800ft

Landing fee   Reciprocals free
Business flights £5.00. All landings free with fuel uplift
Large helicopters/Twin ACFT £10.00

Maintenance   M3 G Fox Engineering
Tel: 01845 597707
Fuel   AVGAS 100LL JET A1

B

ELEVATION	LOCATION	EGPR			BARRA
Sea level 0mb	Foreshore of Traigh Mhor N5701.62.W00726.25	TIR 117.70	340	36.9	− / •• / • − •
PPR		BEN 114.40	193	27.4	− ••• / • / − •

BRR 316

35ft agl •

Terminal

700m x 60m

667m x 46m

846m x 46m

High Water Mark

Public footpath

APP MARKER FACE

101	RWY HDG
B	STRIP CODE
	RED
	WHITE
	BLACK

RWY	SURFACE	TORA	LDA	LIGHTING
07	Sand	700	700	Nil
25	Sand	700	700	Nil
11	Sand	667	617	Nil
29	Sand	667	597	Nil
15	Sand	846	796	Nil
33	Sand	846	776	Nil

	Barra	
FIS	Scottish	
	127.275	
AFIS	118.075	
NDB	BRR 316 range 15nm	

Remarks
PPR is essential in order to obtain information on surface conditions, in addition to other information. The obstacle clearance surfaces of Rwy07/25 are infringed at both ends. A weather minima of 3km visibility and cloudbase of 1000ft aal must be strictly adhered to.

Warnings
The landing and take-off areas may be considerably ridged by hard sand and contain pools of standing water which are hazards to ACFT. The bearing strength, braking action and contamination of the beach is unknown, variable and unpredictable. Some downdraughts may be experienced at the W end of Rwy07/25 in strong wind from the W through S. Rwy07/25 will be marked by black/white boxes on the landward side of Thr on request. The E end of Rwy07/25 is generally unfit for use due to water logging & sand ridging.

Landing fee	£10.65 inc VAT up to 3000kgs booked in advance, VFR cash/cheque on the day
Maintenance	Nil
Fuel	Nil
Operator	HIAL Barra Aerodrome North Bay Castle Bay Isle of Barra Western Isles PA80 5XY **Tel:** 01871 890283 **Tel:** 01871 890212 (PPR) **Fax** 01871 890220
Restaurants	Heathbank Hotel (4 miles) May to Sept only, Craigard/Castlebay Hotels (12 miles) open all year
Taxis Hatchers G. Campbell	**Tel:** 01871 810486 **Tel:** 01871 810216
Weather Info	AirSc GWC

Operating Hrs Mon-Fri 0830-1100 1300-1630 Sat: 0945-1145 (Summer) Winter + 1Hr Tide permiting & by arrangement

Circuits Variable

ELEVATION	LOCATION	**EGNL**	**BARROW (Walney Island)**

47ft	1.5nm NW of	DCS 115.20	183	35.7	– • • / – • – • / • • •
2mb	Barrow in Furness	WAL 114.10	001	44.5	• – – / • – – / • – • •
	N5407.87.W00315.81				
PPR	**Diversion AD**				

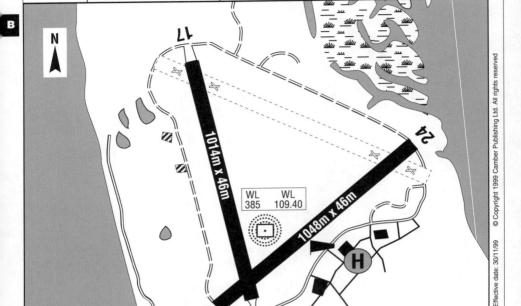

RWY	SURFACE	TORA	LDA	LIGHTING
06	Asphalt	1020	1020	Thr Rwy PAPI 4° LHS
24	Asphalt	1014	966	Thr Rwy PAPI 3.5° LHS
17	Asphalt	1014	1014	Thr Rwy PAPI 4° RHS
35	Asphalt	1014	1014	Thr Rwy PAPI 3° LHS

Walney	
A/G	123.20
NDB	WL 385 on A/D*
DME	WL 109.40**
*range 15 nm	
**DME: zero range at Thr06 & 35 only	

Remarks
**PPR strictly by telephone. Non-radio ACFT not
accepted**. U/L AD. AD closed to all traffic except home
based ACFT and gliders at weekends, Bank Holidays and
other notified periods. Landings absolutely prohibited when
AD is closed.

Warnings
Glider launching takes place on the AD.

Operator	GEC Marine (VSEL)
	Barrow/Walney Island Aerodrome
	Cumbria LA14 1AB
	Tel: 01229 470087/471407
	Fax: 01229 470619

Restaurants	Nil at A/D.
	Ferry Hotel restaurant 20 minutes walk

Taxis	
Acacia Cars	**Tel: 01229 830055**
D&S Contracts	**Tel: 01229 822020**
Car Hire	
Avis	**Tel: 01229 829555**
Hertz	**Tel: 01229 836666**

Operating Hrs	Available on request
Circuits	Variable
Landing fee	£5.00 per half tonne +VAT
Maintenance	Nil
Fuel	AVTUR

Weather Info	M* AirN MWC

ELEVATION	LOCATION		BATTLEFLAT FARM
525ft 17mb	2nm S of Coalville N5241.83 W00121.02		
PPR			

TNT 115.70	157	24.5	– / – • / –
DTY 116.40	348	32	– • • / – / – • –

B

N

60

470m x 12m

< <

27

6' hedge

Crops

B591

30' powerline
pole & tree

Gap in hedge

Crops

Crops

6' hedge

A/C
parking

Twy

Ponds

To industrial
estate

Little Battleflat
Farm

Sand quarry

Coalville to Leicester railway (in cutting)

Large pre-cast concrete
plant with stock yard

RWY	SURFACE	TORA	LDA	LIGHTING		Non Radio	
09/27*	Grass	470x12	U/L	Nil	APP	119.65 (East Mids)	
*27 has displaced landing Thr of **m					ATIS	128.225 (East Mids)	

Remarks
Good flat strip with clear approach to Rwy09. Obstructions on Rwy27 approach see warnings. Good visual aids to location are white farm buildings S of Rwy27 Thr and Coalville-Leicester railway which crosses Rwy27 approach. Also sand quarry and large concrete works with stock yard SSW of AD.

Warnings
There is a 30ft power line and tree bordering the farm track which crosses Rwy27 Thr. B591 borders the strip to N, crops are grown to the Rwy edges. The AD is beneath the East Midlands CTZ, (Class D 2500ft base). **Noise:** Please avoid local habitation. Please fly over local industrial estate to minimise disturbance.

Operator	Mrs J Lees Little Battleflat Farm Ellistown Leicester LE67 1FB **Tel:** 01530 832567
Restaurant	Nil
Taxi/Car Hire	
Weather Info	AirCen MWC

Operating Hrs	SR-SS
Circuits	1000ft QFE See Warnings
Landing Fee	Nil
Maintenance Fuel	Nil Nil

ELEVATION	LOCATION				BAXTERLEY
420ft 14mb	4.5nm SE of Tamworth N5234.00 W00136.00				
PPR		HON 113.65	013	13	••••/– – –/– •
		TNT 115.70	181	29	– /– •/–

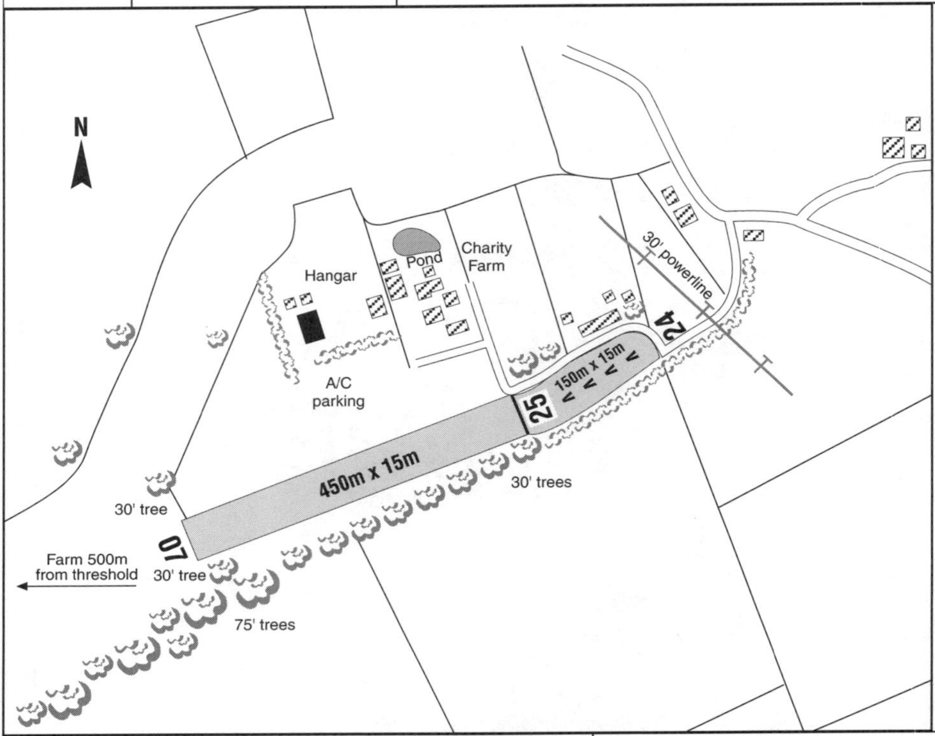

N

Hangar

Pond

Charity Farm

30' powerline

24

150m x 15m

25

A/C parking

450m x 15m

30' trees

30' tree

Farm 500m from threshold

07

30' tree

75' trees

RWY	SURFACE	TORA	LDA	LIGHTING
07/25*	Grass	450x15	U/L	Nil

Plus *150x15m dogleg orientated 240 degrees

Baxterley
A/G   120.30 (only monitored during events)

Remarks
PPR by telephone. Situated close to NE corner of Birmingham CTR. Visitors advised to contact Birmingham APP (118.05). Organised Fly-ins and events during summer months. Check aviation press for details.

Warnings
There are 30ft agl powerlines 70m from the 25 Thr (measured from beginning of dogleg extension). Mature trees to South of Rwy that may cause turbulence, they decrease in size from Rwy07 Thr towards Rwy25. Occasional model aircraft activity. **Noise:**Please avoid local habitation, particularly the farm 500m out Rwy07 approach.

Operator	Ken Broomfield Charity Farm Baxterley Warwickshire **Tel:** 01827 874572 **Fax:** 01827 874898 (Operates as voice info line on fly-in days)
Restaurant	Nil
Taxi/Car Hire	Nil
Weather Info	AirCen MWC

Operating Hrs	SR-SS
Circuits	South at 1000ft QFE Caution: close proximity of Birmingham CTR
Landing Fee	Nil
Maintenance Fuel	Nil MOGAS available by prior arrangement

BECCLES

ELEVATION	LOCATION
80ft 3mb	2nm SE of Beccles N5226.11 E00137.07
PPR	

BKY 116.25	**068**	**63**	— • • • / — • — / — • — —
CLN 114.55	**028**	**39**	— • — • / • — • • / — •

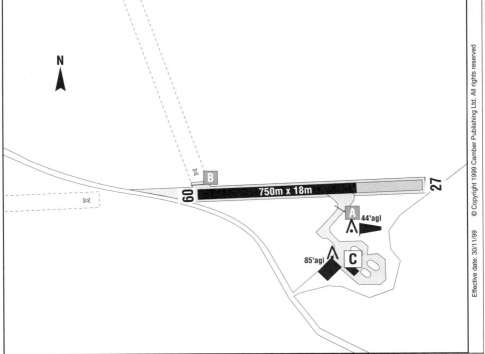

RWY	SURFACE	TORA	LDA	LIGHTING			
09	Concrete/Grass	695	695	Nil		***Beccles***	
27*	Concrete/Grass	695	626	Nil	**A/G**	**134.60**	

*Rwy27 first 250m grass

Remarks
AD on part of old WWII AD. All other hard surfaces not available to ACFT.

Warnings
44ft agl. anemometer mast adjacent to windsock. 85ft agl mast on hangar roof. Helicopters should confirm to circuit pattern. **Noise:** Avoid overflying local villages.

Operator	Mr RD Forster, Rain Air Ltd Beccles Airfield, Beccles LN34 7TE **Tel: 07767 827172**
Restaurant	Tea, Coffee and light snacks available
Taxi/Car Hire Gold Taxi	**Tel**: 01502 711611
Weather Info	AirS BNMC

Operating Hrs	0900-SS (Local)
Circuits	09 RH 27 LH 1000ft agl
Landing Fee	Single £5 Twin £10
Maintenance **Fuel** available during full opening hours	Rainair **Tel:** 07767 827172 AVGAS 100LL

ELEVATION	LOCATION	EGSB				BEDFORD (Castle Mill)
70ft 2mb	2nm ENE of Bedford N5208.60.W00024.37	BKY 116.25	303	19.6	– • • • / – • – / – • – –	
		DTY 116.40	100	26.1	– • • / – / – • – –	
PPR		BNN 113.75	017	25.6	– • • • / – • / – •	

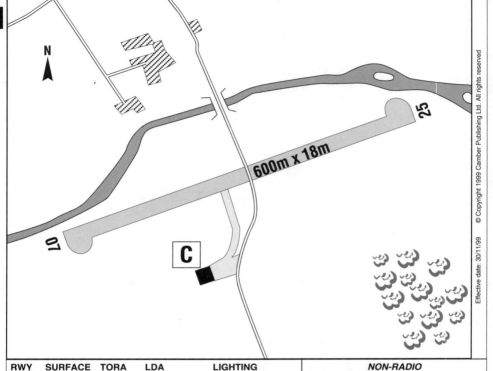

600m x 18m

RWY	SURFACE	TORA	LDA	LIGHTING			
07/25	Grass	600x18	U/L	Nil			

NON-RADIO

APP   Cranfield 122.85
      Useful weather info from
      Cranfield ATIS 121.875

Remarks
PPR by telephone 48hrs notice before arival required.
U/L AD. Use at pilots own risk.
Warnings
Liable to flooding in winter. AD situated 1nm N of Danger
Area D206. Powerline on 25 Approach 600m from Thr.

Operator	Millair Services Limited Bedford (Castle Mill) Aerodrome Risinghoe Castle Mill Goldington Road Bedford MK41 0HY **Tel:** 01234 262441 **Fax:** 01234 273357
Restaurants	Nil
Taxis **Car Hire** National	Arrangement on arrival **Tel:** 01234 269565
Weather Info	AirCen BNMC

Operating Hrs	SR-SS
Circuits	To the S to avoid built-up area
Landing fee	Nil
Maintenance	Millair (Aero engine rebuild specialists)
Fuel	Nil

B

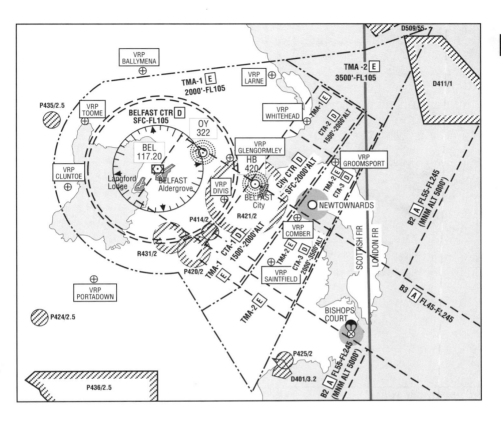

Visual Reference Points (VRPs)

VRP	VOR/VOR	VOR/NDB	VOR/DME FIX
Ballymena N5451.80 W00616.40	BEL R360°/MAC R220°	BEL R360°/HB 325°M	BEL 360°/12nm
Cluntoe (Disused A/D) N5437.23 W00632.03	BEL R264°/ MAC R220°	MAC R220°/ OY 262°M	BEL 265°/11nm
Divis N5436.45 W00600.57	BEL R119°/DUB R015°	BEL R119°/HB 270°M	BEL 119°/8nm
Glengormley(M2 J 4) N5440.83 W00558.90	BEL R089°/TRN R234°	BEL R089°/ HB 325°M	BEL 089°/9nm
Larne N5451.20 W00549.52	BEL R057°/MAC R197°	MAC R197°/OY 050°M	BEL 057°/18nm
Portadown N5425.50 W00626.85	BEL R215°/DUB R002°	DUB R002°/OY 225°M	BEL 215°/16nm
Toome (Disused A/D) N5445.47 W00629.67	BEL R309°/MAC R223°	MAC R223°/OY 292°M	BEL 309°/11nm

ELEVATION	LOCATION	**EGAA**	**BELFAST (Aldergrove)**
267ft 9mb **PPR**	11.5nm NW of Belfast. N5439.45.W00612.93	**BEL 117.20** on A/D – • • • / • / • – • •

Effective date: 30/11/99

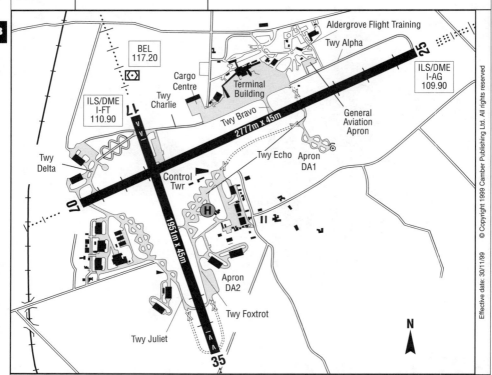

RWY	SURFACE	TORA	LDA	LIGHTING
07/25	Asphalt	2777	2777	Ap Thr Rwy PAPI 3° LHS
17	Asphalt	1798	1798	Ap Thr Rwy PAPI 3° LHS
35	Asphalt	1890	1798	Ap Thr Rwy PAPI 3° LHS

Aldergrove	
ATIS	128.20
APP	120.90 121.50 (O/R)
RAD	120.90 120.00
VDF	120.90
TWR	118.30
GND	121.75
FIRE	121.60
ILS/DME	I-AG 109.90 Rwy25 I-FT 110.90 Rwy17
NDB*	OY 322 range 15nm * NDB OY 253°/4.29nm to Thr25
VOR/DME	BEL 117.20

Remarks

PPR to non-radio ACFT. Pilots must present ACFT and contents to police on arrival from and prior to departure for international flights. ACFT using Belfast International Airport are to carry third party insurance cover of not less than £500,000. Twy J unlicenced for civil use. ACFT below 2000kg AUW will park, normally self-manoeuvring on the GA apron, or as directed. Certain customs facilities available. Eurojet handle all GA ACFT over 2 tonnes Tel 02894 422888 Ext 4040/4041 Fax 02894 422640. Aldergrove Flight Training Centre handle all GA ACFT under 2 tonnes Tel 02894 423747 Fax 02894 423777

Warnings

Severe bird hazard during autumn and winter months; pilots will be advised by ATC. Langford Lodge U/L AD with crossed Rwy07/25 and 03/21 situated 3nm SW of Aldergrove. Helicopters frequently operate at low level south of Rwy25, but will remain at least 250m from that Rwy until further cleared by ATC.

B

Operating Hrs	H24
Circuits	LH except Rwy25
Landing fee	Under 2mt or flights within 185km £12.75

parking £10.20(per 24Hrs) +VAT

Maintenance	Woodgate Air Maintenance
	Tel: 02894 422017
Fuel	JET A1 AVGAS 100LL
	(0900-1700 local daily)

Out of Hrs by prior arrangement with
Aldergrove Flight Training Centre **Tel:** 02894 423747
or Executive Air Service **Tel:** 02894 422478

Operator   Northern Ireland Airports Ltd
Belfast International Airport Belfast BT29 4AB
Tel: 02894 22152/422955 Ext. 255 (ATC/Flight Planning)
Tel: 02894 22888 Ext. 2288 (Duty Ops)
Fax: 02894 423883
Telex: 747980 NATS 747535 CIVILAIR

Restaurant   Buffet and bars available at terminal

Taxis
Available at Terminal. Buses every half hour
Car Hire
Avis	**Tel:** 028944 22333
Europcar	**Tel:** 028944 23444
Hertz	**Tel:** 028944 22533

Weather Info   M T9 T18 Fax 228 A VSc BEL

TMA- Class E Airspace, CTR Class D Airspace
Normal CTA/CTR Class D Airspace rules apply
1. Flight within the Belfast Aldergrove CTR shall not take place without permission of ATC, giving details of position level and track. A listening watch shall also be maintained whilst complying with any instructions from ATC.
2. Beware of AD Langford Lodge 3nm SW of Aldergrove and ensure that you are landing at the correct AD.

B

ELEVATION	LOCATION	EGAC				BELFAST (City)
15ft 1mb	East side of Belfast Docks N5437.08.W00552.35 **Diversion AD**		BEL 117.20	110	12.6	− • • • / • / • − • •

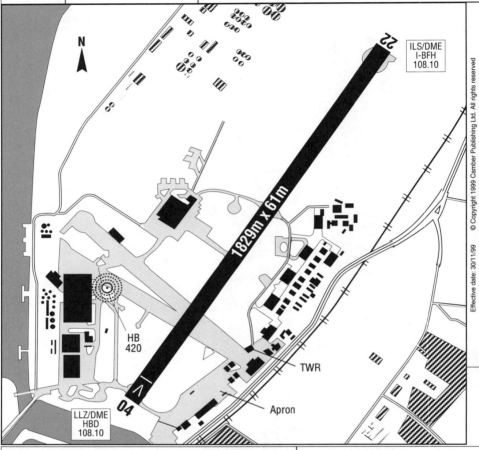

RWY	SURFACE	TORA	LDA	LIGHTING
04	Concrete	1829	1737	Ap Thr Rwy PAPI 3° LHS
22	Concrete	1767	1767	Ap Thr Rwy PAPI 3° LHS

	Belfast
ATIS	136.625
APP	130.85 121.50 (O/R)
RAD	134.80
TWR	130.75 121.50 (O/R)
NDB	HB 420 (on A/D)*
LLZ/DME	HBD 108.10 Rwy04
ILS/DME	I-BFH 108.10 Rwy22
	* range 15nm

Remarks
ACFT departing under IFR will be given individual clearances to take into account any applicable Noise Preferential Routes. SE Twy available for use by ACFT with wingspan less than 25m. Ground handling facilities available during published summer Hrs on Saturdays but only to 1530 on Saturdays in winter. The Twy leading from the southwest end of Rwy04/22 to the apron is not suitable for use by ACFT having a wingspan exceeding 31.5m. Parking is by marshalling assistance, there are no apron guidelines. Customs: 24H PPO for non-EEC movements. Preference Rwy22 for landing, 04 for Departures.

Visual Arrivals: Rwy22, not below 2500ft QNH until established on final approach at 5nm. Rwy04 not below 1500ft QNH before established on final approach at 5nm.

Departures: Rwy22, maintain Rwy heading to 1500ft QNH before turning. Rwy04, track 037°M to 1500ft QNH before turning.

Warnings
AD located within restricted area R421. Many obstacles on approach to Rwy04.

Operating Hrs	
Mon-Sat 0530-2030 Sun 0715-2030(Summer)	
Winter + 1Hr and by arrangement	

Circuits	04 LH 22 RH 1500ft QNH
Landing fee	On Application
Maintenance	Nil
Fuel	AVTUR(JP1) AVGAS 100LL
	– avl published Hrs

Operator Belfast Harbour Airport Services Ltd
Belfast City Airport
Sydenham By-Pass Belfast BT3 9JH Northern Ireland
Tel: 02890 454871 (ATC)
Tel: 02890 458578 (Handling)
Fax: 02890 731557 (ATC)
Fax: 02890 738455 (Admin)

Restaurants	Buffet and bar at Terminal

Taxis	Airport Taxi Rank
Car Hire	
Avis	**Tel:** 02890 420404
National	**Tel:** 02890 739400
Europcar	**Tel:** 02890 450904
Hertz	**Tel:** 02890 732451

Weather Info	M T9 Fax 232 BEL

CTA/CTR-Class D Airspace

Normal CTA/CTR Class D Airspace rules apply

B

Visual Reference Points (VRPs)

VRP	VOR/VOR	VOR/NDB	VOR/DME
Comber N5433.05 W00544.75	TRN R223°/IOM R317°	TRN R223°/HB 136°M	BEL 119°/18nm
Groomsport N5440.50 W00537.08	TRN R223°/IOM R328°	IOM R328°/HB 075°M	BEL 094°/21nm
Saintfield N5427.62 W00549.97	TRN R222°/IOM R309°	IOM R309°/HB 176°M	BEL 138°/18nm
Whitehead N5445.17 W00542.57	TRN R230°/IOM R328	IOM R328°/HB 043M	BEL 080°/19nm

| 10ft
0mb | 4nm N of Limavady
(Disused AD)
N5506.00.W00658.05 | BEL 117.20 | 325 | 38 | – • • • / • / • – • • |
| PPR | | MAC 116.00 | 255 | 47 | – – / • – / – • – • |

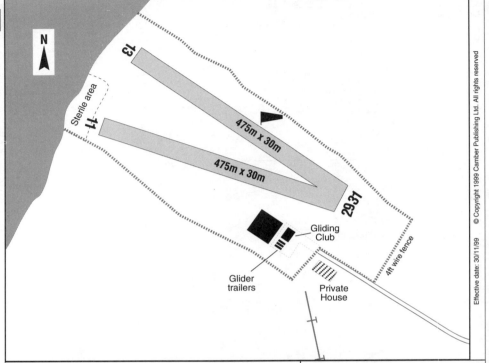

Effective date: 30/11/99

RWY	SURFACE	TORA	LDA	LIGHTING
13/31	Grass	475x30	U/L	Nil
11/29	Grass	475x30	U/L	Nil

Bellarena Base

A/G 130.10
**Used during glider operations
If no response make blind calls**

Remarks
PPR by telephone essential. Primarily a gliding site but occasional visits by light ACFT welcome at own risk. The Rwys are not marked but are the best runs on a large field of coastal turf. Although we quote Rwy widths the large run-off area make these figures academic! The turf is regularly grazed by sheep.

Warnings
The AD is surrounded to the landward by a wire fence 4ft high. Sheep graze the AD during the week. Glider launching by aerotow please keep a good lookout for tugs & gliders. High ground 1263ft amsl 1.8nm to E & SE.

Operating Hrs 0930 (local) to 30mins
after SS-Sat/Sun & PH
7 day ops through Easter week & 1 week in July

Circuits
No overhead joins circuits LH at 1000ft QFE

Landing fee Nil

Maintenance
Nil but possible hangarage for visitors in emergencies
Fuel Nil

Operator Ulster Gliding Club Bellarena Airfield
County Londonderry Northern Ireland
Tel: 02877 750301
(Clubhouse manned at weekends)

Restaurants/Accomodation There are a number of restaurants in Limavady & local hotels & B&B's

Taxis
Tel: 028977 750561
Tel: 028977 750489
Car Hire **Tel:** 02870 343654

Weather Info AirN BEL

ELEVATION	LOCATION				
675ft 22mb	2.5nm NE of Torrington N5058.57 W00405.73 **Diversion AD**	**BHD 112.70**	331	41.5	– • • • / • • • • / – • •
PPR		**BCN 117.45**	220	62.5	– • • • / – • – • / – •

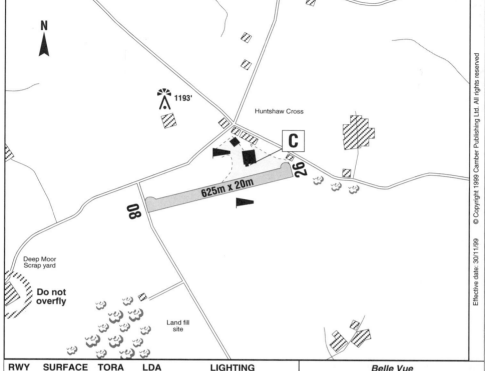

N
∧ 1193'
Huntshaw Cross
C
26
625m x 20m
08
Deep Moor Scrap yard
Do not overfly
Land fill site

RWY	SURFACE	TORA	LDA	LIGHTING			
08/26	Grass	625x20	U/L	Nil			

	Belle Vue
A/G	123.575

*Rwy26 Thr sometimes displaced by 100m
•Electric fence sometimes adjacent to Rwy on S side

Remarks
PPR by telephone. Rwy26 Thr sometimes displaced by 100m. Microlight activity. Visiting ACFT welcome at pilots own risk. Microlights with cruise speed above 45kts permitted. Taxy on the Rwy unless otherwise directed. Eaglescott AD, gliding parachuting, microlights and fixed wing activity 5nm SE avoid ATZ unless transit authorised. Camping and caravanning available

Warnings
Caution: Radio mast with guy lines 537agl (1193ft amsl), 300m N of AD. Beware of grazing sheep. APP to Rwy08 should be sufficiently high to give good clearance of public road close to Thr. **Noise:** Avoid overflying all settlements and farms within 3nm, particularly scrapyard 0.75nm SW of 08 Thr (see map). Dep climb out on Rwy heading 2nm to clear area.

Maintenance	Nil
Fuel	MOGAS available 1nm distance

Operator Mr DR Easterbrook, Belle Vue Aerodrome, Yarnscombe, Barnstaple North Devon EX31 3ND
Tel/Fax: 01805 623113
Mobile: 07831 194530
Tel: 01363 773767 (Jim Gale, Wingnuts Flying Club)

Restaurants Self service refreshments at AD
B&B within 1km details available from operator

Taxis/Car Hire Details available from operator

Weather Info AirSW BNMC

Operating Hrs Mon-Sat 0800-2100 or SS
Sun/PH 0900-1800 landing only until 2100

Circuits LH 1000ft QFE

Landing fee £2.50

ELEVATION	LOCATION				
55ft 2mb	2.3nm NE of Sandown (Isle of Wight) N5040.68.W00106.55 **Diversion AD**	SAM 113.35	157	19	••• / •– / ––
PPR		MID 114.00	224	29.1	–– / •• / –• •
		SFD 117.00	269	47	••• / •• –• / –••

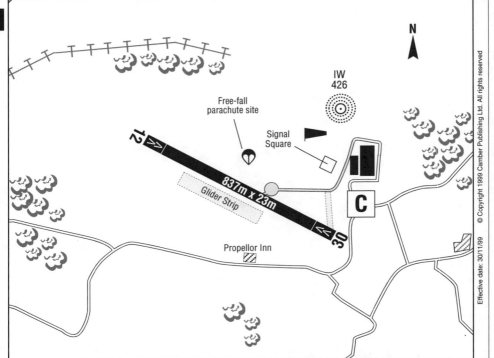

RWY	SURFACE	TORA	LDA	LIGHTING
12	Concrete	837	775	Thr Rwy APAPI 4° LHS
30	Concrete	837	781*	Thr Rwy APAPI 4° LHS 699*(night)

* Night landing Thr is 82m upwind of day marked Thr

	Bembridge
AFIS	123.25
A/G*	123.25
	* when U/L
NDB	IW 426**
	** on A/D range 15nm

Remarks
Non-radio ACFT not accepted. When gliders are operating, join by over-flying the AD at 1500 ft QFE on the Rwy QDM. When overhead the upwind end of the Rwy turn left/right (depending on circuit direction) to level at circuit height (1000ft QFE) on crosswind leg prior to turning downwind. U/L with no Fire Cover as shown below. Certain customs facilities available.

Warnings
Manufacturers' demonstration flights may take place without notice at any time including weekends, during daylight Hrs, within 1.5nm of the AD boundary and up to 3000 ft agl. Visiting ACFT must be prepared to remain clear until advised. There are trees and rising ground within the approach area to Rwy30. Glider activity at times, mainly weekends.

Operating Hrs Mon-Thurs Sat 0800-1800
Fri 0800-11.45 Sun 0900-1800 (Local)

Circuits 12 LH 30 RH 1000ft QFE
Gliders will be flying a circuit opposite to this

Landing fee	Single £10-£15 Twin £20-£25 inc VAT Touch & go 50% disc
Maintenance	Nil
Fuel	AVGAS 100LL JET A1
	by prior arrangement during operational Hrs
Operator	Pilatus Britten-Norman Ltd Bembridge Airport Isle of Wight PO35 5PR **Tel:** 01983 871538 (PPR) **Tel/Fax:** 01983 871566
Restaurants	
	Propeller Inn (bar snacks) at AD Tel: 01983 873611
Taxis	
Ralphs Taxis	**Tel:** 01983 811666
Car Hire	
Avis	**Tel:** 01983 615522
Weather Info	AirS BNMC

ELEVATION	LOCATION	EGPL			BENBECULA

ELEVATION	LOCATION				
19ft 1mb	West Side of Isle of Benbecula N5728.65.W00721.98	TIR 117.70	355	61.2	– / • • / • – •
		STN 115.10	231	57.80	• • • / – / – •
PPR		BEN 113.95	On A/D		– • • • / • / – •

B

18
24
N
1220m x 46m
1656m x 46m
BEN 113.95
06
36
Light a/c parking
Twr

RWY	SURFACE	TORA	LDA	LIGHTING
06	Bitumen	1656	1534	Ap Thr Rwy PAPI 3°LHS
24	Bitumen	1506*	1506	Ap Thr Rwy PAPI 3°LHS
18/36**	Asphalt	1220	1220	Nil

*170m starter extension available on request
**100m starter extension on Rwy36

Benbecula	
APP/TWR	119.20
AFIS	119.20
Fire	121.60
VOR/DME	BEN 113.95

Remarks
PPR 3hrs notice required. Built in tie-downs on the north section of the main apron. Low intensity battery edge lights available Rwy18/36 for air ambulance or SAR ACFT only Rwy18/36 not available to ACFT greater than 5700kg unless Rwy06/24 is not available or surface wind conditions dictate.

Warnings
All Twys closed except between Thr of Rwy06 and apron. Rwy06 end lights visible for last 50m of landing run only. Grass areas soft and unsafe. Only marked Twys to be used.

Maintenance	Nil
Fuel	AVTUR JET A1 Mon-Fri 0800-1530 (Local)

Loganair Fuels **Tel:** 01870 603147 **Fax:** 01870 602714

Operator	HIAL Benbecula Aerodrome Balvanich Isle of Benbecula Western Isles HS7 5LW **Tel:** 01870 602051 **Fax:** 01870 602278

Restaurants	Light refreshments available at AD

Cafe/Bar accommodation at Dark Isle Hotel by taxi

Taxis
Buchanan's	**Tel:** 01870 602277
MacVicar's	**Tel:** 01870 602307
Maclennan's	**Tel:** 01870 602191

Car Hire
Maclennan Bros	**Tel:** 01870 602191
Ask	**Tel:** 01870 602818

Weather Info	M T9 Fax 234 GWC

Operating Hrs
Mon-Fri 0800-1500 Sat 0930-1100 (Summer)
Mon-Fri 0900-1600 Sat 1130-1300 (Winter) & by arrangement

Circuits

Landing fee	£10.65 inc VAT ACFT under 3MT VFR cash/cheque on day

ELEVATION	LOCATION	**EGUB**	**BENSON**

ELEVATION	LOCATION		
203ft 7mb	11nm SE of Oxford N5136.98.W00105.75	CPT 114.35 037 9.0	− • − • / • − − • / −
PPR **MILITARY**		BNN 113.75 257 21.5	− • • • / − • / − •

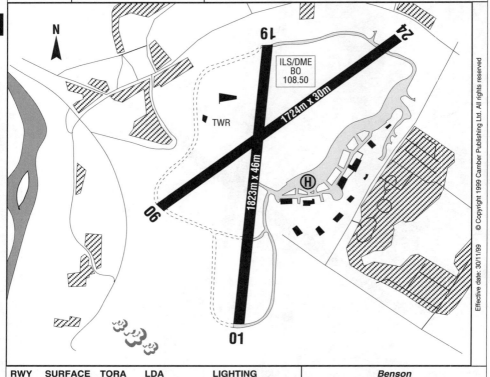

RWY	SURFACE	TORA	LDA	LIGHTING
01/19	Asph/Con	1823	1823	Ap Thr Rwy PAPI 3°
06/24*	Asph/Con	1724	1643	Nil

*06/24 for use by Benson based ACFT only

	Benson
MATZ	120.90
APP	127.15 122.10
RAD	120.90 127.15 122.10
TWR	130.25
ILS	BO 108.50 Rwy19

Remarks
PPR 24Hrs notice required for private ACFT. VFR arrivals below 3000ft are to contact Benson APP at least 5nm before MATZ boundary or to be under control of Brize Radar. After landings & before take-off pilots must report personally to operations. No visitors outside Hrs 0830-1700. Visual aid to location: Ibn BO Red. ACFT to use Twys east side Rwy01/19 only. Ground handling facilities available 0800-1730 Mon-Fri for visiting ACFT. Visitors restricted to landings and take-offs only.

Warnings
Serious risk of bird strikes. Regular glider & helicopter activity in the MATZ. High traffic density due to Oxford AIAA. Do not climb above 4000ft QNH until clear of N boundary Awy G.1. South of Benson, base 4500ft. London QNH. Intensive MATZ crossing traffic. Public road, controlled by traffic lights, crosses the undershoot of Rwy 150m from Thr. Avoid over-flying the villages of Benson, Ewelme and Wallingford. Caution, fixed wing and rotary activity takes place outside published Hrs.

Circuits	01 RH 19LH
Landing fee	£7.56 per 500kgs +VAT & £8.50 insurance
Maintenance Fuel	Nil AVGAS 100LL AVTUR FS11 by arrangement
Operator	RAF Benson, Oxon OX9 6AA **Tel: 01491 837766 Ext 7555/7487**
Restaurants	
Taxis/Car Hire	
Weather Info	AirSE BNMC

Operating Hrs	Mon-Fri 0700-1630 (Summer) Winter + 1Hr

ELEVATION	LOCATION	**EGNY**	**BEVERLEY (Linley Hill)**

ELEVATION	LOCATION		
3ft 0mb	4nm NE of Beverley N5353.92.W00021.72	OTR 113.90 329 15	– – – / – / • – •
PPR	**Diversion AD**	GAM 112.80 035 42	– – • / • – / – –

B

Map labels:
N
12
H
720m x 30m
30
Emergency Vehicle Access Only
Drainage Dykes
A/C Parking
C
No Parking
Car Park
Private Land
100ft agl power line

RWY	SURFACE	TORA	LDA	LIGHTING		Beverley	
12	Grass	720	639	Nil	A/G	123.05	
30	Grass	720	720	Nil			

Remarks
PPR. Non-radio ACFT not accepted. Licensed AD, but not available for public transport flights required to use a licensed AD. ACFT to join overhead at 1500 ft QFE. Due to the proximity of electric transmission line no right base join for Rwy12. Avoid over-flying Leven village 1.5nm east of the AD. Dept from Rwy12 turn left before reaching Leven village. No right turns due to possible conflict with SAR helicopter activity.

Warnings
Displaced Thr Rwy12. Rwy QDM markings appear before the displaced Thr arrow and marked Thr. Power line 100ft AAL crosses extended Rwy centreline 1200m 300°M from the ARP. Pilots using Rwy12 must have visual contact with the power line before starting final approach. A dyke 30m before Rwy30 Thr marked with red and white warning markings. A second dyke runs parallel to Rwy30 23m from the right-hand edge.

Landing fee	Single £5.00 Twin £10.00 inc VAT
Maintenance	Nil
Fuel	AVGAS 100LL
Operator	Hull Aero Club Linley Hill Airfield Leven, North Humberside HU17 5LT **Tel/Fax: 01964 544994**

Restaurants
Tea & coffee and sweets avl in club house

Taxis
| Alpha | **Tel: 01482 881461** |
| Bradcabs | **Tel: 01482 868396** |

Car Hire
| Andrews | **Tel: 01482 867360** |
| Beverly Ford | **Tel: 01482 866900** |

Weather Info AirN MWC

Operating Hrs 0800-2100 or SS (Summer)
0900-SS (Winter)

Circuits All circuits to the North to avoid Leconfield ATZ, 12 LH, 30 RH, 1000 ft QFE

ELEVATION	LOCATION					BIDFORD
135ft 4mb	4nm E of Evesham N5208.03.W00150.97	HON 113.65	212	15	••••/–––/–•	
PPR		DTY 116.40	268	27	–••/–/–•––	

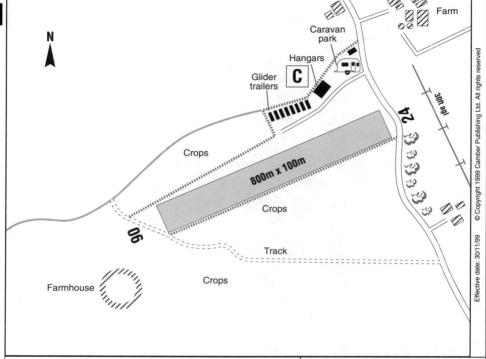

RWY	SURFACE	TORA	LDA	LIGHTING			
							Bidford Base
06/24	Grass	800x100	U/L	Nil		A/G	129.975 (Gliding Freq)

Remarks
PPR essential by telephone for daily gliding briefing.
Gliding site Aerotow only. Powered visitors should keep a
good lookout for gliders ensuring their operations are not
obstructed. Avoid overflying local villages.

Warnings
There are power lines 300m from Thr Rwy24. The AD is
situated within Restricted area R204 which is applicable to
helicopters only. Crops are grown up to the S of the AD.
Mandatory noise abatement procedures: see website for
details at airplan.u-net.com; December amendments

Operating Hrs   0800-SS (local)

Circuits   To south at 1000ft QFE Avoid overflying
Bidford-on-Avon when downwind or departing Rwy06

Landing fee   Nil

Maintenance
Bidford Gliding Centre (Gliders & powered ACFT)
Tel/Fax: 01789 490174
Fuel   Nil

Operator   Mr & Mrs Inglis, Bidford Gliding Centre
Bidford Airfield
Bidford-on-Avon
Warwickshire B50 4PD
Tel: 01789 772606(AD)
Tel/Fax: 01789 490174 (Maintenance)

Restaurants/Accomodation
Cafe & camping on site

Taxis   **Tel:** 01789 262600
Car Hire   **Tel:** 01905 792307

Weather Info   AirCen BNMC

ELEVATION	LOCATION	EGKB				BIGGIN HILL
600ft 20mb	3nm SSE of Bromley N5119.85 E00001.94	BIG 115.10 OCK 115.30 LAM 115.60	On A/D 090 197	18 19.6	— • • • / • • / — — • — — — / — • • — • / — • — • — • • / • — / — —	

B

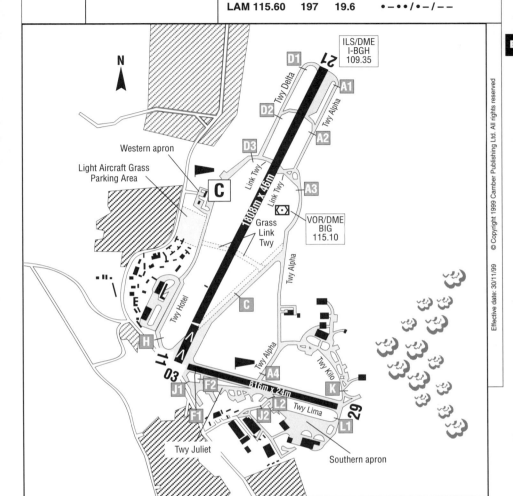

RWY	SURFACE	TORA	LDA	LIGHTING
03	Concrete	1778	1558	Thr Rwy APAPI 4° LHS
21	Concrete	1678	1678	Ap Thr Rwy PAPI 3° LHS
11/29	Asphalt	816	816	Nil

	Biggin
ATIS	121.875
APP	129.40
RAD*	Thames 132.70
VDF	134.80 129.40
TWR	134.80
	* Inbound IFR flights requiring a radar service
VOR/DME	BIG 115.10 on AD
ILS/DME	I-BGH 109.35 Rwy21

Remarks
AD not available to non-radio ACFT or microlights. Airport rules and conditions of use are available from the operator. When taking off, going around or making touch and goes, remain at, or below, 500ft QFE until the upwind end of the Rwy. If joining the circuit do so at, not below, 1000ft QFE across the upwind end of the Rwy in use. Helicopters PPR. To avoid noise sensitive areas surrounding the airport helicopters must conform to normal fixed wing Dept and circuit procedures unless otherwise instructed by ATC.

Warnings
Microlight flying is prohibited at this airport. Aerobatic manoeuvres and low fly pasts are prohibited unless participating in an organised flying display. Light ACFT must follow the noise abatement Dept routes published by the AD authority. Special Note: Helicopters should at all times avoid over-flying highly noise-sensitive areas of housing adjacent to airport to NW, NE and SW.

B

Operating Hrs
Mon-Fri 0630-2000 Sat Sun & PH 0800-1900 (Summer)
Mon-Fri 0730-2100 Sat Sun & PH 0900-2000 (Winter)

Circuits
03/11 LH 21/29 RH 1000ft. QFE day and night

| Landing fee | Up to 0.8 tonnes £14.30 plus VAT |
| | 0.8-1.7 tonnes £17.00 plus VAT |

Maintenance
Shipping & Airlines Ltd	**Tel:** 01959 573404
Falcon Flying Services	**Tel:** 01959 575923
Fuel	AVGAS 100LL AVTUR JET A1
	Tel: 01959 574737

Operator	Regional Airports Ltd
	Biggin Hill Airport, Kent TN16 3BN
	Tel: 01959 574677 (ATC) 571111
	(Admin.) 574679 (Handling)
	Fax: 576404 (Ops)
	Telex: 957045 BIGGIN G

| Restaurants | Restaurant/refreshments available at A/D |

Taxis
Luxury Cars	**Tel:** 01959 574677 01860 379109
Car Hire	
Budget Rent-a-Car	**Tel:** 0208 464 7736

| Weather Info | M T9 Fax 236 A BNMC |

Visual Reference Points (VRPs)
Sevenoaks
N5116.60 E00010.90

VFR Dept Routes
Light twins and singles only
Rwy 21 Depts to East, South, Northeast; avoid built up areas. Keep school and silos on left hand side. Straight ahead for 2nm then left turn. Depts to West, North, straight ahead for 1nm then turn right. Keep school on left hand side.
Rwy 03 Depts to East, South, Northeast; straight ahead for 1.5nm then right turn. Caution; ACFT joining deadside 03/21 at ALT 1600ft. Avoid Farnborough and Downe. Depts to North and West; straight ahead for 1nm then left turn. Avoid built up areas.
Rwy 29 Depts to South, East; straight ahead for 1nm then left turn. Keep silos on left hand side. Caution; ACFT joining deadside 11/29 at ALT 1600ft. Depts to North, Northeast; straight ahead for 1nm right turn. Avoid Leaves Green. Depts to West; straight ahead for 1nm then turn on track.
Rwy 11 all directions; straight ahead for 1nm then left or right on track. Avoid Cudham, Downe, Biggin Hill. Caution; if turning West or South due to ACFT joining deadside 11/29 at ALT 1600ft.

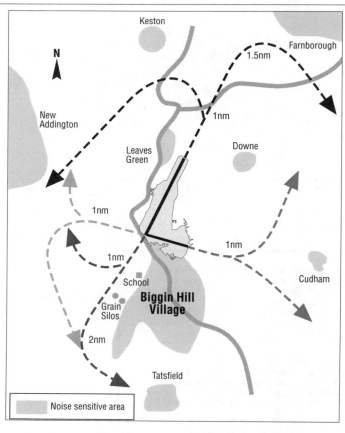

ELEVATION	LOCATION	**EGBB**				**BIRMINGHAM**
325ft	5.5nm ESE of					
11mb	Birmingham	HON 113.65	337	6.6	•••• / – – – / – •	
	N5227.23.W00144.88	DTY 116.40	312	28.5	– •• / – / – • – –	
PPR						

B

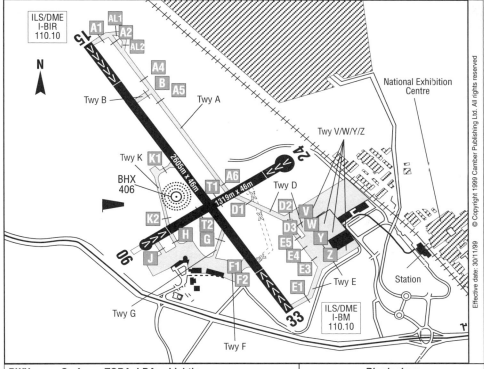

RWY	Surface	TORA	LDA	Lighting
06	Asphalt	1260	1025	Ap Thr Rwy APAPI 3.5° LHS
24	Asphalt	1315	1188	Ap Thr Rwy APAPI 3.5° LHS
15	Asphalt	2575	2279	Ap Thr Rwy PAPI 3° LHS
33	Asphalt	2600	2304	Ap Thr Rwy PAPI 3° LHS

	Birmingham
ATIS	126.275
APP	118.050
VDF	118.050 121.500 (O/R)
RAD	118.050 131.325
TWR	118.30 121.500 (O/R)
GND	121.80
FIRE	121.6
	VDF is not to be used for en-route navigation except in an emergency
ILS/DME	I-BM 110.10 Rwy33
	I-BIR 110.10 Rwy15
NDB	BHX 406 on A/D, range 25nm

Remarks

PPR to non-radio ACFT. Hi-Vis. Use of the airport for training purposes is subject to the approval of the Airport Managing Director & ATC. Training ACFT must climb straight ahead to 1000ft aal before turning, unless otherwise instructed by ATC. Training flights including ILS go-arounds by ACFT not based at Birmingham, likely to cause nuisance to surrounding area, are prohibited between 1800-0800 (Local). ACFT must not join the final approach track to any Rwy below 1500ft aal, unless they are propeller driven ACFT whose MTWA does not exceed 5700kg in which case the minimum height is 1000ft aal. Helicopter Operations: Helicopters to land as instructed by ATC. Visual aids to location: IBn BM Green. Mandatory handling for GA ACFT.

Warnings

TwyC restricted to use by ACFT with a maximum wing span of 39m. TwyD to rear of stands 44-51 restricted to ACFT with max wing span of 38.5m.

B

Operating Hrs	H24

Circuits
Variable circuits 1000ft QFE for light ACFT

Landing fee	Up to 1MT £12.60
	Up to 1.5MT £18.90
	Up to 2MT £25.20
	Up to 3MT £33.63 all +VAT & parking

Maintenance	Available plus hangarage
Fuel	Arrange through handling agents AVGAS

100LL (24 hour Bowser) AVTUR JET A1

Operator	Birmingham International Airport Plc.
	B.I.A. Birmingham B26 3QJ
	Tel: 0121 782 8802 (Airport)
	Tel: 0121 780 0906 (ATC)
	Tel: 0121 767 7139 (Ops Duty Manager)
	Fax: 0121 767 5511 (Airport)

Restaurants
Restaurant, buffet and bar available at Terminal

Taxis
Available at Terminal Also MAGLEV system
Car Hire

Avis	**Tel:** 0121 782 6183
Hertz	**Tel:** 0121 782 5158
Europcar	**Tel:** 0121 782 6507

Weather Info	M T9 T18 Fax 238 A VS MWC

Ground Movement
An ATC Ground Movement Control (GMC) service operates 0700-2100 (Local) on 121.80. On the manoeuvring area, pilots will be cleared under general direction from GMC and are reminded of the importance of maintaining a careful lookout at all times. ATC instructions will normally specify the taxi route to be followed. All operators making requests for taxying or towing clearance to GMC should state their location in the initial call. Mandatory handling is required for all visiting business and General Aviation ACFT. Handling Agencies:
Execair **Tel:** 0121 7821999 **Fax:** 0121 7821899
Midland Airport Services
Tel: 0121 7677715
Servisair **Tel:** 0121 767772 **Fax:** 0121 7827766
British Awys **Tel:** 0121 7677518 **Fax** 0121 7677590

Noise Abatement Procedure
All ACFT using the airport shall be operated in a manner calculated to cause the least disturbance practicable in areas surrounding the airport. Unless otherwise instructed by ATC, ACFT shall not descend below 2000ft before intercepting the glide path nor fly below the glide path thereafter. An ACFT approaching without assistance from ILS or radar must follow a descent path not lower than if following the ILS glide path.

CTACFTTR CLASS D AIRSPACE
Normal CTA/CTR Class D Airspace rules apply.
Clearance for SVFR below 1500ft QNH will not be given in the sector enclosed by the bearings 245°T and 360°T from the airport. This is the main built-up area of Birmingham.

ELEVATION	LOCATION	**EGLK**				**BLACKBUSHE**
329ft 11mb	8.5nm SE by S of Reading N5119.43.W00050.85	OCK 115.30	280	14.9	– – – / – • • / – • –	
PPR	**Diversion AD**	CPT 114.35	131	17.3	– • – • / • – – / –	

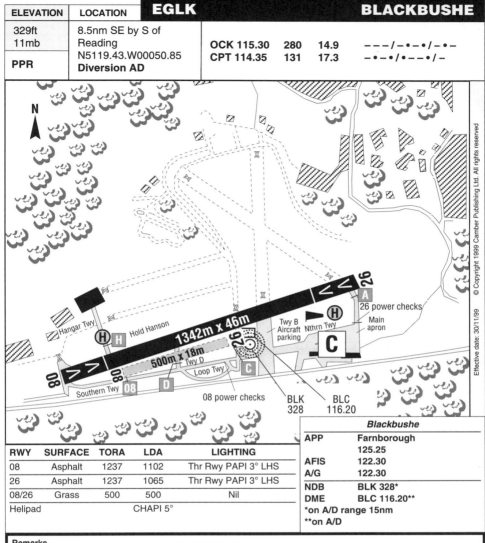

26 power checks

08 power checks

BLK 328   BLC 116.20

RWY	SURFACE	TORA	LDA	LIGHTING
08	Asphalt	1237	1102	Thr Rwy PAPI 3° LHS
26	Asphalt	1237	1065	Thr Rwy PAPI 3° LHS
08/26	Grass	500	500	Nil
Helipad		CHAPI 5°		

	Blackbushe
APP	Farnborough 125.25
AFIS	122.30
A/G	122.30
NDB	BLK 328*
DME	BLC 116.20**
*on A/D range 15nm	
**on A/D	

Remarks
PPR by telephone or radio. Visual Aids to location: Abn White flashing. On PHs the AD is not available for ACFT required to use a licensed AD. approaching Blackbushe remain North of the M3 to avoid ACFT using Farnborough. For noise abatement remain well clear of Yately to the North East and Hartley Witney West of the AD. Pilots are responsible for their passengers whilst on the airside of this airport. Due to planning restrictions the following ACFT may not land at this AD: Cessna Skymaster (C336/337/L); Dornier 28D Sky Servant (D08D/L); Gates Learjet 23,24,25,28,29 (LR23,24,25,28/L,29/M); Piaggio P166 (P166/L).

Warnings
The AD is frequently used outside the published Hrs of operation by fixed and rotary wing ACFT. Pilots operating at any time in the vicinity of the AD should therefore call Blackbushe AFIS/A/G to check if the AD is active. Pilots are further cautioned that no reply does not necessarily imply no traffic in the ATZ, and a very careful lookout should be maintained. Avoidance of the ATZ if at all possible is preferable. Because of increased helicopter activity, helicopter specific lighting aids have been installed on the northern Twy at the western end of the AD. These consist of Helipad, illuminated Tee and CHAPI 5.0° (Air Hanson's Helipad and APP. lights, plus lead-in strobes). Fixed-wing pilots should ignore indications from this lighting. An additional AD beacon situated on the roof of a hangar (287°, 0.3nm from the ARP) may be illuminated, but only outside notified AD Hrs. A section of disused Rwy01/19, to the south of Rwy 08/26, is marked as a Twy and the most southerly portion as an ACFT parking area. The grassed surface south of Rwy 08/26 between Twys C and D is unsuitable for use by certain types of helicopter due to its poor grading. Pilots are cautioned to positively ascertain that the grading of this area is suitable for their operational requirements. Visual glideslope guidance signals for both Rwy08 and 26 are visible to the south of the extended Rwy centrelines where normal obstacle clearance is not guaranteed. They should not be used until aligned with the Rwy. A public footpath crosses the centre of the AD from south east to north west. Fuel not normally available on Public Holidays. Caution large concentrations of birds on and in the vicinity of AD.

B

Operating Hrs	0700-1700 (Summer) 0800-1700 (Winter) and by arrangement

Circuits All circuits to the South of the AD
Single engined ACFT 800ft QFE
Twin engined and executive ACFT 1200 ft QFE
At night circuit height for all ACFT is 1000 ft QFE

Landing fee Single from £17.00 inc.VAT
Discount available for fuel uplift and club ACFT or PFA/AOPA
members with card Single £9.00 inc VAT

Maintenance
Air Hanson Ltd **Tel:** 01252 890089
Fuel AVGAS 100LL AVTUR JET A1

Operator Blackbushe Airport Ltd
Blackbushe Airport
Camberley, Surrey
Tel: 01252 879449 (Management and Admin)
Tel: 01252 873338 (Tower) **Fax** 01252 874444

Restaurants Club facilities

Taxis
A2B Taxis **Tel:** 01276 64488/64499
Car Hire
Avis **Tel:** 01344 417417
Europcar **Tel:** 01276 451570

Weather Info AirSE BNMC

Blackbushe Circuit Diagram

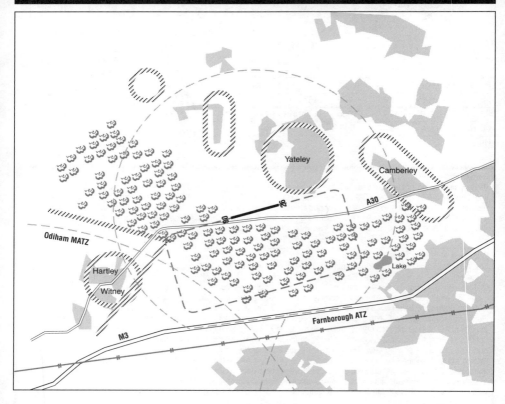

ELEVATION	LOCATION	EGNH				BLACKPOOL
34ft 1mb	2.6nm SSE of Blackpool N5346.29.W00301.71	WAL 114.10	016	23.1	• – – / • – / • – • •	
PPR		MCT 113.55	319	37.2	– – / – • – – • / –	

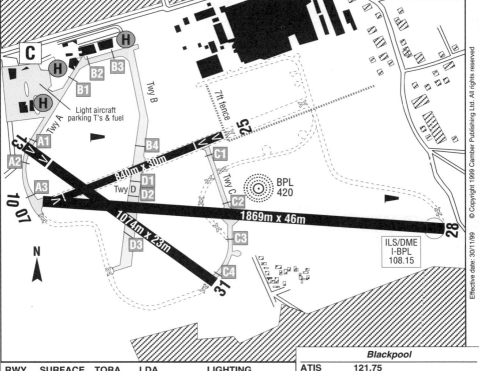

Labels within chart: C, H, H, H, B2, B3, B1, B4, A1, A2, A3, C1, D1, D2, C2, C3, D3, C4, Twy A, Twy B, Twy C, Twy D, Light aircraft parking T's & fuel, 7ft fence, 25, 13, 10 07, 31, 28, 840m x 30m, 1074m x 23m, 1869m x 46m, BPL 420, ILS/DME I-BPL 108.15, N

RWY	SURFACE	TORA	LDA	LIGHTING
07	Asphalt	780	770	Nil
25	Asphalt	840	750	Nil
10/28	Asphalt	1869	1869	Ap Thr Rwy PAPI 3°
13	Asphalt	1074	924	Ap Thr Rwy PAPI 4°
31	Asphalt	1074	1074	Ap Thr Rwy PAPI 3.25°

Blackpool	
ATIS	121.75
APP/RAD	119.95
VDF/Hmr	118.40 135.95
TWR	118.40
ILS/DME	I-BPL 108.15 Rwy28
NDB	BPL 420.0*
	*on A/D range 15nm

Remarks

PPR to non-radio ACFT. Hi-Vis. All inbound ACFT to make initial call to APP. Landing and taxiing on grass areas by fixed-wing ACFT is prohibited. The portion of Twy which passes between the hangars and the ACFT parking area is only suitable for ACFT with wingspan of up to 19m. ACFT using this airport are to carry 3rd Party Insurance cover of at least £1,000,000. ACFT using Blackpool Airport do so in accordance with Blackpool Airport terms and conditions, (available on Application). Two self parking stands are provided adjacent to terminal. Seven parking T's for light ACFT are provided on the western apron adjacent to the fuel farm. Grass parking known as FYLDE PARK is provided to the N of Rwy13 undershoot.

Warnings

In conditions of moderate/heavy rain and a southerly crosswind standing water may persist from the Thr of Rwy28 for a distance of 150 metres on the south side reducing the surface friction coefficient. Rwy13/31 lighting is at full width not useable full width (23m).

Operating Hrs & by arrangement	0600-2000 (Summer) 0700-2100 (Winter)

Circuits	25/28/31 RH
Landing fee	0-500kgs £5.50 501-1000kgs £11.00 1001-1500kgs £16.50 inc. VAT PFA discount £2.00 on the above rates with membership card
Maintenance	Westair Tel: 01253 404925
Fuel	AVGAS 100LL AVTUR JET A1
Operator	Blackpool Airport Ltd Blackpool Airport Blackpool Lancs FY4 2QY **Tel:** 01253 343434 **Fax:** 01253 405009 **Tel:** 01253 342483 (ATC) **Fax:** 01253 402004 (ATC)
Restaurants	Bar/Cafe in terminal
Taxis	Black Taxi freephone in Terminal
Car Hire Avis Hertz	**Tel:** 01253 397771 **Tel:** 01253 404021
Weather Info	M T9 Fax 242 A VN MWC

B

Helicopter Operations

Two helicopter approach aiming points marked with an 'H' are located 140 metres west of the ATC Tower (H north) and 100 metres from the end of Twy 02 (H south).

Arrival Procedures - VFR Helicopters arriving from the south will be routed abeam St Annes Pier to enter the ATZ not above 500ft QFE and route to H south prior to further clearance to requisite parking area.

Helicopters arriving from the north and east quadrants will route via the Fleetwood-Kirkton Railway. M6 or the M55 to approach the airport via the Gasometers on the western edge of the M55, prior to crossing the ATZ not above 500ft QFE to H north.

Helicopters wishing to approach at 1500ft or above will join overhead at 1500ft QFE, descend on the dead side prior to proceeding to H north or H south.

Dept Procedures:- Westward helicopters will remain below 500ft QFE until at least 5nm west (the Holyhead QNH will be furnished) north and eastwards: helicopters will clear the ATZ not above 500ft QFE on track of 071°M, via the Gasometers, and then route either via the M55, the Kirkham-Fleetwood railway northwards to Heysham, or the M6 Motorway. Southwards and southwestwards route seawards via abeam St Annes Pier not above 500ft QFE until clear of ATZ. Helicopter captains are warned about proximity of Warton MATZ, radio masts 700ft at Inskip, radio mast adjacent to gasometers in NE quadrant at 300ft amsl, military low level activity in Irish Sea. Captains will not overfly the ICI complex at Thornton.

VFR Flights

The following locations are established as VFR reporting points:

Approaching south:	Marshside
Approaching southeast:	Warton AD
Approaching east:	Kirkham
Approaching east northeast:	Inskip
Approaching northeast:	Poulton
Approaching north:	Fleetwood

Pilots approaching from the west should contact ATC at 5nm range. All VFR flights should leave the zone tracking to/from these locations.

Arriving ACFT must contact Warton APP (125.925) in the first instance.

Visual Reference Points (VRPs)

Fleetwood Golf Course
N5355.13 W00302.72
Inskip disused A/D
N5349.63 W00250.05
Kirkham
N5346.95 W00252.28
Marshside
N5341.78 W00258.23
Poulton Railway Station
N5350.90 W00259.42

ELEVATION	LOCATION	EGLA				BODMIN

ELEVATION	LOCATION			
625ft 21mb	3.5nm NE of Bodmin N5029.98.W00439.95 **Diversion AD**	BHD 112.05	284	45.1	— • • • / • • • • / — • •
PPR		LND 114.20	066	43.1	• — • • / — • / — • •

Aerodrome chart showing runways: A30 (T), N, 21, 14, 480m x 18m, 03, 610m x 18m, 32, C, Fuel, Apron Grass/Asphalt

RWY	SURFACE	TORA	LDA	LIGHTING		Bodmin	
03/21	Grass	480	480	Nil	APP	St. Mawgan 126.50	
14	Grass	598	598	Nil	A/G	122.70	
32	Grass	610	540	Nil			

Remarks
Not available for public transport passenger flights required to use a licensed AD. Not available for use at night by flights required to use a licensed AD. Rwys are marked with end corner markings and centreline markings. Customs facilities available by arrangement.

Warnings
Use of the AD is limited to ACFT below MTWA of 2490kgs (5500lbs). The AD is convex making it impossible to see the Rwy stop-ends from the take-off position. Due to hilly site and proximity of both the North and South coasts which cause sea breezes, extreme windshear and downdraughts may be encountered at any time, even in light winds. Extreme caution must be taken when taxying to the apron and refuelling area, centreline to obstructions is 8m at the minimum width of the Twy.

Maintenance	Bodmin Light Aero Services
Tel: 01208 821535	Hangarage also available
Fuel	AVGAS 100LL

Operator	Cornwall Flying Club Ltd Bodmin Airfield Cardinham, Bodmin, Cornwall PL30 4BU **Tel:** 01208 821419 **Fax:** 01208 821711

Restaurants	Pilot's Shop/Bar 7 Days Kitchen 10.00-14.30 Vending Machine (tea/coffee/sandwiches)

Taxis	
Bodmin Taxi Serv.	**Tel:** 01208 731000
Car Hire	
Westend Motors	**Tel:** 01208 751656

Weather Info	AirSW BNMC

Operating Hrs	0830-1930 (Summer) 0900-1730 or SS (Winter) and by arrangement
Circuits	03/32 LH 21/14 RH 800 ft QFE
Landing fee	Single £6.00 inc VAT

ELEVATION	LOCATION	EGDM		BOSCOMBE DOWN

ELEVATION	LOCATION			
407ft 13mb	1.5nm SE of Amesbury N5109.13.W00144.84	SAM 113.35	312 19.4	• • • / • — / — —
PPR MILITARY		CPT 114.35	232 28.3	— • — • / • — — • / —

B

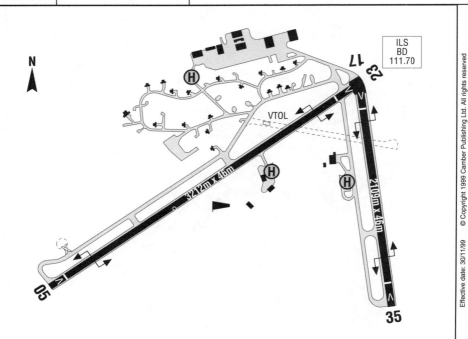

```
ILS
BD
111.70
```

VTOL

3212m x 46m

2105m x 46m

Effective date: 30/11/99

© Copyright 1999 Camber Publishing Ltd. All rights reserved

RWY	SURFACE	TORA	LDA	LIGHTING
05	Asphalt	3212	3209	Ap Thr Rwy PAPI 3°
23	Asphalt	3212	3109	Ap Thr Rwy PAPI 3°
17/35	Asphalt	1913	1913	Ap Thr Rwy PAPI 3°

Boscombe	
APP/MATZ/ LARS	126.70 130.00
VDF	126.70
TWR	130.75
TACAN	BDN 108.20
ILS	BD 111.70 Rwy23

Remarks
PPR from HQ Flying Division, Ext. 2058/2700. Practice diversion PNR by ATC Ext. 3246/2114. Pilots operating over Salisbury Plain must, before recovery to Boscombe Down, establish RT contact for Radar Sequencing and avoidance of circuit traffic. All visiting ACFT to call at min. 20nm. All procedures within 10nm and below 3000ft are flown on Boscombe QFE.

Warnings
Intensive test flying takes place at this AD. Be aware also of close proximity of 'Salisbury Plain' Danger Areas D123, D124, D125, D126 - DACS Salisbury Ops 122.75. After dark up to 2359 Hrs Mon-Fri MATZ may contain unlit ACFT, also AD and obstruction lights may be extinguished during flying. Light ACFT, glider and helicopter flying in daylight outside AD Hrs. Radiation hazard (525ft radius up to 500ft agl extends to within 500ft of Rwy05/23). Possible inadvertent actuation of electrically initiated explosive devices. RAF type B barriers installed for all Rwys. Arrester gears are fitted 435m from 05 Thr, 372m from 23 Thr, 273m from 17 Thr, 427m from 35 Thr. Rwy05/23 overrun cable normally up. Rwy17/35 both cables normally down.

Operating Hrs
Mon-Thu 0730-1600 Fri 0730-1500 (Summer) Winter + 1Hr

Circuits	Variable
Landing fee	£7.56 per 500kgs +VAT & £8.50 insurance
Maintenance Fuel	Nil AVGAS 100LL AVTUR JET A1 with FS11 AVPIN

Operator MOD(PE) Boscombe Down
Salisbury, Wiltshire SP4 0JF
Tel: 01980 663051/2 (PPR thru Ops)
Tel: 01980 662700 (PPR outside normal Ops Hrs)

Restaurants

Taxis/Car Hire

Weather Info	M T Fax 244 BNMC

Visual Reference Point (VRP)
Alderbury   N5102.90 W00143.90

ELEVATION	LOCATION			
8ft 0mb **PPR**	1.5nm W of Boston N5258.48.W00004.27	**GAM 112.80**	126 37	− − • / • − / − −

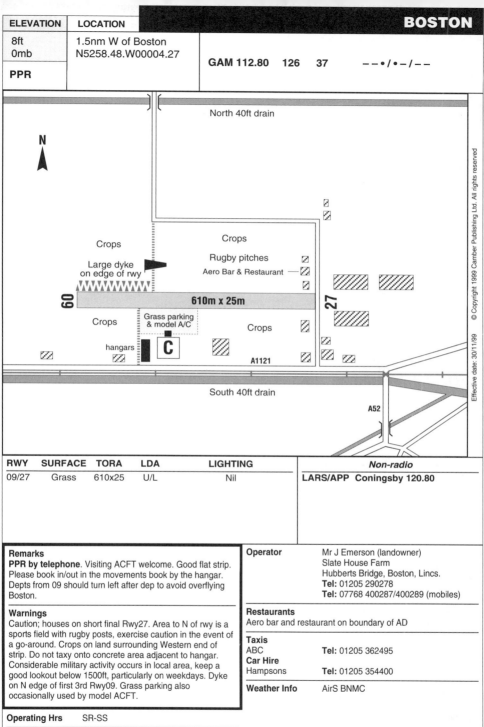

North 40ft drain

N

Crops

Crops

Rugby pitches

Aero Bar & Restaurant

Large dyke
on edge of rwy

09 · 610m x 25m · **27**

Crops

Grass parking
& model A/C

Crops

hangars · **C**

A1121

South 40ft drain

A52

Effective date: 30/11/99

RWY	SURFACE	TORA	LDA	LIGHTING
09/27	Grass	610x25	U/L	Nil

Non-radio
LARS/APP Coningsby 120.80

Remarks
PPR by telephone. Visiting ACFT welcome. Good flat strip. Please book in/out in the movements book by the hangar. Depts from 09 should turn left after dep to avoid overflying Boston.

Warnings
Caution; houses on short final Rwy27. Area to N of rwy is a sports field with rugby posts, exercise caution in the event of a go-around. Crops on land surrounding Western end of strip. Do not taxy onto concrete area adjacent to hangar. Considerable military activity occurs in local area, keep a good lookout below 1500ft, particularly on weekdays. Dyke on N edge of first 3rd Rwy09. Grass parking also occasionally used by model ACFT.

Operating Hrs	SR-SS

Circuits
1000ft QFE please be considerate of local habitation

Landing fee	£5.00

Maintenance	Nil
Fuel	Nil

Operator
Mr J Emerson (landowner)
Slate House Farm
Hubberts Bridge, Boston, Lincs.
Tel: 01205 290278
Tel: 07768 400287/400289 (mobiles)

Restaurants
Aero bar and restaurant on boundary of AD

Taxis
ABC **Tel:** 01205 362495
Car Hire
Hampsons **Tel:** 01205 354400

Weather Info
AirS BNMC

BOUGHTON (North)

ELEVATION	LOCATION
70ft 2mb	4nm SSW of RAF Marham N5235.52 E00030.95
PPR	

BKY 116.25   029   39.5   — • • • / — • — / — • — —

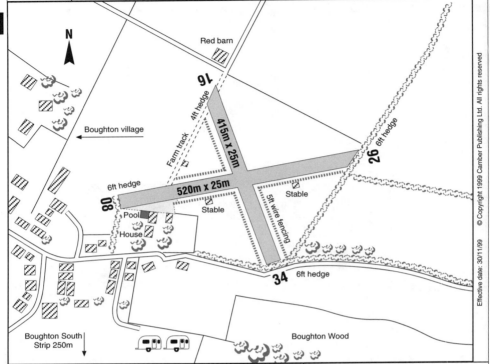

Effective date: 30/11/99

RWY	SURFACE	TORA	LDA	LIGHTING
08/26	Grass	520x25	U/L	Nil
16/34	Grass	415x25	U/L	Nil

Non-Radio

APP   (Marham) 124.15

Remarks
PPR by telephone. Visiting pilots welcome at own risk.
Noise: Avoid overflight of Boughton and Stoke villages.

Warnings
AD situated within Marham MATZ. Arriving and Departing
ACFT contact Marham APP 124.15. Rwys are bordered by
5ft wire fence. A 6ft hedge runs across Thr26. Sheep graze
AD.Caution: There is another Boughton AD (single Rwy) to S.

Operator   Mr P Coulten
Oxborough Road, Boughton, Kings Lynn, Norfolk
Tel: 01366 500315 (Home)
Tel: 01945 582891 (Office)

Restaurants   Tea & coffee available at the farmhouse

Taxi
Transport can be arranged with prior notice
Car Hire

Weather Info   AirS BNMC

Operating Hrs	SR-SS
Circuits	See remarks
Landing fee	Nil
Maintenance	Nil
Fuel	Nil

B

ELEVATION	LOCATION	EGSN				BOURN
225ft 7mb	7nm W of Cambridge N5212.62.W00002.57		BPK 117.50	010	28.2	– • • • / • – – • / – • –
	Diversion AD		BKY 116.25	350	14.2	– • • • / – • – / – • – –
PPR			CFD 116.50	073	22.7	– • – • / • • – • / – • •

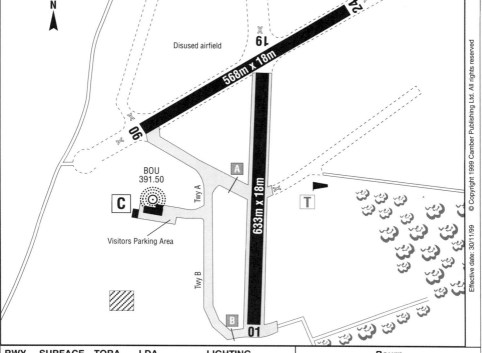

RWY	SURFACE	TORA	LDA	LIGHTING
01/19	Bitumen	633	633	Nil
06/24	Bitumen	568	568	Nil

	Bourn
A/G	129.80
NDB	BOU 391.5* on A/D range 15nm

Remarks
PPR by telephone. The licensed area is situated on a war-time AD on which non-aviation activities also take place. Not available for use by public transport passenger flights required to use a licensed AD or at night.

Warnings
There are a number of other licensed ADs in the vicinity and intensive gliding with winch launching cables to 2000ft agl takes place at Gransden Lodge 3nm south-west of Bourn.

Maintenance	Nil
Fuel	Nil
Operator	Rural Flying Corps, Bourn Aerodrome Bourn, Cambridgeshire CB3 7TQ **Tel/Fax:** 01954 719602 **Fax:** 01767 640652

Restaurants
Light snacks and refreshments available at the AD

Taxis	Arrangement on arrival or
M Nelson	**Tel:** 01589 558735
Car Hire	Arrangement on arrival or
Avis	**Tel:** 01223 212551
National	**Tel:** 01223 365438

Weather Info   AirCen BNMC

Operating Hrs   0830-1700 (Summer)
0930-1700 or SS (Winter)
and by arrangement. Closed PH

Circuits   Variable 1000ft QFE

Landing fee   Single £5.00 Twin £10.00
Microlight £1.00 inc VAT
Classic & interesting ACFT free at discretion of duty instructor

B

Effective date: 30/11/99   © Copyright 1999 Camber Publishing Ltd. All rights reserved

B

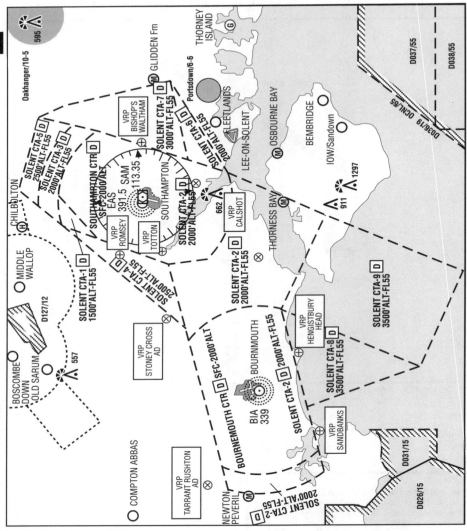

Visual Reference Points (VRPs)

VRP	VOR/NDB	VOR/DME
Hengistbury Head N5042.72 W00144.93	SAM R230°/BIA 142°M	SAM 230°/21nm
Sandbanks N5041.00 W00156.83	No suitable VOR/NDB	SAM 239°/28nm
Stoney Cross (disused A/D) N5054.70 W00139.42	SAM R262°/BIA 045°M	SAM 262°/12nm
Tarrant Rushton (disused A/D) N5051.00 W00204.70	SAM R261°/BIA 300°M	SAM 261°/28nm

ELEVATION	LOCATION	EGHH	BOURNEMOUTH (Hurn)

ELEVATION	LOCATION		
36ft 1mb	3.5nm NNE of Bournemouth N5046.80 W00150.55 **Diversion AD**	SAM 113.35 46 21.5 ●●●/●–/––	
PPR			

B

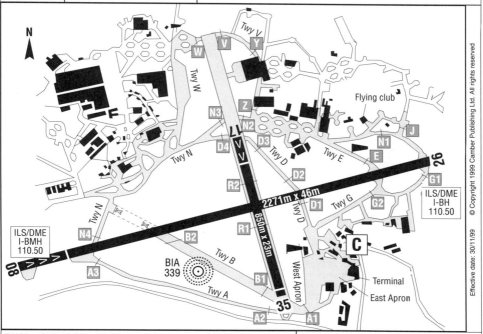

RWY	SURFACE	TORA	LDA	LIGHTING
08	Asphalt	2271	1838	Ap Thr Rwy PAPI 3° LHS
26*	Asphalt	2026	1970	Ap Thr Rwy PAPI 3° RHS
17**	Asphalt	800	750	Thr Rwy APAPI 3° LHS
35**	Asphalt	750	800	Thr Rwy APAPI 3° LHS

*2211m available on request. 3 Deps only between 0730-0900 1600-1800
**17/35 not available when vis/RVR is 1500m or less or there is a tailwind component

Bournemouth	
ATIS	121.950
APP	119.625
RAD	119.625 118.650
TWR	125.600
GND	121.700
ILS/DME	I-BH 110.50 Rwy26
ILS/DME	I-BMH 110.50 Rwy08
NDB	BIA 339*
	*on A/D range 20nm

Remarks

PPR to non-radio and light ACFT. Hi-Vis clothing to be worn on apron, escorts may accompany no more than 3 persons who do not have Hi-Vis clothing. It is prohibited to taxy any ACFT on the U/L part of the AD where vehicles operate on the road system. In these areas towing only approved subject to look-outs. ACFT Be55 and smaller may request to park W side of main apron S of stand A3 (Short stay), asphalt or grass areas S of TwyG long or short stay. ACFT to be parked at least 25m from Twy edge. Pilots to state parked position on initial contact with ATC. Pilots can book out at the Flight Clearance Office adjacent to E apron and by Tel: 01202 364150. Book out via RTF not permitted. Flight plans to be filed at Flight Clearance Office in the main terminal in person. All visiting GA pilots are to record Tel No, address, name of pilot and duration of stay on booking in at the Operations Centre. Duration of stay must also be passed to ATC on arrival. Prop swinging may only be carried out as a 2-person operation, this is to include PIC and person familiar with prop swinging procedures. All ACFT MTWA 3 tonnes or greater intending to park on the E or W apron require marshaller guidance before leaving the apron taxi-lane for stand positioning.

Warnings

With the exception of the Bravo Twy all Twys are only 15 metres wide and so are not suitable for use by ACFT with a wheelbase that exceeds 18 metres or a wheel span greater than 9 metres. The SE Twy is routed through the apron area. The entire area bounded by the stop bar for Rwy35 to the S and by a single yellow painted line near the Control tower to the N is designated as apron area for air traffic control purposes. Pilots are to exercise caution in this area, and when using the NE Twy, due to movements of pedestrians and vehicles. The displaced Thr for Rwy35 should not be crossed below 30 feet.

B

Operating Hrs	0530-2030 (Summer) 0630-2130 (Winter) and by arrangement
Circuits	ACFT less than 5700kgs 1000ft. All other ACFT/jet ACFT 1500ft. After 2030 (L) all ACFT 1500ft QFE
Landing fee	On application (payable at terminal info desk)
Maintenance	Available Full up to 5700kg MAUW
Fuel	AVGAS 100LL AVTUR Jet A-1

Refuelling facilities available daily 0700-2130 with
Shell **Tel:** 01202 575037
and by prior arrangement only outside thesee times with
Esso **Tel:** 01202 594000

Operator	Bournemouth Int Airport Plc Christchurch, Dorset BH23 6SE **Tel:** 01202 364150 (ATC/Ops/FBU) **Tel:** 01202 364119 (Admin) **Tel:** 01202 364176 (Ops) **Fax:** 01202 364159 (FBU)
Restaurants	Cafeteria bar and buffet at terminal
Taxis United	At terminal or **Tel:** 0800 304555
Car Hire Avis Hertz	**Tel:** 01202 293218 **Tel:** 01202 291231
Weather Info	M T9 Fax 246 A VS BNMC

CTR–Class D Airspace
Normal CTA/CTR Class D Airspace rules apply

ELEVATION	LOCATION				BREIGHTON

ELEVATION	LOCATION			
20ft 1mb **PPR**	5nm ENE of Selby N5348.12 W00054.85 **Diversion AD**	**OTR 113.90** **GAM 112.80**	289 008	29.4 31.2

OTR: – – – / – / • – •
GAM: – – • / • – / – –

B

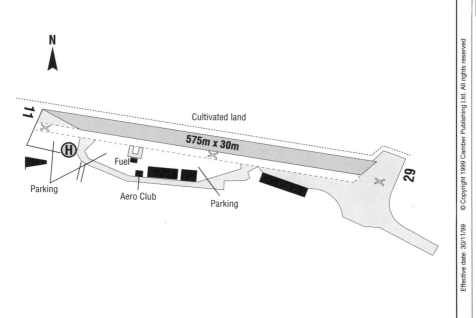

N

11

Cultivated land

575m x 30m

(H)

Fuel

Parking

Aero Club

Parking

29

RWY	SURFACE	TORA	LDA	LIGHTING		Breighton	
11/29	Grass	575	575	Nil	A/G	129.80	

Remarks
U/L AD situated at SW corner of disused military AD. Home of vintage and classic ACFT. Visiting ACFT, including non radio, welcome on prior permission and at pilot's own risk. Live side join required due to frequent aerobatic activity on N side of Rwy centreline. Vintage & Classic ACFT especially welcome.

Warning
Power cables on W APP. Special rules apply on display days. Avoid over-flying the villages of Breighton and Bubwith. **No overhead joins.**

Operating Hrs
Mon-Fri 0730-SS Sat-Sun 0900-SS (Summer)
Mon-Fri 0830-SS Sat-Sun 1000-SS (Winter)

Circuits
29 LH 11 RH 700 QFE all circuits are in the S

Landing fee Nil

Maintenance	
Real Aeroplane Co Fuel	**Tel:** 01757 289065 AVGAS 100LL JET A1
Operator	Real Aeroplane Company Ltd. The Aerodrome, Breighton, Selby, Yorks YO8 7DH **Tel:** 01757 289065
Restaurants	Refreshments & food at weekends
Taxis **Car Hire** National	On request through AD **Tel:** 01904 612141
Weather Info	AirN MWC

ELEVATION	LOCATION	BRIMPTON (Wasing Lower Farm)				
210ft 7mb	5.5nm ESE of Newbury N5123.03.W00110.35 **Diversion AD**	SAM 113.35	018	27.0	···/·−/−−	
PPR		MID 114.0	318	29.0	−−/··/−··	
		CPT 114.35	168	6.0	−·−·/·−−·/−	

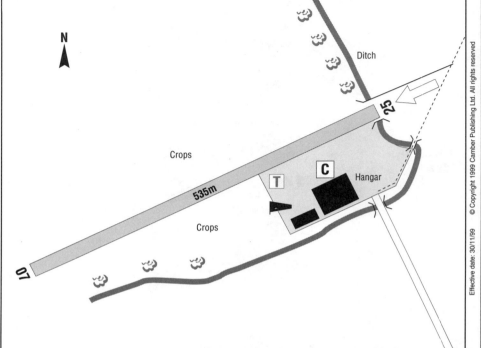

RWY	SURFACE	TORA	LDA	LIGHTING
07	Grass	535m	U/L	Nil
25*	Grass	635m	U/L	Nil

*Rwy Thr displaced 100m from Eastern AD boundary

Brimpton

A/G   **135.125**
Not always manned.
If not follow proc. in 'warning'

Remarks
PPR strictly by telephone.

Warnings
AD is situated just within the NW edge of the Atomic Weapons Establishment Restricted Area R101/2.4 and operates under a Special Exemption. All approaches to the field must be from the North. Flying south of the field below 2400ft AGL prohibited unless landing or taking-off. Avoid over flying the villages of Brimpton, Aldermaston, Woolhampton and local habitation.

Operator	Sylmar Aviation & Services Ltd Kennet House 77-79 Bath Road Thatcham, Berks RG18 3 BD **Tel:** 01635 866088 **Tel:** 01635 863433 / 07836 775557 (Alan House Chairman) **Tel:** 0118 971 3822 (Clubhouse)
Restaurants	Light snacks available in the clubhouse
Taxis **Car Hire** National	Various local firms **Tel:** 01635 582525
Weather Info	AirSW BNMC

Operating Hrs	0830-dusk (local)
Circuits	07 LH 25 RH 800ft QFE
Landing fee	Single £4.00 Twin £7.00
Maintenance **Fuel**	Limited Nil

ELEVATION	LOCATION	**EGGD**		**BRISTOL**

ELEVATION	LOCATION
622ft 21mb	7nm SW of Bristol N5122.96.W00243.15
PPR	

BCN 117.45 140 28.7   — • • • / — • — • / — •

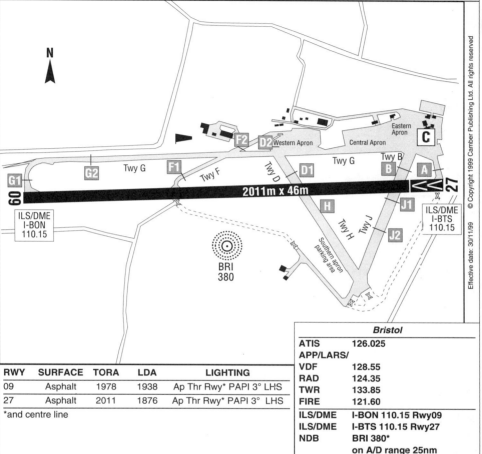

RWY	SURFACE	TORA	LDA	LIGHTING
09	Asphalt	1978	1938	Ap Thr Rwy* PAPI 3° LHS
27	Asphalt	2011	1876	Ap Thr Rwy* PAPI 3° LHS

*and centre line

	Bristol
ATIS	126.025
APP/LARS/ VDF	128.55
RAD	124.35
TWR	133.85
FIRE	121.60
ILS/DME	I-BON 110.15 Rwy09
ILS/DME	I-BTS 110.15 Rwy27
NDB	BRI 380*
	on A/D range 25nm

Remarks
Non-radio ACFT not accepted. Training is not permitted under any circumstances between the Hrs of 2200-0700 daily. See also 'Booking & Training Procedures'. Propeller driven ACFT of more than 5700kg MTWA must not join the final approach track to any Rwy at a height of less than 1000ft QFE. Parking and start up procedure for all ACFT on central, western and eastern aprons is under the guidance of the apron marshaller following clearance from ATC. Grass areas are unsuitable for parking of ACFT. Helicopter Operations: A helicopter training area is designated S of Rwy09/27. Handling required for all visiting ACFT Tel: Servisair 01275 472776 Fax: 01275 474514. Bristol Flight Centre Tel: 01275 474501 Fax: 01275 474851. GA ACFT will normally self-park and start-up on western apron and be handled by Clifton operations (130 625).

Warnings
Ground signals not displayed, except light signals. Hot air balloon activity takes place in VMC and daylight Hrs from a site 4.5nm NE of the AD and downwind of the site. Balloons may be observed passing below the CTA or if radio equipped, within the CTR/CTA. Pilots will be notified by ATC of known balloon activity which may affect their flights. Glider and hang glider activity takes place along the Mendip hills, to the south of the AD. ATC will only be notified of such activity when gliders and hang gliders are operating within designated areas within the CTR/CTA and so pilots may not always receive warning of the activity. ACFT using Bristol Airport are to carry 3rd party insurance cover of not less than £500,000. Bird scaring is carried out on a regular basis but birds may not always be detected on the extreme western end of the AD and on the approaches and Dept tracks of all Rwys. Pilots must conform to the noise abatement techniques laid down for the type of ACFT and operate so as to cause the least disturbance practicable in areas surrounding the airport.

B

Operating Hrs	H24

Circuits   Variable 1000ft QFE for non-jet ACFT
Rwy09 normally RH only but ATC may vary
Rwy27 normally LH

Landing fee	On Application

Maintenance
Global Trading   **Tel:** 01275 472484
Fuel   AVGAS 0800-2000 (Local)
Surcharge APPlies outside these Hrs AVGAS through
Bristol Flight Ctr   **Tel:** 01275 474601
AVTUR JET A1 Mon-Fri 0500-0130 Sat-Sun 0500-2300

Operator	Bristol Airport Plc
	Bristol Airport, Bristol BS48 3DY
	Tel: 01275 474444
	Fax: 01275 474800 / 474482 (ATC)
	Telex: 449295 AIRPORT BRISTOL

Restaurants
Restaurant refreshments and club facilities available
Duty-Free Shop & 24hr (airside) bar

Taxis
Airport Taxis Ltd   **Tel:** 01275 474812
Car Hire
Avis   **Tel:** 01275 472613
Europcar   **Tel:** 01275 474623
Hertz   **Tel:** 01275 472807

Weather Info	M T9 T18 Fax 252 A VS BCFO

Booking & Training Procedures
A booking system operates for instrument training. Training periods can be booked by Application to ATC. Filing of a flight plan does not constitute a booking and failure to make a booking may result in the ACFT being refused use of the facilities. Pilots are to inform ATC of booking cancellations. Circuit training by non-Bristol based ACFT is only available by prior arrangement with ATC. Booking procedures for all circuit training ACFT may be introduced by ATC during busy periods. Circuit direction for all training ACFT will be varied by ATC for air traffic and noise nuisance avoidance purposes.

CTA/CTR-Class D Airspace
Normal CTA/CTR Class D Airspace rules apply.

Visual Reference Points (VRPs)

VRP	VOR/NDB	VOR/DME
Bath N5122.70 W00221.42	BCN R126°/LA 244°M	BCN 126°/40nm
Cheddar Reservoir N5116.78 W00248.08	BCN R152°/BRI 212°M	BCN 152°/32nm
Chew Valley N5119.50 W00235.70	BCN R139°/BRI 130°M	BCN 139°/35nm
Churchill N5120.00 W00247.60	BCN R148°/BRI 230°M	BCN 148°/29nm
Clevedon N5126.35 W00251.08	BCN R143°/LA 267°M	BCN 143°/23nm
East Nailsea N5125.80 W00244.10	BCN R137°/BRI 352°M	BCN 137°/26nm
Hanham N5126.93 W00230.95	BCN R125°/BRI 066°M	BCN 125°/32nm
Portishead N5129.70 W00246.42	BCN R132°/BRI 348°M	BCN 132°/23nm
Radstock N5117.53 W00226.92	BCN R135°/LA 236°M	BCN 135°/40nm
Weston-Super-Mare N5120.70 W00258.33	BCN R159°/BRI 262°M	BCN 159°/25nm

Note: ACFT entering the Controlled Airspace via Portishead, Radstock or Cheddar VRP's may be required to hold at East Nailsea, Churchill or Chew Valley VRPs as appropriate.

B

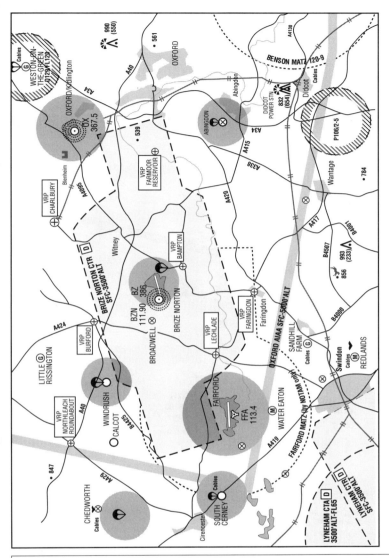

Visual Reference Points

VRP	VOR/VOR	VOR/NDB	VOR/DME FIX
Bampton N5143.50 W00132.80	CPT R324°/DTY R215°	CPT R324°/BZ 129°M	CPT 324°/19nm
Burford N5148.40 W00138.20	CPT R325°/DTY R225°	CPT R325°/BZ 344°M	CPT 325°/24nm
Charlbury N5152.30 W00128.90	CPT R341°/DTY R221°	CPT R341°/BZ 035°M	CPT 341°/25nm
Faringdon N5139.30 W00135.20	CPT R310°/DTY R214°	CPT R310°/BZ 179°M	CPT 310°/17nm
Farmoor Reservoir N5145.20 W00121.40	CPT R347°/DTY R213°	CPT R347°/BZ 093°M	CPT 347°/17nm
Lechlade N5141.60 W00141.40	CPT R309°/DTY R221°	CPT R309°/BZ 229°M	CPT 309°/21nm
Northleach Roundabout N5150.25 W00150.15	CPT R317°/DTY R237°	CPT R317°/BZ 306°M	CPT 317°/31nm

ELEVATION	LOCATION	**EGVN**	**BRIZE NORTON**

ELEVATION	LOCATION			
288ft 10mb	12nm W of Oxford N5145.00.W00135.02	CPT 114.35	322	21.0	– • – • / • – – • / –
PPR Military		DTY 116.40	211	31.6	– • • / – / – • – –

B

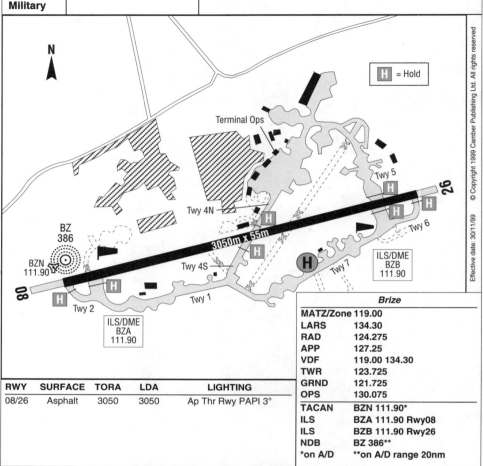

H = Hold

Terminal Ops

N

BZ 386

BZN 111.90

3050m x 55m

Twy 4N

Twy 4S

Twy 1

Twy 2

Twy 5

Twy 6

Twy 7

26

08

ILS/DME BZB 111.90

ILS/DME BZA 111.90

RWY	SURFACE	TORA	LDA	LIGHTING
08/26	Asphalt	3050	3050	Ap Thr Rwy PAPI 3°

Brize

MATZ/Zone	119.00
LARS	134.30
RAD	124.275
APP	127.25
VDF	119.00 134.30
TWR	123.725
GRND	121.725
OPS	130.075
TACAN	BZN 111.90*
ILS	BZA 111.90 Rwy08
ILS	BZB 111.90 Rwy26
NDB	BZ 386**
*on A/D	**on A/D range 20nm

Remarks
PPR 24Hrs notice required. Located within the Brize Norton CTR. No visiting ACFT between 1700-0800 daily (Local). No 180 degree turns on the Rwy. Rwy26 Visual circuits should avoid Cotswold Wildlife Park, Shilton, Witney. Rwy08 visual circuits avoiding Witney. Light ACFT will normally be rtequired to enter or leave the Brize Norton CTR via Burford or Faringdon VRP's. Arriving ACFT are to proceed at 1000ft QFE directly from the VRP's to base leg, or as directed by ATC. Light ACFT can expect to see vehicular traffic crossing at the upwind end of the Rwy.

Warnings
Free fall parachuting takes place up to FL 150 SR-SS. ACFT with wingspan greater than 61m are not permitted to use Twy1.

Operating Hrs
Mon-Fri 0800-1700 (Summer) 0900-1800 (Winter)

Circuits	Variable 1000ft QFE
Landing fee	£7.56 per 500kgs +VAT & £8.50 insurance

Maintenance	Nil
Fuel	AVTUR FS11
Operator	RAF Brize Norton, Oxon OX8 3LX **Tel:** 01993 842551 Ext.7551 (Ops) **Tel:** 01993 842551 Ext.7433 (PPR) all private & charter ACFT **Tel:** 01993 845886 (Brize Norton Flying Club)

Restaurants	
Taxis/Car Hire	
Weather Info	M T Fax 254 BNMC

CTA/CTR-Class D Airspace
Normal CTA/CTR Class D Airspace rules apply.
To assist Brize Radar in ensuring access to its airspace pilots should make an R/T call when 15nm or 5 minutes flying time from the zone boundary, whichever is the earlier.

ELEVATION	LOCATION	EGNB	BROUGH
12ft / 0mb	8nm W of Hull / N5343.25.W00033.83		
PPR			

GAM 112.80   032   29.6   − − • / • − / − −
OTR 113.90   280   16.7   − − − / − / • − •

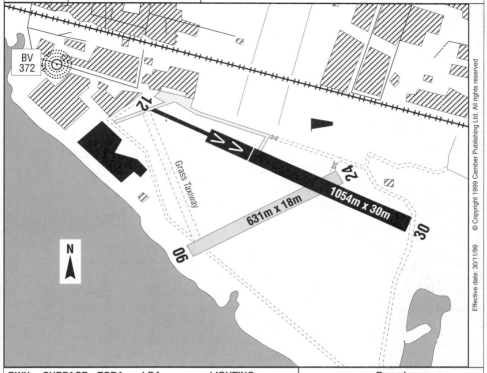

RWY	SURFACE	TORA	LDA	LIGHTING
06	Grass	631	571	Nil
24	Grass	571	571	Nil
12/30	Asphalt	1054x30	*U/L	APP Rwy

*Including 192m x 18m starter extension Rwy12

	Brough
A/G	Brough 130.55
NDB	*BV 372 on AD range 15nm

*Available Mon-Fri 0730-1600 (Summer)
Winter +1hr

Remarks
Not normally available to visiting ACFT. Normally only available to Bae authorised pilots. Brough A/G station not normally manned.

Warnings
A public footpath crosses the midpoint of Rwy06/24. Ships in estuary cross undershoot of Rwy06.

Operator	British Aerospace
	Military Aircraft & Aerostructures
	Brough, East Yorkshire HU15 1EQ
	Tel: 01482 666900 Ext.3111 (BAe)
	Tel: 01482 663730 (The Flying Club)

Restaurants
Ferry Inn   Brough Village (10 min walk)
Buccaneer Inn   Brough Village

Taxis
Cottacars   **Tel: 01482 844466**
Car Hire

Weather Info   AirN MWC

Operating Hrs	Available on request
Circuits	06/30 LH 24/12 RH
Landing fee	Nil
Maintenance	Nil
Fuel	Nil

ELEVATION	LOCATION				BRUNTINGTHORPE
467ft 16mb	6nm S of Leicester N5229.22 W00107.84 **Diversion AD**	DTY 116.40	003	18.4	– • • / – / – • – –
PPR		HON 113.65	074	21.0	• • • • / – – – / – •

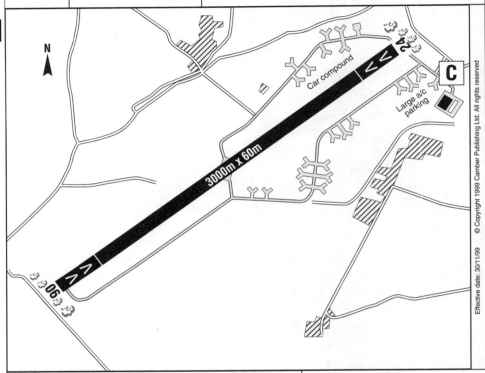

RWY	SURFACE	TORA	LDA	LIGHTING		Bruntingthorpe	
*06/24	Asphalt	2630	2630	Nil	A/G	122.825* * By arrangement	

*3000x60m with displaced Thrs

Remarks
PPR by telephone. U/L AD, used intensively by the motor industry for vehicle proving. Extensive long term parking/storing facilities available for large ACFT. ACFT museum, unique collection of Cold War jets open Sun 1000-1600.

Warnings
Earth banks with trees up to 40' close to both Thrs. **Noise:** Do not overfly local villages.

Operator	C Walton Ltd Bruntingthorpe Aerodrome Lutterworth, Leics LE17 5QN **Tel:** 01162 478030 **Tel:** 01162 478494 (Security) **Fax:** 011624 478031
Restaurants	Pubs 10 minutes walk in Bruntingthorpe village
Taxis/Car Hire	By arrangement on arrival
Weather Info	AirCen MWC

Operating Hrs	Available on request
Circuits	Avoid overflying habitation
Landing fee	On application
Maintenance	Nil
Fuel	Nil

ELEVATION	LOCATION					BUTE
50ft 1mb	1nm SW of Kingarth N5545.00 W0503.00					
PPR		GOW 115.40	255	21.5	– – • / – – – / • – –	
		TRN 117.50	349	27.5	– / • – • / – •	

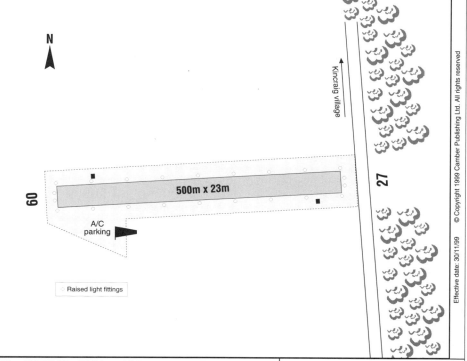

500m x 23m

A/C parking

60

27

N

Kincraig village

○ Raised light fittings

RWY	SURFACE	TORA	LDA	LIGHTING	Non-Radio
09	Grass	500x23	U/L	Rwy.Thr.APAPI 4.5 LHS	**Lighting control**
27	Grass	500x23	U/L	Rwy.Thr.APAPI 5.0 LHS	**130.65 – See remarks**

Remarks
Available to visiting ACFT at Pilots own risk during daylight hours only. AD lighting not available for visitors but provided for Loganair Air Ambulance operations only.

Warnings
Rwy27 approach is through a gap cut in an extensive stand of trees. High ground to SE to 516ft amsl. Strip slopes down from Rwy27 to Rwy09 with 1 degree gradient. Caution AD light fittings raised above Rwy surface. Sector Safety Altitude for AD of 3600ft (NE sector). 2600ft (SE sector). 3900ft (SW sector) 3500ft (NW sector). *Remember- these figures are for the guidance of Air ambulance experienced pilots. Visitors should exercise extreme caution.* There is Class E airspace, Scottish TMA with base 3000ft QNH to E of the AD.

Operator	Mr N Mellish, Bute Estate Ltd Estate Office, High Street, Rothesay Isle of Bute PA20 9AX
Tel: 01700 502627 Mon-Fri 0900-1700 (local) **Fax**: 01700 502353	
Restaurant	Within walking distance of Kingarth village
Taxi/Car Hire	Nil
Weather Info	AirSC GWC

Operating Hrs	SR-SS
Circuits	Circuits to the North
Landing Fee	Nil
Maintenance Fuel	Nil Nil

ELEVATION	LOCATION	EGCK		CAERNARFON

ELEVATION	LOCATION			
1ft 0mb	3.5nm SW of Caernarfon N5306.11.W00420.23	**WAL 114.10**	**255**	**46.3** • – – / • – / • – • •
PPR	**Diversion AD**			

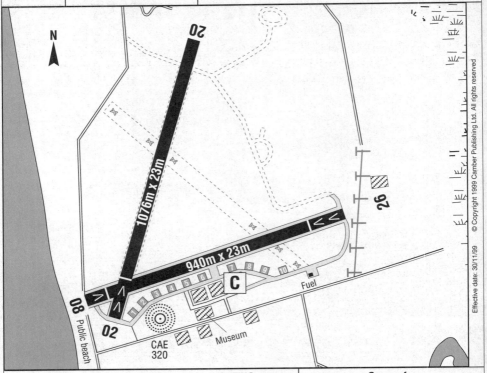

RWY	SURFACE	TORA	LDA	LIGHTING
08	Asphalt	920	885	Nil
26	Asphalt	910	820	Nil
02	Asphalt	1076	1000	Nil
20	Asphalt	1000	1076	Nil

	Caernarfon	
APP	**Valley 134.35**	
APP	**Llanbedr 122.50**	
A/G	**122.25**	
NDB	**CAE 320*** *on A/D range 15nm	

Remarks
Arriving ACFT from S and SE call Llanbedr and subsequently call Valley unless otherwise instructed at least 5 minutes before ETA Caernarfon ATZ boundary. Join the circuit at 1300ft QFE. No taxiing on grass surfaces. Certain customs facilities available. Departing ACFT, unless otherwise instructed should call Valley immediately after take-off. **Noise:** avoid overflight of caravan site close to 26 Thr.

Warnings
The AD is in the vicinity of the Valley CMATZ. Extensive high ground to the S and E of the AD. TV mast 1983ft AMSL 5nm S of A/D. Transient obstacles, vehicles (16ft) on road across Rwy02 APP centreline.

Maintenance	
CAMCO	**Tel:** 01286 830782
Fuel	AVGAS 100LL AVTUR JET A1 with oils W100 & W80

Operator	Air Caernarfon Ltd Caernarfon Airport Caernarfon, Gwyedd LL54 5TP **Tel:** 01286 830800/830475 **Fax:** 01286 830280

Restaurants	Dakota Restaurant & Coffee Shop

Taxis	
Ivans Cabs	**Tel:** 0378 753170
Car Hire	AD will assist

Weather Info	AirN MWC

Operating Hrs 0800-1530 (Summer) 0900-1630 (Winter) up to SS by arrangement U/L

Circuits 02/26 RH 08/20 LH 800ft QFE

Landing fee Single £10.00 £5.00 to PFA members Twin £15.00 Microlight £2.50

ELEVATION	LOCATION	**EGSC**				**CAMBRIDGE**
50ft 2mb	1.5nm E of Cambridge N5212.30.E00010.50	CLN 114.55	306	41.8	−•−•/•−•••/−•	
PPR	**Diversion AD**	BKY 116.25	023	13.6	−•••/−•−/−•−−	
		CFD 116.50	080	30.0	−•−•/••−•/−••	

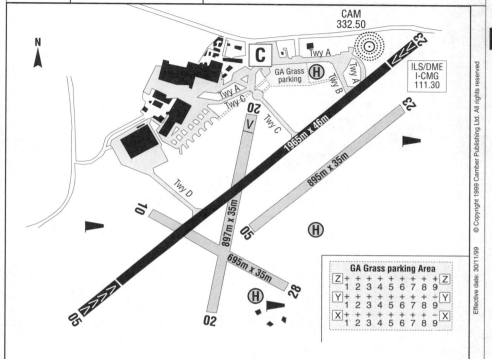

RWY	SURFACE	TORA	LDA	LIGHTING
05	Asphalt	1852	1668	Thr Rwy PAPI 3° LHS
23	Asphalt	1893	1748	Ap Thr Rwy PAPI 3° LHS
02	Grass	808	897	Nil
20	Grass	897	808	Nil
05/23	Grass	895	895	Nil
10/28	Grass	695	695	Nil

	Cambridge
APP	123.60
RAD	124.975
VDF	123.60
TWR	122.20
NDB	CAM 332.50*
ILS/DME	I-CMG 111.30 Rwy23**
	*on A/D, range 15nm
	**on A/D

Remarks
Not available to non-radio ACFT or Microlights. Avoid over-flying Cambridge below 2000ft. Rwy control signals may be received from orange/white caravan. Prefered Rwy Arr 23, Dept 05. ACFT approaching asph Rwy05/23 not below PAPI glideslope from 1000ft. Parallel Rwy ops may be in progress. Rwy05/23 grass go-arounds remain S of Rwy05/23 grass centreline. ACFT require minimum £500K 3rd party insurance cover. A security charge may be levied for secure parking. ACFT taxying on grass to keep to Twys. Long grass is unsuitable for manoeuvring.

Operator	Marshall Aerospace The Airport Cambridge CB5 8RX **Tel:** 01223 293737 (ATC) **Tel:** 01223 373737 (Admin) **Fax:** 01223 373502 **Telex** 81208 MARFLY CAMBRIDGE
Restaurants	Coffee Bar and restaurant available
Taxis Camtax	**Tel:** 01223 313131
Car Hire Hertz Avis	**Tel:** 01223 212551 **Tel:** 01223 365438
Weather Info	M T9 Fax 256 BNMC

Operating Hrs and by arrangement	0800-1700 (Summer) 0900-1800 (Winter)
Circuits	20/23/28 LH 02/05/10 RH 800ft QFE
Landing fee	£13.50 inc VAT up to 1.5MT pay on day
Maintenance **Fuel**	Available & hangerage (by arrangement) JET A1 Mon-Fri 0800-1630 (Local) and by arrangement AVGAS 100LL 0800-1800 (Local)

Minimum noise procedure
05 RTO climb ahead thru 500ft QFE before turning
05 LTO climb ahead thru 2000ft QFE before turning
23 LTO climb ahead thru 500ft QFE before turning
23 RTO climb ahead thru 2000ft QFE before turning

ELEVATION	LOCATION	**EGEC**			**CAMPBELTOWN**
44ft 2mb **PPR**	3nm WNW of Campbletown N5526.17.W00540.79	**TRN 117.50**	292	31.7	– / • – • / – •

C

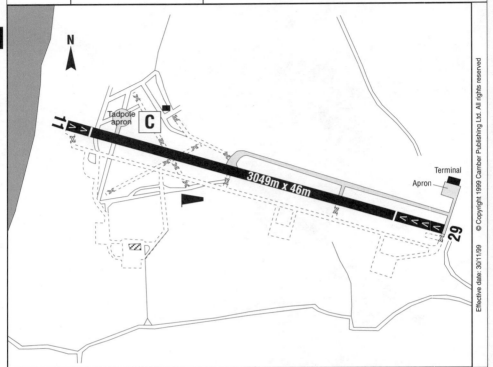

Tadpole apron · C · 3049m x 46m · Terminal · Apron · 11 · 29

RWY	SURFACE	TORA	LDA	LIGHTING
11	Con/Asph	2899	2727	Ap Thr Rwy PAPI 3°
29	Con/Asph	2899	2497	Ap Thr Rwy PAPI 3°

Campbeltown	
AFIS	**125.90**
VOR/DME	**MAC 116.00**

Remarks
PPR. Non-radio ACFT not accepted. Circling is not permitted S of AD. The first 402m of Rwy29 is sterile for landing. The first 322m of Rwy11 is sterile for landing. No ground signals. Fuel and long stay on the apron.

Warnings
There is a serious risk of bird strikes. High ground 1159ft amsl 135°T/4nm & 1465ft amsl 230°T/ 5nm.

Maintenance	Nil
Fuel	AVGAS 100LL by arrangement or within 15 mins of request **Tel:** 01586 552372 Out of Hrs **Tel:** 01586 553786 **Fax:** 01586 553486
Operator	HIAL Campbeltown, Argyll PA28 6NU **Tel:** 01586 553797 **Fax:** 01586 553759
Restaurant	Snack machine in terminal
Taxis DAVAAR	**Tel:** 01586 551122
Car Hire Campbeltown	**Tel:** 01586 552020
Weather Info	M T Fax 366 GWC

Operating Hrs	Mon-Fri 0645-1745 (Summer) Winter +1hr. Hrs may change due to tidal variation at Barra
Circuits	11 LH 29 RH 1500ft QFE
Landing fee	£10.65 inc.VAT up to 3MT VFR cash or Cheque on day

Effective date: 30/11/99 © Copyright 1999 Camber Publishing Ltd. All rights reserved

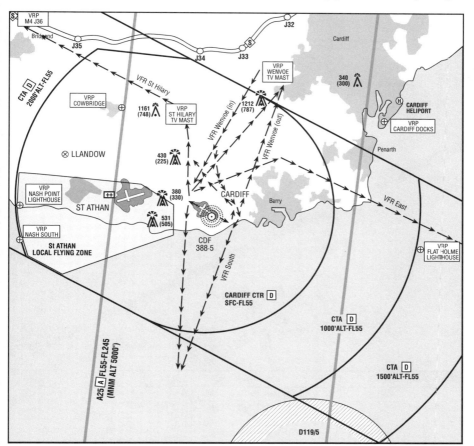

Visual Reference Points (VRPs)

VRP	NDB/DME	VOR/DME
Cardiff Docks N5127.40 W00309.10	CDF 066°M/*I-CWA(I-CDF) 8nm	BCN 172°/17nm
Cowbridge N5127.60 W00326.23	CDF 322°M/*I-CWA(I-CDF) 5nm	BCN 207°/17nm
Flat Holm Lighthouse N5122.55 W00307.13	CDF 102°M/*I-CWA(I-CDF) 8nm	BCN 171°/22nm
M4 J36 N5131.93 W00334.40	CDF 318°M/*I-CWA(I-CDF) 11nm	BCN 230°/16nm
Minehead N5112.35 W00328.50	CDF 209°M/*I-CWA(I-CDF) 12nm	BCN 199°/32nm
Nash Point Lighthouse N5124.08 W00333.33	CDF 278°M/*I-CWA(I-CDF) 7nm	BCN 214°/22nm
Nash S (on St Athan C/L 1nm S of Nash Point) N5122.88 W00333.45	CDF 270°M/*I-CWA(I-CDF) 8nm	BCN 213°/23nm
St Hilary TV Mast ** N5127.45 W00324.18	CDF 332°M/*I-CWA(I-CDF) 4nm	BCN 203°/17nm
Wenvoe TV Mast*** N5127.60 W00316.95	CDF 032°M/*I-CWA(I-CDF) 4nm	BCN 188°/16nm

Note:

* DME frequency-paired with ILS gives zero range indication from the Thr of the Rwy with which it is associated

** Caution to be exercised when routing via St Hilary TV mast 1164ftamsl/745ft agl.

*** Caution to be exercised when routing via Wenvoe TV mast 1212ftamsl/787ft agl.

ELEVATION	LOCATION	**EGFF**			**CARDIFF**

ELEVATION	LOCATION		
220ft 8mb	8.5nm SW of Cardiff N5123.80.W00320.60		
PPR		BCN 117.45 195 19.5	– • • • / – • – • / – •

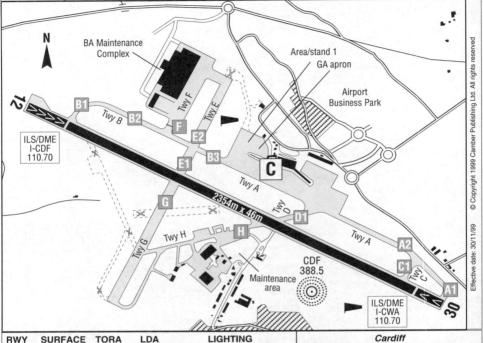

RWY	SURFACE	TORA	LDA	LIGHTING
12	Asphalt	2354	2134	Ap Thr Rwy PAPI 3° LHS
30	Asphalt	2354	2201	Ap Thr Rwy PAPI 3° LHS

	Cardiff
ATIS	119.475
APP/LARS	125.85
RAD	125.85 124.10
VDF	125.85
TWR	125.00
ILS/DME	I-CDF 110.70 Rwy12
ILS/DME	I-CWA 110.70 Rwy30
NDB	CDF 388.50*
	*on A/D, range 20nm

Remarks

PPR to non-radio ACFT. All training in Cardiff CTR/CTA is PPR from Cardiff APP. A helicopter set-down point, marked with an 'H', is situated on the parallel twy to the W of stand 2. ACFT will be allowed to ground taxi or hover taxi to the helicopter alighting pad located to the W of the Western pier, as instructed by ATC. Flight clearance is located on the first floor of the Control Tower building. Access from airside is via the domestic pier. Flight clearance is a self-briefing facility with AIS and full Met info. Landing fees can be paid at the Bureau De Change between 0800-1700 Monday to Friday, otherwise at the Information Desk in the terminal. Also at Cardiff-Wales flying Club on the S side of the airport

Warnings

Possible turbulence on short finals when landing on Rwy30 in strong W to S winds. Due to proximity of RAF St Athan (3nm W) overhead joining will not normally be approved. When inbound to Rwy12 or outbound from Rwy30 at Cardiff be aware of the close proximity of RAF St Athan and the St Athan Local Flying Zone to the Cardiff arrival/departure tracks. VFR flights to/from Cardiff Airport may be required to enter/leave the CTR at VRPs which avoid the St Athan Local Flying Zone. ACFT must be operated to cause the least disturbance practicable to areas surrounding the airport. Single engine ACFT should avoid overflying the chemical complex at Barry.

Circuits	30 RH 12 LH or as instructed by ATC
Landing fee	On application

Maintenance LAM **Tel:** 01446 710106
Fuel AVGAS 100LL AVTUR JET A1 AVGAS
JET A1 by arrangement with Air BP daily 0600-2245
AVGAS 0900-1800 (local) Cardiff Aeronautical
Tel: 01446 711987/02920 513223 (outside Hrs)

Operator	Cardiff International Airport Ltd Rhoose Barry, S Glamorgan CF6 9BD

Tel: 01446 712562 (ATC) / 711111 (Airport Auth)
Fax: 01446 711838 (ATC) / 711675 (Airport Auth)
Telex: 498235 ATC 497720 CWLAPT (Airport Auth)

Restaurants	G/A CTR on S side Licensed Buffet and Cafeteria in Terminal

Taxis
Cardiff Airport Taxis **Tel:** 01446 710693
Frequent buses to/from Cardiff & Barry
Car Hire
Hertz   **Tel:** 01446 711722

Operating Hrs	H24	Weather Info	M T9 T18 Fax 258 A VS BNMC

CTA/CTR – Class D Airspace
Normal CTA/CTR Class D Airspace rules apply.

The attention of pilots is drawn to the close proximity of St
Athan AD and Local Flying Zone. Pilots entering or leaving
Cardiff CTR VFR may be required to do so avoiding the St
Athan Local Flying Zone.

c

Cardiff Standard Visual Routes

VFR Flights
VFR clearance in the Cardiff CTR will be given for flights operating in VMC. Routeing instructions and/or altitude restrictions may be specified in order to integrate VFR flights with other trafic. Pilots are reminded of the requirements to remain in VMC at all times and to comply with the relevant parts of the Low Flying Rules, and must advise ATC if at any time they are unable to comply with the clearance instructions issued.
VFR Routes to/from Cardiff
a In order to intergrate VFR flights to/from Cardiff with the normal flow of IFR traffic, a number of standard routes are established along which ATC VFR clearances will be issued subject to the conditions specified above. These routes are defined by prominent ground features and are detailed below.
b In order to reduce RTF congestion, the standard outbound and inbound visual routes are allocated route designators. Pilots are to ensure that they are familiar with the route alignment and altitude restrictions proir to departure/entering the CTR.

Standard Outbound Visual Routes

Exit point		Rwy		Max Alt	Route Designator	Route
Bridgend	12/30	1500ft			**VFR St Hilary**	Route N of St Hilary TV mast & leave the CTR to the W via Bridgend.
NE Flat Holm Lighthouse	12/30	1500ft			**VFR E**	Route N of Barry then N of Flat Holm Island, leaving the CTR to the E.
N Minehead	12/30	1500ft			**VFR S**	Route towards Minehead & leave the CTR to the S.
W Cardiff	12/30	1500ft			**VFR Wenvoe**	Route towards & to the E of Wenvoe TV mast and leave the Docks CTR to the NE.

Standard Inbound Visual Routes

Entry point	Rwy	Max Alt	Route Designator	Route
NE CTR	12/30	1500ft	**VFR Wenvoe**	At the CTR boundary, route towards and to the W of the Wenvoe TV mast then as directed by 'Cardiff Tower'.
			Remarks:	ACFT may be held at the Wenvoe VRP.
All other inbound VFR Routes	12/30	1500ft	**VFR** (followed by appropriate VRP designator)	The words 'VFR' followed by one of Cardiff's notified VRP's will mean: to route from CTR boundary towards the nominated VRP.
			Remarks:	ACFT may be held at the appropriate VRP.

ELEVATION	LOCATION	CARK (Grange-over-Sands)
17ft 0mb **PPR**	7nm S of Lake Windermere N5409.87.W00257.53	**POL 112.10** 316 39 •– –•/– – –/•–•••

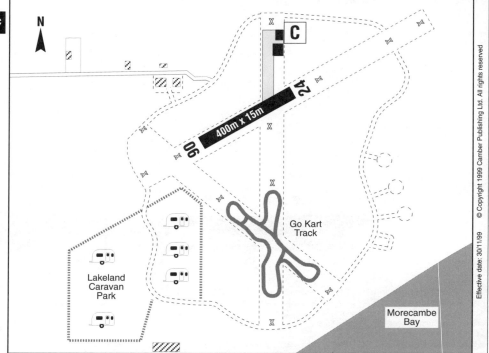

RWY	SURFACE	TORA	LDA	LIGHTING		
06/24	Asphalt	400x15	U/L	Nil		*Cark Drop Zone*
Rwy24 200m overrun					**A/G**	**129.90**
Rwy surface rough						**See remarks**

Remarks
PPR by telephone. Primarily a parachute centre but light ACFT welcome at own risk. Parachutists exit free-fall up to FL140. Parachutes open from 2200ft down. Radio usually manned only at weekends. If no reply please make blind calls.

Warnings
The two other Rwys are fenced off & unusable. Portions of WW II Rwy06/24 are overgrown & unusable but serviceable portion is clearly visible. Windsock at weekends only. Occasionally livestock on AD. power lines 550m from Thr Rwy06. Please avoid local habitation.

Operator	N W Parachute Centre Cark Airfield, Moore Lane, Flookburgh Grange-over-Sands, Cumbria
Tel: 01539 558672 (PPR AD weekends) **Tel:** 01772 720848 (PPR weekdays Mr Prince)	
Restaurants	Snacks at weekends
Taxis **Car Hire**	**Tel:** 01539 533792 Nil
Weather Info	AirN MWC

Operating Hrs	SR-SS
Circuits	No overhead joins Circuits over the sea at 1000ft QFE
Landing fee	Single £5 Twin £10 Microlight £2.50
Maintenance **Fuel**	Nil Nil

ELEVATION	LOCATION	EGNC				CARLISLE

ELEVATION	LOCATION
190ft	5nm NE by E of Carlisle
6mb	N5456.25.W00248.55
PPR	

TLA 113.80	158	38.5	− / • − • • / • −
DCS 115.20	061	22.4	− • • / − • − • / • • •
NEW 114.25	268	38.8	− • / • / • − −

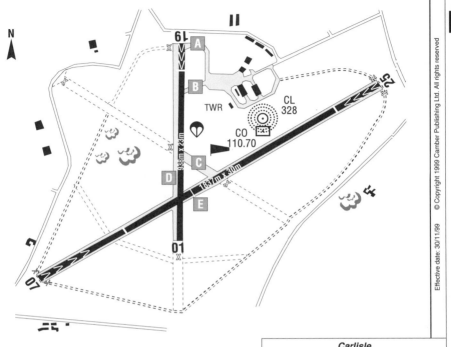

TWR

CL 328

CO 110.70

Effective date: 30/11/99

RWY	SURFACE	TORA	LDA	LIGHTING
01	Asphalt	803	803	Nil
19	Asphalt	938	809	Nil
07	Asphalt	1659	1321	Thr Rwy PAPI 3.5° LHS
25	Asphalt	1714	1469	APThr Rwy PAPI 3.25° LHS

Carlisle

APP/VDF/TWR	123.60
A/G	123.60 (weekends)
NDB	CL 328*
DME	CO 110.70**
	*on A/D range 20nm
	**Zero range at Thr25 only

Remarks
PPR to multi-engined aeroplanes and all ACFT at weekends. AD is not available to non-radio ACFT. Visual aids to location: Ibn Green CL. Certain customs facilities available.

Warnings
Danger Area D510 5nm NE of AD. DAAIS available from Carlisle APP. The ends of TORA/ED/LDA on Rwy07 and 25 are shown by red edge lights only. The red lights across the Rwys mark the end of useable pavement. The only useable Twys are from the apron to the Rwy19 Thr and the disused Rwy13/31 that links 01/19 with 07/25. Parachuting takes place on the AD normally during daylight Hrs Mon-Fri evenings and Sat.

Operating Hrs Mon-Fri 0830-1900
Sat-Sun 0900-1700 or SS (Local & by arrangement)

Circuits Variable

Landing fee On application

Maintenance	Limited
Fuel	AVGAS 100LL AVTUR JET A1 by prior arrangement
Operator	City and County Borough of Carlisle Carlisle Aerodrome, Cumbria CA6 4NW **Tel:** 01228 573629 (ATC) **Tel:** 01228 573641 (Admin) **Fax:** 01228 573310 **Telex:** 64476
Restaurants	Refreshments available at airport
Taxis Radio Taxis	**Tel:** 01228 27575
Car Hire Hertz National	**Tel:** 01228 512529 **Tel:** 01228 42707
Weather Info	M T9 Fax 262 MWC

Visual Reference Points (VRPs)

Gretna	N5459.73 W00304.05
Haltwistle	N5458.13 W00227.73
Penrith	N5439.87 W00245.02
Wigton	N5449.48 W00309.67

ELEVATION	LOCATION				
350 ft 12mb **PPR**	4.5nm SSW of Duns N5542.45.W00222.64 **Diversion AD**	SAB 112.50 TLA 113.80	213 077	13.3 35.5	••• / • – / – ••• – / • – •• / • –

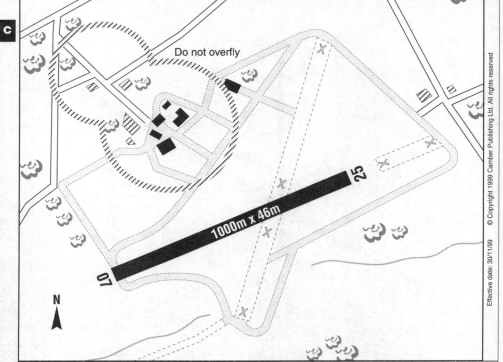

Do not overfly

1000m x 46m

07   25

N

RWY	SURFACE	TORA	LDA	LIGHTING		Non Radio	
07/25	Asphalt	1000m	U/L	Nil	FIS	Scottish 119.875	
Rwy surface poor							

Remarks
PPR essential. Light ACFT accepted at the pilot's own risk. There is microlight activity on AD.

Warnings
Rwy and AD surface rough. AD used for farming –beware of animals on the Rwy. A fence crosses E end of Rwy.

Operator	Mr AR Trotter Charterhall, Duns, Berwickshire **Tel:** 01890 840301 **Fax:** 01890 840651 **E-mail**: meadowhed@aol.com
Taxis Robertson **Car Hire**	**Tel:** 01361 882340
Weather Info	AirSc MWC

Operating Hrs	SR-SS
Circuits	07 RH 25 LH 1000ft QFE
Landing fee	£10
Maintenance Fuel	Nil Nil

ELEVATION	LOCATION	**CHATTERIS**
5ft 0mb	2nm N of Chatteris N5229.12.E00005.43	
PPR		**BKY 116.25** **006** **29.5** — • • • / — • — / — • — —

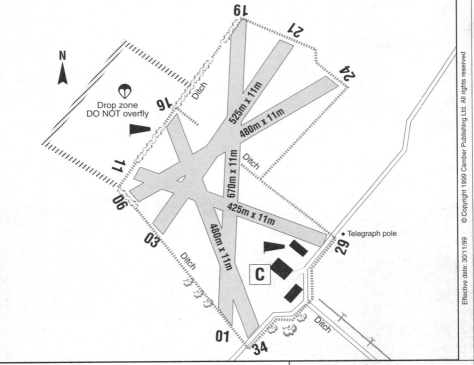

C

RWY	SURFACE	TORA	LDA	LIGHTING
01/19	Grass	670x11	U/L	Nil
06/24	Grass	480x11	U/L	Nil
03/21	Grass	525x11	U/L	Nil
16/34*	Grass	480x11	U/L	Nil
11/29*	Grass	425x11	U/L	Nil

*Microlight use only

Chatteris

A/G	**129.90** **Only manned during** **parachuting**

Remarks
PPR strictly by telephone due to parachuting ops.
Parachutists free-fall from FL150. Microlights also operate
SR-SS. Please avoid overflight of local habitation.

Warnings
Do not overfly the drop zone at any time. Telegraph pole on
short final Rwy29. Public road crosses the undershoot
Rwy29, please be aware of vehicles & pedestrians. AD is in
an area of intense military low flying, keep a good lookout at
all times.

Maintenance	Nil
	Hangarage overnight by prior arrangement
Fuel	AVGAS 100LL by arrangement only
Operator	Chatteris Leisure Ltd Chatteris Airfield, Stonea March Cambridgeshire PE15 0EA **Tel:** 01725 513330 (PPR Weekends) **Tel:** 01354 740810 (PPR Weekdays) **Fax:** 01354 740406 **Email:** chatpara@aol.com
Restaurants	Café at AD Thu-Sun 0800-2000 (local)
Taxis Car Hire	**Tel:** 01354 658083 **Tel:** 01354 652361
Weather Info	AirS BNMC

Operating Hrs	SR-SS
Circuits	19/21/24 LH 01/03/06 RH at 700ft QFE No deadside
Landing fee	Light ACFT £5 Microlight £3 except where reciprocal arrangement exists

ELEVATION	LOCATION		
100ft 3mb	1.5nm NNE of Chichester N5051.55.W00045.55	GWC 114.75	On A/D	— — • / • — — / — • — •
PPR	**Diversion AD**	MID 114.00	209 12.7	— — / • • / — • •
		SAM 113.35	109 22.8	• • • / • — / — —

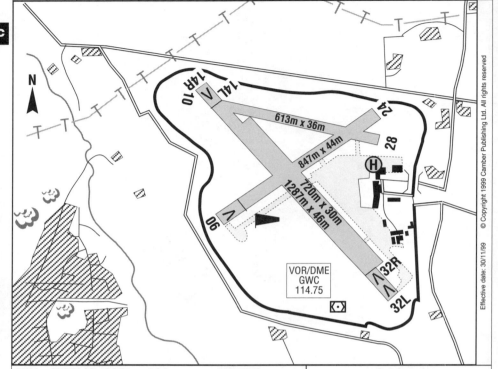

RWY	SURFACE	TORA	LDA	LIGHTING
06	Grass	847	708	Nil
24	Grass	837	837	Nil
14L/32R	Grass	720	720	Nil
14R/32L	Grass	1213	1040	Thr Rwy APAPI 3° LHS
10/28	Grass	613	613	Nil

	Goodwood
LARS	**Dunsfold 135.175**
VDF	**122.45**
AFIS	**122.45**
VOR/DME	**GWC 114.75*** *on A/D

Remarks

PPR by telephone. Instrument training must be approved by ATC. **Noise**: Rwy06 landing. No low APP over built up areas in undershoot. Rwy24 take-off. Turn right avoid built up area, maintain heading to circuit height. No practice EFATO until W of A286 road. Landing: No low APP over E Lavant. Light ACFT land beyond intersection Rwy10/14. 14L/14R take-off, turn L 10° asap after dep to avoid overflying schools & houses on dep path with no practice EFATO until well clear. Rwy32 take-off, turn R 20°, avoid East Lavant, no practice EFATO until well clear of village. Rwy28 take-off maintain Rwy hdg until clear of Lavant village.

Warning

When Rwys06/24 and 10/28 are in use for fixed-wing circuits, opposite direction helicopter circuits will be flown from the Thr of Rwy32L. An arrester bed of shingle is at end Rwy14R. When relief Rwy14L/32R is in use Thr will be marked with black and white markers. The motor racing track on the perimeter is in constant use during daylight Hrs and is not to be used for taxying ACFT at any time.

Circuit	06/14/10 LH 22/28/32 RH ACFT 1200ft QFE Heli 900ft QFE
Landing fee	PA28 £13.57 inc VAT
Maintenance	Goodwood ACFT Maintenance **Tel:** 01243 781934
Fuel	AVGAS 100LL AVTUR JET A1
Operator	Goodwood Motor Racing Co Ltd Chichester (Goodwood) Aerodrome Nr Chichester, W Sussex PO18 0PH **Tel:** 01243 755060 (Admin) **Tel:** 01243 755061 (ATC) **Fax:** 01243 755062 (ATC)
Restaurants	On AD by motor circuit pits and in Goodwood Flying Club
Taxi Dunnaways	**Tel:** 01243 782403
Car Hire National	**Tel:** 01243 202426
Wessex Car Rental	**Tel:** 01243 779977
Weather Info	AirSE BNMC

Operating Hrs	Feb-Mar 0900-1700 0900-1600 (Winter) and by arrangement

ELEVATION	LOCATION	**CHILBOLTON (Stonefield Park)**
292ft 10mb	5nm SSE of Andover N5108.13 W00125.28	SAM 113.35 348 11.5 ••• / • – / – –
PPR		CPT 114.35 204 22 – • – • / • – – • / –

Industrial park

N

C

(H)

Aircraft parking

Crops

411m x 18m

24

06

Crops

Powerline 24'

Footpath to PH

Noise Exclusion Zone

RWY	SURFACE	TORA	LDA	LIGHTING
24	Grass	411	384	Nil
06	Grass	384	411	Nil

Rwy24 has 2% upslope

	Non-Radio
APP	**Boscombe 126.70** **Micro: 129.825** **(Common freq.)**

Remarks

PPR by telephone Microlights, Paramotors, & Helicopters operate. AD close to boundary of Middle Wallop MATZ. In/Outbound ACFT call Boscombe App/Zone 126.70. Telephone available from Industrial site office. Microlights may use 129.825. All flights must be logged in control portacabin facing the strip & landing fees (sealed envelope) in box by flight log.

Warnings

Preferred APP is from S & E. Usual circuit joining procedure is not available owing to noise sensitive areas and proximity to Middle Wallop. It is permissable to join overhead. Not above 1000ft QFE owing to MATZ stub. Fly circuit as if making a go-around. If satisfied direction of landing is known, join Downwind, Base or, final as convenient keep good lookout for any other traffic. Microlights on final make slow steep tight APP. Light ACFT beware of Microlights making tight circuits. Army helicopters on low level exercises in area of AD. CAUTION: 24ft high power line crosses 24 APP short final. Top of tree to left of Thr is above power line. Public road crosses 24 APP on very short final. NOISE: Do not overfly Radio Telescope site & Chilbolton village to N. DO NOT overfly farm Sside of A30. Circuit to S extend base/crosswind leg to line of trees S of A30. Turn base/crosswind leg before B3240/A30 junc. to keep all noise sensitive areas inside circuit. Caution; miniature rifle range E of B3240/A30 junc., do not overfly below 500ft QFE.

Operating Hrs	0800-2100 (local) No night flying No flying training
Circuits	24 LH 06 RH 900ft QFE
Landing fee	£2.50
Maintenance	M3 Hants Light Plane Services **Tel: 01264 860056**
Fuel	Nil
Operator	Stonefield Park & Chilbolton Flying Club **Tel: 01428 723966** (Mr M Treveil) PPR
Restaurants Leckford Hutt Pub	Walking distance **Tel: 01264 810738**
Weather Info	AirSW BNMC

ELEVATION	LOCATION			
448ft 14mb	1nm E of Chirk N5257.00.W00303.00	WAL 114.10	179	27.5 • – – / • – / • – ••
PPR				

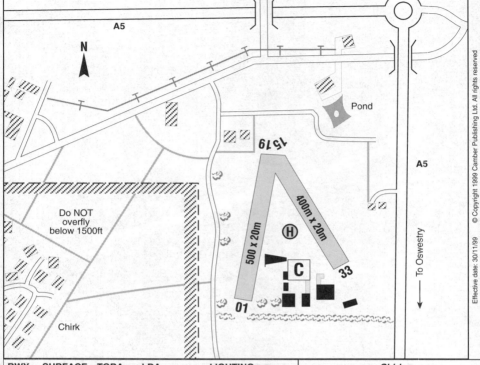

A5

N

Pond

A5

To Oswestry

Do NOT overfly below 1500ft

15/19

500 x 20m

400m x 20m

(H)

C

33

01

Chirk

RWY	SURFACE	TORA	LDA	LIGHTING
01/19	Grass	500x20	U/L	Nil
15/33	Grass	400x20	U/L	Nil

	Chirk
LARS	Shawbury 120.775
A/G	129.825

Remarks
Primary a microlight AD but STOL ACFT welcome at pilots own risk. Rwys have no designator markings or edge marks but AD is easily identifiable by white concrete 'H' in the centre of the AD.

Warnings
Rwy01 has slight downslope. Sheep may be grazing if microlights are not active. **Noise:** Area to the W of AD is particulary noise sensitive and should not be overflown below 1500ft.

Operator	Mr R Everitt, 3 School Lane St Martins, Shropshire **Tel:** 01691 774137
Restaurants	Café on AD Mon-Fri
Taxis/Car Hire	
Weather Info	AirCen MWC

Operating Hrs	PPR
Circuits	15/19 LH 01/33 RH at 600ft QFE
Landing fee	Nil
Maintenance Fuel	BMAA & PFA types Nil

ELEVATION	LOCATION	EGXG				CHURCH FENTON
29ft 1mb	4nm SE of Tadcaster N5350.06.W00111.73		OTR 113.90	288	39.6	– – – / – / • – •
PPR MILITARY			POL 112.10	086	32.6	• – – • / – – – / • – ••

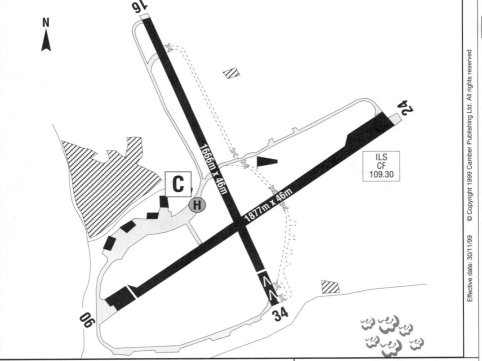

RWY	SURFACE	TORA	LDA	LIGHTING
06	Asph/Con	1711	1711	Ap Thr Rwy PAPI 3°
24	Asph/Con	1829	1829	Ap Thr Rwy PAPI 3°
16	Asphalt	1666	1666	Thr Rwy PAPI 3°
34	Asphalt	1666	1466	Thr Rwy PAPI 3°

Fenton	
MATZ/APP	126.50
PAR	123.30
TWR	122.10
ILS	CF 109.30 Rwy24

Remarks
PPR by telephone. Satellite AD to Linton-on-Ouse. Intensive flying at this AD due to the flying training school. Displaced threshold on Rwy06/34. Visual aids to location: Ibn CF Red.

Warnings
Public road (controlled by traffic lights) crosses final APP to Rwy06 225m from Thr. Civil AD – Sherburn-in-Elmet – 3nm to SW.

Operator	RAF Church Fenton Tadcaster, N Yorks LS24 9SE
	Tel: 01347 848261 Ext 7491/2 (PPR Linton-on-Ouse)
Restaurants	Nil
Taxis Windmill	**Tel:** 01937 232979
Car Hire National (Leeds)	**Tel:** 01132 777957
Weather Info	AirN MWC

Operating Hrs (Summer)	Mon-Thu 0730-1615 Fri 0730-1600 Winter + 1Hr and as required by RAF
Circuits	24/34 RH 06/16 LH 1000ft QFE
Landing fee	£7.56 per 500kgs +VAT & £8.50 insurance
Maintenance	Nil
Fuel	JET A1 AVGAS 100LL by arrangement (limited quantities)

ELEVATION	LOCATION	EGAE	City of Derry (Eglinton)
23ft 1mb **PPR**	7nm ENE of Londonderry N5502.57.W00709.67	MAC 116.00 255 56.5 – – / • – / – • – • BEL 117.20 315 39.0 – • • • / • / • – • •	

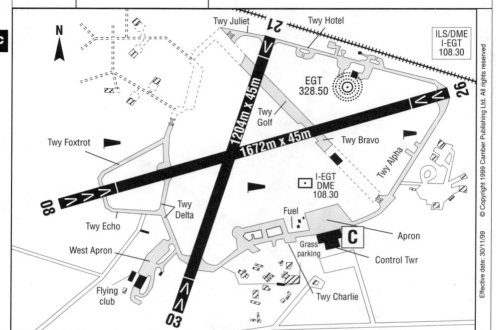

RWY	SURFACE	TORA	LDA	LIGHTING
08	Asphalt	1542	1266	Thr Rwy PAPI 3.5° LHS
26	Asphalt	1589	1459	Ap Thr Rwy PAPI 3° LHS
03	Asphalt	1203	1086	Thr Rwy PAPI 4° LHS
21	Asphalt	1204	1191	Thr Rwy APAPI 4° LHS

	Eglinton
APP	123.625
VDF	123.625
TWR	134.15
FIRE	121.60
ILS/DME	I-EGT 108.30 Rwy26
NDB	EGT 328.5 on A/D range 25nm

Remarks
ACFT unable to communicate by radio subject to ATC approval. Single engine ACFT should avoid over-flying a chemical plant 2-3nm W of AD below 1500ft. All ACFT using City of Derry Airport must have Third Party liability insurance cover of at least £1,000,000. Proof of this insurance should be available for inspection at any time. The use of City of Derry Airport is subject to the published terms and conditions, (available on request). Visual aid to identification: Abn, white flashing.

Warnings
Large congregations of sea-birds in the APP area to Rwy26. Pilots are reminded of the close proximity of Ballykelly 5nm ENE of this AD. Ballykelly is close to the final APP centreline to Rwy26 and rwy lighting may be displayed there. Pilots should positively identify Eglinton before committing the ACFT to land. The APP lighting for Rwy26 extends over water and reflections of the crossbar and centre-line lights may be seen.

Landing fee	Single club & private £7.22 +VAT Multi club & private £14.44 +VAT
Maintenance	Available
Fuel	AVGAS 100LL AVTUR JET A1
Operator	Derry City Council, City of Derry Airport Airport Road, Eglinton Londonderry, N Ireland BT47 3PY **Tel:** 02871 810784 (ATC) **Fax:** 02871 811426 (Admin) **Fax:** 02871 812152 (ATC)
Restaurant	Snack bar in main Terminal
Taxis	Available at Terminal
Car Hire	
Avis	**Tel:** 02871 811708
Ford Rent a Car	**Tel:** 02871 360420
Weather Info	M T9 Fax 354 BEL

Visual Reference Points (VRPs)

Buncrana	N5508.00 W00727.40
Coleraine	N5507.90 W00640.30
Dungiven	N5455.70 W00655.50
Moville	N5511.40 W00702.40
New Buildings	N5457.50 W00721.50

Operating Hrs   Mon-Fri 0800-2045
(PPR for non-scheduled ops 0800-1015, 1715-2045),
Sat 0800-1545, Sun 1115-2045

Circuits   03/21 1200ft 08 1000ft for LH & 1200ft
RH circuits 26 1200ft LH & 1000ft RH

ELEVATION	LOCATION	EGSQ				CLACTON
32ft 1mb	2nm W of Clacton (1nm W of Clacton pier) N5147.10.E00107.73	CLN 114.55	194	4.0	− • − • / • − • • / − •	
PPR	Diversion AD	LAM 115.60	081	37.3	• − • • / • − / − −	
		BKY 116.25	111	41.5	− • • • / − • − / − • − −	

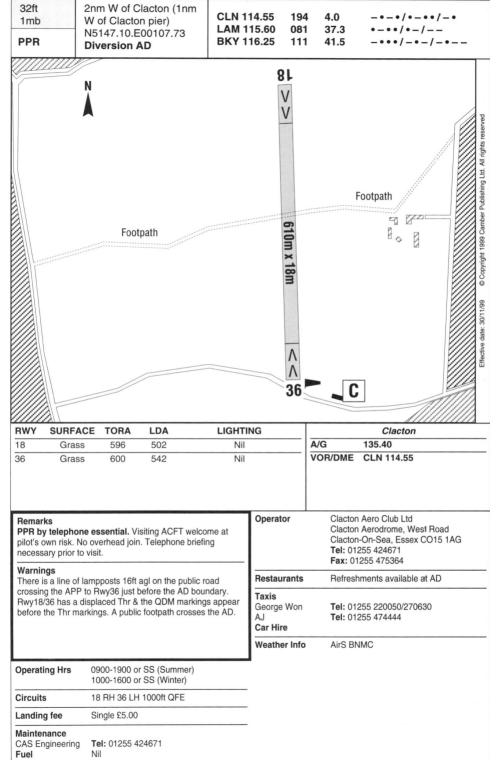

N

18

V V

610m x 18m

Footpath

Footpath

∧ ∧

36

C

RWY	SURFACE	TORA	LDA	LIGHTING		Clacton	
18	Grass	596	502	Nil	A/G	135.40	
36	Grass	600	542	Nil	VOR/DME	CLN 114.55	

Remarks
PPR by telephone essential. Visiting ACFT welcome at pilot's own risk. No overhead join. Telephone briefing necessary prior to visit.

Warnings
There is a line of lampposts 16ft agl on the public road crossing the APP to Rwy36 just before the AD boundary. Rwy18/36 has a displaced Thr & the QDM markings appear before the Thr markings. A public footpath crosses the AD.

Operator	Clacton Aero Club Ltd Clacton Aerodrome, West Road Clacton-On-Sea, Essex CO15 1AG **Tel:** 01255 424671 **Fax:** 01255 475364
Restaurants	Refreshments available at AD
Taxis George Won AJ Car Hire	**Tel:** 01255 220050/270630 **Tel:** 01255 474444
Weather Info	AirS BNMC

Operating Hrs	0900-1900 or SS (Summer) 1000-1600 or SS (Winter)
Circuits	18 RH 36 LH 1000ft QFE
Landing fee	Single £5.00
Maintenance CAS Engineering Fuel	**Tel:** 01255 424671 Nil

ELEVATION	LOCATION				**CLENCH COMMON**
623ft 20mb	2nm S of Marlborough N5123.37.W00143.94	SAM 113.35	334	30	••• / • – / – –
PPR		CPT114.35	256	20.5	– • – • / • – – • / –

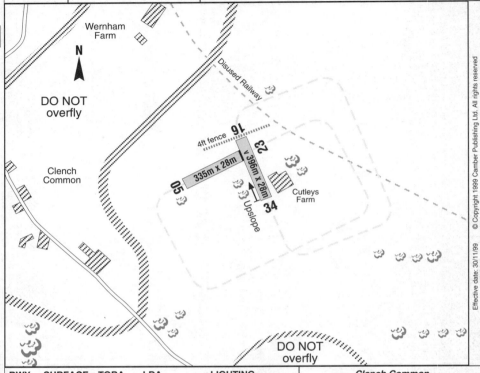

RWY	SURFACE	TORA	LDA	LIGHTING			
05/23	Grass	335x28	U/L	Nil		A/G	**129.825**
16/34	Grass	396x28	U/L	Nil			**If no reply please make**
Upslope on first third Rwy34							**blind circuit calls**

Clench Common

Remarks
PPR by telephone Primarily a microlight school but STOL light ACFT welcome at own risk. AD is close to the southern boundary of the Lyneham CTR (123.40).

Warnings
There is a 4ft high fence close to Rwy16 Thr. Trees close & right of Rwy05 Thr may cause windshear or turbulence on very short final.
Noise: Avoid overflight of Clench Common village and Wernham Farm

Operator	Graham Slater (GS Aviation) Clench Common Airfield Nr Marlborough, Wiltshire SN8 4NZ **Tel:** 01672 515535 **Tel:** 07831 350928 (mobile) **Fax:** 01672 511574 **E-mail:** gsaviation@aol.com
Restaurants	Hot drinks available
Taxis	**Tel:** 01672 511088
Car Hire	**Tel:** 01672 511088
Weather Info	AirSW BNMC

Operating Hrs	Mon-Sat 0800-2100 Sun 0900-2000 or SS (local) whichever earliest
Circuits	05/34 RH 16/23 LH join overhead at 1500ft QFE then descend to 500ft QFE on deadside
Landing fee	£3
Maintenance Fuel	Workshop facilities for microlights MOGAS (local garage by arrangement)

ELEVATION	LOCATION		CLUTTON HILL FARM

ELEVATION	LOCATION
600ft 20mb	5nm WSW of Bath N5120.57.W00231.22
PPR	

BCN 117.45	135	36	– • • • / – • – • / – •
CPT 114.35	263	49.5	– • – • / • – – • / –

c

N

6ft hedge

25

Steep escarpment

590m x 27m

A/c parking

Track

Wessex Aircraft Maintenance

07

Upslope

PH Hunters Rest

DO NOT overfly Clutton village 0.5nm

RWY	SURFACE	TORA	LDA	LIGHTING
07/25	Grass	590x27	U/L	Nil

	Non-radio
APP	**Bristol 128.55**
ATIS	**Bristol 126.025**

Remarks

PPR by telephone. Microlights not accepted. Visiting ACFT are welcome at pilots own risk. This AD is in a very noise sensitive area and extreme care should be taken to avoid overflight of local villages, particularly Clutton to the SW. Useful Weather Info can be obtained from Bristol ATIS (126.025). The Bristol CTA (Base 1500ft) lies over the AD. Arriving/departing ACFT must call Bristol APP (128.55).

Warnings

There is a marked upslope at the W end of the Rwy & steep escarpment up to 07 Thr. The combination of this may be a marked roll-over effect for 25 departures. Trees are close to the N side of the Rwy25 Thr, they may generate turbulence & obscure your view of the rwy when downwind for 07.

Operator Owned	Mr SJ Wilcox (Wessex Aero Group) Mr Tony Appleyard, Clutton Hill Farm Clutton, Bristol, Bath & NE Somerset **Tel:** 01761 452991 (Answerphone & Fax) **Tel:** 07850 223455 (Mobile)
Restaurants Hunters Rest	**Tel:** 01761 452303
Taxis **Car Hire**	**Tel:** 01761 417166 Nil
Weather Info	AirSW BNMC

Operating Hrs	SR-SS
Circuits	08LH, 26RH, 600ft QFE
Landing fee	£5
Maintenance	Wessex Aero Maintenance **Tel:** 01761 452991
Fuel	Nil

ELEVATION	LOCATION			
720ft 24mb	5nm S of Sheffield N5318.28 W00125.83	TNT 115.70	035	17.3	– / – • / –
PPR		GAM 112.80	280	18.0	– – • / • – / – –

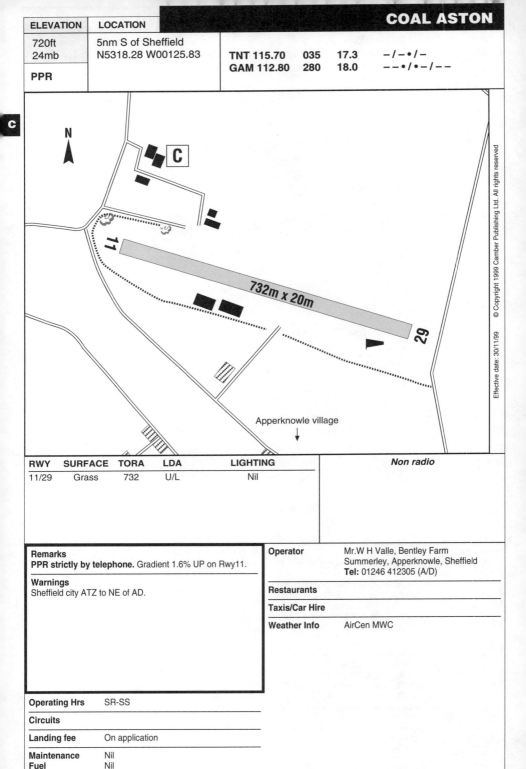

732m x 20m

Apperknowle village

RWY	SURFACE	TORA	LDA	LIGHTING	Non radio
11/29	Grass	732	U/L	Nil	

Remarks
PPR strictly by telephone. Gradient 1.6% UP on Rwy11.

Warnings
Sheffield city ATZ to NE of AD.

Operator	Mr.W H Valle, Bentley Farm Summerley, Apperknowle, Sheffield **Tel:** 01246 412305 (A/D)
Restaurants	
Taxis/Car Hire	
Weather Info	AirCen MWC

Operating Hrs	SR-SS
Circuits	
Landing fee	On application
Maintenance Fuel	Nil Nil

ELEVATION	LOCATION	**EGUO**				**COLERNE**

ELEVATION	LOCATION				
593ft 19mb **PPR**	4.5nm NE of Bath N5126.45 W00216.80	CPT 114.35 SAM 113.35	270 314	40 41.5	– • – • / • – – • / – • • • / • – / – –

C

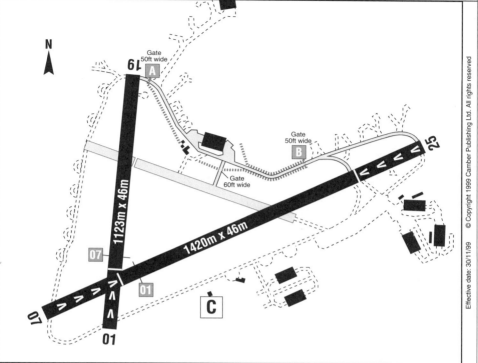

RWY	SURFACE	TORA	LDA	LIGHTING
07	Asphalt	1664	1422	Nil
25	Asphalt	1664	1344	Nil
01	Asphalt	1095	895	Nil
19	Asphalt	1095	1086	Nil

Colerne
APP/LARS (Lyneham) 123.40
APP/TWR 122.10

Remarks
PPR strictly by telephone. RAF AD with pilot training. Special arrival procedures for helicopters details sought with PPR.

Warnings
Rwy07/25/01 have displaced landing Thr. AD borders on W edge of Lyneham CTR. ACFT approaching/departing from/to S call Bristol APP, (128.55). Turbulence expected in any wind conditions. Obstructions are within approach areas up to 604ft amsl. No traffic lights on AD. Perimeter track and high sided vehicles may cross the undershoot of Rwy01/07 without warning. Garston Farm AD is within AD circuit. Obstructions in the circuit are not lit. HIRTA D1616 may affect avionics within ATZ. Twy between A & B has reduced wingtip clearance due to security fencing and two gates 50ft wide.

Maintenance	Nil
Fuel	AVGAS 100LL strictly by prior arrangement
Operator	RAF Colerne, Wiltshire **Tel:** 01225 743240 Ext 5338 (PPR)
Restaurants	Nil
Taxi Grahams **Car Hire**	 **Tel:**07850 874141 Nil
Weather Info	AirSW BNMC

Operating Hrs	As required by RAF operations
Circuits	Instructed by ATC at 1000ft QFE
Landing Fee	£7.56 + VAT per 500kgs & £8.50 Insurance charge

ELEVATION	LOCATION				COLONSAY (Machrins)
24ft 1mb	W side of Colonsay Island N5603.45.W00615.62	TIR 117.70 MAC 116.00	151 340	34.1 43.0	– / • • / • – • – – / • – / – • – •
PPR					

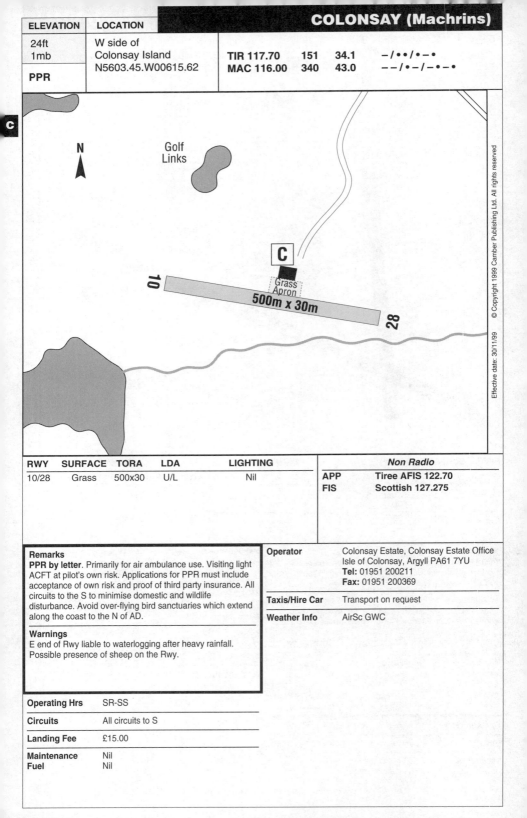

N

Golf Links

C

Grass Apron

10

500m x 30m

28

RWY	SURFACE	TORA	LDA	LIGHTING
10/28	Grass	500x30	U/L	Nil

	Non Radio
APP	Tiree AFIS 122.70
FIS	Scottish 127.275

Remarks

PPR by letter. Primarily for air ambulance use. Visiting light ACFT at pilot's own risk. Applications for PPR must include acceptance of own risk and proof of third party insurance. All circuits to the S to minimise domestic and wildlife disturbance. Avoid over-flying bird sanctuaries which extend along the coast to the N of AD.

Warnings

E end of Rwy liable to waterlogging after heavy rainfall. Possible presence of sheep on the Rwy.

Operator	Colonsay Estate, Colonsay Estate Office Isle of Colonsay, Argyll PA61 7YU **Tel:** 01951 200211 **Fax:** 01951 200369
Taxis/Hire Car	Transport on request
Weather Info	AirSc GWC

Operating Hrs	SR-SS
Circuits	All circuits to S
Landing Fee	£15.00
Maintenance Fuel	Nil Nil

ELEVATION	LOCATION	EGYC		COLTISHALL

EGYC **COLTISHALL**

ELEVATION	LOCATION
66ft 2mb	7.5nm NNE of Norwich N5245.30.E00121.44
PPR MILITARY	

CLN 114.55   012   54.6   — • — • / • — • • / — •

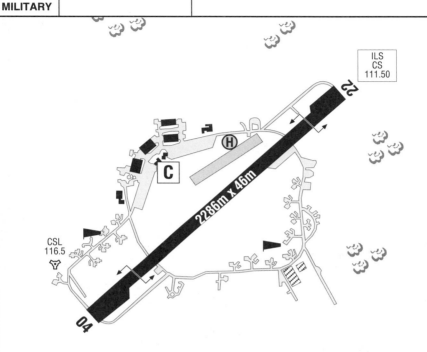

ILS
CS
111.50

2286m x 46m

22

04

CSL
116.5

CSL
116.5

C

RWY	SURFACE	TORA	LDA	LIGHTING
22	Asphalt	2286	2286	Thr Rwy PAPI 3°
04	Asphalt	2286	2286	Ap Thr Rwy PAPI 3°

Arrester gear 390m from both Thrs

Coltishall

APP/MATZ /LARS	**125.90**
PAR	**123.30**
TWR	**122.10/142.295**
TACAN	**CSL 116.50 on A/D**
ILS	**CS 111.50 Rwy22**

Remarks
PPR 24Hrs required. Hang gliding and parascending takes place outside normal A/D Hrs.
Visual aid to location: IBn CS Red.

Warnings
Nearby Norwich airport (216°/5nm from Coltishall) also has Rwy04/22. ATZ active H24.

Operator	RAF Coltishall **Tel:** 01603 737361 Ext.7205/7543
Restaurants	
Taxis/Car Hire	
Weather Info	M T BNMC

Operating Hrs
Mon-Thu 0730-1630 Fri 0730-1600 (Summer) + 1Hr Winter

Circuits	1500ft QFE
Landing fee	£7.56 per 500kgs +VAT & £8.50 insurance
Maintenance	Nil
Fuel	AVTUR Jet-A1

ELEVATION	LOCATION	**EGHA**	**COMPTON ABBAS**
810ft 27mb	2.7nm S of Shaftesbury N5058.03.W00209.22 **Diversion AD**	SAM 113.35 277 30.5	••• / • – / – –
PPR			

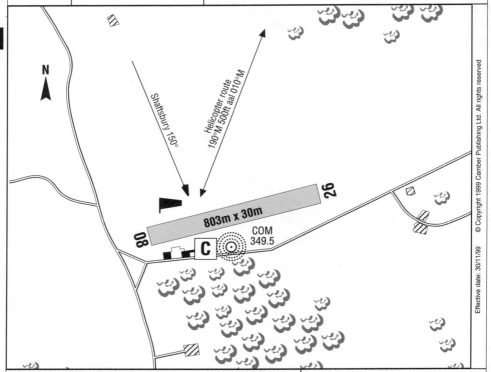

RWY	SURFACE	TORA	LDA	LIGHTING
08/26	Grass	803	803	Nil

	Compton
A/G	**122.70**
NDB	**COM 349.5*** ***on A/D range 10nm**

Remarks
AD is not available at night by flights required to use a licensed AD. ACFT to clear left after landing on Rwy26 and right after landing on Rwy08. Overflights not below 3000ft altitude. Radar assistance available on weekdays only from Boscombe Down on 126.70 or Yeovilton on 127.35. ACFT arriving from the E via 'SAM' can track SAM R281° outbound to Shaftesbury (SAM DME 32.5nm) then track 150° to Compton Abbas. White strobe flashes when visibility is less than 10kms.

Warnings
Noise abatement departures in force. Avoid over-flying villages around the AD. Ground to the N of the Rwy has a steep slope gradient. Turbulence & windshear will be experienced with southerly winds above 10kts. Particularly affected are Rwy08 arrivals in SE winds & climb out Rwy26 with S or SW winds.

Maintenance	Fixed wing Rotary Avionics **Tel:** 01747 812128 Hangerage available
Fuel	AVGAS 100LL
Operator	Compton Abbas Airfield Ltd Compton Abbas Airfield Ashmore, Salisbury, Wiltshire SP5 5AP **Tel:** 01747 811767 **Fax** 01747 811161
Restaurant	Licensed restaurant & bar at AD (1000-SS daily), available for corporate entertainment.
Taxis A+B **Car Hire**	**Tel:** 01722 744744 Operator can arrange on request
Weather Info	AirSW BNMC

Operating Hrs	0900-1700 (local) or SS whichever is earlier
Circuits	08 LH 26 RH 800ft QFE
Landing fee	£7.00 all types

ELEVATION	LOCATION	EGXC		CONINGSBY
25ft 1mb	10nm NW of Boston N5305.58 W00009.96		**GAM 112.80 117 30**	− − • / • − / − −
PPR			**CGY 111.10 (Tacan) on A/D**	− • − • / − − • / − • − −

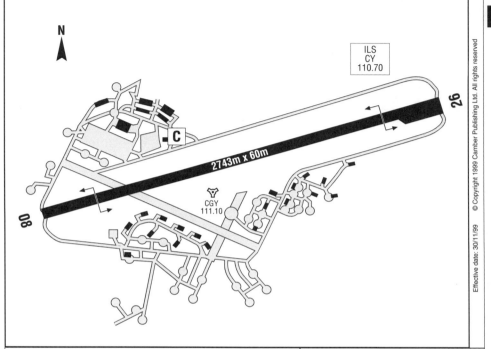

RWY	SURFACE	TORA	LDA	LIGHTING
08	Asphalt/Concrete	2743	2743	Ap Thr Rwy PAPI 2.5
26	Asphalt/Concrete	2743	2791	Ap Thr Rwy PAPI 2.5

Both 200m Concrete section in from Thr

Arrester gear 396m in from both Thrs. Both cables up unless otherwise notified

Coningsby	
APP/LARS	120.80
PAR	(Talkdown) 123.30
TWR	119.975 120.80 122.10
GND	122.10
ILS	CY 110.70 Rwy26
TACAN	CGY 111.10 on A/D

Remarks
PPR strictly by telephone. RAF AD within active MATZ. Based jet ACFT carry out high energy manoeuvers within the vicinity of the AD. Civil visiting ACFT accepted only by telephone permission, may be subject to refusal or specified arrival conditions. Traffic is particularly severely restricted when Rwy08 in use. Aid to location. I Bn CY Red

Warnings
Caution. Arrester cables. Be sure you have identified their position and land beyond. Do not overfly Woodhall Spa Engine De-Tuner. Avoid by 1000ft agl by 0.6nm radius. Danger of severe turbulence.

Operators	RAF Coningsby Woodhall Spa, Lincclnshire **Tel**:01526 342581 (Ext.2061/2)
Restaurants	
Taxi/Car Hire	
Weather Info	AirS BNMC

Operating Hrs	0800-1700 Mon-Fri (Local) ATZ operational H24
Circuits	26 LH 08 RH 1000ft QFE
Landing Fee	£7.56 + VAT per 500kgs & £8.50 Insurance charge
Maintenance Fuel	Not normally available to Civil visitors AVGAS 100LL JET A1 strictly by prior arrangement

ELEVATION	LOCATION	EGWC				COSFORD
271ft 9mb	7nm NW of Wolverhampton N5238.40.W00218.33	**HON 113.65**	**312**	**29.1**	•••• / – – – / – •	
PPR MILITARY		**TNT 115.70**	**229**	**33.8**	– / – • / –	

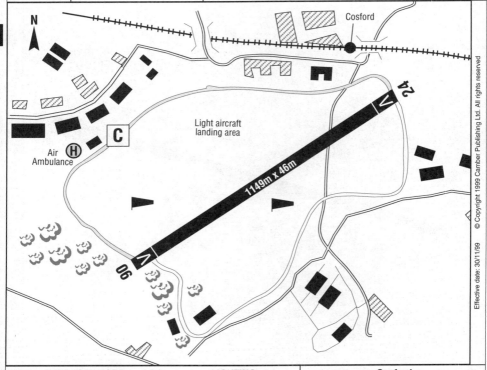

N

Cosford

Light aircraft landing area

C

Air Ambulance (H)

24

1149m x 46m

06

RWY	SURFACE	TORA	LDA	LIGHTING		*Cosford*	
24	Asphalt	1149	1119	Nil	**APP/TWR**	**128.825**	
06	Asphalt	1149	1126	Nil	**GND**	**121.95**	

Remarks
Ab initio pilot training takes place here. A/D closed for lunch at indeterminate times. Minimum manning during continuous operations. No APP facilities available. No civil ACFT accepted Sat/Sun

Warnings
Glider activity outside published Hrs and at weekends. Railway embankment 20ft aal, 274m before Rwy24 Thr. Ravine 91m before Rwy06 Thr. Air ambulance activity H24. Grass Rwys used by light ACFT and gliders are marked by white strips on one side. Caution full obstacle clearance criteria not met on APP. Up to 12 light ACFT operating at any one time.

Operator	RAF Cosford, Wolverhampton W Midlands WV7 3EX **Tel:** 01902 372393 Ext. 7567/7582
Restaurants	In the Aerospace Museum
Taxis/Car Hire	
Weather Info	AirCen MWC

Operating Hrs	0800-1730 (local) daily
Circuits	
Landing fee	£7.56 +VAT per 500kgs & £8.50 insurance
Maintenance	Nil
Fuel	AVGAS 100LL by arrangement

ELEVATION	LOCATION	**COTTERED AIRFIELD (Buntingford)**		
390ft 13mb	5nm SE of Baldock N5157.50 W00006.00	BKY 116.25	250	6.5	— • • • / — • — / — • — —
PPR		BPK 117.50	005	12	— • • • / • — — • / — • —

125ft agl transmission lines

N

100ft agl transmission lines

Slight downslpoe

500m x 20m

Crops

a/c parking

25

A507

A

B

07

Cottered village →

© Copyright 1999 Camber Publishing Ltd. All rights reserved

Effective date: 30/11/99

RWY	SURFACE	TORA	LDA	LIGHTING
07/25	Grass	500x20	U/L	

Slight downslope on Rwy25

APP (Luton) 129.55
Luton ATIS 120.575
Weather info from Luton ATIS

Remarks
PPR by telephone. Visiting ACFT operate at own risk.
Noise: Do not overfly Cottered village to the SE of AD. Strip width is given as 20 metres there is a wider section at the midpoint and to the S of Thr07.

Warnings
AD is situated below Luton CTA (base 2500ft QNH). There are trees and farm buildings close to the Thr25. A farm track runs down N side of strip and branches across Thr07. There are 100ft agl transmission line parallel to AD 80m to the N side with a second line 1000 metres further to the N. Crops are grown close to the strip edge.

Operator	Kingsley Brothers, Childs Farm Cottered, Buntingford, Herts **Tel**:01763 281256 **Fax**: 01763 281652
Restaurants	Bull Pub Cottered Village
Taxi/Car Hire	Nil
Weather Info	AirSE BNMC

Operating Hrs	SR-SS
Circuits	1000ft QFE
Landing fee	£6.00
Maintenance **Fuel**	Nil Nil

ELEVATION	LOCATION	**EGBE**				**COVENTRY**

ELEVATION	LOCATION
281ft 9mb	3nm SSE of Coventry N5222.18.W00128.78
PPR	**Diversion AD**

HON 113.65	090	7	••••/ – – –/ – •
DTY 116.40	317	17.6	– ••/ – / – •– –

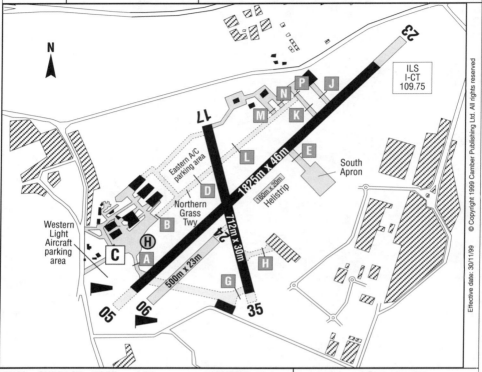

Effective date: 30/11/99

RWY	SURFACE	TORA	LDA	LIGHTING
05	Asphalt	1615	1795	Ap Thr Rwy PAPI 3° LHS
23	Asphalt	1825*	1615	Ap Thr Rwy PAPI 3° LHS
17	Asphalt	486	712	Nil
35	Ashpalt	712	486	Nil
06	Grass	500	400	Nil
24	Grass	400	490	Nil

*Includes 210m block paved starter extension

Coventry	
APP/TWR	**119.25**
ATIS	**126.05**
RAD	**122.00**
VDF	**119.25 122.0 124.80**
TWR	**119.25 124.80**
GND	**121.7**
NDB	**CT 363.50***
ILS	**I-CT 109.75 Rwy23**

*232/3.25 to Rwy23 range 20nm

Remarks
PPR to non-radio ACFT & weekend visitors. Circuit and instrument training can be pre-booked with ATC. Instrument training not available at weekends and subject to certain conditions, more details on request. Non-radio ACFT join overhead at 1500ft QNH (1231ft QFE). Helicopter training flights operating at 700ft QFE and below might not comply with normal R/T procedure. Helicopter circuits will normally operate from a grass area (as directed by ATC) circuit height 700ft QFE (except at night when main Rwy is used). 'Book-out' transit flights by reporting to the Flight Briefing Office or by telephoning ATC. 'Booking-out' by radio is not allowed. An ATC GMC service in use during busy periods when notified by NOTAM. Taxi instructions will be given under general direction from GMC (or Tower), a careful lookout should be maintained at all times. ATC instructions will normally specify the taxi route to be followed. Light ACFT are to self manoeuvre for parking, according to ATC instructions. The western light ACFT park is delineated by paving markers to preserve ILS integrity. Park to the N of these markers. Visual aids to location: Ibn Green CT.

Warnings
Adhere to standard RTF procedures. ACFT with a wingspan in excess of 18m require marshalling when taxying. Regular bird scaring. Rwy shoulders liable to waterlogging; ACFT to cross Rwys where indicated by marker boards.

Operating Hrs	Mon 0530-2359 Tue-Fri H24
(PPR 1900-0600) Sat 0001-1900 Sun 0730-2000 (Summer)	
Mon 0630-2359 Tue-Fri H24	
(PPR 2000-0700) Sat 0001-2000 Sun 0830-2100 (Winter)	

Circuits　　　　05/35 RH 23/17 LH Circuits to the S/E
at 1000ft QFE

Landing fee　　On application

Maintenance　　Atlantic Aero Engineering
Tel: 02476 307566
Fuel　　　　　　AVGAS 100LL AVTUR JET A1
Oils: W80 W100 S100 & Mobil Jet Oil II

Operator　　　　West Midlands International Airport Ltd
Coventry City Council, Coventry Airport
Baginton, Coventry CV8 3AZ
Tel: 02476 301717
Fax: 02476 639451(ATC)

Restaurants　　Licensed Buffet and Cafeteria in Terminal

Taxis
Allen's　　　　　　**Tel:** 02476 555555
Car Hire
Avis　　　　　　　**Tel:** 02476 225500
National　　　　　**Tel:** 02476 677042
Hertz　　　　　　　**Tel:** 02476 251741

Weather Info　　M T9 Fax 266 MWC

Visual Reference Points (VRPs)
Bitteswell (disused A/D)
N5227.47 W00114.78
Cement Works
N5216.35 W00123.07
Draycott Water
N5219.57 W00119.58
Nuneaton (disused A/D)
N5233.90 W00126.88

C

EGTC — CRANFIELD

ELEVATION	LOCATION				
364ft 12mb	7nm SW of Bedford N5204.33.W00037.00 **Diversion AD**	CFD 116.50	On A/D		– • – • / • • – • / – • •
PPR		BNN 113.75	358	20.8	– • • • / – • / – •
		DTY 116.40	116	19.4	– • • – / – / – • – –

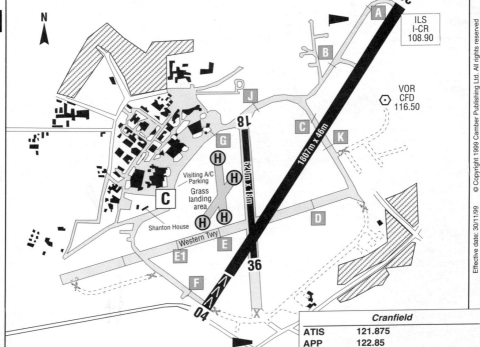

ILS I-CR 108.90

VOR CFD 116.50

1807m x 46m

	Cranfield
ATIS	121.875
APP	122.85
VDF	122.85
	134.925 121.5
TWR	134.925 122.85
ILS	I-CR 108.90 Rwy22
NDB	CIT 850*
VOR	CFD 116.50**

*217/3.69 to A/D **on A/D

RWY	SURFACE	TORA	LDA	LIGHTING
04	Asphalt	1807	1602	Nil
22*	Asphalt	1680	1680	Ap Thr Rwy PAPI 3° LHS
18/36	Asphalt	620	620	Nil

*Only Rwy22 licensed for night use
Rwy08/26 now withdrawn and used as a Twy

Remarks
PPR to non-radio ACFT and instrument training, instrument test and circuit training flights. Slots are allocated by ATC and must be adhered to. PPR granted on day of flight only. No dead side due to helicopter circuits on all Rwys. All VFR traffic to join via VRP's. Rwy18 for use of light ACFT by day only. All helicopters must request start up clearance. Avoid over-flying all buildings and structures 1500m W of the disused Rwy below 500ft QFE. Customs 24 Hrs' notice required.

Warnings
Intensive flight training takes place at AD. The S 300m of Rwy18/36 is unfit for use. Helicopter operations take place on the grass area NW of main Rwy intersection. All fixed wing ACFT entering/exiting the grass via N Twy to use concrete entry/exit points.

Operating Hrs
Mon-Fri 0730-1800 Sat-Sun & PH 0900-1700 (Summer),
Mon-Fri 0830-1900 Sat-Sun & PH 0900-1800 (Winter)
Extensions by arrangement **Tel:** 01234 750111 (Ext. 3175)

Circuits	Fixed-wing day 800ft QFE night 1200ft QFE
Landing fee	On application

Maintenance	Various
Fuel	AVGAS 100LL AVTUR JET A1

Operator	Cranfield Institute of Technology Cranfield, Bedfordshire MK43 0AL

Tel: 01234 754784 (Admin) **Tel:** 01234 754761 (ATC)
Tel: 01234 750661 (Handling) **Fax:** 01234 754785 (ATC)
Fax: 01234 751805 (Admin) **Fax:** 01234 751731 (Handling)
Telex 825072 CITECHC

Restaurants	Shanton House chinese restaurant open 1200-1400 1800-2300 daily
Taxis Car Hire	**Tel:** 01234 750005
Budget	**Tel:** 01908 217733
Hertz	**Tel:** 01908 374492
Weather Info	M T9 Fax 268 A BNMC

Visual Reference Points (VRPs)
Olney Town
N5209.20 W00042.10
Stewartby Brickworks
N5204.40 W00031.05
Woburn Town
N5159.40 W00037.15

ELEVATION	LOCATION	**EGYD**		**CRANWELL**

ELEVATION	LOCATION
218ft 7mb	9nm NE of Grantham N5301.82.W00028.99
PPR MILITARY	

GAM 112.8	137	22.5	− − • / • − / − −
TNT 115.70	098	42.7	− / − • / −

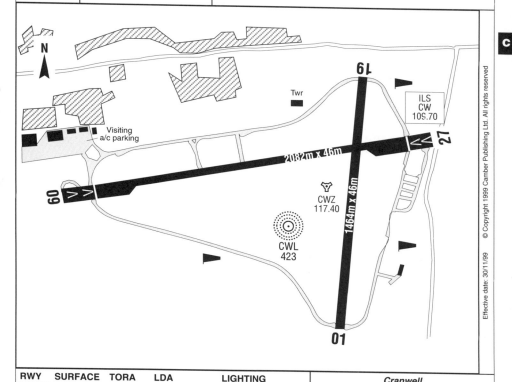

RWY	SURFACE	TORA	LDA	LIGHTING
09	Asph/Con	2082	1918	Ap Thr Rwy
27	Asph/Con	2082	1989	Ap Thr Rwy PAPI 3°
01/19	Asph/Con	1464	1464	Thr Rwy PAPI 3°

CRANWELL N

RWY	SURFACE	TORA	LDA	LIGHTING
07	Grass	1100	963	Nil
25	Grass	1100	1100	Nil

	Cranwell
ATIS	135.675
MATZ/APP	119.375
	(A/G outside Ops Hrs)
PAR	123.30
TWR	122.10
TACAN	CWZ 117.40 on a/d
ILS	CW 109.70 Rwy27
NDB	CWL 423 on a/d Rng 25nm

Remarks

The grass AD to the N of the main AD is for glider ops only. ACFT inbound to either Cranwell or Barkston Heath are to call Cranwell MATZ 119.375 at least 5nm before the boundary of the Cranwell/Barkston Heath CMATZ. Visual aids to location: Abn White; Ibn CW Red. ACFT must adhere to slot times. Light ACFT may operate outside normal operating times using 119.375 as A/G freq.

Warnings

Public roads cross the APP to all Rwys. Motorised glider towing up to 3000 ft and winch launching up to 2000 ft takes place on the grass AD to the N of the main AD during daylight Hrs, evenings & weekends.

Operating Hrs	As required for 3FTS operations (ATZ H24)
Circuits	Variable except Rwy01/09 RH
Landing fee	£7.56 +VAT per 500kgs & £8.50 insurance
Maintenance	Nil
Fuel	AVGAS 100LL AVTUR FS11
	By arrangement with min notice of 24 Hrs and max uplift of 500 Imp Galls
Operator	RAF Cranwell, Sleaford, Lincs NG34 8HB **Tel:** 01400-261201 Ext. 7377
Restaurants	
Taxis/Car Hire	
Weather Info	AirCen MWC

CROFT FARM (Defford)

ELEVATION	LOCATION		
70ft 2mb	0.5nm SE of Defford disused AD N5205.13.W00208.15	HON 113.65 232 24	••••/–––/–•
PPR		DTY 116.40 265 38.5	–••/–/–•––

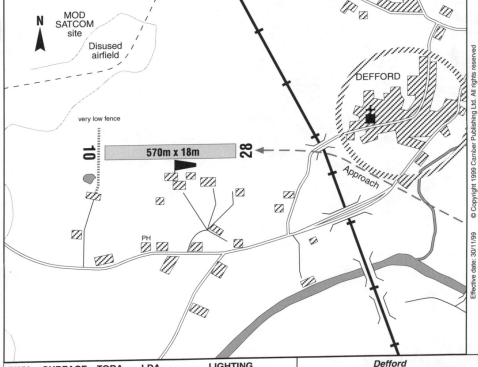

RWY	SURFACE	TORA	LDA	LIGHTING
10/28	Grass	570x18	U/L	Nil

Strip marked by reflective edge markings

	Defford
A/G	119.10 **Please make routine circuit calls**

Remarks
PPR by telephone. Visiting ACFT welcome at pilots own risk.

Warnings
Strip may be soft in winter after heavy rain. Low fence by Rwy10 Thr. Avoid overflying the SatCom site N of AD and the villages of Defford and Eckington.

Operator	Mr CH Porter, The Croft Farm Defford, Worcester WR8 9BN **Tel: 01386 750400** **Tel: 07767 606172**
Restaurants	Pub 400m from AD
Taxis	
Pershore Priv. Hire	**Tel: 01386 561060**
Eckington Taxis	**Tel: 01386 750407**
Car Hire	
PJ Nichols	**Tel: 01386 555555**
Brendon Motors	**Tel: 0800 614809**
Weather Info	Air Cen BNMC

Operating Hrs	SR-SS
Circuits	1000ft QFE
Landing fee	Nil but donations to: Mission Aviation Fellowship gratefully received
Maintenance	Nil
Fuel	Nil

ELEVATION	LOCATION				CROMER (Northrepps)
188ft 6mb	2nm SE of Cromer N5254.09.E00119.73	CM 313.5	158	1.9	— • — • / — —
PPR	**Diversion AD**	CLN 114.55	010	63.0	— • — • / • — • • / — •

C

N

Crossdale Street

81

V

C

493m x 23m

Crops

Crops

36

DO NOT overfly Northrepps

Avoid Bridge Farm (1000m SE)

RWY	SURFACE	TORA	LDA	LIGHTING
18/36	Grass	493x23	U/L	Nil
1.8% upslope Rwy36				

	Non radio
	Cromer Micro 129.825
APP	**Norwich 119.35**
LARS	**Coltishall 125.90**
	Useful wx information
	Norwich ATIS 128.625

Remarks
Light ACFT & helicopters welcome at pilots own risk. Extensive microlight activity at AD. Intensive military & civli low flying in the area including off-shore civil helicopters, throughout the week. Occasional banner towing and model ACFT flying. **Noise:** Avoid overflight of Northrepps, Crossdale Street & Bridge Farm below 500ft QFE. All visiting ACFT must book in and out. If field unmanned book in box outside wooden shed

Warnings
Departures are normally restricted to Rwy18 which has a 1.8% downslope and public road close to Thr. Public footpath close to Thr Rwy36. SAR helicopters may operate from AD. Heavy SAR helicopter landing area on Rwy, users must be prepared for AD to be unavailable to fixed wing ACFT at short notice.

Maintenance	Nil
Fuel	AVGAS 100LL by arrangement MOGAS
Operator	Chris Gurney, Heath Cottage Northrepps, Cromer, Norfolk NR27 9LB **Tel:** 01263 513015 **Fax:** 01263 515516 **Mobile:** 07860 466484
Restaurants	Light refreshments available on AD Pub & hotel in village 5min walk
Taxis A1 Cabs **Car Hire**	**Tel:** 01263 513371 and bikes available on request
Weather Info	AirS BNMC

Operating Hrs	SR-SS
Circuits	36 LH 18 RH 600 QFE
Landing fee	Private £4 Microlights £2 Commercial on application

ELEVATION	LOCATION	**EGSO**				**CROWFIELD**
201ft 7mb	4nm ESE of Stowmarket N5210.27 E00106.66	CLN 114.55	359	19.3	–•–•/•–••/–•	
PPR		BKY 116.25	079	40.6	–•••/–•–/–•––	
		LAM 115.60	052	47.8	•–••/•–/––	

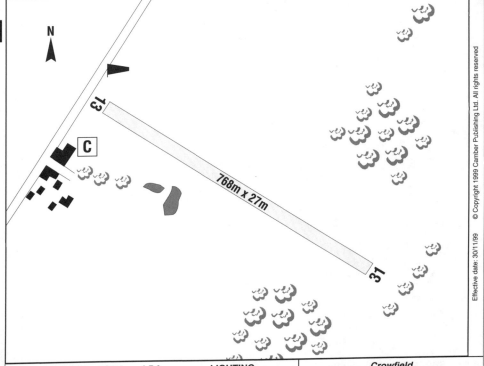

Runway labels: 13, 768m x 27m, 31

C

RWY	SURFACE	TORA	LDA	LIGHTING
31	Grass	768	741	Nil
13	Grass	768	768	Nil

U/L AD

	Crowfield
APP	**Wattisham MATZ** **125.8**
A/G	**122.775**

Remarks
PPR by telephone only. No multi engined ACFT. No singles more than 180hp or 1200kgs AUW. No single seaters, Gliders, Microlights or Helicopters. Total daily movements restricted. Arrivals must contact Wattisham APP on 125.8 when at least 15nm from Wattisham. Departures, unless otherwise instructed by Wattisham, must fly not above 800ft QFE while under Wattisham MATZ stub and remain at that height until clear of Wattisham MATZ. Contact Wattisham ASAP after takeoff.

Warnings
Please operate with consideration, this AD is in an extremely noise sensitive area.

Operator	Mr A C Williamson, Crowfield Aerodrome Coddenham Green, Ipswich Suffolk IP6 9UN **Tel:** 01449 711017 **Fax:** 01449 711054
Restaurants	Coffee & tea available
Taxis Stowmarket **Car Hire**	By arrangement or **Tel:** 01449 677777 By arrangement
Weather Info	AirS BNMC

Operating Hrs	0700-1900 (Summer) 0900-1800 or SS (Winter)
Circuits	31 variable 13 LH 800ft QFE
Landing fee	£5
Maintenance Fuel	Nil AVGAS 100LL Oils W100 W80 100 80

ELEVATION	LOCATION				CROWLAND (Spalding)

ELEVATION	LOCATION			
10ft 0mb	4nm of Spalding (On Spalding/Crowland road) N5242.53 W00008.57	BKY 116.55	355	43.8	– • • • / – • – / – • – –
PPR		GAM 112.80	145	45.1	– – • / • – / – –

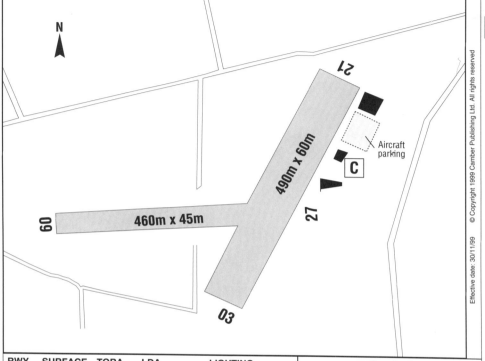

N

21

490m x 60m

27

03

60 460m x 45m

Aircraft parking

C

C

RWY	SURFACE	TORA	LDA	LIGHTING
03/21	Grass	490x60	U/L	Nil
09/27	Grass	460x45	U/L	Nil

	Crowland
APP	Cottesmore MATZ/LARS 130.20
A/G	Crowland Radio 130.10 or 130.40 (Glider ops)

Remarks
PPR by telephone. Visitors welcome at pilot's own risk. Good approaches. Frequent aero-tow glider flying. RAF Wittering MATZ panhandle begins 5nm WSW of Crowland. If windsock and signal square 'T' indicate different Rwys, be guided by the wind.

Warnings
Intensive military low-flying activity Mon-Fri in the vicinity. Mast 200 ft agl situated S of Crowland. AD surface rough in places.

Operator	Peterborough & Spalding Gliding Club Postland, Crowland, Lincs **Tel:** 01733 210463 **Tel:** 01832 280087 **Tel:** 01933 274198 (CFI)

Restaurants
Light refreshments when gliding in progress

Taxis Car Hire	**Tel:** 01775 711122

Weather Info	AirS BNMC

Operating Hrs	SR-SS
Circuits	Powered ACFT LH Gliders RH 800ft QFE
Landing fee	Nil
Maintenance Fuel	Nil Nil

ELEVATION	LOCATION	EGDR			CULDROSE

ELEVATION	LOCATION
267ft 9mb	1nm SE of Helston N5005.17.W00515.34
PPR MILITARY	

LND 114.20   109   15   • — • • / — • / — • •

C

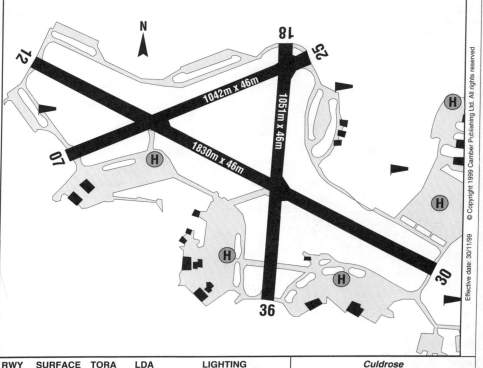

Effective date: 30/11/99

RWY	SURFACE	TORA	LDA	LIGHTING
07/25	Asphalt	1028	1028	Ap Rwy PAPI 3°
12/30	Asphalt	1830	1830	Ap Rwy PAPI 3°
18/36	Asphalt	1051	1051	Ap Rwy PAPI 3°

Culdrose	
MATZ/	
LARS/APP	**134.05**
PAR	**123.30 122.1**
SRE	**134.05 122.1**
TWR	**122.10 123.30**

Remarks
PPR 24 Hrs required. Inbound ACFT to contact Culdrose APP at 20nm. Radar letdown mandatory. Visual aids to location: Ibn CU Red. AD name displayed.

Warnings
High intensity helicopter operations in the area and at Predannack. Glider launching at weekends and evenings. More than one Rwy may be used simultaneously. No visual signals.

Operator	RNAS Culdrose, Helston Cornwall TR12 7RH **Tel:** 01326 574121 Ext. 2415 (ATC) PPR from Ops Ext. 2620
Restaurants	
Taxis/Car Hire	
Weather Info	M T Fax 272 BNMC

Operating Hrs	Mon-Thu 0730-1600 or SS Fri 0730-1300 or SS (Summer) + 1Hr Winter
Circuits	Helicopter circuits LH & RH no deadside
Landing fee	£7.56 per 500kgs +VAT & £8.50 insurance
Maintenance **Fuel**	Nil AVGAS 100LL AVTUR JET A1 By arrangement

ELEVATION	LOCATION	EGPG				CUMBERNAULD

350ft
12mb

PPR

16nm NE of Glasgow
N5558.50.W00358.47
Diversion AD

TLA 113.80 331 35.5 — / • – • • / • —
GOW 115.40 076 17.0 — — • / — — — / • — —

N

CBN 374   CBN 117.55

C B A

26

08

820m x 23m

West Apron

C

Main Apron   East Apron

RWY	SURFACE	TORA	LDA	LIGHTING
08	Asphalt	820	820	Thr Rwy APAPI 4° LHS
26	Asphalt	820	820	Ap Thr Rwy APAPI 3° LHS

	Cumbernauld
AFIS/AG*	120.60
NDB	CBN 374.0
DME	CBN 117.55
	on A/D range 25nm
	*at weekends

Remarks
Certain customs facilities available. In IFR, suitably equipped ACFT may let down at Edinburgh and proceed to Cumbernauld VMC. Visual aids to location: white strobe on roof of Control Tower, available on request.

Warnings
The AD is situated under the Scottish TMA. Traffic in transit should anticipate local circuit activity at this AD. Microlight flying takes place at this AD.

Operator

Cumbernauld Airport Ltd
Duncan Macintosh Road, Ward Park
North Cumbernauld, G68 0HH
Tel: 01236 722100
Tel: 01236 722822(ATC)
Fax: 01236 781646

Restaurant Cafe and licensed bar available at the AD

Taxis
Eastfield **Tel:** 01236 730009
Car Hire
National **Tel:** 01786 470123

Weather Info AirSc GWC

Operating Hrs	0730-1930 (Summer) 0800-1700 (Winter) & by arrangement
Circuits	26 RH 08 LH 1000ft QFE
Landing fee	Single £12 Twin £30.00 +VAT
Maintenance	Cormack Aircraft Services Ltd **Tel:** 01236 722100
Fuel	AVGAS 100LL AVTUR JET A1

0800-1600 daily, VISA/Mastercard accepted

ELEVATION	LOCATION			
800ft 26mb	8nm SW of Newcastle Airport N5456.03.W00150.73	**NEW 114.25**	**225**	**8** — • / • / • — —
PPR				

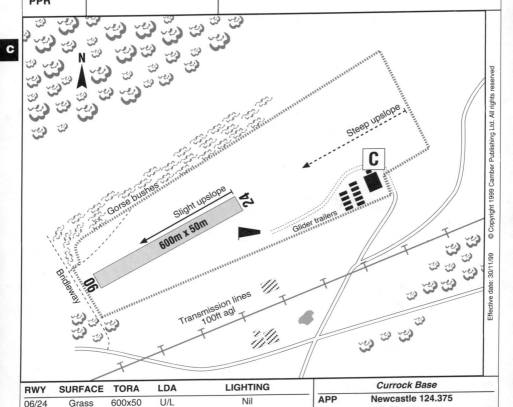

RWY	SURFACE	TORA	LDA	LIGHTING
06/24	Grass	600x50	U/L	Nil

	Currock Base
APP	Newcastle 124.375
A/G	130.10

Remarks
PPR by telephone Primarily a gliding site but light ACFT welcome at pilot's own risk. Only part of large grass area is suitable for light ACFT landing/take-off runs to WSW with 24 Thr abeam the windsock. The AD is situated within Newcastle CTR, clearance to enter must be obtained from APP 124.375.

Warnings
Rwy24 has slight upslope, Steep slope area E of Rwy24 Thr may cause turbulence on short final. Gliders launch with winch and aerotow. Launch positions may not be co-located. Sheep graze when gliding is not in progress.

Operator	Northumbria Gliding Club Ltd Currock Hill Chopwell, Newcastle NE17 7AX **Tel:** 01207 561286 **Fax:** 01207 562078

Restaurants
Tea & coffee available when gliding in progress
Luigis   **Tel:** 01207 561208 (5min walk)

Taxis	**Tel:** 0191 413 1143
Car Hire	Nil

Weather Info   AirN MWC

Operating Hrs	Sat-Sun & Wed 0900-SS (local) also by arrangement
Circuits	Powered ACFT to S at 1000ft QFE gliders variable
Landing fee	Private £5 Commercial £10
Maintenance Fuel	Nil AVGAS 100LL by prior arrangement

ELEVATION	LOCATION					DAVIDSTOW MOOR

ELEVATION	LOCATION				
969ft 33mb	3nm ENE of Camelford N5038.25.W00437.13 **Diversion AD**	BHD 112.05	295	44.8	– •• / •••• / – ••
PPR		LND 114.20	059	49.0	• – •• / – • / – ••

D

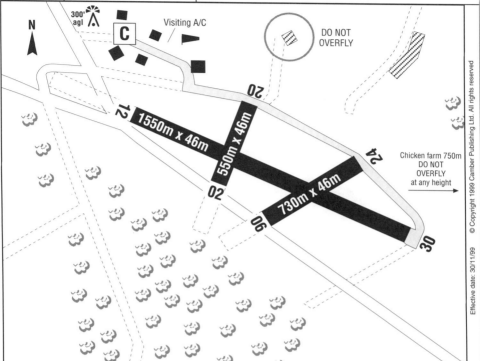

RWY	SURFACE	TORA	LDA	LIGHTING
12/30	Concrete	1550x46	U/L	Nil
06/24	Concrete	730x46	U/L	Nil
02/20	Concrete	550x46	U/L	Nil

Non radio

LARS	St Mawgan 126.50
Microlights may monitor 129.825	

Remarks

PPR by telephone. Situated on unfenced moorland. Windsock displayed when flying in progress. Beware of livestock and people on Rwys. Gliding at weekends. Microlight activity at any time. No flying within 1/2nm radius of farm approx 1.5 miles E of AD at N5038.45 W00434.30.

Warning

A road running SE/NW bisects the AD. Only Rwy to NE of road are useable. Radio TWRs 236ft aal in NW corner of the AD, 200m from signals square. Do not overfly villages to NW of AD.

Operator	Moorland Flying Club, Davidstow Airfield Camelford PL32 9YF **Tel:** 01840 261517 **Fax:** 01840 213844 **Email:** mfc@avnet.co.uk
Restaurants	Available in Camelford 1m NW
Taxis Car Hire	**Tel:** 01840 213867
Weather Info	AirSW BNMC

Operating Hrs	0800-1700 (Summer) 0900-1800 (Winter)
Circuits	All to S
Landing fee the local area	No charge for flyers spending money in
Maintenance **Fuel**	For microlights MOGAS

DEANLAND (Lewes)

ELEVATION	LOCATION
60ft 2mb	5nm E of Lewes N5052.73.E00009.38
PPR	

SFD 117.00   **015**   **7.5**   • • • / • • – • / – • •

D

N

457m x 27m

24

06

RWY	SURFACE	TORA	LDA	LIGHTING
06/24	Grass	457x27	U/L	Rwy

	Deanland
A/G	129.725 **not always manned**

Remarks
PPR by telephone. No weightshift Microlights. Available for single-engined ACFT only. Considerate pilots welcome at own risk but ACFT performance must be compatible with the length of the strip and pilot must have short field experience. Do not over-fly any local houses, the caravan park and village of Ripe. Arrivals: large circuits with a minimum of 1.5nm final maintaining the Rwy centreline. Under no circumstances cut the corners. Departures: Climb accurately maintaining Rwy centreline for 1.5nm before turning on track. Under no circumstances make early turns. No local or training flights. Please enter flight details in movements book at the 'Control Point'. ACFT insurance must cover operational risks at strips.

Warnings
After prolonged or heavy rainfall the Rwy can become waterlogged, please check by phone. Make blind calls if radio unmanned.
Caution: Private strip 1nm from end of Rwy24 to SW

Operating Hrs   SR-SS

Circuits   O6 LH 24 RH 1000ft QFE

Landing Fee	No charge to private (non business) flights but donations to World Wildlife Fund please (Panda in Control Point)
Maintenance	Nil
Fuel	Nil
Operator	Messrs Brook & Price, Deanland Airfield c/o DJ Brook, BCL House, Gatwick Road Crawley, Sussex RH10 2AX

Tel: 01323 811410 (AD)
Tel: 07785 316368 **Tel:** 01273 400768
Tel: 01903 774379 **Fax:** 01293 429836

Restaurant
Coffee/Tea available from machine in Control Point

Taxis	
Becks	**Tel:** 01273 483838
Car Hire	Nil

Weather Info	AirSE BNMC

ELEVATION	LOCATION				
328ft 11mb	4nm E of Corby N5230.37.W00035.35	DTY 116.40	049	27.1	– • • / – / – • – –
PPR		BKY 116.25	328	39.0	– • • • / – • – / – • – –
		CFD 116.50	007	26	– • – • / • • – • / – • •
		HON 113.65	084	40	• • • • / – – – / – •

DEENETHORPE

RWY	SURFACE	TORA	LDA	LIGHTING
04/22	Asphalt	1200x23	U/L	Nil

Deenethorpe

APP/LARS	Cottesmore 130.20
A/G	127.575 by arrangement

Remarks
PPR by telephone. ACFT arr and dep are advised to contact Cottesmore MATZ. ACFT should avoid over flying Deene Park (1.5nm W of AD) below 2000ft. Join overhead at 2000ft. Visiting ACFT must carry third party insurance cover of not less than £500,000

Warnings
Rwy04 Thr inset by 400m, Rwy22 Thr by 237m. Microlights operate outside AD Hrs. Beware close proximity of Lyveden gliding site.

Operator	Mr API Campbell, Estates Office Deene Park, Corby Namptonshire NN17 3EW **Tel:** 01780 450361 **Fax:**01780 450282
Restaurants	
Taxis/Car Hire	
Weather Info	AirCen MWC

Operating Hrs	Sat-Sun PH 0800-1630 (Summer) Sat-Sun PH 0900-SS (Winter) Other Hrs strictly PPR
Circuits	LH 800ft
Landing Fee	Single £5.00, Twin £10.00, penalty for no PPR
Maintenance	Nil
Fuel	Nil

Effective date: 30/11/99   © Copyright 1999 Camber Publishing Ltd. All rights reserved

D

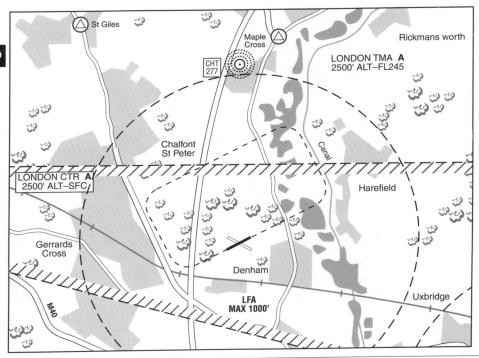

Visual Reference Point (VRP)

	VOR/DME	
Maple Cross	BNN 167/6.1	BPK 248/16.5
N5137.77 W00030.25		
Chalfont St Giles	BNN 190/5.6	BPK 253/18.5
N5138.03 W00034.02		

Flight without compliance to IFR within the Denham ATZ is permitted subject to the following conditions:

1 ACFT must remain clear of cloud and in sight of the surface.
2 Fly NOT above 1000ft QNH
3 Minimum flight visibility 3km
DO NOT proceed S of the A40

Pilots flying in the ATZ are responsible for providing their own separation from other ACFT flying in the relevant airspace.

Joining Procedures
THERE ARE NO OVERHEAD JOINS
Rwy06
Join via Chalfont St Giles (N5138.03 W00034.02) directly to base leg to the E of the A413 to avoid Gerrards Cross.
Rwy24
Join via Maple Cross (N5137.77 W00030.25) directly to base leg over the lakes to avoid Harefield.
Joining traffic MUST establish radio contact with Denham at 10nm range & then report at St Giles or Maple Cross as appropriate to rwy in use.

Circuit Traffic
Circuit traffic should stay S of Hogtrough Wood to avoid a noise sensitive area in Chalfont St Peter. Additional restrictions apply to twin engined ACFT & helicopters.

Departure Procedures
Rwy06
Turn left over the lakes to avoid Harefield.
Rwy24
After take-off continue straight ahead until past the houses on the right, then turn right before the A413 to avoid overflying Gerrards Cross.

ELEVATION	LOCATION	**EGLD**				**DENHAM**
249ft 8mb	1.5nm E of Gerrards Cross N5135.30.W00030.78	**LON** 113.60	347	6.4	• — • • / — — — / — •	
PPR	**Diversion AD**	**BNN** 113.75	175	8.3	— • • • / — • / — •	
		LAM 115.60	267	25.0	• — • • / • — / — —	

D

N

RWY	SURFACE	TORA	LDA	LIGHTING
06	Asphalt	737	701	Thr Rwy APAPI 4.5° LHS
24	Asphalt	727	675	Thr Rwy APAPI 4.5° LHS
12	Grass	439	428	Nil
30	Grass	540	380	Nil

Denham

A/G /AFIS	130.725

Remarks

PPR. non-radio ACFT not accepted. Visual aids to location: Name displayed. Obligatory third party insurance £500,000 minimum. ID beacon green, DN.
Noise: Fly circuits tight, as safety allows. Rwy24 deps. Climb ahead past houses on right, turn right before A413, to avoid Gerrards Cross. Rwy06 deps. Turn left over lakes to avoid Harefield. Rwy24 arr. From Maple Cross fly base leg over lakes avoiding Harefield. Rwy06 arr. From Chalfont St Giles fly base leg E of A413 avoiding Gerrards Cross. In circuit stay S Hogtrough Wood avoid noise sensitive area Chalfont St Peter.
Additional restrictions for twins & helicopters at weekends.

Warnings

A public road, adjacent to the AD boundary, crosses the extended centre-line of Rwy24. Do not descend below the glide-path, nor touchdown before the Thr. Visual glideslope guidance signals for Rwy06 are visible to the left of the extended centreline where normal obstacle clearance is not guaranteed. They should not be used until the ACFT is aligned with the Rwy.

Landing fee	Up to 1 tonne £9.50 inc.VAT
Maintenance	Denham Aircraft Maintenance **Tel: 01895 834187**
Fuel	AVGAS 100LL AVTUR JET A1 by arrangement
Operator	Bickerton's Aerodromes Ltd Denham Aerodrome Uxbridge, Middlesex UB9 5DE **Tel: 01895 832161 (Admin) Tel: 01895 833236 (A/G Radio) Fax: 01895 833486**
Restaurant	Restaurant and club facilities available
Taxis Harefield Cars	**Tel: 01895 824024**
Car Hire National Lordship Motors	**Tel: 01753 534442 Tel: 01753 883120**
Weather Info	AirSE BNMC

Operating Hrs	0800-1630 or SS (Summer) 0900-1730 or SS (Winter) and by arrangement
Circuits	06 LH 24RH 12/30 vari Max 750ft QFE (1000ft QNH)

ELEVATION	LOCATION				
175ft	6nm SW of Derby	TNT 115.70	176	12.0	– / – • / –
6mb	N5251.58.W00137.05	HON 113.65	011	29.7	• • • • / – – – / – •
PPR		GAM 112.80	226	35.2	– – • / • – / – –

Effective date: 30/11/99

456m x 20m
602m x 20m
528m x 20m

Aircraft Parking

C

RWY	SURFACE	TORA	LDA	LIGHTING
23	Grass	445	341	Nil
05	Grass	356	430	Nil
10	Grass	276	306	Nil
28	Grass	293	291	Nil
17	Grass	525	No landing	Nil
35	Grass	No take-off	540	Nil

	Derby
APP	E Midlands 119.65
A/G	118.35

Remarks

PPR. Non-radio ACFT not accepted. Not available at night or to Public Transport flights required to use a licensed AD. Special arrival and departure procedures apply, which can be obtained when telephoning for PPR. Overhead joins are not permitted, Derby is under the E Midlands CTA (base 1500ft AMSL over the AD). Avoid over-flying local villages.

Warnings

A power line 100ft aal crosses Rwy23 APP 1200m from touchdown. Trees on the APP to 23 may cause turbulence and block the view of approaching ACFT to ACFT on the GND. There are no QDM marks on the Rwys. The thresholds are marked by red and white wing bars. Due to short LDA's on 28/10 and 23/05 an early go around decision is vital. DO NOT attempt to land long!

Operating Hrs

Mon-Sat 0800-1600 Sun & PH 0830-1600 (Summer)
Mon-Sat 0900-SS Sun & PH 0930-SS (Winter)

Circuits	05 LH 23 RH 1000ft QFE
Landing fee	Single £5.00 Twin/Heli £10.00 inc VAT

Maintenance	Airspeed Aviation Shop
	Tel: 01283 733803
Fuel	AVGAS 100LL
Operator	Derby Aero Club, Derby Aerodrome Hilton Road, Egginton Derby DE65 6GU
	Tel: 01283 733803
	Fax: 01283 734829
Restaurants	Tea & Coffee in the club house

Taxis
Stretton — Tel: 01283 511876
A1 — Tel: 01283 838383

Car Hire
Hertz — Tel: 01332 205215
National — Tel: 01332 382251

Weather Info	AirCen MWC

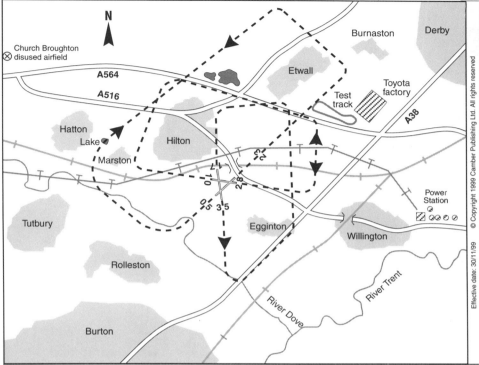

Rwy23
Turn crosswind S of river Dove but before Rolleston
Turn downwind at small lake between Hatton & Marston
Turn baseleg between Burnaston & Etwall
Final APP will overfly Toyota test track

Rwy05
Turn Crosswind abeam Toyata factory pass between
Burnaston & Etwall
Turn downwind to remain W of Hilton
Turn baseleg by initially turning at small lake to remain clear
of Hatton & Marston, then follow course of river Dove to final
remaining clear of Rolleston

Rwy28
Turn crosswind before Marston but remain W of Hilton
Turn downwind following course of A564
Turn Baseleg at Toyota test track
Continue to final

Rwy10
Turn Crosswind abeam Toyota test track
Turn downwind following course of A564
Turn baseleg W of Hilton & E of Marston
Continue to final

Rwy17 (Departures Only)
Turn crosswind at river Dove, intercept A38 to avoid Egginton
Turn downwind to toyota test track
Then leave circuit

Rwy35 (Landing Only)
Turn crosswind to avoid Etwall
Turn downwind at Toyota test track
Then leave the circuit

ELEVATION	LOCATION	EGXD	DISHFORTH

ELEVATION	LOCATION
117ft 4mb	3.5nm E of Ripon N5408.23.W00125.22
PPR MILITARY	

POL 112.10   051   33.9   •——•/———/•—••

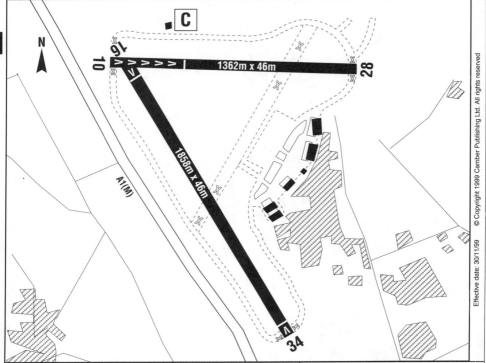

RWY	SURFACE	TORA	LDA	LIGHTING
16	Asphalt	1858	1716	Thr Rwy PAPI 3°
34	Asphalt	1858	1782	Ap Thr Rwy PAPI 3°
10	Asphalt	1362	936	Nil
28	Asphalt	1362	1362	Nil

Dishforth

MATZ	Leeming 127.75
APP	Topcliffe 125.00
TWR	Dishforth 122.10
A/G	130.1 (Glider Ops)

Remarks

This AD is a satellite for Linton-on-Ouse. Pilots should contact Leeming MATZ before entering the area. Avoid overflying Boroughbridge and Kirby Hill.

Warnings

High intensity military flying during operational Hrs. Glider flying outside AD Hrs, evenings and weekends. Army helicopter operations may take place at any time.

Operator	RAF Dishforth, Thirsk, North Yorks
Tel:	01347 848261 Ext.7491/2 (PPR thru Linton-on-Ouse)
Tel:	01347 832521 (AD)
Restaurants	
Taxis/Car Hire	
Weather Info	AirN MWC

Operating Hrs	Mon-Fri 0830-1700 and as required by RAF
Circuits	10/16 RH 28/34 LH 1000ft QFE
Landing fee	£7.56 per 500kgs +VAT & £8.50 insurance
Maintenance	Nil
Fuel	JET A1 (not normally available to civil visitors)

ELEVATION	LOCATION					
3ft 0mb	1nm S of Dornoch N5752.14.W00401.32 **Diversion AD**	**INS 109.20**	011	19.6	••/−•/•••	
PPR		**WIK 113.60**	228	45.8	•−−/••/−•−	

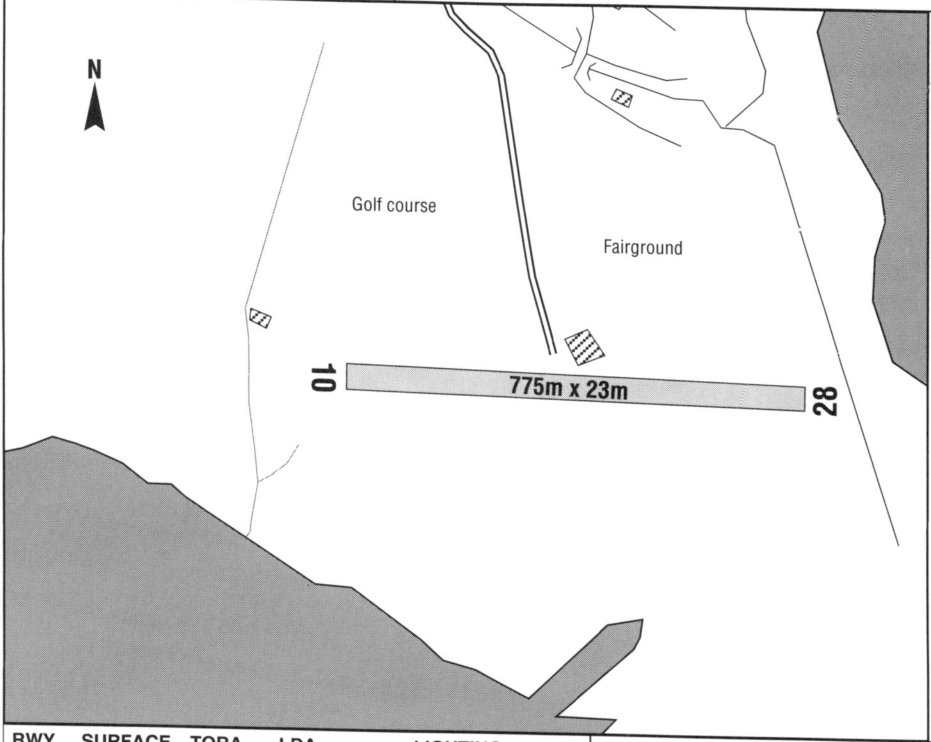

DORNOCH

Effective date: 30/11/99

N

Golf course

Fairground

10

775m x 23m

28

RWY	SURFACE	TORA	LDA	LIGHTING		
10/28	Grass	775x23	U/L	Nil		

Non radio

APP | Lossiemouth
LARS 119.35

Remarks
PPR prospective visitors must telephone Council Offices. Dornoch during office Hrs. Tel: 01862 810491.
An entry/exit lane is established from the Danger Area boundary S to the AD via Embo from the surface to 1000ft amsl. There is a telephone at the AD.

Warnings
AD situated near W edge of Danger Area D703. DAAIS Tain Range 122.75. Landing strip is marked by 3ft high posts 90m either side of Rwy centre line.

Operator The Highland Council Area Manager Roads and Transport, Victoria Road Brora, Sutherland KW9 6QN
Tel: 01862 812000
Tel: 01408 623400 (Area Roads and Transport Mgr)
Fax: 01408 621118

Restaurants Nil at AD
Royal Golf Hotel **Tel:** 01862 810283
Matlin House **Tel:** 01862 810335

Taxis
John Gordon **Tel:** 01862 810503
Car Hire
John Gordon **Tel:** 01862 810503

Weather Infos AirSc GWC

Operating Hrs	SR-SS
Circuits	
Landing fee	On application
Maintenance	Nil
Fuel	Nil

ELEVATION	LOCATION				
150ft 5mb	7nm SE of Oxford N5139.85 W00107.56	CPT 114.35	020	11	— • — • / • — — • / —
PPR		BNN 113.75	265	22	— • • • / — • / — •

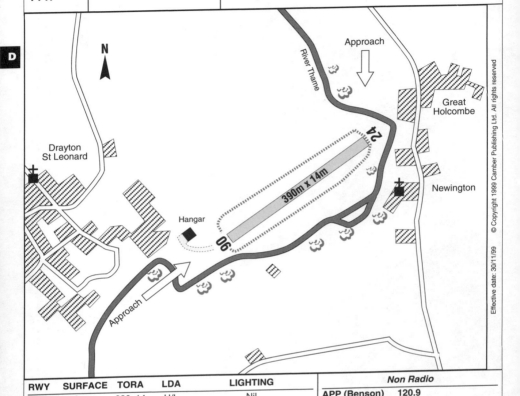

RWY	SURFACE	TORA	LDA	LIGHTING		
06/24	Grass	390x14	U/L	Nil	**APP (Benson)**	120.9

Non Radio

Operating Hrs	SR-SS
Circuits	See Local procedures/Noise
Landing Fee	Nil
Maintenance	Nil
	Limited outside parking available by arrangement
Fuel	Nil
Operator	Mr George Farrant, Manor Cottage Drayton St.Leonards, Wallingford Oxfordshire OX10 7BE **Tel:** 01865 891717/890223 **Fax:** 01865 400064
Restaurants	Nil
Taxis/Car Hire	Nil
Weather Info	AirSE BNMC

Remarks
PPR by telephone. Microlight AD but STOL aircraft and experienced pilots welcome at pilots own risk. AD located in Benson MATZ. The circuit passes over Drayton St.Leonard at 1200ft QNH.

Warnings
Electric fences surround AD sides and thresholds. When cattle are not grazing in the adjacent field Thr fences can be removed to provide extensions on Rwy24 & 06 for take-off only. AD is prone to flooding after heavy precipitation. Caution, parachuting takes place at Chalgrove, 2nm ENE. **Local procedures/Noise:** Inbound ACFT should contact Benson APP (120.9) before entering the MATZ or telephone Benson ATC, (01491 837766 Ext7555/7487. Departures telephone Benson before take-off. To avoid local noise sensitive areas and to avoid conflict with Benson circuit Arrivals are to follow these procedures. Do not carry out overhead joins or circuits. If safety allows carry out a direct approach from a long final. APP Rwy24 offset to N to avoid Newington, The farm to the W, & the farm on the hill. Approach Rwy06 should be slightly right of centreline to avoid Drayton St.Leonard. Departures Rwy06. ASAP after take-off turn left onto N. Rwy24. ASAP after take-off turn left onto 220° to avoid Drayton St.Leonard.

ELEVATION	LOCATION				
17ft 0mb	0.5nm S of Dundee N5627.15.W00301.55				
PPR		SAB 112.50	326	42.6	••• / • − / − •••
		PTH 110.40	095	11.5	• − − • / − / ••••

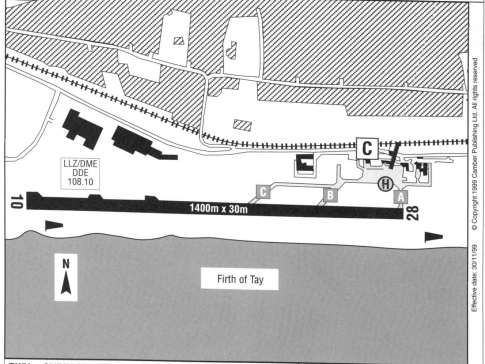

LLZ/DME
DDE
108.10

10

1400m x 30m

28

C   B   A   H   C

N

Firth of Tay

Effective date: 30/11/99

RWY	SURFACE	TORA	LDA	LIGHTING
10	Asphalt	1319	1400	Ap Thr Rwy PAPI 3.7° LHS
28	Asphalt	1319	1400	Thr Rwy PAPI 3.25° LHS

Dundee

APP	Leuchars MATZ 126.50
APP/TWR	122.90
LLZ/DME	DDE 108.10 Rwy10
NDB	DND 394.00* *102/2.63 to Thr10

Remarks

PPR to non-radio ACFT and all training flights. ACFT departing to N on Rwy10 are to climb straight ahead to 2000ft before setting course. Because view from Control TWR is restricted local movements to the N of the AD are not permitted. Pilots should avoid flying over Nine-Wells Hospital which is 1.2nm bearing 306°T from the AD. Parachuting takes place at Errol. Visual aids to location: Ibn Green DN. Link C only available to ACFT 5700kgs or less.

Warnings

AD is in the vicinity of Leuchars MATZ. Birds are a constant hazard at this AD. An additional PAPI system set for 5.25° is located on the right-hand side of Rwy10 and 28. This system is available by prior arrangement.

Operating Hrs

Mon-Fri 0545-1930 Sat-Sun 0800-1600 (Summer)
Mon-Fri 0645-2030 Sat-Sun 0930-1600 (Winter)
and by arrangement

Circuits	10 RH 28 LH 1000ft QFE
Landing fee	Single £7 inc VAT

Maintenance	Tayside Aviation **Tel:** 01382 644577 **Fax:** 01382 644531
Fuel	AVGAS 100LL AVTUR JET A1
Operator	Dundee City Council, Dundee Airport Riverside Drive, Dundee DD2 1UH **Tel:** 01382 643242 (APT) **Tel:** 01382 669414 (ATC) **Fax:** 01382 641263 **Telex:** 76431
Restaurant	Coffee Bar in Clubhouse
Taxis	**Tel:** 01382 515573
Car Hire	
National	**Tel:** 01382 224037
Mitchells	**Tel:** 01382 223484
Weather Info	M* T9 GWC

Visual Reference Points (VRPs)

Broughty Castle
N5627.75 W00252.18

ELEVATION	LOCATION	EGTU				DUNKESWELL
850ft 28mb	14nm NE of Exeter N5051 60.W00314.08	BHD 112.05	026	29.8	– • • • / • • • • / – • •	
		SAM 113.35	272	71.6	• • • / • – / – –	
PPR						

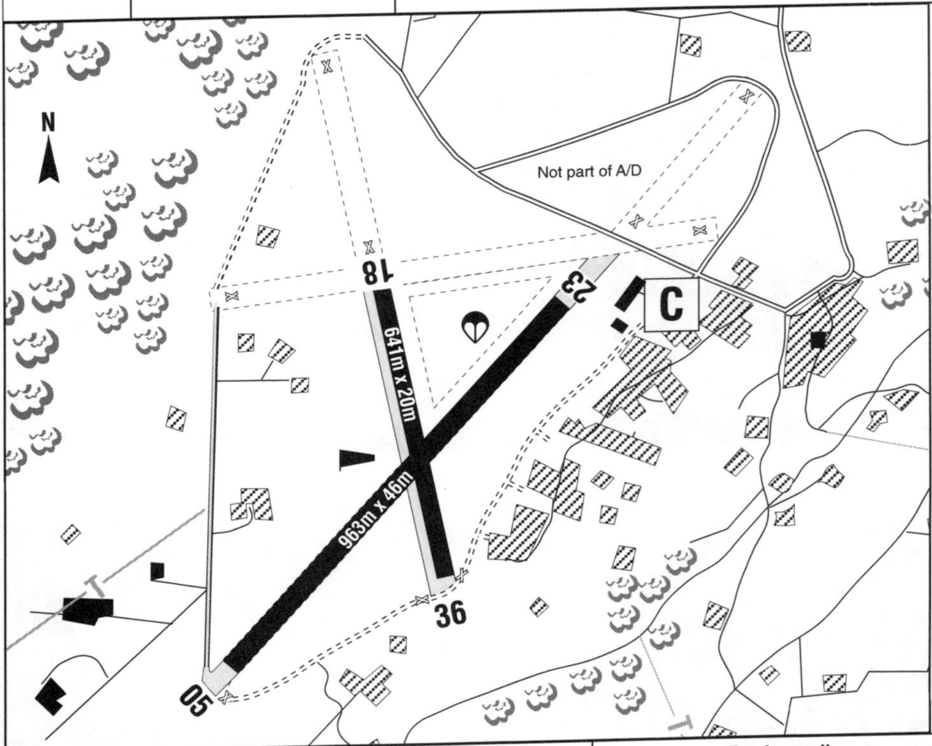

Not part of A/D

N

18

23

C

641m x 20m

963m x 46m

36

05

Effective date: 30/11/99

RWY	SURFACE	TORA	LDA	LIGHTING
05	Asphalt	963	963	Goosenecks for
23	Asphalt	963*	963	emergency use only
18/36	Asphalt	641	641	

* starter extension of additional 150m available on request

	Dunkeswell
APP	Exeter 128.15
A/G	123.475

Remarks
U/L at night. Avoid overflying Dunkeswell below 500ft QFE.
Three masts inside AD boundary are not a hazard but pilots should be aware.

Warnings
Gliders WSW of AD. Free-fall parachuting from up to FL150 on AD. Sheep grazing adjacent to Rwy. Pilots should positively identify Rwy23 displaced Thr before committing ACFT to finals. Only use established Twys or Rwys for taxy, peri-track is unsuitable. Large paved area to NE not part of AD.

Operating Hrs
0800-1800 or SS+30 whichever is earlier (Summer)
0900-1800 or SS+30 whichever is earlier (Winter)

Circuits	05/36 RH 18/23 LH
Landing fee	Single £7.50 Twin £3.50 +VAT per half metric tonne or part thereof

Maintenance	Devon School of Flying Tel: 01404 891643 Also limited hangerage available
Fuel	AVGAS 100LL
Operator	Air Westward Ltd, Dunkeswell Nr Honiton, Devon EX14 0RA Tel: 01404 891643/891271 Fax: 01404 891024
Restaurants	Club facilities & refreshments at AD
Taxis Canns Cosy Cars Car Hire Hillside Garage	Tel: 01404 43440 Tel: 01404 42389
Weather Info	T9 BNMC

D

ELEVATION	LOCATION		
490ft 16mb	2nm ESE of Ballymena N5450.87 W00612.38	**DUNNYVADDEN**	
PPR		BEL 117.20 011 11.5 − • • • / • / • − • •	

RWY	SURFACE	TORA	LDA	LIGHTING
13*/31	Grass	540x11m	U/L	Nil

*Rwy13 upslope

Dunnyvadden

APP	(Aldergrove) 120.90
A/G	122.30

Useful weather info on
Aldergrove ATIS 128.20

Remarks

PPR strictly by telephone. Visitors welcome at own risk. Telephone briefing for first time visitors is mandatory.Pilots/ACFT must be experienced/suitable for operating from a short strip. Microlight activity at AD. Quarry 1 nm SE of AD on final for Rwy31 is a good locator Also wind farm 4.5nm SE on Elliot's Hill (1158ft amsl).This AD is not notified as a designated point of entry/exit for N I. under the Prevention of Terrorism Act but this can be arranged by RUC Tel: 02890 650222.

Warnings

Parts of AD are prone to waterlogging after heavy rain - enquire when telephoning for PPR. Crosswind and terrain/tree induced turbulence/rotor are often a problem. Beware of trees on both APP Rwy31 has a 4ft fence at threshold. Rwy13 has telephone wires across approach. Farm road crosses strip at midpoint - beware loose stones. Keep a good lookout for slow-moving farm vehicles especially where they might be partially obscured by the trees.

Landing fee	Nil
Maintenance **Fuel**	Nil possible hangarage by prior arr MOGAS limited supplies by prior arr
Operator	Christine Goodwin, Dunnyvadden Aerodrome, Craigadoo Rd, Ballymena, Co. Antrim, BT42 4RS

Tel/Fax: 02825 650002
E-mail: chrisgoodwin@dunnyvadden.freeserve.co.uk

Restaurants

Taxis **CarHire**	Operator can provide info Nil
Weather Info	AirN BEL

Operating Hrs   SR-SS

Circuits

Standard overhead join then LH at 1000ft QFE

ELEVATION	LOCATION				
172ft 5mb	8nm S of Guildford N5107.03.W00032.13	**MID 114.00**	045	5.1	– – / •• / – •
	Diversion AD	**MAY 117.90**	289	25	– – / • – / – • – –
PPR		**OCK 115.3**	202	12	– – – / – • – • / – • –

Link Twy

1880m x 45m

N

25

07

C

RWY	SURFACE	TORA	LDA	LIGHTING
07	Asphalt	1880	1718	Ap Thr Rwy PAPI 3° LHS
25	Asphalt	1735	1735*	Ap Thr Rwy PAPI 3° LHS

* Night only 1695m by day

	Dunsfold
APP	**135.175**
LARS	**135.175**
RAD	**135.175 125.55**
VDF	**135.175 124.325**
TWR	**124.325**

Remarks
Available only to civil ACFT on British Aerospace business.

Warnings
Flight testing high performance jet ACFT takes place at AD. LARS available freq.135.175. Single engine jet ACFT unable to engage the arrester barrier will not be permitted to take-off from Rwy07. At both ends Rwy07/25 width is twice that of the associated edge lights due extra pavement one side. Rwy centreline lighting not installed pilots must ensure they are correctly lined up, especially at night, when Rwy is contaminated, or low visibility. Avoid overflying villages Cranleigh & Dunsfold in VMC. No flying below 1000ft QFE within 5nm a/d except take-off/landing.

Operating Hrs
Mon-Fri 0700-1730 Sat-Sun by arrangement (Summer)
Mon-Fri 0800-1830 Sat-Sun by arrangement (Winter)
Mon-Fri out of Hrs by arrangement

Circuits	07 RH 25 LH 1000ft QFE unless ATC instuct otherwise
Landing fee	£12 per metric tonne +VAT

Maintenance	Nil
Fuel	AVGAS 100LL AVTUR Jet A1
Operator	British Aerospace (Military ACFT & Aerostructures) Dunsfold Aerodrome, Godalming Surrey GU8 4BS **Tel:** 01483 272121 **Tel:** 01483 265279 (ATC) **Fax:** 01483 200341
Restaurant	
Taxis/Car Hire	
Weather Info	M* AirSE BNMC

D

ELEVATION	LOCATION	**EGSU**			**DUXFORD**

ELEVATION	LOCATION				
125ft	8nm S of Cambridge	CLN 114.55	296	40.0	− • − • / • − • • / − •
4mb	N5205.45.E00007.92	CFD 116.50	092	27.2	− • − • / • • • − • / − • •
PPR	**Diversion AD**	BKY 116.25	029	6.7	− • • • / − • − / − • − −

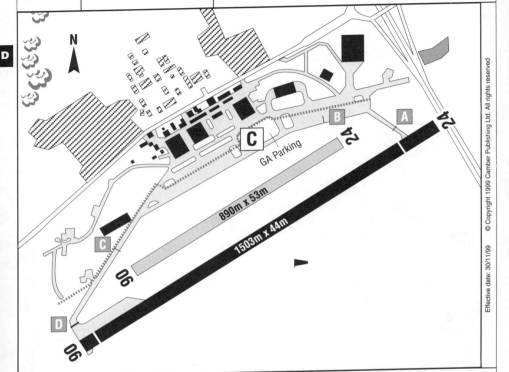

RWY	SURFACE	TORA	LDA	LIGHTING
06	Asphalt	1348	1348	Nil
24	Asphalt	1453	1353	Nil
06/24	Grass	890	890	Nil

	Duxford
AFIS	122.075

Remarks

PPR by telephone only during the winter period. Powered ACFT circuits (from grass or paved Rwys) are normally to the S. Pilots should avoid over-flying the nearby villages of Duxford, Fowlmere or adjacent bird sanctuary, Thriplow, Whittlesford and the chemical works at Whittlesford. Certain customs facilities available. Visiting ACFT must carry proof of £500, 000 minimum insurance. Inbounds should avoid penetrating Stanstead CTZ & Wethersfield gliding site

Warnings

Thr to Rwy24 (Asphalt) displaced 150m. Combined AD Traffic Zone with Fowlmere. Circuit patterns are mutually agreed between the two ADs so it is essential that pilots obtain a briefing from Duxford before departure whether inbound or outbound. When Fowlmere is open, ACFT departing Duxford to the W should contact Fowlmere as soon as possible after take-off. ACFT arriving from the W should make normal contact with Fowlmere before entering the ATZ. Pilots of ACFT who are required to use a licensed AD are cautioned that the taxyways are not suitable for wingspan over 23m. ACFT should use Twys with extreme caution due to the reduced obstacle clearance. Caution: High powered ACFT may be carrying out high energy manoevers at any time. **Noise:** 06 dept. continue straight ahead 2nm before turning on course. 24 arr. position for 2nm final.

Operating Hrs

0900-1700 or SS whichever earlier (Summer)
1000-1600 or SS which ever earlier (Winter)

Circuits	Variable no overhead joins
Landing fee	On application
Maintenance	Aircraft Restoration Co Tel: 01223 835313
Fuel	JET A1 AVGAS 100LL 1000-1600 (Local) & by arrangement

Operator

Imperial War Museum/Cambridgeshire County Council
Duxford Airfield, Cambridgeshire CB2 4QR
Tel: 01223 833376 (ATC)
Fax: 01223 833376 (ATC)

Restaurant	Restaurant at AD

Taxis
Sawston Taxis **Tel:** 01223 833838
Car Hire
Autorent **Tel:** 01223 835288
National **Tel:** 01223 365438

Weather Info	AirCen BNMC

ELEVATION	LOCATION	**EGHU**	**EAGLESCOTT**
655ft 22mb	6nm ESE of Torrington N5055.70.W00359.37		
PPR	**Diversion AD**		

N5055.70.W00359.37 — **Diversion AD** — BHD 112.05   336   37   — • • • / • • • • / — • •

CAA radar station

N

600m x 18m

17

26

08

35

A

B

T

C

Aircraft parking area

Emergency Rwy Unlicensed

RWY	SURFACE	TORA	LDA	LIGHTING		*Eaglescott*	
08/26	Grass	600	600	Nil	A/G	123.0	

An additional 120m at the E end and 180m at the W end of Rwy give a total overrun of 900m. Emergency crosswind strip doubling as a Twy, 35/17 is also available for light ACFT but is U/L.

Remarks
PPR by telephone. Not available at night for flights required to use a licensed AD or for public transport passenger flights required to use a licensed AD. Non-radio ACFT must contact the AD prior to visiting in order to obtain details of parachuting activity. All ACFT should avoid flying low over Burrington RAD Station (adjacent to the NE boundary) and over-flying local villages.

Warnings
Gliding by aerotow takes place at the AD using the area to the right of the Rwy in use. Parachuting up to FL150 takes place at the AD. Microlight flying takes place at the AD.

Operator   Devon Airsports Ltd, Eaglescott Airfield
Burrington, Umberleigh
N Devon EX37 9LQ
Tel: 01769 520404

Restaurants
Golf Club restaurant village cafe/restaurant in Atherington (Sunday lunches recommended)

Taxis
Barum Cabs   **Tel:** 01271 24444
Car Hire   **Tel:** 01271 42746

Weather Info   AirSW BNMC

Operating Hrs	1100-1900 (Summer) 1100-SS (Winter) and by arrangement
Circuit	LH for conventional fixed-wing ACFT RH for gliders and microlights 800ft QFE
Landing fees	Single £3 (£5 from inside Devon), Twin £7.50, Heli £5.00
Maintenance	Nil
Fuel	AVGAS 100LL MOGAS

ELEVATION	LOCATION	**EGSR**				**EARLS COLNE**
225ft 8mb	3nm SE of Halstead N5154.83.E00040.97	CLN 114.55	288	17.5	– • – • / • – • • / – •	
PPR		LAM 115.60	055	25.6	• – • • / • – / – –	

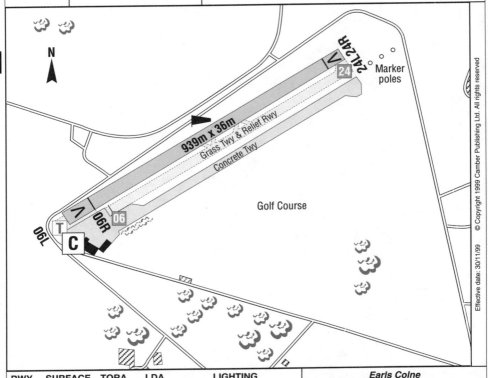

939m x 36m
Grass Twy & Relief Rwy
Concrete Twy

Marker poles

Golf Course

RWY	SURFACE	TORA	LDA	LIGHTING		*Earls Colne*
06L	Grass	866	767	Nil	A/G	122.425
24R	Grass	840	767	Nil		

A licensed relief Rwy may be in operation S of and parallel to 06L/24R. When in use it will be marked by black and white Thr markers, the inoperable Rwy will be marked with white crosses.

Remarks
Not available at night for flights required to use a licensed AD. Noise abatement: 24R departures, climb ahead to 900' QNH before turning. 06 departures, keep left of marker poles & climb to 700ft QNH before turning. Certain customs facilities available.

Warnings
Avoid over-flying Earls Colne village. At entry to parking area distance between Twy centre-line and parked ACFT is only 8m. Visiting pilots should obtain a briefing on Twy procedures and taxi with extreme caution. Use only grass surfaces. Power lines cross Rwy06L/R APP. Pilots should not land before the displaced Thr.

Operator	Bulldog Aviation Ltd The Barn, Over Hall Hill, Earls Engaine Colchester, Essex CO6 2NS **Tel:** 01787 223943 **Fax:** 01787 224246 **Tel:** 01787 223676 (Essex Flying School)

Restaurant
Leisure complex on AD swimming pool gymnasium 18 hole golf course & driving range **Tel:** 01787 224466
Drapers Hotel   **Tel:** 01787 223666

Taxis/Car Hire
Yellowline   **Tel:** 01376 322771

Weather Info   AirCen BNMC

Operating Hrs	0900-1800 (Summer) 0900-SS (Winter)
Circuits	24 LH 06 RH
Landing fees	Single £8.00 Twin/Heli £11.00
Maintenance Fuel	Euroair Tech Servs. **Tel:** 01787 224988 AVGAS 100LL

ELEVATION	LOCATION				
115ft 4mb	2.5 nmS of North Berwick N5600.07.W00243.99	SAB 112.50	294	18	••• / • — / — •••
PPR		TLA 113.80	041	36.5	— / • — •• / • —

E

Aerodrome chart showing runways 11/29 (450m x 12m), 08/26 (250m x 8m), West Fortune, Dingleton, Merryhatton, East Fortune, Public Road, Model aircraft flying, Cemy, Gilmerton House, Museum of Flight.

RWY	SURFACE	TORA	LDA	LIGHTING
11/29	Grass/Conc	450x12	U/L	Nil
08/26	Grass/Conc	250x8	U/L	Nil

	E Fortune Micro
A/G	129.825

Remarks
PPR by telephone. Primarily a microlight AD but light ACFT welcome. The useable portion of this wartime AD is clearly marked out in the NW corner. Do not use other parts of the AD which are the property of other landowners. The AD is the home of the Museum of Flight which is a short walk down the perimeter track.

Warnings
Caution; a public road crosses the wartime Rwy close to 29 Thr. There is considerable military low flying in the vicinity.
Noise: Please follow circuit pattern marked on AD chart. Do NOT overfly Sunday market on E portion of AD. during Sunday Market PPR may be refused to visitors. Model ACFT flying takes place on E portion of AD.

Maintenance	Nil
Fuel	MOGAS available in emergency
Operator	Mr G Douglas East of Scotland Microlights, East Fortune **Tel:** 01620 880332 (AD) **Tel:** 01875 820102 (Mr Douglas)
Restaurants	Light snacks available most days Restaurant in museum complex
Taxis/Car Hire	Nil
Weather Info	AirSC GWC

Operating Hrs	SR-SS
Circuits	Join overhead at 1000ft QFE circuit S at 500ft QFE Please follow tight circuit procedure on diagram
Landing fee	Nil donations gratefully received

ELEVATION	LOCATION	**EGNX**		**EAST MIDLANDS**

ELEVATION	LOCATION			
310ft 10mb	7nm SE of Derby N5249.86.W00119.60 **Diversion AD**	TNT 115.70 143 18.3 GAM 112.80 212 30.3		– / – • / – – – • / • – / – –
PPR				

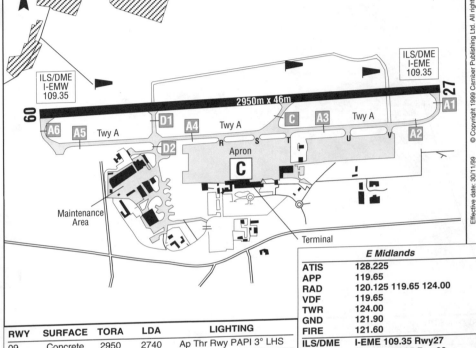

	E Midlands	
ATIS	128.225	
APP	119.65	
RAD	120.125 119.65 124.00	
VDF	119.65	
TWR	124.00	
GND	121.90	
FIRE	121.60	
ILS/DME	I-EME 109.35 Rwy27	
ILS/DME	I-EMW 109.35 Rwy09	
NDB	EME353.5*	
NDB	EMW 393.0**	
*EME: 273/4.3 to Thr27		
**EMW: 093/3.91 to Thr09		

RWY	SURFACE	TORA	LDA	LIGHTING
09	Concrete	2950	2740	Ap Thr Rwy PAPI 3° LHS
27	Concrete	2950	2790	Ap Thr Rwy PAPI 3° LHS

Remarks

PPR to non-radio ACFT. Use of a handling agent is mandatory when using the main apron. Handling services available from: British Midland Tel 01332-852204 Fax 01332-811416, Donington Aviation Tel 01332-811004 Fax 01332-812726, Servisair Tel 01332-812278 Fax 01332-811904. Corporate Handling Tel: 01332 811179 Fax: 01332 811139 .Overnight parking on the main apron is limited and requirements should be notified early to handling agents. Pilots must ensure that, as far as practicable, ACFT are operated in a manner calculated to cause the least disturbance in areas surrounding the airport. Training flights are subject to approval and acceptance by ATC, but permission will not be given for any such flights by any type of ACFT between 2300 and 0700 (Local). Operators wishing to take advantage of rebated fees and charges for training must make an application for training rebates in advance to the Airport Authority.

Warnings

Interference to magnetic compasses may be experienced by ACFT taxiing or holding in the areas of the QDM figure at the Thr of Rwy27 and over the final 100m of Twy A S of the Thr of Rwy27. Carry out any pre take-off check of Heading Indicator against magnetic compass alternative. Avoid making final turn on APP to Rwy27 over Kegworth village. Between April and September when grass cutting is taking place in the areas immediately adjacent to the Rwy, circuit flying by light ACFT on Tuesdays between 0830 and 1800 (Local) will not be permitted. In Spring and Autumn bird concentrations may be present on all areas under agricultural use on the APP to Rwy09/27. In conditions of moderate to heavy rain, and particularly associated with a southerly wind, pilots are advised that temporary standing water may occur on the southside of Rwy09/27. A pyrotechnic factory is situated approximately 3nm N of the AD. Rockets, carrying flares of up to 150,000 candela deployed on parachutes, may be tested up to a height on 1000 ft agl by day and night. A flare stack is situated at Chellaston. The stack is 36 ft agl and the flare is 20 ft in length. ACFT must not descend below ILS GP on final APP. Turbulence may be expected on Rwy09 APP in strong N or NE winds. This maybe accompanied by associated downdraughts.

Operating Hrs	H24
Circuits	Variable at the discretion of ATC

Landing fee
On application Reduced rates for light ACFT handled by Corporate Handling **Tel:** 01332 811179

Maintenance
Hunting **Tel:** 01332 810910
Fuel Thru mandatory handling agent
AVGAS 100LL 0800-1800 (Local)daily at other times
Donnington Aviation **Tel:** 01332 811004
AVTUR JET A1 H24

Operator East Midlands Airport Ltd
Castle Donington, Derby DE74 2SA
Tel: 01332 852852
Fax: 01332 852823 (ATC)
Tel: 01332 850393 (General)
Tel: 0891 517567 (Airport Met Information)
E-mail:atsm@Emidsairport.demon.co.uk

Restaurants Refreshments available at Airport
Restaurant at Donington Thistle Hotel

Taxis	Available at terminal
Airport	**Tel:** 01332 814225
Donnington	**Tel:** 01332 810146
Car Hire	
Avis	**Tel:** 01332 811403
National	**Tel:** 01332 382251
Hertz	**Tel:** 01332 811726

Weather Info MT9 T18 Fax247 A VM VN BNMC

Helicopter Arrival VFR
Helicopters must APP from N or S, remaining clear of the APP and climb-out of Rwys 09/27, not below 500ft QFE or at height/altitude assigned by ATC. Do not ovefly Castle Donington to N or Diseworth to S.
Arrivals from N must obtain specific clearance to cross Rwy09/27 prior to crossing AD boundary, and on crossing boundary are to descend towards the allocated apron stand without overflying equipment or occupied stands
Arrivals from S must join close base leg, (RB09, LB27) or as directed by ATC. Descend along Rwy or safe path parallel S of Rwy or as directed by ATC. GND or air taxi to parking areas as instructed, following Twys.
Helicopter Departure VFR
Depart as cleared by ATC. Depts must obtain specific clearance to cross Rwy09/27, which must be made at right angle to Rwy. departures to S must ground or air taxi to Rwy, then on ATC clearance, climb above Rwy to 500ft initially, turning S only when clear of all airport buildings. On reaching airport boundary comply with ATC instructions regarding heading/route & height/altitude.

CTA/CTR Class D Airspace
Normal CTA/CTR Class D Airpsace rules apply.

Entry/Exit lanes are established to permit ACFT to operate to and from E Midlands Airport in IMC, but not under IFR.
1. Long Eaton
2. Shepshed Lane
(Both are 3nm wide centred on the M1 motorway)
Use of the lanes is subject to SVFR clearance. ACFT must remain clear of cloud and in sight of the surface not above 2000ft (QNH).

E

Visual Reference Points (VRPs)

VRP	VOR/VOR	VOR/NDB	VOR/DME
Bottesford** N5257.88 W00046.90	TNT R103°/HON R045°	TNT R103°/EME 066°M	TNT 103°/33nm/ GAM 167°/20nm
Church Broughton* N5253.17 W00141.90	TNT R190°/HON R362°	TNT R190°/EME 285°M °	TNT 190°/10nm
Markfield (M1 J22) * N5241.73 W00117.55	TNT R152°/HON R038°	DTY R352°/EME 208°M	HON 038°/24nm/ DTY 352°/32nm
Measham (M42 J11)* N5241.33 W00132.88	TNT R173°/HON R017°	HON R016°/EME 240°M	HON 017°/20nm/ DTY 337°/34nm
Melton Mowbray*** N5244.37 W00053.57	TNT R128°/HON R055°	HON R055°/ DTY R 018°	HON 055°/36nm/ DTY 018°/35nm
Trowell (M1 Services) N5257.70 W00116.50	TNT R115°/HON R026°	TNT R116°/EME 345°	TNT 116°/16nm/GAM 215°/22nm

Notes: * Below 2500ft QNH.
** Pilots routing via Bottesford should avoid over-flying the area around Langar AD, which is designated an area of intense parachuting activity.
*** If routing via Melton Mowbray be advised of the TV mast at Waltham on the Wold, 1466ft amsl.

ELEVATION	LOCATION	EGED		EDAY

20ft
1mb

PPR

On Isle of Eday
N5911.48.W00246.43

WIK 113.60   021   45.1   • – – / • • / – • –

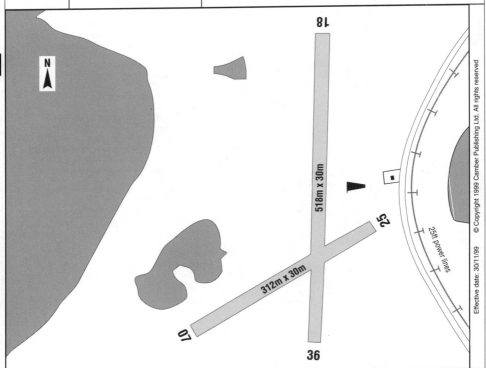

RWY	SURFACE	TORA	LDA	LIGHTING
18/36	Grass	518	518	APAPI 4.5 on request
07/25	Grass	312	312	Nil

Non-radio

APP   Kirkwall 118.30

Remarks
Licensed for day use. Windsock displayed. Visual aids to location: Flashing beacon on terminal building available on request.

Warnings
Rwy07/25 may become soft and waterlogged after periods of continuous rainfall, particularly at W end.

Operator   Orkney Islands Council Council Offices
Kirkwall, Orkney, Scotland
Tel: 01856 873535
Fax: 01856 876094

Restaurants
Blett Boathouse   **Tel:** 01857 622248

Taxis
Mr A Stewart   **Tel:** 01857 622206
Car Hire

Weather Info   AirSc GWC

Operating Hrs	By arrangement
Circuits	
Landing fee	Nil
If fire cover provided then £16.09 +VAT
Maintenance	Nil
Fuel	Nil

© Copyright 1999 Camber Publishing Ltd. All rights reserved
Effective date: 30/11/99

E

Effective date: 30/11/99

E

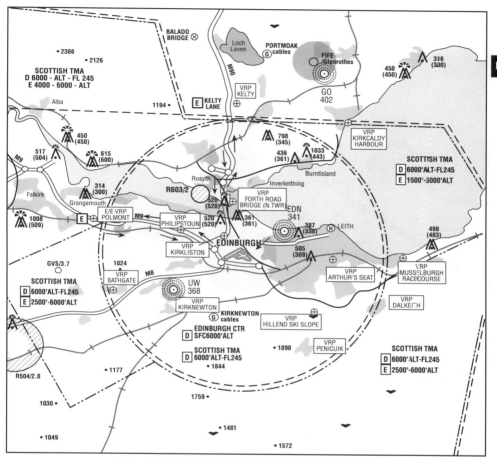

ELEVATION	LOCATION	EGPH	EDINBURGH
135ft 5mb **PPR**	5nm W of Edinburgh N5557.15.W00321.77	TLA 113.80 006 27.0 GOW 115.40 090 36.7	– / • – • • / • – – – • / – – – / • – –

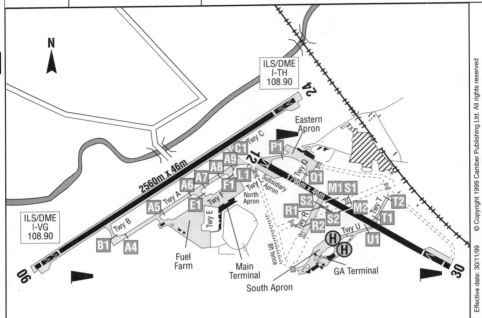

RWY	SURFACE	TORA	LDA	LIGHTING
06/24*	Asphalt	2560	2347	Ap Thr Rwy PAPI 3° LHS
12**	Asphalt	1796	1796	Ap Thr Rwy PAPI 3° LHS
30**	Asphalt	1796	1734	Ap Thr Rwy PAPI 3.5° LHS

*06/24 PPR 0800-1000 for training flights
**12/30 avail Mon 0630-2100 closed at all other times due parked ACFT

Edinburgh	
ATIS	132.075
APP	121.20 130.40*
RAD	128.975 121.20
VDF	121.20 118.70
TWR	118.70 121.20 121.50
GND	121.75

*130.40 for gliders transiting the CTR.

ILS/DME	I-VG 108.90 Rwy06
ILS/DME	I-TH 108.90 Rwy24
NDB	EDN 341**
NDB	UW 368***

**EDN: 245/2.8 to Thr24
***UW: 065/4.5 to Thr06

Remarks

PPR to non-radio ACFT. All GA must make prior arrangements with a handling agent for GND handling of all flights. Due to ltd parking space ALL ACFT are PPR with their handling agent. Approved handling agents: Execair Tel: 0131 344 3146 or Serviceair Tel: 0131 333 3111. GA requiring Customs/Immigration require prior permission from AD operations (Tel: 0131 344 3139) to avoid congestion on apron. All other GA ACFT may be required to go directly to GA terminal for off-loading/loading of passengers. Permission MAY be given for parking on the main apron for off-loading passengers interlining etc. BUT ACFT must move to GA apron ASAP. Transport to & from the main terminal is via your handing agent or alternatively through Ext.3159/3213. Long stay ACFT may be required to use the subsidiary apron.

Warnings

There is a large bird population around the airport and hence increased bird activity in the lower airspace, together with visible evidence of deterrent activity in the form of shell crackers being fired. All ACFT must be operated in a manner calculated to cause the least disturbance practicable in areas surrounding the airport. For visual approaches to Rwy06/24: Propeller driven ACFT whose MTWA does not exceed 5700kg will not join final below 1000ft QFE.Twy P closed Tue-Fri: 0500-0730, 1730-2000. Flying club ACFT will be escorted by ops if operating during these times.

Operating Hrs	H24
Circuits	
Landing fee	BAA Rates
Maintenance	ACFT Engineers Ltd **Tel:** 0131 333 4150
Fuel	AVGAS 100LL AVTUR JET A1

AVGAS Edinburgh Refuelers **Tel:** 0131 339 4990
0600-2230(Local) and by arrangement (Execair) H24
(Pentland Aviation)

Operator	Edinburgh Airport Ltd

Edinburgh Airport, Lothian EH12 9DN
Tel: 0131 344 3139 (Ops)
Tel: 0131 317 7638 (ATC)
Fax 0131 317 7638 (ATC)
Fax: 0131 333 5055 (EAL)

Restaurant
Restaurants/buffet/bars available at Terminal

Taxis	Available at Terminal
Car Hire	
Avis	**Tel:** 0131 333 1866
Europcar	**Tel:** 0131 333 2588
Hertz	**Tel:** 0131 333 1019
Alamo	**Tel:** 0131 333 5100

Weather Info M T9 T18 Fax 276 A VSc GWC

CTR – Class D Airspace
Normal CTA/CTR Class D Airspace rules apply
1. SVFR flight clearance may be given in the Edinburgh CTR subject to traffic limitations; normally when the MET reports indicate IMC within the zone or when the pilot is unable to maintain VMC.
2. Due to the nature of the terrain in the vicinity, a PAD service will not normally be provided.
3. Pilots are reminded that SVFR clearances only apply to flight within the CTR.
4. Entry/Exit lanes are established to permit ACFT to operate to and from Edinburgh in IMC but not under IFR. These are:
(a) Polmont lane.
(b) Kelty lane.
Both these lanes are 3nm wide and use is subject to ATC clearance, irrespective of weather conditions. ACFT must remain clear of cloud, in sight of the surface and not above 2000ft QNH. Minimum visibility is 3km. ACFT using the lanes shall keep the centre-line on the left.
Pilots are responsible for maintaining adequate clearance from the ground and other obstacles.
SVFR clearances may not be confined to the Entry/Exit lanes described above.
5. During the day, non-radio ACFT may fly in the CTR provided they have previously obtained permission and maintain VFR.

E

Visual Reference Points (VRPs)

VRP	VOR/VOR	VOR/NDB	VOR.DME
Arthur's Seat N5556.63 W00309.70	GOW R090°/TLA R019°	TLA R019°/EDN 123°M	SAB 281°/32nm
Bathgate N5554.17 W00338.42	TLA R344°/GOW R092°	TLA R344/EDN 255°M	GOW 092°/27nm
Cobbinshaw Reservoir N5548.47 W00334.00	TLA R345°/GOW R103°	TLA 345°/EDN 229°M	TLA 345°/19nm
Dalkeith N5553.60 W00304.10	TLA R028°/SAB R274°	TLA R028°/EDN 131°M	TLA 028°/26nm
Forth Road Bridge, (N Twr) N5600.37 W00324.23	GOW R083°/TLA R003°	PTH R189°/EDN299°M	SAB 285°/41nm
Hillend Ski Slope N5553.30 W00312.50	TLA R018°/SAB R274°	SAB R274°/EDN 160°M	TLA 018°/24nm
Kelty N5608.08 W00323.25	TLA R004°/SAB R295°	SAB R295°/EDN 346°M	GOW 072°/39nm
Kirkcaldy Harbour N5606.83 W00309.00	TLA R016°/SAB R297°	SAB R297°/EDN 035°M	GOW 077°/46nm
Kirkliston N5557.33 W00324.18	TLA R002°/GOW R087°	GOW R087°/EDN 257°M	GOW 087°/35nm
Kirknewton N5553.25 W00325.08	GOW R094°/TLA R360°	GOW R094°/EDN 225°M	GOW 094°/35nm
Musselburgh N5556.83 W00302.42	TLA R027°/SAB R281°	TLA R027°/EDN 109°M	TLA 027°/29nm
Penicuik N5549.92 W00313.42	GOW R099°/TLA R018°	GOW R099°/EDN 173°M	GOW 099°/41nm
Philipstoun (M9 J2) N5558.90 W00330.72	GOW R084°/TLA R355°	GOW R084°/UW 227°M	GOW 084°/32nm
Polmont N5559.33 W00341.00	TLA R345°/SAB R282°	TLA R345°/EDN 279°M	GOW 080°/27nm
W Linton N5545.17 W00321.45	TLA R005°/SAB R262°	SAB R262°/EDN 196°M	TLA 005°/15nm

ELEVATION	LOCATION			
226t 7mb	3nm S of RAF Wattisham N5204.52 E00058.68			
PPR		CLN 114.55	338	15	–·–·/·–··/–·
		LAM 115.60	053	40.5	·–··/·–/––

E

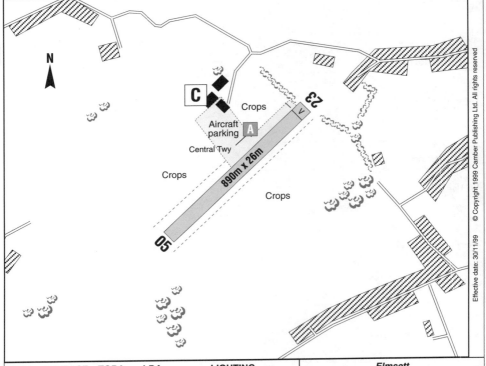

RWY	SURFACE	TORA	LDA	LIGHTING
05*	Grass	799	799	Thr Rwy LITAS
23	Grass	799	775	Thr Rwy LITAS

* 1.8% upslope

	Elmsett
APP	Wattisham 125.80
A/G	130.90

Remarks

PPR by telephone. Non-radio ACFT not accepted. Due to planning constraints visitors may be refused. AD within Wattisham MATZ, (high intensity helicopter operations). Elmsett local flying area established within 2nm radius of AD EXCLUDING portion within Wattisham ATZ.
Arrival procedures – Contact Wattisham APP 125.80 at least 15nm from Wattisham. If no radio contact: **1** remain VFR not above 800ft agl within Wattisham MATZ/Elmsett LFA. **2** Route not above 800ft agl via RAYDON disused AD, (N5200.01 E00100.00) or Copdock jct A12/A14.
Departure procedures – 1 Contact Wattisham APP 125.80 ASAP after departure. Do NOT climb above 800ft agl without clearance from Wattisham. **2** If no contact with Wattisham, then route not above 800ft agl via RAYDON disused AD.

Warnings

Rwy lighting stands proud of surface exercise caution vacating Rwy. Crops up to edge of Rwy S side. Mill approx 100ft high close to left of short final Rwy23. DO NOT overfly local villages, particularly Aldham, Elmsett & Hadleigh town. Public right of way crosses APP Rwy23 70m from Thr. Taxying beyond hold A not permitted when ACFT are taking-off or landing.

Operating Hrs	0800-1600 (Summer) 0900-1700 (Winter)
Circuits	05 RH 23 LH 800ft QFE
Landing fee	On application
Maintenance Fuel	Poplar Aviation AVGAS 100LL
Operator	Mr TD Gray, Poplar Aviation Ltd Poplar Hall Farm, Elmsett Ipswich, Suffolk IP7 6LN **Tel:** 01473 824116 **Fax:** 01473 822896
Taxis/Car Hire	By arrangement
Weather Info	AirS BNMC

ELEVATION	LOCATION	EGTR				ELSTREE
334ft 11mb	2.6nm E of Watford N5139.35.W00019.55		BPK 117.50	240	9.9	– • • • / • – – • / – • –
	Diversion AD		BNN 113.75	122	9.4	– • • • / – • / – •
PPR			BUR 117.10	062	15.3	– • • • / • • – / • – •

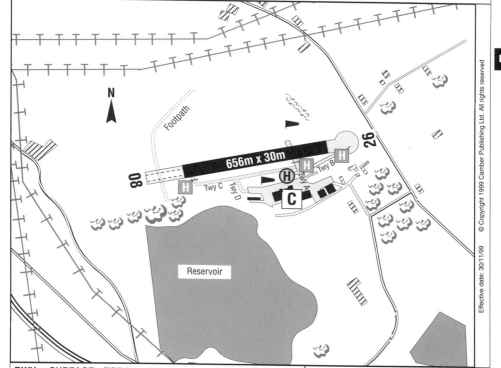

E

RWY	SURFACE	TORA	LDA	LIGHTING
08	Asphalt	656	656	Rwy
26	Asphalt	656	656	Thr Rwy LITAS 4.5° LHS

Pavement at W end provides 174x18 U/L stopway

Elstree

A/G/AFIS* 122.40

* AFIS available Fri-Sun 0800-SS

Remarks
PPR. Not available to non-radio ACFT. Licensed for night use on Rwy26 only. Terms and conditions of use are available on request from the AD operator. Cessna 336 and 337 ACFT not accepted at Elstree due to high noise level. Specific helicopter Arr/Dep Routes. The only helicopters permitted to carry out circuit training are Robinson R22s operated by Cabair Group. Helicopter circuit height is 750 ft QFE or below to the N of the AD. Visual aids to location: Ibn Green EL, Abn White flashing.

Warnings
Distance between Twy centreline & parked ACFT can be as little as 10.5m. Taxi with extreme caution.
Noise abatement procedures: Rwy26 after Take-off maintain rwy heading until power cables, then turn right approx. 20° aim midway between Bushey & N Bushey. For S, start turning left at cemetery, follow fields around Bushey. For N continue straight ahead until above 900ft QFE. before turn on track. Rwy08 after take-off maintain rwy heading for 1nm, avoid flying N of the Rwy extended centreline.

Circuits	Variable See Remarks re Helicopters
Landing fee	On application
Maintenance	Cabair **Tel:** 0208 953 3586
Fuel	JET A1 AVGAS 100LL
Operator	Montc'are Shipping Co. Ltd Elstree Aerodrome, Borehamwood Hertfordshire WD6 3AR **Tel:** 0208 953 7480 (ATC) **Fax:** 0208 207 3691
Restaurants	Licensed restaurant at the AD
Taxis Allied	**Tel:** 01923 232505
Car Hire National	Available on request **Tel:** 01923 233340
Weather Info	AirSE BNMC

Operating Hrs 0800-SS (Summer) 0900-SS (Winter) and by arrangement

ELEVATION	LOCATION	EGAB	ENNISKILLEN (St Angelo)
155ft 5mb PPR	4.5nm N of Enniskillen N5423.93.W00739.12 **Diversion AD**	BEL 117.20 261 52	− • • • / • / • − • •

Labels on map: 15 · 1326m x 30m · ENN 116.75 · Military compound · C · Fuel · EKN 357.50 · H · 33 · 112' aal · Church

RWY	SURFACE	TORA	LDA	LIGHTING
15	Asphalt	1236	1286	PAPI 3.5° LHS
33**	Asphalt	1326	979	PAPI* 4.25° LHS

*Rwy 33 PAPI only to be used once aligned with Rwy
** Includes 100m starter extension

St Angelo	
A/G	123.20
NDB	EKN 357.50 on A/D range 15nm
DME	ENN 116.75 on A/D

Remarks
Not available to ACFT unable to communicate by radio unless the pilot has obtained specific prior permission.

Warning
The Twys parallel to and on both sides of Rwy15/33 are unusable.

Operator	St Angelo Aviation Fermanagh District Council Enniskillen, Co Fermanagh, N Ireland **Tel:** 02866 328282/322771 **Fax:** 02866 322024

Restaurants
Tea and Coffee facilities courtesy of Mr Ron Patton

Taxis
Call a Cab   **Tel:** 02866 324848
Star   **Tel:** 02866 323232
Car Hire
Lochside Garages Ltd   **Tel:** 02866 324366
Country Cars   **Tel:** 02866 322727

Operating Hrs 0800-1600 (except Mondays*) (Summer)
0900-1700 (except Mondays*) (Winter) and by arrangement.
*Operations Mondays only by PPR

Weather Info	AirN BEL

Circuits	15 RH 33 LH
Landing fee	Private ACFT Single £5.00 Twin £10.00
Maintenance	Nil
Fuel	JET A1 AVGAS 100LL

E

Effective date: 30/11/99

E

RWY	SURFACE	TORA	LDA	LIGHTING			Enstone
08/26	Asphalt	1100x40	U/L	Nil	A/G		129.875
*08/26	Grass	800x50	U/L	Nil			

*Gliders only unless authorised by Enstone Eagles Gliding Club

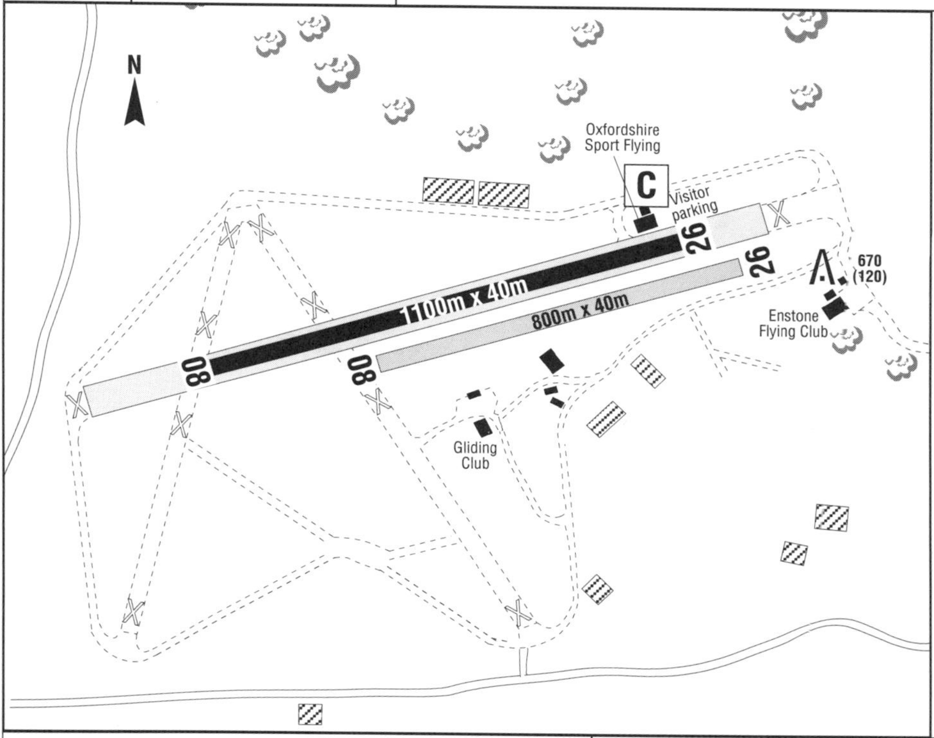

Remarks

PPR by telephone or radio. Circuits: 600ft QFE for motor gliders, 800 ft QFE for Group A ACFT. Variable direction, powered ACFT to the N, gliders to the S of the Rwy08/26. No departures before 0800 or after 1930 or SS whichever is earlier.

Warnings

Rwys15/33 and 02/20 are not usable. Gliders, Motor Gliders, Light ACFT and Microlights operate from this AD. Radio mast 120ft aal (670ft amsl) in SE corner of the AD. Avoid over-flying the noise sensitive villages of Great Tew, Little Tew, Sandford St Martin, Enstone and Church Enstone and Heythrop College.

Operator	Oxfordshire Sport Flying Club Ltd Enstone Aerodrome, Church Enstone Oxon OX7 4NP **Tel:** 01608 677208 **Tel:** 01608 678741 (Microlights)
Restaurants	Cafe on A/D (Mon-Fri) Little Chef on A44 & the Crown Inn Church Enstone
Taxis Aston Cars Car Hire Europcar	Tel: 01869 340460 Tel: 01295 51787
Weather Info	AirCen BNMC

Operating Hrs	0730-SS (Summer) 0830-SS (Winter*) and *1930 by arrangement
Circuits	See Remarks
Landing fees	Single £6.00 Twin £12.00 inc VAT
Maintenance Fuel	Available AVGAS 100LL/Shell Oil

ELEVATION	LOCATION
197ft 7mb	7nm N of Morpeth N5516.84.W00142.82
PPR	

NEW 114.25	005	14.9	− • / • / • − −
TLA 113.80	110	58	− / • − • • / • −
SAB 112.50	161	41	• • • / • − / − • • •

E

N

19/14

26

08

490m x 20m

600m x 43m

32

610m x 45m
550m x 25m

A/c grass parking

A1(M)

01

C

DO NOT overfly

DO NOT overfly Eshott Hall & village

RWY	SURFACE	TORA	LDA	LIGHTING
01/19	Asphalt	610x45	U/L	Nil
01/19	Grass	550x25	U/L	Nil
08/26	Asphalt	490x20	U/L	Nil
14/32	Asphalt	600x43	U/L	Nil

Eshott

APP	Newcastle 124.375
A/G	122.850

Remarks
PPR important to ring for joining instructions. Avoid over-flying Felton village to N and farm buildings and houses in the immediate area.

Warnings
Asphalt E of intersection 08/26 and 14/32 is a go-kart racing track and not useable by ACFT. A fence runs along the E side of Rwys14/32 separating the AD from the go-kart track. Intense microlight activity, contact Newcastle APP for information.

Operator	Eshott Airfield Ltd Bocken Field, Felton Northumberland NE65 9QJ

Tel: 01670 825427 (Operator Mr R Rhodes)
Tel: 01670 787881 (AD)
Tel: 0797 4768148 (Mobile)

Restaurants/Accomodation
Cafe on AD at weekends
B&B   **Tel:** 01670 787056 Mr & Mrs Armstrong

Taxis/Car Hire	AD operator will advise
Weather Info	AirN MWC

Operating Hrs	0900-1900 (local)
Landing fee	Light ACFT £3.00 microlights free overnight parking £2.50
Circuits	01/08/14 RH 19/26/32 LH
Maintenance **Fuel**	Nil MOGAS by arrangement

ELEVATION	LOCATION	EGTE				EXETER

ELEVATION	LOCATION				
102ft 3mb	4nm NE of Exeter N5044.07.W00324.83	BHD 112.05	014	20.5	− • • • / • • • • / − • •
PPR		BCN 117.45	192	59.3	− • • • / − • − • / − •

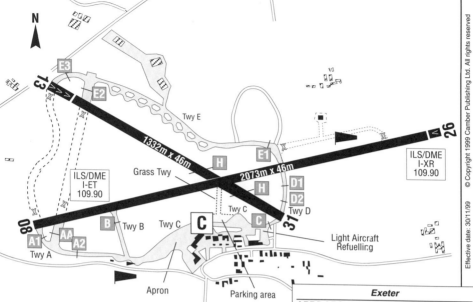

Effective date: 30/11/99

RWY	SURFACE	TORA	LDA	LIGHTING
08	Asphalt	2047	2037	Ap Thr Rwy PAPI 3° LHS
26	Asphalt	2073	2037	Ap Thr Rwy PAPI 3.5° LHS
13	Asphalt	1332	1196	Nil
31	Asphalt	1210	1210	Nil

Exeter

APP/LARS	128.15
RAD	128.15 119.05
VDF	128.15
TWR	119.80
ILS/DME	I-XR 109.90 Rwy26
ILS/DME	I-ET 109.90 Rwy08
NDB	EX 337* range 15nm *EX 261/4.12 to Thr26

Remarks

PPR non-radio ACFT not accepted. Light ACFT pilots beware of elevated Rwy lights and PAPI 08/26. Rwy13/31 not available at night. Twys are only 15m wide and thus not suitable for use by ACFT whose wheel base exceeds 18m and whose wheelspan is greater than 9m. Nern Twys limited to light single and twin engined ACFT with wingspan not exceeding 15m. Fuelling: for AVGAS 100LL ACFT with a wing span exceeding 15m must be marshalled into position for fuelling. Max. of 2 ACFT at fuelling apron at any one time. ACFT must call ATC prior to leaving fuelling apron. Hi-vis

Warnings

Public road crosses final APP for Rwy13 (137m from Thr). Rwy02/20 not in use. Pilots must ensure at all times that ACFT are operated to cause the least disturbance practicable in areas surrounding the airport, particularly the City of Exeter. ACFT approaching without assistance from RAD shall follow a descent path no lower than the normal APP path indicated by the PAPIs.

Operating Hrs (*subject to excess charge)
Mon 0001-0100 0700-2359 Tue-Fri 0001-0200 0700-2359 PPR before 0800 & after 2000
*Ops outside Mon-Fri 0800-1900 Sat-Sun 0900-1700 (Winter)
Mon 0600-2359 Tue-Fri 0001-0100 0600-2359 Sat 0001-0100 0530-2000 PPR before 0700 & after 1900
*Ops outside Mon-Sat 0700-1900 Sun 0800-1900 (Summer)

Landing fee	On application
Maintenance Iscavia **Fuel**	JEA (Engineering) Ltd Tel: 01392 362415 AVGAS 100LL AVTUR JET A1
Operator	Exeter & Devon Airport Ltd Exeter Airport, Exeter, Devon EX5 2BD

Tel: 01392 367433 **Telex:** 42648
Fax: 01392 364593 (Airport Auth) **Fax:** 01392 366170 (ATC)
Email: exeterair@eclipse.co.uk

Restaurant	Bar/Buffet facilities available
Taxis **Car Hire** Europcar Hertz Avis	Available at Terminal Tel: 01392 75398 Tel: 01392 57791 Tel: 01392 59713
Weather Info	M T9 Fax 278 BNMC

Visual Reference Points (VRPs)
Axminster	N5046.90 W00259.90
Crediton	N5047.43 W00339.08
Cullompton	N5051.47 W00323.63
Exmouth	N5037.48 W00324.13
Topsham	N5041.38 W00328.82

E

FADMOOR (Moors National Park)

ELEVATION	LOCATION
780ft 26mb	4.5nm N of Wombleton N5418.52.W00058.43
PPR	

OTR 113.90	325	48	− − −/−/• − •
POL 112.10	055	52	• − −•/− − −/• −••

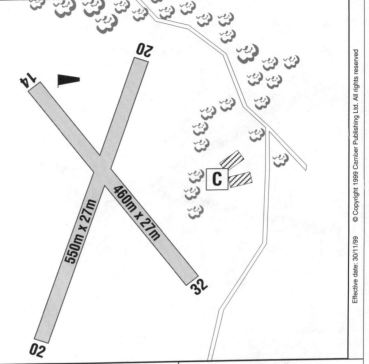

RWY	SURFACE	TORA	LDA	LIGHTING
02/20	Grass	550	550	Nil
14/32	Grass	460	460	Rwy on request

Note: Rwy02 or 32 preferred for landing.

Non-radio

Remarks
PPR visiting ACFT accepted on agricultural business.
Pilots should have experience in grass field landings. AD situated on crown of hill, on edge of escarpment, at southern edge of moorland. ground slopes away from all thresholds. Self contained holiday flat available for rent from operator on AD phone number.

Warnings
All Rwys except Rwy14 are uphill. Beware of low flying military ACFT above and below AD level.

Operator	PH Johnson, Fadmoor Kirkbymoorside, Yorks YO6 6JH **Tel:** 01751 431171 (AD) **Tel:** 07702 641732 (Mobile) **Fax:** 01751 432727
Restaurants Plough Royal Oak	 **Tel:** 01751 431515 **Tel:** 01751 431414
Taxis/Car Hire	On request
Weather Info	AirN MWC

Operating Hrs	Mon-Sat SR-SS Closed Sundays
Circuits	
Landing Fee	On application
Maintenance **Fuel**	Nil limited hangerage AVGAS 100LL

ELEVATION	LOCATION				
223ft 7mb	On Fair Isle N5932.15.W00137.68 **Diversion AD**	SUM 117.30	214	23.1	•••/••–/––
PPR		KWL 108.60	056	51.9	–•–/•––/•–••

RWY	SURFACE	TORA	LDA	LIGHTING
06/24	Gravel	486	486	Nil

	Non Radio
APP	Sumburgh 123.15
A/G	118.025 (PPR SR-SS)

Remarks

Ground falls away very steeply approx 30m beyond each Rwy end. Care should be taken to anticipate sudden wind changes which might result in a touchdown short of the thresholds. The Rwy surface is prone to moss growth almost exclusively on the E end and may be slippery in patches, particularly when wet. Accommodation available at the Fair Isle Observatory Lodge, E of AD. A/G 118.025 is SR-SS only subject to PPR and as required for emergency use.

Warnings

Turbulence can be expected with a westerly wind. Avoid low flying over islands or cliffs. Rwy is banked above surrounding land. Weather conditions can change rapidly. Pilots can arrive, having had a favourable met. report, to find the Isle shrouded in fog/low cloud. Bird hazard, May-Aug particularly on 06 APP.

Maintenance	Nil
Fuel	Nil
Operator	The National Trust for Scotland Fair Isle, Shetland ZE2 9TU **Tel:** 01595 760224 (Mr D Wheeler) **Fax:** 01595 760252
Restaurants	Food and accomodation available at the Fair Isle Observatory Lodge **Tel:** 01595 760258
Taxis/Car Hire J Stout	**Tel:** 01595 760222
Weather Info	AirSc GWC

Operating Hrs	SR-SS
Circuits	06 RH 24 LH
Landing fee	Single £10 Twin £15 inc VAT

ELEVATION	LOCATION				
80ft 3mb	2nm N of Woking N5120.88.W00033.53 **Diversion AD**	OCK 115.30	317	5.0	– – –/– • – •/– • –
PPR		LON 113.60	207	9.0	• – • •/– – –/– •

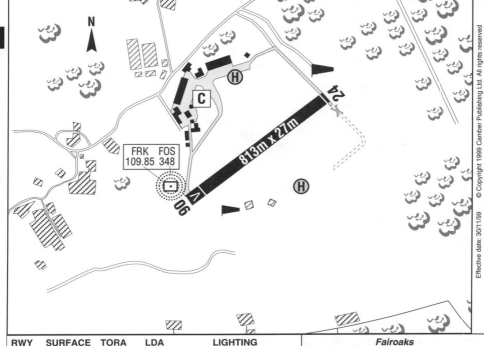

© Copyright 1999 Camber Publishing Ltd. All rights reserved

Effective date: 30/11/99

RWY	SURFACE	TORA	LDA	LIGHTING
06	Asphalt	800	747	Thr Rwy APAPI 3.5°
24	Asphalt	813	800	Thr Rwy APAPI 3.5°

	Fairoaks
AFIS/A/G	123.425
NDB DME	FOS 348* FRK 109.85** *on A/D range 8nm **on A/D

Remarks
PPR non-radio ACFT. Microlights not accepted. Not available on PH's for flights which require a licensed AD except by prior arrangement. Airside passengers are pilots responsibility. Visual aid to location: Abn flashing white. New visitors should obtain a telephone briefing.

Warnings
The AD is located just inside the southern boundary of the London Control Zone - special procedures apply. The grass areas are subject to waterlogging. Due to a hump on the Rwy Rwy24 red end lights are visible only for the last 150m of LDA. The last 3 Rwy edge lights are cautionary yellow. Exercise caution when taxiing through the apron/parking areas due to reduced wingtip clearances. Pilots of ACFT whose wingspan exceeds 15m should satisfy themselves that they have adequate clearance. The Twy to the SE of Rwy24 Thr is not available to ACFT required to use a licensed AD. Other ACFT should only use this Twy with the permission of AD management. A public footpath crosses the AD close to the Thr of Rwy24. Helicopter training takes place at this AD. The AD is frequently used outside published Hrs, pilots in the vicinity should call Fairoaks to determine if it is active. **Noise:** Inbound, do not overfly Knaphill below 1500ft QNH & avoid properties to NE of AD below 1000ft QFE.

Operating Hrs
Mon-Sat 0700-1700 Sun & PH 0900-1700 (Summer)
Mon-Sat 0800-1800 Sun & PH 1000-1800 (Winter)
(Local) Daily by arrangement 0700-2200

Circuits	Variable

Landing fee	On application

Maintenance
Mann Aviation	**Tel:** 01276 857441
Fuel	AVGAS 100LL AVTUR JET A1
	All aviation oils

Operator	Fairoaks Airports Ltd
	Fairoaks Airport, Chobham
	Woking, Surrey GU24 8HX
	Tel: 01276 857700 (Admin)
	Tel: 01276 857300 (ATC)
	Fax: 01276 856898
	Telex: 859033 FKSATC

Restaurants   Five Oaks Coffee Shop. The control TWR
can help with food and accomodation requirements

Taxis
Chobham Cars	**Tel:** 01276 855151
Chris Edwards	**Tel:** 07973 307255
Joan Anderson	**Tel:** 01932 344282
Car Hire	
Moores Car Rental	**Tel:** 01276 857557

Weather Info	M* AirSE BNMC

Fairoaks ATZ and Local Flying Area

Within the Local Flying Area (2nm radius centred on the AD) flights may take place without compliance with IFR requirements subject to the following conditions.
1. ACFT to remain below cloud and in sight of the GND.
2. Maximum altitudes 800ft (QNH) when London Heathrow Rwy23 is in use. Otherwise maximum altitude is 1500ft (QNH).
3. Minimum visibility is 3km.
ACFT must not enter the Fairoaks ATZ without permission, even if operating on an SVFR clearance in the London CTR.
4. Inbound traffic approaching from the S must remain W of the M25 whilst within the Fairoaks Local Flying Area.
5. Pilots of ACFT flying in the Local Flying Area are responsible for providing their own separation form other ACFT operating in the same airspace.

F

ELEVATION	LOCATION	EGLF	FARNBOROUGH (Civil)

ELEVATION	LOCATION				
237ft 8mb	1nm NNW of Aldershot N5116.55.W00046.58	OCK 115.30	268	12.3	– – – / – • – • / – • –
PPR		MID 114.00	343	14.6	– – / • • / – • •
		CPT 114.35	132	20.9	– • – • / • – – • / –

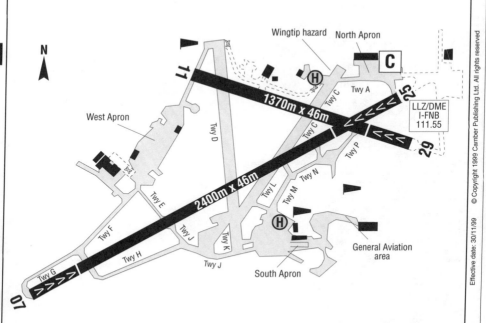

Wingtip hazard   North Apron

C

Twy A

Twy C

H

LLZ/DME
I-FNB
111.55

1370m x 46m

West Apron

Twy D

Twy C

Twy C

Twy P

25

29

Twy L   Twy N

Twy M

2400m x 46m

Twy E

H

Twy F

Twy J

Twy K

General Aviation
area

Twy G

Twy H

Twy J

07

South Apron

RWY	SURFACE	TORA	LDA	LIGHTING
07*	Con/Asph	2400	2080	Ap Thr Rwy PAPI 3.5°
25*	Con/Asph	2400	2074	Ap Thr Rwy PAPI 3.5°
11	Asphalt	1370	1370	Thr Rwy PAPI 3.5°
29	Asphalt	1370	1110	Thr Rwy PAPI 3.5°

*Rwy07/25 friction surface no tight turns on asphalt section

	Farnborough
LARS/RAD	125.25
APP	134.35
PAR	130.05
TWR	122.50
OPS	Farnborough Business Aviation Farnboro EXEC 130.375
LLZ/DME	I-FNB 111.55 Rwy25

Remarks
Noise abatement- all departures are to use maximum climb until ACFT reaches initial clearance level. Mandatory handling through FBA Tel: 01252 524440. Pilots must book out by phone. Helicopter landing area on disused N/S Rwy between S apron and intersection of Twy J & K.

Warnings
Minimum obstacle clearance to Rwy07/25 is not provided by PAR or PAPIs at less than 1nm from the Thr. Intensive and varied aviation activity takes place outside published AD Hrs during periods when ATC not operating. Danger Areas D132, D133A and D133 are within 3nm E of the AD boundary. Free-fall parachuting takes place at Queens Parade 1nm SE of ARP. Traffic carrying out instrument approaches to Rwy28 at Odiham will pass approximately 1.5nm S of Farnborough AD at 1900ft QNH or lower. Single engined jet ACFT may not depart Rwy07. A/f will close prior to 2200 Mon-Fri when no operations expected.

Operating Hrs	Mon-Fri 0600-2100 Sat-Sun & PH 0700-1900 & by arrangement (Summer) Winter + 1Hr
Circuits	1000ft QFE day 1500 ft QFE night

Landing fees	Minimum charge including Nav and handling £30 +VAT
Maintenance	Farnborough Aviation Services **Tel: 01252 524440**
Fuel	AVGAS 100LL AVTUR JET A1
Operator	COMAX, Control Tower, Farnborough Airport, Hampshire GU14 6TD **Tel: 01252 526015 (ATC)** **Tel: 01252 524440 (PPR)** **Fax: 01252 526024** Telex 858981 FNBAPT Farnborough Business Centre
Restaurants	Many pubs within walking distance
Taxis/Car Hire	Can be arranged on arrival at Airport
Weather Info	M T9 Fax 282 BNMC

Visual Reference Points (VRPs)
Alton	N5109.12 W00057.97
Bagshot	N5120.95 W00041.95
Farnborough Rly Stn	N5117.78 W00045.30
Guildford	N5114.37 W00035.10
Hook	N5116.77 W00057.72

F

ELEVATION	LOCATION	EGMF **FARTHING CORNER (Stoneacre Fm)**
420ft 14mb	4nm S of Gillingham N5119.83.E00036.07	DET 117.30 005 1.9 — •• / • / —
PPR		BIG 115.10 094 21.2 — ••• / •• / — — •

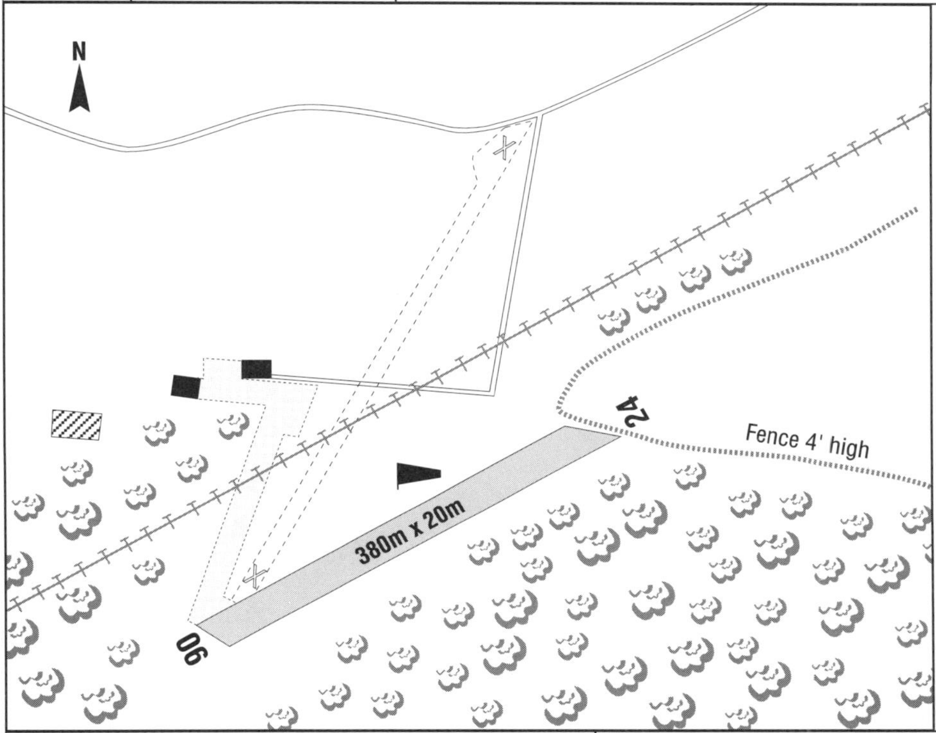

380m x 20m

06 / 24

Fence 4' high

F

RWY	SURFACE	TORA	LDA	LIGHTING
06/24	Grass	380x20	U/L	Nil

Non-radio

Make advisory calls to Rochester 122.25 Local traffic listens out on this frequency

Remarks
PPR strictly by telephone. Avoid over-flying farmhouse 400 yards to the E of Rwy. All final APP to Rwy24 are to be made between farmhouse and Thr.

Warnings
Turbulence on APP to both ends of Rwy. Detling VOR is 1.25nm to the S. Power lines up to 110ft agl run parallel to the strip between 80 and 100m to N W of the strip. The GND in the immediate undershoot area of Rwy06 falls away steeply.

Operator	Harry Folds, Stoneacre Farm Matts Hill Road, Hartlip Sittingbourne Kent ME9 7XA
	Tel: 01634 389757 (A/F) Medway Flight Training **Fax:** 01634 264011 (A/F)
Restaurants	Nil
Taxis/Car Hire	Can be arranged locally
Weather Info	AirSE BNMC

Operating Hrs	SR-SS
Circuits	24 LH 06 RH
Landing fee	£2.00
Maintenance	Available
Fuel	AVGAS 100LL limited to emergency only

ELEVATION	LOCATION	
771ft 25mb **PPR**	4nm NE of Sidmouth N5044.15.W00311.46 **Diversion AD**	BHD 112.05 035 24 $-\bullet\bullet\bullet/\bullet\bullet\bullet\bullet/-\bullet\bullet$

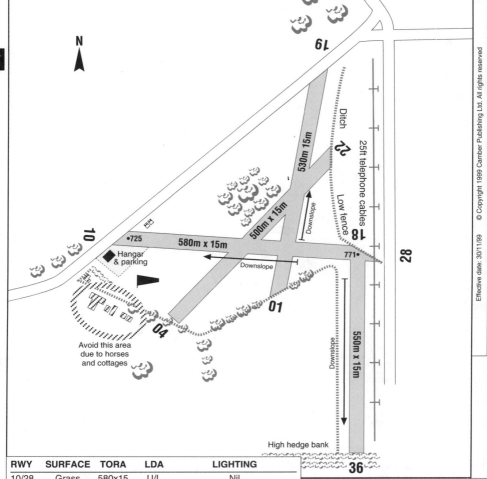

RWY	SURFACE	TORA	LDA	LIGHTING
10/28	Grass	580x15	U/L	Nil
18/36	Grass	550x15	U/L	Nil
01/19	Grass	530x15	U/L	Nil
04/22	Grass	500x15	U/L	Nil

	Non-radio
APP	**Exeter 128.15**

Remarks
PPR may regretfully be denied as visiting ACFT are limited by planning permission. There is an annual fly-in (usually August) associated with Devon Strut of the PFA which is well worth a visit. See aviation press for details.

Warnings
Sheep may be grazing. There are numerous hazards (mostly minor) relating to most Rwys which should be considered. Please study the AD diagram closely.
Noise: Avoid local habitation, particularly area SW of AD

Maintenance	Nil
Fuel	Nil
Operator	Jean & Terry Case, Moorlands Farm Sidbury, Sidmouth, Devon EX10 0QW **Tel/Fax:** 01395 597535
Restaurants/Accomodation	Numerous local hotels & B&B's
Taxis/Car Hire	Locally by arrangement
Weather Info	AirSW BNMC

Operating Hrs	SR-SS
Circuits	1000ft QFE
Landing fee	Nil

ELEVATION	LOCATION				FELTHORPE

ELEVATION	LOCATION				
120ft 4mb	4nm NW of Norwich Airport N5242.35.E00111.57	CLN 114.55	005	51	– • – • / • – • • / – •
PPR		BKY 116.25	048	59.5	– • • • / – • – / – • – –

© Copyright 1999 Camber Publishing Ltd. All rights reserved

Effective date: 30/11/99

F

Map labels:
- N (compass)
- Felthorpe village
- Avoid Felthorpe village
- 16
- 23
- 436m x 28m
- 487m x 26m
- 05
- 34
- Crops (×4)
- Aircraft parking
- T
- Route via quarry
- Avoid Taverham, The Garden Centre & Thorpe Marriott
- Taverham

RWY	SURFACE	TORA	LDA	LIGHTING
16/34	Grass	436x28	U/L	Nil
05/23	Grass	487x26	U/L	Nil

	Felthorpe
APP	Norwich 119.35
AG	123.50 (Not always manned)

Remarks
PPR by telephone. Visiting ACFT welcome at pilots own risk. Windsock and landing T displayed. Due to close proximity of Norwich Airport all ACFT call Norwich APP on 119.35

Warnings
Trees at boundry may cause tubulence, even in light wind and also obscure view of ACFT in circuit when departing. **Avoid;** overflying Felthorpe village to NE &Taverham to SSE, also Taverham nursery between AD & village. Busy public road on two sides of AD. Space between Rwys cultivated, agricultural workers & machinery may be present. Clubhouse open weekends.

Operating Hrs	SR-SS
Circuits	05/16 RH 23/34 LH Overhead joins 1000ft QFE circuit 500ft QFE
Landing fee	Nil
Maintenance **Fuel**	Nil Nil

Operator	Felthorpe Flying Group Ltd Norman Dean (Secretary) 12 Aspen Way, Cringleford Norwich NR4 6UA **Tel:** 01603 867691 (AD) **Tel:** 01603 504865 (Secretary) **Tel:** 01603 755317 (Chairman)
Restaurant	Norwich approx 15mins drive
Taxis Olivers Travels HP Private Hire **Car Hire** National	 **Tel:** 01603 261010 **Tel:** 01603 897261 **Tel:** 01603 631912
Weather Info	AirS BNMC

ELEVATION	LOCATION	EGCL				FENLAND

ELEVATION	LOCATION				
8ft 0mb **PPR**	6nm SE of Spalding N5244.35W00001.78 **Diversion AD**	BKY 116.25	360	44.8	— • • • / — • — / — • — —
		GAM 112.80	140	46.5	— — • / • — / — —
		DTY 116.40	055	51.6	— • • / — / — • — —

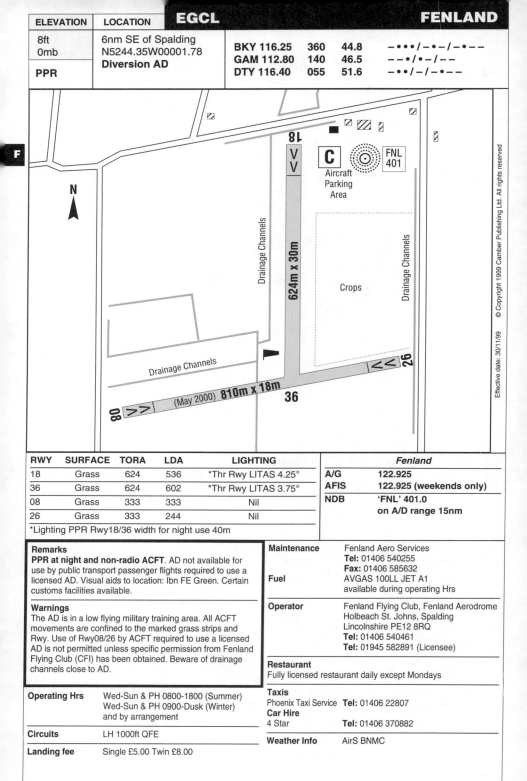

RWY	SURFACE	TORA	LDA	LIGHTING
18	Grass	624	536	*Thr Rwy LITAS 4.25°
36	Grass	624	602	*Thr Rwy LITAS 3.75°
08	Grass	333	333	Nil
26	Grass	333	244	Nil

*Lighting PPR Rwy18/36 width for night use 40m

	Fenland
A/G	122.925
AFIS	122.925 (weekends only)
NDB	'FNL' 401.0 on A/D range 15nm

Remarks
PPR at night and non-radio ACFT. AD not available for use by public transport passenger flights required to use a licensed AD. Visual aids to location: Ibn FE Green. Certain customs facilities available.

Warnings
The AD is in a low flying military training area. All ACFT movements are confined to the marked grass strips and Rwy. Use of Rwy08/26 by ACFT required to use a licensed AD is not permitted unless specific permission from Fenland Flying Club (CFI) has been obtained. Beware of drainage channels close to AD.

Maintenance	Fenland Aero Services **Tel: 01406 540255** **Fax: 01406 585632**
Fuel	AVGAS 100LL JET A1 available during operating Hrs
Operator	Fenland Flying Club, Fenland Aerodrome Holbeach St. Johns, Spalding Lincolnshire PE12 8RQ **Tel: 01406 540461** **Tel: 01945 582891 (Licensee)**
Restaurant	Fully licensed restaurant daily except Mondays

Operating Hrs	Wed-Sun & PH 0800-1800 (Summer) Wed-Sun & PH 0900-Dusk (Winter) and by arrangement
Circuits	LH 1000ft QFE
Landing fee	Single £5.00 Twin £8.00

Taxis
Phoenix Taxi Service **Tel: 01406 22807**
Car Hire
4 Star **Tel: 01406 370882**

Weather Info AirS BNMC

ELEVATION	LOCATION
860ft 28mb	1.5nm SE of Loch Insh N5706.00.W00353.08
PPR	

FESHIEBRIDGE (Aviemore)

INS 109.20	177	27	••/−•/•••
ADN 114.30	263	52	•−/−••/−•

Caution terrain shielding

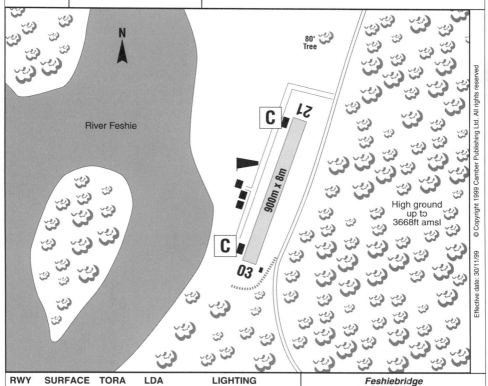

RWY	SURFACE	TORA	LDA	LIGHTING
03/21	Grass	900x8	U/L	Nil

Slight upslope in last 25% Rwy21

Feshiebridge

130.1 Glider common freq

Remarks
PPR by telephone. Primarily a gliding field with both winch and aerotow. Powered ACFT welcome. AD situated in stunning countryside but due consideration should be given for mountain weather and turbulence. Parking by the control caravan parked at appropriate landing Thr. Pilots are welcome to camp on the AD.

Warnings
Caution turning off strip: Rwy smooth but lower than surrounding land with varying 'kerb effect' up to approx. 15cm (6"). There is an 80ft tree on centreline approx. 250m Rwy21Thr, also low fence crosses 25m away from Rwy21 APP Thr. Give priority to gliders, they may block the rwy for short periods during launch and retrieval. Information is passed by control on glider common freq. 130.10. Make normal circuit calls on this freq. High GND up to 3668ft immediately to E and heavily wooded areas close to E & SE.

Maintenance	Nil
Fuel	Nil

Operator	Cairngorm Gliding Club Miss J Williamson (Landowner) Balnespick, Kincraig, Kingussie, Inverness **Tel: 01540 651246** (Land owner) **Tel: 01540 651317** (AD) **Mobile: 07770 454593**

Restaurant	Tea & coffee available at control

Aviemore Tourist Board **Tel: 01479 810363**
(for restaurants/accommodation etc.)

Taxis	**Tel: 01479 810118**
Car Hire Budget	**Tel: 01463 713333**

Weather Info	AirSc GWC

Operating Hrs	SR-SS

Circuits	21 RH 03 LH

Gliders use left and right circuit on both Rwys

Landing fee	£10 inc. day membership to club

ELEVATION	LOCATION					FETLAR
270ft 9mb PPR	1nm NW of Houbie Isle of Fetlar Shetlands N6036.23.W00052.33	SUM 117.35	022	45.5	•••/••–/––	

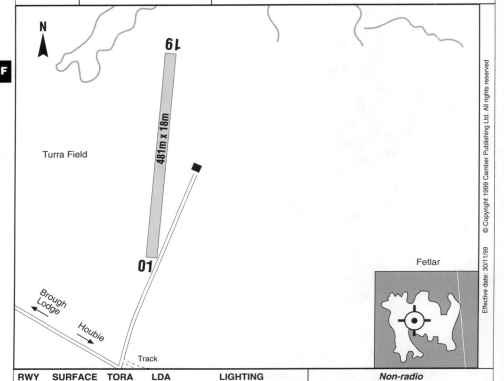

Turra Field

481m x 18m

19

01

Brough Lodge

Houbie

Track

Fetlar

RWY	SURFACE	TORA	LDA	LIGHTING			
01/19	Rolled mortar	481x18	U/L	Nil		**Non-radio**	
					APP	Sumburgh 123.15	

Remarks
PPR by telephone. The AD is available for visiting ACFT We strongly advise that visitors also contact Loganair (Tel: 01595 840246) to establish the operating times of their services. As there is extremely limited off-Rwy parking, your ACFT could obstruct the Rwy for essential services (see warnings). A windsock is provided with PPR.

Warnings
Although the Rwy has no gradient the surface is rough and could cause prop-strike to nosewheel ACFT with little prop clearance. Parking off-Rwy should only be attempted with extreme care, after first investigating on foot. The highest point on the Island (Vord Hill 522ft amsl) is 1.5nm out close to left of 19 APP. The AD is on common land and sheep may stray onto the Rwy at any at any time. Moss growth may affect braking action.

Maintenance	Nil
Fuel	Nil
Operator	Fetlar Development Group Fetlar Aerodrome, Shetland ZE2 9DJ **Tel:** 01957 733267 (Mr R Leaper)

Restaurants/Accomodation
B&B	**Tel:** 01957 733227 (Mrs L Boxall) (10min walk from AD)

Taxis/Car Hire Nil
Mr Leaper can provide transport by arrangement

Weather Info AirSC GWC

Operating Hrs	SR-SS
Circuits	1000ft QFE
Landing fee	Nil

ELEVATION	LOCATION	EGPJ				FIFE (Glenrothes)

ELEVATION	LOCATION			
399ft 13mb	2nm W of Glenrothes N5611.00.W00313.22 **Diversion AD**	TLA 113.80	014	41.3	–/•–••/•–
PPR		SAB 112.50	304	37.8	•••/•–/–•••
		PTH 110.40	170	16.3	•–––•/–/••••

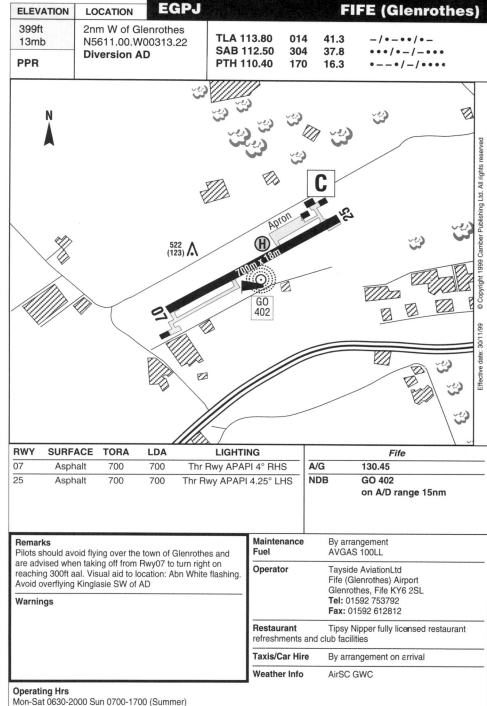

RWY	SURFACE	TORA	LDA	LIGHTING		Fife	
07	Asphalt	700	700	Thr Rwy APAPI 4° RHS	A/G	130.45	
25	Asphalt	700	700	Thr Rwy APAPI 4.25° LHS	NDB	GO 402 on A/D range 15nm	

Remarks
Pilots should avoid flying over the town of Glenrothes and are advised when taking off from Rwy07 to turn right on reaching 300ft aal. Visual aid to location: Abn White flashing. Avoid overflying Kinglasie SW of AD

Warnings

Maintenance	By arrangement
Fuel	AVGAS 100LL
Operator	Tayside AviationLtd Fife (Glenrothes) Airport Glenrothes, Fife KY6 2SL **Tel:** 01592 753792 **Fax:** 01592 612812
Restaurant	Tipsy Nipper fully licensed restaurant refreshments and club facilities
Taxis/Car Hire	By arrangement on arrival
Weather Info	AirSC GWC

Operating Hrs
Mon-Sat 0630-2000 Sun 0700-1700 (Summer)
PPR 0900-1800 (Winter) and by arrangement

Circuits	25 LH 07 RH

Landing fees   Single £8.00 Twin £16.00
Commercial Twin £32 inc.VAT Light Commercial Twin £16
Free landing fee for users spending same amount in restaurant

ELEVATION	LOCATION	**EGTG**		**FILTON**

ELEVATION	LOCATION	EGTG	FILTON
226ft 8mb	4nm N of Bristol N5131.17.W00235.42	**BCN 117.45 121 28.0**	− • • • / − • − • / − •
PPR			

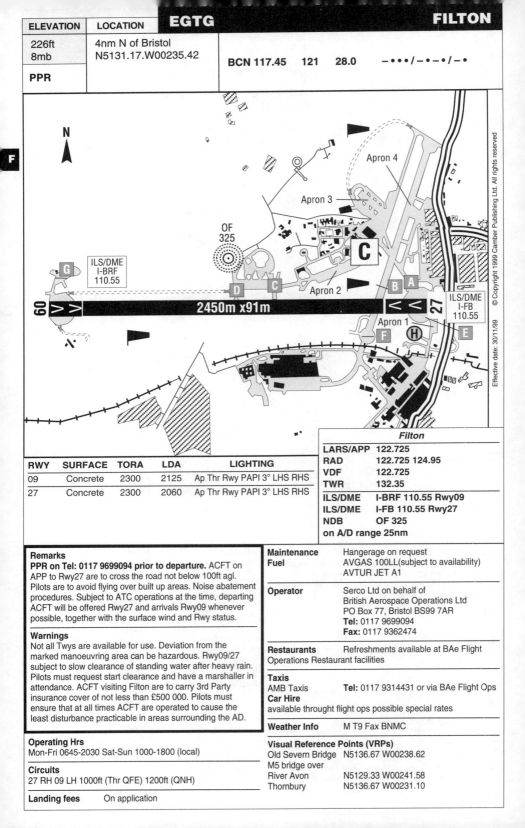

Apron 4

Apron 3

OF 325

ILS/DME I-BRF 110.55

G

D   C

Apron 2

C

B A

ILS/DME I-FB 110.55

60   V V   2450m x91m   < <   27

Apron 1

F   (H)   E

RWY	SURFACE	TORA	LDA	LIGHTING
09	Concrete	2300	2125	Ap Thr Rwy PAPI 3° LHS RHS
27	Concrete	2300	2060	Ap Thr Rwy PAPI 3° LHS RHS

	Filton
LARS/APP	**122.725**
RAD	**122.725 124.95**
VDF	**122.725**
TWR	**132.35**
ILS/DME	**I-BRF 110.55 Rwy09**
ILS/DME	**I-FB 110.55 Rwy27**
NDB	**OF 325**
on A/D range 25nm	

Remarks
PPR on Tel: 0117 9699094 prior to departure. ACFT on APP to Rwy27 are to cross the road not below 100ft agl. Pilots are to avoid flying over built up areas. Noise abatement procedures. Subject to ATC operations at the time, departing ACFT will be offered Rwy27 and arrivals Rwy09 whenever possible, together with the surface wind and Rwy status.

Warnings
Not all Twys are available for use. Deviation from the marked manoeuvring area can be hazardous. Rwy09/27 subject to slow clearance of standing water after heavy rain. Pilots must request start clearance and have a marshaller in attendance. ACFT visiting Filton are to carry 3rd Party insurance cover of not less than £500 000. Pilots must ensure that at all times ACFT are operated to cause the least disturbance practicable in areas surrounding the AD.

Operating Hrs
Mon-Fri 0645-2030 Sat-Sun 1000-1800 (local)

Circuits
27 RH 09 LH 1000ft (Thr QFE) 1200ft (QNH)

Landing fees
On application

Maintenance	Hangerage on request
Fuel	AVGAS 100LL(subject to availability) AVTUR JET A1
Operator	Serco Ltd on behalf of British Aerospace Operations Ltd PO Box 77, Bristol BS99 7AR **Tel:** 0117 9699094 **Fax:** 0117 9362474
Restaurants	Refreshments available at BAe Flight Operations Restaurant facilities
Taxis **AMB Taxis** **Car Hire**	**Tel:** 0117 9314431 or via BAe Flight Ops available throught flight ops possible special rates
Weather Info	M T9 Fax BNMC

Visual Reference Points (VRPs)
Old Severn Bridge	N5136.67 W00238.62
M5 bridge over River Avon	N5129.33 W00241.58
Thornbury	N5136.67 W00231.10

ELEVATION	LOCATION				FINMERE
405ft 14mb	2.5nm WSW of Buckingham N5159.13.W00103.36	**DTY 116.40**	175	12	– • • / – / – • – –
PPR	**Diversion AD**	**BNN 113.75**	315	24	– • • • / – • / – •

F

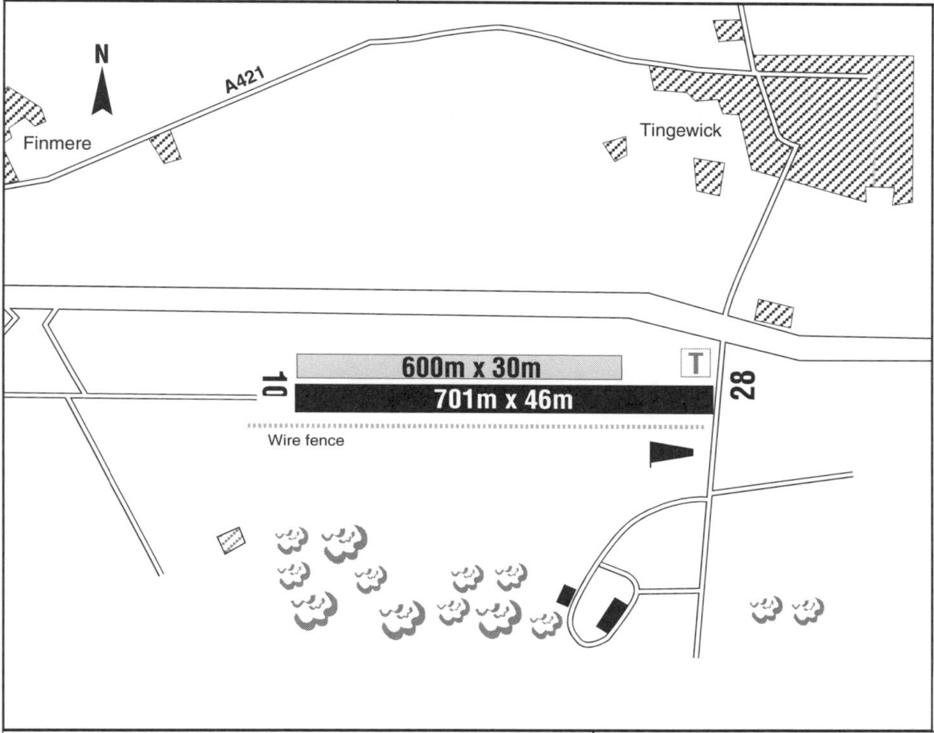

N

A421

Finmere

Tingewick

600m x 30m

10

701m x 46m

28

T

Wire fence

RWY	SURFACE	TORA	LDA	LIGHTING		*Non Radio*
10/28	Asphalt	701	701	Nil		
10/28	Grass	600	600	Nil		

Remarks
PPR by telephone. Visiting light ACFT welcome at pilot's own risk. U/L AD.

Warnings
Power cables to S and W of Rwy. Barbed wire and netting fence along S side of Rwy. Surface best at E end of Rwy. One low level circuit should be made prior to landing in order to permit lorries and model ACFT to clear the Rwy. Do not over-fly the market which is held adjacent to the AD on Sundays. Do not over-fly villages of Tingewick and Finmere.

Operator	Mrs PJ Knapton, 23 Gorrell Close Tingewick, Bucks MK18 4FL **Tel:** 01280 848589
Restaurants Royal Oak	Nil at A/D **Tel:** 01280 848373 (Tingewick)
Taxis A.K.Cars Buckingham Taxis **Car Hire** Bucks Self Drive	**Tel:** 01280 817338 **Tel:** 01280 812038 **Tel:** 01280 822493
Weather Info	AirCen BNMC

Operating Hrs	Available on request
Circuits	28 LH 10 RH
Landing fee	Nil
Maintenance **Fuel**	Nil Nil

F

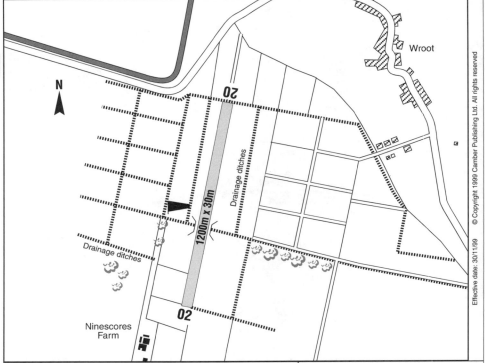

N

20

1200m x 30m

Drainage ditches

Drainage ditches

Wroot

02

Ninescores
Farm

RWY	SURFACE	TORA	LDA	LIGHTING	Non-Radio
02/20	Grass	1200x30	U/L	Nil	**LARS (Humberside) 124.67**

Remarks
PPR by telephone. No Microlights. Visiting ACFT welcome at pilots own risk. Rwy is flat and well maintained with no approach hazards. Windsock displayed. Avoid overflight of village of Wroot NE of AD.

Warnings
Drainage ditch close to Rwy20 Thr. Sandtoft ATZ NE of AD. Occasional military low flying activity takes place in the vicinity of the AD (mainly weekdays).

Operator	Philip Hopkins & Sons, Ninescores Farm Finningley Yorkshire DN9 3DY **Tel:** 01302 770274 **Mobile:** 07836 659322 **Fax**: 01302 772800
Restaurants	Bawtry or Epworth
Taxi John's. **Car Hire**	 **Tel:**01427 873103 Nil
Weather Info	AirN MWC

Operating hours	SR-SS
Circuits	LH 1000ft QFE
Landing Fee	Nil
Maintenance **Fuel**	Nil Nil

ELEVATION	LOCATION		**FISHBURN**
377ft 12mb	2.5nm NNW of Sedgefield N5441.30.W00127.85		
PPR			

NEW 114.25 165 22.7 — • / • / • — —
DCS 115.20 098 63.6 — • • / — • — • / • • •

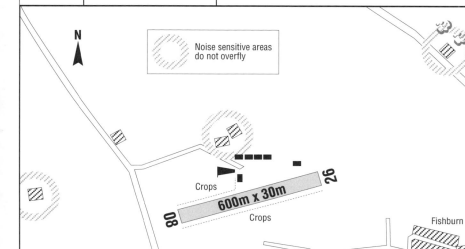

Effective date: 30/11/99

F

RWY	SURFACE	TORA	LDA	LIGHTING
08/26	Grass	600x30	U/L	Nil

	Fishburn
APP	**Teesside 118.85**
A/G	**118.275**

Remarks
PPR by telephone. Situated N of the Teesside CTR.
Helicopters now accepted.

Warnings
Join circuit from N only; avoid overflying local habitation –
local area is noise sensitive. 1.6% upslope Rwy26. Crops
grown right up to Rwy edge.

Operator Bill Morgan, West House Farm
Fishburn, Co Durham
Tel: 0191 3720213 (Operator)
Tel: 0191 3770213 (AD)
Fax: 01913 3720213

Restaurants
Snacks and hot drinks available in caravan

Taxis
Ron's   **Tel:** 01740 621862
Car Hire
Avis   **Tel:** 01325 368800
National   **Tel:** 01325 353659

Weather Info   AirN MWC

Operating Hrs   Mon-Sat 0800-2030
Sun 0930-2030 (local) (Last take-off 2000)

Circuits   08 LH 26 RH 800ft QFE

Landing fee   Single £2.00 Twin £5.00
No fee with fuel uplift of 40ltrs or more

Maintenance   Available in emergency
Fuel   AVGAS 100LL

ELEVATION	LOCATION					
150ft 5mb	Nr Hametown Isle of Foula SE coast Shetland N6007.33.W00203.12	**SUM 117.35**	**309**	**28**	●●●/●●–/––	
PPR						

FOULA

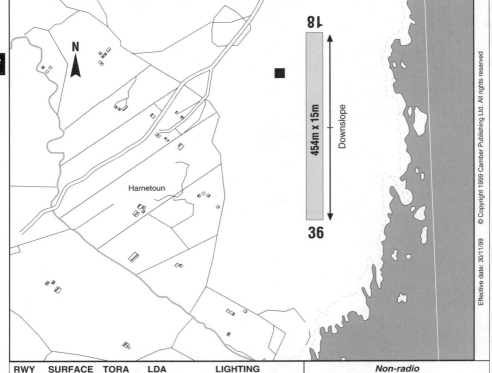

18

454m x 15m   Downslope

36

Hametoun

N

RWY	SURFACE	TORA	LDA	LIGHTING		
18/36	Gravel	457x18	U/L	Nil		

45m overun at S end

	Non-radio
APP	**Sumburgh 123.15**

Remarks
PPR contact Airstrip Trust 01595 753233. Visiting ACFT accepted. We strongly advise that visitors contact Loganair (Tel: 01595 840246) to check details of their services (currently 7 a week). There is no off-Rwy parking so visiting ACFT will constitute an obstruction to vital local services (see warnings).

Warnings
This AD is extremely hump backed giving rise to possible optical illusion on APP and roll-out. The paved surface is rough and could cause prop-strike to nosewheel ACFT with little prop clearance. The AD is prone to severe turbulence, particularly in crosswinds. There are soft sections of the paved surface at the rwy midpoint on either side of the centreline, ACFT should avoid turning here to prevent surface damage. High GND 0.5nm W of AD (814ft amsl) & 1.5nm NW (1373ft amsl). AD is on common land and sheep may stray onto strip at any time. High risk of birdstrike in summer. Moss may effect braking. No windsock. **Important:** ACFT parked on strip restrict scheduled & ambulance services – consult with Loganair.

Operating Hrs	SR-SS
Circuits	1000ft QFE
Landing fee	Nil
Maintenance **Fuel**	Nil Nil
Operator	Mrs Isobel Holbourn, Foula Airstrip Trust **Tel:** 01595 753233
For assistance in the event of an emergency: Island Fire Service**Tel:** 01957 753227	
Restaurants	
Taxis/Car Hire	Nil
Weather Info	AirSC GWC

ELEVATION	LOCATION	**EGMA**			**FOWLMERE**

ELEVATION	LOCATION
124ft 4mb	7.5nm SSW of Cambridge N5204.65.E00003.70
PPR	**Diversion AD**

CLN 114.55	294	42.5	— • — • / • — • • • / — •
CFD 116.50	094	24.8	— • — • / • • • — • / — • •
BKY 116.25	004	5.3	— • • • / — • — / — • — —

F

Bird Reserve

N

C

A

Grass Twy

C

25

B

704m x 30m

07

X

X

© Copyright 1999 Camber Publishing Ltd. All rights reserved

Effective date: 30/11/99

RWY	SURFACE	TORA	LDA	LIGHTING
07/25*	Grass	704	704	Nil

*An extra 150m of unmarked Rwy is available at the E end of 07/25 for take-offs on 25 and landings & take-offs on 07 by ACFT not required to use a licensed AD.

Fowlmere

Combined ATZ see Remarks
APP	**Essex Rad 120.625**
AFIS	**Duxford 122.075**
A/G	**120.925**

Remarks
PPR may be denied, severe planning restrictions, Singles 241 BHP max No helicopters, microlights or twins. No overhead joins, please ring for briefing. Avoid making a low APP to Rwy25 due public road, flying over Fowlmere village & built up areas in the vicinity. Bird reserve 700m NW of AD. Fowlmere is close to Duxford (Fowlmere is 2.5nm WSW of Duxford) & both ADs operate under a Combined AD Traffic Zone (CATZ) with Duxford as the controlling authority. An ACFT shall not fly, take off or land within the Fowlmere ATZ unless the pilot has contacted the AFIS unit at Duxford. The pilot of an ACFT flying within the Fowlmere ATZ should maintain a continuous watch on the Duxford frequency 122.075. Position and height should be communicated to Duxford on entering the CATZ and prior to leaving it. Join via Royston Rwy25: follow railway NE between Melbourne & Meldrith keep N of bird sanctuary, turn right base between Fowlmere & Thirplow. Rwy07: Royston direct to long final.

Warnings
Back tracking is necessary for entry/exit on Rwy07/25. Pilots should not take-off or land while this is in progress. ACFT holding at the marked holding points will be clear of the Rwy and strips. Daily movements strictly ltd. Outside parking restricted. Strict compliance with noise abatement.

Operating Hrs	Closed Mondays Tue-Fri 0800-1200 Sat-Sun 0800-1400 (Summer) Winter + 1Hr
Circuits	07 LH 25 RH 800ft QFE
Landing fees	Single £10.00
Maintenance **Fuel**	Modern Air AVGAS 100LL by arrangement
Operator	Modern Air Ltd, Fowlmere Aerodrome Royston, Herts SG8 7SJ

Tel: 01763 208281 **Fax:** 01763 208861
Tel: 01223 833376 (Duxford ATC)

Restaurants
Sheen Mill	**Tel:** 01763 261393 (Melbourn)
Maguires	**Tel:** 01763 208444 (Fowlmere)

Taxis
Meltax	**Tel:** 01763 244444

Car Hire
Kirkham Cars	**Tel:** 01763 261116
Ford	**Tel:** 01763 242084

Weather Info	AirS BNMC

ELEVATION	LOCATION		
86ft 3mb	7nm E of York N5358.83.W00051.85 **Diversion AD**	OTR 113.90 307 32	– – – / – / • – •
PPR		POL 112.10 077 46.1	• – – • / – – – / • – • •
		GAM 112.80 010 41.5	– – • / • – / – –

F

Effective date: 30/11/99

H.M. Prison

N

Pond

Crops

Crops

Aircraft parking

Asphalt Twy

772m x 20m

400m x 25m

04 07

16

22

25

34

RWY	SURFACE	TORA	LDA	LIGHTING
04/22	Grass	772	772	Nil
*16/34	Asphalt	700x25	U/L	Nil
*07/25	Grass	400x25	U/L	Nil

*Primarily used as Twy only available with PPR from AD manger

	Full Sutton
A/G	132.325
	Mandatory radio

Remarks
PPR. Non–radio ACFT not accepted. Radio use is mandatory. Visual aid to location 4 large grain silos E of AD. AD not available to Public Transport flights which require a licensed AD. The signal square by the Control TWR is primarly for microlights only.

Warnings
AD is within Restricted Area R315 (applies to helicopters only). **Do not overfly the prison** on the N side of the AD under any circumstances. Deps. Rwy22, fly between two pig farms on climbout. Power cables cross APP to 22, do not land short of displaced Thr. Intensive gliding at Pocklington, 4nm SE of AD. High GND (up to 807ft amsl) starting 4nm E of AD. Microlight flying takes place on AD on Rwy16/34 or 07/25.

Operating Hrs
Tue-Fri 0800-1800 Sat-Sun 0900-SS (Summer)
Tue-Fri 0900-1700 Sat-Sun 0900-SS (Winter)

Circuits	04 RH 22 LH 800ft QFE
Landing fee	Single £3.00 Twin £10.00

Maintenance	RH Aviation Tel: 01759 372849
Fuel	AVGAS 100LL available by arrangement
Operator	Full Sutton Flying Centre Ltd Full Sutton Airfield, Stamford Bridge York YO4 1HS **Tel:** 01759 372717 **Tel:** 01759 373277 (Club) **Fax:** 01759 372991
Restaurants	Bar in flying club.Tea & coffee weekdays
Taxis Hessles's Cabs	**Tel:** 01759 303176
Car Hire Avis National	**Tel:** 01904 610460 **Tel:** 01904 612141
Weather Info	AirN MWC

ELEVATION	LOCATION				GARSTON FARM
600ft 20mb	1nm NNW of Colerne AD N5127.60.W00218.00	BCN 117.45 CPT 114.35	119 272	40 40.5	– • • • / – • – • / – • / – • – • / • – – • / –
PPR					

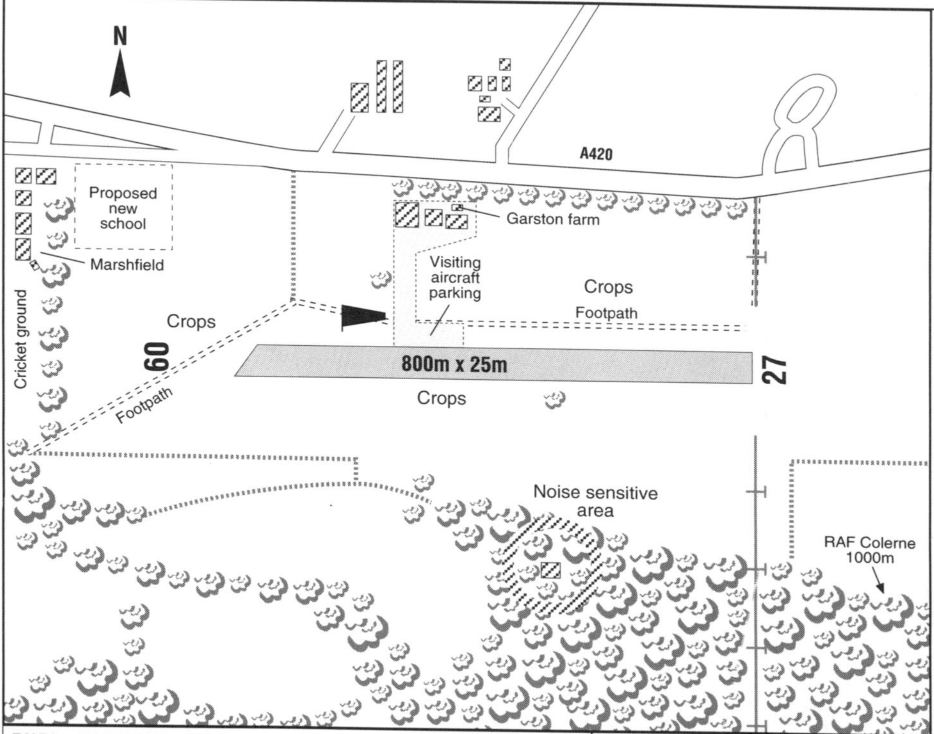

Map labels: N, A420, Proposed new school, Marshfield, Cricket ground, Crops, 60, Footpath, Garston farm, Visiting aircraft parking, Crops, Footpath, 800m x 25m, Crops, 27, Noise sensitive area, RAF Colerne 1000m

RWY	SURFACE	TORA	LDA	LIGHTING
09/27	Grass	800x25	U/L	Nil

Non-radio

APP	Colerne 122.10

Remarks
PPR by telephone. Visitors welcome at pilots own risk. Well maintained flat strip.

Warnings
AD situated within the Colerne ATZ. Arriving ACFT must contact Colerne TWR (122.10). Departures must call before take-off. Wires approach the 27 Thr from N & S but are underground 50m either side of the Thr. Wooded area to the S of Rwy may cause turbulence at low levels. NO right turns Rwy27 departure (due school). Right of way crosses Thr of Rwy09 and Twy. **Noise:** Do not overfly Marshfield to the W of AD.

Operator	Mr M. Ball, Garston Farm Marshfield Nr Chippenham, Wilts SN14 8LH **Tel**: 01225 891418 **Tel**: 0790 1755312 (mobile)
Restaurants	3 pubs in village
Taxis Grahams	**Tel**: 07850 874141
Car Hire	Nil
Weather Info	AirSW BNMC

Operating Hrs	SR-SS

Circuits
N at 1000ft QFE Downwind 09 to be extended to avoid village

Landing fee

Maintenance	Nil
Fuel	Nil

G

ELEVATION	LOCATION				
90ft 3mb	1nm S of Upminster N5131.80 E00014.78	LAM 115.60	158	8	• – • • / • – / – –
PPR		BIG 117.30	038	14.5	– • • • / • • / – – •

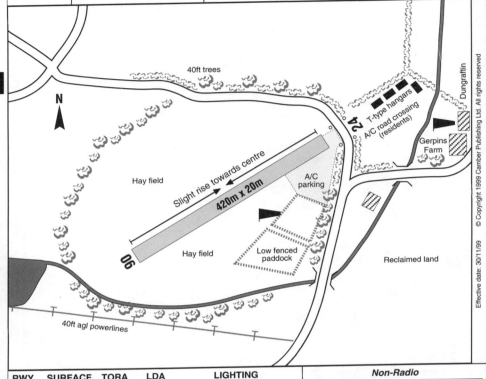

RWY	SURFACE	TORA	LDA	LIGHTING	Non-Radio
06/24	Surface	420x20	U/L	Nil	APP/LARS (Thames) 132.70

Remarks

PPR by telephone. Visiting ACFT welcome at pilots own risk. AD situated on reclaimed land and old gravel workings close to M25. Residents hangars and operators house across the lane from AD.

Warnings

AD close to edge of London City CTR (class D). Controlling authority is Thames Radar, (132.70). Also under the London TMA, (class A). Base 2500ft QNH. Long grass, grown for Hay may be present up to Rwy edge. AD slightly convex in configuration. Caution: This AD is NOT Damyns Hall, which is approx 700m to the ENE.

Operator	Mr Derek Izod, Dungraftin, Gerpins Lane Upminster RM14 2XR **Tel:** 01708 250315
Restaurants	Huntsman & Hounds or The Optimist within 10 mins walk.
Taxis/Car Hire	Nil
Weather Info	AirSE BNMC

Operating Hrs	SR-SS
Circuits	06 LH 24 RH
Landing Fee	Nil
Maintenance Fuel	Nil Nil

ELEVATION	LOCATION			
46ft 2mb PPR	1.5nm S of Village N5539.20.W00545.47 **Diversion AD**	**MAC 116.00** 001 13.0	– – / • – / – • – •

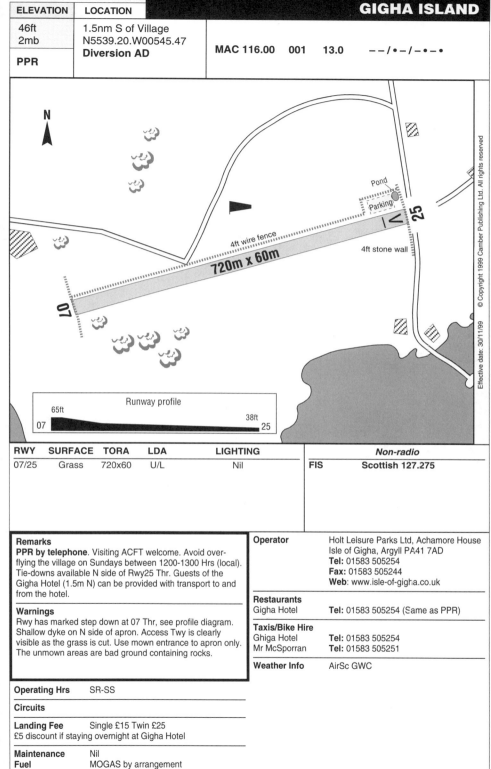

720m x 60m

07

25

4ft wire fence

4ft stone wall

Pond

Parking

N

Runway profile
65ft
07
38ft
25

RWY	SURFACE	TORA	LDA	LIGHTING		
07/25	Grass	720x60	U/L	Nil		

	Non-radio
FIS	**Scottish 127.275**

Remarks
PPR by telephone. Visiting ACFT welcome. Avoid over-flying the village on Sundays between 1200-1300 Hrs (local). Tie-downs available N side of Rwy25 Thr. Guests of the Gigha Hotel (1.5m N) can be provided with transport to and from the hotel.

Warnings
Rwy has marked step down at 07 Thr, see profile diagram. Shallow dyke on N side of apron. Access Twy is clearly visible as the grass is cut. Use mown entrance to apron only. The unmown areas are bad ground containing rocks.

Operator	Holt Leisure Parks Ltd, Achamore House Isle of Gigha, Argyll PA41 7AD **Tel:** 01583 505254 **Fax:** 01583 505244 **Web**: www.isle-of-gigha.co.uk
Restaurants Gigha Hotel	**Tel:** 01583 505254 (Same as PPR)
Taxis/Bike Hire Ghiga Hotel Mr McSporran	**Tel:** 01583 505254 **Tel:** 01583 505251
Weather Info	AirSc GWC

Operating Hrs	SR-SS
Circuits	
Landing Fee	Single £15 Twin £25
£5 discount if staying overnight at Gigha Hotel	
Maintenance	Nil
Fuel	MOGAS by arrangement

Effective date: 30/11/99

G

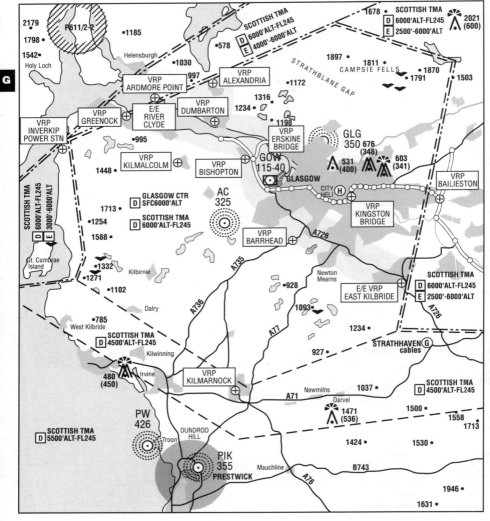

ELEVATION	LOCATION	EGPF			GLASGOW
26ft 1mb	6nm W of Glasgow N5552.32.W00426.00	GOW 115.40 TRN 117.50 TLA 113.80	On A/D 027 312	 35.6 40.5	– – • / – – – / • – – – / • – • / – • – / • – • • / • –

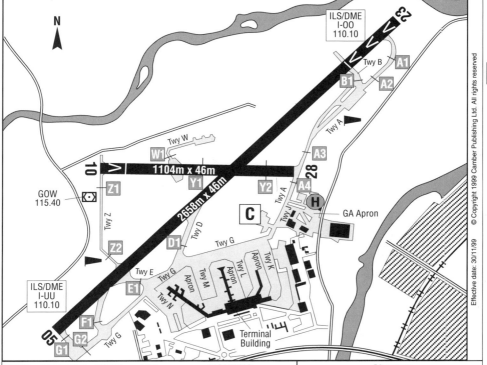

GOW 115.40
ILS/DME I-OO 110.10
Twy B A1
B1 A2
Twy A
A3
1104m x 46m W1 Y1
GOW 115.40
Z1 Y2 A4
2658m x 46m
Twy Z H GA Apron
Z2 C
D1 Twy G
Twy D
Twy E Twy G
E1 Twy M Twy L Apron Twy K
Twy N
F1
ILS/DME I-UU 110.10
05 G2 G1 Twy G
Terminal Building

RWY	SURFACE	TORA	LDA	LIGHTING
05	Asphalt	2658	2658	Ap Thr Rwy PAPI 3°
23	Asphalt	2658	2353	Ap Thr Rwy PAPI 3°
10	Asphalt	1104	1042	Thr Rwy PAPI 3°
28	Asphalt	1104	1104	Thr Rwy PAPI 3°

Glasgow

ATIS	129.575
APP	119.10
RAD	119.10 119.30 121.30
TWR	118.80
GMC	121.70**
FIRE	121.60

**GMC:
Mon-Fri 0630-2030
Sat-Sun 0900-1900 (Winter)
0530-1930 Daily (Summer)

VOR/DME	GOW 115.40***
NDB	GLG 350****
NDB	AC 325*****
ILS/DME	I-UU 110.10 Rwy05
ILS/DME	I-OO 110.10 Rwy23

***GOW on A/D
****233/4 to Thr23
range 15nm
***** 053/4.34 to Thr05
range 25nm

Remarks

Use governed by Scottish CTR regulations . Filing a flight plan does not constitute permission to use Glasgow Airport. All pleasure, training & non-business GA traffic subject to prior notification to ATC Tel: 0141 8878918. Operators must make prior arrangements with handling agent for GND handling all flights. GA handing by Execair on 122.35 or Tel: 0141 8878348. Use of airport for training purposes is subject to Operations Directors permission, Glasgow Airport Ltd., ATC Tel: 0141 8878918. Visiting GA ACFT including international arrivals will be parked on GA Park, Stand 35. Pilots of international arriving and departing GA ACFT are responsible for presenting their passengers to Customs and Immigration. Transport to and from the Customs Office will be provided by a Handling Agent.

Warnings

No GND signals except light signals. Large Whooper swans up to 12kgs are present around the airport from September to April. Flocks of up to 100 birds may fly at heights up to 500ft. The main flying activity of the swans is usually confined to short periods around dawn and dusk and ATC will endeavour to advise their presence when airborne. Hang Gliding takes place within the Glasgow CTR up to 2500ft amsl (occasionally 3000ft with ATC permission) and sites are considered active during all daylight hours. Pilots inbound to or outbound from the airport must operate ACFT so as to cause the least disturbance practicable to the areas in and around the airport.

Operating Hrs	H24 with all flights subject to approval
Circuits	
Landing fees	BAA rates
Maintenance	Available
Fuel	AVGAS 100LL AVTUR JET A1
	arranged by mandatory handling agent
Operator	Glasgow Airport Ltd
	Paisley, Strathclyde PA3 2ST
	Tel: 0141 8871111 (Airport)
	Tel: 0141 8878914 (NATS)
	Tel: 0141 8408029 (ATC)
	Tel: 0141 8879319 (AIS)
	Fax: 0141 8484586 (Airport)
	Telex: 776613 (Airport) 778219 (NATS)
Restaurant	Restaurant buffet and bars in Terminal
Taxis	Available at Terminal
Car Hire	
Avis	**Tel:** 0141 887 2261
Hertz	**Tel:** 0141 887 2541
Weather Info	M T9 T18 Fax 286 A VSc GWC

Helicopter Operations

Helicopters are not to move out of the alighting and parking area without obtaining taxi instructions from ATC. Glasgow-based helicopters will park on the old Loganair taxiiway. Visiting helicopters will normally be allocated a stand on the W apron (Stands 31-34). Helicopters, inbound and outbound, are to avoid over flying airport buildings whenever possible. CASEVAC helicopters will be directed by ATC to alight on the main apron taxiiway, then to GND taxy to an ACFT stand.

Use of Rwys

Rwy10/28 may be used at night by ACFT up to ATP size but only when the crosswind component on Rwy05/23 is greater than that specified in the ACFT's operations data manual. A Rwy lighting system including PAPI set at 5.25° can be made available at thirty minutes notice. Rwy10/28 is not available when low visibility procedures are in force.

GND Movement Control

GMC is responsible for:
The surface movement of all ACFT on the Manoeuvring area excluding the Rwy(s) in use.
Passing Air Traffic Control clearances to ACFT.
Passing parking instructions to all ACFT. All ACFT making requests for taxying or towing clearance on the GMC frequency should state their location in the initial call.

CTR-Class D Airspace

Normal CTA/CTR Class D Airspace rules apply

1 These rules do not apply to non-radio ACFT by day provided they have obtained permission and maintain 5km visibility 1500m horizontally and 1000ft vertically away from cloud.
2 SVFR clearances may be given that are not confined to Entry/Exit lanes.
3 When operating on a SVFR clearance, pilots must remain clear of cloud in sight of the surface and remain in flight conditions that will ensure they can determine their flight path and remain clear of obstacles.
4 Due to the nature of the terrain, a RAD service will not normally be provided to ACFT on a SVFR clearance.
5 SVFR clearance only applies to the CTR.
6 Entry/Exit lanes are established to permit ACFT to operate to and from Glasgow in IMC, but not under IFR, these are a) Clyde lane, b) Alexandria lane, c) Barrhead E Kilbride Lane. All these lanes are 3nms wide and use of the lanes is subject to ATC clearance and radio contact with Glasgow App. ACFT must remain clear of cloud and in sight of the surface not above 2000ft. Minimum visibility is 3km. ACFT must keep the lane centre-line on the left, unless otherwise instructed.

Visual Reference Points (VRPs):

VRP	VOR/VOR	VOR/NDB	VOR/DME FIX
Alexandria N5559.33 W00434.58	GOW R334°/TRN R010°	TRN R010°/GLG 302°M	GOW 334°/8nm/ TRN010°/41nm
Ardmore Point N5558.28 W00441.95	GOW R312°/TRN R011°	GOW R312°/GLG 290°M	GOW 312°/10nm
Baillieston N5551.17 W00405.37	TLA R317°/GOW R101°	TLA R317°/AC 088°M	GOW101°/12nm
Barrhead N5548.00 W00423.50	TRN R031°/TLA R303°	TLA R303°/GLG 200°M	GOW 163°/5nm/TRN031°/32nm
Bishopton N5554.13 W00430.10	GOW R322°/TUR R021°	GOW R322°/GLG 263°M	GOW 322°/3nm
Dumbarton N5556.67 W00434.10	GOW R324°/TRN R017°	GOW R324°/GLG 285°M	GOW 324°/6nm/TRN 017°/39nm
E Kilbride N5545.83 W00410.33	TRN R044°/TLA R306°	TRN R044°/GLG 156°M	GOW131°/11nm
Erskine Bridge N5555.22 W00427.77	GOW R355°/TRN R023°	GOW R355°/GLG 273°M	GOW 355°/3nm
Greenock N5556.83 W00445.08	GOW R300°/TRN R008°	TRN R008°/GLG 282°M	GOW300°/11nm
Inverkip Pwr Stn N5553.90 W00453.20	GOW R283°/TRN R001°	TRN R001°/GLG 272°M	GOW283°/15nm
Kilmacolm N5553.67 W00437.65	TRN R015°/GOW R289°	TRN R015°/GLG 266°M	GOW 289°/6nm/TRN 015°/35nm
Kilmarnock N5536.75 W00429.90	GOW R193°/TRN R035°	GOW R193°/NGY 343°M	GOW 193°/16nm
Kingston Bridge N5551.37 W00416.18	GOW R104°/TRN R034°	GOW R104°/GLG 158°M	GOW 104°/nm/TRN 034°/37nm

GLENFORSA (Mull)

ELEVATION	LOCATION				
15ft 0mb **PPR**	1nm E of Salen on Isle of Mull N5631.04.W00554.85 **Diversion AD**	**TIR 117.70**	097	31.7	– / • • / • – •

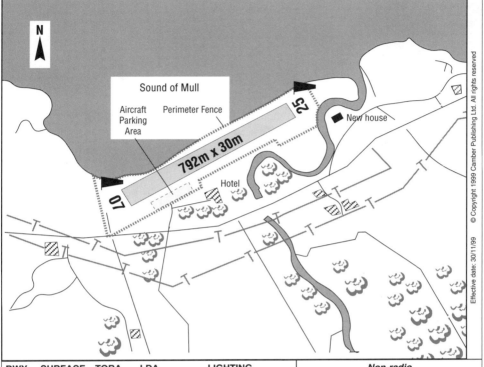

RWY	SURFACE	TORA	LDA	LIGHTING
07/25	Grass	792x30	U/L	Nil

Use S side of Rwy only because of poor drainage

	Non-radio
FIS	**Scottish 127.275**

Remarks
PPR 24Hrs notice required. Avoid overflying Glenforsa Hotel and village of Salen, also large new structure just S of Rwy25 Thr. For advisory WX actuals and information on state of strip Tel: 01680 300402. On rare occasions pilots are not met at the AD; please leave flight details at the adjacent caravan.

Warnings
Rwy designators still show 08/26. 07 requires a curved APP to keep clear of high GND to W. There is also high GND to the S.E. close to the AD. Sheep graze from Oct-Apr on the strip. Keep a lookout for microlight activity at any time.

Operator	Argyll and Bute Council DS Howitt, AD Bungalow, Salen Isle of Mull PA72 6JN **Tel:** 01680 300402 (AD) **Tel:** 01680 812487
Restaurants Glenforsa Hotel	**Tel:** 01680 300377 (by AD)
Taxis R Atkinson **Car Hire** Mull Travel	**Tel:** 01680 300441 **Tel:** 01680 812487
Weather Info	AirSc GWC

Operating Hrs	By arrangement
Circuits	Over sea at 800ft QFE
Landing fee	Available on request with PPR
Maintenance **Fuel** James Knight or at Oban	Nil AVGAS 100LL **Tel:** 01680 812475 **Tel:** 01631 710384

ELEVATION	LOCATION	EGBJ			GLOUCESTERSHIRE

ELEVATION	LOCATION				
95ft 3mb	3.5nm W of Cheltenham N5153.65.W00210.03	HON 113.65	220	33.5	••••/−−−/−•
		CPT 114.35	310	42.6	−•−•/•−−•/−
		BCN 117.45	081	42.1	−•••/−•−•/−•

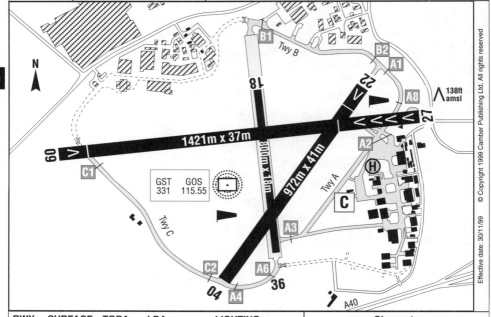

RWY	SURFACE	TORA	LDA	LIGHTING
04	Asphalt	972	972	APAPI 4.5° LHS
22	Asphalt	972	895	APAPI 3.5° LHS
09	Asphalt	1279	1161	Thr Rwy PAPI 3° LHS PAPI 5.3° RHS
27	Asphalt	1345	1027	Ap Thr Rwy PAPI 3.5° LHS 5.3° RHS
18/36	Asphalt	800	800	Nil

Gloucester	
ATIS	127.475
APP	125.65
RAD	120.975*
VDF	125.65 122.90
TWR	122.90
FIRE	121.60
*RAD not continuously manned	
NDB	GST 331**
DME	GOS 115.55***
**on A/D range 25nm	
***Co-located with NDB	

Remarks

PPR at all times for instrument training. Non-radio ACFT not accepted. Permission to use the AD outside scheduled hours to be obtained from ATC. T/O on Rwy09 or Rwy27 climb on Rwy heading to 1500ft QFE before turning. APP will only provide AFIS to ACFT within 10nm of AD & only if traffic conditions permit. VFR ACFT outside this parameter are requested not to call Gloster. Visual aids to location: lbn Green GO. **Noise:** Rwy18, turn left 20° after departure. Rwy27 turn right 10° on crossing upwind end of Rwy to avoid housing estate, a left turn can be made after passing 700ft QFE.

Warnings

The S Twy between Rwy09 & 04 Thr is edge-marked white reflective discs. The entry/exit curves to the Rwys are marked by green reflective studs. Due to extensive standing water Rwy04/22 may not be usable after periods of heavy/prolonged rain.

Operating Hrs

Mon-Fri 0730-1830 Sat-Sun 0800-1830 (Summer)
Mon-Fri 0830-1930 Sat-Sun 0900-1800 (Winter)
and by arrangement

Circuits

04/09/18 LH 22/27/36 RH
fixed wing above 1000ft QFE Heli 750ft QFE max

Landing fee	£12 up to 1.5MT inc.VAT £7.05 inc.VAT with +40ltrs fuel uplift
Maintenance Fuel	Available. Also limited hangerage AVGAS 100LL AVTUR JET A1
Operator	Gloucestershire Airport Ltd Gloucestershire Aerodrome Cheltenham, Gloucestershire GL51 6SR **Tel:** 01452 857700 **Fax:** 01452 715174
Restaurants	Refreshments and Club facilities at A/D
Taxis	
Associated Taxis **Tel:** 01242 523523	
Car Hire	
National	**Tel:** 01452 421133
Weather Info	M T9 Fax 288 A BNMC

ELEVATION	LOCATION	GREAT MASSINGHAM				
295ft 10mb	10nm E of Kings Lynn N5246.73.E00040.35					
PPR	**Diversion AD**	**BKY 116.25**	**029**	**52.0**	— • • • / — • / — • — —	

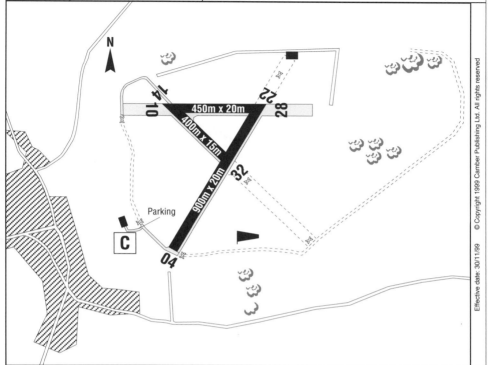

RWY	SURFACE	TORA	LDA	LIGHTING
04/22	Concrete	900x20	U/L	Nil
10/28	Concrete	450x20	U/L	Nil
14/32	Concrete	400x15	U/L	Nil

	Non radio
LARS	**Marham 124.15**

Remarks
PPR by telephone, non-radio ACFT not accepted. WW II AD. Radio contact with Marham essential (when open) due to proximity to Marham MATZ. No signals square. Avoid overflying Great Massingham and other local villages. ACFT parking next to hangar at SW corner of AD. Visiting pilots requested to complete movements book in control hut adjacent to hangar. No training flights permitted.

Warning
Agricultural operations may temporarily block Rwys. Caution; pedestrians – perimeter track is a public footpath.

Operator	OC Brun, Great Massingham Airfield Great Massingham, Kings Lynn, Norfolk **Tel:** 01485 520257 **Fax:** 01485 520234
Restaurants	
Taxis Geoff's Taxis Silverlink **Car Hire**	**Tel:** 01553 772616 **Tel:** 01485 520938
Weather Info	AirS BNMC

Operating Hrs	SR-SS
Circuits	04 RH 22 LH
Landing fee	Singles £5.00 Multi £10.00
Maintenance **Fuel**	Nil Nil

G

ELEVATION	LOCATION				GREAT ORTON

ELEVATION	LOCATION	
234ft 7mb	5nm WSW of Carlisle N5452.53 W00304.58	DCS 115.20 050 13 – •• / – • – • / •••
PPR		

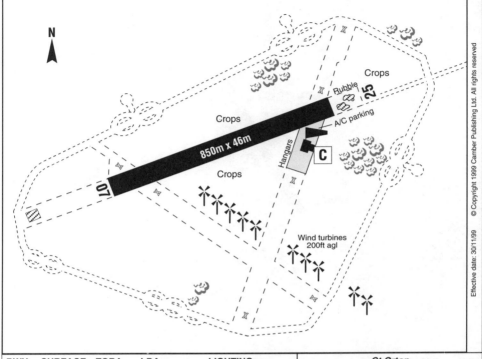

850m x 46m

Effective date: 30/11/99

RWY	SURFACE	TORA	LDA	LIGHTING
07/25	Concrete	850x46	U/L	Nil

Gt.Orton

A/G　　　　**129.825***
Microlight common freq
Which is also used by
Kirkbride 2.5nm to E

Remarks
PPR by telephone. WW II AD all other portions of the manouevering area are not suitable for ACFT use. Visitors welcome at pilots own risk. AD used for Microlight and Gyroplane training.

Warnings
Large wind turbines up to 200ft agl on N edge of disused Rwy13/31.

Operator	Great Orton Solway Light Aviation Ltd
	Tel: 017684 83859 (Roger Savage) **E-mail**: rogsavage@aol.com
Restaurants	Nil
Taxis/Car Hire	Nil
Weather Info	AirN MWC

Operating Hrs	SR-SS
Circuits	Join overhead at 1500ft 25 LH 800ft QFE, 07 LH 500ft QFE
Landing Fee	On application
Maintenance	Nil Residential or temporary hangarage available
Fuel	MOGAS by arrangement only

ELEVATION	LOCATION	GREENLANDS (Emlyn's Field)

ELEVATION	LOCATION
588ft 19mb	4nm WSW of Holywell N5317.40 W00319.50
PPR	

WAL 114.10   232   10.5   • – – / • – / • – • •

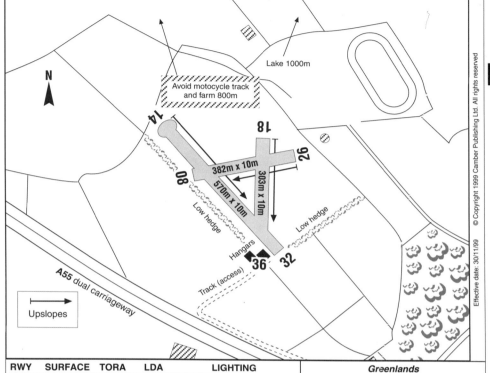

Effective date: 30/11/99

G

Lake 1000m

Avoid motocycle track and farm 800m

14

18

26

80

382m x 10m

570m x 10m

303m x 10m

Low hedge

Low hedge

N

36

32

Hangars

Track (access)

A55 dual carriageway

Upslopes

RWY	SURFACE	TORA	LDA	LIGHTING
14/32	Grass	570x10	U/L	Nil
08/26	Grass	382x10	U/L	Nil
18/36	Grass	303x10	U/L	Nil

Upslope on Rwy14/26/18 Rwy14 Thr marked with red square

Greenlands

A/G	129.825*, 129.975**

*Microlight common
frequency please make
Blind calls Also used by Gliders
**Glider common frequency

Remarks
PPR by telephone. Microlights operate from AD. Visiting ACFT welcome at pilots own risk. Aid to location-small lake to N and A55 dual carriageway to S. Windsock occasionally displayed on S AD boundary.

Warnings
AD is convex, this may cause turbulence/roll-over on approaches. Noise: Avoid overflight of local habitation, particularly the Farmhouse & Motorcycle track 800m N of AD.

Operator	Mr Richard Jones

Rhedyn, Coch, Rhuallt, St.Asaph, Denbighshire LL17 0TT
Tel: 01745 584051

Restaurant/Accommodation
Travellers Inn   **Tel:** 01352 720251 (200m from the AD)

Taxi/Car Hire	Nil
Weather Info	AirN MWC

Operating Hrs	SR-SS
Circuits	Overhead join circuits to N at 500ft QFE
Landing Fee	Nil
Maintenance	Nil
Fuel	MOGAS provided in cans by prior arrangement

Effective date: 30/11/99

ELEVATION	LOCATION	**EGJB**		**GUERNSEY**

ELEVATION	LOCATION		
336ft 11mb	2.5nm WSW of St Peter Port N4926.10.W00236.12	GUR 109.4 On A/D	– – • / • • • / • – •
PPR	**Diversion AD**	JSY 112.20 307 25.3	• – – – / • • • / – • – –

G

- N
- GUR 109.40
- ILS I-UY 108.10
- ILS I-GH 108.10
- 60
- 1463m x 45m
- 27
- C
- B
- East Link
- A2
- A1
- (H)
- D1 D2
- Aero Club
- West grass parking
- C
- South grass parking

RWY	SURFACE	TORA	LDA	LIGHTING
09	Asphalt	1453	1453	Ap Thr Rwy PAPI 3° LHS
27	Asphalt	1463	1453	Ap Thr Rwy PAPI 3° LHS

Remarks

Use governed by regulations applicable to Channel Islands CTR. IMC flight to Guernsey by ACFT not equipped with ADF or VOR is by prior permission only. All ACFT visiting Guernsey are required to have third party liability insurance cover of at least £500 000. Proof of this insurance should be available for inspection whilst the ACFT is at Guernsey Airport. Model ACFT flying at Chouet Headland takes place up to 400ft amsl on any day of the year during daylight hours. All training must be booked in advance with ATC **Tel:** 01481 237766 Ext. 2130. Light ACFT grass parking to W of control TWR. Terminal building pedestrian access via path on S edge of grass parking area. **Not** across W apron. **Noise:** 09/27 climb straight ahead thru 1500ft agl before turning on course.

Warnings

Flight is not permitted at a height of less than 2000ft agl within 3nm of N4952.83 W00221.67 on the island of Sark except with the permission of the States Board of Administration. All ACFT are to avoid over flying the Princess Elizabeth hospital (3.5nm ENE of the AD) at less than 1000ft agl. Light ACFT grass parking areas on the W side of the control TWR. All chocks and picketing blocks should be removed to the edge of the parking area after use. Downdraught or turbulence may be experienced on APP to either Rwy in strong winds from any direction due to local terrains cliffs and valleys. Landing Rwy27 in strong SE-SW winds, buildings induce turbulence & windshear. All aircrew & passengers must carry a means of identification to gain access airside. Due to coastal location birds are a hazard most of year, particularly during migration season.

	Guernsey
ATIS	109.40*
APP	128.65
RAD	118.90 124.50
VDF	128.65 124.50
TWR	119.95
GND	121.80
	*ATIS: ON GUR VOR
VOR/DME	GUR 109.40
ILS	I-UY 108.10 Rwy09
ILS	I-GH 108.10 Rwy27
NDB	GRB 361** range 30nm
	**GRB 093/1.08 to Thr09

Operating Hrs
0515-2000 (Summer)
0615-2100 (Winter) and by arrangement.

Circuits   700ft QFE

Landing fee
£8.30 per 1000kgs or part thereof
(flights over 55nm)
£6.75 per 1000kgs or part thereof
(flights over 55nm)
£5.25 per1000kgs or part thereof (local flights)
Fuel uplift discounts – Single £6.00 Twin £12

Maintenance
ACFT Servicing (Guernsey) **Tel:** 01481 265750
Fuel AVGAS 100LL AVTUR JET A1

Operator	States of Guernsey Airport Guernsey, Channel Isles **Tel:** 01481 237766 **Fax:** 01481 239595
Restaurant	Buffet at Terminal
Taxis Harlequin	**Tel:** 01481 239511
Car Hire Avis Europcar	**Tel:** 01481 235266 **Tel:** 01481 237638
Cycle Hire Rentabike W Coast	**Tel:** 01481 249311 **Tel:** 01481-253654
Weather Info	M T9 Fax 292 A JER

Guernsey Control Zone

Unless otherwise authorised, a pilot who intends to fly in the Guernsey CTR must:

1. Contact Jersey Zone for entry into the Channel Islands Control Zone, giving details of the ACFT position, level and track.
2. Obtain permission for the flight.
3. Maintain a listening watch on the appropriate frequency.
4. Comply with any instructions from ATC.
5. An ACFT shall not fly below 2000ft within 5nm of the AD, unless permission has been obtained.
6. SSR transponder equipment is mandatory within the Channel Islands Control Zone.
7. In the event of radio failure the pilot should leave the Control Zone by maintaining track 225° T from overhead Guernsey Airport at 2000ft.
8. A VFR lane is established between GUR & ALD for traffic routing between the airports. The lane is 5nm either side of a line joining the airports, with a maximum alt of 2000ft, subject to ATC clearance.

G

Channel Island Visual Reference Points

VRP	VOR/DME
Alderney NDB N4942.53 W00211.98	JSY 353°/30nm, GUR 048°/23nm, SAM 209°/82nm
Cap de la Hague N4943.00 W00156.00	JSY 012°/30nm, GUR 061°/31nm, SAM 202°/78nm
Carteret Lighthouse N4922.00 W00148.00	JSY 052°/13nm, GUR 102°/32nm
Casquets Lighthouse N4943.00 W00222.00	JSY 341°/33nm, GUR 033°/19nm, SAM 213°/84nm
Cap de Flamanville N4931.00 W00153.00	JSY 024°/19nm, GUR 084°/28nm
Corbiere Lighthouse N4911.00 W00215.00	JSY 258°/8nm, GUR 142°/21nm, DIN 353°/36nm
E of Iles Chausey N4853.00 W00139.00	JSY 147°/26nm, GUR 136°/50nm, DIN 048°/25nm
Granville N4850.00 W00139.00	JSY 150°/28nm, GUR 138°/52nm, DIN 053°/22nm
Ile de Brehat N4851.00 W00300.00	JSY 244°/44nm, GUR 208°/39nm, DIN 292°/40nm
Miniquiers N4857.00 W00208.00	JSY 197°/17nm, GUR 153°/35nm DIN 358°/22nm
N E Point (of Guernsey) N4930.42 W00230.52	JSY 318°/25nm, GUR 045°/5.6nm N4930.48 W00230.43
St Germain N4914.00 W00138.00	JSY 091°/16nm, GUR 112°/40nm, DIN 028°/42nm
S E Corner (of Jersey) N4910.00 W00202.00	JSY 176°/3nm, GUR 130°/28nm, DIN 007°/35nm
W of Minquiers N4857.00 W00218.00	JSY 216°/19nm, GUR 162°/32nm, DIN 343°/23nm

ELEVATION	LOCATION	**EGBO**				**HALFPENNY GREEN**

ELEVATION	LOCATION		
293ft 10mb	5nm E by S of Bridgenorth N5231.05.W00215.58	**HON 113.65** 300 24.0	•••• / − − − / − •
PPR		**TNT 115.70** 220 38.3	− / − • / −

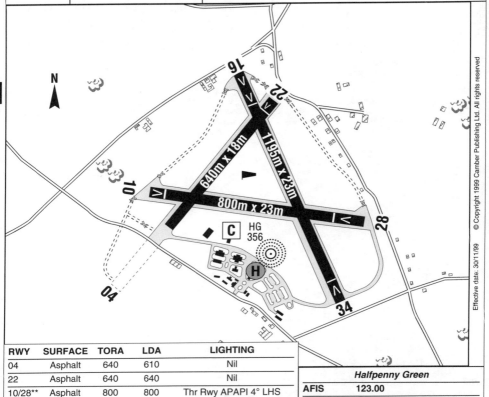

RWY	SURFACE	TORA	LDA	LIGHTING
04	Asphalt	640	610	Nil
22	Asphalt	640	640	Nil
10/28**	Asphalt	800	800	Thr Rwy APAPI 4° LHS
16	Asphalt	1104	1000	Rwy* LITAS 4.25°
34	Asphalt	1082	1000	Rwy*

*Portable lighting
**Additional starter extn 120x33m available at either end

	Halfpenny Green
AFIS	123.00
NDB	**HG 356**
on A/D range 10nm	

Remarks

PPR. Microlights not accepted. Excess charges levied against ACFT landing without permission from operator. Rwy16/34 closed to all traffic PH's, from end scheduled hrs Sun to 0900 Tue, also closed November/December after scheduled hrs Fri to 0900 Sun, due to markets. Non-radio ACFT will not be accepted on these days. Rwy34 not available to ACFT required to use a runway licensed for landing at night. Pilots are responsible for their passengers whilst airside at this airport. AD not available for use by microlight ACFT. Visual aids to location: Abn White flashing. IBn flashing green HG.

Warnings

Twy adjacent control TWR, semi width restricted 13m N side &14.5m S side. Helicopters circuits RH 800ft QFE, joining ACFT keep above 1300ft QFE deadside. Rwy10/28 lighting outside hrs for police ops. only.

Operating Hrs   0800-1630 (Summer)
0900-1730 or SS (Winter) and by arrangement

Circuits

Landing Fee

Singles (up to 2500 lbs) £13.00/£15 at weekends others on application. Fixed wing half price with fuel uplift. Surcharge for landing out of hrs. Helis free with fuel uplift

Maintenance
MAM   **Tel: 01384 221302**
Fuel   AVGAS 100LL AVTUR JET A1
         Oil W80 W100.80 100 by arrangement

Operator   Bobbington Estates Ltd
Halfpenny Green Aerodrome, Bobbington, Stourbridge
W Midlands DY7 5DY
Tel: 01384 221350 (Admin) Tel: 01384 221378 (ATC)
Fax: 01384 221514 (ATC)
Tel: 0800 600 900 (Talking pages A/D details)

Restaurants   High Flyers in TWR - 0900-1730 7day

Taxis	
Albro	**Tel: 01902 22525**
3Cs	**Tel: 01384 77772**
Car Hire	
Europcar	**Tel: 01902 453544**

Weather Info   AirCen MWC

ELEVATION	LOCATION		
370ft 12mb	3.5nm SE of Aylesbury N5147.55.W00044.27	**BNN 113.75** 305 8.0 – • • • / – • / – •	
PPR MILITARY		**CPT 114.35** 050 25.5 – • – • / • – – • / –	

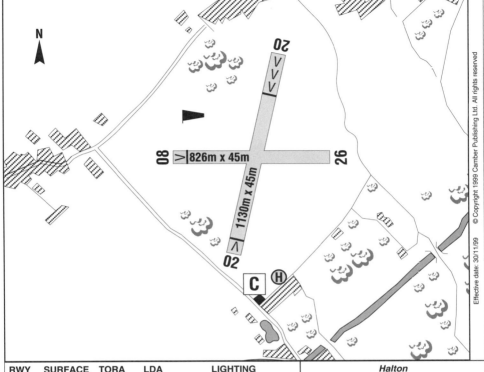

826m x 45m
1130m x 45m

RWY	SURFACE	TORA	LDA	LIGHTING		*Halton*	
02	Grass	1130	1100	Nil	**APP**	**Luton 129.55**	
20	Grass	1130	840	Nil	**A/G**	**130.425***	
08	Grass	826	762	Nil		***If no contact transmit**	
26	Grass	826	826	Nil		**intentions blind and**	

Rwys have white sideline markers

*If no contact transmit intentions blind and proceed with caution

Remarks

PPR 24Hrs notice required. Pilots of visiting ACFT should obtain a briefing on arrival procedure by telephone. Light ACFT may operate daily. Avoid over-flying hospital 1.5nm S of AD. Inbound ACFT will be requested to route via LAKES VRP (2nm NE) Rwy20/26 or TERRICK VRP (2nm SW) Rwy02/08 min height 1500ft QFE.

Warnings

Unmarked obstacles protrude through the 1 in 25 APP plane on all approaches (cables up to 1500ft QFE), consult AD. Intensive motor and winch gliding the AD is divided into powered ACFT and glider areas by a line of markers.

Maintenance	Nil
Fuel	Nil

Operator	RAF Halton, Aylesbury Buckinghamshire HP22 5PG

Tel: 01296 623535 Ext.6367/6211 (PPR 0800-1700, Mon-Fri) Ext. 6409/6178 (PPR Sat, Sun & PH)
Tel: 01296 622697 (Halton Flying Club)
PPR compulsory thru RAF

Restaurants

Taxis/Car Hire

Weather Info	AirCen BNMC

VRP's
Lakes	N5148.60 W00040.97
Terrick	N5145.97 W00047.14

Operating Hrs	Mon-Fri 0700-1900 or SS (Summer) Winter + 1Hr

Circuits	20/26 RH 02/08 LH 1000ft QFE

no overhead/deadside joins. Gliders operate mirror circuit

Landing fee	£7.56 +VAT per 500kgs & £8.50 insurance

H

ELEVATION	LOCATION	HANLEY (Hanley William)

ELEVATION	LOCATION
645ft 21mb	12nm W of Worcester N5217.98.W00228.22
PPR	**Diversion AD**

HON 113.65   269   30   •••• / – – – / – •
BCN 117.45   045   45.3   – ••• / – • – • / – •

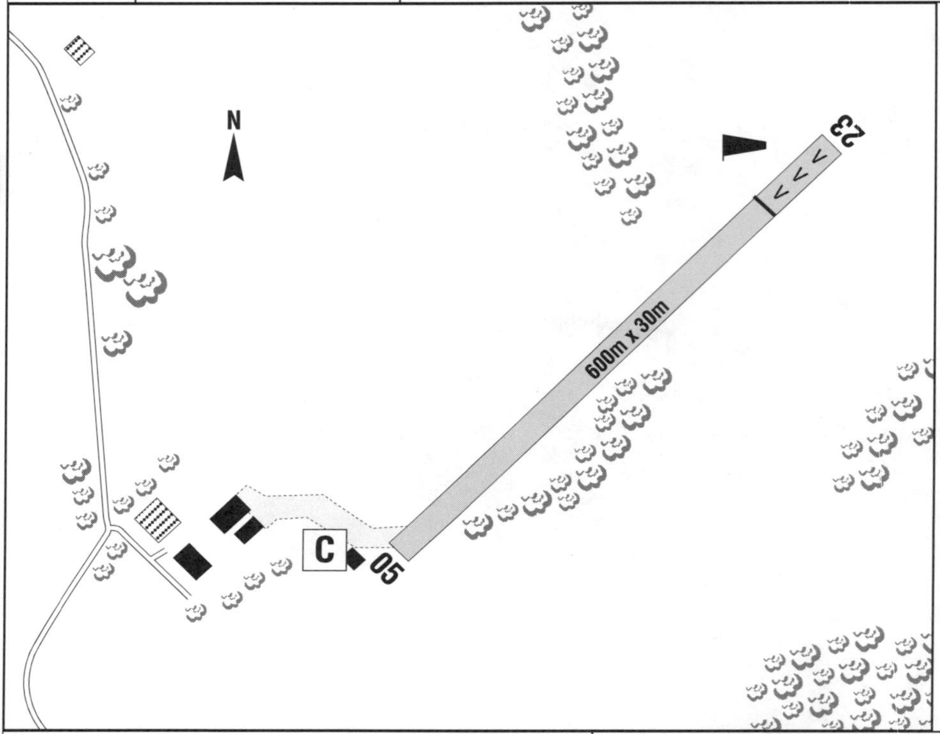

Effective date: 30/11/99

H

600m x 30m

C 05

23

RWY	SURFACE	TORA	LDA	LIGHTING		Non Radio
05/23	Grass	600x30	U/L	Nil		

Rwy23 displaced 100m due to 18% upslope. Displacement end marked by 2 white chevrons

Remarks
PPR by telephone. AD on top plateau with steep upslope E end Rwy. Surface slightly undulating. Considerate visitors welcome at own risk, third party insurance mandatory. Camping/overnight stay available.

Warnings
Strong southerly winds cause turbulence on Rwy23 APP due to local geography. **Noise:** Please be considerate of local habitants, avoid overflying local houses & maintain Rwy centreline on APP/departure.

Operator	Geoff & Angela Bunyan,
Hanley House Farm, Hanley William
Tenbury Wells, Worcestershire WR15 8QT
Tel/Fax: 01886 853410

Restaurants	Light refreshments on site
The Fox Inn	**Tel:** 01886 853219
Tally Ho Inn	**Tel:** 01886 853241
Upper Sapey Golf Club	**Tel:** 01886 853506

Taxis
Swan Cabs	**Tel:** 01584 810310
Car Hire	
Dunley Service Sta.	**Tel:** 01299 827867

Weather Info	AirN MWC

Operating Hrs	0900-SS
Circuits	LH 800ft QFE but can vary (details with PPR)
Landing fee	Donations to hospital charity welcomed
Maintenance **Fuel**	Nil Nil

HARDWICK (Norwich)

ELEVATION	LOCATION				
78ft 00mb	10nm S of Norwich N5228.54.W00119.42	CLN 114.55	012	38	–•–•/•–••/–•
PPR		BKY 116.25	061	54	–•••/–•–/–•––

N
Trees 30ft agl
13
Crops
Crops
1300m x 40m
Crops
Crops
Oaktree
Farm
31

Effective date: 30/11/99

H

RWY	SURFACE	TORA	LDA	LIGHTING
13/31	Concrete	1300x40	U/L	Nil

Non Radio

Remarks
PPR essential. Light ACFT welcome at pilots own risk. ACFT parking/storage available on short or long term basis. All ACFT avoid overflying local villages.

Warnings
Noise: Rwy13 turn left on to heading 100° as soon as practicable after take-off. Rwy31 turn right on to heading 330° as soon as practicable after take-off.

Operating Hrs	SR-SS
Circuits	13 LH 31 RH 1000ft QFE
Landing fee	Nil
Maintenance	Nil
Fuel	Nil

Operator	North London Aviation Supplies Ltd **Tel:** 020 89950 1724 **Fax:** 020 8386 7823
Restaurants	
Taxis/Car Hire	by arrangement
Weather Info	AirS BNMC

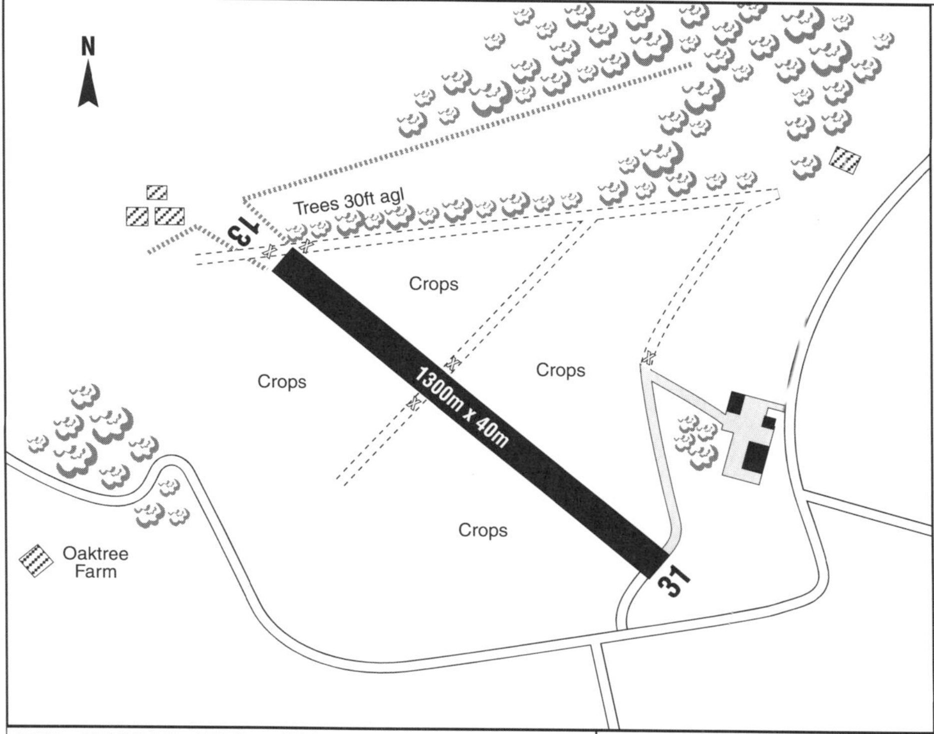

ELEVATION	LOCATION			
155ft 5mb	2nm N of Haverfordwest N5150.02.W00457.63	STU 113.10	170	10.1	••• / – / •• –
PPR	**Diversion AD**	BCN 117.45	284	63.4	– ••• / – • – • / – •

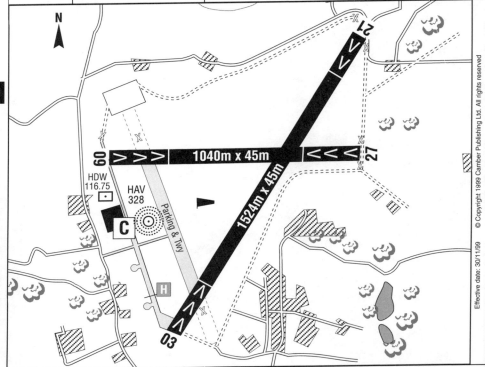

RWY	SURFACE	TORA	LDA	LIGHTING
03	Asphalt	1269	1202	Thr Rwy APAPI 3.5° LHS
21	Asphalt	1262	1269	Thr Rwy APAPI 3.5° LHS
09	Asphalt	1040	800	Nil
27	Asphalt	1010	800	Nil

	Haverfordwest
A/G	122.20
NDB	HAV 328 on A/D range 10nm
DME	HDW 116.75 on A/D

Remarks
AD U/L weekends. Visual aids to location: Ibn HW Green.

Warnings
A third disused Rwy is not available except as a Twy between Rwy04 & 09 Thrs and as an ACFT parking area. Microlight flying takes place on the AD. Microlights to fly RH circuits.

Operator
Pembrokeshire County Council Department Area Office
County Offices, Fishguard Road, Haverfordwest
Dyfed SA62 4BN
Tel: 01437 764551 (Operator)
Tel: 01437 765283 (PPR ATC)
Tel: 01437 760822 (PPR W/E)
Fax: 01437 769246

Restaurants
Hot snacks & drinks (Mon-Fri)

Taxis
Rocky's Taxis   **Tel:** 01437 764822
Car Hire
Days Drive   **Tel:** 01437 760860

Weather Info   AirS BNMC

Operating Hrs   Mon-Fri 0815-1530 (Summer)
Mon-Fri 0915-1630 (Winter)
except PH also by arrangement. PPR weekends

Circuits   LH but microlights RH

Landing fee   Singes £8.00 inc.VAT

Maintenance
Prestige   **Tel:** 01437 766126
Fuel   AVGAS 100LL & Oil. AVTUR JET A1

ELEVATION	LOCATION	EGNR				HAWARDEN

ELEVATION	LOCATION
35ft 1mb	3.5nm WSW of Chester N5310.68.W00258.67
PPR	**Diversion AD**

WAL 114.10	163	13.9	•– –/•–/•–••
MCT 113.55	254	28.0	– –/–•–•/–

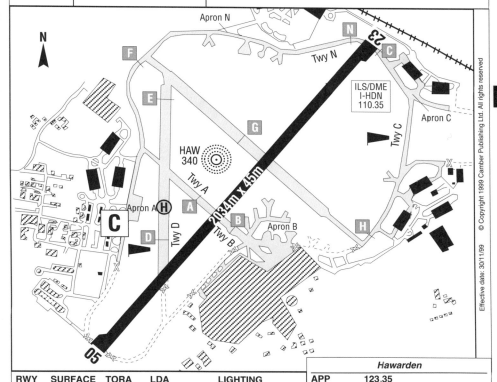

RWY	SURFACE	TORA	LDA	LIGHTING
05	Asphalt/concrete	1962	1662	Ap Thr Rwy PAPI 3.5° RHS
23	Asphalt/concrete	2034	1732	Ap Thr Rwy PAPI 3° LHS

Hawarden	
APP	123.35
RAD	130.25*
VDF	123.35 130.25
TWR	124.95

*SRA only when directed by APP

ILS/DME	Rwy23 I-HDN 110.35
NDB	HAW 340 on A/D range 25nm

Remarks
PPR non-radio ACFT not accepted.
Noise: avoid overflight of local habitation below 1500ft.

Warnings
Test flying takes place (including outside promulgated hours of ATC). Pilots are reminded of the proximity of Restricted Area R311, 5nm N of the AD. compass deviation likely on new portion Rwy05/23 due steel reinforcement. Glider activity at Sealand 3nm NNE weekends up to 3000ft agl.

Maintenance	Hawarden Air Services Tel: 01244 538568
Fuel	AVGAS 100LL AVTUR JET A1 By prior arrangement only
Operator	Bae (Airbus Division) Hawarden Airport Broughton, Clwyd, N Wales CH4 OBA **Tel:** 01244 522012 (ATC) 522013 (PPR) **Fax:** 01244 523035

Restaurants

Taxis
Airport Service	**Tel:** 01244 346550
Abbey Taxis	**Tel:** 01244 311804
Dee Cars	**Tel:** 01244 671671

Car Hire
Avis Rent-a-Car	**Tel:** 01244 311463
National	**Tel:** 01244 390008

Weather Info   M T9 MWC

Operating Hrs
Mon-Fri 0700-1800 Sat-Sun 0830-1500 (Summer)
Mon-Fri 0800-1900 Sat-Sun 0930-1600 (Winter)

Circuits	05 RH, 23 LH, 1000ft QFE
Landing fee	Up to 1500kgs £15 inc.VAT 1500-2000kgs £20.00 +VAT

ELEVATION	LOCATION			
11ft 0mb	12.5nm E of Doncaster N5329.42 W00049.79			
PPR		GAM 112.80 026 14 OTR 113.90 248 28	– – • / • – / – – – – – / – / • – •	

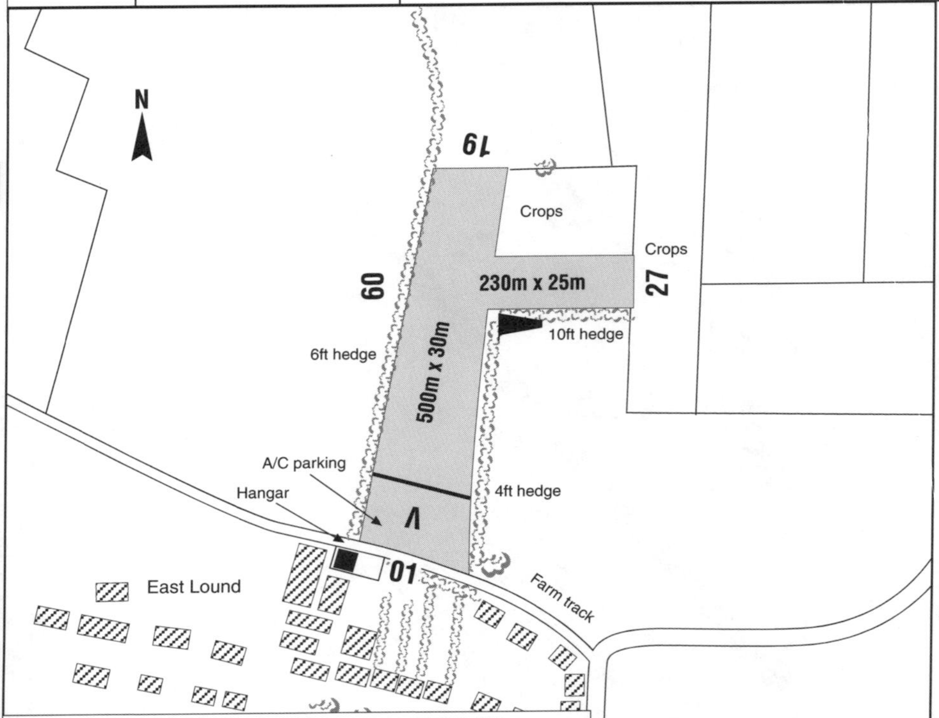

H

RWY	SURFACE	TORA	LDA	LIGHTING
01	Grass	500	400	Nil
19	Grass	400	500	Nil
27/09*	Grass	230x25	Nil	

All Rwy U/L Dimensions calculated by operator.
Displaced Thr is to avoid houses & trees on Rwy01 short final
*Rwy09 not available for takeoff or landing.

Non Radio

LARS (Waddington) 127.35

Remarks **PPR essential by telephone**	
Warnings Please avoid very low overflight of houses on short final Rwy01 both on approach Rwy01 or departing Rwy19. AD slightly undulating. Rwy09 not available for takeoff or landing. Avoid obstructing the farm track which crosses the extreme S edge of AD. Windsock in corner of hedge at junction of Rwy27/09-01/19. Noise: Avoid overflying local villages.	

Operator	Mr J D Bingham, Haxey Airfield East Lound, Doncaster Tel: 01427 752291
Restaurant	Nil
Taxi/Car Hire	Nil
Weather Info	AirN MCW

Operating Hrs	SR-SS
Circuits	Overhead join 01 LH 19/27 RH
Landing Fee	Nil
Maintenance Fuel	Nil Nil

HAYDOCK PARK (Newton-le-Willows)

ELEVATION	LOCATION				
80ft 2mb	4nm NNW of Warrington N5328.53.W00237.30	MCT 113.55	302	14.8	– – / – • – • / –
PPR		WAL 114.10	082	18.4	• – – / • – / • – • •

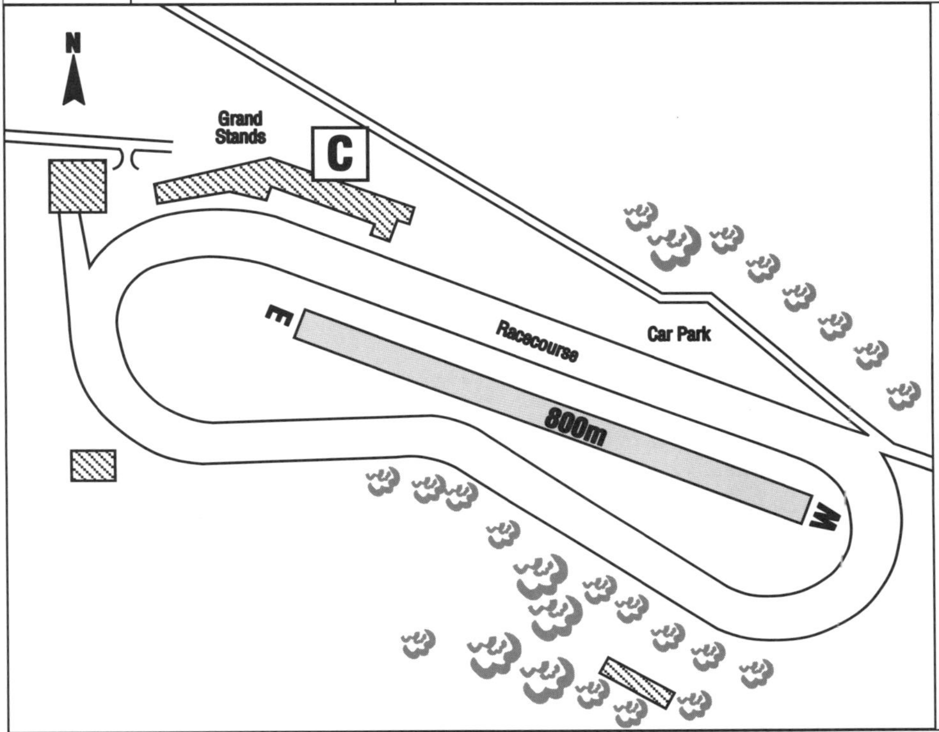

H

RWY	SURFACE	TORA	LDA	LIGHTING
E/W	Grass	800	U/L	Nil

	Non-radio
APP	Manchester 119.40
ATIS	Manchester 128.175

Remarks
PPR essential. AD situated in the Low Level Route within the Manchester CTR. Primarily for use on racedays when all landings must be made half an hour before the first race. Light ACFT may be accepted on non racedays at pilot's own risk. Windsock displayed on racedays and when given sufficient prior notice. Limited helicopter servicing on race days.

Warnings
Care should be taken over rough GND, particularly at each end of Rwy. Parascending on own racedays.

Operator	The Haydock Park Racecourse Ltd Newton-Le-Willows Merseyside WA12 0HQ

Tel: 01942 725963 Ext.208 (0900-1700 Mon-Fri)
Fax: 01942 270879

Restaurants

Taxis/Car Hire

Weather Info	AirCen MWC

Operating Hrs	Available on request
Circuits	
Landing fee	Light ACFT £10.00 plus VAT Nil on racedays
Maintenance	Limited helicopter facilities race days
Ground Zero	**Tel:** 0161 799 6967
Fuel	Helicopter fuel available on race days

ELEVATION	LOCATION				
170ft 5mb	4nm N of Hitchin N5201.17.W00018.10	BKY 116.25	282	13.5	$-\bullet\bullet\bullet/-\bullet-/-\bullet--$
PPR					

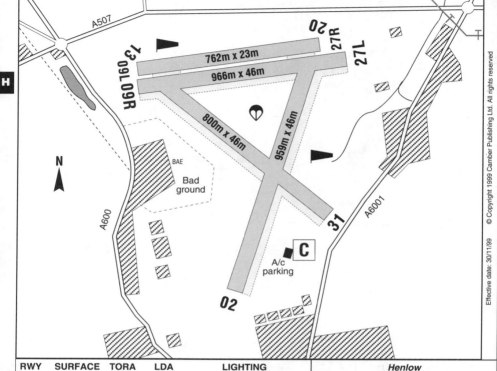

RWY	SURFACE	TORA	LDA	LIGHTING
02/20	Grass	959	959	Nil
09L/27R	Grass	762	762	Nil
09R/27L	Grass	966	966	Nil
13/31	Grass	800	800	Nil

Rwys have white edge markings

Henlow

APP	Luton 129.55
A/G	121.10*

* If no contact transmit normal calls blind & proceed with caution

Remarks

PPR 48 Hrs notice by telephone. Civil flying training organisation operating on an RAF AD. Visitors PPR O.C. flying, or station duty officer 48hrs beforehand and must obtain arrival briefing from flying club. **Arrivals** Std OH join. During gliding route via local VRPs: Blue Lagoon 140m/2.25nm (brick pit with blue water). Chicksands 300m/2.5nm (Aerial farm NW edge Shefford). Water TWR 060m/3.5nm (light concrete structure). **Departures** Normal procedure except:Rwy02 No left turns before 700ft QFE. Rwy31 at 300ft QFE, turn left, track 295m until clear of ATZ.

Warnings

considerable ATC flying, some model ACFT flying & free-fall parachuting. Grass area consolidated with metal tracking that protrudes in places, remain within Rwys & Twys. Do not overfly the BAE complex or AD rifle range.

Maintenance	Nil
Fuel	AVGAS 100LL
Operator	RAF Henlow Bedfordshire **Tel:** 01462 851515 Ext.7432 (PPR) **Tel:** 01462 851936 (flying club)
Restaurant	Cafe & pub food in Henlow village
Taxis/Car Hire	By arrangement
Weather Info	AirCen BNMC

Operating Hrs	0830-SS daily (Local)
Circuits	LH except 13 (RH) & 27R (variable) 1000ft QFE
Landing fee	£7.56 per 500kgs + VAT & £8.50 insurance

ELEVATION	LOCATION		
184ft 6mb	4.5nm SSE of Wincanton N5059.30 W00221.52 **Diversion AD**	SAM 113.35 278 37.5	••• / • − / − −
		BHD 112.05 057 56	− ••• / •••• / − ••
		BCN 117.45 149 56	− ••• / − • − • / − •

RWY	SURFACE	TORA	LDA	LIGHTING
07/25	Asphalt/Concrete	750x26	U/L	Nil

	Henstridge
A/G	130.25
LARS	Yeovilton APP 127.35

Remarks
Situated close to Yeovilton MATZ panhandle please call Yeovilton APP on 127.35. Visiting ACFT welcome. Rwy07/25 can be identified by the Concrete 'dummy deck' in the middle. All other Rwys are unuseable.

Warnings
Keep a good lookout for high speed military ACFT and high intensity helicopter operations associated with Yeovilton. Caution, Power cables 20ft agl cross 07 final APP 230m from the Thr. There is a fence 50m from the 07 Thr.

Operator	Henstridge Airpark Ltd
	Henstridge Airfield, Somerset BA9 0T
Tel: 01963 364231	
Fax: 01963 364232	
E-mail: wings@henstridge.freeserve.co.uk	
Web: http://www.avnet.co.uk/ktallent/henstridge/	

Restaurant	Hot & cold food available at AD

Taxis	
Honeycomb	**Tel:** 01935 813853
Car Hire	Courtesy car available by arrangement

Weather Info	AirSW BNMC

Operating Hrs
0900-2000 arrivals after 1830 phone for PPR (Summer)
0900-SS (Winter)
and by arrangement (local)

Circuits	N at 800ft QFE
Landing fee	Singles £7 Twins £12
Maintenance	Maintenance and Hangarage available
Fuel	AVGAS 100LL JET A1

ELEVATION	LOCATION				HERMITAGE (Sherborne)

ELEVATION	LOCATION		
325ft 10mb	5nm S of Sherborne Dorset N5051.88.W00229.28	SAM 113.35 268 44 BHD 112.05 058 47.5	•••/•–/–– –•••/••••/–••
PPR			

H

Middlemarsh Common Wood

Pasture

Low angled approach

Hay grass

Dip

Downslope

495m x 22m

Hay grass

Pasture

Parking

Hardy's Copse

Williford House Farm

DO NOT overfly village to SW

DO NOT overfly Hurdley Farm

26

08

RWY	SURFACE	TORA	LDA	LIGHTING			
08/26	Grass	495	450	Nil		**LARS**	*Non-radio* Yeovilton 127.35
U/L AD							

Remarks

PPR by telephone. Private farm strip operated under '28 day rules'. Light single-engine ACFT welome. Sheltered parking & tie down. Many facilities available from the operators & locally see Restaurants. Trout & course fishing in well stocked lakes close to farm.

Warnings

Rwy undulates, high at E and centre, low to W. Trees to N & S at centre section generate slight down rotor in Nerly winds. High GND 1.5nm S rising to 860ft amsl. Rwy08 APP should be offset to the N to avoid trees close to Thr. **Noise:** Do not overfly Hurdley Farm & village to SW (see diagram).

Operator	Mike & Rachel Rudd
	Williford House Farm, Hermitage, Dorchester DT2 7BB
Tel/Fax: 01963 210739	

Restaurants
Snacks by arrangement & en-suite B&B at farmhouse
Camping at farm also choice of local sites

Taxis	Call out from Sherborne (15min)
Car Hire	Loan of car 'at cost' by arrangement to visit places of interest coast & pubs

Weather Info   AirSW BNMC

Operating Hrs	SR-SS
Circuits	Overhead join circuit to N 08 LH 26 RH at 800ft QFE
Landing fee	£3 upkeep contributions appreciated
Maintenance	Nil
Fuel	MOGAS by prior arrangement AVGAS 100LL available at Compton Abbas (073°M/14nm)

ELEVATION	LOCATION				
505ft 17mb	2nm W of Brackley 5201.75.W00112.48	**HINTON IN THE HEDGES**			
PPR	**Diversion AD**	DTY 116.40 BNN 113.75	207 311	9.5 29.8	– • • / – / – • – – – • • • / – • / – •

H

RWY	SURFACE	TORA	LDA	LIGHTING		*Hinton*
06/24	Asphalt	700x18	U/L	Nil	**A/G**	**119.45**

Remarks
PPR by telephone. Visitors welcome Gliding and parachuting daily throughout the year.

Warnings
Rwy06/24 has new surface, strip on N side of original centreline. Gliding and parachuting daily throughout the year. Avoid overflying villages and habitation in vicinity of AD.

Operating Hrs	SR-SS
Circuits	Variable
Landing fee	Donations welcome
Maintenance	Holdcroft Aviation **Tel:** 01295 810287 **Fax:** 01295 812247
Fuel	AVGAS 100LL

Operator	Mr RB Harrison, Walltree House Farm Steane Brackley Nants
	Tel: 01295 811235 (PPR) **Tel:** 01295 812300 (Hinton Skydiving) **Tel:** 01295 811056 (Gliding club) **Tel:** 01295 812775 Flight Training (Tom Eagles) **Fax:** 01295 811147 (owner) **Fax:** 01295 812400 (Hinton Skydiving)
Restaurants	Light refreshments in clubhouse Accomodation available at Walltree Farm on AD
Taxis PJ Cars **Car Hire**	**Tel:** 01280 704330
Weather Info	AirCen BNMC

ELEVATION	LOCATION	EGNA	HUCKNALL
281ft 9mb	5nm NNW of Nottingham N5300.85.W00113.10	TNT 115.70 104 16.5 –/–•/– HON 113.65 028 42.7 ••••/–––/–•	
PPR			

Effective date: 30/11/99

RWY	SURFACE	TORA	LDA	LIGHTING
04/22	Grass	730	730	Nil
11*	Grass	865	776	Nil
29	Grass	776	776	Nil

* Rwy11 89m starter extension available

Hucknall	
A/G	130.80

Remarks
PPR by telephone. Open weekends only to visiting ACFT. This AD is available Saturday and Sunday only. AD is not available for public transport passenger flights required to use a licensed AD.

Warnings
Hard Rwy08/26 is disused. Mast 530ft amsl. 280°T/1.4nm. Mast 530ft amsl. 275°T/1.9nm. Rwy29 Thr low fence.

Operating Hrs Mon-Fri closed to visiting ACFT
Sat-Sun 1000-1800 or SS (Winter)
Sat-Sun 0900-1700 or SS (Summer)

Circuits

Landing fee On application

Maintenance Nil
Fuel AVGAS 100LL
available by prior arrangement only

Operator Merlin Flying Club Rolls Royce Ltd
Aero Division, Hucknall
Nottingham NG15 6EU
Tel: 0115 964 2495/2539

Restaurants Tea & coffee available

Taxis
Streamline **Tel:** 0115 947 3031
Car Hire
National **Tel:** 0115 950 3385

Weather Info AirCen MWC

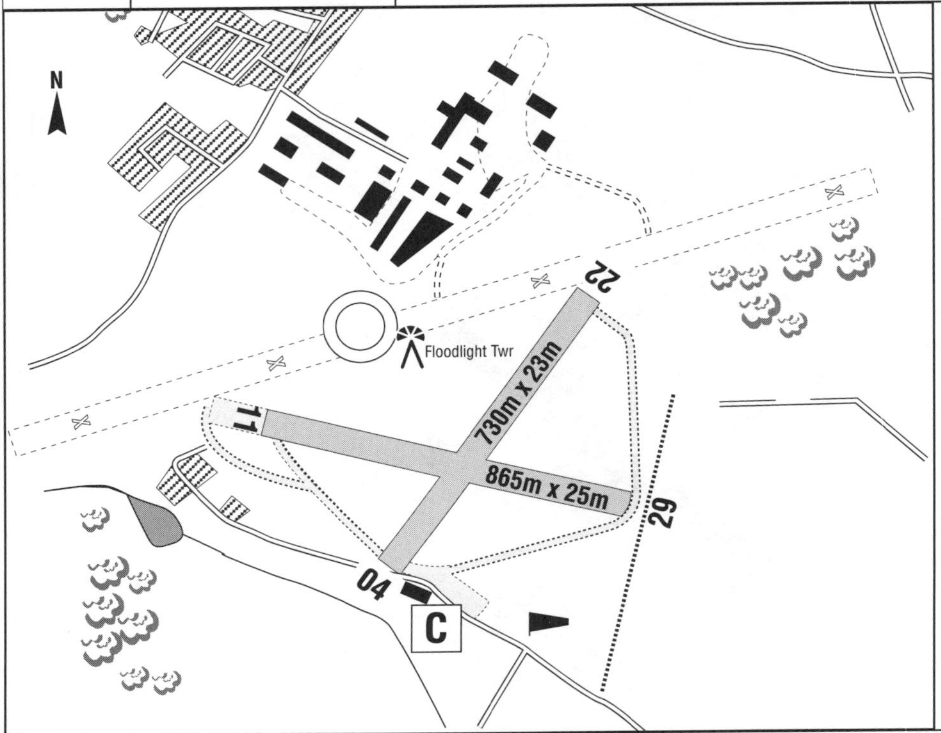

ELEVATION	LOCATION	EGND	HUDDERSFIELD (Crosland Moor)
825ft 28mb	1.5nm of Huddersfield N5337.28 W00149.72		
PPR			

POL	112.10	133	12.2	•– –•/ – – –/ •–••
MCT	113.55	050	22.1	– –/ –•–•/ –
GAM	112.80	308	37.6	– –•/ •–/ – –

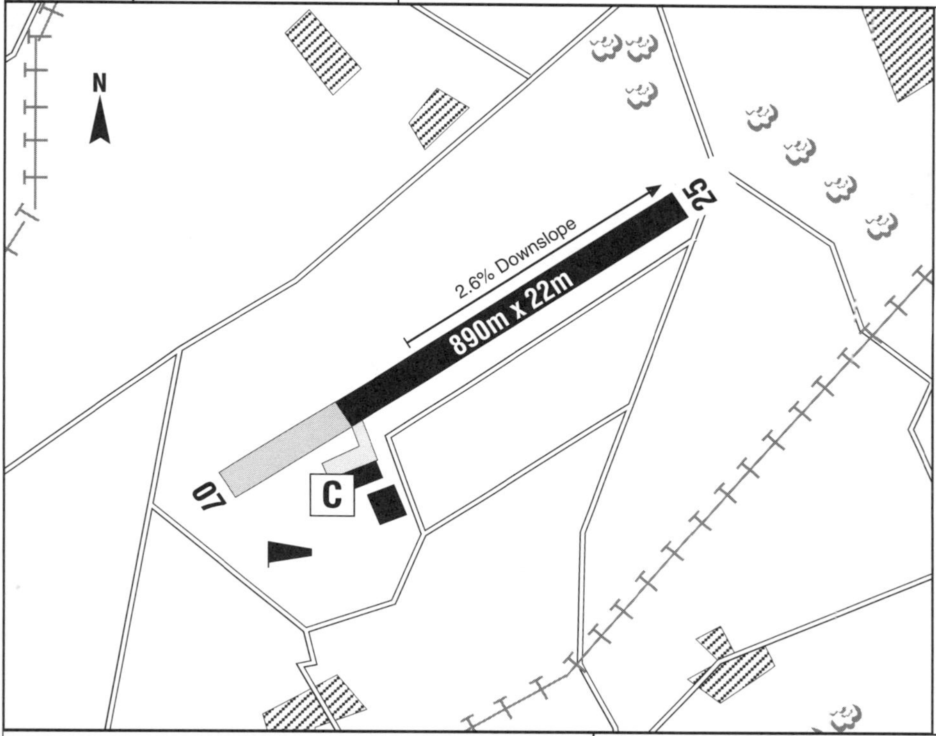

N

↑ N

2.6% Downslope

890m x 22m

25

07

C

Effective date: 30/11/99

H

RWY	SURFACE	TORA	LDA	LIGHTING
07/25	Asph/Grass*	890	890	Nil
*640m asphalt 250m grass				

Huddersfield

A/G	122.20	
	Not usually manned	

Remarks

PPR by telephone. U/L AD. Use restricted to ACFT up to 2730kg AUW. Avoid low flying over houses and hospital 0.5m from Thr of Rwy25. Whenever possible land and take-off of Rwy25. When Rwy25 is in use pilots are advised to land well beyond the Thr.

Warnings

Emley Moor TV mast (concrete) 1924ft amsl 6nm E. Holme Moss TV mast 2490ft amsl 5nm to S. Radio masts 1614ft amsl 2.5nm to NW. Rwy gradient - 2.6% down on Rwy07 from start of asphalt. Possible downdrafts overhead quarry 100m from Thr 25.

Operator	J Witham, Huddersfield Aviation Ltd
	The Airfield, Crosland Moor, Huddersfield HD4 7AG
	Tel: 01484 645784/654473
Restaurants	Refreshments available
Taxis	
GT	**Tel:** 01484 534565
Car Hire	
National	**Tel:** 01484 455050
Europcar	**Tel:** 01484 513353
Weather Info	AirCen MWC

Operating Hrs	SR-SS
Circuits	LH 1000ft QFE
Landing fee	Single £5 twin £10
Maintenance	Nil
Fuel	AVGAS 100LL

HULL (Mount Airy)

ELEVATION	LOCATION				
460ft 15mb	8nm WNW of Hull N5346.30.W00034.62	OTR 113.90	290	17	– – – / – / • – •
PPR		GAM 112.80	029	32	– – • / • – / – –

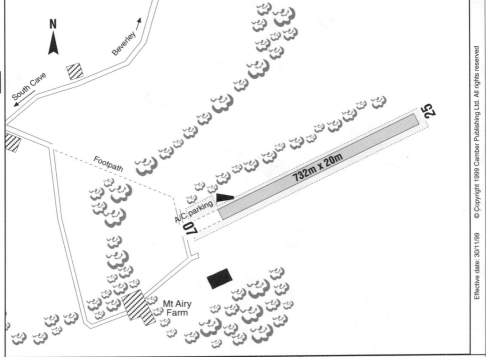

RWY	SURFACE	TORA	LDA	LIGHTING
07/25	Grass	732x20	U/L	Nil

Rwy25 has a 2.3° down gradient

	Non-radio
LARS	Humberside APP 124.675

Remarks
PPR. Visitors welcome at pilots own risk. Pilots of visiting ACFT must obtain a briefing on landing and take-off procedures. This is available by telephone from the AD operator at weekends.

Warnings
Caution, the steeply rising GND and trees on the W boundary produce roll-over which should be anticipated at any time but particularly with strong winds. A public footpath crosses the undershoot of Rwy07, 95 metres short of the Thr. Radio masts 208ft agl are close to the N of 25 APP 1300m from the Thr. Low flying high speed military ACFT may be encountered in the vicinity of the AD. Avoid overflying the village of South Cave which is to the W of the AD.

Operator	N&L May, Mount Airy Farm South Cave, Hull HU15 2BD **Tel:** 01430 422395/422973 (Operator)
Restaurants	Food available in South Cave (1.25nm)

Taxis
Courtesy Car usually available or taxi arranged

Car Hire	
National	**Tel:** 01482 343223

Weather Info	AirN MWC

Operating Hrs	No takeoff before 0800 and after 2000 daily Landings are permitted
Circuits	RH 07 LH 25 at 1000ft QFE
Landing fee	Singles £3 Twins £5 Business use £5
Maintenance Fuel	Can be arranged on a call-out basis Nil

ELEVATION	LOCATION	EGNJ	HUMBERSIDE
122ft 3mb	10nm W of Grimsby N5334.47.W00021.05		

OTR 113.90	235	11.3	− − − / − / • − •
GAM 112.80	055	27.8	− − • / • − / − −

H

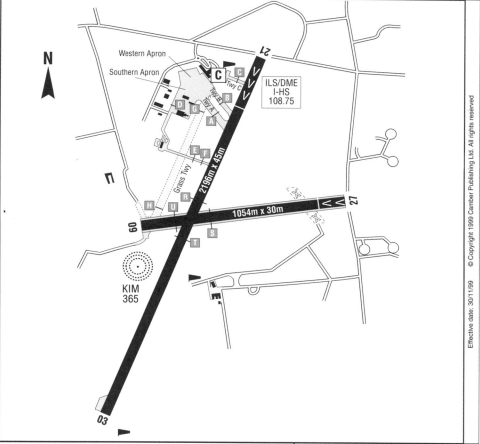

RWY	SURFACE	TORA	LDA	LIGHTING
03	Asphalt/Concrete	2070	2068	Ap Thr Rwy PAPI 3° LHS
21	Asphalt/Concrete	2196	1950	Ap Thr Rwy PAPI 3° LHS
09	Asphalt/Concrete	994	994	Nil
27	Asphalt/Concrete	1034	920	Nil

Humberside	
ATIS	124.125
APP/LARS	124.675
RAD	124.67 123.15
TWR	118.55
FIRE	121.60
NDB	KIM 365*
ILS/DME	I-HS 108.75 Rwy21
*KIM On A/D range 15nm	

Remarks

Non-radio ACFT not accepted. Hi-vis. Training flights subject to ATC approval. Helicopters to land as instructed by ATC. Helicopters operating to and from main apron are to avoid over-flying buildings on the Sern edge of apron. Taxiiway to the light ACFT parking area and maintenance area is routed behind the apron area and marked with a single yellow centreline, exercise caution in this area due to movement of vehicles and personnel. Pilots and passengers of ACFT arriving from foreign countries (including European Union) are to enter the terminal only through the international arrivals hall. Handling Servisair Tel 01652 688491, Fax 01652 688060

Warnings

Avoid rifle range 340°T/1350m from the ARP below 500ft agl. D306 is located at DME range 15.5nm or the extended centreline of Rwy21. ACFT must not establish on the ILS localiser Rwy21 until DME range is 12nm unless ATC advise that D306 is not active. ACFT using Humberside International Airport must carry 3rd party insurance cover of not less than £500,000. Light ACFT pilots should be aware of the possible effect of rotor downwash generated by large helicopters operating through the main apron area.

Operating Hrs
Sun-Fri 0530-2045 Sat 0530-1700 (Summer) Winter + 1Hr
and by arrangement

Landing fee	On application

Maintenance
Bostonair	**Tel:** 01652 680411
Fuel	AVGAS 100LL AVTUR JET A1
	Tel: 01652 682044

Operator	Humberside International Airport Ltd
	Humberside Airport, Kimmington
	Ulceby, S Humberside DN39 6YH
	Tel: 01652 688456 (admin)
	Tel: 01652 682022 (ATC)
	Fax: 01652 680244 (ATC)
	Fax: 01652 680524 (Admin)

Restaurant	Licensed buffet in Terminal

Taxis	Available at Terminal

Car Hire
| Hertz | **Tel:** 01652 688414 |
| Europcar | **Tel:** 01652 680338 |

Weather Info	M T9 Fax 296 A MWC

Visual Reference Points (VRPs)
Immingham Docks	N5337.01 W00010.10
N Tower Humber Bridge	N5342.95 W00027.08
Caistor	N5329.52 W00019.10
Brigg	N5333.07 W00028.10
Laceby Crossroads	N5332.03 W00010.60
Elsham Wolds	N5336.42 W00026.10

ELEVATION	LOCATION	**HUSBANDS BOSWORTH (Rugby)**			
505ft 16mb	8.5nm NE of Rugby N5226.23.W00102.32	HON 113.65	085	23.5	••••/– – –/– •
PPR		DTY 116.40	013	16	– ••/– /– • – –

Sand Quarry

A50

N

Club House

Caravans

Fuel

1

2

4ft fence

10

1200m x 90m

28

Crops

WW2 control twr

(H)

1 West launch point
2 East launch point

H

RWY	SURFACE	TORA	LDA	LIGHTING	**Husbands Bosworth**
10/28	Grass	1200x90	U/L	Nil	**Launch point 129.975**

Remarks
PPR by telephone. Primarily gliding site with winch & aerotow launching. Cables up to 3000ft agl.

Warnings
Use extreme vigilance – intensive gliding. Although launch point may not acknowledge, please make circuit calls. give preference to aerotow ACFT. Concrete track crosses AD. Police helicopter may lift from helipad on old S portion of AD without warning. **Noise:** Dept Rwy28 turn left towards lake & climb to lake before turning on course. Dept Rwy10 turn on course before Sibbertoft village but do not overfly farmhouses E of AD.

Operator	The Soaring Centre
	Husbands Bosworth Airfield, Lutterworth, Leicestershire
	Tel: 01858 880429 (AD)
	Tel: 01858 880521 (Office)
Restaurants	Refreshments & comprehensive accomodation list available at AD. Local B+B's in Sibbertoft village (2 miles)
Mary Hart	**Tel:** 01858 880886
Archway Farmho.	**Tel:** 01858 525623 (Mrs Boulton)
Taxis	
A&B Murphy's	**Tel:** 01858 410210/410776/434935
ACE Cabs	**Tel:** 01858 462233
Weather Info	AirCen MWC

Operating Hrs	SR-SS daily May-Sept W/E only Oct-Apr
Circuits	To south 1000ft QFE
Landing fee	£5
Maintenance	Storey ACFT Servs.**Tel:** 01858 880807
Fuel	AVGAS 100LL by arrangement only

INSCH

ELEVATION	LOCATION				
500ft 17mb	2nm SW of Insch N5718.68.W00238.80	**INS 109.20**	**116**	**47.4**	•• / — • / •••
PPR		**ADN 114.30**	**277**	**12.2**	• — / — •• / — •

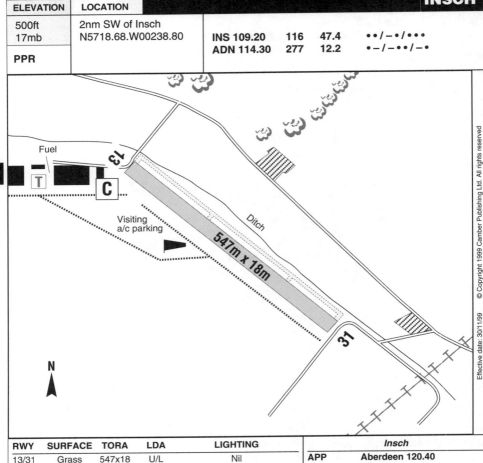

RWY	SURFACE	TORA	LDA	LIGHTING
13/31	Grass	547x18	U/L	Nil

	Insch
APP	**Aberdeen 120.40**
A/G	**129.825**

Remarks
High GND around circuit may cause localised wind effects.
Avoid over-flying Auchleven village 0.5nm E of AD or the
castle to NW. Caution, microlights.

Warnings
Military ACFT avoiding the Aberdeen CTZ tend to overfly.
Pilots are advised to keep a good lookout and call Aberdeen
for traffic information. DO NOT continue if cars are crossing
Rwy31, wait until clear. Power cables 10ft aal 174m before
Rwy31 Thr.

Operator	Ken Wood, Insch Aerodrome Auchleven, Insch Aberdeenshire AB5 6PL **Tel:** 01464 820422 (home) **Tel:** 01464 820003 (AD) **Tel:** 07831 412619 (mobile)
Restaurants	Nil
Taxis/Car Hire	Available through AD
Weather Info	AirSc GWC

Operating Hrs	By arrangement
Circuits	1000ft AGL variable direction for noise abatement
Landing fee	Donation by pilot
Maintenance	Nil
Fuel	AVGAS 100LL by arrangement

ELEVATION	LOCATION	**EGPE**	**INVERNESS**
31ft 1mb **PPR**	7nm NE of Inverness N5732.40.W00403.00		

INS 109.20	On A/D		•• / − • / •••
ADN 114.30	292	59.2	• − / • • / − •
WIK 113.60	218	62.9	• − − / • • / − • −

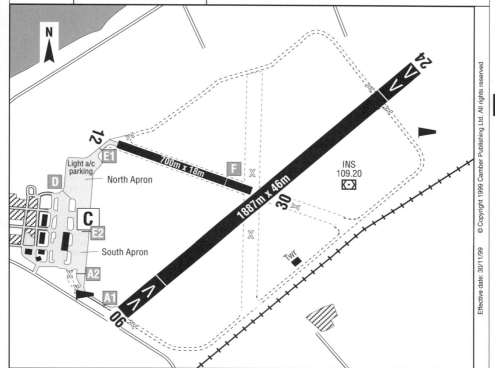

RWY	SURFACE	TORA	LDA	LIGHTING
06	Asphalt	1887	1664	Ap Thr Rwy PAPI 3° LHS
24	Asphalt	1765	1765	Ap Thr Rwy PAPI 3° LHS
12/30	Asphalt	700	700	Nil

	Inverness
APP	**Lossiemouth 119.35**
TWR/	
VDF	**122.60**
FIRE	**121.60**
VOR/DME	**INS 109.20 on A/D**

Remarks
No GND signals except light signals. Lossiemouth provides a RAD service for Inverness traffic.

Warnings
Agricultural work takes place on the grass areas throughout the year. Exercise caution when taxying to hangars No.1 and 2 due to the close proximity of an adjacent security fence. The Twy between the N end of the S apron and Thr12 is available for use only by ACFT with wingspan less than 36m. Use of the Twy between the N and S aprons is limited to ACFT with a wing span of less than 24m. Exercise caution as this AD has a year round deer hazard, particularly around dawn and dusk. Patrols are mounted whenever the presence of deer is known or anticipated, but pilots are requested to report to ATC the location of any animals on the AD. Birds are a constant hazard especially during migration. TV Masts 1074ft amsl 5.6nm to N & 1495ft amsl 8nm to WNW. High GND to S 1500ft. amsl.

Operating Hrs Mon-Fri 0545-2100 (Summer)
Mon-Fri 0645-2200 Sat 0645-1915 Sun 0745-2200 (Winter) and by arrangement

Circuits

Landing fee £10.65 inc VAT ACFT under 3MT VFR cash/cheque on day

Maintenance	Merlin Maintenance **Tel:** 01667 462642
Fuel	AVGAS 100LL (**Tel:** 01667 462664):

0800-1500 (Summer), +1hr (Winter).
JET A1 Mon-Fri 0545-1830, Sat 0545-1800, Sun 0800-1830 (Winter); Daily 0500-1730 (Summer)
Fuel available out of Hrs on payment of surcharge

Operator	HIAL Inverness, Inverness AD
	Invernesshire IV1 2JB
	Tel: 01667 464000/464293 (ATC)

Fax: 01667 462041 (Admin), **Fax:** 01667 462586 (ATC)

Restaurants	Refreshments and Bar

Taxis	Available at the terminal
Car Hire	
AVIS	**Tel:** 01667 462787
Europcar	**Tel:** 01667 462374

Weather Info	M T9 Fax 298 VSc GWC

Visual Reference Points (VRPs)

Invergordon	N5741.53 W00410.05
Lochindorb	N5724.17 W00342.95
Tomatin	N5700.03 W00359.50
Dores	N5722.92 W00419.92
Dingwall	N5735.97 W00425.53

ELEVATION	LOCATION	**EGPI**					**ISLAY**
54ft 2mb	4.5nm NNW of Port Ellen N5540.92.W00615.40		**MAC 116.00**	317	23.7	– – / • – / – • – •	
PPR			**TIR 117.70**	166	53.0	– / • • / • – •	

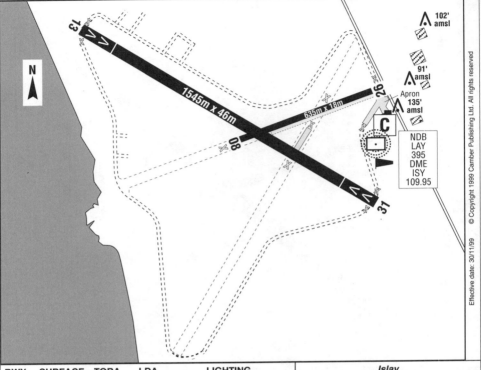

Effective date: 30/11/99

RWY	SURFACE	TORA	LDA	LIGHTING
13	Asphalt	1395*	1245	Ap Thr Rwy APAPI 3° LHS
31	Asphalt	1380	1245	Thr Rwy APAPI 4° LHS
08	Asphalt	635	635	Nil
26	Asphalt	635	575	Nil

*includes unlit 150m starter extension

	Islay
FIS	**Scottish 127.275**
AFIS	**123.15**
NDB	**LAY 395***
DME	**ISY 109.95**
	***on A/D range 20nm**

Remarks
PPR by telephone. Pilots should only call Islay Information when within 10nm radius of the AD and below 3000ft.

Warnings
Do not land short of sterilisation markings. Perimeter track is permanently closed. No GND signals except light signals. Increased numbers of deer can be found on the AD & large flocks of geese in area between Oct & Mar. Rwy26 displaced Thr due being near uncontrolled public road 260ft NE of Rwt13 touchdown point. Uncontrolled public crossing at Rwy31 Thr and 700m from Rwy08 Thr. Do not taxi or park on grass area unless marshalled by AD staff. The grass areas are soft and unsafe only marked Twy to be used.

Operating Hrs
Mon-Fri 0815-1715 Sat 1000-1100 (Summer)
Mon-Fri 0915-1715 Sat 1100-1200 (Winter)
and by arrangement

Landing fee £10.65 inc.VAT ACFT under 3MT VFR cash/cheque on day

Maintenance Nil
Fuel AVGAS 100LL (check availability)

Operator Highlands and Islands Airports Ltd Islay
AD Isle of Islay Argyll PA42 7AS Scotland
Tel: 01496 302361
Fax: 01496 302096

Restaurants
Hot snacks at terminal Restaurants in Port Ellen

Taxis	**Tel:** 01496 302155
Carmichael	**Tel:** 01496 810380
Car Hire	
Mackenzie	**Tel:** 01496 850200
Bowmore Car Hire	**Tel:** 01496 810206
Bike Hire	**Tel:** 01496 302560

Weather Info M* T9 GWC

Visual Reference Points (VRPs)
Mull of Oa	N5535.50 W00620.30
N Coast	N5556.00 W00609.90
Port Ellen	N5538.00 W00611.40
Rhinns Point	N5540.40 W00629.10

ELEVATION	LOCATION	**EGNS**	**ISLE OF MAN (Ronaldsway)**
55ft 2mb	6nm SW of Douglas N5405.00 W00437.45		
PPR			

IOM 112.20	087	4.9	•• / – – – / – –
WAL 114.10	317	67.3	• – – / • – / • – ••

Terminal — Apron — C — Northern Twy — Central Twy — Western Twy — 17 — 21 — 1245m x 46m — 1753m x 46m — Central Twy — Southern Twy — 08 — 15 — 26 — 35 — 03 — 1km x 46m

N

RWY 359

ILS/DME I-RY 110.90

Effective date: 30/11/99

RWY	SURFACE	TORA	LDA	LIGHTING
03	Asphalt	1255	1199	Thr Rwy PAPI 3° LHS
21	Asphalt	1225	1225	App Thr Rwy PAPI 3.5° LHS
08	Asph/Conc	1630	1462	App Thr Rwy PAPI 3° LHS
26	Asph/Conc	1753	1612	Ap Thr Rwy PAPI 3° LHS
17*	Asphalt	903	787	Thr Rwy
35*	Asphalt	-	898	Thr Rwy

*Not available by night for ACFT required to use a licensed AD

	Ronaldsway
APP	120.85
RAD	120.85
	118.2* 125.30*
VDF/	120.85 118.90
TWR	118.90
FIRE	121.60
NDB	CAR 366.5 range 25nm
NDB	RWY 359**
ILS/DME	I-RY 110.90 Rwy26

*RAD: When directed by ATC only
**on A/D range 20nm

Remarks

PPR for non-radio ACFT. Use governed by regulations applicable to the Isle of Man CTR/CTA. Instrument training is subject to prior permission from ATC. Pilots and passengers of private and charter ACFT arriving from or departing to Great Britain, the Republic of Ireland or the Channel Islands must report immediately on arrival and immediately before departure to a Police Examining Officer in the designated security area. As extensions to airport Hrs are frequent, pilots intending to transit the Isle of Man CTR outside published airport Hrs are strongly advised to contact Ronaldsway APP. Pilots of helicopters should APP & land in accordance with ATC instructions. The southern Twy between Rwy03 and Rwy26 is to be used only by light ACFT. A holding bay, situated adjacent to the northern holding point of Rwy26, is available for the use of light ACFT. Pilots should enter this bay when requested by ATC. Light ACFT are to land and take off on the Rwy, no other landing area is available. Rwy35 is not available for take-off. On departure all propeller driven ACFT must climb straight ahead to at least 500ft and must have passed the AD boundary before commencing any turn.

Warnings

No GND signals except light signals. Bird scaring takes place using pyrotechnics. Windshear exists on short final for Rwy08 in SE winds. There is a possibility of turbulence on all Rwys during strong wind conditions. Rwy21: due to high GND to the left of the APP for Rwy21, pilots must establish on the Rwy centreline before descending on the PAPI glidepath. The apron flood lighting to the W of the apron area is 7m from the edge of the useable paved apron area. If self parking in this area exercise extreme caution in respect of wingtip clearance. Marshaller available on request. Pilots must ensure that ACFT are operated in a manner calculated to cause the least disturbance practicable in areas surrounding the airport, particularly near Castletown.

Operating Hrs
Mon-Sat 0515-1945 Sun 0600-1945 (Summer)
Mon-Sat 0615-2045 Sun 0700-2045 (Winter)
and by arrangement

Circuits

Landing fee
£12.44 up to 1999kgs, £24.89 2000-3000kgs
+VAT (cash on day)

Maintenance   Woodgate Aviation
Hangerage by arrangement with local companies
Fuel   AVGAS 100LL AVTUR JET A1
Oil Grades W100 W80 Facilities available between 0700-2030
local & by arrangement with Manx Petroleums
Tel: 01624 821681

Operator
The Isle of Man Department of Transport-Airports Division
Isle of Man Airport, Ballasalla, Isle of Man IM9 2AS
Tel: 01624 821600 (Airport)
Tel: 01624 821625 (FBU)
Tel: 01624 821642 (MET)
Fax: 01624 821611 (Airport)
Fax: 01624 821627 (ATC)
Fax: 01624 821626 (FBU)
Fax: 01624 821646 (MET)

Restaurants   Buffet and bar at terminal
La Rosette Ballasalla, Silverburn Lodge, Ballasalla

Taxis   Available at terminal
Car Hire
Athol Car Hire   Tel: 01624 822481
Mylchreests   Tel: 01624 823533

Weather Info   M T9 Fax 322 VN IOM

**The Isle of Man Control Zone (CTR) & Control Area (CTA)
are notified as Class D Airspace**
Normal CTA/CTR Class D Airspace rules apply
SVFR within the zone in IMC or night will be given subject to
traffic conditions.

Visual Reference Points (VRPs)

VRP	VOR/NDB	VOR/DME Fix
Laxey	IOM R059°/CAR 037°M	IOM 059°/16nm
N5413.45 W00424.06		
Peel	IOM R022°/CAR 311°M	IOM 022°/10nm
N5413.20 W00441.30		

ELEVATION	LOCATION						**ISLE OF SKYE (Broadford)**
34ft 1mb	On the Isle of Skye N5715.19.W00549.68						
PPR		STN 115.10	179	58.4	••• / – / – •		
		BEN 114.40	113	51.6	– ••• / • / – •		

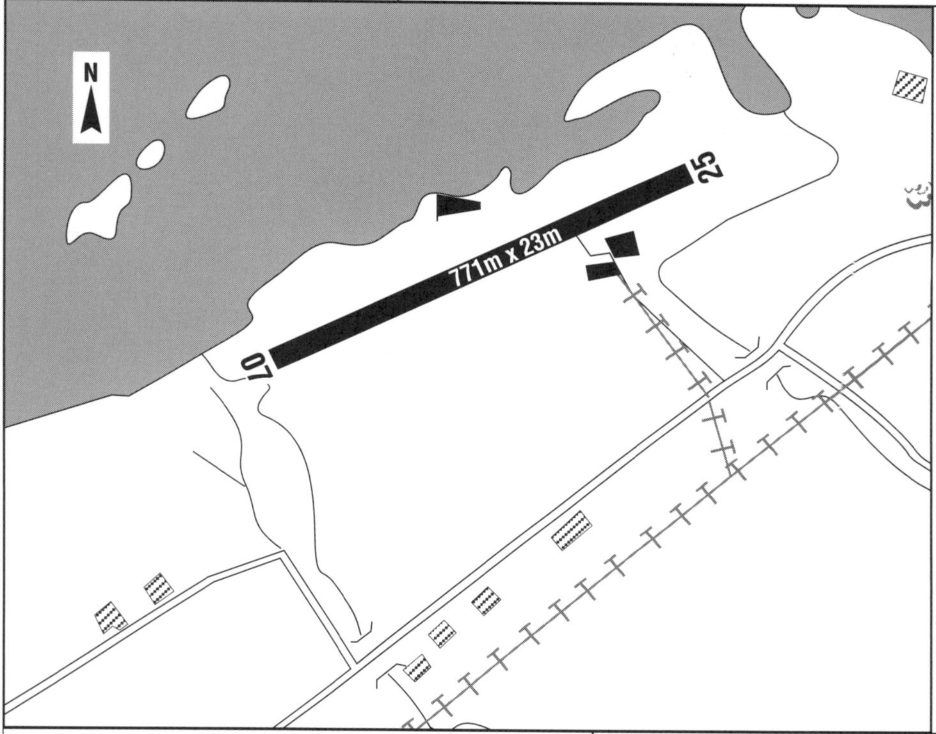

RWY	SURFACE	TORA	LDA	LIGHTING			
07/25	Asphalt	771x23	U/L	Only emergency			

Non-radio

FIS   **Scottish 127.275**
Heli ops may monitor
130.65

Remarks
PPR 24 Hrs notice required.

Warnings
Motorcycle riding tests take place occasionally on the Rwy.
Road cones are used to delineate the test course. Helicopter
operations take place at the AD and local areas up to 2000ft
within a radius of 25nm, radio watch on 130.65. The
windsock pole 6m high is located 40m N of Rwy centreline.
High GND up to 2405ft to the E and W of AD.

Operator
Highland Regional Council Department of Road & Transport
Regional Buildings, Glenurquhart Road Inverness IV3 5NX
Tel: 01478 612727 (Divisional Engineer)
Tel: 01463 702604 (Area Road & Transport)
Fax: 01478 612255 (Area Road & Transport)
Fax: 01463 702606 (Regional Buildings)

Restaurants
Broadford Hotel   **Tel:** 01471 822204 (Bar meals)
Claymore Restaurant   **Tel:** 01471 882333 (Broadford)

Taxis
Waterloo   **Tel:** 01471 822630 (Broadford)
Car Hire
Sutherland's Garage **Tel:** 01471 822225 (self drive)

Weather Info   AirSc GWC

Operating Hrs	SR-SS
Circuit	
Landing fee	on application
Maintenance	Nil
Fuel	Nil

ELEVATION	LOCATION	EGHN	ISLE OF WIGHT (Sandown)
60ft 2mb	5nm SE of Newport N5039.17.W00110.92	SAM 113.35 166 19.1 GWC 114.75 238 20.2	•••/•–/–– ––•/•––/–•–•
PPR			

884m x 40m

05   23

Public footpath

Grass Twy

C

N

RWY	SURFACE	TORA	LDA	LIGHTING
05	Grass	884	775	Nil
23	Grass	884	884	Nil

	Sandown	
A/G	123.50	

Remarks
PPR by telephone.

Warnings
Either Rwy or Twy maybe withdrawn or dimensions changed at short notice. Black & white wing bars mark the landing Thr. Rwy05 QDM markers located before start of Rwy. Caution: taxi with care at all times due to undulating GND in some parts of Twy, active public footpath crosses Rwy 200m upwind of Rwy05 Thr. ATZ overlaps Bembridge ATZ, it may be nessary to contact Bembridge after take-off/arrival for transit clearance. Maintain rwy heading 1nm before turn en-route. Avoid local towns & villages below 1500ft QNH

Operator	Isle of Wight Airport Ltd
	Isle of Wight Airport, Sandown, Isle of Wight PO36 9PJ
Tel: 01983 405125	
Fax: 01983 406117	
Restaurant	Cafe at AD
Taxis	
Lake	**Tel:** 01983 402641
Car Hire	
SW Rentals	**Tel:** 01983 864263
Weather Info	AirS BNMC

Operating Hrs	0800-1700 (Summer) 0900-1700 or SS whichever is earlier (Winter) and by arrangement
Circuit	05 LH 23 RH 1000ft QFE 1060ft QNH
Landing fee	Single £8 Twin £14 inc VAT
Maintenance	Vectis Aviation Services **Tel:** 01983 405520
Fuel	AVGAS 100LL cheque/cash only

ELEVATION	LOCATION	**EGJJ**			**JERSEY**
277ft 9mb	4nm WNW of St Helier N4912.18.W00211.73 **Diversion AD**	JSY 112.20	268	5.8	• – – – / • • • / – • – –
PPR		GUR 109.40	137	20.0	– – • / • • – / • – •

N

ILS/DME
I-DD
110.30

ILS/DME
I-JJ
110.90

1706m x 46m

27

09

B1 B2 B3 C1 C2 D E F G A H J1 J2 K C

A/C Parking

Light A/C Parking

RWY	SURFACE	TORA	LDA	LIGHTING
09	Asphalt	1706	1645	Ap Thr Rwy PAPI 3° RHS
27	Asphalt	1645	1554	Ap Thr Rwy PAPI 3° RHS

Jersey	
ATIS	129.725
ZONE	125.20 120.45
APP	120.30
RAD	118.55 120.30 125.20 120.45
TWR	119.45
GND	121.90
FIRE	121.60
ILS/DME	I-JJ 110.90 Rwy09
ILS/DME	I-DD 110.30 Rwy27
NDB	JW 329* range 25nm * 087/0.6 to 09

Remarks

PPR for SVFR flights. Use governed by regulations applicable to Channel Islands CTR. All aircraft using Jersey Airport and its facilities must have third party liability insurance cover of at least £500,000. Proof of this insurance should be available for inspection. Ground signals other than light signals and letter C not displayed. Visiting light parked as directed by ATC. All occupants are required to be transported to the terminal building by courtesy bus service for Customs and Immigration facilities. All occupants must remain with their aircraft until the transport bus arrives. Handling fees will be collected by Aviation Beauport at checkpoint 2 on departure. All commercial and executive operators must nominate a handling agent. Tel: Airport admin 01534 492000

Remarks for propeller-driven aircraft: Rwy27: Take-off; Climb to at least 500ft aal before turning on to a heading and avoid over-flying land below 1000ft aal. Landing; Maintain at least 1000ft aal until intercepting the ILS glidepath or PAPI indication and thereafter descend on the facility. If under 5700kg and making a visual approach, land must not be overflown below 500ft agl until on final approach. Rwy09: Take-off; Climb straight ahead to a minimum of 500ft aal before turning and climb as rapidly as safe to not less than 1000ft agl. Landing. Maintain at least 1000ft aal until intercepting the ILS glidepath or PAPI indication and thereafter descend on the facility. If under 5700kg and making a visual approach, land must not be overflown below 500ft agl until on final approach. Light aircraft parking area S of 27 Twy. Pilots must exercise caution when manoeuvring in this area due to rutted ground. A/D not to be nominated as an alternate at weekends, May-Oct.

Warnings

All surface movement of aircraft subject to ATC authority, including start-up, push-back and taxi clearance. Turbulence and variable wind conditions may be caused by nearby cliffs on final approach and landing Rwy 09. Blasting takes place infrequently on any weekday at quarries adjacent to the airport bearing 042°T 1.36nm from the ARP.

J

Operating Hrs	0600-2030 (Summer) 0700-2100 (Winter) and by arrangement

Circuits
Whenever cloudbase permits maintain at least 1000ft QFE and make the majority of the circuit over the sea.

Landing fee	On application
Maintenance	Jersey Aircraft Maintenance **Tel:** 01534 45124 Channel Islands Aero Servs **Tel:** 01534 42373

Fuel   AVGAS 100LL AVTUR JET A1 Refuelling not available after 1930 (L) for AVGAS 100LL or after 2100 (L) for AVTUR JET A1 except by special arrangement through airport switchboard

Operator   States of Jersey
States of Jersey Airport Jersey, Channel Islands
Tel: 01534 492000
Tel : (01534 47415 when ATC is not manned)
Fax: 01534 46831(Admin)
Fax: 01534 41094(ATC)
Telex: 4192332 AIRHJER G

Restaurant	Restaurant & buffet in terminal
Taxis/Car Hire	Available at terminal
Weather Info	M T9 Fax 324 A VS JER

Channel Islands Control Zone (Class A) and Jersey Control Zone (Class D)
Normal CTA/CTR Class D Airspace rules apply
In the event of radio failure whilst within the Jersey Zone, the aircraft should proceed to overhead Jersey Airport at 2000ft and then leave the Zone tracking 225°T.
Carriage of SSR transponders is mandatory within the Channel Islands Control Zone. PPR for SVFR flight is required at all times. Mode 'A' for SVFR, Mode 'A+C' for IFR flights.

Channel Island Visual Reference Points

VRP	VOR/DME
Alderney NDB N4942.53 W00211.98	JSY 352°/30nm, GUR 048°/23nm
Cap de la Hague N4943.00 W00156.00	JSY 012°/30nm, GUR 061°/31nm
Carteret Lighthouse N4922.00 W00148.00	JSY 052°/13nm, GUR 102°/32nm
Casquets Lighthouse N4943.00 W00222.00	JSY 341°/33nm, GUR 033°/19nm
Cap de Flamanville N4931.00 W00153.00	JSY 023°/19nm, GUR 084°/28nm
Corbiere Lighthouse N4911.00 W00215.00	JSY 258°/8nm, GUR 142°/21nm, DIN 353°/36nm
E of Iles Chausey N4853.00 W00139.00	JSY 146°/26nm, GUR 135°/50nm, DIN 048°/25nm
Granville N4850.00 W00139.00	JSY 150°/28nm, GUR 138°/52nm, DIN 053°/22nm
Ile de Brehat N4851.00 W00300.00	JSY 243°/44nm, GUR 208°/39nm, DIN 298°/40nm
Miniquiers N4857.00 W00208.00	JSY 196°/17nm, GUR 153°/35nm DIN 359°/22nm
N E Point (of Guernsey) N4930.42 W00230.52	JSY 318°/25nm, GUR 045°/5.6nm
St. Germain N4914.00 W00138.00	JSY 091°/16nm, GUR 112°/40nm, DIN 028°/42nm
S E Corner (of Jersey) N4910.00 W00202.00	JSY 176°/3nm, GUR 130°/28nm, DIN 008°/35nm
West of Miniquiers N4857.00 W00218.00	JSY 216°/19nm, GUR 162°/32nm, DIN 342°/23nm

ELEVATION	LOCATION				
435ft 14mb	5nm SW of Cirencester N5140.04 W00203.42 **Diversion AD**	DTY 116.40	232	46.5	— • • / — / — • — —
		CPT 114.35	294	33	— • — • / • — — — • / —
PPR		BCN 117.45	100	45	— • • • / — • — • / — •

RWY	SURFACE	TORA	LDA	LIGHTING
09	Asphalt	1833x46	U/L	Ap Thr Rwy PAPI 3°LHS*
27	Asphalt	1833x46	U/L	Nil
13/31	Asphalt	941x46	U/L	Nil
04/22	Grass	380x20	U/L	Nil
09/27	Grass	450x20	U/L	Nil
13/31	Grass	450x20	U/L	Nil

*AD lighting available on request

	Kemble
A/G*	118.90 Kemble info 118.90
LARS	Brize 134.3 *AFIS at W/E

Remarks
AD is multi-use. Look out for microlights & model ACFT. All visitors welcome. Please book-in and pay landing fees in the Control TWR coffee bar

Warnings
Rwys prone to standing water after heavy rain. Oaksey Park AD is 2.5nm to SE, keep good lookout for their traffic. AD may be closed for special events, PPR telephone call will provide information. Turbulence likely on APP Rwy27 with N or S wind. Do not overfly the villages of Kemble and Rodmartin.

Maintenance
Aero Developments **Tel:** 01285 770291
Aerostone Eng. **Tel:** 01285 771070
Delta Jets **Tel:** 01285 770917
Eagles Aviation **Tel:** 01285 771020
Fuel Avgas 100LL & Jet A1
0900-1700 (Daily) **Tel:** 01285 770917

Operator Kemble Airfield Management Ltd
The Control Tower, Kemble Airfield, Cirencester
Glos GL7 6BA
Tel: 01285 771177
Fax: 01285 771177

Restaurant Tower coffee bar
for delicious bacon butties & light refreshments

Taxis/Car Hire
Station **Tel:** 01285 770717

Weather Info AirSW BNMC

Operating Hrs 0800-1700 (Summer)
0900-1700 (Winter)

Circuits LH all Rwys unless advised
1200ft QFE ACFT 800ft microlights 500ft Helicopters

Landing fee Single £8 Twin/Heli £10
Microlights £5

KINGSMUIR (Sorbie)

ELEVATION	LOCATION				
387ft 12mb **PPR**	3.5nm SE of St. Andrews N5616.15 W00245.05	**TLA 113.80**	030	51	– / • – • • / • –

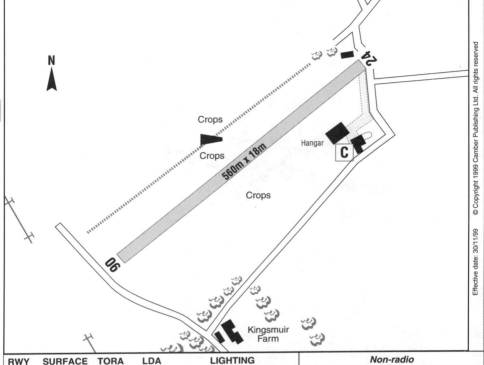

RWY	SURFACE	TORA	LDA	LIGHTING
06/24	Grass	560x18	U/L	Nil

First 25% of Rwy06 has transverse slope from right to left

	Non-radio
APP	**Leuchars 126.50**

Remarks
AD close to SE boundary of Leuchars MATZ. Overnight parking is available at owners own risk. Visiting ACFT welcome subject to PPR. Rwy has white flush edge markings but no Thr designators.

Warning
An access road crosses Thr24. Beware flocks of crows congregate on cut portion of strip. Occasional model ACFT activity on Thr06.

Operator	David and Violet Smith **Tel: 01333 310619**
Restaurants	Nil
Taxis/Car Hire	Nil
Weather Info	AirSC GWC

Operating Hrs	Available on request
Circuits	06 RH 24 LH
Landing fee	No set charge but donations to upkeep gratefully accepted
Maintenance	Nil
Fuel	Mogas available in emergency

ELEVATION	LOCATION	EGQK	KINLOSS
22ft 0 mb **PPR** **Military**	2.5nm NE of Forres N5738.96 W00333.64	**INS 109.20** 074 17 ••/ – •/ • ••	

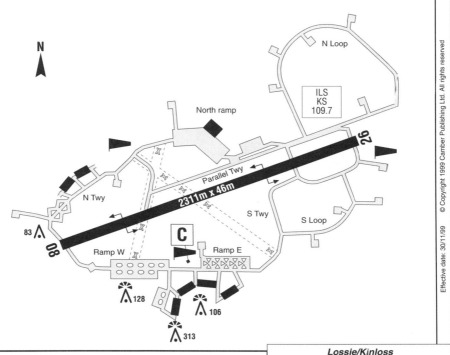

K

N Loop

ILS
KS
109.7

North ramp

26

Parallel Twy

2311m x 46m

N Twy

S Twy   S Loop

83

08

Ramp W   Ramp E   C

128   106   313

RWY	SURFACE	TORA	LDA	LIGHTING
08/26	Asphalt/Concrete	2311	2311	Ap Thr Rwy PAPI 3° LH

Arrester gear normal ops App cable DOWN overun cable UP.
26.704m 08. 498m from landing Thr.

Lossie/Kinloss

APP (Lossie) 119.35
PAR (Lossie) 123.30
TWR (Kinloss) 122.10

TACAN KSS 109.80 (On A/D)
NDB KS 370 (Range 20nm On A/D)
ILS   KS 109.70 Rwy26

Remarks
PPR by telephone essential. RAF AD used by heavy ACFT situated in combined MATZ with Lossiemouth, (who are the controlling authority). Lossie also provide LARS service within the local area of Intense aerial activity. **Noise:** Langcot House (N side of Rwy08 Thr) and Binsness House (270°/2.5nm) may not be overflown. Overflight of Forres and Findhorn prohibited. Rwy26 VFR deps maintain Rwy heading to 1000ft QFE before turning.

Warnings
Inbound ACFT must contact Lossie APP at 50nm if approaching at medium/high level and at 20nm when approaching from low level. Caution: Bird hazard, Geese activity may be encountered within 10nm of the AD from Sept-Apr. Glider flying activity on the AD Sat-Sun and public holidays.

Maintenance Fuel	Not normally available to civil visitors AVGAS 100LL JET A1 by prior arrangement
Operator	RAF Kinloss Forres **Tel: 01309 672161 Ext 7609**
Taxi/Car Hire	Nil
Weather Info	M T Fax326 GWC

Operating Hrs	H24
Circuits	As instructed by ATC
Landing Fees	£7.56 per 500kgs + VAT & £8.50 insurance charge

ELEVATION	LOCATION				KIRKBRIDE
38ft 1mb	9.5nm W of Carlisle N5452.94 W00312.32	DCS 115.20	032	11	– • • / – • – • / • • •
PPR					

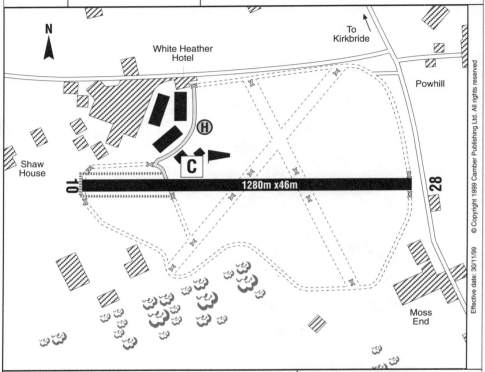

RWY	SURFACE	TORA	LDA	LIGHTING
10/28	Asphalt	1280x46	U/L	Nil

Rwy surface good. All other Rwys disused

	Kirkbride
APP	**Carlisle 123.60**
A/G	**129.825**
	not always manned
	– make blind calls

Remarks
PPR by telephone .Visiting ACFT are welcome at own risk. ACFT must carry third party insurance. Microlight activity at all times.

Warnings
There is considerable military low flying activity weekdays. HGV's may use AD manoeuvring area to access storage facilities on the AD. Masts: (TV) 3nm SE of AD (1985ft amsl, 1034ft agl), 3.5nm S (1753ft amsl, 561ft agl) & at Anthorn disused AD 2.5nm NW (778ft amsl, 561ft agl). Do not overfly Kirkbride village. Only one Twy useable. A wire fence 4ft high runs across Thr10 on both sides of Rwy up to first Twy intersection.

Operator	White Heather Hotel Kirkbride, Cumbria
	Tel: 01697 351373 (Hotel for PPR)
	Tel: 01697 351006 (Lorton Aero Club)
	Tel: 0410 672087 Lorton Aero Club Mobile)
	Tel: 01697 342142 (John Plaskett Club co-ordinator)

Restaurants	Accomodation & meals available at White Heather Hotel

Taxis	**Tel:** 01697 343148
Car Hire	Nil

Weather Info	AirN MWC

Operating Hrs	AD manned at weekends but available during week
Circuits	Overhead join then LH at 1000ft QFE
Landing fee	Nil
Maintenance	Nil
Fuel	Nil

ELEVATION	LOCATION				
135ft 4mb	1nm S of Kirkbymoorside N5415.00 W00057.00	**OTR 113.90**	323	45	– – – / – / • – •
PPR		**GAM 112.80**	005	58	– – • / • – / – –
		POL 112.10	059	51	• – – • / – – – / • – • •

K

Kirbymoorside

30ft powerlines on high ground

50ft trees

22

Slingsby factory

Track crosses Rwy

735m x 20m

50ft trees

04

N

RWY	SURFACE	TORA	LDA	LIGHTING
04	Grass	718	539	Nil
22	Grass	539	525	Nil

Slingsby

LARS (Linton)	129.15
A/G	129.90

Remarks
PPR by telephone. U/L AD. Use of AD is restricted to visitors to Slingsby Aviation and company flight tests or by prior arrangement. Operations at pilots own risk. Noise: Avoid overflight of local habitation.

Warnings
There are domestic powerlines on high ground on short final Rwy22. Trees close to APP may cause turbulence. After heavy/prolonged precipitation AD may be boggy. Considerable military low-level activity in the area. Wombleton AD is 1.5nm to the SW.

Operator Slingsby Aviation Ltd
Kirkbymoorside, Yorkshire YO62 6EZ
Tel: 01751 432474
Fax: 01751 431173

Restaurant/Accomodation
George & Dragon Hotel **Tel:** 01751 433334
Kings Head Hotel **Tel:** 01751 431340
Fox & Hounds Hotel **Tel:** 01751 731577 (Sinnington, approx 3nm from factory)

Taxi/Car Hire

Weather Info AirN MWC

Operating Hrs	PPR
Circuits	04 RH 22 LH
Landing fee	advised with PPR
Maintenance Fuel	Slingsby Aviation AVGAS 100LL by arrangement only

ELEVATION	LOCATION	**EGPA**				**KIRKWALL**

ELEVATION	LOCATION			
50ft 2mb	2.5nm SE of Kirkwall N5857.80 W00254.30	KWL 108.60	On A/D	– • – / • – – / • – ••
		WIK 113.60	019 30.5	• – – / •• / – • –
PPR		SUM 117.35	230 74.2	••• / •• – / – –

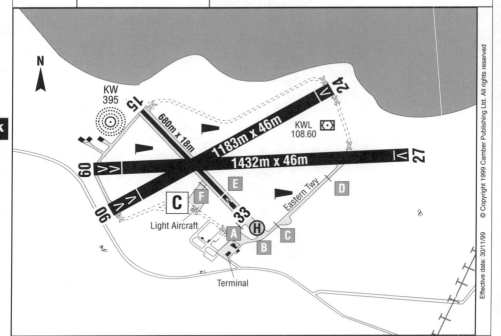

RWY	SURFACE	TORA	LDA	LIGHTING
06*	Asphalt	1168	1031	Nil
24*	Asphalt	1084	1078	PAPI 3°
09	Asphalt	1400	1289	Thr Rwy PAPI 3.5°
27	Asphalt	1365	1320	Ap Thr Rwy PAPI 3.25°
15	Asphalt	560	560	Nil
33	Asphalt	680	560	Nil

* Limited for use by ACFT of 5700kg or less

Kirkwall

APP/TWR	118.30
FIRE	121.60
VOR/DME	KWL 108.60 on A/D
NDB	KW 395*
	*on A/D range 40nm

Remarks
Rwy33 has displaced Thr. The E Twy is the only portion of Twy available for use by ACFT requiring a licensed AD. Grass areas soft and unsafe only marked Twy to be used. Perimeter Twy is not available to ACFT requiring a licensed AD.

Warnings
Grass areas outside strip are unfit for transit of ACFT because of open drains. An uncontrolled road is located 61m from Rwy06 and 91m from Rwy09 landing thresholds. A section of 549m in length, on Rwy15/33, commencing at the SE end of the Rwy, has a down gradient of 1 in 50 (1.1%). AD is subject to waterlogging. Rwy27, severe turbulence may be encountered on short final during periods of strong SW to NW winds. Security post 3m high at edge of apron adjacent to passenger gate.

Operating Hrs   Mon-Fri 0645-1745
Sat 0800-1645 Sun 0900-1100(Summer) +1Hr (Winter) and by arrangement

Landing fee	£10.65 inc.VAT up to 3MT VFR cash/cheque on day
Maintenance	Available (Loganair)
Fuel	AVGAS 100LL AVTUR JET A1 Oil **Tel: 01856 872415**
Operator	Highland and Island Airport Ltd Kirkwall Airport, Kirkwall, Orkney Islands KW15 1TH **Tel:** 01856 872421 Ext.130 **Fax:** 01856 875051
Restaurants	Light refreshments at AD
Taxis	
Brass's	**Tel:** 01856 850750
Craigie's Garage	**Tel:** 01856 872817
Car Hire	
National	**Tel:** 01856 875500 **Fax:** /874458
Weather Info	M T9 Fax 328 GWC

Visual Reference Points (VRPs)
Foot	N5901.72 W00248.38
Lamb Holm Island	N5853.23 W00253.60
Stromberry	N5901.82 W00256.02

ELEVATION	LOCATION				
290ft 9mb	4.5nm SE of Oswestry N5249.30 W00259.30	WAL 114.10	177	35.5	• – – / • – / • – • •
		TNT 115.70	258	50	– / – • / –
PPR		SWB 116.8	285	12	• • • / • – – / – • • •

KNOCKIN (Oswestry)

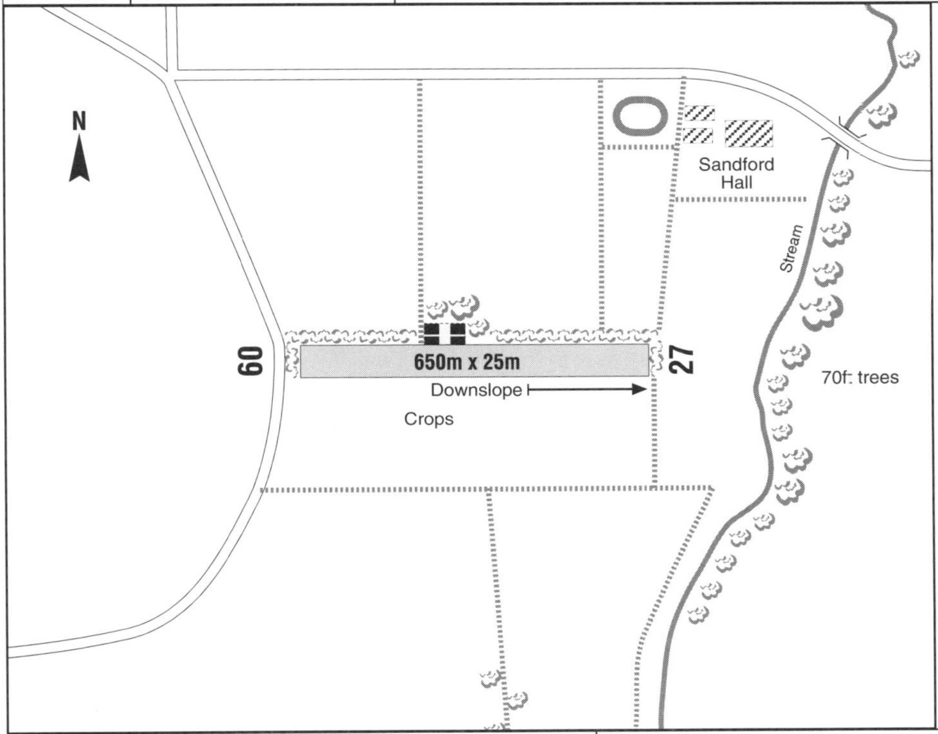

K

N ↑

Sandford Hall

Stream

60 | 650m x 25m | 27
Downslope →
Crops

70f: trees

RWY	SURFACE	TORA	LDA	LIGHTING
09/27	Grass	650x25	U/L	Nil

	Non-radio
LARS	**Shawbury 120.775**

Remarks
PPR by telephone. Well prepared grass strip. Light ACFT visitors welcome at own risk.

Warnings
6ft hedgerow runs along the N edge of strip & crosses both thresholds. A conifer tree on N edge of strip adjacent to hangars. Downslope in final 1/3rd Rwy09. A copse of mature trees bordering a stream crosses Rwy27 final APP approx 250m from Thr. Power cables 30ft cross Rwy27 final 400m from Thr.

Operator	Mr TR Jones, Sandford Hall
	West Felton, Oswestry SK11 4EX
	Tel: 01691 610888 (PPR during office Hrs)
	Tel: 01691 610206 (PPR evenings)
	Fax: 01691 610144
Restaurants	Nil
Taxis	**Tel:** 01691 650651
Car Hire	Nil
Weather Info	AirN MWC

Operating Hrs	SR-SS
Circuits	As you wish but please avoid local habitation
Landing fee	Nil
Maintenance	Nil
Fuel	Nil

ELEVATION	LOCATION				LAMB HOLM
65ft 2mb	4nm S of Kirkwall Airport N5853.18.W00253.60	KWL 108.60	187	4.5	– • – / • – – / • – • •
PPR	Diversion AD	WIK 113.60	022	26	• – – / • • / – • –

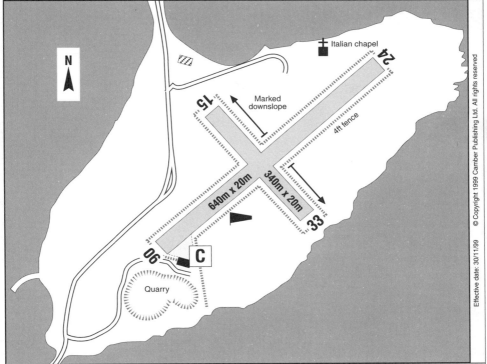

Effective date: 30/11/99

L

RWY	SURFACE	TORA	LDA	LIGHTING
06/24*	Grass	640x20	U/L	Nil
15/33**	Grass	340x20	U/L	Nil

* Fence to fence distance 06/24 658m
** Rwy15/33 severe hump-back
only use when strong winds preclude Rwy06/24

Lamb Holm

APP	Kirkwall 118.30
A/G*	129.825 (Microlight Ops)

* Not continuously manned

Remarks
PPR by telephone. Visiting ACFT welcome own risk. AD close to southern boundary Kirkwall ATZ., inbound make initial call to Kirkwall. Kirkwall town centre approx 7 miles by road. Italian chapel (hand painted to resemble a basilica by Italian prisoners of War) is short walk.

Warning
Width of strip between fencing is 40m, 20m Rwy & 10m each side rough grass. 20ft electricity pole (no wires), 120m from Thr Rwy15. 4ft boundry fence, wooden poles & barbed wire surrounds AD. Please avoid overflying St. Mary's village 1nm to NW of AD.

Operator	Tom Sinclair, Tighsith Holm Orkney Islands KW17 2RX
Tel: 07803 088938 (days)	
Tel/Fax: 01856 781310 (Home/evenings)	
Restaurants	15mins walk across causeway food and accomodation (have been known to discount for pilots)
Commodore Motel **Tel:** 01856 781319	
Taxis Andersons	(also mini-bus hire) **Tel:** 01856 781237 (days) **Tel:** 01856 781267 (evenings)
Car Hire National	**Tel:** 01856 875500 **Fax:** /874458
Weather Info	Kirkwall info. M T9 Fax 328 GWC

Operating Hrs	SR-SS
Circuits	6/15 RH 24/33 LH
Landing fee	Donations to upkeep gratefully accepted
Maintenance	Nil
Fuel	Mogas available from garage (1mile walk) or by arrangement

ELEVATION	LOCATION	LAMBLEY (Jericho Farm)			
300ft 10mb	4nm NE of Nottingham N5300.55 W00103.48				
PPR		TNT 115.70	103	23	– / – • / –
		GAM 112.80	200	16.8	– – • / • – / – –

L

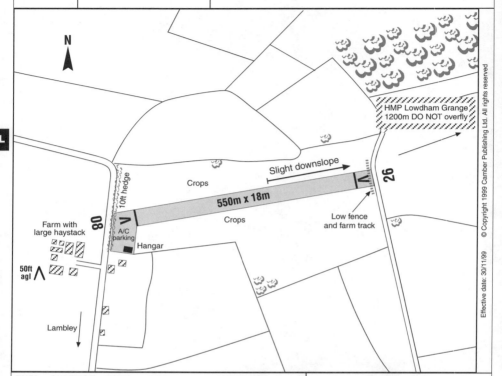

N

Crops

HMP Lowdham Grange 1200m DO NOT overfly

Slight downslope

550m x 18m

26

10ft hedge

Crops

Low fence and farm track

08

A/C parking

Farm with large haystack

Hangar

50ft agl

Lambley

RWY	SURFACE	TORA	LDA	LIGHTING			
08/26	Grass	550	550	Nil			
Rwy26 has slight upslope in first third							

	Lambley Radio
APP	(East Midlands) 119.65
APP	(Newton) 119.125
A/G	123.05*
*Only occasionally manned	

Remarks
PPR essential. Visiting ACFT welcome at pilots own risk. Rwy has white side markers. Windsock may be displayed close to hangar.

Warnings
Rwy surface may become boggy after prolonged rainfall. Low fence and farm track at the Rwy26 Thr. Public road and 10ft hedge at 08 Thr. The AD is situated close to a number of AD in busy airspace. Hucknall ATZ, (active only at weekends), is close to the W. (Freq:130.80). RAF Newton ATZ to SE operate daily, (Freq:119.125). RAF Syerston ATZ, to the E military gliding school operates daily. A good lookout is strongly recommended. Noise:Please avoid local habitation and the villages of Lambley & Woodborough. DO NOT OVERFLY HMP LOWDHAM GRANGE which is approx 1200m out to N of Rwy26 approach.

Maintenance	Nil
Fuel	Nil
Operator	Mr John Hardy, Jericho Farm Green Lane, Lambley, Nottinghamshire NG4 4QE
Tel: 0115 9313530 (Home/Office)	
Tel: 0115 9313639 (Hangar)	
Tel: 07768 726279 (Mobile)	
Restaurant	Pub 800yds in village
Taxi/Car Hire	Nil
Weather Info	AirCen MWC

Operating Hours	SR-SS
Circuits	LH 800ft QFE
Landing Fee	Available on request

ELEVATION	LOCATION	EGHC	LANDS END (St Just)
401ft 13mb	5nm W of Penzance N5006.16.W00540.23 **Diversion AD**		
PPR		LND 114.20 220 2.4 • — • • / — • / — • •

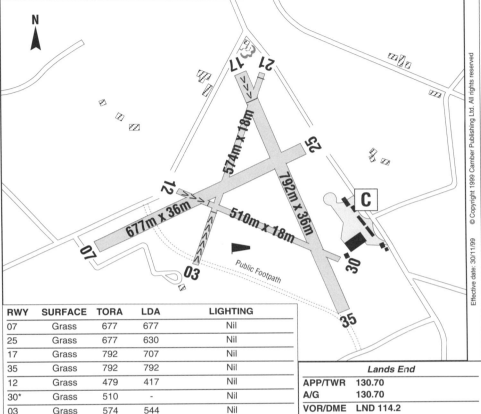

RWY	SURFACE	TORA	LDA	LIGHTING
07	Grass	677	677	Nil
25	Grass	677	630	Nil
17	Grass	792	707	Nil
35	Grass	792	792	Nil
12	Grass	479	417	Nil
30*	Grass	510	-	Nil
03	Grass	574	544	Nil
21	Grass	574	436	Nil

* Rwy30 not available for ACFT requiring a licensed Rwy for landing

Lands End	
APP/TWR	130.70
A/G	130.70
VOR/DME	LND 114.2

Remarks
PPR by telephone. Entire grass area is maintained and useable. Rwys17/35 & 07/25 are sufficiently wide to allow differential use of each side of the Rwy to conserve the grass surfaces. Pilots may be asked to use the Rwy (left or right) in order to achieve this. Schedule flights to the Scillies operate using transit lane SFC-2000ft QNH. Avoid over flying St Just village.

Warning
Some parts of the manoeuvring area are undulating. Mast to right of Rwy21 APP, range 1nm, extending to 286ft aal. A public footpath crosses the AD from NW to SE, entering near Rwy12 Thr, crossing Rwy07/25 and leaving near Rwy03 Thr.

Operating Hrs
Mon-Sat 0800-1700 Sun 0800-1600 (Summer)
0900-1700 or SS (Winter)
and by arrangement

Circuits
LH 1000ft QFE

Landing fee
Single £7.50 Twin £15 inc.VAT

Maintenance
Westward	**Tel:** 01736 788771
Fuel	AVGAS 100LL Oil 80 W80 W100

Operator Westward Airways Ltd
Land's End Aerodrome, St Just, Cornwall TR19 7RL
Tel: 01736 788771 (Operator)
Tel: 01736 788944 (ATC)
Fax: 01736 788366

Restaurant Restaurant and club facilities available

Taxis
Tom's Taxis	**Tel:** 01736 871442
Stone's Taxis	**Tel:** 01736 63400

Car Hire
Tuckers	**Tel:** 01736 629880

Weather Info AirSW BNMC

ELEVATION	LOCATION				LANGAR
109ft 4mb	10nm ESE of Nottingham N5253.63 W00054.27	GAM 112.80	182	23.0	– – • / • – / – –
PPR	**Diversion AD**	TNT 115.70	116	29.0	– / – • / –

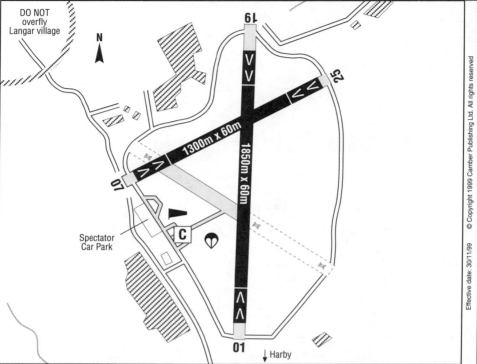

RWY	SURFACE	TORA	LDA	LIGHTING
01/19	Asphalt	1850x60	U/L	Nil
07/25	Asphalt	1300x60	U/L	Nil

	Langar
APP	**Cottesmore MATZ** **130.20**
Para Base	**129.90**

Remarks
PPR vital in order to obtain briefing on parachuting operation for the day Visiting ACFT welcome. Contact Langar at least 5nm from AD for joining information - normally a straight-in APP or base leg join. Disused Rwy13/31 is available as Twy.

Warnings
Do not overfly the AD – intensive para-dropping up to FL150 daily. **Noise:** Do not overfly Langar village 1nm NW of AD or Harby 1nm S.

Operating Hrs
Mon-Sat 0900-2000 Sun 1000-2000 (Summer)
Mon-Sat 0900-SS Sun 1000-SS (Winter)

Circuits	See jioning procedures
Landing fee	Single £2.00 Twin £5.00 No charge if on BPS business
Maintenance	Nil
Fuel	AVGAS 100LL for emergency use only

Operator	British Parachute Schools **Tel/Fax: 01949 860878**
Restaurants	Cafe open weekends
Taxis Bingham **Car Hire**	**Tel: 01949 839000**
Weather Info	AirCen MWC

Langar Joining Proceedures
ACFT MUST NOT overfly the airfield.
Arriving ACFT should call Langar Para Base 129.90 at least 8nm from AD.
Straight approach or base leg join will be given.
Holding Patterns
If joining from north:
LH orbit on GAM 182r 20D 1500ft QNH (3.5nm N of Langar)
If joining from south:
LH orbit on TNT 296r 33D 2000ft QNH (3.5nm SE of Langar)

ELEVATION	LOCATION	EGHL				LASHAM

ELEVATION	LOCATION				
618ft 21mb	5nm SE of Basingstoke N5111.17 W00101.83 **Diversion AD**	GWC 114.75	338	22.4	− − • / • − • / − • − •
PPR		CPT 114.35	164	19.6	− • − • / • − − • / −
		SAM 113.35	045	18.2	• • • / • − / − −

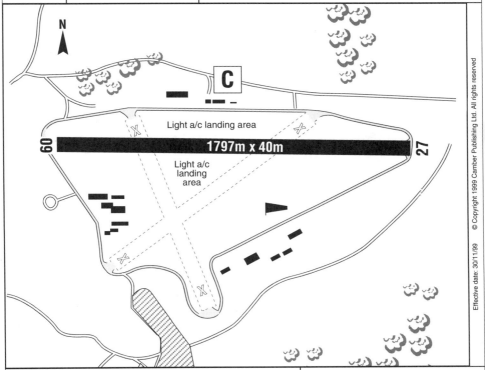

N

C

Light a/c landing area

60

1797m x 40m

27

Light a/c landing area

L

RWY	SURFACE	TORA	LDA	LIGHTING
09/27	Asphalt	1797x40	U/L	Nil

Rwy not normally available. Landing on grass only.

APP	**Farnborough 125.25** **for Odiham MATZ** **clearance**
A/G	**Lasham 129.875** **make joining and circuit calls**

Remarks
PPR strictly by telephone. This AD is only available to persons having business with Lasham Gliding Society. Certain customs facilities are available. Light ACFT must use grass area N of main Rwy or centre triangle dependant on Rwy in use. Visiting pilots & passengers are required to become temporary members, indemnifying the society of all liability.

Warnings
Extreme caution due to cables winch launching to 3000ft agl. Parts of the AD surface are unsuitable for the movement of ACFT. Intense gliding activity takes place.

Operator	Lasham Gliding Society Ltd
	Lasham Aerodrome, Lasham, Alton, Hants GU34 5SS **Tel:** 01256 381322
Restaurant	Clubhouse facilities available at AD
Taxis	
Alton	**Tel:** 01420 84455
Ames	**Tel:** 01420 83309
Car Hire	
National	**Tel:** 01256 477777
Weather Info	AirSE BNMC

Operating Hrs	Strictly PPR
Circuits	
Landing fee	Single £10 Others £20 per tonne

Maintenance
Three counties   **Tel:** 01256 381330
Fuel   Nil

ELEVATION	LOCATION	EGKH	LASHENDEN (Headcorn)

ELEVATION	LOCATION				
72ft 2mb	8nm S of Maidstone N5109.41 E00038.50 **Diversion AD**	DET 117.30	173	9.0	– •• / • / –
PPR		MAY 117.90	071	21.5	– – / • – / – • – –
		DVR 114.95	275	27.0	– •• / ••• / – • – •

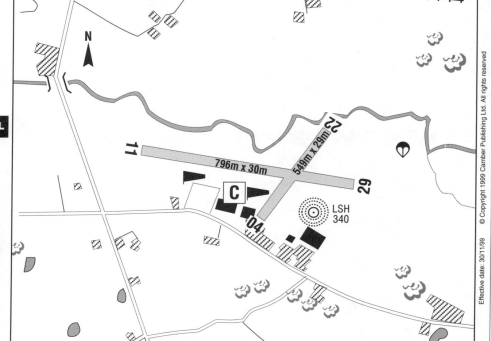

796m x 30m — 11 / 04 / 22 / 29
549m x 29m
C
LSH 340
N

RWY	SURFACE	TORA	LDA	LIGHTING		*Lashenden*	
11/29	Grass	796	796	Nil	**A/G**	122.00	
04/22	Grass	549x29	U/L	Nil	**NDB**	LSH 340	

Remarks
Not available for use at night by flights required to use a licensed AD. Rwy04/22 not available to ACFT flying for public transport or flying instruction.

Warnings
Helicopters must obtain clearance before engaging rotors. Free-fall parachuting takes place up to FL150. Helicopters may not operate & no overhead joins when parachuting in progress. All ACFT must avoid over-flying local villages. No marked Twys. Taxy to S of Rwy, due to poor condition & undulating surface of AD.

Operating Hrs
0800-SS (Summer) 0900-SS (Winter) and by arrangement

Circuits
LH 1000ft QFE Rotary LH 11 RH 29 at 700ft QFE

Landing fee   Single £5.00 £10 Twin

Maintenance   Available
Fuel   AVGAS 100LL, Jet A1
for emergencies or business users only
Oil 80 W80 100 W100

Operator   Mr JPA Freeman
The Aerodrome, Headcorn, Ashford, Kent TN27 9HX
Tel: 01622 890226 01622 890236 (Out of Hrs)
Fax: 01622 890876
Telex: 966127

Restaurant
Cafe available at AD   **Tel:** 01622 890671
George & Dragon   **Tel:** 01622 890239 (Pub B+B)

Taxis
MTC   **Tel:** 01622 890003
Car Hire
National   **Tel:** 01622 684844

Weather Info   AirSE BNMC

ELEVATION	LOCATION		LEDBURY (Velcourt)
250ft 8mb	3nm SW of Ledbury N5200.17 W00228.50	**HON 113.65** 241 37	••••/–––/–•
PPR		**BCN 117.45** 066 33	–•••/–•–•/–•

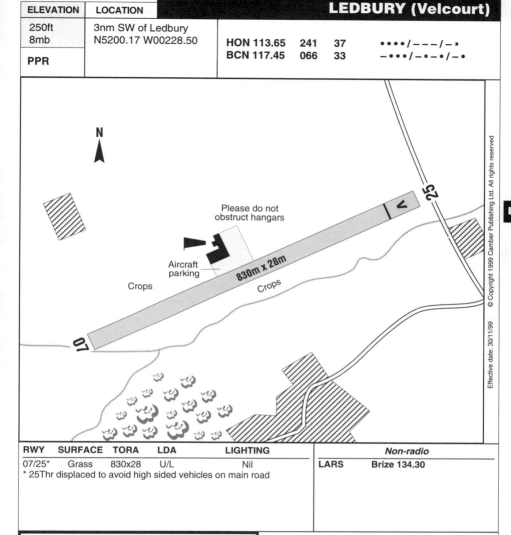

Effective date: 30/11/99

Please do not obstruct hangars

Aircraft parking

Crops

Crops

830m x 28m

25

07

RWY	SURFACE	TORA	LDA	LIGHTING		Non-radio	
07/25*	Grass	830x28	U/L	Nil	**LARS**	**Brize 134.30**	

* 25Thr displaced to avoid high sided vehicles on main road

Remarks
PPR by telephone. Visitors welcome PPR at own risk. Windsock on roof of hangar at rwy mid-point. Smooth surface on regularly cut Rwy.

Warnings
Crops grow to edge of strip. 30ft power lines cross 25 APP 300m from Thr. Trees SW of Rwy07 can cause turbulence on final in SE wind. TV mast 1210amsl, (540agl) 2nm W AD. Hangar close to mid point of strips N edge.

Operator Mary Alexander, Bromesberrow Estate
c/o Robert Killen, Chartered Surveyors, Littlemead, Tortworth Wotton-under-Edge, Glos GL12 8HB
Tel: 01531 660207/660286 (Office Hrs please)
Fax: 01531 660307

Restaurant	Nil

Taxis
Wyvern (Ledbury) **Tel:** 01531 633001
Ames **Tel:** 01420 83309
Car Hire

Weather Info AirSW BNMC

Operating Hrs	SR-SS
Circuits	LH 1000ft QFE
Landing fee	Nil
Maintenance **Fuel**	Nil Nil

ELEVATION	LOCATION	EGNM			LEEDS BRADFORD

ELEVATION	LOCATION
682ft 23mb	6nm NW of Leeds N5351.95 W00139.63
PPR	

POL 112.10   071   17.5   •––•/–––/•–••

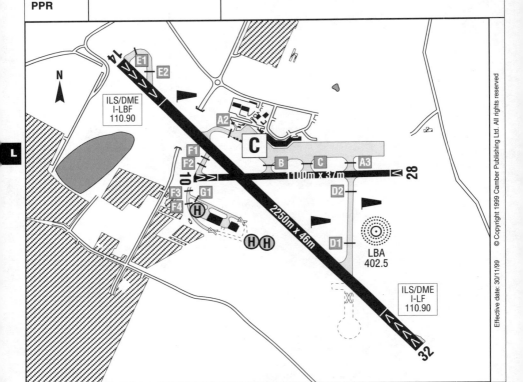

RWY	SURFACE	TORA	LDA	LIGHTING
10*	Asphalt	1052	948	Thr Rwy
28	Asphalt	1052	1004	Thr Rwy PAPI 3° LHS
14	Concrete	2113	1802	Ap Thr Rwy PAPI 3.5° RHS
32	Concrete	2190	1916	Ap Thr Rwy PAPI 3° LHS

* Rwy10 not available for night landings

	Leeds
ATIS	118.025
APP	123.75
RAD	121.05
VDF	123.75
TWR	120.30
FIRE	121.60
NDB	LBA 402.5*
ILS/DME	I-LF 110.90 Rwy32
ILS/DME	I-LBF 110.90 Rwy14
	*on A/D range 25nm

Remarks

PPR to non-radio ACFT.(except by special arr. for maintenance) **microlights not accepted**. Class D Airspace ACFT must have Third Party insurance cover of not less than £1,000,000. All public transport/GA ACFT must designate a handling agent in advance if operating from the main N side apron. Approved handling agents: British Midland 0113 2508194, Servisair 0113 2503251, Nordic Aero 0113 250 1401 (for ACFT with 12 passenger seats or less). Customs during airport Operating Hrs. Helicopters to land as instructed by ATC. Rebated fees for training flights subject to prior written approval from the Airport Authority. A booking slot system is in operation for ACFT using the airport for training Tel: 0113 2504522 (ATC).Pilots transiting the Vale of York AIAA, use LARS offered by Linton or Leeming. Helicopter training is permitted dual only, no circuits.

Warnings

Bird activity noted at this airport - large flocks of Lapwings. ACFT may be delayed while flocks are cleared. The southern Twy is restricted to use by ACFT with a wingspan of 17m or less.

Operating Hrs	H24
	PPR 2200-0600 (Summer) + 1Hr Winter

Circuits

Landing fee	On application

Maintenance	Yorkshire Light Aviation
	Tel: 0113 250 3133
Fuel	AVGAS 100LL AVTUR JET A1

Fuel available by prior arrangement only. AVGAS 100LL only available 0800-1800 or by prior arrangement. **Tel:** 0113 503133 or 01132 501401 (Multiflight) AVGAS not available to ACFT with a wingspan greater than 17m

Operator	Leeds Bradford Int Airport Ltd

Leeds Bradford Int Airport, Yeadon, Leeds
Yorkshire LS19 7TZ
Tel: 01133 2509696 (Admin)
Fax: 01133 2505426 (Admin)
Tel: 01133 913282 (ATC)
Tel: 01133 913287 (flight planning)
Fax: 01133 250 8131
Telex: 557868

Restaurant
Restaurant buffet and bar available at Terminal

Taxis	Available at Terminal
Telecabs	**Tel:** 0113 279 2222
Car Hire	
Avis	**Tel:** 0113 250 3880
Europcar	**Tel:** 0113 250 9066
Hertz	**Tel:** 0113 250 4811

Weather Info	M T9 Fax 334 A VN MWC

CTR/CTA - Class D Airspace
Normal CTR/CTA Class D Airspace rules apply.

Visual Reference Points (VRPs):

VRP	VOR/DME
Dewsbury (DBY)	POL 105°/17nm
N5341.50 W00138.10	
Eccup Reservoir(ECP)	POL 073°/21nm
N5352.27 W00132.60	
Harrogate (HGT)	POL 058°/25nm
N5359.50 W00131.60	
Keighley (KLY)	POL 048°/10nm
N5352.00 W00154.60	

L

ELEVATION	LOCATION	**EGXE**				**LEEMING**

ELEVATION	LOCATION
132ft 5mb	7nm SW of Northallerton
PPR MILITARY	N5417.54 W00132.11

POL 112.10	036	38.5	•—•/———/•—••
NEW 114.25	179	45.0	—•/•/•——

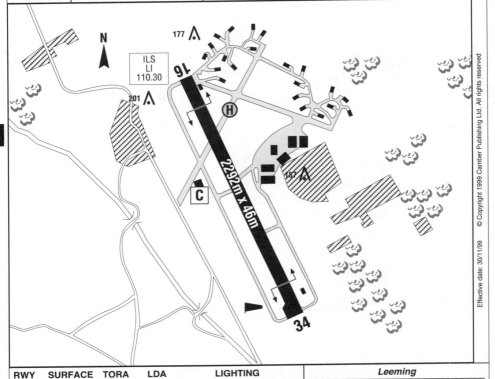

RWY	SURFACE	TORA	LDA	LIGHTING
16/34	Asphalt	2292	2292	Ap Thr Rwy PAPI 3°

Arrester gear 390m from THrs

Leeming	
APP/MATZ /LARS	127.75 123.30
TWR	120.50 122.1
ILS	LI 110.30 Rwy16

Remarks
PPR 24 Hrs required. Resident jet ACFT have priority for takeoff, visiting ACFT may have to break-off APP to permit departures. Limited parking and handling facilities. AD often active at weekends, ATZ active H24. Visual aid to location: IBn LI Red. Station based light ACFT operate outside normal Hrs.

Warnings
Strong possibility of windshear on APP to 16 when wind is more than 10 knots in sector 210°-250°. Glider flying at Catterick and Dishforth outside normal Hrs

Maintenance	Nil
Fuel	AVGAS 100LL AVTUR Jet A1
Operator	RAF Leeming
Tel: 01677 423041 Ext. 2058/2059 (PPR) Ext. 7770 (ATIS)	
Restaurants	
Taxis/Car Hire	
Weather Info	M T Fax 336 MWC

Operating Hrs
Mon-Thu 0700-2259 Fri 0700-1700 Sat-Sun PPR (Summer) + 1Hr Winter
Station based light ACFT operate Sat-Sun 0900-1715

Circuits	Join not below 1000ft QFE
Landing fee	£7.56 +VAT per 500kgs & £8.50 insurance

Effective date: 30/11/99

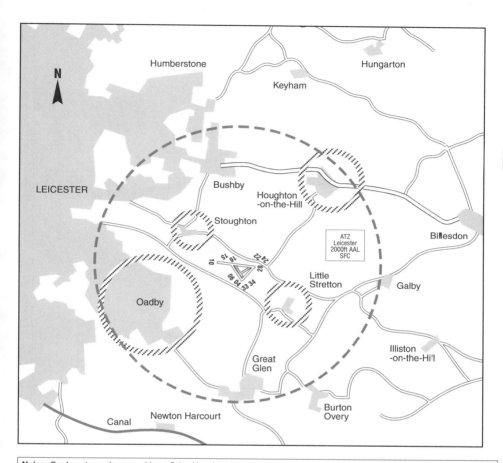

Noise: On departure, please avoid overflying Houghton-on-the-Hill, Little Stretton, Stoughton and Oadby where possible.

ELEVATION	LOCATION	EGBG				LEICESTER
469ft 16mb	4nm ESE of Leicester N5236.47 W00101.92		HON 113.65	063	27.4	• • • • / – – – / – •
PPR	**Diversion AD**		TNT 115.70	144	35.0	– / – • / –

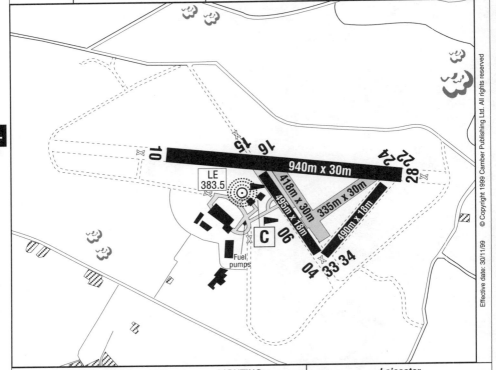

RWY	SURFACE	TORA	LDA	LIGHTING			
10/28	Asphalt	940	940	Thr Rwy APAPI3.25° LHS			
06/24	Grass	335	335	Nil			
16/34	Grass	418	418	Nil			
04/22	Asphalt	490	490	NIL			
15/33	Asphalt	495	495	NIL			

	Leicester
A/G	122.125
NDB	LE 383.5 on A/D range 10nm

Remarks
When using Rwy28, all ACFT are to climb straight ahead maintaining Rwy centre-line to 1000ft before turning. Visual aids to location: Ibn, Green, LE.
Noise: See diagram overleaf.

Warnings
15/33 used for parking when not active. Helicopters to join circuit not above 500ft. Grass Rwys and Twy are subject to waterlogging, especially in winter.

Operating Hrs
0800-1700 (Summer) 0900-1800 (Winter) and by arrangement

Circuits Variable

Landing fee Single £7.50 Twin £20.50 inc VAT
Weekends no charge with fuel uplift over 20ltr or £5 inc.VAT (all ACFT)

Maintenance Fuel	RN Aviation **Tel:** 01162 593629 AVGAS 100LL
Operator	Leicestershire Aero Club Ltd

Leicester Airport, Gartree Road, Leicester LE2 2FG
Tel: 01162 592360
Fax: 01162 592712

Restaurant
Club facilities and bar meals available at AD

Taxis	
ABC	**Tel:** 01162 555111
Car Hire	
National	**Tel:** 01162 510455
Europcar	**Tel:** 01162 538531

Weather Info	AirCen MCW

ELEVATION	LOCATION	EGET		LERWICK (Tingwall)

ELEVATION	LOCATION
43ft 1mb	4nm NW of Lerwick N6011.53 W00114.62
PPR	

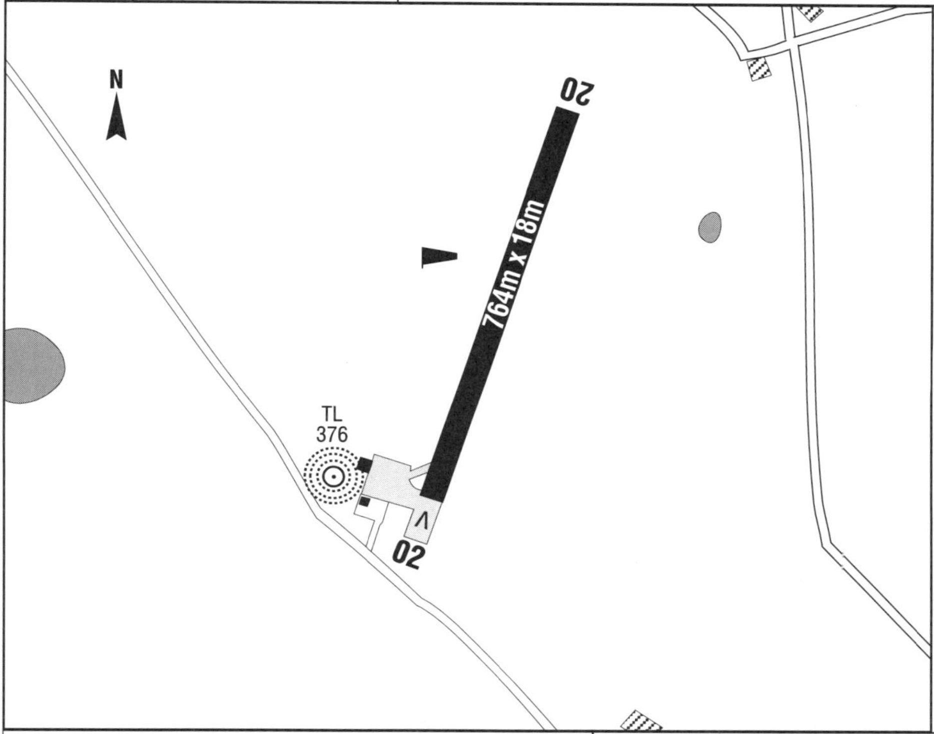

SUM 117.35 012 18.6 ••• / •• − / − −

TL 376

764m x 18m

20

02

N

RWY	SURFACE	TORA	LDA	LIGHTING
02*	Asphalt	764	744	AP Thr Rwy APAPI 4°
20	Asphalt	764	764	Thr Rwy APAPI 4°

*Rwy02 has a displaced Thr.

Tingwall

APP	Sumburgh RAD 123.15
A/G	122.60
NDB	TL 376 On A/D range 25nm

Remarks

Warnings
High GND 449aal 1.25nm to NW

Operator   Shetland Islands Council
Grantfield, Lerwick, Shetland ZE1 0NT
Tel: 01595 744850
Tel: 01595 840306 (AD)
Fax: 01595 694544 (Dept of Roads/Transport)

Restaurants   Bar meals available at Herrislea House within walking distance

Taxis
L Sinclair   **Tel:** 01595 694617
R Greenwald   **Tel:** 01595 692080
Car Hire
J. Leask & Son   **Tel:** 01595 693162
Bolts Car Hire   **Tel:** 01595 692855

Weather Info   AirSc GWC

Operating Hrs
Mon-Fri 0800-1600 (Summer) Mon-Fri 0900-1700 (Winter)

Circuits

Landing fees   Per 0.5 tonne or part: up to 3 tonnes £4.05 3-20 tonnes £8.15. Parking fees: £1.40 per tonne or part thereof for each 24 Hrs or part thereof. All fees +VAT

Maintenance   Nil
Fuel   AVGAS 100LL

ELEVATION	LOCATION			
38ft 1mb	3.5nm NW of St Andrews N5622.37 W00252.11	PTH 110.40	110	17	•–––•/–/••••
PPR MILITARY		SAB 112.50	148	36	•••/•–/–•••

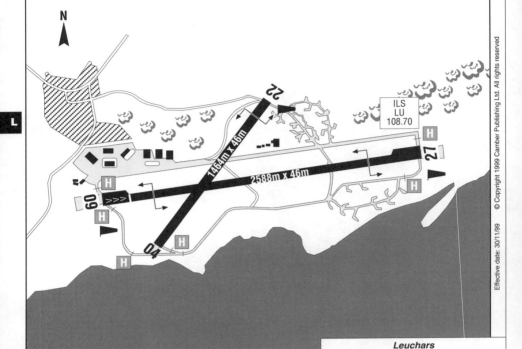

RWY	SURFACE	TORA	LDA	LIGHTING
09	Asphalt/Con	2588	2318	Ap Thr Rwy PAPI 3°
27	Asphalt/Con	2588	2588	Ap Thr Rwy PAPI 2.5°
04	Asphalt	1464	1464	Thr Rwy PAPI 3°
22	Asphalt	1464	1464	Ap Thr Rwy PAPI 3°

Leuchars

APP/MATZ/ LARS	126.50
RAD	123.30
VDF	126.50 122.10
TWR/GND	122.10
TACAN	LUK 110.50
ILS	LU 108.70 Rwy27

Remarks

Military Emergency Diversion AD. All ACFT inbound to Leuchars are to call App on 126.50 before 20nm range. All ACFT to avoid St Andrews by 2000ft/2nm. Light ACFT circuits up to 800ft QFE. Visual aids to Location: Ibn LU Red. Airways traffic request start on 126.50

Warnings

Arrester gear is fitted 396m from Rwy 09/27/22 Thr. There is a possible RAD radiation hazard on the southern Twy between the Thr of Rwy04 & 09. Increased bird hazard on APP to Rwy27, 30 mins either side of sunset (Sep-Mar).

Operator	RAF Leuchars, Fife KY16 0JX
Tel:	01334 839471 Ext.2055

Restaurants

Taxis/Car Hire

Weather Info	M T Fax 338 GWC

Operating Hrs	H24 Movements normally only accepted Mon-Thu 0800-2300 Fri 0800-1700 (local)
Circuits	09 LH 04/22/27 RH
Landing fees	£7.56 +VAT per 500kgs & £8.50 insurance
Maintenance	Nil
Fuel	AVGAS 100LL AVTUR JET A1

ELEVATION	LOCATION	EGXU	LINTON-ON-OUSE

ELEVATION	LOCATION
53ft 2mb	9nm NW of York N5402.95 W00115.17
PPR **MILITARY**	

POL 112.10	064	32.2	• — — • / — — — / • — • •
OTR 113.90	304	45.8	— — — / — / • — •

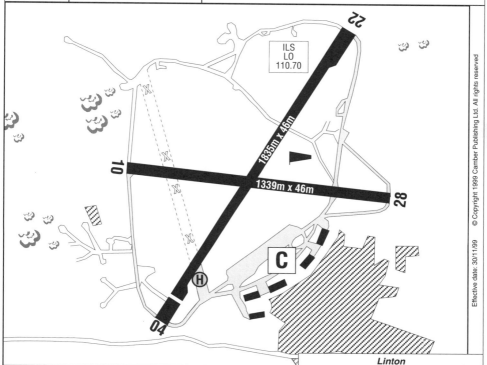

RWY	SURFACE	TORA	LDA	LIGHTING
04	Asphalt	1835	1681	Ap Thr Rwy PAPI 3°
22	Asphalt	1835	1833	Ap Thr Rwy PAPI 3°
*10/28	Asphalt	1339	1339	Thr Rwy PAPI 3°

* Rwy10 only available for landing in an emergency

Linton

APP/MATZ/	
LARS	129.15
RAD	129.15 123.30
TWR	122.10
A/G	129.15 (Glider Ops)
TACAN	LOO 109.00
ILS	LO 110.70 Rwy22

Remarks
First 152m of Rwy04 is sterile. A third Rwy17/35 is closed. Circuit directions and heights are variable. Rwy22 & 28 are RH. Visual aids to Location: Ibn LO Red.

Warnings
Linton is a high intensity flying training school. Two Rwys may be in use at the same time. Glider launching at the AD takes place in the evenings and weekends. Rwy28 – trees 110ft amsl, 130m from Thr 88m left of centre-line. Rwy10 only available for landing in an emergency – trees within APP area up to 143ft amsl.

Operator	RAF Linton-on-Ouse York YO6 2AJ
Tel: 01347 848261 Ext.7491/2 Ext 7327 (ATC) Ext 7467 (ATIS Ansafone)	
Restaurants	
Taxis/Car Hire	
Weather Info	AirN MWC

Operating Hrs
Mon-Thu 0630-1615 Fri 0630-1600 (Summer) + 1Hr Winter

Circuits	04/10 LH 22/28 RH but may vary by ATC
Landing fee	£7.56 +VAT per 500kgs & £8.50 insurance
Maintenance	Nil
Fuel	limited quantities PNR AVGAS 100LL AVTUR JET A1

ELEVATION	LOCATION	EGMJ				LITTLE GRANSDEN

ELEVATION	LOCATION				
250ft 8mb	5nm SE of St Neots N5210.00 W00009.23	BKY 116.25	329	13.2	— • • • / — • — / — • — —
PPR	**Diversion AD**	DTY 116.40	097	34.7	— • • / — / — • — —

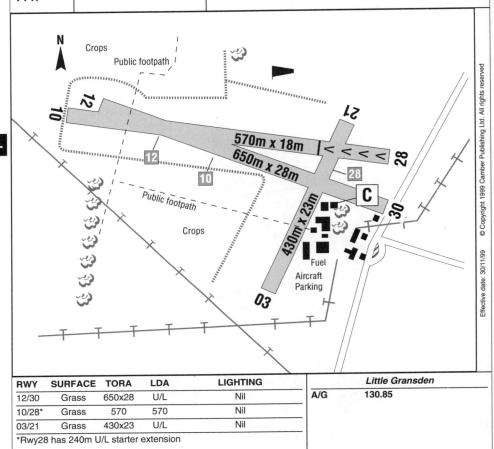

Effective date: 30/11/99

Little Gransden

RWY	SURFACE	TORA	LDA	LIGHTING
12/30	Grass	650x28	U/L	Nil
10/28*	Grass	570	570	Nil
03/21	Grass	430x23	U/L	Nil

*Rwy28 has 240m U/L starter extension

A/G	130.85

Remarks
PPR by telephone essential. Non-radio ACFT not accepted. Not available for public transport flights that require the use of a licensed AD. In the absence of A/G facility, make normal calls. No dead side, all ACFT join downwind to the S or W of AD. Pilots equipped with constant speed propellers should at safest opportunity set power and propellers to cruise climb configuration.

Warnings
Gransden Lodge Gliding AD is located 2500m to the NE. Rwy03/21 is only for use by experienced pilots, marked power lines cross Thr of Rwys03 and 28. Bridle-path crosses Rwy10/28. Rwy03/21 is unmarked and also used as Twys. Avoid over flying The Gransdens, Gamlingay, Hatley Estate and Waresley.

Operating Hrs
Mon-Sat 0830-1830 Sun 0900-1500 (local) and by arrangement

Circuit   03/28/30 LH 10/12/21 RH 800ft QFE

Landing fee   Single £5.00 Free with 50ltr fuel uplift

Maintenance
YAK UK Ltd   **Tel:** 01767 651156 **Fax:** /651157
Fuel   AVGAS 100LL

Operator   Skyline School of Flying Ltd
Fullers Hill, Little Gransden, Sandy, Bedfordshire SG19 3BP
Tel: 01767 651950
Fax: 01767 651157

Restaurants   Tea & coffee available at AD

Taxis
Dereks   **Tel:** 01767 260430
Sandy Cars   **Tel:** 01767 682634
Andys   **Tel:** 01767 260288
Car Hire
Budget   **Tel:** 01223 323838

Weather Info   AirCen BNMC

ELEVATION	LOCATION				LITTLE SNORING

ELEVATION	LOCATION	
196ft 7mb	3nm NE of Fakenham N5251.65 E00054.57	CLN 114.55 358 61.0 — • — • / • — • • / — •
PPR		

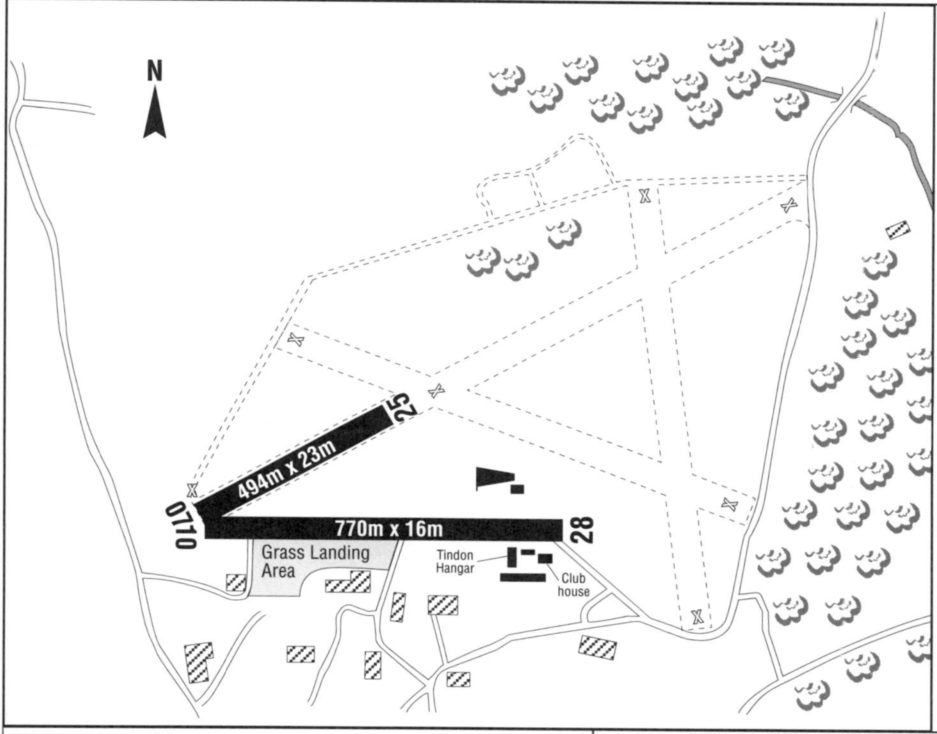

Effective date: 30/11/99

L

Map labels: N, 25, 0710, 494m x 23m, 770m x 16m, 28, Grass Landing Area, Tindon Hangar, Club house

RWY	SURFACE	TORA	LDA	LIGHTING
10/28	Asphalt	770x16	U/L	Nil
07/25	Asphalt	494x23	U/L	Nil

Grass Landing areas:
10/28 approx 390m
07/25 approx 300m

	Non-radio
LARS	Marham 124.15

Remarks
Avoid overflying villages and habitation in vicinity of AD.

Warnings
Uncontrolled vehicles often on AD. Grass landing area for tail wheel ACFT only.

Operator	McAully Flying Group
	Little Snoring Aerodrome, Little Snoring, Fakenham Norfolk NR21 0JR
	Tel: 01328 878470 (Mr T Cushing)
	Tel: 01328 878809 (Tindon Engineering)
Restaurants	Good place for a picnic
Taxis	
Courtesy Cabs	**Tel:** 01328 855500
Car Hire	
Candy	**Tel:** 01328 855348
Weather Info	AirS BNMC

Operating Hrs	SR-SS
Circuits	LH 800ft QFE
Landing fee	Donations please (box nr clubhouse)

Maintenance
Tindon   **Tel:** 01328 878809
Fuel   AVGAS 100LL JET A1
by arrangement from Tindon
during normal working Hrs

LITTLE STAUGHTON

ELEVATION	LOCATION				
225ft 7mb	10nm NE of Bedford N5214.57.W00021.85	**CFD 116.50**	**047**	**14**	— • — • / • • — • / — • •
PPR		**BKY 116.25**	**320**	**22**	— • • • / — • — / — • — —

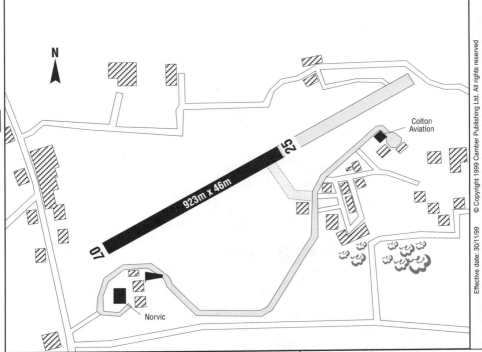

Colton Aviation

923m x 46m

25

07

Norvic

RWY	SURFACE	TORA	LDA	LIGHTING		
07/25*	Asphalt	923x46	U/L	Nil		

*500m starter extention available Rwy25

	Non-radio
A/G	**123.925**

Not always manned make blind calls

Remarks
Strictly PPR. Visiting ACFT should proceed to Colton Aviation. AD is also home of Norvic engineering (Aero engine overhaul).

Warnings
Grass Twy may be boggy when wet. Keep to centre where steel grids provide reinforcement. The grass Twy also leads to the perimeter road which acts as an access track, caution motor vehicles. There is a mast 171ft agl, (331ft amsl) 1500m from the Thr of Rwy25. Caution Gliders may be operating at weekends from Sackville Farm strip 3nm to the WNW, and also from Thurleigh AD.
Noise: avoid overflight of local villages.

Operator	Colton Aviation Ltd
Tel: 01234 376775/376705	
Fax: 01234 376544	

Restaurants	Local pub in village 10mins walk

Taxis		
Anglian St Neots	**Tel:** 01480 75222
Car Hire	
National	**Tel:** 01234 269565

Weather Info	AirCen BNMC

Operating Hrs
0900-2000 daily (Summer) 0900-SS (Winter)

Circuits	07 RH 25 LH

Landing fee	Single £5 Twin £10

No charge if in for maintenance or a fuel stop

Maintenance	Colton Aviation
Fuel	Avgas 100LL

Effective date: 30/11/99 © Copyright 1999 Camber Publishing Ltd. All rights reserved

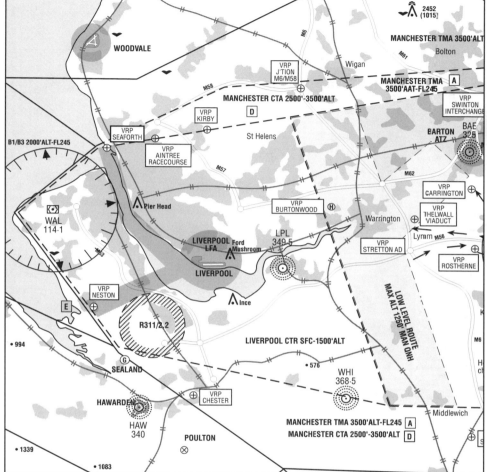

Visual Reference Points (VRPs)

VRP	VOR/VOR	VOR/NDB	VOR/DME
Aintree Racecourse N5328.60 W00256.58	WAL R058°/MCT R291°	MCT R291°/WHI 332°M	WAL 058°/9nm
Burtonwood (disused A/D) N5325.00 W00238.28	WAL R090°/POL R230°	WAL R090°/WHI 001°M	WAL 090°/17nm/ MCT 288°/14nm
Chester N5311.52 W00253.42	WAL R149°/MCT R251°	WAL R149°/WHI 278°M	WAL 149°/15nm/ MCT 251°/24nm
Kirby N5328.80 W00252.90	WAL R065°/MCT R293°	MCT R293°/WHI 337°M	WAL 065°/10nm/ MCT 293°/23nm
Neston N5317.50 W00303.60	WAL R161°/MCT R267°	WAL R161°/WHI 297°M	WAL 161°/7nm/ MCT 267°/29nm
Seaforth N5327.68 W00302.08	WAL R046°/MCT R288°	MCT R288°/ WHI 323°M	WAL 046°/5nm
Stretton (disused A/D) N5320.77 W00231.58	WAL R102°/POL R217°	MCT R271°/WHI 025°M	WAL 104°/22nm/ MCT 273°/9nm

Low Level Route: A proposed re-alignment of the low level route will come into force during 2000. Please watch Notams or our web amendments service for details (www.airplan.u-net.com).

WAL 114.10	116	10.8	•– –/•–/•–••
MCT 113.55	272	21.1	– –/–•–•/–

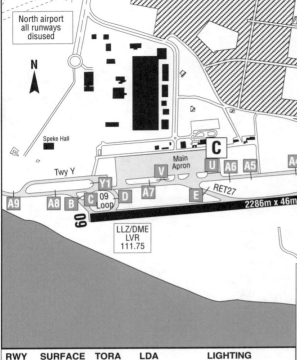

North airport all runways disused

N

Speke Hall

Twy Y

Main Apron

C

Twy Alpha

GA Apron

V U A6 A5 A4 A3 A2

Y1 A7 F G A1

A9 A8 B C D E RET27 RET09 27 Loop

09 Loop 2286m x 46m 27

LLZ/DME LVR 111.75

ILS/DME I-LQ 111.75

Effective date: 30/11/99

L

	Liverpool	
APP	119.85	
RAD	118.45 119.85	
TWR	118.10	
FIRE	121.6	
Handling	Liverpool Aviation Services/Ravenair 131.75 Reed Aviation 122.35 Servisair 130.60	
ILS/DME	I-LQ 111.75 Rwy27	
LLZ/DME	LVR 111.75 Rwy09	
NDB	LPL 349.5* range 25nm *LPL 272/3.88 to Thr27	

RWY	SURFACE	TORA	LDA	LIGHTING
09	Asphalt	2286	2225	Ap Thr Rwy PAPI 3° LHS
27	Asphalt	2286	2286	Ap Thr Rwy PAPI 3° LHS

Remarks

Non-radio ACFT not accepted. Class D Airspace. Await signals from marshaller before proceeding on to apron. Landing and taxiing on grass area not permitted. Circuit training for non-Liverpool based operators is only available by prior arrangement with ATC and is subject to local circuit traffic. For training flights, a booking system is now in operation by ATC. Failure to make a booking may result in the ACFT being refused use of the facilities. Book out by reporting to the flight briefing office in the terminal building or by telephoning details to ATC. Payment of landing fees does not constitute booking out. GA handling available through Liverpool Aviation Services. All ACFT to enter apron through V. ACFT repositioning on the apron require marshaller guidance.

Warnings

Positively identify Rwy27/09 before committing to landing – all Rwys on the N AD are disused. Be aware of Restricted Area R311, 5nm to the SW. Take care when leaving the main apron not to enter the rapid exit turnoff for Rwy27.

Operating Hrs	H24
Circuits	Variable at the discretion of ATC
Landing fee	Single £17.02 +VAT Twin on application

Maintenance

Keenair	**Tel:** 0151 427 3275/7449
Air Nova	**Tel:** 0151 427 8093
LAS	**Tel:** 0151 486 6161
Fuel	AVGAS 100LL AVTUR JET A1

Tel: 0151 4867084 (Depot) **Fax:** 0151 4867720
Payment by cash cheque Esso Exxon carnet 3rd Party cards by prior arrangement or credit card

Handling Liverpool Aviation Services
Tel: 0151 486 6161 **Fax:** 0151 486 5151
Freephone: 0800 368 2680 **Email:** ops@ravenair.co.uk
Reed Aviation **Tel:** 0151 448 0826 **Fax:** 0151 448 0852
Servisair **Tel:** 0151 486 5421 **Fax:** 0151 486 1427

Operator Liverpool Airport PLC
Liverpool Airport, Liverpool L24 1YD
Tel: 0151 288 4000 (Admin) 0151 283 1322 (ATC)
Fax: 0151 288 4000 (Admin) 0151 288 4610(ATC)

Restaurants	Restaurant refreshments in terminal
Taxis	Taxi Rank outside Terminal
Car Hire	
Avis	**Tel:** 0151 486 6686
Hertz	**Tel:** 0151 486 7111
Weather Info	M T9 T18 Fax 342 VN MWC

CTR - Class D Airspace
Normal CTR/CTA Class D Airspace rules apply
1 SVFR clearance will not be given to fixed-wing ACFT if the weather conditions are below 1800m visibility or a cloud base below 600ft.
2 Local flying area. Mersey and Neston Entry/Exit lanes, flight in these areas without compliance with IFR may take place subject to the following:
a) ACFT
b) maximum altitude 1500ft QNH
c) minimum visibility 3km
d) PPR from ATC (Liverpool)

Flights up to 1500ft altitude W of the low level corridor may take place in VMC without compliance with IFR. However, pilots will have to comply (when flying in this area) with Liverpool's Rules which are as follows:
1. Call Liverpool ATC on the appropriate frequency giving details of ACFT position, level and proposed track.
2. Obtain permission for the flight.
3. Maintain a listening watch.
4. Obey any instructions given by Liverpool ATC.
A number of standard routes have been established along which VFR/SVFR clearances will be given.

Noise abatement procedures
ACFT must be operated in a manner calculated to cause the least disturbance practicable in areas surrounding the airport. Inbound ACFT, other than light ACFT flying under VFR or SVFR, shall maintain a height of at least 1500 ft ael until cleared to descend for landing. ACFT approaching without assistance from ILS or RAD must not fly lower than the ILS glidepath. Between 2300 and 0700 (Winter) 2200 and 0600 (Summer), Rwy 09 will only be available for take off when overriding operational considerations necessitate its use. Avoid overflying Speke Hall.

L

ELEVATION	LOCATION	EGOD				LLANBEDR

ELEVATION	LOCATION				
30ft 1mb	3nm S of Harlech N5248.70 W00407.41	WAL 114.10	231	49.8	• – – / • – / • – • •
PPR **MILITARY**		STU 113.10	046	58.5	• • • / – / • • –

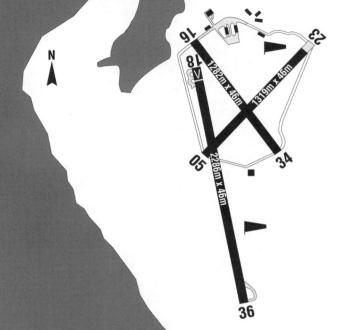

RWY	SURFACE	TORA	LDA	LIGHTING
18	Asphalt	2193	2193	Ap Thr Rwy PAPI 3°
36	Asphalt	2226	2226	Ap Thr Rwy PAPI 3°
05/23	Asphalt	1319	1319	Nil
16/34	Asphalt	1282	1282	Nil

Llanbedr	
APP/RAD/	
VDF	122.50
TWR	122.50

Remarks

PPR 24 Hrs notice in writing required. AD may remain open until 2300. All inbound and transit ACFT to call Llanbedr App at 25nm range or 10 mins ETA.

Warnings

Unmanned target ACFT operating. Main Rwy18/36 obstructed for long periods during target ACFT operations. ACFT wishing to penetrate D202 to call Llanbedr App 122.50. Caution risk of bird strikes. AD Hrs may be changed or ATC services reduced or withdrawn at short notice. Arresting system at the end of Rwys18/36 and 16. Surveillance RAD APP not available to civil ACFT. Rwy05/23 obstructed outside Hrs, to E Rwy16/34. AD sometimes used outside published Hrs. Pilots operating in the vicinity should call on the published frequency to determine whether a/d is active. Vacating Rwy36, follow broken yellow lines to avoid barrier equip. easterly winds make severe low-level turbulence. Use extreme caution if wind in sector 045-135 exceeds 10kts.

Landing fee	£7.56 +VAT per 500kgs & £8.50 insurance
Maintenance **Fuel**	Nil AVGAS 100LL AVTUR FS11 by prior arrangement
Operator RAE, Llanbedr, Gwynedd LL45 2PX **Tel/Fax:** 0134 124 1321 Ext.3022 (PPR Ops) Ext.3246 (ATC)	Serco Skysafe for MOD (PE)
Restaurants	
Taxis/Car Hire	
Weather Info	AirN MWC

Operating Hrs	Mon-Thu 0900-1200 1300-1630 Fri 0900-1200 1300-1600 (local)
Circuit	As much as possible over the sea

ELEVATION	LOCATION	**EGLC**				**LONDON (City)**
16ft 1mb	6nm E of City of London N5130.32 E00003.26					
PPR		BIG 115.10	009	10.1	— • • • / • • / — — •	
		LAM 115.60	208	9.5	• — • • / • — / — —	

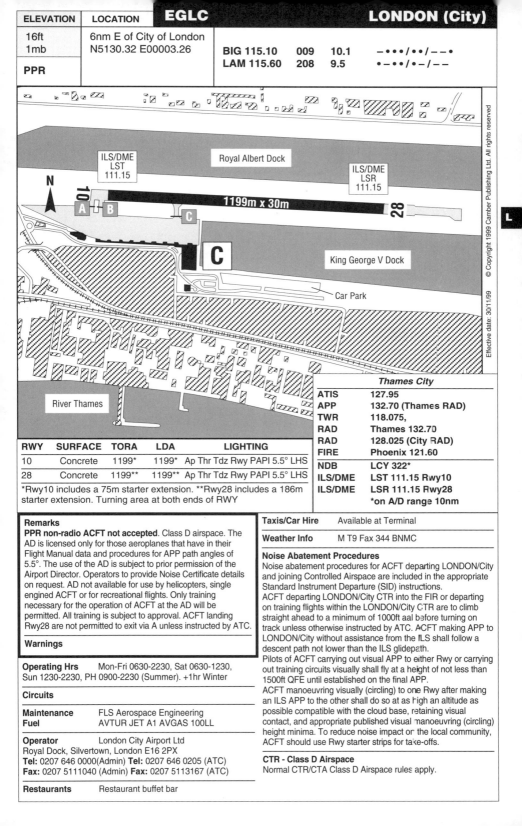

ILS/DME LST 111.15

ILS/DME LSR 111.15

Royal Albert Dock

N

10

A B C

1199m x 30m

28

C

King George V Dock

Car Park

River Thames

			Thames City
ATIS	127.95		
APP	132.70 (Thames RAD)		
TWR	118.075,		
RAD	Thames 132.70		
RAD	128.025 (City RAD)		
FIRE	Phoenix 121.60		
NDB	LCY 322*		
ILS/DME	LST 111.15 Rwy10		
ILS/DME	LSR 111.15 Rwy28		
	*on A/D range 10nm		

RWY	SURFACE	TORA	LDA	LIGHTING
10	Concrete	1199*	1199*	Ap Thr Tdz Rwy PAPI 5.5° LHS
28	Concrete	1199**	1199**	Ap Thr Tdz Rwy PAPI 5.5° LHS

*Rwy10 includes a 75m starter extension. **Rwy28 includes a 186m starter extension. Turning area at both ends of RWY

Remarks
PPR non-radio ACFT not accepted. Class D airspace. The AD is licensed only for those aeroplanes that have in their Flight Manual data and procedures for APP path angles of 5.5°. The use of the AD is subject to prior permission of the Airport Director. Operators to provide Noise Certificate details on request. AD not available for use by helicopters, single engined ACFT or for recreational flights. Only training necessary for the operation of ACFT at the AD will be permitted. All training is subject to approval. ACFT landing Rwy28 are not permitted to exit via A unless instructed by ATC.

Warnings

Operating Hrs
Mon-Fri 0630-2230, Sat 0630-1230, Sun 1230-2230, PH 0900-2230 (Summer). +1hr Winter

Circuits

Maintenance	FLS Aerospace Engineering
Fuel	AVTUR JET A1 AVGAS 100LL

Operator London City Airport Ltd
Royal Dock, Silvertown, London E16 2PX
Tel: 0207 646 0000(Admin) **Tel:** 0207 646 0205 (ATC)
Fax: 0207 5111040 (Admin) **Fax:** 0207 5113167 (ATC)

Restaurants Restaurant buffet bar

Taxis/Car Hire	Available at Terminal
Weather Info	M T9 Fax 344 BNMC

Noise Abatement Procedures
Noise abatement procedures for ACFT departing LONDON/City and joining Controlled Airspace are included in the appropriate Standard Instrument Departure (SID) instructions.
ACFT departing LONDON/City CTR into the FIR or departing on training flights within the LONDON/City CTR are to climb straight ahead to a minimum of 1000ft aal before turning on track unless otherwise instructed by ATC. ACFT making APP to LONDON/City without assistance from the ILS shall follow a descent path not lower than the ILS glidepath.
Pilots of ACFT carrying out visual APP to either Rwy or carrying out training circuits visually shall fly at a height of not less than 1500ft QFE until established on the final APP.
ACFT manoeuvring visually (circling) to one Rwy after making an ILS APP to the other shall do so at as high an altitude as possible compatible with the cloud base, retaining visual contact, and appropriate published visual manoeuvring (circling) height minima. To reduce noise impact on the local community, ACFT should use Rwy starter strips for take-offs.

CTR - Class D Airspace
Normal CTR/CTA Class D Airspace rules apply.

ELEVATION	LOCATION				
196ft 6mb	2.7nm N of Crawley N5108.88 W00011.42	BIG 115.10	220	13.8	— • • • / • • / — — •
		MAY 117.90	309	14.1	— — / • — / — • — —
PPR		MID 114.00	077	17.5	— — / • • / — • •

Effective date: 30/11/99

Map labels: N, Vallance Byways Strip, 553m x 9m, 26, 50ft trees, Old Control Tower, North Terminal Building, South Terminal Building, Cargo Apron, H, Twy 4, Twy 3, Twy 2, Twy 1, Twy 7, Twy 8, Twy 9, Twy 10, Twy A North, Twy A South, Twy Maintenance, C, N, P1, Q1, M1, B2, K1, G1, A5, A1, R1, 26R, 26L, C1, E6, E3, E1, W1, D2, F1, 08L, 08R, 2565m x 45m, 3316m x 46m, ILS/DME I-GG 110.90, ILS/DME I-WW 110.90

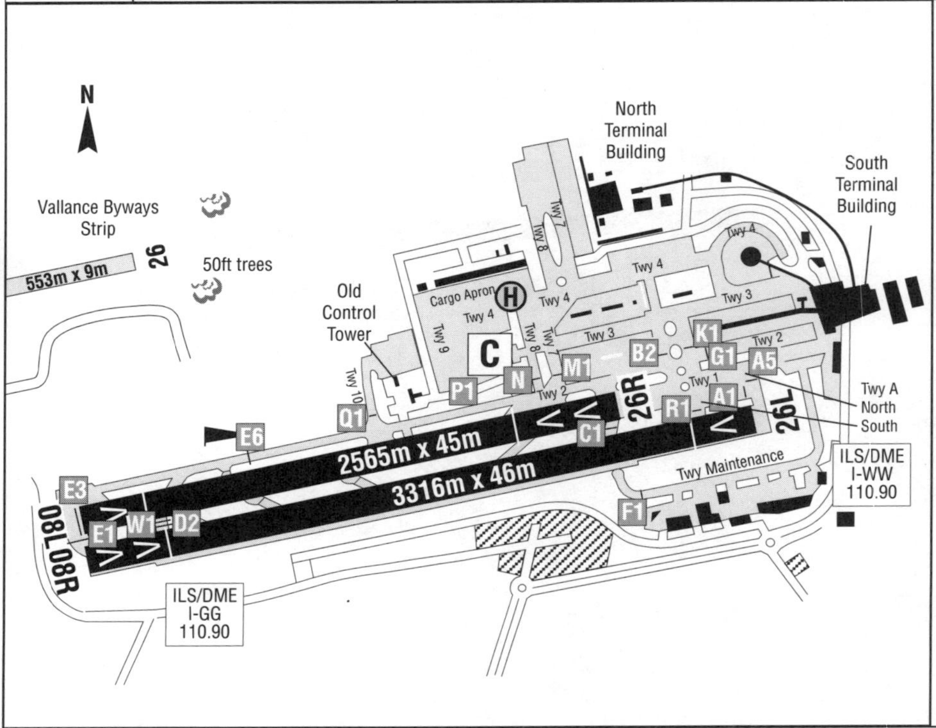

RWY	SURFACE	TORA	LDA	LIGHTING
08R	Asphalt/Concrete	3159	2766	Ap Thr Rwy PAPI 3°
26L	Asphalt/Concrete	3255	2831	Ap Thr Rwy PAPI 3°
08L	Asphalt/Concrete	2565	2243	Ap Thr Rwy PAPI 3°
26R	Asphalt/Concrete	2565	2148	Ap Thr Rwy PAPI 3°

	Gatwick
ATIS	136.525
APP	126.825 118.95
	135.575 129.025
TWR	124.225 134.225
GND	121.80
DELIVERY	121.95
FIRE	121.60
ILS/DME	I-GG 110.9 Rwy08R
ILS/DME	I-WW 110.9 Rwy26L
NDB	GY* 365 range 15nm
NDB	GE** 338 range 15nm
	*GY 082/4.23 Rwy08R/L
	**GE 262/3.96 Rwy26R/L

Remarks

PPR mandatory not more than 10 days, not less than 24 Hrs. Non-radio ACFT not accepted. Use governed by regulations applicable to Gatwick CTR. This airport may be used by executive and private ACFT (general aviation) subject to the following conditions. General aviation operators must notify details of each flight in advance to their nominated handling agent who will obtain permission from apron control Tel: 01293 503089 or Fax 01293 505149. Operators are advised that before selecting Gatwick as an alternate, prior arrangements for GND handling should have been agreed with one of the nominated handling agents. The use of this airport for training is prohibited. Helicopter operations: The helicopter alighting/departing area which is situated at Block 68 is indicated by an H. It is available for daylight use only, but not during periods of low visibility. Helicopters may not carry out direct APP to or take-of from apron areas or Twys. Operator to provide Noise Certificate details on request.

Warnings

In low visibility at night the apron and car park floodlighting may be seen before APP lights on 26L and 26R APP. Except for light signals, GND signals are not displayed. When landing on Rwy26L/R in strong S/SW winds, there is the possibility of building induced turbulence and windshear.

Operating Hrs	H24

Maintenance
Available (by arrangement with local operators)
Fuel   AVTUR JET A1

Operator   Gatwick Airport Ltd
London (Gatwick) Airport, W Sussex RH6 0NP
Tel: 01293 535353 or 0208 6684211 (GAL)
Tel: 01293 575278 (NATS Ltd)
Tel: 01293 575280 (FBU)
Fax: 01293 575204 (NATS Ltd)
Fax: 01293 505093 (GAL)
Telex: 87127 (Nats Ltd) 877725 (GAL)

Handling   GA handling
Interflight   **Tel:** 01293 503201

Restaurants
Restaurants buffets and bars in N and S terminals

Taxis   Available at N and S Terminals
Car Hire
Avis   **Tel:** 01293 529751
Hertz   **Tel:** 01293 530555

Weather Info   M T9 T18 Fax 346 A VM VN BNMC

CTA/CTR Class D Airspace
Normal CTA/CTR Class D Airspace rules apply.
1 VFR ACFT should, whenever possible, avoid flying below 3000ft over towns and other populated areas within the zone. ACFT must also avoid over-flying Crawley.
2 SVFR clearances for flights within the Gatwick CTR can be requested and will be given whenever traffic conditions permit. SVFR clearances will not be granted if the flight visibility is less than 3km or the cloudbase is less than 1000ft.
3 ACFT may be given a RAD service within the zone, if ATC consider it advisable. However pilots must be able to determine their flight path at all times and comply with the low flying rules.

L

Visual Reference Points (VRPs)

VRP	VOR/VOR	VOR/NDB	VOR/DME
Billingshurst N5100.90 W00027.00	MID R113°/GWC R054°	MID R113°/GY 220°M	MID 113°/7nm/
Dorking N5113.62 W00020.10	BIG R249°/LON R166°	BIG R249°/GY 356°M	BIG 249°/15nm/ LON 166°/16nm
Guildford N5114.37 W00035.10	MID R012°/BIG R261°	MID R012°/GY 306°M	MID 012°/11nm
Handcross N5103.17 W00012.13	MID R094°/SFD R328°	MID R094°/GE 220°M	MID 094°/16nm/ MAY 284°/16nm
Haywards Heath N5100.45 W00005.77	MID R102°/SFD R334°	MID R102°/GE 189°M	MID 102°/20nm/ MAY 269°/8nm
Tunbridge Wells N5108.00 E00015.90	BIG R147°/ DET R234°	BIG R147°/GE 101°M	BIG 147°/15nm/ MAY 042°/9nm

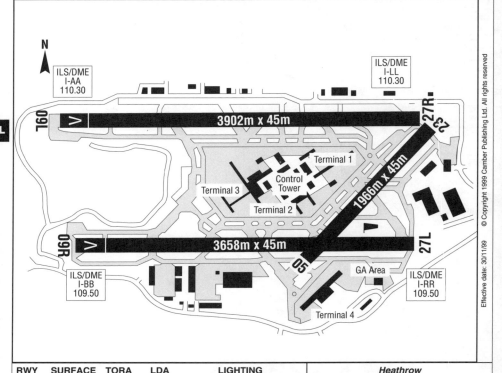

ELEVATION	LOCATION	EGLL		LONDON (Heathrow)

ELEVATION	LOCATION
80ft 3mb	12nm W of London N5128.65 W00027.68
PPR	

LON 113.60   180   1.0   • — • • / — — — / — •

RWY	SURFACE	TORA	LDA	LIGHTING
23	Asphalt	1183	1966	Ap Thr Rwy PAPI 3°
09L	Con/Asph	3902	3597	Ap Thr Rwy PAPI 3°
27R	Con/Asphalt	3902	3902	Ap Thr Rwy PAPI 3°
09R	Con/Asph	3658	3353	Ap Thr Rwy PAPI 3°
27L	Con/Asphalt	3658	3658	Ap Thr Rwy PAPI 3°

Heathrow	
ATIS	123.90
APP	119.725 120.40 127.525 134.975 121.50
RAD	119.90* 125.625
TWR	118.70 118.50 124.475
GND	121.90
DELIVERY	121.975
FIRE	121.60
*SVFR AND HELI FLIGHTS IN CTR	
DME	HTT 110.7 RWY23
NDB	HRW 424**
ILS/DME	I-AA 110.3 RWY09L
ILS/DME	I-BB 109.5 RWY09R
ILS/DME	I-LL 109.5 RWY27L
ILS/DME	I-RR 110.3 RWY27R
** ON A/D RANGE 20NM	

Remarks
PPR mandatory not more than 10 days not less than 24 Hrs. Use governed by regulations applicable to London CTR. IFR procedures apply in all weather conditions. Light single and twin engined ACFT may not use the airport. General and business aviation movements permitted subject to the following conditions. General aviation operators must notify details of each flight in advance to the Manager, Heathrow Airport Operations Centre, Tel: 0208 7455566 or 0208 7457432 or by telex 934892 LHR Limited. Before selecting Heathrow as an alternate, prior arrangements for GND handling should have been agreed with one of the nominated handling agents. The use of this airport for training is prohibited.

Helicopter operations
Helicopter aiming point is located at NE end of Block 97. Helicopters alighting at the aiming point will GND or air taxi to parking areas as directed by ATC. The following conditions and procedures apply to single-engined and light twin-engined ACFT not fully equipped with radio apparatus (including ILS receiver) as specified in the RAC Section but carrying at least the VHF RT frequencies to allow communication with London (Heathrow) Airport APP/Director, TWR and GND Movement Control: the flight must be made on Special VFR clearance under the weather conditions and along the routes specified in the RAC Section. Operator to provide Noise Certificate details on request.
All flights (including Helicopters) are at all times subject to PPR.

Warnings
The letters L H and an arrow pointing to Rwy23 at Heathrow are painted on the gas holder at Southall on its N-E side. When landing on Rwy 27R in strong S/SW winds, beware of the possibility of building induced turbulence and large windshear effects.

Operating Hrs	H24
Circuits	N/A
Landing fees	BAA Plc Airports Rates.
Maintenance	Available (by arrangement)
Fuel	AVTUR JET A1
Operator	London Heathrow Airport

Heathrow Point Middlesex UB3 5AP
Tel: 0208 759 4321 (HAL) 0208 7453328 (NATS)
Tel: 0208 7453368 (Heli route ATC Nats Ltd)
Fax: 0208 7453491/2 (NATS/FBU) 0208 7454290 (HAL)

Restaurants	Restaurants buffets and bars in Terminals
Taxis	Available at Terminals
Car Hire	
Avis	**Tel:** 0208 897 9321
Hertz	**Tel:** 0208 679 1799
Alamo	**Tel:** 0208 897 0536
Weather Info	M T9 T18 Fax 348 A VM VSc BNMC

CTR - Class A Airspace

1. SVFR clearances for flights within the London CTR can be requested and will be given whenever traffic conditions permit. ACFT must be able to communicate on the relevant RT frequencies.
2. SVFR will be restricted to ACFT having an all up weight of 5700kg or less wishing to proceed to an AD within the CTR, or transit the zone at lower levels.
3. SVFR clearance below 1500ft will not be given in the sector enclosed by bearings 020°T and 140°T from LHR, unless otherwise approved.
4. SVFR clearances will not be granted when the visibility is less than 10km or the cloudbase is less than 1200ft.
5. ACFT will be given a RAD service within the zone. However, pilots must remain in conditions such that a flight path can be determined visually. At the same time due regard must be given to the low flying rules, especially the ability to land clear of a built-up area in the event of engine failure.
6. SVFR flights may be subject to delay, and pilots must therefore ensure they have adequate fuel reserves and are able to divert if necessary.

L

Effective date: 30/11/99

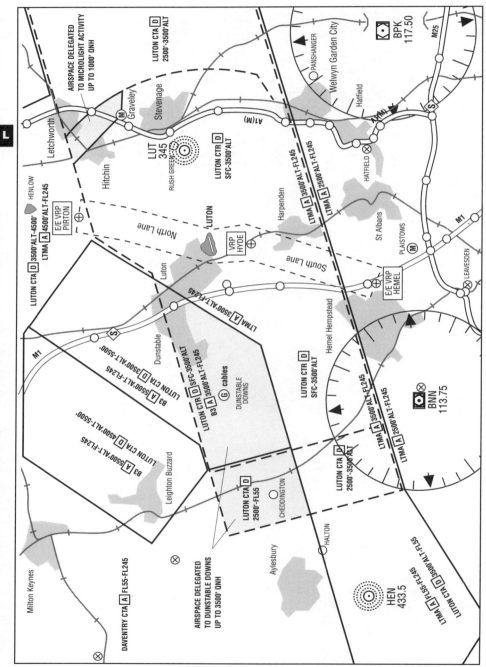

ELEVATION	LOCATION	EGGW	LONDON (Luton)
526ft 18mb	1.5nm E of Luton N5152.47.W00022.12		
PPR		BNN 113.75 041 11.2 — • • • / — • / — • BPK 117.50 313 12.4 — • • • / • — — • / — • —	

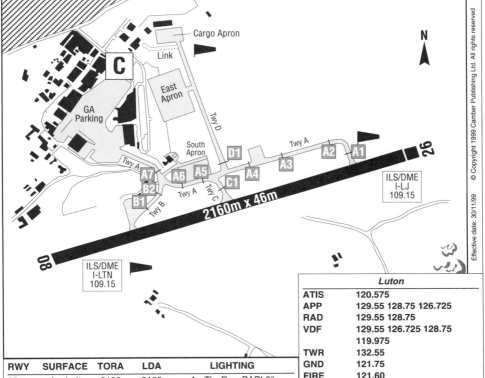

L

Luton	
ATIS	120.575
APP	129.55 128.75 126.725
RAD	129.55 128.75
VDF	129.55 126.725 128.75 119.975
TWR	132.55
GND	121.75
FIRE	121.60
NDB	LUT 345*
ILS/DME	I-LTN 109.15 Rwy08
ILS/DME	I-LJ 109.15 Rwy26 *LUT: 259/3.94 to Thr26 Range 20nm

RWY	SURFACE	TORA	LDA	LIGHTING
08	Asphalt	2160	2160	Ap Thr Rwy PAPI 3°
26**	Asphalt	2160	2075	Ap Thr Rwy PAPI 3°

**Thr Rwy26 displaced by 85m

Remarks
Use governed by regulations applicable to Luton CTR. Non-scheduled commercial executive and private ACFT are subject to PPR. To assist parking arrangements, details of each flight must be notified in advance to the ATC Watch Manager. All GA flights using the main apron must use a handling agent. Handling agents are Magec Aviation Tel: 01582 724182, Servisair Tel: 01582 618603, Metro Aviation Tel: 01582 738322 The airport is available only to qualified pilots. Minimum circuit height for ACFT whose MTWA does not exceed 5700kg (12500lbs) is 1000ft QFE in the vicinity of the Airport. When taking off from Rwy26, if able to turn crosswind by the end of the Rwy confine circuit to the E of the London/Luton railway line.

Warnings
Grass cutting takes place as required during the summer months.

Operating Hrs	H24
Circuits	See Remarks
Landing fee	On application mandatory handling

Maintenance
Magec Aviation Ltd **Tel:** 01582 724182
Fuel AVGAS 100LL
(0600-2359. Other times by arrangement with surcharge).
AVTUR JET A1 Out of Hrs contact
Shell UK Limited **Tel:** 01582 417659

Operator London Luton Airport Ltd
Luton, Bedfordshire LU2 9LY
Tel: 01582 395000 (Switchboard)
Tel: 01582 395256 (Airport Director Passenger Service Duty Officer)
Tel: 01582 395395 (ATC) 01582 395375 (FBU)
Fax: 01582 395499 (FBU) 395205 (Airport Duty Officer) 395313 (Admin/not H24)

Restaurant	Restaurant refreshments and Club facilities available at Airport

Taxis	Available at Terminal
Car Hire	
Alamo	**Tel:** 01582 468414
National	**Tel:** 01582 417723
Europcar	**Tel:** 01582 413438

Weather Info	M T9 T18 Fax 358 A VS BNMC

CTA/CTR Class D Airspace

Normal CTA/CTR Class D Airspace rules apply.

1. Clearances may be requested for SVFR flights within Stansted and Luton Control Zone whenever the traffic situation permits.

2. RAD service may be given whilst within the zone if ATC consider it advisable. However, pilots must remain in conditions such that a flight path can be determined visually. At the same time, due regard must be given to the low flying rules, especially the ability to alight clear of a built-up area in the event of engine failure.

3. To permit ACFT to operate to and from Luton in IMC, but not IFR, the following Entry/Exit lanes have been established:

a) N Lane

b) S Lane

Both lanes are only 1.5nm wide and use is subject to an SVFR clearance from Luton. ACFT must remain clear of cloud and in sight of the surface, not above 1500ft QNH.

Pilots are responsible for their own separation from other ACFT within the lanes and are also responsible for maintaining adequate ground clearance.

SVFR is not compulsory. ACFT can fly VFR in the Luton CTR, subject to ATC clearance.

Visual Reference Points (VRPs)

VRP	VOR/DME	VOR/DME	NDB
Hemel	BPK 276°/12nm	BNN 074°/5nm	LUT 220°M
N5145.37 W00024.97			
Hyde	BPK 304°/11nm	BNN 047°/10nm	LUT 238°M
N5150.65 W00021.97			
Pirton	BPK 332°/16nm	BNN 032°/17nm	LUT 331°M
N5158.30 W00019.90			

ELEVATION	LOCATION	EGMH			LONDON (Manston)
178ft 6mb	2.5nm W of Ramsgate N5120.53 E00120.77 **Diversion AD**		DVR 114.95	002	10.8 — • • / • • • — / • — •
PPR			DET 117.30	090	28.2 — • • / • / —

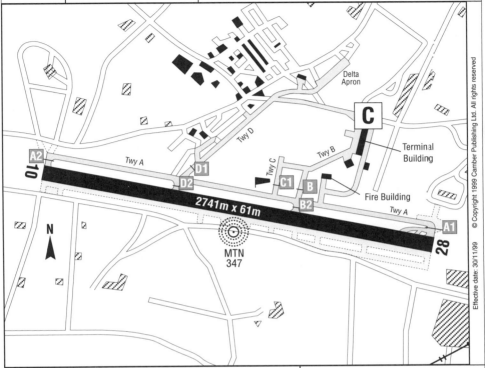

RWY	SURFACE	TORA	LDA	LIGHTING
10/28	Asph/Con	2741	2741	Ap Thr Rwy PAPI 3°

Manston	
LARS	126.35
APP	126.35
RAD	126.35 119.925 129.45
VDF	126.35
TWR	119.275 122.10
NDB	MTN 347 20nm

Remarks
PPR. The sterile areas on the sides of Rwy10/28 are not to be used for taxiing of ACFT. ACFT using Manston are to carry Third Party Insurance cover of not less than £500,000. Visual aids to location: Ibn MN Red. LARS not available at present but is anticipated during 2000.

Warnings
Pilots intending to transit between Twy A and the B, C and D Twys On short final to Rwy28 turbulence may be encountered when surface wind is from NW or SW. Pilots entering the Delta apron use caution, uncontrolled vehicular and pedestrian traffic on apron.

Operator London Manston Airport
PO Box 500, Manston, Ramsgate, Kent CT12 5BS
Tel: 01843 823333 (ATC)
Fax: 01843 821386 (KIA)
Telex: (Civil) 965446 KIAOPS G

Restaurants Restaurant and refreshments available

Taxis
Minicabs **Tel:** 01843 581581
Car Hire
Budget **Tel:** 01843 860310

Weather Info M T15 Fax 372 BNMC

Operating Hrs 0700-2100 (Summer) 0800-2000 (Winter)
and by arrangement

Circuits 28 LH 10 RH 1000ft QFE

Landing fee On application

Maintenance
TG Aviation **Tel:** 01843 823656
Fuel AVGAS 100LL AVTUR JET A1

ELEVATION	LOCATION	**EGSS**			**LONDON (Stansted)**
347ft 11mb	2.5nm ENE of Bishops Stortford N5153.10 E00014.10	BKY 116.25	139	9.0	— • • • / — • — / — • — —
PPR		LAM 115.60	016	14.5	• — • • / • — / — —
		BPK 117.50	062	14.9	— • • • / • — — • / — • —

Effective date: 30/11/99

RWY	SURFACE	TORA	LDA	LIGHTING
05/23	Asphalt	3048	3048	Ap Thr Rwy PAPI 3°

	Stansted/Essex
ATIS	127.175 114.55 (CLN VOR)
APP	120.625
RAD	120.625 Essex Rad
	126.95
TWR	123.80 125.55
GND	121.725
DEL	125.55
FIRE	121.60
ILS/DME	I-SX 110.50 Rwy23
ILS/DME	I-SED 110.50 Rwy05
NDB	SSD 429 (20nm) on a/d

Remarks

PPR not less than 4hrs before intended movement. Non-radio ACFT not accepted. Use governed by regulations applicable to Stansted CTR. Use of a handling agent is mandatory. Pilots of non-commercial (General Aviation) flights arriving from abroad are required to report to Customs at the Designated Customs Clearance Office in the Business Aviation Terminal. The Business Aviation Terminal is manned 0700-2300 (L) daily & available outside Hrs by arrangement with Metro Aviation. The use of the airport for training is subject to prior permission, contact Stansted ATC Tel: 01279 669328 before departure. On Public Holidays flying training is permitted only by ACFT whose MTWA does not exceed 9000kg. A helicopter aiming point is situated in block 100 at the western end of Twy2 and is indicated by "H". The aiming point is unlit and available during daylight Hrs for VFR operations only. Helicopters may arrive or depart from the aiming point and air or ground taxi as directed by ATC. Twy Alpha W is limited to ACFT with a wingspan of 27m or less.

Warnings

Extensive instrument flying takes place in vicinity of airport. Noise: An ACFT using this airport shall maintain as high an altitude as practicable, shall avoid flying over Bishops Stortford, Sawbridgeworth and Stansted Mountfitchet below 2500ft amsl and shall avoid flying over St. Elizabeth's Home below 4000ft amsl.

Operating Hrs	H24

Circuits   Do not descend below 2000ft QNH
downwind and avoid over-flying Great Dunmow and Takeley

Landing fees	BAA Plc Airport Rates

Maintenance   Available (by arrangement)
Fuel   AVTUR JET A1 Water/Meth 45/55/30
N side AVTUR JET A1 available 0700-2300 daily. At other
times a call out charge of £100.00 will be levied unless fuel is
required for medical flight or prior arrangement has been made.
Tel: 01279 663178/9 (Esso)

Operator   Stansted Airport Ltd
Stansted, Essex CM24 1QW
Tel: 01279 680500 (Airport) 01279 669316 (NATS)
Fax: 01279 662066 (SAL) 01279 669339 (NATS)
Fax: 01279 669336 (FBU)

Restaurants	Buffets and bars in Terminal
Taxis/Car Hire	Available at Terminal
Weather Info	M T9 T18 Fax 352 A VM BNMC

GA Handling Agents (Compulsory)
Metro Business Aviation **Tel:** 01279 680167 **Fax:** /681367
Inflite Ltd **Tel:** 01279 680736 **Fax:** /680104
Universal Aviation UK **Tel:** 01279 680349 **Fax:** /680372

CTA/CFR Class D Airspace
Normal CTA/CTR Class D Airspace rules apply
1. Clearances may be requested for SVFR flights within the
Stansted and Luton Control Zone and will be given whenever
the traffic situation permits.
2. RAD service may be given whilst within the zone if ATC
consider it advisable. However, pilots must remain in
conditions such that a flight path can be determined visually.
At the same time due regard must be given to the low flying
rules, especially in the event of engine failure.
3. Stansted VFR arrivals and departures are
cleared normally not above 1500ft QNH by the following
routes:
a) Audley End Railway Station via M11
b) Great Dunmow via A120
c) Puckeridge via A120 avoiding Bishops Stortford
d) Nuthampstead VRP
4. VFR traffic wishing to transit the Stansted zone can expect
a clearance via the routes detailed in 3 a-d Great Dunmow
and either Puckeridge or Nuthampstead routing via the
Stansted overhead not above 2000ft QNH. N.B. Beware of
ACFT in the Nuthampstead circuit up to 1500ft QNH.
5. The following areas are notified for the purposes of the low
flying rule (Rule 5):
a) within 1nm of the A10 and the river Lea from the Ware
(VRP) to the intersection with the M25.
b) within 1nm of the M25 from its intersection with the A10
clockwise to its intersection with the M11
c) within 1nm of the track between Ware and Epping (VRPs)
where the route lies beneath the CTR/CTA.
6. a) For clearance contact Essex Radar giving at least 5min
notice. Do not enter controlled airspace without clearance.
b) Clearance may be subject to delay or re-routing.
c) Pilots are reminded of the close proximity of busy minor AD
adjacent to CTA/CTR periphery.

Visual Reference Points (VRPs)

VRP	VOR/VOR	VOR/DME
Audley End Stn N5200.25 E00012.42	BKY R084°/LAM R009°	BKY 084°/5nm
Braintree N5152.70 E00033.23	BKY R113°/LAM R050°	LAM 050°/20nm
Chelmsford N5144.00 E00028.40	BKY R138°/LAM R070°	LAM 070°/13nm
Diamond Hangar N5152.67 E00014.15		
Epping N5142.00 E00006.67	BKY R177°/BNN R097°	BNN 097°/25nm
Great Dunmow N5152.30 E00021.75	BKY R126°/LAM R033°	BKY 126°/13nm
Haverhill N5204.95 E00026.07	BKY R071°/LAM R025°	LAM 025°/28nm
N end of Hangar 4 N5153.32 E00013.53		
Nuthampsted (Disused A/D) N5159.40 E00003.72	BKY VOR site	LAM 354°/21nm
Puckeridge (A10/A120) N5153.10 E00000.27	BKY R202°/LAM R343°	BKY 202°/7nm
Ware N5148.70 W00001.60	BKY R200°/LAM R330°	LAM 330°/12nm

ELEVATION	LOCATION	LONG ACRES FARM (Sandy)			
80ft 2mb	By A1 close to W of Sandy N5207.44 W00018.35	**CFD 116.5**	077	11.5	− • − • / • • − • / − • •
PPR		**BKY 116.25**	305	16	− • • • / − • − / − • − −

N

60

4ft hedge

550m x 18m

Upslope

27

25ft trees

River Ivel

A1

© Copyright 1999 Camber Publishing Ltd. All rights reserved

Effective date: 30/11/99

L

17

Lake

365m x 18m

C

20ft hedge

35

A603

Sandy

RWY	SURFACE	TORA	LDA	LIGHTING		*Sandy*	
17/35	Grass	365x18	U/L	Nil	**A/G**	**129.825***	
09/27	Grass	550x18	U/L	Nil			

* Microlight common frequency if no answer make blind calls

Remarks
PPR by telephone. Briefing essential. Microlight AD with Ab-initio training but suitable STOL ACFT are welcome at pilots own risk. **Noise:** Do not overfly Sandy to E of AD.

Warnings
Considerable road traffic crosses Rwy35 short final using A603. 25ft trees adjacent to Lake on short final Rwy27, has upslope in final third. There is a 4ft hedge close to the Thr09. Old Warden AD, (Shuttleworth collection) is 2.5nm SSW of AD, has regular air displays during the summer period, particularly at weekends. Sandy TV mast, 972ft amsl, (790ft agl) 2.5nm E of AD.

Operator	Snowy Barton, Long Acres Farm Mogerhanger Road, Sandy, Bedfordshire SG19 1ND **Tel:** 01767 691616
Restaurants	Tea & Coffee available at airfield Little Chef within walking distance adjacent to A1
Taxis Sandy Taxis	**Tel:** 01767 683333
Car Hire	Nil
Weather Info	AirCen BNMC

Operating Hrs	SR-SS
Circuits	35/09 LH 27/17 RH No dead side
Landing fee	Nil
Maintenance	Microlight maintenance available
Fuel	MOGAS available from nearby garage

ELEVATION	LOCATION				**LONG MARSTON**

ELEVATION	LOCATION				
154ft 5mb	3.5nm SW of Stratford-on-Avon N5208.44 W00145.18	**HON** 113.65	199	13.5	•••• / – – – / – •
PPR		**DTY** 116.40	268	24	– •• / – / – • – –

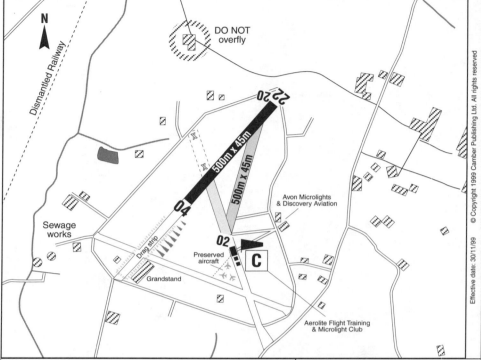

RWY	SURFACE	TORA	LDA	LIGHTING
02/20	Grass	500x45	U/L	Nil
04/22	Asphalt	500x45	U/L	Nil

Long Marston

A/G	129.825
Microlight common frequency	

Remarks

PPR by telephone. Visiting ACFT welcome. AD used for microlighting and occasional motorsport. Avoid overflying HMP Long Lartin, 8nm WSW of AD, Long Marston village to W & farm on chart.

Warnings

Wellesbourne Mountford ATZ 3nm NE.

Operator	Long Marston Airfield Ltd
	Long Marston, Warwickshire
	Tel: 01789 720326 (PPR owner)
	Tel: 01789 299229 (Aerolite Ltd flight training)
	Tel: 0370 680195 (Mobile)
Restaurant	Tea & coffee making facilities
Taxis/Car Hire	Can be arranged locally
Weather Info	AirCen BNMC

Operating Hrs	0900-SS (Local)
Circuits	02/22 RH 04/20 LH 600ft QFE (04/22 500ft QFE)
Landing fee	Nil but £25 without PPR
Maintenance	Microlight available
Fuel	Nil

ELEVATION	LOCATION			**LONG STRATTON**
172ft 5mb	11.5nm SW of Norwich Airport N5229.30 E00113.00	CLN 114.55	008 38	– • – • / • – • • / – •
PPR				

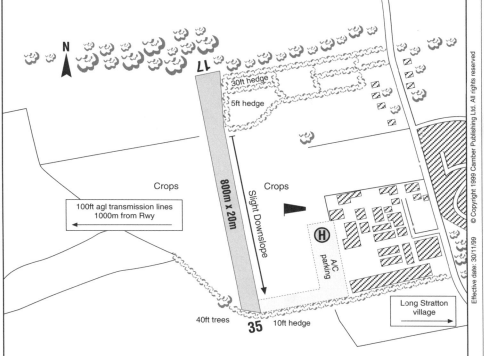

RWY	SURFACE	TORA	LDA	LIGHTING		*Chequair Ops*	
17/35	Grass	800x20	U/L	Nil	A/G	122.95	
AD U/L for fixed wing, Licensed for rotary							

Remarks
PPR strictly by telephone and at pilots own risk. Visitors must have business with Chequair (Operations), SMC Aviation Services or Stratton Motor Co, (Aston Martin Dealership). Noise: Do not overfly the villages of Long Stratton (E) and Wacton (SW).

Warnings
Pilots must receive briefing from Chief Pilot or Ops. Helicopters are to join via reporting points to N & S of AD. Details provided with PPR. National Grid powerline runs 100m W of Rwy 100ft agl.

Operating Hrs
Mon-Fri 0800-1730 Sat 0800-1200(Local) Closed Sunday

Circuits
Fixed wing 35 LH 17 RH Rotary via entry/exit points

Landing fee   £10

Maintenance   JAR 145 fixed & rotary wing limited hangarage available for visiting ACFT and Helicopters by arrangement
Fuel   JET A1

Operator   Chequair Ltd, Tharston Ind Site Chequers Lane, Long Stratton, Norwich NR15 2PE
Tel: 01508 531144 (PPR)
Tel: 01508 530493 (Out of Hrs)
Fax: 01508 531670

Restaurant

Taxi/Car Hire
Available from the operators by arrangement

Weather Info   AirS BNMC

ELEVATION	LOCATION	EGQS			LOSSIEMOUTH
42ft 2mb	4nm N of Elgin N5742.31 W00320.35	INS 109.20 WIK 113.60	074 196	24.8 45.9	•• / – • / ••• • – – / •• / – • –
PPR MILITARY					

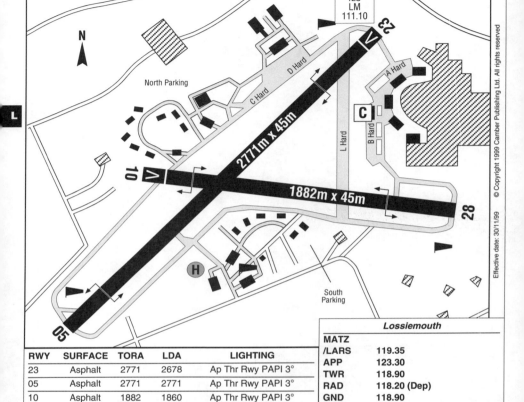

RWY	SURFACE	TORA	LDA	LIGHTING
23	Asphalt	2771	2678	Ap Thr Rwy PAPI 3°
05	Asphalt	2771	2771	Ap Thr Rwy PAPI 3°
10	Asphalt	1882	1860	Ap Thr Rwy PAPI 3°
28	Asphalt	1882	1882	Ap Thr Rwy PAPI 3°

Arrester gear 23/28 426m 05 396m 10 161m from threshold

Lossiemouth	
MATZ /LARS	119.35
APP	123.30
TWR	118.90
RAD	118.20 (Dep)
GND	118.90
ILS	LM 111.10 Rwy23 (no OM)

Remarks
PPR required 24 Hrs. ATZ active H24. Visual aid to location: IBn LM Red. Aerial farm at Milltown disused AD 4nm SE of A/D.

Warnings
Avoid overflying Elgin, Lossiemouth & Gordonstoun school.

Operator	RAF Lossiemouth
Tel: 0134381 2121 Ext. 2051 Ext 7666 (ATIS)	

Restaurants

Taxis/Car Hire

Weather Info	M T Fax 356 GWC

Operating Hrs
Mon-Thu 0700-1500 Fri 0700-1600 + 1Hr Winter

Circuits	Join not below 1000ft QFE
Landing fee	£7.56 +VAT per 500kgs & £8.50 insurance
Maintenance Fuel	Nil AVTUR Jet A1

L

LOUTH HALL FARM (North Reston)

ELEVATION	LOCATION	
4ft 0mb	4nm SE of Louth N5319.50 E00004.40	**OTR 113.90** 168 23 – – – / – / • – • **GAM 112.80** 090 37 – – • / • – / – –
PPR		

Track to North Reston

White hangar

505m x 30m

Slight downslope

Crops

Drainage ditch

Drainage ditch

Drainage ditch

A157

Stream

Dismantled railway

Drainage ditch

Gillwoods Grange

24

06

N

L

© Copyright 1999 Camber Publishing Ltd. All rights reserved

Effective date: 30/11/99

Strip profile

mod | slight | flat

06 _____ **24**

RWY	SURFACE	TORA	LDA	LIGHTING			
06/24	Grass	505x30	U/L	Nil			

	Non-Radio
LARS	(Coningsby) 120.8

Remarks
PPR essential by telephone. Visiting ACFT welcome. AD well prepared but has no facilities. Rwy flat at 24 Thr, has a slight downslope in second third, final 60m has increased downslope. Aid to location; disused railway from Louth to Boston passes close to W of AD. **Noise:** Avoid overflight North Reston to the N of AD.

Warnings
Drainage ditches cross the Thr of both landing directions and run along N side of the strip. Approaches are clear. Gliding activity at Manby & Strubby, (mainly weekends). Crops are grown up to S edge of AD.

Operator	Mr John Read, Hall Farm North Reston, Louth LN11 8JD **Tel:** 01507 450238
Restaurant	Royal Oak Cawthorpe **Tel:** 01507 600750
Taxis Dixon's **Car Hire**	 **Tel:** 01507 603864 Nil
Weather Info	AirN MWC

Operating Hrs	SR-SS
Circuits	1000ft QFE
Landing Fee	Nil
Maintenance **Fuel**	Nil Nil

ELEVATION	LOCATION
60ft 2mb	1.5nm SE of Louth N5321.50 E00002.00
PPR	

GAM 112.80   086   36.5   — — • / • — / — —

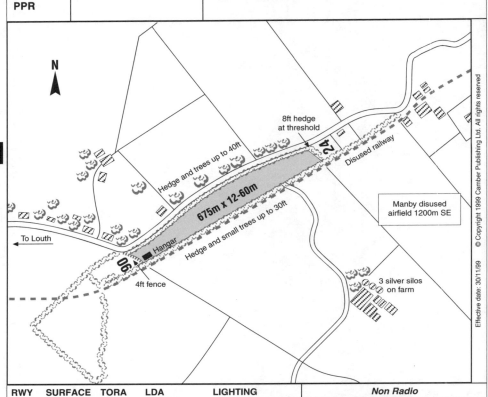

RWY	SURFACE	TORA	LDA	LIGHTING
06/24	Grass	675x12/60	U/L	Nil

Non Radio

LARS (Waddington)	127.35
LARS (Coningsby)	120.80

Remarks
PPR by telephone. AD of variable width between the Louth to Stewton road and the disused, (and removed), Louth to Mablethorpe railway. The witness marks of the old railway track are clearly visible. Visiting pilots are welcome at pilots own risk. This AD is quite unusual in its location and great care should be taken.

Warnings
The AD is bordered by mature hedges and trees which may cause turbulence. The AD has undulations in the centre. Identification of the Thr is particularly important. At 24 Thr the adjoining field is used for paddocks and a hedge across it. The Rwy is TO THE WEST OF THE HEDGE. There is a low fence at the 06 Thr.

Operator	Douglas Electronic Industries Ltd Louth, Lincolnshire **Tel:** 01507 604398/606128
Restaurant	
Taxi/Car Hire	Operator can provide help/assistance
Weather Info	AirN MWC

Operating Hrs	SR-SS
Circuits	As you wish but avoid local habitation 1000ft QFE
Landing Fee	Nil
Maintenance **Fuel**	Nil Nil

ELEVATION	LOCATION			LUDHAM
50ft 1mb **PPR**	11nm ENE of Norwich city centre N5243.10 E00133.07	**CLN 114.55**	020 54.5	— • — • / • — • • / — •

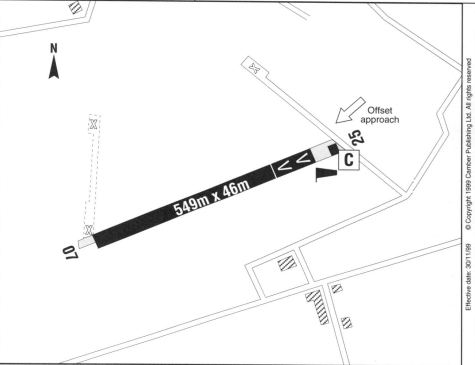

RWY	SURFACE	TORA	LDA	LIGHTING
07	Concrete	420	450	Nil
25	Concrete	549	420	Nil

	Non radio
LARS	**Coltishall 125.90**
APP	**Norwich 119.35**

Remarks
Situated close to the E boundary of the Coltishall MATZ.
Suggest contact Norwich APP on 119.35 as this controller is
at Coltishall during their normal Operating Hrs.

Warnings
Hangar at E end of Rwy necessitates an off-set APP to
Rwy25. Loose stones on Rwy. Large commercial helicopters
operate at low altitudes to the E of the AD following defined
helicopter routes. AD situated in the heart of Broadland,
please fly with consideration.

Operator	Ludham Aerodrome
Tel: 01493 843211 (Mr.R.Collins)	
Tel: 01493 730064 (Ansaphone)	
Fax: 01493 859555	

Restaurant

Taxis/Car Hire

Weather Info   AirS BNMC

Operating Hrs	Available on request
Circuits	07 LH 25 RH 1000ft aal
Landing fee	£5
Maintenance **Fuel**	Available Nil

L

ELEVATION	LOCATION				
455ft 15mb	11nm NW of Hartland Point N5110.20 W00440.23	**BCN 117.45**	243	62.5	– • • • / – • – • / – •
PPR		**BHD 112.05**	321	65	– • • • / • • • • / – • •

N

Ponds

4ft white posts

400m x 28m

24

06

4ft white posts

Acklands Moor

Old Light

Beacon Hill

Shop

Marisco Tavern

(H)

RWY	SURFACE	TORA	LDA	LIGHTING		Non-radio	
06/24	Grass	400x28	U/L	Nil	**FIS**	London Info 124.75	

Remarks
PPR by telephone. Light ACFT welcome at pilots own risk. Rwy has no designators but is marked by 4ft white posts at its edges. The island has many interesting buildings and much wildlife. The Old Lighthouse is close to SW of strip.

Warnings
This is a difficult strip for the experienced pilot only! The rwy is convex in configuration. PPR is essential so that livestock may be moved and a fence taken down to allow rwy use. Advise land 06 if wind conditions allow, the strip is in good condition but bumpy for the first three posts from 06 Thr. A rock is present flush with rwy surface. Please do not low fly in the vicinity of the island to avoid disturbance to bird colonies and possibility of birdstrike. However a flyby is advised to examine strip prior to landing.

Maintenance	Nil
Fuel	Nil

Operator The Lundy Company
Lundy Island, Bristol Channel, North Devon EX39 2LY
Tel: 01237 431831
Fax: 01237 431832

Restaurants Marisco Tavern (within easy walking distance of the strip) B&B sometimes available contact the operator for more information

Taxi/Car Hire	Nil
Weather Info	AirSW BNMC

Operating Hrs	Available on request
Circuits	1000ft QFE

Landing fee Administered by the National Trust.
The landing fee is £10 plus £3.50 National Trust admission waived on production of NT membership card

L

ELEVATION	LOCATION	EGMD				LYD
11ft 0mb	1.2nm E of Lydd N5057.37 E00056.35	LYD 114.05	148	3.5	•—••/—•—•/—••	
	Diversion AD	DVR 114.95	237	19.9	—••/•••—/•—•	
PPR		MAY 117.90	101	31.3	——/•—•/—•——	

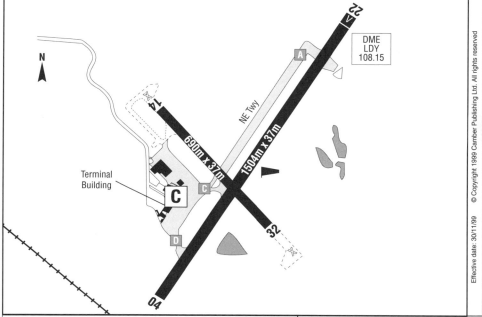

RWY	SURFACE	TORA	LDA	LIGHTING
04	Asphalt	1468	1468	Ap Thr Rwy PAPI 3° LHS
22	Asphalt	1504	1468	Ap Thr Rwy PAPI 3.5° LHS
14/32	Asphalt	690x35	U/L	Nil

Lydd	
AFIS	120.70 131.30
DME 22	LDY 108.15
VOR/DME	LYD 114.05 not on A/D
NDB	LYX 397 – 217/1.17 to ARP Range 15nm

Remarks

Take-offs: Rwy04: Climb straight ahead to 1000ft, or crossing the coast, whichever is sooner, before turning right or left as instructed by ATC. Rwy22: Climb straight ahead to 800ft before turning left or right as instructed by ATC. Landing: Rwy04 & 22. Inbound ACFT maintain as high an altitude as is practicable & maintain altitude 800ft minimum until commencing final APP. ACFT approaching to land without assistance from RAD follow a descent not lower than 3° glideslope or that shown by the PAPIs. Training take-offs involving engine failure practice Not allowed Rwy04. Visual aids to identification: Flashing white strobe. VFR arrival position overhead 1500ft QNH downwind at 1000ft QFE. Deadside joins not permitted due poor visibility from TWR. NE Twy available light singles only during daylight. Caution: Twy 6m wide with uneven edges. Departures Rwy22, power checks hold C, then as instructed. Rwy22 not available to turbine ACFT.

Warnings

Avoid over flying Dungeness Nuclear Power Station 2.5nm SE of the AD below 2000ft. Use of U/L Rwy14/32 is not permitted whilst 04/22 is in operation. Circuits on 14/32 will be prohibited whilst the circuit of 04/22 is active. Extensive firing activity on Lydd ranges (EGD-044) DAAIS available on Lydd info during Ops Hrs, outside Hrs from London INFO 124.6.

Circuits	04/32 RH 14/22 LH
Landing fees	1.1p per kg MAUW +VAT
Maintenance Fuel	Skysure **Tel:** 01797 321444 AVGAS 100LL AVTUR JET A1 Water/Meth
Operator	Lydd Airport Group Ltd,

Lydd Airport, Lydd, Romney Marsh, Kent TN29 9QL
Tel: 01797 320401 320881(ATC) 320401 (Admin)
Fax: 01797 321964(ATC) 321615 (Admin)

Restaurant	Bar restaurant

Taxis	
Shepways	**Tel:** 01679 66842/0836 775014

Car Hire
Sussex Road Garage **Tel:** 01797 362404
Romney Car Hire **Tel:** 01797 363189 **Fax:** 01797 364505

Weather Info	M T9 Fax 362 BNMC

Visual Reference Points (VRPs)

Appledore Rly Stn	N5101.01 E00049.01
Ashford	N5108.80 E00051.91
Folkestone Lighthouse	N5104.55 EC0111.70
Rye	N5057.00 E00044.00

Operating Hrs Daily 0800-2000 (Apr- Sept local)
Sun-Thu 0800-1800 Fri-Sat 0800-1900 (Oct-Mar local)
and by arrangement

Effective date: 30/11/99

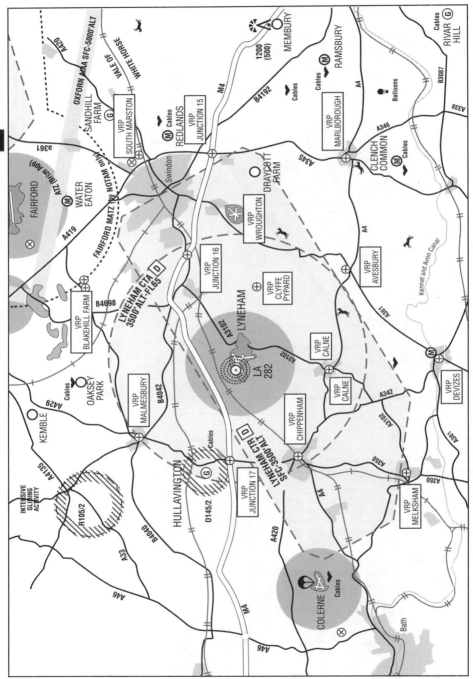

ELEVATION	LOCATION	EGDL				LYNEHAM
513ft 17mb	8nm WSW of Swindon N5130.31. W00159.60	CPT 114.35	277	28.8	– • – • / • – – • / –	
PPR MILITARY		SAM 113.35	329	41.1	• • • / • – / – –	

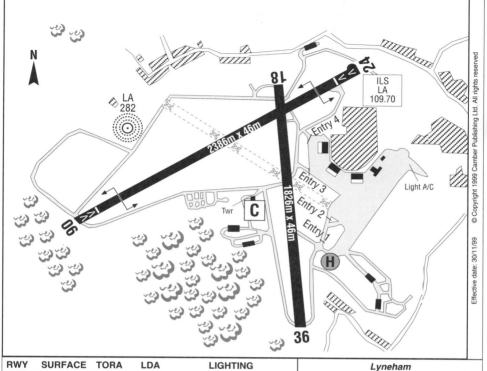

L

RWY	SURFACE	TORA	LDA	LIGHTING
06	Asphalt/conc	2386	2386*	Ap Thr Rwy PAPI 3°
24	Asphalt/conc	2386	2204	Ap Thr Rwy PAPI 3°
18/36	Asphalt/conc	1826	1826	Ap Thr Rwy PAPI 3°

*2235 by night Arrester gear Rwy24 480m Rwy06 510m from THrs

	Lyneham
ZONE/RAD	123.40
APP	118.425 123.40
RAD	123.30
VDF	123.40 118.425
TWR	119.225 122.1
GND	129.475 122.1
TACAN	LYE 109.8 on A/D
ILS	LA 109.70 Rwy24
NDB	LA 282
	on A/D range 40nm

Remarks

PPR 24 Hrs notice required. Class D airspace. Military Emergency Diversion AD. No night stopping for visiting ACFT. ACFT to contact Lyneham App 118.425 at 20nm unless under control of another agency who should be asked to advise Lyneham of the ETA. Instrument APP may be mandatory. ACFT are not to overfly Wroughton hospital below 2000ft. ACFT are not to request start-up unless RAF starter crew are present. After landing and before take-off pilots must report personally to Operations.

Warnings

GND rises sharply from 300ft below A/D to Rwy06 Thr which may cause turbulence and windshear on the APP. Vehicles/pedestrians may be present on the apron not under the control of ATC. Heavy bird concentration in the area at dawn and dusk. Rwy06 PAPI's unreliable, may result in flying beneath actual glidepath.

Maintenance	Nil
Fuel	AVGAS 100LL (72Hrs notice) AVTUR FS11

Operator	RAF Lyneham

Chippenham, Wiltshire, SN15 4PZ
Tel: 01249 890381 Ext.6214 Ext 7308 (ATIS)

Restaurant	
Taxis Car Hire	
Thrifty	**Tel:** 01793 422644
Weather Info	M T Fax 364 BNMC

Operating Hrs	H24
Circuits	06 variable
Landing fee	£7.56 +VAT per 500kgs & £8.50 insurance

Class D Airspace
Normal CTA/CTR Class D Airspace rules apply.
1 Except at night, these rules do not apply to gliders provided
they remain at least 1500m horizontally and 1000ft vertically
away from cloud in a flight visibility of at least 8km.
2. To assist Lyneham RAD in ensuring access to its airspace
pilots should make an R/T call when 20nm or 5 minutes flying
time from the zone boundary, whichever is the earlier.

Visual Reference Points (VRPs)

VRP	VOR/VOR	VOR/NDB	VOR/DME
Avebury N5125.68 W00151.28	CPT R265°/SAM R330°	CPT R265°/LA 135°M	CPT 265°/24nm
Blakehill Farm N5137.00 W00153.10	CPT R293°/SAM R337°	CPT R293°/LA 039°M	CPT 293°/26nm
Calne N5126.20 W00200.30	CPT R268°/SAM R324°	CPT R268°/LA 184°M	CPT 268°/30nm
Chippenham N5127.60 W00207.40	CPT R273°/SAM R321°	CPT R273°/LA 241°M	CPT 273°/34nm
Clyffe Pypard N5129.40 W00153.70	CPT R274°/SAM R332°	CPT R274°/LA 104°M	CPT 274°/25nm
Devizes N5120.80 W00159.30	CPT R258°/SAM R319°	CPT R258°/LA 181°M	CPT 258°/30nm
M4 J 15 N5131.60 W00143.48	CPT R281°/SAM R342°	CPT R281°/LA 089°M	CPT 281°/19nm
M4 J 16 N5132.70 W00151.25	CPT R282°/SAM R336°	CPT R282°/LA 073°M	CPT 282°/24nm
M4 J 17 N5130.88 W00207.30	CPT R277°/SAM R324°	CPT R277°/LA 280°M	CPT 277°/34nm
Malmesbury N5135.10 W00206.20	CPT R284°/SAM R328°	CPT R284°/LA 327°M	CPT 284°/33nm
Marlborough N5125.20 W00143.70	CPT R262°/SAM R337°	CPT R262°/LA 121°M	CPT 262°/19nm
Melksham N5122.50 W00208.30	CPT R263°/SAM R315°	CPT R263°/LA 216°M	CPT 263°/35nm
S Marston N5135.40 W00144.10	CPT R292°/SAM R343°	CPT R292°/LA 069°M	CPT 292°/20nm
Wroughton N5130.55 W00147.98	CPT R277°/SAM R328°	CPT R277°/LA 327°M	CPT 277°/22nm

Effective date: 30/11/99 © Copyright 1999 Camber Publishing Ltd. All rights reserved

Standard Inbound Visual Routes

Entry point	Rwy	Max Alt (QNH)	Route
Stretton	06L	1250ft	From Stretton AD VRP, route via M56, keep motorway on left join left base Rwy06L
		Remarks:	1 Outbound traffic operates N of M56
			2 ACFT may be held at Stretton VRP or Rostherne VRP
Stretton	24R	1250ft	From Stretton AD VRP, route N of M56. Join downwind right-hand Rwy24R
		Remarks:	1 For ACFT inbound from Liverpool only.
			2 ACFT will be held at Stretton VRP if outbound to Thelwall Viaduct VRP is in use.
Swinton	24R	2500ft	From CTR boundary at Swinton VRP, remain E of M62/M63 Motorways.
		Remarks:	1 ACFT may be held at Sale Water Park VRP.
			2 Whenever possible fly between 2000ft and 2500ft. When cloudbase or ATC instruction requires ACFT to be flown at or below 2000ft QNH, contact Barton Radio 122.700 Mhz for transit Through Barton ATZ.
Congleton	24R (Notes 1 & 4)	2500ft	From CTR Boundary E of Congleton VRP, route via the Woodford Entry/Exit Lane (keeping railway line on left) to Woodford AD. Join left base for Rwy24R.
		Remarks:	1 Maximum altitudes 2500ft betwwen CTR Boundary & northern edge of Macclesfield, 1500ft N of Macclesfield to Woodford ATZ southern Boundary.
			2 ACFT may be held by visual reference to ensure that the holding pattern does not deviate to the N, which would come in to conflict with Rwy24R final instrument APP, particularly in a southerly wind.
			3 The Entry/Exit Lane may be under Woodford Control. Pilots should contact Manchester APP on 119.400Mhz initially.
			4 **Warning:** High GND to the E of the Entry/Exit Lane.
			5 ACFT must not leave confines of Entry/Exit Lane without prior ATC co-ordination
			6 ACFT with radio failure inbound to Manchester in Woodford Entry/Exit Lane, or holding at Hilltop, carry out Radio Communication Failure procedure, (ENR 1-2).
Sandbach	06L	1500ft	From Sandbach VRP, follow Crewe-Wilmslow railway line, keep railway line on left At Jodrell Bank VRP, cross railway & route direct Manchester, join right base Rwy06L
		Remarks:	1 ACFT may be held at Sandbach VRP or Jodrell Bank VRP.

Standard Outbound Visual Routes

Entry point	Rwy	Max Alt (QNH)	Route Designator	Route
Thelwall	06L/24R	1250ft	**Thelwall 1 Vis.**	Cross M56 via Warburton Green VRP. Route N of M56 to Thelwall Viaduct VRP, then via low level route.
		Remarks:		1 Avoid overflying Lymm.
				2 Inbound traffic operates S of M56 for Rwy06L.
				3 **Warning:** Traffic in Low Level Route is unknown to ATC.
Carrington	06L/24R	1250ft	**Carrington 1 Vis.**	Cross M56 via Warburton Green VRP. Route N of M56 to abeam Rostherne VRP, then to Carrington VRP
		Remarks:		1 Avoid overflying Dunham Deer Park.
				2 For ACFT routing from Manchester Airport to Barton AD only.
				3 **Warning:** Traffic in Low Level Route is unknown to ATC.
Sandbach	24R	1500ft	**Sandbach 1 Vis.**	Left turn via Jodrell Bank VRP then keep railway line on left to Sandbach VRP
Congleton	06L	2500ft (notes 1, 2 & 6)	**Congleton 2 Vis.**	Right turn after Alderley Edge Hill VRP. Route W then S of Alderley Edge Hill & join Woodford Entry/Exit Lane at Prestbury Station. Keep railway line on left and leave via Congleton VRP.
		Remarks:		1 Max altitude 1500ft between Manchester & N edge of Macclesfield, 2500ft S of N edge to CTR Boundary.
				2 **Warning:** High GND to E of Entry/Exit Lane.
				3 Entry/Exit Lane may under Woodford or Manchester control.
				4 ACFT may be routed direct from Manchester to Prestbury Station, or via Woodford.
				5 ACFT must not leave the Entry/Exit Lane without ATC prior co-ordination.
				6 **Caution:** Alderley Edge 650ft amsl.

M

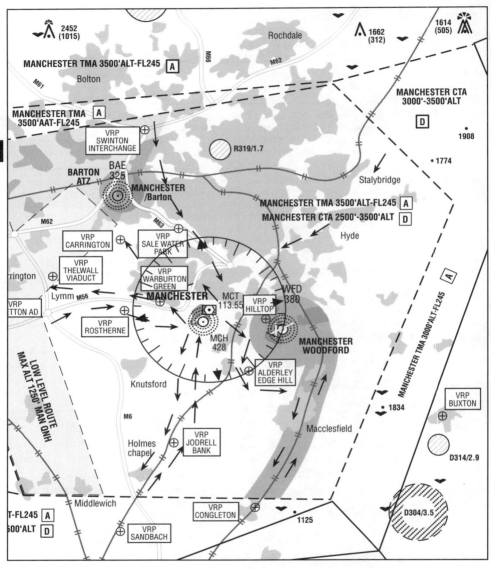

Barton local flying area and Low Level Route:
Proposed changes are to be implemented during 2000, please
check NOTAMS and our amendment service for details.

ELEVATION	LOCATION		
257ft 9mb	7.5nm SW of Manchester N5321.22 W00216.50	MCT 113.55 On AD POL 112.10 201 24.2	– –/– • – •/– • – –•/– – –/• – • •
PPR			

M

Terminal 2
Twy D
Twy N
Twy P
Pier C
Terminal 1
Customs
Twy J
J
24R
JA
ILS/DME I-NN 109.50
Terminal 3
Pier A
H
Twy L
Twy D
Twy Q
G
Pier B
Twy J
Fire Station
Twy K
JB
MCT 113.55
NEA Apron
Twy C
KC
MCH 428
South Bay GA park
Twy A
Twy B
3048m x 46m
BD
B1
Construction zone
ILS/DME I-MM 109.50
AF1
AG1
A1
06L

RWY	SURFACE	TORA	LDA	LIGHTING
06L	Con/Asph	3048	2621	Ap Thr Rwy PAPI 3° RHS
24R	Con/Asph	3048	2865	Ap Thr Rwy PAPI 3° LHS

Manchester	
ATIS	128.175
APP	119.40
RAD	119.40 118.575 121.35
TWR	118.625 121.50(C/R)
GND/DEL	121.70 121.85*
FIRE	121.60
	*when instructed by ATC
VOR/DME	MCT 113.55
NDB	MCH 428**
ILS/DME	I-NN 109.50 Rwy24R
ILS/DME	I-MM 109.50 Rwy06L
	**on AD range 15nm

Remarks

PPR essential. All flights are at all times subject to PPR. The filling of a Flight Plan does constitute PPR. Operation of business and GA ACFT require permission from AD operator in advance obtained as follows: During office Hrs contact ACL Tel: 0161 489 2583/2422 Fax: 0161 489 2470. SITA LONACXH. Outside office Hrs contact AD Ops Tel: 0161 489 3657 Fax: 0161 489 2881. Include following info ACFT owner/operator, type and registration. Flight number (if any), requested time of Arr and Dep at Manchester and nominated handling agent. Use governed by regulations applicable to Manchester CTR. Operators of General and Business Aviation ACFT must obtain PPR from the Airport operator in advance of each movement. Applications for PPR must be made not more than ten days and not less than 24 Hrs before the proposed flight to one of the designated GA Agencies: Air Kilroe Tel: 0161 4362055 Fax: 0161 4991890 Telex: 665525 Company Freq: 122.35. northern Executive Aviation Tel: 0161 4366666 Fax: 0161 4363450 Telex: 668777. Company Freq: 130.65. Before filing Manchester as an alternate, make arrangements for GND handling. Training flights by all ACFT are subject to the approval of the Chief Executive. All initial calls for ATC clearances should be made on 121.70 (Manchester Delivery) between 0700-2200 (Winter) & 0600-2100 (Summer). Outside these Hrs call Manchester GND on 121.70. At all times ACFT must be operated in a manner calculated to cause the least disturbance practicable in areas surrounding the airport. Unless otherwise instructed by ATC, ACFT shall not descend below 2000ft before intercepting the glidepath. ACFT approaching without assistance from the ILS shall follow a descent path no lower than that of the ILS glidepath. On departure from Rwy 24R, avoid over-flying the town of Knutsford.

Warnings

GND signals other than light signals are not displayed. The hard shoulders outboard of the Rwy side stripes have only 25% of the Rwy bearing strengths and should not be used by ACFT turning on the Rwy or when backtracking. Flocks of racing pigeons may cross the AD below 100ft April to September.

Effective date: 30/11/99

Operating Hrs	H24
Circuits	As directed by ATC
Landing fee	On application
Maintenance	Up to B.747 (by arrangement)
Fuel	AVGAS 100LL AVTUR JET A1
Arranged Thru mandatory handling agent	

Operator   Manchester Airport Plc
Manchester Airport, Manchester M90 1QX
Tel: 0161 489 3000 (Airport)
Tel: 0161 489 3331 (Ops duty manager)
Tel: 0161 499 5502 (FPRS)
Tel: 0161 489 3657 (Slot line)
Fax: 0161 499 5504 (Flight plans)

Restaurants	Restaurants buffets and bars (24Hr)
Taxis	Available at Terminal

Car Hire

Avis	**Tel:** 0161 436 2020
Budget	**Tel:** 0161 449 3042
Europcar	**Tel:** 0161 436 2220
Hertz	**Tel:** 0161 437 8208

Weather Info	M T9 T18 Fax 368 A VM VN MWC

Low Level Route Through Manchester Control Zone

This low level route allows ACFT to transit the Manchester CTR without compliance with full IFR procedures. Additionally, to allow ACFT to transit to and from Barton AD, there is a branch route to Barton from the low level corridor.
The rules governing flight within the low level route are as follows:

1. Remain clear of cloud and in sight of the surface.
2. Maximum altitude 1250ft (Manchester QNH).
3. Minimum flight visibility 4km.
4. ACFT must be transiting the CTR, or proceeding directly to or from an AD within the CTR.
5. Pilots using the corridor are responsible for their own separation from other ACFT.
6. The corridor is not aligned with the M6 motorway. The M6 should not be used as a navigational line feature.

VFR/SVFR Flights

VFR and Special VFR clearance for flights within the control zone may be requested and will be given whenever traffic conditions permit. These flights are subject to the general conditions for VFR and Special VFR flight and will normally be given only to helicopters or aeroplanes other than microlights which can communicate with ATC on the appropriate frequencies.
The use of VFR/SVFR clearance is intended to be for the following types of flight:
Light ACFT (less than 5700kg MTOW) which cannot comply with full IFR and wish to transit the zone or proceed to or from an AD within the zone. ACFT using the low level corridor will be considered as complying with a VFR/SVFR clearance.
Special VFR clearance to operate within the Manchester CTR will not be granted to fixed-wing ACFT when:
i) proceeding inbound to Manchester Airport, if the reported weather conditions at the airport are below 2800m visibility or a cloud ceiling of 1000ft.
ii) wishing to depart Manchester Airport if the reported weather conditions at the airport are below 1800m visibility or a cloud ceiling of 600ft.

Visual Reference Points (VRPs)

VRP	VOR/VOR	VOR/NDB	VOR/DME
Alderley Edge Hill N5317.72 W00212.73	MCT R159°/WAL R105°	MCT R159°/WHI 070°M	MCT 159°/4nm
Barton AD N5328.27 W00223.42	MCT R331°/POL R217°	MCT 331°/WHI 031°M	MCT 331°/8nm
Buxton N5315.35 W00154.77	MCT R120°/POL R172°	MCT 120°/WHI 085°M	MCT 120°/14nm
Carrington N5325.70 W00224.47	MCT R314°/WAL R090°	MCT 120°/WHI 085°M	MCT 314°/7nm
Congleton N5309.90 W00210.85	MCT R175°/TNT R295°	MCT R170°/WHI 100°M	MCT 175°/12nm
Hilltop N5320.50 W00210.45	MCT R111°/TNT 318°	MCT R111°/WHI 064°M	MCT 111/3nm
Jodrell Bank N5314.18 W00218.55	MCT R198°/WAL R112°	MCT R198°/WHI 079°M	MCT 198°/7nm
Rostherne N5321.23 W00223.12	MCT R272°/POL R208°	MCT R272°/WHI 045°M	MCT 272°/4nm
Sale Water Park N5326.00 W00218.17	MCT R347°/POL R206°	MCT347°/WHI 042°M	MCT 347°/5nm
Sandbach N5309.00 W00223.62	MCT R206°/WAL R123°	MCT R206°/WHI 109°M	MCT 206°/13nm
Stretton (disused AD) N5320.77 W00231.58	POL R217°/WAL R102°	MCT R271°/WHI 025°M	MCT 271°/9nm
Swinton Interchange N5331.40 W00221.60	MCT R346°/POL R220°	MCT 346°/WHI030°M	MCT 346°/11nm
Thelwall (M6 Viaduct) N5323.43 W00230.42	MCT R288°/POL R219°	MCT R288°/WHI 023°M	MCT 288°/9nm
Warburton Green N5321.50 W00218.90	MCT R277°/POL R202°	MCT R277°/WHI 052°M	MCT 277°/2nm

M

ELEVATION	LOCATION		
73ft 2mb	5nm W of Manchester N5328.28 W00223.35 **Diversion AD**	MCT 113.55 332 8.2 – – / – • – • / –	
PPR		POL 112.10 218 19.3 • – – • / – – – / • – • •	
		WAL 114.10 087 27.0 • – – / • – / • – • •	

Runway markings on map: 14, 20, N60, 27N, 27, 32, 02, 60
- 396m x 32m
- 520m x 18m
- 621m x 32m
- 528m x 32m
- C — Fuel
- A57
- BAE 325
- M62
- N

RWY	SURFACE	TORA	LDA	LIGHTING
09/27S	Grass	621	621	Nil
09/27N*	Grass	518	518	Nil
14/32	Grass	396	396	Nil
02/20	Grass	528	528	Nil

*Temporary Rwy. Marked when in use by white corners and white painted edge markers on the N edge. Barton local flying area & low level route: Proposed changes are to be implemented during 2000, please check NOTAMS & our amendment service for details.

Barton	
A/G AFIS*	122.70
NDB	**BAE 325** on AD range 10nm
*AFIS by arrangement	

Remarks

Within the Manchester CTR. Not available to public transport passenger flights required to use a licensed AD. Avoid flying low over the cemetery to the NE of the AD. In no wind conditions pilots should land and take off to the W. Overhead join not above 1500ft Manchester QNH. ACFT may operate within the Barton local flying area (1.5nm radius from the ARP) without compliance with IFR subject to the following conditions: (1) ACFT to remain below cloud and in sight of the GND. (2) Maximum altitude 1500 ft Manchester QNH. (3) Minimum flight visibility 3km. Pilots of ACFT in the local flying area are responsible for their own separation. A branch route connects the Barton LFA to the Low Level Route Through the Manchester CTR. Flights within the branch route must remain clear of cloud and in sight of GND and operate with a maximum altitude of 1250ft Manchester QNH with a minimum flight visibility of 4km. Visual aids to location. No multi-engined fixed wing ACFT unless in emergency.

Warnings

35ft high lamps on the A57 to the SE and SW of the AD. Areas of soft GND on the manoeuvring area are marked with cones. Surface undulating in places and soft after heavy rain.

Operating Hrs	0800-SS (Summer) 0900-SS (Winter)
Circuits	14/20/27 RH 09/02/32 LH to avoid over-flying Flixton 800ft QFE
Landing fee	Single £5.88 Twin £10.00 + VAT
Maintenance	Light Planes (Lancashire) Ltd **Tel: 0161 707 8644**
Fuel	AVGAS 100LL AVTUR JET A1
Operator	Lancashire Aero Club Manchester/Barton Aerodrome, Liverpool Road Eccles Manchester M22 5PA **Tel: 0161 789 4785, Tel: 0161 787 7326 (ATC) Fax: 0161 787 8782**
Restaurant	LAC Club facilities available at AD
Taxis Road Runner Lyle Cars **Car Hire** National	Arranged on arrival or **Tel: 0161 776 2426** **Tel: 0161 707 4444** **Tel: 0161 834 3020**
Weather Info	AirCen MWC

M

ELEVATION	LOCATION	EGCD	MANCHESTER (Woodford)

ELEVATION	LOCATION		
298ft 10mb	6nm N of Macclesfield N5320.28.W00208.93	MCT 113.55 112 4.2	– – / – • – • / –
PPR		POL 112.10 190 24.4	• – – • / – – – / • – • •

ILS/DME
I-WU
109.15

WFD
380

N

Twy D

C

D

C

Twy C

07

Twy B

B

A

Twy A

2292m x 46m

25

Flight Ops

G. A. Parking

Effective date: 30/11/99

RWY	SURFACE	TORA	LDA	LIGHTING
07	Asphalt	2167	2061	Thr Rwy PAPI 3° LHS
25	Asphalt	2217	1671	Thr Rwy PAPI 3.6° LHS

Woodford	
APP/TWR	120.70
RAD	130.050
FIRE	121.60
ILS/DME	I-WU 109.15 Rwy25
NDB	WFD 380 on A/D range 15nm

Remarks
PPR non-radio ACFT not accepted.

Warnings
The AD is located inside the Manchester Control Zone. An additional set of PAPI on Rwy25, 360m prior to the displaced Thr are solely for test flying purposes. The broken yellow lines are for calibration purposes. The use of mobile phones on the apron area is strictly prohibited.

Operator   AVRO International, Woodford Aerodrome
Chester Road, Bramhall, Stockport, Cheshire SK7 1QR
Tel: 0161 439 5050 Ext.3294 (PPR)
Tel: 0161 439 3383 (ATC)
Fax: 0161 955 3316

Restaurants
Licensed club and VIP suite available Snacks in lounge

Taxis	
	Tel: 0161 456-7099
	Tel: 0161 440-9769
	Tel: 0161 439-9056
Car Hire	Bramhall Self Drive Hire
	Tel: 0161 439-5826

Operating Hrs (Summer)	Sun-Fri 0700-1900 Sat 0900-1500 + 1Hr Winter (Z time) and by arrangement
Circuits	07 RH 25 LH
Landing fee	On request with PPR
Maintenance	Nil
Fuel	AVGAS 100LL AVTUR JET A1

Weather Info   M* AirCen MWC

Local Flying Area
Within a local flying area of 1.5nm radius, centred on the AD VFR/SVFR flights may take place subject to ATC clearance from Manchester/Woodford ATC.

Entry-Exit Lane
An Entry-Exit lane is established 1nm wide aligned on the Congleton-Macclesfield railway from the boundary of the LFA to the southern boundary of Manchester CTR. VFR/SVFR flights may take place subject to ATC clearance & compliance with the following conditions.
1 ACFT using the lane must remain clear of cloud and in sight of the GND & in a flight visibility of **at least 3km.**
2 ACFT using the lane **must comply with the left hand rule** when following the railway line unless otherwise instructed by ATC for separation purposes.
3 Pilots are responsible for maintaining adequate clearance from the GND and other obstacles, & are warned of **high GND to the E** of the lane.
4 ACFT **must not** leave the confines of the lane unless authorised by ATC.
5 Inbound ACFT should make their first call to Woodford APP (120.70) to ascertain the controling agency at the time they wish to join.

It is essential that inbound ACFT follow the flight profile detailed below
Fly not above 2500ft QNH from Congleton to Macclesfield
Fly not above 1500ft QNH from N of Macclesfield to LFA

Woodford Standard VFR Departures
To assist in reducing RTF Workload, Woodford ATC will use the following abreviated phraseology to issue the following departure clearances.

Congleton One VFR Departure Rwy25
A left turn out towards Macclesfield to intercept the Macclesfield-Congleton railway then remain within the confines of the Entry-Exit lane unless otherwise instructed by ATC.

Flight Profile ...ACFT MUST...
Fly not above 1500ft QNH to the N edge of Macclesfield.
Fly not above 2500ft QNH to the Congleton VRP.

Congleton Two VFR Departures Rwy07
A right turn out towards Macclesfield & then as the procedure above.

The Woodford Entry-Exit lane is notified for the purpose of Rule 5 (2)(a). That is…It is NOT obligatory to comply with the '1500ft rule' but essential that the ACFT be flown 'at such a height that would enable the ACFT to alight clear of the congested area in the event of failure of a power unit.

M

VRP	VOR/VOR	VOR/NDB	VOR/DME
Congleton	MCT r175		
N5309.90 W00210.85	TNT R295	MCT R175/WHI 100m	MCT R175/12d

ELEVATION	LOCATION
75ft 2mb	9nm ENE of Downham Market N5238.90 E00033.03
PPR	

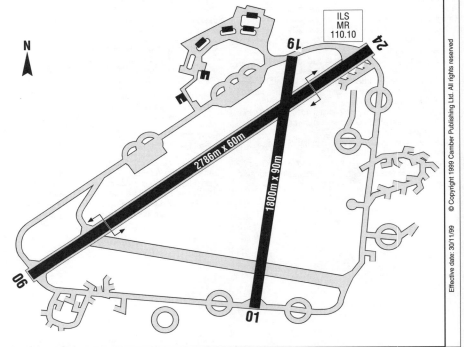

ILS
MR
110.10

2786m x 60m

1800m x 90m

RWY	SURFACE	TORA	LDA	LIGHTING
06/24*	Asphalt/Concrete	2786	2786	Ap Thr Rwy PAPI 2.5
01/19	Concrete	1800	1800	Rwy PAPI 2.5

*Arrester Gear 640m from Thr06 487m from Thr24
Under normal Ops APP cable down Overun cable up

Marham	
APP/LARS	124.15
PAR	(Talkdown) 123.30
TWR	122.10
ILS	MR 110.10 Rwy 24

Remarks
PPR strictly by telephone, 24 hrs notice required. Active RAF AD. Intensive fast Jet operations. Civil visitors may be subject to refusal or individual arrival conditions. Inbound aircraft should call Marham Approach at least 20nm from the airfield. I Bn MR red.

Warnings
Considerable bird activity in vicinity of AD. Glider flying takes place outside normal operating hours. Under normal operations the approach arrester gear is down trampling of the wires by light ACFT constitutes a hazard.

Operator	RAF Marham Downham Market Norfolk
Tel: 01760 337261 (Ext.2044/2058) PPR	
Tel: 01760 337261 (Ext.7282/7412) ATC	
Tel: 01760 337261 (Ext.7888) Answerphone ATIS	

Restaurants

Taxis/Car Hire

Weather Info	M T Fax374 AirS BNMC

Operating Hrs	0800-2359 Mon-Thu 0800-1800 Fri (Local) ATZ active 24hrs
Circuits	24/01 LH 06/19 RH at 1000ft QFE
Landing Fee	£7.56 + VAT per 500Kgs £8.50 insurance charge
Maintenance Fuel	Not available to Civil visitors JET A1 by prior arrangement

ELEVATION	LOCATION				MARSHLAND
-6ft 0mb **PPR**	5nm ESE of Wisbech N5239.50 E00018.00	BKY 116.25	011	40	– • • • / – • – / – • – –

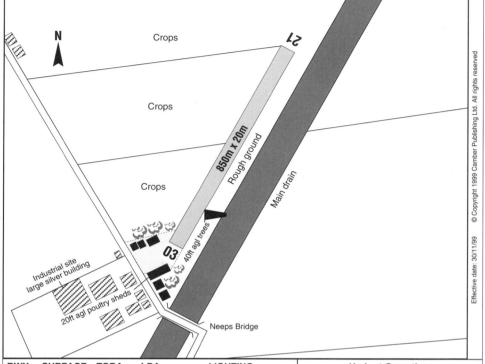

M

RWY	SURFACE	TORA	LDA	LIGHTING
03/21	Grass	850x20	U/L	Rwy

Herbert Operations

APP (Marham)	**124.15**
A/G	**130.375***
	* Not normally manned

Remarks
PPR by telephone. Visiting ACFT welcome at pilots own risk. AD is suitable for light twin ACFT with a good level surface. Close proximity to the main drain and industrial site with large silver roofed building.

Warnings
AD may be soft after prolonged rain or snow. approach to Rwy03 is over group of buildings and trees. Crops are grown up to Rwy on W side.

Operator	RJ Herbert, Harps Hall, Walton Highway Wisbech, Cambs **Tel:** 01945 430365 (Evenings) **Tel:** 01945 430666 (Daytime/weekend)
Restaurant	
Taxi/Car Hire	
Weather Info	AirS BNMC

Operating Hrs	SR-SS
Circuits	LH
Maintenance **Fuel**	Nil AVGAS 100LL by arrangement

ELEVATION	LOCATION		
110ft 3mb	3nm NE of Canterbury N5120.31 E00109.34	DVR 114.95 325 13	— • • / • • • — / • — •
PPR		DET 117.30 090 21	— • • / • / —

M

RWY	SURFACE	TORA	LDA	LIGHTING			
02/20	Grass	550x18	U/L	Nil	APP	*Non-radio* **Manston 119.27**	

Remarks
Strictly PPR by telephone only & at pilots own risk.
ACFT should call Manston TWR 119.27 when inbound & before take-off for flight information. Planning restraints mean that permission to visit this AD may be denied.

Warnings
Do not overfly the village of Hoath & avoid other local habitation. Caution: Buildings on short final to Rwy02. Windsock at northern end of Rwy. Turbulence possible from trees in woodland to W of AD.

Operator   JH Spanton, Maypole Farm
White Horse Cottage, Hoath, Canterbury, Kent CT3 4LN
Tel: 01227 860374/860592 (PPR)
Tel: 01227 860150 (Maypole Flying Club)

Restaurants
Food sometimes available at Prince of Wales pub, Maypole village. Nearest accomodation in Herne Bay (2 miles)

Taxis   **Tel:** 01227 710777
Car Hire

Weather Info   AirSE BNMC

Operating Hrs	0800-2100 (local) or dusk if earlier
Circuits	02 LH 20 RH
Landing fee	Nil
Maintenance Maypole Air Fuel	**Tel:** 01227 860592 (B Mayo) Nil

ELEVATION	LOCATION	**EGVP**	**MIDDLE WALLOP**

ELEVATION	LOCATION
297ft 10mb	5nm SW of Andover N5108.96 W00134.22
PPR MILITARY	

SAM 113.35	330	14	• • • / • − / − −
CPT 114.35	216	24.9	− • − • / • − − • / −

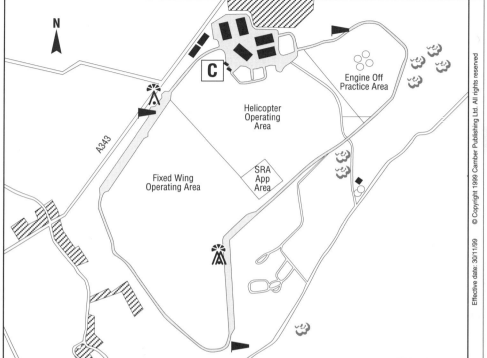

M

RWY	SURFACE	TORA	LDA	LIGHTING
08/26	Grass	732	732	Rwy
13/31	Grass	732	732	Nil
01/19	Grass	732	732	Nil

Wallop

APP/MATZ /TWR	118.275
LARS	Boscombe 126.70

Remarks
PPR by telephone essential 24 Hrs notice required.
Intensive helicopter and fixed wing activity, special
procedures apply. Flying may take place at weekends,
parascending W/E & PH. Frequent night flying. ATZ active
H24. Visual aid to location: IBn MW Red.

Warnings

Operator	Army Air Corps Middle Wallop **Tel:** 01980 674380 (ATC)
Restaurants	
Taxis/Car Hire	
Weather Info	AirSW BNMC

Operating Hrs
Mon-Thu 0730-1600 or SS + 15 min Fri 0730-1500 (Summer)
+ 1Hr Winter

Circuits

Landing Fee	£7.56 +VAT per 500kgs & £8.50 insurance
Maintenance	Military engineers present
Fuel	AVGAS 100LL AVTUR Jet A1

ELEVATION	LOCATION		**MILSON (Cleobury Mortimer)**			
500ft 16mb **PPR**	3nm WSW of Cleobury Mortimer N5221.68 W00232.75	HON 113.65	276	32		••••/ – – –/– •

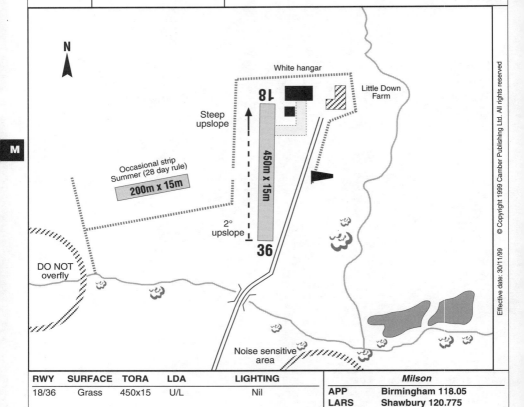

RWY	SURFACE	TORA	LDA	LIGHTING
18/36	Grass	450x15	U/L	Nil

Rwy36 2° upslope increases in last 5%

Milson

APP	**Birmingham 118.05**
LARS	**Shawbury 120.775**
A/G	**129.825**
Microlight common freq	
Useful weather info on	
Birmingham ATIS 126.275	

Remarks

PPR by telephone essential. Pilot/ACFT must be capable of operating from a short strip. Microlight activity at AD. Two white hangars and farm house at N end of strip are good locators. Birmingham ATIS on 126.275 provides useful weather info. Ten resident ACFT. Fly-ins, when daily movement restrictions are relaxed, usually in spring & Aug/Sept. Please sign visiting ACFT movement book situated in box on wall with 'C' on yellow. Occasional military helicopter movements weekdays.

Warnings

Rwy36 has upslope which increases markedly in last portion, land 36, Dep 18 unless wind is extreme. Rwy18 APP area has obstructions & high GND, a long final is recommended for accurate arrival. **Caution:** Clee Hill (1750ft amsl) 2nm NW. Sheep may graze on AD. Strip can be waterlogged in winter. Crosswinds & terrain enduced turbulence are often a problem.

Landing fee	Single £2.00 Microlights £1.00
Maintenance	Nil
Fuel	Nil
Operator	H Thompson, Little Down Farm Milson, Kidderminster, Worcester DY14 0BD **Tel:** 01584 890486 (AD PPR) **Tel:** 01584 811652/890980 (only if absolutely neccesary)
Restaurants	Nil Toilet facilities available
Taxis/Car Hire	
Weather Info	AirN MCW

Operating Hrs   10 flights a day is maximum permissible under planning consent visitor availability Ltd. Arrivals only (no Dep) 1400-1700 (local) on Sun on main N/S strip

Circuits   Show consideration to local habitation avoid houses adjacent to W end of 2 small lakes SE of AD

M

ELEVATION	LOCATION	EGOQ		MONA

ELEVATION	LOCATION
202ft 7mb	2nm W of Llangefni Anglesey N5315.53 W00422.38
PPR MILITARY	

WAL 114.10   266   45.0   • — — / • — / • — • •

M

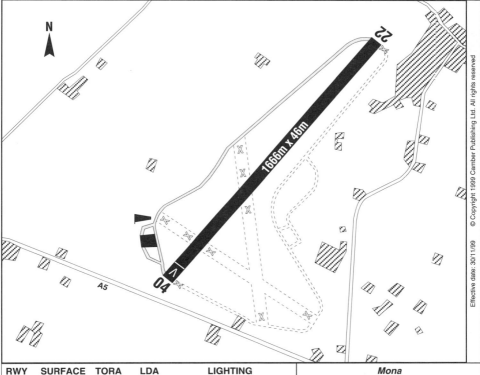

1666m x 46m

22

04

A5

N

RWY	SURFACE	TORA	LDA	LIGHTING
04*	Asphalt	1579	1524	Ap Thr Rwy PAPI 3°
22	Asphalt	1579	1579	Ap Thr Rwy PAPI 3°

* Arrester gear 04 Thr

Mona	
APP/LARS	Valley MATZ 134.35
A/G	122.00

Remarks
PPR during RAF operating hrs. Relief AD to RAF Valley.
PPR obtained through Mona Flying Club evenings & W/ends
during BST. PPL/IMC/Night rating training available through
flying club. Visiting pilots report to flying club near RAF TWR.

Warnings
Visiting ACFT must contact Valley before entering MATZ.
Valley will transfer to Mona Radio. If Valley does not answer
contact Mona Radio direct. DO NOT enter Valley MATZ or
attempt to land if Valley or Mona cannot be contacted.

Landing fee	Members free, visitors MOD rates

information should be requested with PPR

Maintenance	Nil but hangarage available
Fuel	Nil

Operator	RAF Valley/Mona Flying Club

RAF Valley, Holyhead, Gwynedd LL65 3NY
Tel: 01407 762241 Ext.7291 (PPR RAF ops Hrs)
Tel: 01407 720581 (PPR Mona Flying Club Hrs)

Restaurants	Cafe in clubhouse on Sundays
Taxis/Car Hire	Information in clubhouse
Weather Info	AirN MWC

Operating Hrs   RAF: Mon-Fri 0800-1730 (Summer)
Mon-Fri 0800-1700 (Winter)
Mona Flying Club:
Mon-Fri 1800-SS Sat-Sun 0900-1800 (Summer)
Sat-Sun 0900-SS (Winter)

Circuits   04 RH 22 LH join deadside not below
2000ft QFE then fly circuit 800ft QFE. On APP Rwy04 cross
A5 not below 200ft QFE

MONEWDEN (Cherry Tree Farm)

ELEVATION	LOCATION
180ft 6mb	9nm NE of Ipswich N5210.10 E00029.30
PPR	

CLN 114.55   015   19.5   — • — • / • — • • / — •

Crops

40ft tree

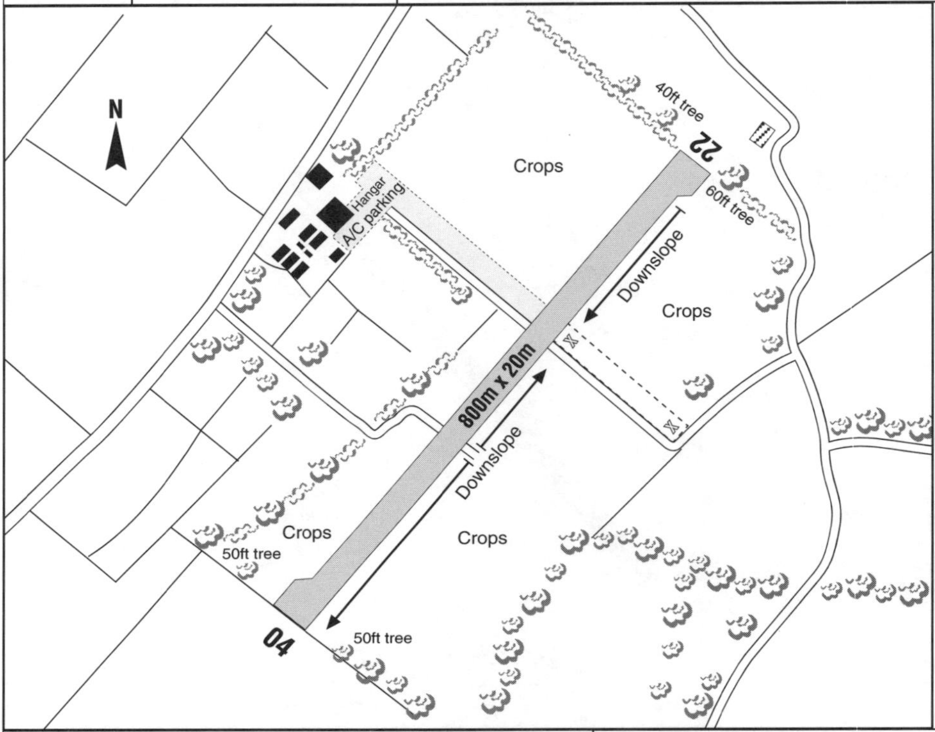

60ft tree

22

Hangar

A/C parking

Downslope

Crops

800m x 20m

Downslope

Crops

Crops

50ft tree

04

50ft tree

N

Effective date: 30/11/99

M

RWY	SURFACE	TORA	LDA	LIGHTING
04/22	Grass	800x20	U/L	Nil

Rwy has undulations

Non-Radio

APP (Wattisham) 125.80

Remarks
PPR by telephone. Visiting ACFT welcome at pilots own risk. Caravan available for hire on AD. Noise: Do not carry out long power checks at Thr22 due to close proximity of house. Do not overfly village church on Sundays.

Warnings
APP to Rwys clear, but trees at Thrs which may cause turbulence. Crops are grown close to S of strip and N of first third Rwy04/22. Irigation pipes present in summer.

Operator	Mr John F Wright, Cherry Tree Farm Monewden, Woodbridge Suffolk **Tel: 01473 737223**
Restaurant	
Taxi/Car Hire	**Tel: 01728 685883** **Tel: 07836 676656** (mobile)
Weather Info	AirS BNMC

Operating Hrs	SR-SS
Circuits	LH 800ft QFE
Landing fee	Nil
Maintenance Fuel	Nil Nil

ELEVATION	LOCATION				MOVENIS
180ft 6mb	4nm NW of Kilrea Northern Ireland N5459.25 W00638.81	BEL 117.20	331	24.5	— • • • / • / • — • •
PPR					

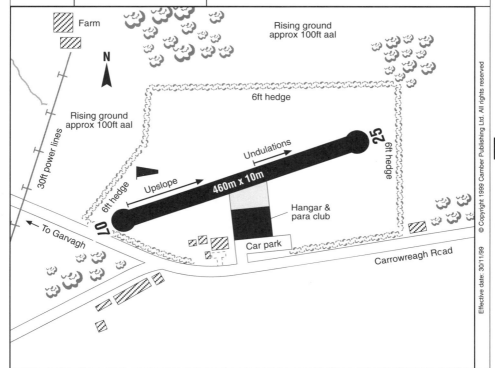

RWY	SURFACE	TORA	LDA	LIGHTING		Movenis Drop Zone	
07/25	Asphalt	460x10	U/L	Nil		A/G	129.90

Remarks

PPR by telephone. Primarily a parachute centre but light ACFT & microlights welcome. Rwy has undulating surface. No Rwy designators. The AD is situated in a very scenic rural area, Although this AD is not notified as a point of entry/exit under the terms of the prevention of terrorism act permission will normally be granted after contact with the Royal Ulster Constabulary (Tel: 02890 650222).

Warnings

Inbound ACFT should call Movenis to ascertain parachuting status; freefall parachuting takes place up to FL120. Parachutists use the nearby drop zone at Garvagh which is marked on CAA 1:500,000 charts. Visiting pilots are requested to avoid transiting this area. The AD is surrounded by a hedge and rolling hills (see diagram).

Operating Hrs   SR-SS

Circuits
Standard overhead join then LH both Rwys

Landing fee   Nil

Maintenance   Nil
Fuel   JET A1 AVGAS 100LL

Operator   Wildgeese Skydiving Centre
Movenis Airfield, 160 Carrowreagh Road, Garvagh
Coleraine BT51 5LQ
Tel: 02829 558609 (PPR)
Fax: 02829 557050

Restaurants/Accomodation
Tea & Coffee at AD. Restaurants & hotel at Garvagh. Accommodation can be provided in the parachute clubhouse for £5 per night. Other neighbouring hotels & B&B's can be recommended.

Taxis/Car Hire   Nil

Weather Info   AirN BEL

ELEVATION	LOCATION	
33ft 1mb	4nm SW of Ballymoney N5501.38 W00635.45	BEL 117.20 337 25 — • • • / • / • — • •
PPR		

M

N

Coleraine 7nm

A54

Kilrea 5nm

4ft fence

18

4ft fence

4ft fence

Access road

420m x 15m

36

4ft fence

RWY	SURFACE	TORA	LDA	LIGHTING		*Mullaghmore*
18/36	Asphalt/Conc	420x15	U/L	Nil	A/G	122.30
					APP	Aldergrove 120.90

50m Grass starter extension Rwy18

Remarks
PPR by telephone. Visitors are welcome at pilots own risk. The operator can provide useful information on local strips that will accept visitors. Although the AD is not notified as a point of entry/exit under the prevention of terrorism act this is easily arranged by telephoning the RUC (02890 650222).

Warnings
Strip is situated in the SE corner of old WW II AD using a portion of the Twy. All other portions of the AD are unusable for ACFT. There is a 4ft fence along the first 40m of Rwy18. Microlight activity, particularly at weekends.

Operator   Microflight Ireland, 67 Main Street
Portrush, Northern Ireland BT56 8BN
Tel: 02870 868002 (AD)
Fax: 02870 824625 (Office)

Restaurants/Accomodation
B&B hotel & restaurant within walking distance from AD

Taxis   Operator can provide help & advice
Car Hire   Nil

Weather Info   AirN BEL

Operating Hrs	SR-SS
Circuits	Standard overhead join. Live side of circuit towards River Bann at 500ft QFE
Landing fee	Nil
Maintenance **Fuel**	Nil possible hangarage by prior arr. MOGAS available from nearby garage

ELEVATION	LOCATION				NAYLAND
180ft 6mb	5nm NW of Colchester N5158.29.E00051.03	CLN 114.55	307	14	— • — • / • — • • / — •
PPR		BKY 116.25	095	30	— • • • / — • — / — • — —

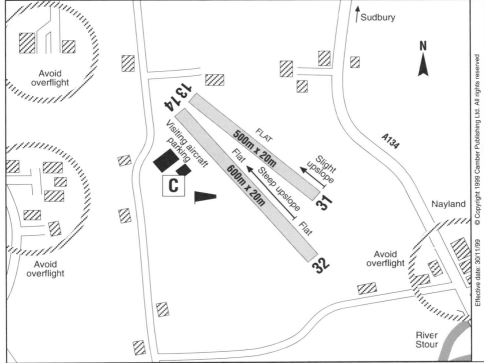

RWY	SURFACE	TORA	LDA	LIGHTING			
14/32	Grass	600x20	U/L	Nil		**APP**	Wattisham 125.80
13/31*	Grass	500x20	U/L	Nil			

Non-radio

*approximate

Remarks
PPR by telephone for briefing essential. Visitors welcome at own risk. Rwy is delineated with white edge markers. Steep upslope on 32. Unless in extreme conditions land 32, Dep 14

Warnings
Noise: Avoid overflight of Nayland to SE, hospital to W and large house to NW (see diagram).

Operator	Mr R Harris, Nayland Flying Group
	Hill Farm, Wiston, Nayland CO6 4NL
	Tel: 01206 262298
	Tel: 07887 594355 (mobile)
Restaurants	Light refreshments available at weekends
Taxis	**Tel:** 01206 262049
Car Hire	**Tel:** 07979 640040 (mobile)
Weather Info	AirS BNMC

Operating Hrs	SR-SS
Circuits	LH at 800ft QFE
Landing fee	£2
Maintenance	**Tel:** 01206 263178 (club room)
	Tel: 01206 230333
Fuel	AVGAS 100LL Cash only

ELEVATION	LOCATION	EGDN			NETHERAVON
455ft 15Mb	5nm N of Boscombe Down N5114.83 W00145.25	CPT 114.35 SAM 113.35	238 323	25 23.5	– • – • / • – – • / – • • • / • – / – –
PPR MILITARY					

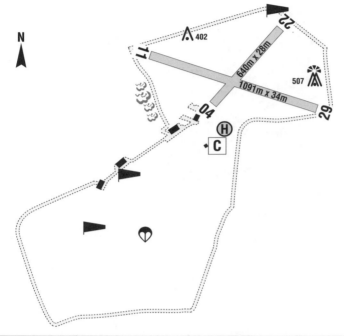

RWY	SURFACE	TORA	LDA	LIGHTING
11/29	Grass	1091x34	Nil	
04/22	Grass	640x28	Nil	

	Netheravon
A/G	(Salisbury Plain) 122.75
AFIS	128.30*
A/G	128.3 (operational Drop Zone) outside ATC hrs

Remarks
PPR essential due to special procedures associated with D128. Military AD Inbound pilots are required to contact Salisbury Plain (122.75) to ascertain range status at least 10nm from the danger area boundary before contacting Netheravon.

Warnings
AD used for parachuting up to FL150. Outside ATC operational hrs parachute Drop zone will operate freq 128.3 using callsign Drop zone. All aircraft must call for start up clearance.

Maintenance	Nil
Fuel	JET A1 by prior arrangement
Operator	MOD (Army) Netheravon Airfield Salisbury Plain, Wilts **Tel:** 01980 678289
Restaurants	
Taxis/Car Hire	
Weather Info	AirSW BNMC

Operating Hrs   Mon-Fri 0800-1700 (Local)
Military useage may be outside these times

Circuits
11/22 LH 29/04 RH Fixed wing circuit height 700ft QFE remaining outside Boscombe MATZ

Landing fee	£7.56 +VAT per 500Kgs & £8.50 insurance

ELEVATION	LOCATION	**EGNF**	**NETHERTHORPE**
250ft 8mb	2.5nm WNW of Worksop N5319.02 W00111.77	GAM 112.80 290 9.2	– – • / • – / – –
PPR	**Diversion AD**	TNT 115.7 052 23.3	– / – • / –

Effective date: 30/11/99

Runways: 450m x 36m (18/06), 382m x 18m (36/24)

Visitor parking

RWY	SURFACE	TORA	LDA	LIGHTING		Netherthorpe	
06	Grass	476*	407	Nil	A/G	123.275	
24	Grass	488*	370	Nil	APP	Sheffield 128.525	
18	Grass	382	357	Nil			
36	Grass	382	309	Nil			
*Includes a 38m starter extension							

Remarks
PPR by telephone. AD not available to public transport flights required to use a licensed airport. Inexperienced pilots and/or unsuitable ACFT may be refused due to short Rwy lengths. ACFT approaching from the N or W should contact Sheffield APP 128.525.

Warnings
At weekends when Rwy06/24 is in use, ACFT may be parked at the southern end of Rwy18/36. Rwy06 gradient 1.9% down. Rwy 06/24/36 have displaced Thr due to proximity of public Rd. Pilots whose APP would result in being below 20ft crossing the road must initiate an immediate missed approach.

Operator   Sheffield Aero Club Ltd
Netherthorpe Aerodrome, Thorpe, Salvin
Worksop, Nottinghamshire
Tel: 01909 475233 (Ops) 473428 (Clubhouse)
Fax: 01909 532413

Restaurant
Restaurant facilities usually available at AD

Taxis
Nunns   **Tel:** 01909 500005
Car Hire
DC Cook   **Tel:** 01142 484484
National   **Tel:** 01142 754111

Weather Info   AirCen MWC

Operating Hrs	0815-SS (Summer) 0915-SS (Winter) and by arrangement
Circuits	06/36 RH 18/24 LH 800ft QFE
Landing fee	Single £5.88 inc VAT PFA members free

Maintenance
Dukeries Aviation   **Tel:** 01909 481802
Fuel   AVGAS 100LL

ELEVATION	LOCATION
250ft 8mb	0.5nm E of Newbury N5123.65 W00118.87
PPR	

NEWBURY RACECOURSE

CPT 114.35   216   6.5   — • — • / • — — • / —

Red flag

11

830m x 30m

29

Golf course

Racecourse

N

RWY	SURFACE	TORA	LDA	LIGHTING
11/29	Grass	830x30	U/L	Nil

ACFT must land on Rwy29 Dept Rwy11
(Rwy has white corner & edge markers)

	Non-radio
LARS	**Brize 134.30** **Farnborough 125.25**

Remarks
PPR by telephone. The AD is strictly ONLY available to those involved or attending race meetings. Open race days only. Pilots should book in & out at the race course office. Comprehensive briefing notes are available on request.

Warnings
Situated in the middle of a golf course but play is suspended race days. ACFT movements are not allowed 30min before the first race until 30min after the final race or when horses are on the track. A red flag is displayed when engines are to be shut-down. There is a copse of mature trees 200m W of Rwy11 Thr. Please avoid built-up areas to W & N.

Operator   Newbury Racecourse PLC
Newbury, Berks RG14 7NZ
Tel: 01635 40015 (PPR Racecourse Office)
Fax: 01635 528354
Email: info@newbury-racecourse.co.uk

Restaurant	Extensive facilities in racecourse stands

Taxis
Baileys of Newbury   **Tel:** 01635 40661
Car Hire   Nil

Weather Info	AirSW BNMC

Operating Hrs
Race days only PPR 1st race 2hrs until SS

Circuits   N 1000ft QFE

Landing fee   Nil However Groundmans fund donations gratefully appreciated (box in racecourse office)

Maintenance   Nil
Fuel   Nil

ELEVATION	LOCATION	**EGNT**	**NEWCASTLE**
264ft 9mb	5nm NW of Newcastle-upon-Tyne N5502.25 W00141.50	**NEW 114.25** **On A/D**	— • / • / • — —
PPR	**Diversion AD**		

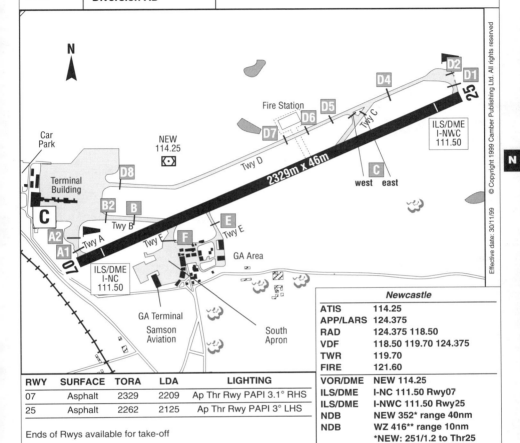

	Newcastle
ATIS	114.25
APP/LARS	124.375
RAD	124.375 118.50
VDF	118.50 119.70 124.375
TWR	119.70
FIRE	121.60
VOR/DME	NEW 114.25
ILS/DME	I-NC 111.50 Rwy07
ILS/DME	I-NWC 111.50 Rwy25
NDB	NEW 352* range 40nm
NDB	WZ 416** range 10nm
	*NEW: 251/1.2 to Thr25
	**WZ: 070/3.9 to Thr07

RWY	SURFACE	TORA	LDA	LIGHTING
07	Asphalt	2329	2209	Ap Thr Rwy PAPI 3.1° RHS
25	Asphalt	2262	2125	Ap Thr Rwy PAPI 3° LHS

Ends of Rwys available for take-off

Remarks
PPR to non-radio ACFT. ACFT must book out by telephone. ACFT towing banners may not operate to or from this airport. The grass verges along the sides of the Rwy and Twys are soft in many places. Hangar entrances should remain unobstructed. In association with the Fire Station and Rwy link road located mid-way along the parallel Twy, two Twy holding points Y and Z are introduced to hold ACFT for AFS deployment. Booking out details should be passed by telephone. All ACFT should have 3rd party liability insurance of at least £1 000 000. All international GA ACFT (including those inbound from or returning to the EU) wishing to use the main apron are required to nominate a handling agent. Handling is provided by NE Aviation & Servisair. For international and GA flights not using the main terminal, Samson Aviation operate a full GA Terminal and will arrange any necessary clearances Tel: 0191 2144111 Fax: 0191 2144112 (Samson Ops freq 130.65). Visual aids to location: Ibn NE Green. Helicopter Ops 1) As directed by ATC; 2) Helicopters must use the Rwy for take-off & landing; 3) Helicopters parking on the S apron at positions PW or PE are restricted to Jet Ranger size and below; 4) Limited helicopter training area available, contact ATC.

Warnings
Gliding takes place at Currock Hill gliding site, 8nm SW of Newcastle Airport from dawn to dusk. ATC will advise when active. ACFT using the ILS in IMC or VMC shall not descend on approach to Rwy25 below 1500ft QFE and on Rwy07 below 2300ft QFE before intercepting the glidepath and shall not thereafter fly below it. ACFT approaching without assistance from radar or ILS shall follow a descent path not lower than the ILS glidepath. ACFT must not join the final APP track to either Rwy at a height of less than 1500ft QFE (1800ft QNH) unless they are a propeller driven ACFT whose MTWA does not exceed 5700kg when the minimum height shall be 1000ft QFE (1300ft QNH). The portion of Twy 3 to the W of the Belman hangar has a maximum wingspan clearance of 17m. When Rwy25 is in use and wind direction is from 160-190° expect turbulence and possible negative gradient.

Operating Hrs	H24
Circuits	Variable as advised by ATC
Landing fee	on application

Maintenance
M3 GA Terminal **Tel:** 0191 214 4111
Fuel
Limited Hrs of availability Not available 1900-0900 daily
AVGAS 100LL
Samson Av **Tel:** 0191 214 4111/4114
JET A1
Air BP **Tel:** 0191 286 0966 Ext 4290
Conoco **Tel:** 0191 286 2252

Operator	Newcastle Int Airport Ltd
	Newcastle Airport, Woolsington
	Newcastle-upon-Tyne NE13 8BZ
	Tel: 0191 286 0966 (Switchboard)
	Tel: 0191 214 3400/3401 (ATIS)
	Fax: 0191 2714742 (ATC)

Restaurant
Restaurant and Club facilities available at Airport

Taxis Available at GA Terminal. Metro link to
Newcastle. GA Terminal has courtesy coach
Car Hire
Hertz **Tel:** 091 286 0966 Ext.4281
Budget **Tel:** 0191 286 0966 Ext.4393
Europcar **Tel:** 0191 286 0966 Ext.4382
Avis **Tel:** 0191 286 0815

Weather Info M T9 T18 Fax 376 A VN MWC

CTR-Class D Airspace
Normal CTA/CTR Class D Airspace rules apply
These rules do not apply by day to non-radio ACFT provided
they have obtained permission and maintain 5km visibility,
1500m horizontally and 1000ft vertically away from cloud, or
for gliders provided they maintain 8km visibility, 1500m
horizontally and 1000ft vertically away from cloud.

Visual Reference Points (VRPs)

VRP	VOR/DME
Bolam Lake	NEW 317°/8nm
N5507.78 W00152.47	
Blaydon	
N5458.10 W00141.62	NEW 183°/4nm
Blyth Power Station	NEW 049°/9nm
N5508.50 W00131.50	
Durham	NEW 170°/16nm
N5446.43 W00134.60	
Hexham	NEW 259°/14nm
N5458.25 W00206.17	
Morpeth Railway Station	NEW 009°/7nm
N5509.75 W00140.97	
Ouston (disused A/D)	NEW 267°/6nm
N5501.50 W00152.52	
Stagshaw Masts	NEW 274°/11nm
N5502.00 W00201.42	
Tyne Bridges	NEW 148°/5nm
N5458.05 W00136.42	

ELEVATION	LOCATION	EGSW		NEWMARKET HEATH

ELEVATION	LOCATION
100ft	1.5nm W of Newmarket
3mb	N5214.50E00022.33
PPR	

| BKY 116.25 | 042 | 19.1 | − • • • / − • − / − • − − |
| CLN 114.55 | 314 | 36.9 | − • − • / • − • • / − • |

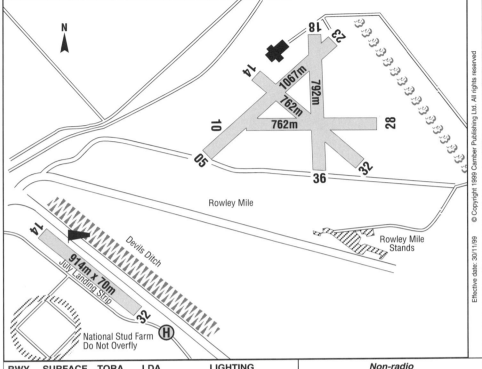

Rowley Mile

Rowley Mile Stands

Devils Ditch

914m x 70m
July Landing Strip

National Stud Farm
Do Not Overfly

RWY	SURFACE	TORA	LDA	LIGHTING
18/36	Grass	792	U/L	Nil
05/23	Grass	1067	U/L	Nil
10/28	Grass	762	U/L	Nil
14/32	Grass	762	U/L	Nil
14/32	Grass	914 July course	U/L	Nil

	Non-radio
APP	Cambridge 123.60
LARS	Lakenheath 128.90

Remarks

PPR open race days only. Run by Jockey club. Visits at pilots own risk. Two separate strips on racecourse. No ops 30mins before first race until 30mins after last race, unless extreme circumstances, via racecourse manager if horses are within parade ring. **Rowley mile landing area:** Only available when racing Rowley mile course, 1200-1800 (local) PPR Tel: 01638 663482 (non race day), /662762 (race day). **July Strip:** Restricted use both race & non-race days. PPR, briefing sheet MUST be obtained prior to arrival Tel: 01638 663482 (Racecourse office) /664151 (Jockey club office). All arrivals Rwy14, all departs Rwy32. **All landing & take-offs banned when yellow or white cross is displayed at S end of strip.** Non race days only July strip is normally available, strictly PPR through Jockey Club estates, 101 High Street, Newmarket, Suffolk Tel: 01638 664151

Warnings
Noise: Stud farms & training facilities in local area. Correct adherence to local restrictions essential.

Operating Hrs	Available on request

Circuits	

Landing fee	Nil race days £20 +VAT non-race days
Maintenance	Nil
Fuel	Nil

Operator	Newmarket Racecourse Trust

Westfield House, The Links, Cambridge Road
Newmarket, Suffolk CB8 8JL
Tel: 01638 663482/664151(non-race days)
Tel: 01638 662762 (during racing)

Restaurants	Racecourse facilities

Taxis	
Chilcots	**Tel:** 01638 663282
Car Hire	
Godfrey Davis	**Tel:** 01223 48198

Weather Info	AirS BNMC

ELEVATION	LOCATION					
200ft 6mb	2.5nm N of Baldock N5201.42 W00009.45	BKY 116.25	288	9.5	— • • • / — • — / — • — —
PPR		BPK 117.50	355	17	— • • • / • — — • / — • —

NEWNHAM (Nr. Baldock)

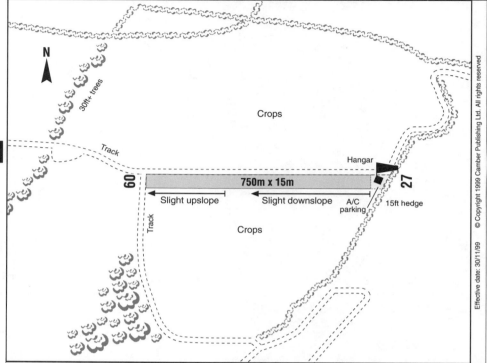

RWY	SURFACE	TORA	LDA	LIGHTING		Non-Radio	
09/27	Grass	750x15	U/L	Nil		APP (Luton)	129.55

Remarks
PPR by telephone. Visiting ACFT and Microlights welcome at pilots own risk. The operator is a BMAA approved inspector and Check pilot, (Flex-wing & 3 Axis) and welcomes fly-in inspections. Noise: Avoid overflight of Newnham village 5nm to the SW.

Warnings
Hedge and hangars in undershoot Rwy27. Caution farm vehicles may use tracks which run along N of AD and across 09 Thr. AD has slight downslope on first 75% of Rwy27. Crops are grown close to strip S edge.

Operator	Kevin Woods, 12 Ennerdale Close Steukeley Meadows, Huntingdon PE18 6UU
Tel: 01480 434439	
Tel: 07801 556665 (Mobile)	
Restaurants	
Taxis/Car Hire	
Weather Info	AirCen BNMC

Operating Hrs	SR-SS
Circuits	As you wish but avoid Newnham
Landing Fee	Nil
Maintenance	Nil
Fuel	MOGAS
by prior arrangement lift can be provided to local garage	

ELEVATION	LOCATION	EGXN				NEWTON

ELEVATION	LOCATION
182ft 6mb	7nm E of Nottingham N5257.99 W00059.37
PPR MILITARY	

GAM 112.80	191	18.8	– – • / • – / – –
TNT 115.70	118	25.0	– / – • / –

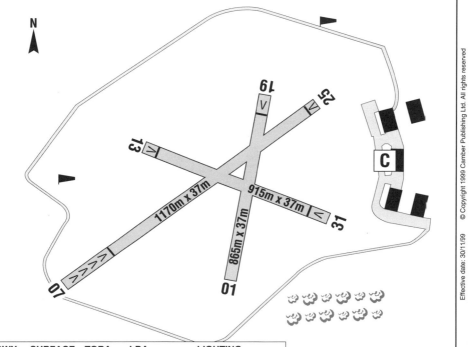

RWY	SURFACE	TORA	LDA	LIGHTING
07	Grass	1170	1090	Nil
25	Grass	1170	940	Nil
01	Grass	865	750	Nil
19	Grass	865	705	Nil
13	Grass	915	815	Nil
31	Grass	915	770	Nil

Newton

APP	119.125
TWR	119.125 122.10
DEP	Waddington 127.35

Remarks
Intensive AB-Initio training No jet ACFT. The Rwys are marked on one side only by 25ft concrete strips. Thresholds marked by red/white marker boards. Visual aids to location: Ibn NW Red.

Warnings
Locally based ACFT give very late finals call. Glider flying takes place Mon-Fri 0630-1700 Sat-Sun 0630-SS, up to 5000ft within 5nm radius of Syerston (N5302 W00055). ATZ permanently active during Operational hours.

Operator	RAF Newton, Nottingham NG13 8HL **Tel:** 01400 261201 Ext.4140 (ATC)
Restaurants	
Taxis/Car Hire	
Weather Info	AirCen MWC

Operating Hrs
0800-1600 (Summer) Daily 0900-1700 (Winter)

Circuits	Variable
Landing fee	£7.56 +VAT per 500kgs & £8.50 insurance
Maintenance	Nil
Fuel	AVGAS 100LL by arrangement

ELEVATION	LOCATION	EGAD				NEWTOWNARDS
9ft	8.5nm E of Belfast					
0mb	N5434.87 W00541.53	**BEL 117.20**	112	19.1	– • • • / • / • – • •	
	Diversion AD	**IOM 112.20**	322	44.8	• • / – – – / – –	
PPR						

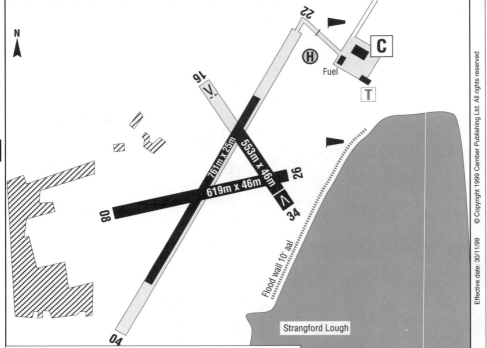

Strangford Lough

Flood wall 10' aal

Fuel

RWY	SURFACE	TORA	LDA	LIGHTING
04	Asphalt	761	761	Thr Rwy APAPI 4.5°
22	Asphalt	761	690	Thr Rwy APAPI 4.5°
16	Asph/Grass**	533	533	Nil
34	Asph/Grass	553	493	Nil
08/26	Asph/Grass	619	U/L	Nil

**Paved strip (345 x 45m) at S E end

Newtownards	
APP	**Belfast (City) 130.85**
A/G	**123.50**

Remarks
Visiting ACFT welcome, not a designated AD under the provention of terrorism act. ACFT operating under restrictions of the act must contact RUC force control Tel: 02890 650222 Ext.22430. Rwy08/26 not available for ACFT required to use a licensed AD. U/L for ACFT exceeding 2730kgs. Visual aids to location: Abn White/Green.

Warnings
Situated on the shore of Strangford Lough with high GND & obstructions to W & N. Belfast (City) CTZ boundary close to N & W. **Obstructions:** Monument (lit) 591ft amsl 267°/0.90nm. HT cables on high GND 232ft aal within 0.5nm Rwy22 approach. Hill 705ft amsl 314°/2.8nm.

Operator	Ulster Flying Club (1961) Ltd
	Newtownards Aerodrome, Portaferry Road, Newtownards County Down, B23 3SG N Ireland
	Tel: 02891 813327
	Fax: 02891 814575
Restaurants	New Dragon Palace (in clubhouse)
	Tel: 02891 816800
	(1230-1400 1700-2330)
Taxis	
SCRABO	**Tel:** 02891 810360
Car Hire	
A1 Car & Van Hire	Tel 02891 464447
	(Duffern Avenue Co. Down)
Weather Info	AirN BEL

Operating Hrs	0800-1630 (Summer) 0900-1730 (Winter)
Circuits	04 RH
Landing fee	Single £10 Twin £25 inc VAT

Maintenance
Kenboag — **Tel:** 02891 811241
Fuel — AVGAS 100LL JET A1 by arrangement

ELEVATION	LOCATION		NORTH COATES

10ft 0mb	6nm SE of Grimsby N5330.25.E00003.73	OTR 113.90 158 12.5 – – – / – / • – •
PPR		

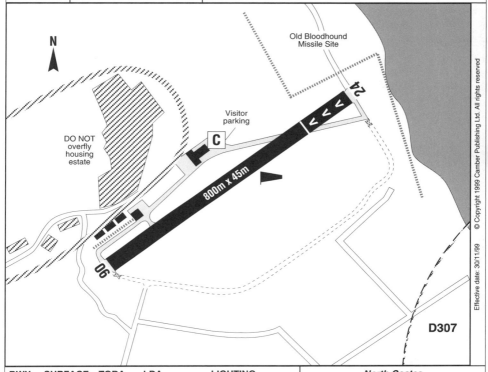

RWY	SURFACE	TORA	LDA	LIGHTING
06/24	Concrete	800x45	U/L	Nil

	North Coates
A/G	**120.15 (Mon-Fri) Inbounds first call Donna Nook Range 122.75**

Remarks
PPR by telephone. Visiting ACFT welcome at pilots own risk. Inbound ACFT must call Donna Nook range on 122.75 at least 5mins or 15nm from N Coates to determine range activity condition. Approach the AD from the W or SW and, if notified that Donna Nook (D307), northerly pattern is active, descend to fly at 500ft on Donna Nook QFE when within 2nm of North Coates. Advise Donna Nook when landing complete. D307 is not active at weekends. This AD has a past stretching from WWI to the 80's when it was a bloodhound missile base. Visitors are allowed to investigate the site.

Warnings
Sea breezes can cause localised wind effects. The perimeter fence restricts Twy width on the extreme W portion of Twy towards Rwy06.
Noise: 24 depts, turn left 10° to avoid North Coates village.

Maintenance Fuel	Limited facilities Hangarage available

Operator   North Coates Flying Club
Tel: 01472 388850 (AD)
Tel: 01472 388824 (site Manager)
Tel: 01472 500144 (Outside Operational hours)
Tel: 01507 358716 Ext 130. (Donna Nook Range)

Restaurants   Accomodation in village
Snack bar only with light refreshments on AD

Taxis/Car Hire   By arrangement

Weather Info   AirN MWC

Operating Hrs	Daily

Circuits   Normally LH 06/34 RH 16/24
Opposite circuits at the weekends when the range is closed.
All at 1000ft aal

Landing fee   on application

ELEVATION	LOCATION	**EGEN**		**NORTH RONALDSAY**

ELEVATION	LOCATION				
40ft 1mb	28nm NE by N of Kirkwall Airport N5922.12 W00226.07	KWL 108.60	038	28.3	– • – / • – – / • – ••
PPR		SUM 117.35	237	46.4	••• / •• – / – –

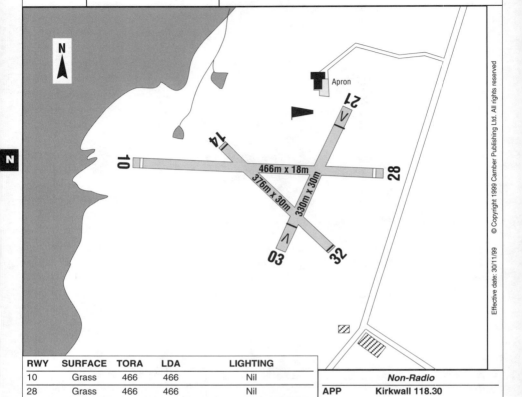

RWY	SURFACE	TORA	LDA	LIGHTING
10	Grass	466	466	Nil
28	Grass	466	466	Nil
14	Grass	336	323	Nil
32	Grass	326	306	Nil
03	Grass	292	277	Nil
21	Grass	295	277	Nil

	Non-Radio
APP	Kirkwall 118.30

Remarks
This AD is used at pilot's own risk. Licensed AD (day use only). Starter extensions of 15m are available on all Rwys.

Warnings
Lighthouse 100ft aal/140ft amsl 2.0nm 051° from ARP.

Operator   Orkney Islands Council Offices
Kirkwall, Orkney Islands
Tel: 01856 873535
Fax: 01856 876094

Restaurants   Meals & accomodation at
North Ronaldsay Bird Sanctuary **Tel:** 01857 633200

Taxis/Car Hire
Garso   **Tel:** 01857 633244
Bike Hire
AD Goods & Servces **Tel:** 01857 633220

Weather Info   AirN GWC

Operating Hrs	SR-SS
Circuits	
Landing fee	£16.47 + VAT
Maintenance **Fuel**	Nil MOGAS (AD Goods & Services) **Tel:** 01857 633220

ELEVATION	LOCATION	EGSX				NORTH WEALD
321ft
11mb	3.5nm SE of Harlow
N5143.30 E00009.25					
PPR	**Diversion AD**	LAM 115.60	005	4.5	• — • • / • — / — —
		BPK 117.50	105	9.8	— • • • / • — — • / — • —

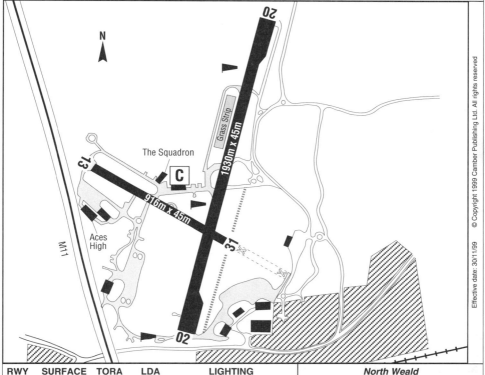

RWY	SURFACE	TORA	LDA	LIGHTING
02/20	Asphalt	1930x45	U/L	Nil
13/31	Asphalt	916x45	U/L	Nil

North Weald

APP	Essex Rad 120.625
A/G	123.525
	Aceair Nth Weald 130.17

Remarks
The AD is situated below the Stansted CTA base 1500ft. Contact must be established with Stansted APP on 120.625 prior to entering Controlled Airspace. Rwy13/31 is to be used only when strong winds preclude the use of Rwy02/20. During Special Event days contact with Stansted Approach is not required except for permission to enter controlled airspace or in an emergency.

Warnings
Gliding, parascending and model ACFT flying take place on the AD. Masts up to 304ft agl/625ft AMSL 1nm E of A/D. 02/20 PCN varies from 5 at 02 Thr 9 at 20 Thr.

Operator Epping Forest District Council
25 Hamnall Street, Epping, Essex CM16 4LX
Tel: 01992 524740 (ATC)
Tel: 01992 524510 (The Squadron)
Fax: 01992 522238 (The Squadron)
Fax: 01992 524047(ATC)

Restaurants	The Squadron on AD bar and restaurant
Taxis
Lawlor Car Services	Can be arranged thru The Squadron or **Tel:** 01992 57888/576094
Car Hire
Hertz	Can be arranged thru The Squadron or **Tel:** 01279 433316
Weather Info	AirSE BNMC

Operating Hrs	0900-1900 or SS
Circuits	02 LH 20 RH
Landing fee	Donation to upkeep
Maintenance	N Weald Flying Services
Tel: 01992 524510
Fuel	AVGAS 100LL JET A1

ELEVATION	LOCATION	EGBK		NORTHAMPTON (Sywell)	
429ft 14mb	5nm NE of Northampton N5218.29 W00047.48	DTY 116.40	063	13.9	– •• / – / – • – –
PPR		HON 113.65	101	31.9	•••• / – – – / – •

Note: Gas Storage Here See Warnings

909m x 30m
528m x 18m
700m x 18m

N

21
15
25
33
07
03

C (H)

NN 378.5

RWY	SURFACE	TORA	LDA	LIGHTING
03/21	Grass	909	909	Thr Rwy LITAS 4° LHS
15/33	Grass	528	528	Nil
07/25	Grass	700	700	Nil

Sywell	
AFIS	122.70
A/G	122.70
NDB	NN 378.50* range 15nm *NN 030/0.2 to Thr03

Remarks
Not available to non-radio ACFT. Helicopter training circuits are opposite to fixed wing circuits and are flown up to 700ft agl on the dead side of the active Rwy. Only Rwy 03/21 is licensed for night use. Visual aids to location: Ibn NN Green.

Warnings
A public road runs along the SE, S and SW boundaries. S edge of Rwy03/21 and N edge of Rwy15/33 are marked by a number of 2m square white GND markers for helicopter operations; fixed wing pilots should disregard. Pilots should note presence of gas storage tanks just NNW of 07 and 03 Thr.

Operating Hrs
Mon-Fri 0800-1800 or SS Sat-Sun 0800-1700 or SS (Summer) 0900-1700 or SS (Winter) and by arrangement

Circuits Fixed Wing 07/ 21/33 RH 03/15/25 LH
1000ft Helicopters see Remarks

Landing fee Single/Heli £9.00 Twin from £15
Microlight £7.00 inc VAT
Special rates at certain times

Maintenance
Taylor **Tel:** 01604 492160
Fuel AVGAS 100LL JET A1 (credit cards accepted) Rotors running refuel available H24 from Sloane Helicopters **Tel:** 01604 790595 **Fax;** 01604 790988

Operator Sywell Aerodrome Ltd
Sywell Aerodrome, Northampton NN6 0BT
Tel: 01604 644917(ATC)
Tel: 01604 491112 (admin)
Fax: 01604 499210 (ATC)

Restaurants Restaurants & refreshments available
Aviator Hotel **Tel:** 01604 642111

Taxis **Tel:** 01604 38888
Car Hire
National **Tel:** 01604 259101

Weather Info AirCen BNMC

ELEVATION	LOCATION	EGWU	NORTHOLT
124ft 4mb	2nm E by N of Uxbridge N5133.18.W00025.09		

LON 113.60	030	4.2	• – • • / – – – / – •
BNN 113.75	161	11.5	– • • • / – • / – •

PPR MILITARY

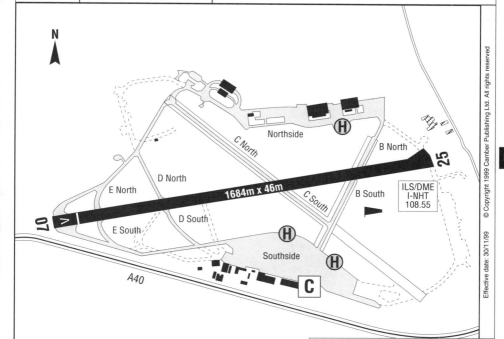

Effective date: 30/11/99

Northside

B North

25

ILS/DME I-NHT 108.55

C North

D North

E North

1684m x 46m

C South

B South

D South

E South

07

Southside

H

H

H

A40

C

RWY	SURFACE	TORA	LDA	LIGHTING
07	Asphalt	1684	1592	Ap Thr Rwy PAPI 3°
25	Asphalt	1684	1702	Ap Thr Rwy PAPI 3°

Nolt	
ATIS	125.125
APP	126.45
RAD	130.35 125.875
VDF	126.45
TWR	120.675
GND	124.975
DEPS	120.325
ILS/DME	I-NHT 108.55 Rwy25

Remarks
Located within the London CTR. Pilots must be familiar with the Northolt procedures and noise abatement regulations. PPR for all private, executive and charter flights. 24 Hrs notice required for all flights. Between 0800-2000 Sat Sun civil ACFT will only be accepted when AD is planned to be open for military movements. Flight plans showing previously arranged alternatives are to be filed for each flight. Civilian movements at Northolt are limited to 28 per day. Single-engined ACFT are not permitted to land at Northolt. Non airways inbound to Northolt should work from NW: London RAD 135.150 From NE: Essex RAD 120.625. Visual location aids: Ibn NO Red.

Warnings
Rwy usage dictated by Heathrow. In certain circumstances pilots may have to accept a tailwind.

Maintenance	Nil
Fuel	JET A1

Operator RAF Northolt, West End Road Ruislip, Middx HA4 6NG
Tel: 0208 845 2300 Ext.4233
Fax: 0208 841 9307

Restaurants

Taxis/Car Hire

Weather Info AirSE BNMC

Operating Hrs	0700-1900 (Summer) + 1Hr Winter PPR by 1400 previous day
Circuits	25 RH 07 LH 1000ft QNH
Landing fees	£7.56 per 500kgs + VAT & £8.50 insurance

ELEVATION	LOCATION
117ft 4mb	2.8nm N of Norwich N5240.56 E00116.96
PPR	

CLN 114.55   010   49.9   — • — • / • — • • / — •

	Norwich	
ATIS	128.625	
APP	119.35	
RAD	119.35* 128.325	
TWR	124.25	
FIRE	121.60	

* Available during opening hours of
RAF Coltishall

ILS/DME	I-NH 110.90 Rwy27
NDB	NH 371.5* range 20nm
NDB	NWI 342.5 on A/D range 20nm

*NH 273/3.2 to Thr27

RWY	SURFACE	TORA	LDA	LIGHTING
09/27	Asph/Con	1842	1842	Ap Thr Rwy PAPI 3° LHS
04/22*	Asph/Con	1285	1285	Thr Rwy PAPI LHS

*Licensed for visual day use only

Remarks

PPR to non-radio ACFT. ACFT must contact Norwich Approach at least 10 mins before ETA. RAF Coltishall 5nm NE of Norwich generates high intensity jet traffic & early information of ACFT approaching Norwich is vital to co-ordinate traffic. Helicopters land as ATC instruct. Light ACFT & microlight activity at Felthorpe AD occasionally with increased activity during summer. ACFT operating for hire or reward must be handled by Norwich Airport Ltd. Avoid over-flying residential area SW. Visual aids: Ibn NH Green. ACFT book out by telephone to avoid delay. Proof of third party insurance cover of not less than £1m must be available for inspection. Light helicopters not required to use rwys but operations should avoid disturbance to local residential areas.

Warnings

Both ends Rwy09/27 width is twice that of associated edge lights due to extra pavement on one side. Rwy centreline lighting not installed, pilots should ensure they are correctly lined up, especially at night, when Rwy is contaminated, or in low visibility. Circuit/instrument training 0700-1930 (local), outside these hrs extension charges. Use Rwy04/22 only when Rwy09/27 unavailable/dangerous thru wind turbulence. **Noise:** Deps, climb Rwy heading thru 1000ft QFE, then turn on course unless ATC instruct otherwise.

Operating Hrs
Sun-Fri 0530-2130 Sat 0530-1900 (Summer)
Winter +1hr & by arrangement

Circuits	As instructed by ATC
Landing fee	On application
Maintenance Fuel	Available AVGAS 100LL AVTUR JET A1

Operator	Norwich Airport Ltd, Norwich NR6 6JA

Tel: 01603 411923 (Admin) **Fax:** 01603 487523 (Admin)
Tel: 01603 420641 (ATC) **Tel:** 01603 420636 (Ops)

Restaurants	Restaurant/bar & cafeteria services

available in terminal & at flying club

Taxis	Available during Airport opening hours
Car Hire	
Avis	**Tel:** 01603 416719
Europcar	**Tel:** 01603 400280
Hertz	**Tel:** 01603 404010

Weather Info	M T9 Fax 378 VS BNMC

ELEVATION	LOCATION	EGBN				NOTTINGHAM

ELEVATION	LOCATION
138ft	3nm SE of Nottingham
5mb	N5255.20 W00104.75
PPR	**Diversion AD**

TNT 115.70	116	22.8	– / – • / –
GAM 112.80	199	22.0	– – • / • – / – –

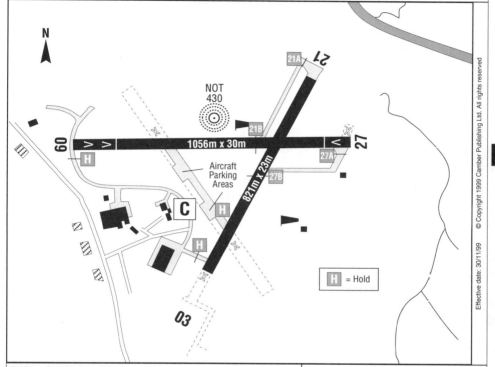

NOT 430

1056m x 30m

821m x 23m

Aircraft Parking Areas

H = Hold

RWY	SURFACE	TORA	LDA	LIGHTING
03/21	Asphalt	821	821	Nil
09	Asph/Con	989(day)	837(day)	-
09	Asph/Con	837(night)	837(night)	Thr Rwy LITAS 3.5°
27	Asph/Con	975(day)	929(day)	-
27	Asph/Con	837(night)	837(night)	Thr Rwy LITAS 3.75°

	Nottingham
APP	**East Midlands 119.65**
A/G	**122.80**
NDB	**NOT 430**
	on A/D range 10nm

Remarks
PPR to non-radio ACFT. AD is situated close to the East Midlands CTR and under the E Midlands CTA (base 2500ft AMSL). Contact East Midlands Approach for transit. Visual aids to location: Ibn NT Green.

Warnings
Chimney 205ft aal/343 ft amsl 1.4nm 285° from the ARP. The Rwy end lights for Rwy27 are located at the end of the declared TORA. In an emergency pilots should be aware that there is a further 150m of usable Rwy beyond the lighting.

Maintenance	
Trueman	**Tel: 0115 982 6090**
Fuel	AVGAS 100LL JET A1

Operator Truman Aviation Ltd, Nottingham Airport
Tollerton, Nottingham NG12 4GA
Tel: 0115 9811327 (ATC) 0115 9815050
Fax: 0115 9811444

Restaurant	Club facilities at AD

Taxis	Arranged locally
Car Hire	
National	**Tel:** 0115 950 3385

Weather Info	AirCen MWC

Operating Hrs
Mon-Fri 0800-1700 Sat 0800-1800 Sun 0900-1800 (Summer)
Mon-Sat 0900-1700 Sun 1000-1700 Thu 1700-2000 (Winter)
and by arrangement with 24 Hrs notice

Circuits	800ft QFE

Landing fee	Single £10.00 Twin £14.00 inc VAT

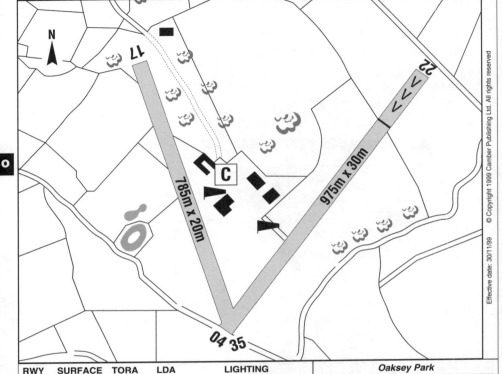

RWY	SURFACE	TORA	LDA	LIGHTING
*17/35	Grass	785x20	U/L	Nil
22/04	Grass	975x30	U/L	Nil

* Rwy17/35 emergency use only

	Oaksey Park
APP	**Lyneham 123.40**
A/G	**122.775**

Remarks

Strict PPR by telephone. Visitors welcome at own risk. ACFT must be kept to the mown strips and manoeuvring areas. Heavy, wet land may prevail during some winter months making the AD unusable. Visiting pilots must avoid noise-sensitive areas of local villages and avoid over-flying local farms and houses. Standard circuit joining and departure must be obeyed at all times. No low flying or beat-ups. New clubhouse.

Warnings

200Kv National grid line 1.75km E of AD, on APP to Rwy22.

Operator	Mr MC Woodhouse Oaksey Park Airfield
	Oaksey, Malmesbury, Wilts SN16 9SD
	Tel: 01666 577130 (Operator)
	Tel: 01666 577152 (AD)
	Fax: 01666 577169
Restaurants	Good pubs in Oaksey village
Taxis **Car Hire**	**Tel:** 01285 650850
Weather Info	AirSW BNMC

Operating Hrs	0700-2100 or SR-SS
Circuits	04 RH 22 LH 1000ft QNH
Landing Fee	Single £5 Twin/Heli £10 +VAT
Maintenance **Fuel**	Nil hangarage available to visiting ACFT AVGAS 100LL

ELEVATION	LOCATION		
20ft 1mb **PPR**	5nm NE of Oban N5627.81.W00523.98	**TIR 117.70** **101** **48.8** – / • • / • – •	

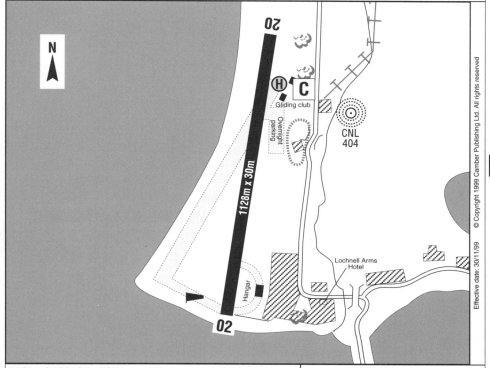

RWY	SURFACE	TORA	LDA	LIGHTING
02/20	Asphalt	1128x30	U/L	Nil

Oban Radio

FIS	Scottish 127.275
A/G	118.05
NDB	CNL 404

Remarks
AD is increasingly active with light ACFT & light/heavy helicopters. Weather actuals may be obtained on 01631 710384.

Warnings
Glider launching takes place at the AD. Microlight flying takes place at the AD. High ground 990 ft aal/1010 ft amsl 1nm to N and NNE of AD respectively. Gliders are operating when a double cross is displayed N of disused Rwy04/22

Operating Hrs   SR-SS

Circuits   Powered ACFT to W gliders to E

Landing fee   Single £8 Twin £12 inc.VAT
Public transport £4.90 per 500kgs AVW +VAT

Maintenance   Nil
Fuel   AVGAS 100LL JET A1 H24 7-days
Tel: 01631 710384 (AD)
Tel: 01631 720215 (office) 07770 620988 (mobile)

Operator   Total Logistics Concepts, Oban Airport
Oban, Argyll, Scotland PA34 4AR
Tel/Fax: 01631 710384 (PPR)
Tel/Fax: 01631 710888
Tel: 01631 720215 (Out of Hrs)
Tel: 07770 620988 (Mobile)

Restaurants   Light refreshments at AD
Lochnell Arms   **Tel:** 01631 710408

Taxis
Tel: 01631 562834
Tel: 01631 563784

Car Hire
Tel: 01631 566476
Tel: 01631 563519

Weather Info   AirSc GWC
Also observed actuals from AD
Tel: 01631 710384

ELEVATION	LOCATION	**EGVO**					**ODIHAM**

ELEVATION	LOCATION				
405ft 14mb	8nm SW of Aldershot N5114.05 W00056.57	**MID 114.00**	315	16	– – / •• / – ••
PPR MILITARY		**OCK 115.30**	262	18.9	– – – / – • – • / – • –

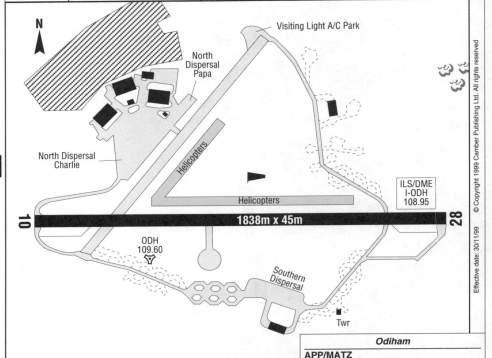

Visiting Light A/C Park
North Dispersal Papa
North Dispersal Charlie
Helicopters
Helicopters
ILS/DME I-ODH 108.95
10
1838m x 45m
28
ODH 109.60
Southern Dispersal
Twr

RWY	SURFACE	TORA	LDA	LIGHTING
10	Asphalt	1838	1836	Ap Thr Rwy PAPI 3°
28	Asphalt	1838	1838	Ap Thr Rwy PAPI 3°

Odiham	
APP/MATZ /LARS	Farnborough 125.25
TWR	122.10
AFIS	122.10*
	* Local helis receive AFIS on TWR Freq
TACAN	ODH 109.60
ILS/DME	108.95, I-ODH Rwy28

Remarks
PPR 24 Hrs notice required. Intensive helicopter activity, special procedures apply. Inbound helicopters to route via 'N Gate' (M3 junction 2nm N of A/D). ATZ active H24. Visual aid to location: IBn OI Red.

Warnings
Glider flying weekends, and summer evenings Mon, Tue & Fri.

Operator	RAF Odiham **Tel:** 01256 702134 Ext.7254
Restaurants	
Taxis/Car Hire	
Weather Info	M T 382 BNMC

Operating Hrs
Mon-Fri 0700-1600 (Summer) + 1Hr Winter

Circuits	Variable for heli fixed wing to S
Landing fee	£7.56 per 500kgs +VAT & £8.50 insurance
Maintenance Fuel	Nil AVTUR Jet A1

ELEVATION	LOCATION	EGSV	OLD BUCKENHAM

ELEVATION	LOCATION		
180ft 6mb	12nm SW of Norwich City centre N5229.83 E00103.06	CLN 114.55 358 39	— • — • / • — • • / — •
PPR			

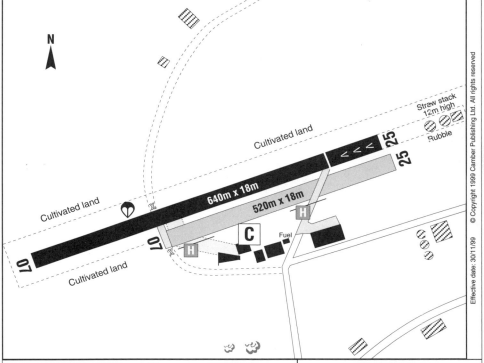

RWY	SURFACE	TORA	LDA	LIGHTING
07	Tarmac	640	640	Nil
25	Tarmac	800	640	Nil
07/25	Grass	520	U/L	Nil

Rwy25 (Tarmac) has 160m concrete starter extension

	Old Buckenham
LARS	Lakenheath 128.90
A/G	124.40

Remarks
PPR by telephone. Microlights not accepted. Recently developed AD with many new facilities. Tarmac Rwy constructed on the wartime Rwy & partly beyond the old perimeter track. Flying training, ACFT hire & sales available. Please avoid overflying villages of Old Buckenham, (1nm SSW) of AD & town of Attleborough, (2nm NW of AD).

Warnings
No ACFT movements 2000-0700 (local) on any day. Tacolneston TV mast, (735ft amsl) 3nm ENE. Considerable gliding activity at Tibbenham, 4nm SE. Disused section short of Rwy25 starter extension, rubble piles & up to 12m high straw stacks. Freefall parachuting Sr-SS Mon-Fri & PH up to FL150.

Operating Hrs
Mon-Sat & PH 0800-SS Sun 0900-1700 (Summer)
Mon-Sat & PH 0900-SS Sun 1000-SS (Winter)
also by arrangement

Circuits
07 LH 25 RH 1000ft QFE

Landing fee
Single below 1500kgs £4.26 above 1500kgs £8 or £2.50 with fuel uplift Twin below 3000kgs £8 above 3000kgs by arrangement All prices +VAT

Maintenance
Norfolk Light Aviation **Tel:** 01953 861051
Fuel   AVGAS 100LL

Operator
Touchdown Aero Centre Ltd
Old Buckenham Airfield, Abbey Road, Old Buckenham
Norfolk NR17 1PU
Tel: 01953 860806
Fax: 01953 861212

Restaurants
Restaurant & bar in clubhouse
Hot meals snacks Sunday lunches
Sun-Thu 0900-1800 Fri-Sat 0900-2100 (local)

Taxis
A+G   **Tel:** 01953 453134

Car Hire
Dingles   **Tel:** 01953 452274 (AD pick-up)

Weather Info
AirS BNMC

ELEVATION	LOCATION	EGLS			OLD SARUM

ELEVATION	LOCATION				
285ft 9mb	2nm NNE of Salisbury N5105.93 W00147.05 **Diversion AD**	SAM 113.35	302	18.7	••• / • – / – –
PPR		CPT 114.35	227	31.8	– • – • / • – – • / –

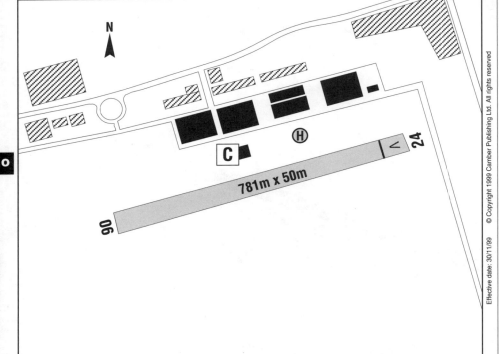

781m x 50m

RWY	SURFACE	TORA	LDA	LIGHTING
06	Grass	781	781	Nil
24	Grass	781	731	Nil

	Old Sarum
APP	**Boscombe Down MATZ** **126.70**
A/G	**123.20**

Remarks

PPR to non-radio ACFT. AD is not available at night by ACFT required to use a licensed AD or for public transport passenger flights required to use a licensed AD. Arriving pilots must establish contact with Boscombe Down (126.70) before entering the MATZ, at VRP Alderbury (155°M 4nm from AD). When Boscombe Down is closed standard overhead join at Old Sarum. Circuit direction when Boscombe Down is open, Rwy 06 RH, Rwy 24 LH. Circuit direction when Boscombe Down is closed, Rwy06 LH, Rwy24 RH.

Warnings

The AD is located within the Boscombe Down MATZ. Danger Area D127 is located 2nm to the E of the AD. Due to a hump on the Rwy, pilots of ACFT with low eye level should exercise caution. Pilots should avoid flying low level over Salisbury. Helicopters may operate to the S of the Rwy.

Operating Hrs 0900-1800 (Licensed) After 1800 up to 2000 or SS whichever is the earlier (U/L) (Summer 0830-1730 or SS whichever is the earlier (Winter)

Circuits Variable dependent on Boscombe Down (see Remarks) 800ft QFE

Landing fee Free to members
Single £7.00 Twin £14.00 Microlights £4.00 inc VAT

Maintenance Old Sarum Engineering
Tel: 01722 410711
Fuel AVGAS 100LL

Operator Megastream Ltd, Hangar 3
Old Sarum Aerodrome, Salisbury, Wiltshire SP4 6BJ
Tel: 01722 322525 (Flying club)
Fax: 01722 323702

Restaurants Old Sarum Restaurant on the AD
Various others in Salisbury within 2 miles

Taxis On request or
Salisbury Taxis **Tel:** 01722 334343
Car Hire On request or
Budget **Tel:** 01722 3364444

Weather Info AirSE BNMC

Visual Reference Points (VRPs)
Alderbury N5102.90 W00143.90

ELEVATION	LOCATION				**OTHERTON**

ELEVATION	LOCATION
340ft 11mb	1.5nm SE of Penkridge N5242.49 W00205.56
PPR	

TNT 115.70   222   26   – / – • / –
HON 113.65   328   26.5   • • • • / – – – / – •

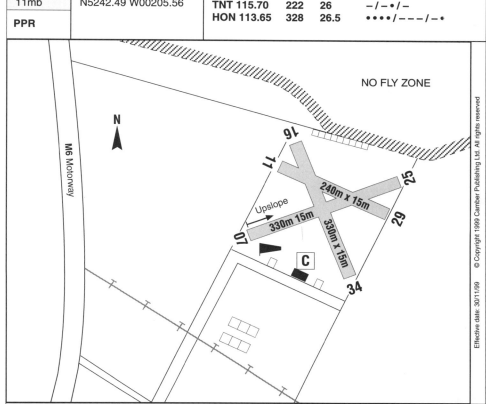

RWY	SURFACE	TORA	LDA	LIGHTING
07*/25	Grass	330x15	U/L	Nil
11/29	Grass	240x15	U/L	Nil
16/34	Grass	330x15	U/L	Nil

*Rwy07 has 2% upslope for first 80m

Otherton

A/G   129.825

Microlight common freq not always manned

Remarks
PPR by telephone MICROLIGHTS ONLY Microlight training school operated by Staffordshire Microlight Centre. Training Tue-Sun. Radio only occasionally manned mainly weekends. Visitors should keep a good lookout for non-radio aircraft in circuit.

Warnings
Noise: All arrivals into overhead at 1000ft QFE from at least 2nm out from E or W. All circuits S only at 500ft QFE. Direction; 07/11 16 RH 25/29/34 LH. Keep circuits tight. Departures: Climb in overhead to min 1200ft QFE then depart to E or W maintaining heading until at least 2nm from AD before turning on course. Do not overfly Penkridge town, the village, farm buildings to N of AD, or Gailey lake wildlife reserve and farm to S.

Maintenance	Nil
Fuel	MOGAS by arrangement with the operator. (Not Mondays).
Operator	Staffordshire Microlight Centre **Tel:** 07831 811783 (Airfield) **Tel/Fax:** 01543 673075 (Evenings) **Tel:** 07973 940222 (Briefing at any time)
Restaurant	Self-service hot drinks available in the clubhouse most days
Taxi Penkridge Cabs **Car Hire**	**Tel:** 01785 712589 Nil
Weather Info	AirCen MWC

Operating Hrs
Mon-Sat 0800-2000 Sun 0900-1700 (Local)

Circuits   See Warnings

Landing fee   £2

ELEVATION	LOCATION				OUT SKERRIES
20ft 0mb	Nr Bruary Out Skerries Shetland N6025.54.W00044.80	SUM 117.35	032	37	● ● ● / ● ● – / – –
PPR					

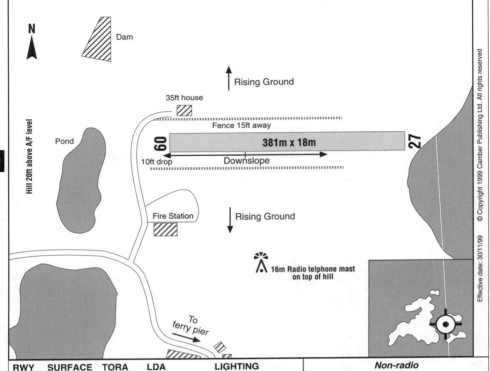

RWY	SURFACE	TORA	LDA	LIGHTING		Non-radio	
09/27	Gravel/Asphalt	381x18	U/L	Nil		APP	Sumburgh 123.15

Remarks
PPR by telephone essential. Visiting ACFT accepted. We recommend visitors contact Loganair (Tel: 01595 840246) to ascertain when their service operates. There is no off-Rwy parking visiting ACFT will constitute an obstruction to vital local services.

Warnings
Rwy surface is poor & uneven fenced on both sides. Due to uneven surface there is danger of prop-strike to nosewheel ACFT with little prop clearance. Rwy profile is hump-backed. The hamlet of Bruray is close to SW of AD. Moss may affect braking action.
Important: ACFT parked on strip restrict scheduled & ambulance services – consult with Loganair.

Operator
Tel: 01806 515235 (Alice Arthur PPR)

Restaurants/Accomodation
Alice Arthur can provide B&B

Taxis/Car Hire Nil

Weather Info AirSc GWC

Operating Hrs	SR-SS
Circuits	1000ft QFE
Landing fee	£3
Maintenance Fuel	Nil Nil

ELEVATION	LOCATION	EGTK				OXFORD

ELEVATION	LOCATION			
270ft 9mb	6nm NW by N of Oxford N5150.20 W00119.18 **Diversion AD**	DTY 116.40	207	22.0	– •• / – / – • – –
PPR		BNN 113.75	288	29.4	– ••• / – • / – •

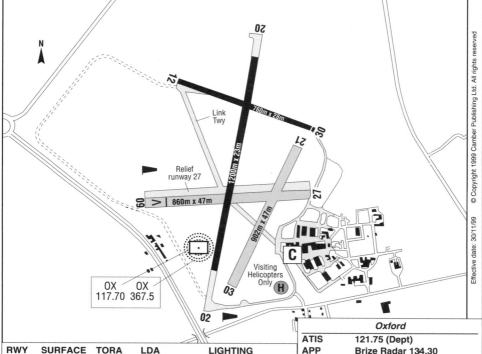

OX 117.70   OX 367.5

RWY	SURFACE	TORA	LDA	LIGHTING
02	Asphalt	1200	1200	Ap Thr Rwy PAPI 3.5° LHS
20	Asphalt	1200	1200	Thr Rwy PAPI 3° LHS
03/21	Grass	902	902	Nil
09	Grass	860	764	Nil
27	Grass	860	860	Thr Rwy APAPI 3° LHS
12/30	Asphalt	760	760	Nil

	Oxford
ATIS	121.75 (Dept)
APP	Brize Radar 134.30
APP/VDF	125.325
TWR/AFIS	118.875
GND	121.95
DME	OX 117.70 on A/D
NDB	OX 367.5 on A/D range 25nm
	*AFIS: Sat/Sun & PH

Remarks

PPR by telephone only Sat/Sun & PH. Rwy03/21 not available due parked ACFT. All departing fixed-wing ACFT climb straight ahead to 1000ft QNH before turning crosswind, endeavour to complete this before the Mercury satellite station. Rwy20 visual Dep turning left should climb ahead until clear to S of Yarnton village, remaining clear of the Brize CTR. Subject to Rwy & circuit direction pilots should avoid noise sensitive areas of Begbroke, Bladon, Blenheim Palace, Kidlington, Woodstock, Yarnton and Thrupp. Whenever possible ACFT joining the circuit should plan to join on base leg or via straight in APP giving way to traffic already in circuit. A relief Rwy is established N parallel & adjacent to Rwy09/27. Rwy, 40m wide, marked white corners & yellow reflective markers on N side. Declared distances for Rwy09/27. Pilots may be asked to use this Rwy at certain times by ATC. Rwy09 thr. displaced 120m (indicated by black & white markers). Visual aids to location: Ibn KD Green.

Warnings

Rwy20 downslope of 2.25% over last 200m SW end. Twys Rwy02 thr. to Rwy09 thr. disused. Helicopter training takes place in designated areas on AD. Jet fuel installation N of tower, infringes western Twy, ACFT winspan over 18m; exercise caution.

Operating Hrs	Mon-Fri 0700-1630 Sat-Sun & PH 0730-1600 (Summer) + 1Hr Winter and by arrangement
Circuits	Variable fixed-wing ACFT 1200ft QFE
Landing fee	Single £12.50 Twin on application

Maintenance
CSE   **Tel:** 01865 844227
Fuel   AVGAS 100LL AVTUR JET A1

Operator   CSE Aviation Ltd, Oxford Airport Kidlington, Oxford OX5 1RA
Tel: 01865 844272 (ATC) /841234 (Ops)
Tel: 01865 844267 (PPR w/e) **Fax:** 01865 841807

Restaurants	Restaurant/refreshments

Taxis
James Cars   **Tel:** 01865 375742
Car Hire
Godfrey Davis   **Tel:** 01865 246373
Target Car&Van Hire **Tel:** 01865 379691

Weather Info	M* A AirCen BNMC

ELEVATION	LOCATION	EGLG				PANSHANGER

ELEVATION	LOCATION				
250ft 8mb	2.5nm W of Hertford N5148.15.W00009.08 **Diversion AD**	BPK 117.50	329	3.7	– • • • / • – – • / – • –
PPR		BNN 113.75	078	15.2	– • • • / – • / – •

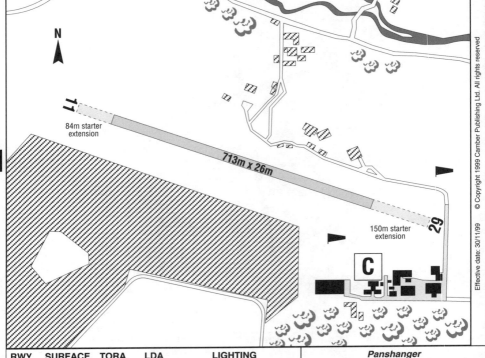

84m starter extension

713m x 26m

150m starter extension

C

RWY	SURFACE	TORA	LDA	LIGHTING
11	Grass	797	713	Nil
29	Grass	863	713	Nil

Starter extensions: Rwy11 84m Rwy29 150m

	Panshanger
APP	Luton 129.55
A/G	120.25

Remarks
Rwy29 Noise Abatement: After take-off turn right overfly golf clubhouse, turn to Rwy QDM until passing prominent white building (school). turn right, fly to square wood approx 0.5 nm, turn downwind between Tewin and Tewin Wood.

Warnings
Luton CTR is 1nm to the N and the ATZ passes into the Luton CTR. Pilots are to obtain a departure briefing to avoid noise sensitive areas.

Operator	Professional Flight Management Ltd
	Panshanger Airfield, Cole Green, Hertford, Herts SG14 2NH
Tel: 01707 391791	
Fax: 01707 392792	

Restaurants	Snacks at A/D

Taxis	
Castle	**Tel:** 01992 501002
County	**Tel:** 01992 504111
Car Hire	
Europcar	**Tel:** 01438 715888
Hertz	**Tel:** 01707 331433

Weather Info	AirSE BNMC

Operating Hrs	0900-SS Winter and Summer

Circuits
11 LH 29RH 800ft QFE standard overhead joins

Landing fee	Singles/Heli £10 Twins £10

Maintenance	PSF ACFT Engineering
Fuel	AVGAS 100LL

ELEVATION	LOCATION		PAPA STOUR

ELEVATION	LOCATION
82ft 2mb **PPR**	Isle of Papa Stour Shetland Isles N6120.13.W00145.18

SUM 117.35   341   30   ••• / •• – / – –

N

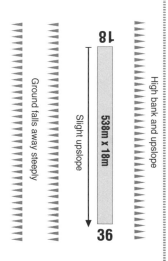

Ground falls away steeply

Slight upslope

538m x 18m

18

36

High bank and upslope

Fence and stone wall

P

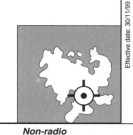

RWY	SURFACE	TORA	LDA	LIGHTING
18/36	Grass/Stones	538x18	U/L	Nil

Non-radio	
APP	**Sumburgh 123.15**
APP	**Scatsa* 123.60**
	*Primary contact during operating Hrs:
	0730-1700 (W) 0630-1600 (S) Mon-Fri

Remarks
PPR by telephone. Visiting ACFT accepted. We recommend visitors seek up-to-date AD condition advice from Loganair (Tel: 01595 840246).

Warnings
The Rwy surface is rough & could cause prop-strike to nosewheel ACFT with little prop clearance. The Rwy profile has a slight up gradient from 18 to 36 Thr. The Rwy is constructed on the side of a hill with an upslope to E & downslope to W. White inset edge markings are somewhat overgrown. Expect severe turbulence on short final to 18 as you cross the cliffs. Caution: standing water after heavy rain. The AD is common land & sheep may stray across the strip at any time. **Important:** ACFT parked on strip restrict scheduled & ambulance services – consult with Loganair.

Operator	
Tel: 01595 873229 (Ted Gray for PPR)	
Restaurants	
Taxis/Car Hire	Nil Only 1.5nm of road on island
Weather Info	AirSc GWC

Operating Hrs	SR-SS
Circuits	1000ft QFE
Landing fee	Nil
Maintenance	Nil
Fuel	Nil

ELEVATION	LOCATION	EGEP				PAPA WESTRAY
91ft 3mb **PPR**	22nm N of Kirkwall Airport N5921.06.W00254.01	**KWL 108.60** **SUM 117.35**	**008** **245**	**23.5** **58.3**	— • — / • — — / • — • • • • • / • • — / — —	

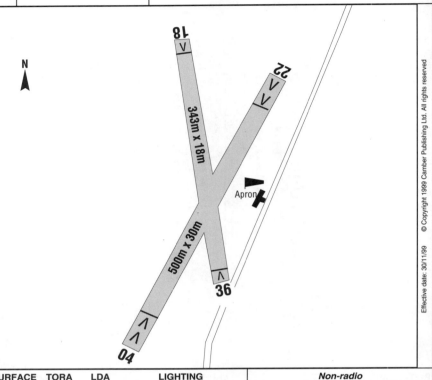

343m x 18m

500m x 30m

Apron

RWY	SURFACE	TORA	LDA	LIGHTING
04/22*	Grass	520	500	Nil
18**	Grass	383	323	Nil
36**	Grass	386	323	Nil

* Starter extension of 20m available at both ends of Rwy
**Starter extension of 40m Rwy18 & 43m Rwy36

	Non-radio
APP	**Kirkwall 118.30**

Remarks
PPR from OIC. Licensed AD, available at pilot's own risk.
Windsock displayed. For Rwy conditions contact AD
Manager on Tel: 01857 644232.

Warnings

Operator	Orkney Islands Council Offices Kirkwall, Orkney **Tel:** 01856 873535 **Fax:** 01856 876094
Restaurants	Nil
Taxis Beltane House Hotel **Car Hire**	Free guest transport to & from **Tel:** 01857 644267
Weather Info	AirSc GWC

Operating Hrs	SR-SS
Circuits	
Landing fee	Nil Fire cover £16.09 +VAT if req
Maintenance **Fuel**	Nil Nil

ELEVATION	LOCATION	EGFP	PEMBREY

ELEVATION	LOCATION
18ft 0mb	6nm WNW of Llanelli N5142.48.W00418.44
PPR	

| BCN 117.45 | 275 | 39 | — • • • / — • — • / — • |
| STU 113.10 | 129 | 31.5 | • • • / — / • • — |

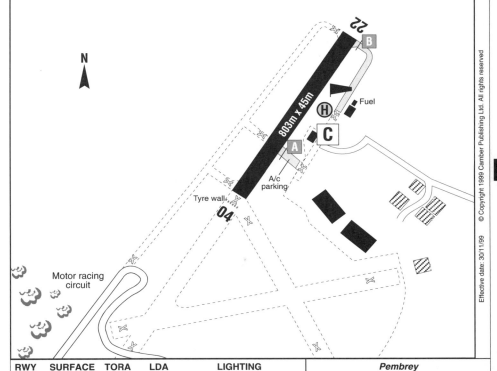

N

803m x 45m

22

B

Fuel

H

C

A

A/c parking

04

Tyre wall

Motor racing circuit

P

RWY	SURFACE	TORA	LDA	LIGHTING
04/22	Concrete	803	803	Nil

Pembrey

DAAIS	Pembrey range 122.75*
AFIS/A/G	124.40
	*See warnings

Remarks
PPR by telephone, non-radio ACFT not accepted.
Located within D118, special procedures apply (see warnings). The active portion is the NE corner of the ex-RAF AD. Visitors welcome. Many local attractions of natural & historical significance. Cefn Sidan Beach (Blue flag 20min walk) & Ashburnham Golf Club 2 miles. 6 berth caravan for hire on AD. Visiting ACFT must carry third party & public liability insurance.

Warnings
Access to Pembrey penetrates D118 active Mon-Fri 0800-1700. Inbounds must call Pembrey Range on 122.75 10nm before DA boundary. Inbounds may be instructed to hold if the range is hot. Non-radio ACFT not accepted. Vehicles cross at mid-point.

Operating Hrs
Daily 0900-1730 or SS. PPR Mon-Fri not required W/E

Circuits Variable

Landing fee Up to 1000kgs £6 1001-1500kgs £12 1501-2000kgs £15 2001-3000kgs £22 3001-4000kgs £30 Inc.VAT

Maintenance	Available also hangarage
Fuel	AVGAS 100LL

Operator	Cpt Winston Thomas, Pembrey Airport
	Pembrey, Carmarthenshire, Wales SA16 0HZ
Tel: 01554 891534	
Fax: 01554 891388	

Restaurants	Available on AD at weekend snacks
during the week	

Hotel accommodation
Gwenllian Court	**Tel:** 01554 890217
Ashburnham Hotel	**Tel:** 01554 834455
Diplomat Hotel	**Tel:** 01554 756156

Taxis	**Tel:** 01554 890111
Car Hire	Can be provided by operator

Weather Info	AirS BNMC

ELEVATION	LOCATION	EGTP	PERRANPORTH
330ft 11mb	1.5nm SW of Perranporth N5019.90.W00510.66	LND 114.20 062 21.5 • — • • / — • / — • • BHD 112.05 272 65.0 — • • • / • • • • / — • •	
PPR			

Effective date: 30/11/99

Map labels: GLIDING AREA, 860m x 18m, 600m x 27m, UNLICENSED, GLIDING AREA, 618m x 46m, 19, 23, 27, 01, 09, 05, Apron, C, Do not overfly (×4)

RWY	SURFACE	TORA	LDA	LIGHTING
05	Asphalt	940*	799	Nil
23	Asphalt	799	799	Nil
09	Asphalt	750**	750	Nil
27	Asphalt	750	750	Nil
01/19	Asphalt	600x27	U/L	Nil

* includes a 204m starter extension
** includes a 129m starter extension

	Perranporth	
APP	Culdrose	134.05
APP	St Mawgan	126.50
A/G		119.75
	Glider Ops	130.10

Remarks

Pilots should avoid flying directly over St. Agnes, Perranporth and settlements to the S of the AD. These areas are particularly noise sensitive. After take-off, when practicable, reduce to climb power and turn to track out over the sea to at least 1500ft QNH before proceeding on course. Pilots arriving from the E should first make contact with St. Mawgan on 126.50. ACFT under the control of Culdrose are by agreement permitted to fly in the ATZ at 2000ft QFE & above during Culdrose ATC Hrs of watch. Accordingly ACFT should not fly within the Perranporth ATZ above 1000ft without clearance from either Culdrose ATC or via relay from Perranporth.

Warnings

Gliding takes place at the AD. When gliding is taking place fixed wing ACFT should make wide circuits. The AD is located within the Culdrose AIAA. Rwy 01/19 is available for ACFT not required to use a licensed AD. For noise abatement, land 19 and take-off 01 – beware of windshear in NW wind. Some parts of the manoeuvring area prone to loose gravel. It is also used for taxiing by ACFT using other Rwys. Only the hard Twys from the apron to the Rwy05 hold and Rwy27 hold are useable.

Operating Hrs	Wed-Sun 0915-1600 or SS Mon-Tues by arr (Winter) 0800-1600 (Summer) daily
Circuits	To N of AD 19RH 01LH 1000ft QFE
Landing Fee	On application
Maintenance	By arrangement
Fuel	AVGAS 100LL
Operator	Perranporth Airfield Ltd

The Airfield, Higher Trevellas, St Agnes, Cornwall TR5 0XS
Tel: 01872 552266
Tel: 01872 573368 (Tourist Info)
Fax: 01872 261126 (operator)

Restaurants	Hotels in Perranporth
Taxis Atlantic	Tel: 01872 572126
Car Hire TMS	Tel: 01872 225511
Weather Info	AirSW BNMC

ELEVATION	LOCATION	EGPT			PERTH (Scone)

ELEVATION	LOCATION			
397ft	3nm NE of Perth	PTH 110.40	VOR on A/D	• — — • / — / • • • •
13mb	N5626.35.W00322.33	SAB 112.50	318 50.3	• • • / • — / — • • •
PPR	**Diversion AD**	GOW 115.40	054 49.0	— — • / — — — / • — —

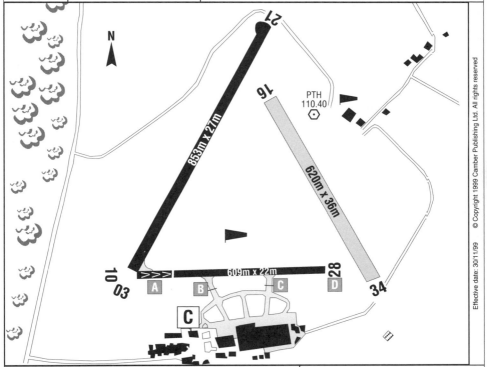

RWY	SURFACE	TORA	LDA	LIGHTING
03/21	Asphalt	853	853	Thr Rwy PAPI 3°
10	Asphalt	609	466*	Nil
28	Asphalt	466	609	Nil
16/34	Grass	620	620	Nil

*Displaced landing Thr

	Perth
A/G	119.80
VOR	PTH 110.40 on A/D

Remarks
PPR non-radio ACFT not accepted.

Warnings
When taking off from Rwy28 there may be severe down draughts and turbulence in the vicinity of the line of trees that form an obstacle (70ft agl) across the Rwy centreline at 910m beyond the start of TORA.

Maintenance
AST Engineering **Tel:** 01738 552311
Tayside **Tel:** 01738 553757
Fuel AVGAS 100LL JET A1

Operator Scottish Aero Club/Tayside Aviation
Tel: 01738 553357
Fax: 01738 553097

Restaurants Restaurant & Club facilities available

Taxis
David Rhind **Tel:** 01738 536098
Car Hire
Struans **Tel:** 01738 445566

Weather Info AirSC GWC

Operating Hrs
0800-1530 (Summer) Winter +1hr (daylight hrs)

Circuits 03/10/16 LH 21/28/34/ RH

Landing fee Single/Private/Club £8.00 Twin £16.00 (Cash)

ELEVATION	LOCATION	EGSF	PETERBOROUGH (Conington)

ELEVATION	LOCATION		
26ft 1mb	7nm S of Peterborough N5228.08.W00015.07 **Diversion AD**	BKY 116.25　343　31.0	− • • • / − • − / − • − −
PPR		DTY 116.40　067　35.9	− • • / − / − • − −

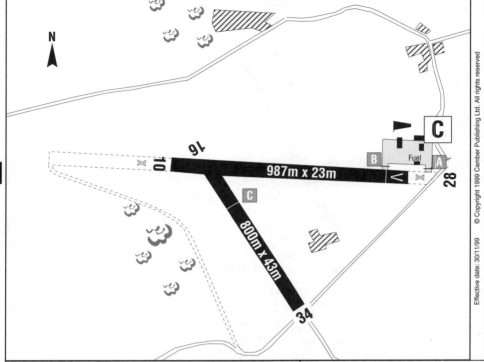

Effective date: 30/11/99

RWY	SURFACE	TORA	LDA	LIGHTING
10	Asphalt	957	957	Thr Rwy LITAS 3.25°
28	Asphalt	987	876	Thr Rwy LITAS 3.25°
16	Asphalt	800	U/L	
34	Asphalt	800	U/L	

	Conington
A/G	129.725

Remarks
PPR non-radio ACFT not accepted. All pilots must avoid over-flying village to the S of the AD. Visual aids to location: Ibn PB Green, AD is 1nm E of A1 N/S dual carriageway

Warnings
Avoid Sibson AD (7nm NW)

Operating Hrs
Mon-Fri 0830-1800 Sat Sun 0900-1800 (Summer)
Mon-Fri 0830-1700 Sat Sun 0900-1700 (Winter)

Circuits　1000ft QFE
Mon-Fri before 1700 (1800 Summer) 10 RH 28 LH
Mon-Fri after 1700 (1800 Summer) 10 LH 28 RH

Landing fee　Single £10 (weekday) £7.00 (Weekend) inc.VAT. Twin available on request

Maintenance	CAA & AOC Inc. Avionics M3 App
Klingair	**Tel:** 01487 832022
Fuel	AVGAS 100LL AVTUR JET A1

Operator　Klingair Ltd
Peterborough Business Airfield, Holme
Peterborough PE7 3PX
Tel: 01487 832022 (PPR)
Tel: 01780 410576 (Out of Hrs)
Fax: 01487 832614

Restaurants　Club facilities with members bar
Light snacks available. Closed Tue-Wed

Taxis	
Anglis	**Tel:** 01733 66661
Car Hire	On request or
Avis	**Tel:** 01733 349489

Weather Info　AirCen BNMC

ELEVATION	LOCATION	EGSP	PETERBOROUGH (Sibson)

ELEVATION	LOCATION
100ft 3mb	6nm W of Peterborough N5233.35.W00023.18
PPR	**Diversion AD**

DTY 116.40	055	34.9	– • • / – / – • – –
BKY 116.25	339	37.7	– • • • / – • – / – • – –

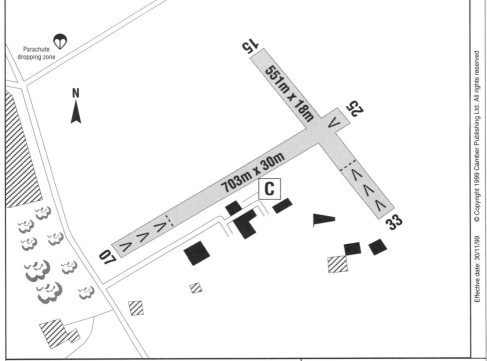

RWY	SURFACE	TORA	LDA	LIGHTING
07	Grass	703	411	Nil
25	Grass	703	613	Nil
15	Grass	551	551	Thr Rwy APAPI 4° LHS
33	Grass	551	424	Thr Rwy APAPI 4° LHS

	Sibson
APP	**Cottesmore MATZ** **130.20**
A/G	**122.30**

Remarks
PPR by telephone. Non-radio ACFT not accepted. Not available to public transport passenger flights required to use a licensed AD. There is no overhead joining and no deadside. Inbound ACFT to call Cottesmore MATZ/LARS on 130.20 when no less than 15nm from Wittering. If no R/T contact is made during opening Hrs for Wittering, ACFT must avoid the Wittering MATZ except for that part which lies S of Sibson, and must descend to the Sibson circuit height before entering. Transiting fixed & rotary wing ACFT may not penetrate the ATZ whilst parachuting is in progress. Helicopters may not operate in the ATZ whilst parachuting is in progress. Visual aids to location: Abn White flashing.

Warnings
Free-fall parachuting up to FL120. Visiting pilots to contact A/G station to ascertain the latest situation. Do not overfly the field. Power lines on approach to 25. Surface can become boggy in winter.

Landing fee	Single £7.00 Twin £14.00
	Microlights £3.00 Unless reciprocal arrangement exists

Maintenance	Available (CAA-approved)
Fuel	AVGAS 100LL Oils W80 80 W20/50

Operator Walkbury Flying Club, S bson Aerodrome
Wansford, Peterborough PE8 6NE
Tel: 01832 280289/280203
Fax: 01832 280289

Restaurants	Available at AD Thu-Sun 1200-1400 1900-2000

Taxis	**Tel:** 01733 254633
Car Hire	
Avis	**Tel:** 01733 349489
Hertz	**Tel:** 01733 273543

Weather Info	AirCen BNMC

Operating Hrs 0700-1900 (Summer) 0800-SS (Winter) (local) and by arrangement

Circuits 15/25 LH 07/33 RH 800ft QFE

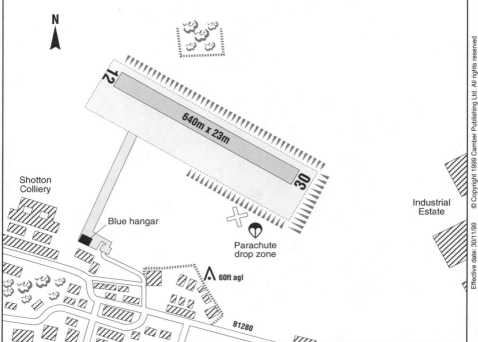

RWY	SURFACE	TORA	LDA	LIGHTING			
12/30	Grass	640x23	U/L	Nil			

Peterlee Drop Zone

APP	Newcastle 124.375
APP	Teeside 118.85
A/G	129.90

Remarks

PPR by telephone. AD operated primarily as parachute centre with free-fall operations up to FL150. Visiting ACFT welcome with PPR & at own risk. AD constructed on a disused colliery site with slight downslopes on E side of Rwy & S end. Rwy has white edge markers & Rwy designators.

Warnings

AD situated on reclaimed land may be waterlogged after heavy rain, Please avoid overflying Peterlee & the village of Shotton Colliery. AD situated close to N edge of Teeside CTZ, (Teeside APP 118.85).

Operator	Peterlee Parachute Centre
	Peterlee Airfield, Shotton Colliery, Co Durham
	Tel: 0191 517 1234
	Tel: 0191 526 0752

Restaurants	Canteen Sat-Sun & PH

Taxis	Locally
Car Hire	Nil

Weather Info	AirN MWC

Operating Hrs	0830-2030 local daylight Hrs only
Circuits	12 LH, 30 RH 1000ft, N of AD only
Landing fee	Nil with fuel uplift
Maintenance	Nil
Fuel	AVGAS 100LL when parachute centre open

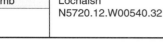

ELEVATION	LOCATION					
80ft 3mb	3.5nm NE of Kyle of Lochalsh N5720.12.W00540.32	INS 109.20 STN 115.10 BEN 114.40	266 172 105	54.0 54.8 55.4	••/–•/••• •••/–/–• –•••/•/–•	

PLOCKTON

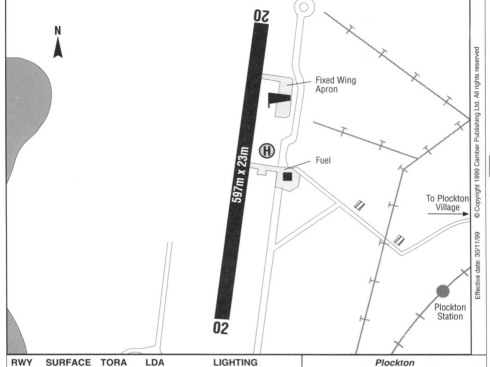

P

RWY	SURFACE	TORA	LDA	LIGHTING		
02/20	Asphalt	597x23	U/L	Nil		

	Plockton
A/G	122.375

Remarks
Visitors welcome. Camping on-site.

Warnings
There is a ridge of high GND up to 140ft amsl 500m to the E and up to 400ft amsl 500m to the SE. Helicopter operations take place at the AD and local areas up to 2000ft within a radius of 25nm.

Operator   ND Aviation
Plockton, Ross-Shire, Highland Region
Tel: 01599 544398
Tel: 0378 478542 (mobile)
Fax: 01599 544413

Restaurants/accomodation
The Haven   **Tel:** 01599 544223
Plockton Hotel   **Tel:** 01599 544274
Plockton Inn   **Tel:** 01599 544222

Taxis
Kyle Taxi   **Tel:** 01599 534323
Car Hire
F&F Motors   **Tel:** 01599 584114

Weather Info   AirSc GWC

Operating Hrs	24Hrs
Circuits	
Landing fee	Highland Regional Council rates
Maintenance **Fuel**	Nil Hangarage available AVTUR JET A1 100LL Cash/cheque Please check availability

ELEVATION	LOCATION	EGHD	PLYMOUTH (City)
474ft 16mb PPR	3.5nm NNE of Plymouth N5025.37.W00406.37 **Diversion AD**	BHD 112.05 280 23.6	– • • • / • • • • / – • •

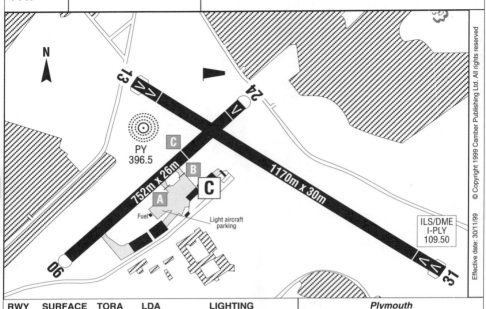

RWY	SURFACE	TORA	LDA	LIGHTING
06 RHS	Asphalt	752	752	Ap Thr Rwy APAPI 3.75
24	Asphalt	752	714	Ap Thr Rwy PAPI 3.5° LHS
13	Asphalt	1105	1038	Thr Rwy PAPI 3.75° LHS
31	Asphalt	1100	1055	Ap Thr Rwy PAPI 3.5° LHS

Plymouth	
APP	133.55
VDF	133.55 122.60
TWR	118.15
FIRE	121.60
ILS/DME	I-PLY 109.50 Rwy31
NDB	PY 396.50 on A/D range 20nm

Remarks

PPR strict non-radio ACFT not accepted. PPR by telephone during the following periods: Mon-Fri 2000-2230, W/E & PH all day, (Winter). Mon-Fri 2000-2300, W/E & PH all day (Summer). Rescue & Police helicopter flights may take place at any time outside Hrs. Rwy31 is used preferential Rwy in zero wind conditions. Rwy06/24 may be used when crosswinds preclude the use of Rwy13/31 for the ACFT type. Helicopter training is prohibited. No circuit training flights during PPR Hrs.Light ACFT parking is normally on the W end of the main apron but subject to ATC requirements. Light ACFT and helicopters may be directed to park on adjacent grass areas. Start up clearance must be requested from ATC. ACFT are to be operated so as to cause the least disturbance practicable in areas surrounding the airport. Aerobatic manoeuvres and low fly pasts are prohibited at this airport unless the ACFT is participating in an organised flying display. Visual aid to location: White Strobe.

Warnings

Signals for Rwy06 are visible at night in an area N of the extended centreline where normal obstacle clearance is not guaranteed. Not to be used for approach slope guidance until ACFT is aligned with the Rwy. Surface gradients in excess of 2.4% are present in the S W corner of the AD. In strong winds windshear and turbulence may be experienced on the approach and climbout from all Rwys. Downdraughts and sudden changes in W/V are possible in light wind conditions.

Circuits	06/13 LH 24/31 RH or as directed by ATC 800ft QFE
Landing fee	Available on request
Maintenance Plymouth Exec Fuel	**Tel:** 01752 786611 AVGAS 100LL AVTUR JET A1
Operator	Plymouth City Airport Plc

Crownhill, Plymouth, Devon PL6 8BW
Tel: 01752 772752 (ATC)
Fax: 01752 770160 (ATC)
Fax: 01752 795590 (Brymon Ops)

Restaurants	Available at the terminal
Taxis	Available at terminal
Car Hire Europcar	**Tel:** 01752 779967
Weather Info	M T9 Fax 386 BNMC

Visual Reference Points (VRPs)

Avon Estuary	N5017.00 W00353.00
Ivy Bridge	N5024.08 W00355.10
Saltash	N5024.07 W00413.07
Yelverton	N5029.07 W00404.15

Operating Hrs 0530-2130 (Summer)
0630-2230 (Winter)
See remarks for PPR periods

ELEVATION	LOCATION				POCKLINGTON
87ft 3mb	10nm ESE of York N5355.50.W00047.77	OTR 113.90	304	28.1	– – – / – / • – •
PPR		GAM 112.80	013	39.0	– – • / • – / – –
		POL 112.10	082	47.6	• – – • / – – – / • – • •

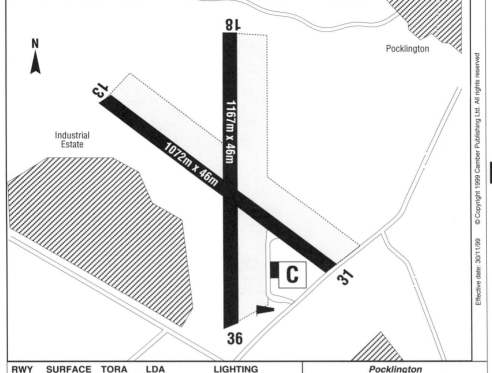

RWY	SURFACE	TORA	LDA	LIGHTING			
13/31	Asphalt	1072x50	U/L	Nil		*Pocklington*	
13/31	Grass	1072x25	U/L	Nil	A/G	**130.10 129.90**	
18/36	Asphalt	1167x50	U/L	Nil		**(Glider operations)**	
18/36	Grass	1167x25	U/L	Nil			

Asphalt Rwys in poor condition but considered safe for landing & take-off

Remarks
Operated by the Wolds Gliding Club Ltd. Primary use for gliding operations. Situated within the Vale of York AIAA, pilots are advised to use the LARS of Linton Approach 129.15. Joining Instructions: During gliding activity plan circuit on Rwy in use by gliders regardless of wind direction. Orbit the AD at about 1000ft aal, keeping well outside the traffic pattern, to indicate intention to land. When the Rwy & approach are clear of gliders, land on asphalt or grass Rwy & backtrack to glider launch point. With no glider activity, check windsock, select Rwy and land on either Rwy. Taxy to hangar area. Avoid over-flying the villages of BARMBY MOOR (NW of AD) & POCKLINGTON.

Warnings
Lookout for gliders. DO NOT join overhead below 2000ft agl when gliding is in progress due to cables.

Maintenance	Nil
Fuel	AVGAS 100LL
Operator	Wolds Gliding Club Ltd, The Airfield Pocklington, East Yorkshire YO4 2NR **Tel:** 01759 303579
Restaurant The Feathers	**Tel:** 01759 303155
Taxis Hessels	**Tel:** 01759 303176
Car Hire National	**Tel:** 01904 612141
Weather Info	AirN MWC

Operating Hrs	SR-SS
Circuits	Variable no overhead joins
Landing fee	Private £5.00 Commercial £10.00

ELEVATION	LOCATION	**EGHP**	**POPHAM**

ELEVATION	LOCATION
550ft 18mb	8.5nm NNE of Winchester
PPR	N5111.66.W00114.17 **Diversion AD**

SAM 113.35	021	14.9	•••/•−/−−
MID 114.00	295	24.5	−−/••/−••
CPT 114.35	187	17.8	−•−•/•−−•/−

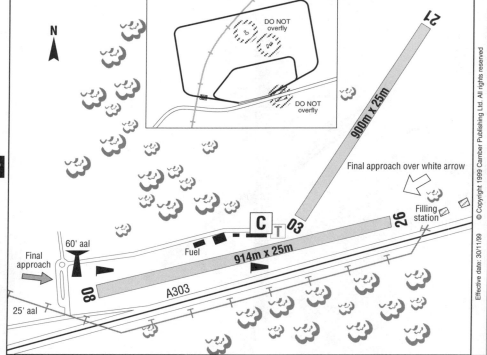

Final approach over white arrow

RWY	SURFACE	TORA	LDA	LIGHTING		*Popham*	
08/26	Grass	914	U/L	Nil		A/G	129.80
03/21*	Grass	900	U/L	Nil			

*Use restricted to certain dates check in advance

Remarks
PPR to non-radio ACFT. ACFT within 4500lbs MAUW welcome at pilots own risk. Approaches Rwy08/26 offset, 26 over white arrow avoiding bungalow & filling station, 08 over silver grain silos avoiding houses W of AD.

Warnings
Caution: Water tower 60ft aal close N of 08 Thr. Thr downslopes: Rwy08 approx 1%, Rwy26 approx 3.3%. Microlight activity at AD. During week extensive military flying in local area, mainly helicopters & C130 ACFT often low level & very close to the AD.

Operator Charles Church (Spitfires) Ltd
Popham Airfield, Winchester, Hampshire SO21 3HB
Tel: 01256 397733
Fax: 01256 397114

Restaurants
Hot & cold refreshments available 10am-5pm daily

Taxis
Grassbys Taxis **Tel:** 01256 465000
Car Hire
Martins Autorent **Tel:** 0800 174949

Weather Info AirSE BNMC

Operating Hrs	0830-1730
Circuits	All circuits to the N. 800ft QFE
Landing fee	£4 non-members. Free to Members
Maintenance	Wiltshire ACFT Maintenance **Tel:** 01256 398372
Fuel	AVGAS 100LL (cash/cheque only)

ELEVATION	LOCATION				
66ft	1nm NE of Prestwick	TRN 117.50	038	13.5	– / • – • / – •
2mb	N5530.47.W00435.20	GOW 115.40	200	22.3	– – • / – – – / • – –
PPR		TLA 113.80	279	41.9	– / • – • • / • –

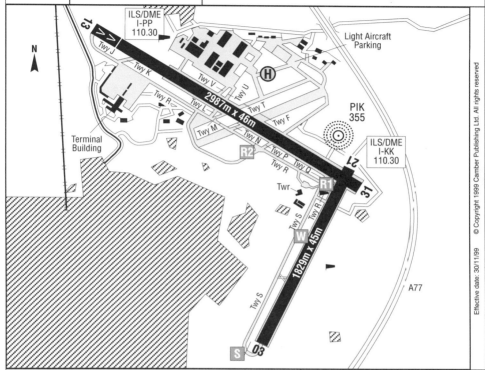

RWY	SURFACE	TORA	LDA	LIGHTING
13	Con/Asph	2987	2743	Ap Thr Rwy PAPI 3° LHS
31	Con/Asph	2987	2987	Ap Thr Rwy PAPI 3.5° LHS
03*	Asphalt	1829	1829	Thr Rwy
21	Asphalt	1829	1829	Thr Rwy PAPI 3.5° LHS

* Rwy03 additional 160m starter strip available

	Prestwick
ATIS	127.125
APP	120.55 121.50(O/R)
RAD	120.55 119.45
	121.50 (O/R)
TWR	118.15 121.80
FIRE	121.60
ILS/DME	I-PP 110.30 Rwy13
ILS/DME	I-KK 110.30 Rwy31
NDB	PW* 426 range 15nm
NDB	PIK** 355 range 30nm
	*PW 135/2.96 to
	Thr Rwy13
	**ABM Thr Rwy31

Remarks

PPR via ATC. Operators should make prior arrangements for GND handling of non-scheduled flights. Training flights PPR from ATC. In VMC, or when following a non standard instrument departure, avoid flying over Troon. ACFT shall maintain as high an altitude as practicable. If approaching without assistance from ILS or RAD fly not lower than the ILS glidepath. Operation in visibility of 600m or less not permitted. Only marked twys to be used. Rwy 03/21 associated twy available from link Sierra but limited to ACFT with a max. wing span 12m. Helicopter operations: The helicopter area in the N corner of Apron C is designated as a manoeuvring area. Helicopters may taxy between this area and the military parking circles. Civil helicopters are normally allocated a stand on the main apron. They are to operate to/from the main aprons A/B by approaching to/from the main Rwy block 11 or Twy block 16 as directed by ATC.

Warnings

If carrying out circuits on Rwy03/21 be warned of rising GND to the N E. Bird hazard assessed as 'moderate' and severe during migratory periods, Oct/Nov and Mar/Apr. Except for light signals, GND signals are not displayed. Traffic flow management of inbound, outbound & local ACFT may be applied without notice. Twys L, N & P are not to be used at night or in low vis. Twys S L & P suitable for light ACFT only.

Operating Hrs	H24
Circuits	See Warnings
Landing fee	Light ACFT £35.00 minimum charge
Maintenance	Available
Fuel	AVGAS 100LL AVTUR JET A1

Operator
Glasgow Prestwick International Airport Ltd
Aviation House, Prestwick, Scotland KA9 2PL
Tel: 01292 511000 (Switchboard)
Tel: 01292 511107 (PIK ATC)
Tel: 01292 511026 (PIK Handling)
Fax: 01292 511106 (PIK Ops)
Fax: 01292 475464 (PIK ATC)

| **Restaurants** | Restaurant buffet and bars in terminal |

Taxis   Available at terminal or on request
Courtesy coach available to/from railway station
Car Hire
Avis   **Tel:** 01292 77218
Hertz   **Tel:** 01292 79822 Ext.3080

| **Weather Info** | M T9 T18 Fax 388 A VSc GWC |

Booking Out
Pilots **must** book out by telephone – payment of landing fee
does not constitute booking out. Pilots attempting to book out
by RT may force delays.

Visual Reference Points (VRPs)
Culzean Bay/Castle
N5522.17 W00446.08
Cumnock
N5527.33 W00415.45
Heads of Ayr
N5525.97 W00442.78
Irvine Harbour
N5536.50 W00440.90
Kilmarnock
N5536.75 W00429.90
Pladda
N5525.58 W00507.07
W Kilbride
N5541.13 W00452.08

P

ELEVATION	LOCATION	**RAYNE HALL FARM (Braintree)**
225ft 7mb	1.3nm W of Braintree N5153.23.E00031.42	BKY 116.25 116 18 — • • • / — • — / — • — —
PPR		

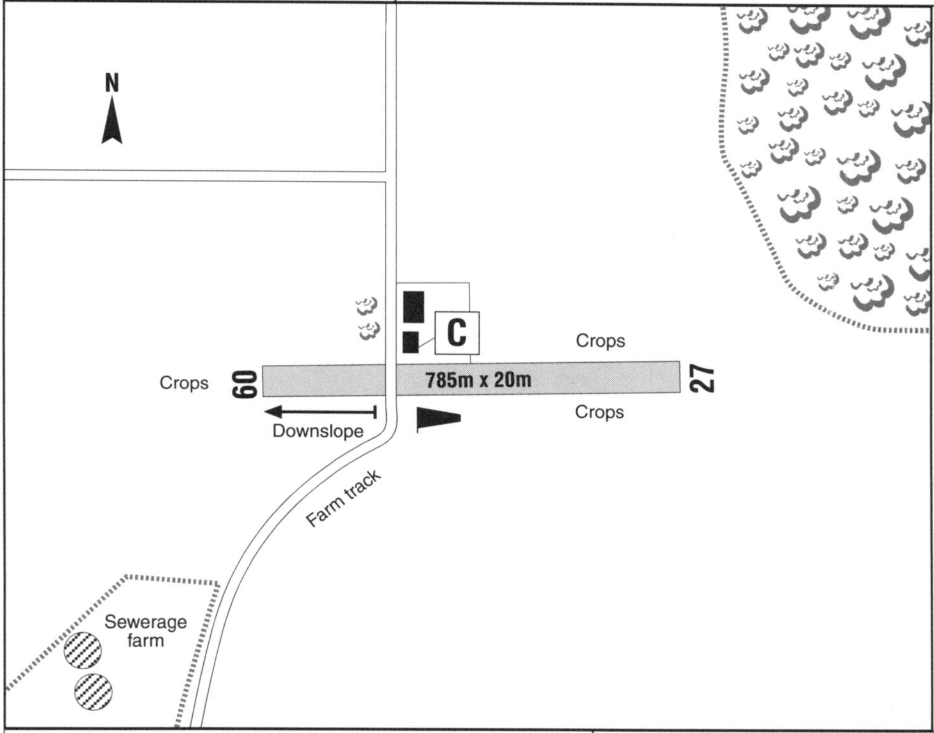

N

Crops

60 785m x 20m **27**

Crops

Crops

Crops

Downslope

Farm track

Sewerage farm

C

Effective date: 30/11/99

R

RWY	SURFACE	TORA	LDA	LIGHTING			Rayne
09/27	Grass	785x20	U/L	Nil		APP	Essex Radar 120.625
Rwy27 has marked downslope after road crossing						A/G	130.775

Remarks
PPR by telephone. Visitors welcome at pilots own risk. Clubhouse at weekends. Picnic table adjacent parking area. Situated under Stansted CTA (base 2000ft QNH). Useful Weather Info can be obtained from Stansted ATIS 127.175. Microlights operate from AD. The Rwy has white edge & corner markings.

Warnings
Andrewsfield ATZ boundary close to E of AD. Caution; crops grow up to edge of strip. Farm road crosses the Rwy midpoint loose stones may be encountered when crossing the road. Rwy27 has marked downslope after crossing the road. Avoid overflying local habitation.

Operator	Mr DS McGregor, Rayne Hall Farm
	Braintree, Essex CM7 5BT
	Tel/Fax: 01376 321899 (Operator)
	Tel: 01376 346217 (AD)
	Tel: 07850 921961 (mobile)
Restaurants	Nil
Taxis	
T&M Taxis	**Tel:** 01376 347888
Car Hire	
Weather Info	AirCen BNMC

Operating Hrs	Available on request
Circuits	To the N. 1000ft QFE
Landing fee	£4
Maintenance	Nil
Fuel	Nil

ELEVATION	LOCATION	EGKR				REDHILL
221ft	1.5nm SE of Redhill	**BIG** 115.10	228	9.6	– • • / • • / – – •	
7mb	N5112.82.W00008.32	**OCK** 115.30	120	12.8	– – – / – • – • / – • –	
PPR	**Diversion AD**	**DET** 117.30	264	28.2	– • • / • / –	

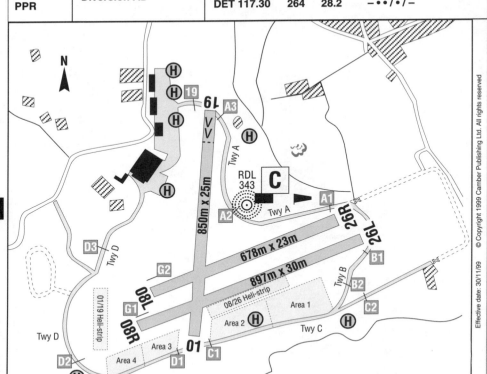

RWY	SURFACE	TORA	LDA	LIGHTING
01	Grass	850	850	Nil
19	Grass	850	699*	Nil
08R	Grass	897	897	Thr Rwy APAPI 4.25° LHS
26L	Grass	897	897	Thr Rwy APAPI 3.5° LHS
08L/26R	Grass	678	678	Nil

*Landing Thr of Rwy19 is displaced by 151m

	Redhill
TWR	120.275
AFIS	120.275
NDB	RDL 343
	on A/D range 10nm

Remarks

PPR by telephone. No flexwing microlights. AD based microlights only. Rwy08R/26L licensed for night use by all ACFT. No deadside, helicopters circuit pattern opposite to fixed-wing ACFT. ACFT to leave or join circuit via VRP's. Fixed wing ACFT will join at 1300ft QFE. If required to join overhead enter the ATZ on the Rwy QDM within the fixed wing circuit area. When instructed descend to circuit height and join visual pattern. Dep fixed wing will maintain 1500ft QNH until VRP. Helicopters to join at 1000ft QFE from VRP directly into the circuit. Dep helicopters will maintain 1200ft QNH until passing appropriate VRP. Fixed-wing ACFT confined marked Rwy/Twy & grass areas N of Rwy08R/26L. Due to intensive helicopter operations fixed-wing ACFT are not to vacate Rwy until instructed by ATC. ACFT operating visual circuit avoid over-flying built-up areas within ATZ. All fixed-wing circuit training is PPR by telephone. AD has both fixed lit & portable helipads. Visual aid to location: Abn White flashing.

Warnings

The aerodrome is subject to waterlogging. The surface slopes up 10ft from the centre to the W boundary. Intensive helicopter operations. Helicopters may not comply with standard R/T procedures. The markings on the S taxiway relate to helicopter operations. The landing Thr of Rwy19 is displaced by 151m in order to give sufficient clearance over high GND and traffic using the perimeter road. It is dangerous to attempt to land short of the marked displaced Thr.

Operating Hrs	0800-1900 (Summer) 0900-1700 (Winter)
Circuits	Variable Fixed wing/Heli 1000ft QFE
See Remarks	

Maintenance
Redhill Engineering **Tel:** 01737 822959
Fuel AVGAS 100LL AVTUR JET A1

Landing fee Single £12.50 + VAT, Twin under 1500kg
£14.69 2000kg £20.33 2500kg £27.38 inc VAT

Operator	Redhill Aerodrome Ltd

Terminal Building, Redhill Aerodrome, Surrey RH1 5YP
Tel: 01737 823377 (Admin/ATC) **Tel:** 01737 823518 (Fuel)
Fax: 01737 823640

Restaurant	Cafe in Redhill Aviation

Taxis

Bellfry Cars	**Tel:** 01737 766111
Roadrunners	**Tel:** 01737 645555
Car Hire	See companies listed for London (Gatwick)

Weather Info	AirSE BNMC

VRP's

Junction	N5115.82 W00007.62
(Jct M23/M25)	
Godstone	N5114.90 W00004.03
(Jct A25/B2236)	
North Point	N5115.03 W00008.33
(Mercers Lake)	
East Point	N5113.12 W00003.60
(Roman Rd/Rwy line)	
West Point	N5113.53 W00013.03
(Western tip of Reigate)	

Redhill Circuit Diagram
Although the Redhill ATZ is within the GATWICK CTR a local flying area has been established which permits operations within this area without reference to GATWICK ATC. Such flights may ONLY be made during the Hrs of watch of REDHILL ATC.

Area A
1 Clear of cloud and in sight of the surface in minimum flight visibility, (for fixed wing ACFT), of 3km.
2 Fly not above 1500ft QNH.

Flight in circuit must not proceed beyond
W: A23 Redhill-Horley road.
E: Outwood-Bletchingley road.
S: Picketts & Brownslade farms.

Area B
Fly NOT ABOVE 1500ft QNH
All ACFT must obtain clearance from Redhill ATC at least 5min before ETA. (This includes ACFT which have initially contacted Gatwick ATC)
Arriving & departing ACFT must do so N of Gatwick CTR. Outbound ACFT will not normally be routed via VRP being used by inbound ACFT.
Ensure you are familiar with joining/departing procedures detailed in this section.

Helicopter Joining Procedures
Unless otherwise instructed by ATC, ACFT should join overhead at 1200ft QFE, descending within the helicopter circuit area to circuit height. Helicopters may be required to route via the "Sand Pit" VRP. ATC may permit direct arrivals from the N when Rwy 08, 19 or 26 are in use. Joins via the "Sand-Pit" are not permitted when Rwy 01 is in use. When Rwy 01/19 is in use, ATC may instruct helicopters joining from the E to route via the eastern boundary at 500 ft QFE. Helicopter Departing Procedures: Unless otherwise instructed by ATC helicopters will depart from the helicopter circuit. routing as instructed and climbing to 1400 ft QNH. ATC may permit departures direct from other positions on the aerodrome.

Fixed Wing ACFT Joining Procedures
Two visual reporting points are available to ATC for use by fixed wing ACFT; Motorway Junction (M23/M25) and Godstone (A25 roundabout). If required to join overhead - position to overfly the aerodrome at 1000 ft QFE on the Rwy QDM remaining within the fixed wing circuit area. When abeam the upwind end of the Rwy in use turn left or right (depending on circuit direction), descend to 800ft QFE on the crosswind leg to be level prior to turning downwind.

Noise:
Always use best rate of climb. ACFT departing Rwy26 must not commence right turn until past Brookside Farm. Avoid overflying S Nuffield & E Surrey Hospital.

R

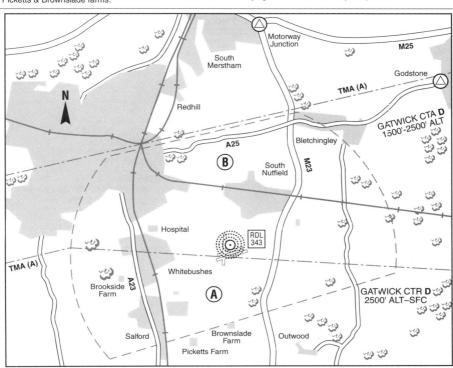

ELEVATION	LOCATION				
275ft 9mb	4.5nm E of Oswestry N5250.50.W00255.83	SWB 116.80 WAL 114.10	290 173	11 34	•••/•−−/−••• •−−/•−/•−••
PPR					

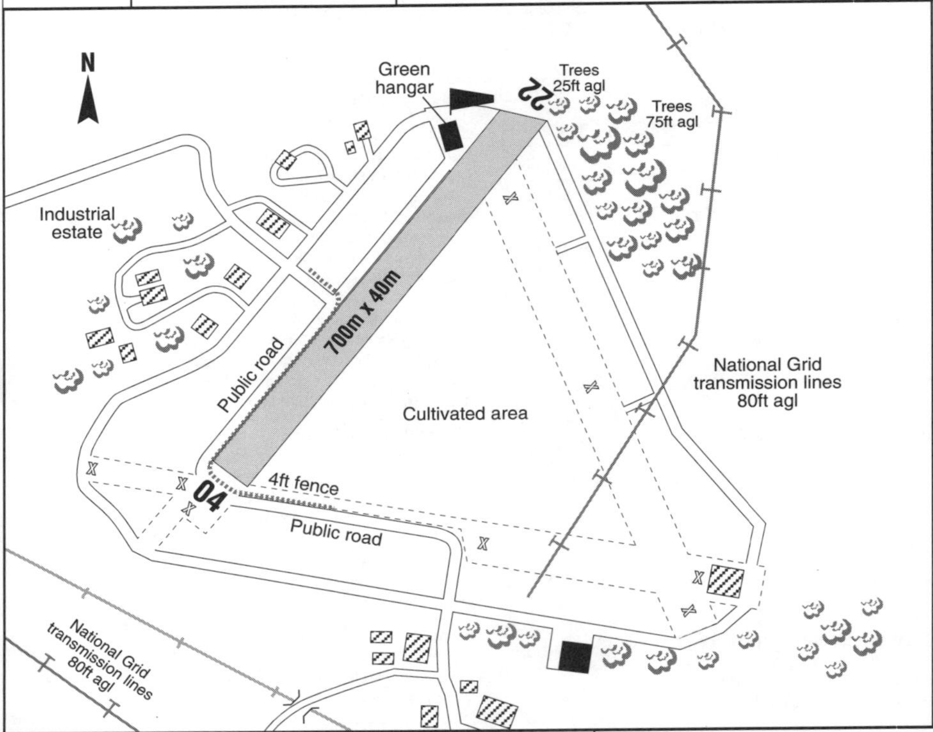

N
Green hangar
Trees 25ft agl
22
Trees 75ft agl
Industrial estate
700m x 40m
Public road
National Grid transmission lines 80ft agl
Cultivated area
4ft fence
04
Public road
National Grid transmission lines 80ft agl

Effective date: 30/11/99

RWY	SURFACE	TORA	LDA	LIGHTING
04/22	Asphalt	700x40	U/L	Nil

Rednal

LARS	**Shawbury 120.775**
A/G	**118.175 & UNICOM**

Remarks
PPR by telephone or fax. Established on W portion of WWII AD. All other Rwys are unavailable. Visiting ACFT welcome at own risk. Windsock at W end of green hangar. Grass Rwy on E side of asphalt Rwy is unuseable!

Warnings
National grid power lines & pylons cross both approaches 80ft aal. A public road crosses 04 Thr & runs along W side for half Rwy length.
Caution: A 4ft wire fence divides the road from the active Rwy. A copse of mature trees, 25ft aal, encroach on the E side of 22 final APP. Avoid overflight of local habitation.

Operating Hrs	SR-SS
Circuits	Join on E side at 1500ft QFE then circuits to E at 800ft QFE
Landing fee	Nil
Maintenance	Nil
Fuel	Nil

Operator Roger Reeves
The Classic & Vintage Aeroplane Co
Moss House, Malpas, Cheshire SY14 7JJ
Tel: 01948 860111 (Office for PPR)
Tel: 01691 610507 (AD not normally manned)
Fax: 01948 860222 (Office PPR if no tel answer)

Restaurants/Accomodation
Travelodge **Tel:** 01691 658178 (Oswestry 2m)
Queens Head 1m – good food (no accom.)

Taxis
Berwin Cars **Tel:** 01691 652000
Car Hire Nil

Weather Info AirN MWC

ELEVATION	LOCATION	EGNE		RETFORD (Gamston)

ELEVATION	LOCATION			
87ft 3mb	2nm S of Retford N5316.83.W00057.08	GAM 112.80	on A/D	− − • / • − / − −
		OTR 113.90	236 39.1	− − − / − / • − •
PPR		POL 112.10	129 49.8	• − − • / − − − / • − • •

Aerodrome chart. Runway 1203m x 30m (03/21), Runway 799m x 18m (14/32). Engine run-up area. Access points A, B, C. GAM 112.80.

RWY	SURFACE	TORA	LDA	LIGHTING
03	Asphalt	1203	1203	Thr Rwy APAPI 3.5° LHS
21	Asphalt	1203	1203	Thr Rwy APAPI 3° LHS
*14/32	Asphalt	799x18	U/L	Nil

An additional U/L 240m starter extension 03/21 available
* 50m starter extension available 14/32

	Gamston
A/G	130.475
VOR/DME	GAM 112.80 on A/D

Remarks
Pilots are to contact the A/G station 10 minutes before ETA. PPR by R/T acceptable. Visiting ACFT will be asked to park on numbered stands marked by yellow boards on the taxiway edges.

Warnings
Pilots taxiing for take-off on Rwy21 at night should not back track further than the red Rwy end lights. The Rwy edge lights are positioned at the edge of the hard surface at a width of 46m. Rwy03/21 is side striped at 30m. Glider launching takes place on Rwy14/32 at weekends. Access to and from Rwy03/21 is via points A and B only.

Operating Hrs
Mon-Fri 0700-1700 Sat-Sun & PH 0800-1700 (Summer)
Mon-Fri 0800-1800 Sat-Sun & PH 0900-1800 (Winter)
& by arrangement

Circuits

Landing fee
Single £8 Heli £6.30 Twin £4.75 per half tonne +VAT

Maintenance
	Tel: 01777 838595	
Vallely	**Fax:** 01777 838775	
Fuel	AVGAS 100LL AVTUR JET A1	

Operator
Gamston Aviation Ltd
Retford/Gamston Airport, Retford, Nottingham DN22 0QL
Tel: 01777 838593 (Ops/ATC)/838521 (Outside Ops Hrs)
Fax: 01777 838035

Restaurants
Refreshments available at aerodrome
Local pubs within 1.5 miles

Taxis
Discount with B J's **Tel:** 01777 228999/01860 876766
Car Hire On request

Weather Info
AirCen MWC

ELEVATION	LOCATION	RHEDYN COCH (Emlyn's Other Field)			
650ft 21mb	3nm SE of Prestatyn N5316.58 W00322.07				
PPR		WAL 114.10	237	10.5	•−−/•−/•−••
		MCT 113.55	268	40	−−/−•−•/−

R

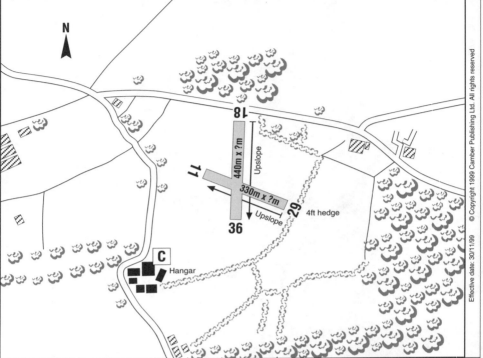

RWY	SURFACE	TORA	LDA	LIGHTING		*Rhedyn Coch*
18/36	Grass	440	U/L	Nil	A/G	129.825*
11/29	Grass	330	U/L	Nil		• Microlight common freq
Rwy have no markings ID by witness marks on large field						Make blind calls

Remarks
PPR by telephone. Visiting STOL ACFT and microlights welcome at pilots own risk. Rwys are large part of field which allows run off to either side.

Warnings
This is a difficult AD to locate, particularly during the winter when there is little aviation use. There is high ground up to 998ft amsl 0.25nm W of AD. There are wood plantations close to AD, particularly on Rwy18 APP which may cause turbulence. There are upslopes on Rwy29 & 18. Do not overfly local habitation.

Operator	R Emlyn Jones
Rhedyn Coch, Rhault, St Asaph, Denbigshire	
Tel: 01745 584051 (home)	
Tel: 07880 733274 (mobile)	

Restaurant	Tea & coffee available
Taxi/Car Hire	
Weather Info	AirCen MWC

Operating Hrs	SR-SS
Circuits	Join overhead 1500ft QFE Descend quietly to 600ft QFE 36/18/11 LH 29 RH
Landing Fee	Donations welcome
Maintenance Fuel	Nil MOGAS available on request

ELEVATION	LOCATION	**EGTO**				**ROCHESTER**
436ft 16mb	1.5nm S of Rochester N5121.12.E00030.20					
	Diversion AD					
PPR		DET 117.30	317	4.6	— • • / • / —	
		BIG 115.10	089	18.6	— • • • / • • / — — •	
		MAY 117.90	040	24.7	— — / • — / — • — —	

RWY	SURFACE	TORA	LDA	LIGHTING
02L	Grass	827	827	Thr Rwy APAPI 4° LHS
20R	Grass	827	827	Ap Thr Rwy APAPI 3.5° LHS
02R	Grass	690	690*	Nil
20L	Grass	690	690*	Nil
16	Grass	773	689	Nil
34	Grass	966	773	Nil

*Additional 35m is available on request to the AD management. Taxi on prepared and marked areas only

	Rochester
AFIS	122.25
NDB	RCH 369 on A/D range 10nm

Remarks
A relief Rwy02R/20L has been established parallel to Rwy02/20 used when main Rwy is under maintenance. Rwys and Twys may be restricted or withdrawn at short notice due to surface conditions. Pilots should obtain latest info before arrival. ACFT requiring a night licensed aerodrome cannot use this Rwy. ACFT using Rochester Airport are required to have 3rd Party Liability Insurance in the sum of at least £500,000. Proof of this insurance should be available for inspection at any time ACFT is at Rochester Airport. Visual aids to location: Abn White flashing. Aerodrome name displayed.

Warnings
A road used by vehicular traffic runs E/W immediately to the S of the take-off Thr of Rwy34. Visual glideslope signals for Rwy 20R are visible to the E of the extended Rwy centreline where normal obstacle clearance is not guaranteed. They should not be used until the ACFT is aligned with the extended Rwy centreline.

Operating Hrs
Mon-Fri 0700-1700 Sat-Sun 0730-1600 (Summer)
Mon-Fri 0800-1800 Sat-Sun 0830-1700 (Winter)

Circuits	Variable to avoid over-flying built up areas: 16/20 RH 02/34 LH
Landing fee	Single £6.00 Twin £10.00 inc VAT

Maintenance
GEC	**Tel:** 01634 816130
Fuel	AVGAS 100LL AVTUR JET A1

Operator GEC Marconi Avionics Ltd
Rochester Airport, Chatham, Kent ME5 9SD
Tel: 01634 816132/816127 (AD Manager)
Fax: 01634 816193

Restaurants	Forte Post House Restaurant Several pubs nearby

Taxis
Medway	**Tel:** 01634 848848
Volkes	**Tel:** 01634 222222/843601

Car Hire
Kenning	**Tel:** 01634 845145

Weather Info	AirSE BNMC

ELEVATION	LOCATION		RODDIGE
171ft 6mb	3nm NE of Lichfield N5242.80.W00144.63	TNT 115.7 192 21 HON 113.65 357 21.5	– / – • / – • • • • / – – – / – •
PPR			

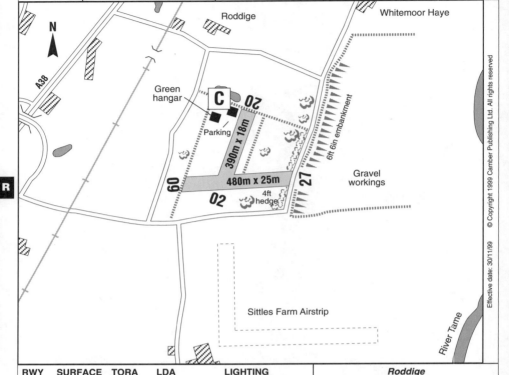

RWY	SURFACE	TORA	LDA	LIGHTING		Roddige	
02/20	Grass	390x18	U/L	Nil	A/G	129.825	
09/27	Grass	480x25	U/L	Nil			

Remarks
PPR by telephone. Primarily a microlight training AD but light ACFT and pilots with STOL capability welcome with PPR and at own risk. **Noise:** Please avoid overflight of local habitation.

Warnings
A 4ft hedge crosses Rwy27 Thr & a 6.5ft embankment screening gravel workings on the opposite side of the road from the Thr. Caution: Do not confuse Roddige with Sittles Farm strip to S on opposite side of hedge.

Operator	Mr Shea, The Microlight School
	Roddige Lane, Fradley, Lichfield WS13 8QS
	Tel: 01283 792193
	Tel: 0467 474847 (mobile)

Restaurants	Tea & coffee

Taxis	**Tel:** 01543 254999
Car Hire	**Tel:** 01543 254825

Weather Info	AirCen MWC

Operating Hrs	0930-dusk (local)
Circuits	Join overhead at 1500ft QFE then circuit at 800ft QFE
Landing fee	Nil

Maintenance
Limited microlight Hangarage & maintenance
Fuel MOGAS

ELEVATION	LOCATION					ROSSENDALE (Lumb)

ELEVATION	LOCATION
990ft 33mb	3.5nm South of Burnley N5343.21 W00215.10
PPR	

POL 112.10	263	5.5	•−−•/−−−/•−••
MCT 113.55	006	22	−−/−•−•/−

Moorland

Track

Stone wall

400m x 18m

Upslope

Marked upslope

Silver hangar

Red hangar

Middle Bank Top Farm

Lumb village →

R

RWY	SURFACE	TORA	LDA	LIGHTING
12/30	Grass	400x18	U/L	Nil

Rwy30 has steep upslope in first quarter lessening in last portion but still marked

	Non-Radio
LARS (Warton)	129.525

Remarks
PPR by telephone. AD situated in high moorland with surrounding high ground. Aid to location; two T type hangars on AD one silver, one red. AD situated underneath the Manchester TMA, base 3500ft QNH. Windsock is displayed when AD in use.

Warnings
AD not for the novice, Upslope Rwy30 means this is preferred Rwy in all but severe winds from S or E. Waterlogging after prolonged wet weather. AD sometimes difficult to locate as it is cut for sileage. A tractor path crosses 12 Thr Local weather effects should be considered due to high elevation of AD. Winter precipitation of rain at your AD is likely to produce snow at Lumb! Also low cloud and increased surface wind effects.

Operator	Mr S Walmsley, Middle Bank Top Farm

Lumb-in-Rossendale, Lancashire BB4 9NF
Tel: 01706 216564
Tel: 01706 227667 (Mr R Legge if no contact at above number)

Restaurant	
Taxis/Car Hire	
Weather Info	AirCen MWC

Operating Hrs	SR-SS
Circuits	
Landing Fee	Nil
Maintenance	Nil
Fuel	Nil

ELEVATION	LOCATION	**EGDX**	**ST ATHAN**
163ft 6mb	3nm W of Cardiff Airport N5124.29.W00326.15	**BCN 117.45** 205 20.1	— • • • / — • — • / — •
PPR MILITARY			

RWY	SURFACE	TORA	LDA	LIGHTING
08	Asphalt	1825	1825	Thr Rwy PAPI 3°
26	Asphalt	1825	1825	Ap Thr Rwy PAPI 3°

Arrester gear 390m from 08/26 Thrs

	St Athan
APP	**Cardiff 125.85**
TWR	**122.10**
ATIS	**Cardiff 119.475**
TACAN	**SAT 114.80 on A/D**

Remarks
PPR 24 Hrs noticed required. AD is within Cardiff CTR. Light ACFT & glider flying Wed evening & weekends. Avoid overflying St Athan village. ATZ active H24.

Warnings
Beware mis-identifying AD Cardiff airport (Rwy12/30 & 03/21) is just 3nm E of A/D. Windshear hazard on 26 in strong NW winds. No Twy lighting N of Rwy. ACFT using 122.10 use full callsign due frequency congestion. VFR recovery procedures in force. Ask for info.

Operator	RAF St Athan Tel: 01446 798798 Ext.8282
Restaurants	
Taxis **Car Hire** National	**Tel:** 01222 496256 (Cardiff)
Weather Info	AirS BNMC

Operating Hrs
Mon-Thu 0730-1600 Fri 0730-1500 (Summer) + 1Hr Winter

Circuits	08 RH 26 LH 1000ft QFE Do not join on deadside
Landing fee	£7.56 per 500kgs +VAT & £8.50 insurance
Maintenance Fuel	Nil AVGAS 100LL AVTUR Jet A1

ELEVATION	LOCATION	**EGDG**	**ST MAWGAN**
390ft 13mb	3.5nm ENE of Newquay N5026.43.W00459.72		
PPR MILITARY		**LND 114.20 060 30.6 • — • • / — • / — • •**	

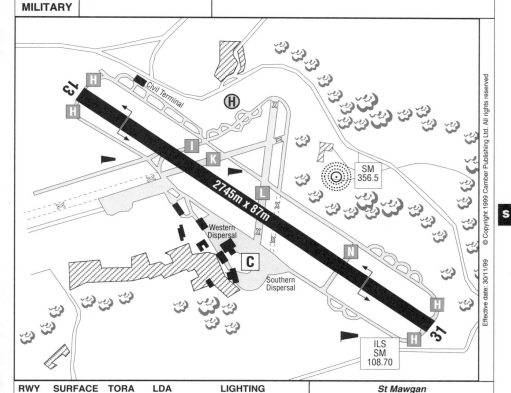

RWY	SURFACE	TORA	LDA	LIGHTING
13/31	Asph/Con	2745	2745	Ap Thr Rwy PAPI 3°
Reduced dimensions for ACFT unable to trample arrester gear				
13		2230	2230	
31		2325	2325	

St Mawgan	
APP/MATZ/	
LARS	126.50
RAD	125.55 123.30
VDF	126.50 125.55
TWR	123.40 122.10
TACAN	SMG 112.60 on A/D
ILS	SM 108.70 Rwy31
NDB	SM 356.5 on A/D

Remarks
Civil ACFT wishing to operate at weekends must request PPR not later than 1800hrs Friday. Civil Flight Plans must be sent to Ops for processing EGDGYXYW. All inbound ACFT to contact St. Mawgan on 125.55 at 20nm. RADAR approach may be mandatory. Avoid overflying Carnantion House 400m NE of AD.Visual aid to location: Ibn SM Red.

Warnings
Risk of bird strikes. Pilots unfamiliar with the area should note that St Eval disused AD lies 3nm N of St Mawgan. The standard arrester gear cable configuration is overshoot cable up, APP cable down.

Maintenance	Nil
Fuel	AVTUR JET A1

Operator   RAF St Mawgan
Newquay, Cornwall TR8 4HP
Tel: 01637 872201 Ext.2045/6
Civilian handling by Brymon Airways
Tel: 01637 860551

Restaurants

Taxis/Car Hire

Weather Info	M T Fax 392 BNMC

Operating Hrs	Civil Ops 0630-2130 daily
	Mon-Thur 0600-2259 Fri-Sun 0550-2100 (Summer) + 1Hr Winter

Circuits	No deadside
	Fixed wing to the S 1000ft QFE

Landing fee	£7.56 per 500kgs +VAT & £8.50 insurance

S

ELEVATION	LOCATION				ST MICHAELS
16ft 0mb	7nm NNW of Preston N5350.71 W00246.96	POL 112.10 MCT 113.55	290 332	25.5 35	• – – • / – – – / • – • • – – / – • – • / –
PPR					

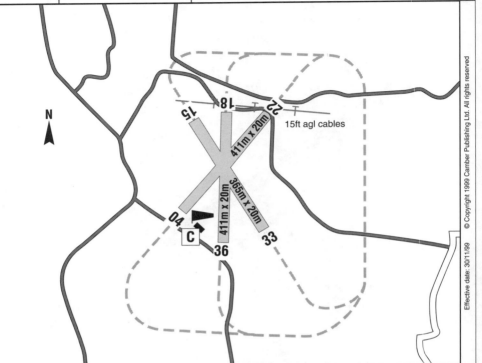

15ft agl cables

RWY	SURFACE	TORA	LDA	LIGHTING			
04/22	Grass	411	U/L	Nil	**A/G**	**St Michaels** **129.825***	
18/36	Grass	411	U/L	Nil			
15/33	Grass	365	U/L	Nil		***Microlight common freq***	

Remarks
PPR by telephone. Microlight school which is particularly active at weekends. Please be considerate of ab-initio students. Although Rwys are marked by cut grass strips, all the field is useable. Take-offs are resticted to the Rwys. Student pilots are encouraged to land into wind and not stick blindly to cut Rwys.

Warnings
Occassionaly waterlogged after heavy winter rain/snow. Grass may be long at sides of cut Rwys in summer. Telephone poles and wires 15ft on Rwy22 Thr. Dyke 10ft on W of AD. Noise: Avoid overflight of local habitation.

Operator	Graham Hobson

Northern Microlight School
2 Ashlea Cottage, Bilsborrow, Preston PR3 0RT
Tel: 01995 641058 (Office)
Tel: 01995 640713 (AD)

Restaurant	Self brew tea & coffee available
Taxis	

Available by phone from club caravan at AD
Car Hire

Weather Info	AirN MWC

Operating Hrs	SR-SS
Circuits	Join overhead at 1500ft QFE Circuits E at 500ft QFE
Landing Fee	£3.00 for as many landings as required in any 1 day
Maintenance	Nil
	Overnight parking available at owners risk
Fuel	MOGAS available by arrangement

ELEVATION	LOCATION	**SACKVILLE FARM (Riseley)**		
250ft 8mb **PPR**	2nm N of Bedford Thurleigh disused airfield N5215.87.W00029.08	BKY 116.25	313	26 — •••/—•—/—•——

Crops

13

N

Upslope ⊢

730m x 23m

C

31

Aircraft
parking

Riseley
village

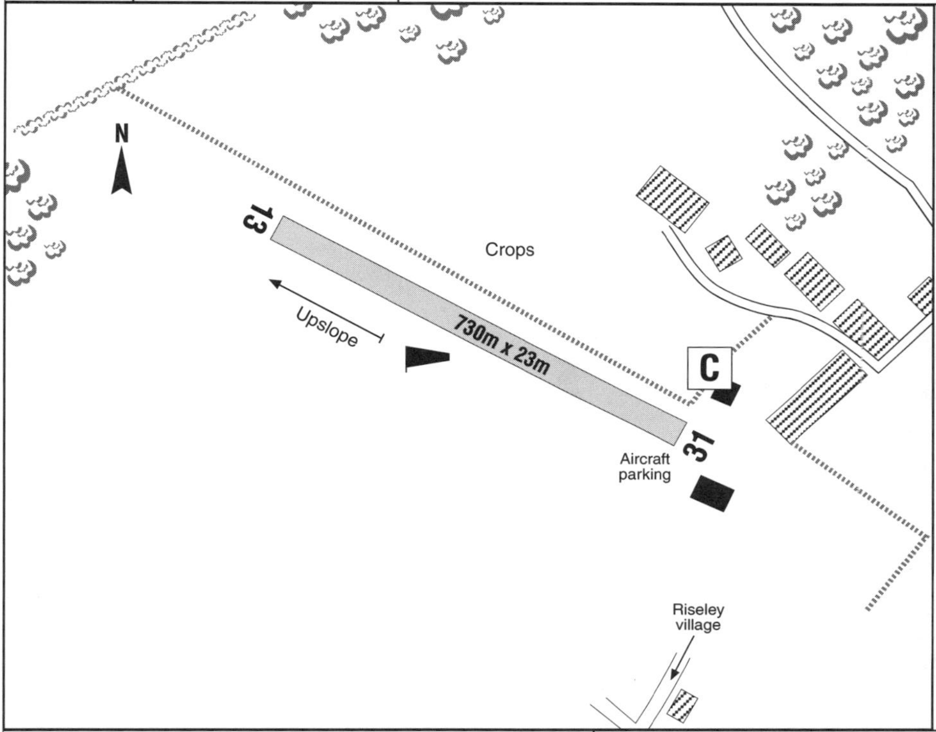

Effective date: 30/11/99

S

RWY	SURFACE	TORA	LDA	LIGHTING			
13/31	Grass	730x23	U/L	Nil		*Non-radio*	
Rwy31 has upslope in final third					**APP**	Cranfield 122.85	

Remarks
PPR by telephone. Primarily a gliding site but power pilots welcome at own risk. Glider launching is carried out most weekends by winch & aerotow.
Visitors are invited to try gliding.

Warnings
PPR is essential for briefing & removal of livestock from strip. Do not overfly Riseley village S of strip.

Operator   Mr T Wilkinson Sackville Lodge Farm
Riseley, Bedfordshire
Tel: 01234 708877 (AD PPR)
Fax: 01234 708862

Restaurants   Tea coffee & snacks weekends
Fox & Hounds in Riseley village approx 10mins walk

Taxis   **Tel:** 01234 750005
Car Hire
National   **Tel:** 01234 269565 (Bedford)

Weather Info   AirCen BNMC

Operating Hrs	SR-SS
Circuits	13 LH 31 RH 1000ft QFE
Landing fee	Nil
Maintenance **Fuel**	Nil Nil

ELEVATION	LOCATION				
480ft 16mb	7nm NE of Melton Mowbray N5249.77.W00042.65	GAM 112.80	168	28.5	– – • / • – / – –
PPR		DTY 116.40	024	42	– • • / – / – • – –

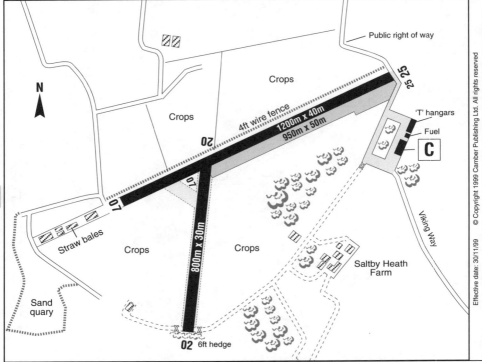

RWY	SURFACE	TORA	LDA	LIGHTING
07/25	Conc/Asphalt	1200x45	U/L	Nil
07/25	Grass	950x50	U/L	Nil
02/20*	Concrete	800x30	U/L	Nil

*Rwy surface rough

Saltby Base

LARS	Cottesmore 130.20
A/G	130.10*
	*Not always manned
	If no answer make
	normal circuit calls

Remarks
PPR by telephone. Primarily a gliding site but light ACFT welcome at own risk. Operated by Buckminster Gliding Club on lease from Buckminster Estates. Due to rural nature/gliding tasks PPR may be denied. Gliders launch by aerotow & winch, priority should be given to gliding activity. Keep a good lookout at all times. Considering the 07/25 surface dates to 1945 it is in excellent condition. A public right of way crosses 25Thr

Warnings
There is a wire fence along the N side of hard Rwy07/25. Crops grow up to S edge of grass Rwy07/25. Waltham-on-the-Wold TV mast (1487ft amsl, 1050ft agl) 3.5nm out on 07 APP. Cottesmore MATZ 1.5nm SSE Inbound/outbound ACFT call Cottesmore on 130.20. Due to cables NO overhead joins.
Noise: Please avoid overflying local villages.

Maintenance	Nil
Fuel	AVGAS 100LL by prior arrangement

Operator	Buckminster Gliding Club Saltby Airfield

Sproxton Road, Skillington, Grantham, Lincolnshire NG33 5HL
Tel: 01476 860385
Tel: 01476 860947
E-mail: gliding@saltby.freeserve.com
www.btinternet.com/~buckminster.gc

Restaurants	Snacks tea & coffee at gliding club
Taxis/Car Hire	Nil
Weather Info	AirCen MWC

Operating Hrs	SR-SS

Circuits	No overhead joins join downwind LH

circuit all Rwys at 1000ft QFE. Glider circuits variable

Landing fee	Nil

ELEVATION	LOCATION	EGES				SANDAY

ELEVATION	LOCATION				
66ft 2mb	20nm NNE of Kirkwall Airport N5915.01.W00234.60	KWL 108.60	037	20.0	— • — / • — — / • — • •
PPR		SUM 117.35	235	54.4	• • • / • • — / — —

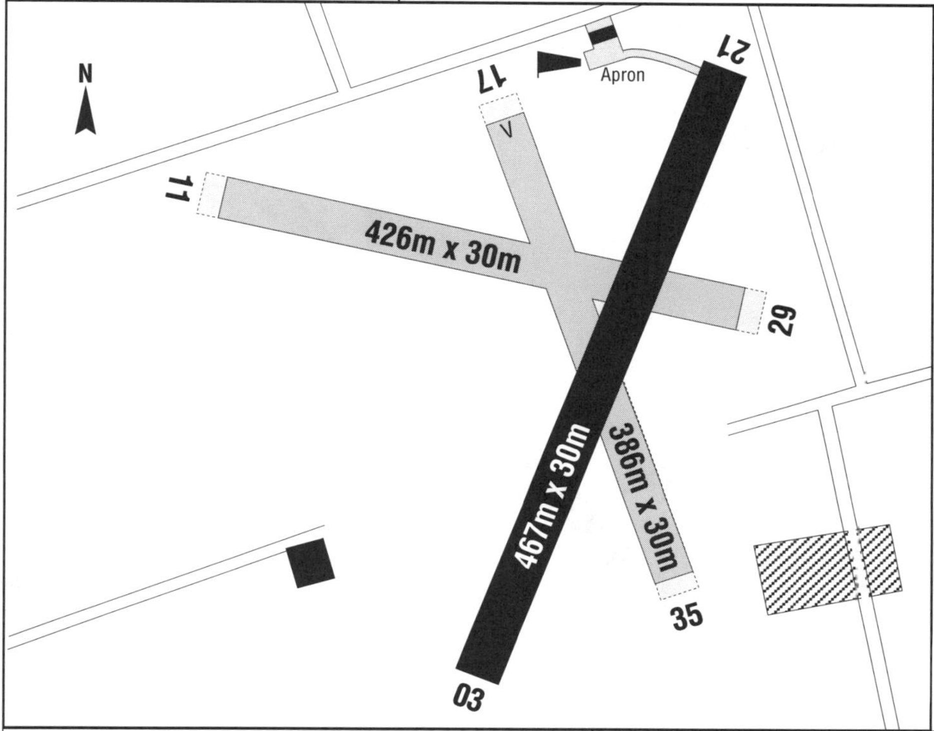

N

17

11

21

Apron

V

426m x 30m

29

467m x 30m

386m x 30m

35

03

© Copyright 1999 Camber Publishing Ltd. All rights reserved

Effective date: 30/11/99

S

RWY	SURFACE	TORA	LDA	LIGHTING
03	Compacted Stone	467	467	Nil
21	Compacted Stone	467	467	Nil
11/29	Grass	426	396	Nil
17/35	Grass	378	366	Nil
Starter extension of 15m available on all Rwys				

	Non-Radio
APP	Kirkwall 118.30

Remarks
Visiting ACFT accepted at pilot's own risk. Windsock displayed. Scheduled Air Service daily Mon-Sat.

Warnings

Operator   Orkney Islands Council Offices
Sanday Aerodrome, Kirkwall, Orkney KW15 1NY
Tel: 01856 873535 (PPR)
Fax: 01856 876094

Restaurants
Belsair Hotel   **Tel:** 01857 600206

Taxis
Kettletoft Garage   **Tel:** 01857 600321
Quivals Garage   **Tel:** 01857 600418
Car Hire
Kettletoft Garage   **Tel:** 01857 600321
Quivals Garage   **Tel:** 01857 600418 (also bikes)

Weather Info   AirSc GWC

Operating Hrs	SR-SS
Circuits	
Landing fee	Nil
Maintenance **Fuel**	Nil Nil

ELEVATION	LOCATION	**EGCF**	**SANDTOFT**

ELEVATION	LOCATION		
11ft 0mb **PPR**	7nm SW of Scunthorpe N5333.58.W00051.50 **Diversion AD**	**GAM 112.80** 017 16.9 **OTR 113.90** 258 28.2	– – • / • – / – – – – – / – / • – •

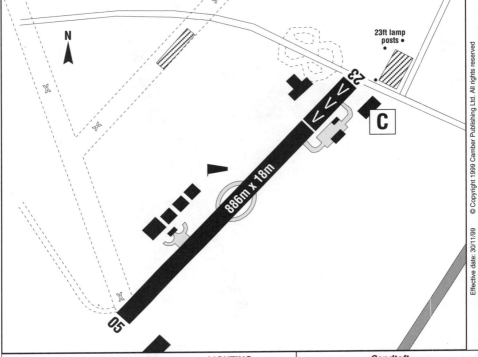

886m x 18m

Effective date: 30/11/99

23ft lamp posts •

RWY	SURFACE	TORA	LDA	LIGHTING
05	Asphalt	786(day)	786(day)	Thr Rwy
05	Asphalt	696(night)	696(night)	Thr Rwy
23	Asphalt	866(day)	696(day)	Thr Rwy APAPI 4° LHS
23	Asphalt	696(night)	696(night)	Thr Rwy APAPI 4° LHS

	Sandtoft
LARS	**Humberside 124.675**
A/G	**130.425**

Remarks
PPR non-radio ACFT. Local flying area NE of AD clear of built-up areas. Rwy05 is not licensed for night use.

Warnings
Street lights on road at 23 Thr. Please avoid over-flying the village of Belton to the E.

Operator	Imperial Aviation, Sandtoft Aerodrome
	Belton, Doncaster, South Yorkshire DN9 1PN
	Tel: 01427 873676 (A/D)
	Fax: 01427 874656

Restaurant
Restaurant and bar available at AD 0900-2300

Taxis	
Alan	**Tel:** 01427 875675
John	**Tel:** 01427 873103
Jim	**Tel:** 01427 874569
Car Hire	
Europcar	**Tel:** 01724 840655/843239

Weather Info	AirN MCW

Operating Hrs	0800-1700 (Summer) 0900-SS (Winter)
Circuits	05 LH 23 RH 800ft QFE
Landing fee	Single £5, Twin £10, Microlight £2.50, Heli £10.00, inc.VAT
Maintenance	Nil
Fuel	AVGAS 100LL JET A1

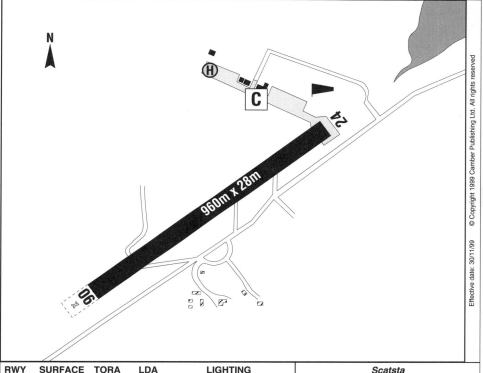

S

RWY	SURFACE	TORA	LDA	LIGHTING
06	Asphalt	960	960	Ap Thr Rwy PAPI* 4° LHS
24	Asphalt	960	960	Ap Thr Rwy PAPI* 3.25° LHS

* PAPI 5.3° RHS available by arrangement

Scatsta	
APP/TWR	**123.60**
RAD	**122.40**
FIRE	**121.60**
NDB	**SS* 315.50 range 25nm** ***SS 242/2.7 to Thr24**

Remarks
PPR non-radio ACFT not accepted. No training flights.
Pilots are to avoid over-flying the oil terminal area. Visual aids
to location: Strobe alignment beacons for App. to Rwy06.

Warnings
Pilots are warned that there is an area of bad GND in the
strip near Rwy06 Thr on S side suitably marked with 'bad
GND' markers. Unpaved surfaces are liable to be soft,
particularly after periods of heavy rain. High GND in vicinity
of the AD. Do not overfly oil terminal area. Taxiway S side of
main apron has semi-width of only 6.6m. Rwy lights 15in
above agl.

Operator   Serco Ltd, on behalf of Bristow Helicopters
Scatsta Aerodrome, Brae, Shetland ZE2 9QP
Tel: 01806 242791
Fax: 01806 242110

Restaurants

Taxis
W Hurson   **Tel:** 01806 522550
G Johnson   **Tel:** 01806 522443
Car Hire
Bolts Car Hire   **Tel:** 01595 692855

Weather Info   M T9 Fax 394 GWC

Visual Reference Points (VRPs)
Brae   N6023.82 W00121.23
Fugla   N6026.95 W00119.43
Hillswick   N6028.55 W00129.32
Voe   N6021.00 W00115.97

Operating Hrs	Mon-Fri 0630-1600 (Summer) + 1Hr Winter and by arrangement
Circuits	To the N
Landing fee	On application
Maintenance **Fuel**	Nil AVTUR JET A1 (2 Hrs PNR)

ELEVATION	LOCATION	EGHE	SCILLY ISLES (St Mary's)

ELEVATION	LOCATION		
116ft 4mb **PPR**	1nm E of Hugh Town N4954.80.W00617.52 **Diversion AD**	LND 114.20 249 28.6	• — •• / — • / — ••

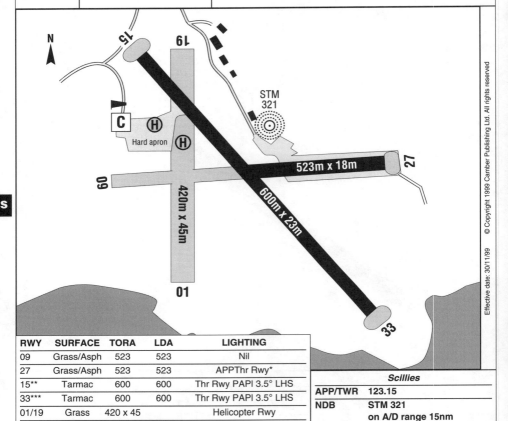

RWY	SURFACE	TORA	LDA	LIGHTING
09	Grass/Asph	523	523	Nil
27	Grass/Asph	523	523	APPThr Rwy*
15**	Tarmac	600	600	Thr Rwy PAPI 3.5° LHS
33***	Tarmac	600	600	Thr Rwy PAPI 3.5° LHS
01/19	Grass	420 x 45		Helicopter Rwy

* Two lights each side on asphalt section only
** A starter extension of 13m is available.
*** A starter extension of 38m is available

	Scillies	
APP/TWR	123.15	
NDB	STM 321	
	on A/D range 15nm	

Remarks
PPR strictly by telephone. Non-radio ACFT not accepted.
Flight plans should be filed for all flights to and from Scilly
Isles/St. Mary's. Visual aid to location: Ibn Green SC.

Warnings
Pilots should exercise extreme caution when landing or
taking off at this AD, which is markedly hump-backed. The
gradients increase to as much as 1 in 13 at Rwy ends. Pilots
are warned of the different braking characteristics of the
grass/asphalt sections of Rwy10/28. A perimeter road runs
around the N part of the AD and vehicular traffic is liable to
cross the APP to Rwy15. The coastal footpath crosses the
APP to Rwy33. Pilots should exercise great care when using
the Rwy33 end turning circle due to reduced clearance to the
SSE where a granite outcrop is present. Microlight activity
may take place outside published Hrs. This AD is closed to
ACFT on Sundays and pilots should not attempt to land.

Operating Hrs
Mon-Thu 0730-1900 Fri-Sat 0730-1930 (Summer)
Mon-Fri 0830-1230 & 1330-1700 Sat 0830-1230 (Nov-13 Feb)
& 1400-1700 (14 Feb-21 Mar) (Winter)

Circuits

Landing fee	Single £14.10 Twin £20.57 inc VAT
Maintenance	Nil
Fuel	Nil

Operator	Council of the Isles of Scilly

St. Mary's Airport, St Mary's, Isles of Scilly TR21 0NG
Tel: 01720 422677 Ext.132 (ATC)
Fax: 01720 422226

Restaurants	Buffet and bar available at the Airport

Taxis	
Pauls	**Tel:** 0374 299885
Scilly Cabs	**Tel:** 01720 422901
	Tel: 0836 253063 (mobile)
Car Hire	Nil

Weather Info	M T9 Fax 396 BNMC

Visual Reference Points (VRPs)
Pendeen Lighthouse	N5009.88 W00540.30
St Martins Head	N4958.05 W00615.95

ELEVATION	LOCATION	EGSJ				SEETHING
130ft 4mb	9nm SSE of Norwich N5230.65.E00125.03 **Diversion AD**		CLN 114.55	018	40.9	— • — • / • — • • / — •
PPR						

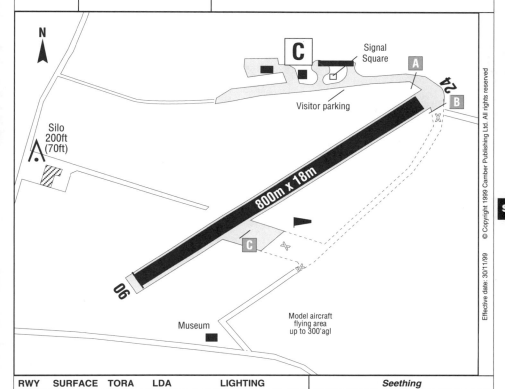

RWY	SURFACE	TORA	LDA	LIGHTING		Seething	
06/24	Asphalt	800	800	Thr Rwy		A/G	122.60

Remarks
AD not available for public transport passenger flights required to use a licensed AD. AD is not available at night to ACFT required to use a licensed AD. Pilots are requested to avoid over-flying surrounding villages below 1000ft. Pilots taking-off to leave the circuit from Rwy24 should climb straight ahead to 500ft before turning. If using Rwy06, turn right 10° on passing over the 24 Thr and climb to 500ft before turning. Flying activity may take place outside published Operating Hrs.

Warnings
Agricultural vehicles and equipment may be crossing close to the Thr of Rwy24. Silo 70ft aal/200ft amsl, 0.13nm 277° from ARP. Model ACFT flying at weekends.

Operating Hrs	0800-SS (Summer) 0900-SS (Winter)

Circuits	06 RH 24 LH 1000ft

Landing fee Business flights Single £6.00 Twin £12.00
For GA ACFT no landing fees but a donation to the group to assist in Rwy maintenance would be appreciated

Maintenance
Seething Aviation **Tel:** 01508 558013
Fuel AVGAS 100LL (limited)

Operator Waveney Flying Group
Seething Aerodrome, Brooke, Norwich NR15 1EL
Tel: 01508 550453 (A/D)
Tel: 01502 711852 (PPR out of Hrs)
Fax: 01508 550453

Restaurants Snacks available at the AD

Taxis
Bungay **Tel:** 01502 712625
Car Hire
Godfrey Davis **Tel:** 01603 45798

Weather Info AirS BNMC

ELEVATION	LOCATION	**EGOS**				**SHAWBURY**

ELEVATION	LOCATION				
249ft 8mb	6nm NNE of Shrewsbury N5247.89.W00240.08	**WAL** 114.10	162	39.4	• – – / • – / • – • •
PPR **MILITARY**		**MCT** 113.55	210	36.6	– – / – • – • / –

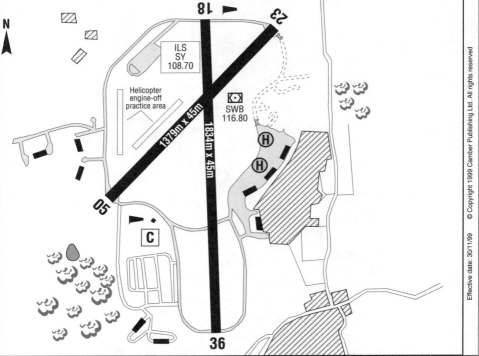

RWY	SURFACE	TORA	LDA	LIGHTING
18/36	Asph/Con	1834	1834	Ap Thr Rwy PAPI 3°
05/23	Asph/Con	1379	1379	Thr Rwy PAPI 3°

Shawbury	
APP/MATZ/ **LARS**	120.775
RAD	123.30
TWR	122.10
ILS	SY 108.70 Rwy18
VOR/DME	SWB 116.8

Remarks
Visual location aids: Ibn SY Red. Visiting pilots intending to operate out of Shawbury are to contact Shawbury Operations.

Warnings
Helicopters operate within 50m of either side of the active Rwy below 1500ft. Go arounds to be made down the full length of the Rwy. All ATC services may be provided by student controllers under supervision. PAPI Rwy18 coincides with ILS touchdown only. PAR approach will result in incorrect PAPI indications.

Operator RAF Shawbury
Shrewsbury, Shropshire SY4 4DZ
Tel: 01939 250351 Ext.7227 (ATIS on Ext 7574)

Restaurants

Taxis/Car Hire

Weather Info M T Fax 398 MWC

Operating Hrs	Mon-Fri 0700-1600 (Summer) Mon-Fri 0800-1700 (Winter)
Circuits	05/36 RH 18/23 LH no dead side 1500ft QFE
Landing fee	£7.56 per 500kgs +VAT & £8.50 insurance
Maintenance	Nil
Fuel	AVTUR JET A1

ELEVATION	LOCATION	**EGSY**		**SHEFFIELD CITY**
231ft 7mb	3nm ENE of Sheffield city centre N5323.66 W00123.31	**TNT** 115.70	032 22	– / – • / –
PPR		**GAM** 112.8	298 18	– – • / • – / – –

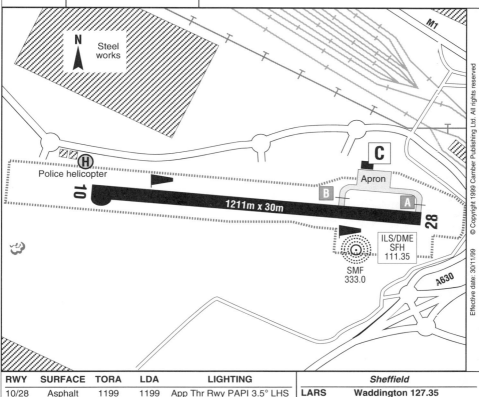

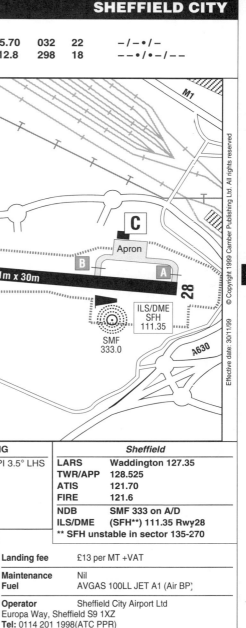

Effective date: 30/11/99

RWY	SURFACE	TORA	LDA	LIGHTING
10/28	Asphalt	1199	1199	App Thr Rwy PAPI 3.5° LHS

Sheffield

LARS	**Waddington 127.35**
TWR/APP	**128.525**
ATIS	**121.70**
FIRE	**121.6**
NDB	**SMF 333 on A/D**
ILS/DME	**(SFH**) 111.35 Rwy28**
** SFH unstable in sector 135-270	

Remarks

PPR by telephone. Non-radio ACFT not accepted. AD NOT available to single engined ACFT (single engine helicopters acceptable). No non-radio ACFT.Training ACFT accepted subject to time slot. Slots must be adhered to. Visual approaches/circuit training MUST maintain 1500ft QFE until established on final. Minimum £1 million third party insurance compulsory. Noise: departing ACFT use full length of Rwy. Helicopters MUST arrive/dept via (N) Tinsley Power Station & E of steel works, (S) Tinsley Park golf course. Very short taxi ride to Meadowhall shopping centre.

Warnings

Turbulence in strong SW wind effects APP & climb out Rwy28. AD in highly populated & industrial area. Major obstacles: Chimney 405ft amsl 259/2.33nm. Mast 559ft amsl 044°/1.92nm. Steel works 332ft amsl (lit) 0.24nm N of Rwy. High GND 372ft amsl (lit) S of Rwy. Rwy28 Papis subject to inaccuracies in wet ground conditions.

Landing fee	£13 per MT +VAT
Maintenance	Nil
Fuel	AVGAS 100LL JET A1 (Air BP)
Operator	Sheffield City Airport Ltd
Europa Way, Sheffield S9 1XZ	
Tel: 0114 201 1998(ATC PPR)	
Fax: 0114 201 1888 (ATC)	
Restaurants	Cafe in terminal
Taxis/Car Hire	Available on request in terminal
Weather Info	AiCen MCW **Tel:** 0114 201 5545

Visual Reference Points (VRP's)

Barnsley Rwy Station	N5333.27 W00128.65
Old Coates	N5323.52 W00107.11
Chesterfield Rwy Station	N5314.25 W00125.22
Redmires Res	N5321.92 W00136.42

Operating Hrs Mon-Fri 0530-1930 Sat 0530-1430 Sun & PH 0930-1930 (Summer) + 1Hr Winter and by arrangement

Circuits As instructed by ATC1500ft QFE

ELEVATION	LOCATION	EGCJ				SHERBURN-IN-ELMET
26ft 1mb	5.5nm W of Selby N5347.28.W00113.10 **Diversion AD**	OTR 113.90	284	40.1	– – – / – / • – •	
		POL 112.10	091	31.4	• – – • / – – – / • – • •	
PPR		GAM 112.80	348	31.9	– – • / • – / – –	

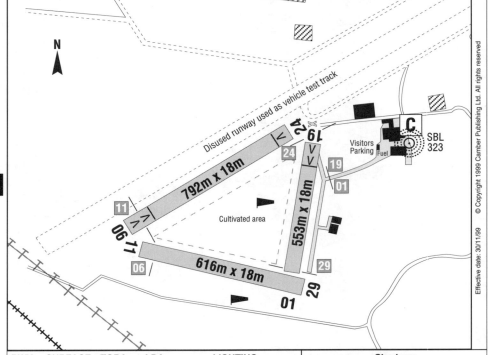

Disused runway used as vehicle test track

N

792m x 18m

553m x 18m

616m x 18m

06 11 / 24 / 19 24 / 11 / 06 / 29 / 01

Cultivated area

Visitors Parking   Fuel   SBL 323   C

RWY	SURFACE	TORA	LDA	LIGHTING
01	Grass	553	553	Nil
19	Grass	553	520	Nil
11/29	Grass	616	616	Nil
06	Grass	730	673	Nil
24	Grass	700	700	Nil

	Sherburn
APP	Fenton MATZ 126.50
APP	Linton MATZ 129.15
A/G	122.60
NDB	SBL 323 on A/D range 10nm

Remarks

This AD is situated within the Church Fenton MATZ. AD is not available for use by public transport passenger flights required to use a licensed AD. Inbound ACFT are to contact Fenton MATZ 126.50 when at 15nm or 5 mins flying time from the MATZ boundary and are to enter MATZ at 1500ft on the Sherburn QFE. If unable to make contact with Fenton APP, pilots are to contact Sherburn Radio 122.6 or Linton MATZ 129.15 and advise inability to contact Fenton. Departing ACFT are to contact Fenton MATZ 126.50 before leaving the Sherburn circuit and are to leave the MATZ below 1500ft QFE.

Warnings

Paved Rwy N of grass Rwys is closed to ACFT. It is used as a vehicle test track. ACFT must not overfly the villages of Sherburn-in-Elmet, S Milford, Monk Fryston or Hambleton.

Maintenance	Sherburn Engineering Tel: 01977 685296
Fuel	AVGAS 100LL

Operator	Sherburn Aero Club Ltd

Sherburn-in-Elmet Aerodrome, Lennerton Lane
Sherburn-in-Elmet, Leeds, West Yorkshire LB25 6JE
Tel: 01977 682674
Fax: 01977 683699

Restaurants	Bar & Café

Taxis
Speedway	**Tel:** 01977 681381
Windmill	**Tel:** 01937 232979
Car Hire	
National	**Tel:** 0113 277 7957

Weather Info	AirN MWC

Operating Hrs	0830-SS (Summer) 0900-SS (Winter)

Circuits
01/19 variable 24/29 LH 06/11 RH 1000ft QFE

Landing fee	Single £3.00 Twin £6.00 No charge with fuel uplift

S

Sherburn-in-Elmet Circuits

Rwy06/24
06 Right hand: Taxi out along Rwy29. After departure turn right, not above 500ft QFE. Turn base leg before Monk Fryston. Turn final no further W than Sherburn by-pass. DO NOT overfly S Milford.
24 Left hand: Turn left onto HDG 190°, when height & speed permit turn crosswind before S Milford. Turn downwind before Monk Fryston. DO NOT extend downwind due Church Fenton circuit. DO NOT overfly farmhouse at N Sweeming. After landing exit along Rwy11.

Rwy11/29
11 Right hand: Taxi out along Rwy24. Turn crosswind before Hambleton. Turn downwind N of Monk Fryston. Turn base leg W of S Milford, DO NOT overfly built up areas on APP. Complete final turn not below 400ft QFE. DO NOT overfly S Milford or Lumby
29 Left hand: After departure climbout between Sherburn & S Milford. DO NOT overfly S Milford or Lumby. Turn base leg before Hambleton. After landing exit along Rwy06.

Rwy01/19
01 Left hand: After departure turn left crosswind at 400ft or abeam factory (whichever is first). Continue to 700ft QFE max. until downwind. DO NOT overfly Sherburn or S Milford downwind leg. Turn base leg before Monk Fryston.
19 Right hand: Turn crosswind before Monk Fryston. DO NOT overfly S Milford or Sherburn on downwind leg. Turn base leg no further N than abeam factory.

S

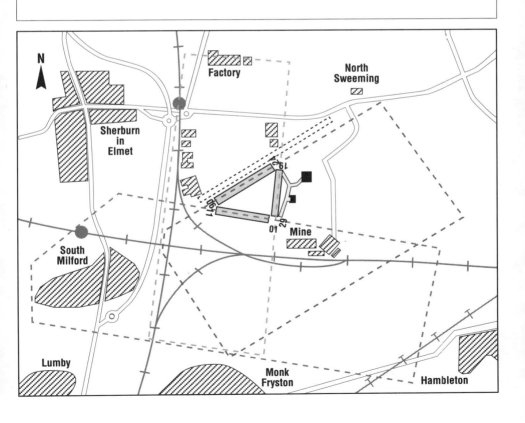

ELEVATION	LOCATION	EGBS				SHOBDON

ELEVATION	LOCATION				
318ft 11mb	6nm W of Leominster N5214.48.W00252.88 **Diversion AD**	HON 113.65	267	45.6	••••/–––/–•
PPR		BCN 117.45	029	34.0	–•••/–•–•/–•

S

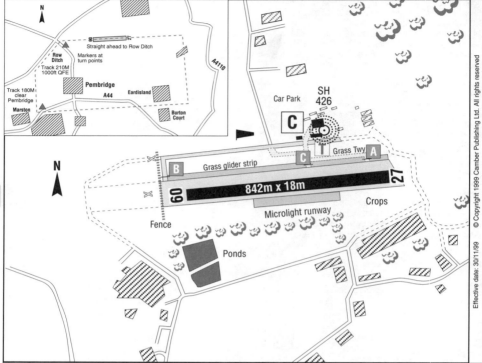

Straight ahead to Row Ditch — Markers at turn points — Row Ditch — Track 210M 1000ft QFE — Pembridge A44 — Eardisland — Track 180M clear Pembridge — Marston — Burton Court — A4110 — Car Park — SH 426 — C — Grass Twy — A — B — Grass glider strip — C — 60 — 842m x 18m — 27 — Crops — Microlight runway — Fence — Ponds

RWY	SURFACE	TORA	LDA	LIGHTING
09	Asphalt	842	842	Thr Rwy
27	Asphalt	842	842	Thr Rwy APAPI 3.5° LHS

	Shobdon
A/G /AFIS	123.50
NDB	SH 426 on A/D range 10nm

Remarks

Warnings
Note that parallel asphalt Twy and W access Twy are suitable only for ACFT with a wing span less than 8m and wheel span less than 4.5m. Deviation from the marked movement area can be hazardous. When Rwy27 is in use, gliders land on the grass strip to the N of Rwy. Grass microlight strip 380m S of main Rwy09/27. Fence 4.5ft high, 97m W of Rwy09 Thr. During heavy rain the Rwy is liable to have patches of standing water. Pilots should use the centre of the Rwy at night as the outer sections are rough.

Operating Hrs Nov-Mar 0900-1630, Apr 0800-1700, May-Aug 0800-1850, Sep-Oct 0800-1700, daily

Circuits
Powered ACFT wide 09 RH 27 LH 1000ft QFE
Microlight/Heli using microlight strip tight 800ft QFE (helis) 500ft QFE (micros)
Overhead joins 1500ft QFE min deadside. Descend to circuit height S of Rwy, see noise chart.

Landing fee	Single £7.00 Twin £14.00 Microlight £2
Maintenance	Shobdon ACFT Maintenance **Tel:** 01568 708855
Fuel	AVGAS 100LL JET A1

Operator	Herefordshire Aero Club Ltd

Shobdon Aerodrome, Leominster, Hereford HR6 9NR
Tel: 01568 708369
Fax: 01568 708935

Restaurants	Cafe at AD

Bateman Arms pub, Shobdon

Taxis
Markham's **Tel:** 01568 708208
Car Hire
Watson's Leominster **Tel:** 01568 612060

Weather Info AirN MWC

ELEVATION	LOCATION	EGKA				SHOREHAM
7ft 0mb	1nm W of Shoreham-by-Sea N5050.07.W00017.67	SFD 117.00	291	16.4	••• / •• – • / – ••	
		MID 114.00	141	18.1	– – / •• / – ••	
PPR		MAY 117.90	240	18.9	– – / • – / – • – –	

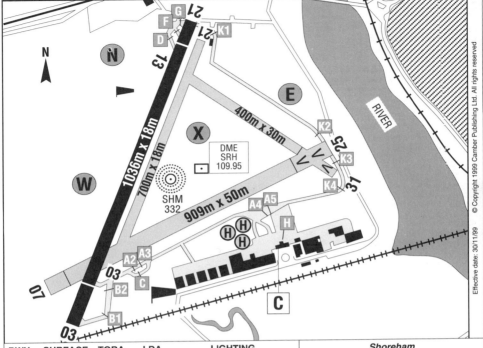

RWY	SURFACE	TORA	LDA	LIGHTING
03	Asphalt	960	871	Thr Rwy PAPI 3.5° LHS
21	Asphalt	916	865	Thr Rwy PAPI 4.5° LHS
07	Grass	877*	877	Nil
25	Grass	894	794	Nil
13	Grass	400	400	Nil
31	Grass	400**	400	Nil

*Additional 60m grass available daylight only PPR
**Additional 130m grass starter extension available

Shoreham	
ATIS	132.40
APP**	123.15
VDF	123.15
TWR	123.15 125.40
A/G*	123.15
DME	SRH 109.95
NDB	SHM 332 on A/D range 10nm

*Mon-Sat 08-09 (W) 07-08 (S)
**APP service limited pilots advised to check availability

Remarks

PPR for non-radio ACFT and Microlights. Unless otherwise instructed, join the circuit by over-flying the AD at 2000ft aal, descend to circuit height on the dead side of the Rwy in use and join the circuit by crossing the upwind end. More than one Rwy may be in use at any one time. Rwy03/21 will always be preferred subject to operational limitations. ACFT Dept Rwy21 should avoid over-flying as much of the built-up area to the S as practical. Noise abatement techniques should be practised at all times, the area to the E and W being particularly sensitive. Training: Touch and go training is not permitted on Sundays or before 1000 and after 1800 local time Monday to Saturday. Rwy13/31 is not available for 'touch and go' landing. Visiting ACFT may not carry out touch and go training. Only Rwy03/21 may be used for practice engine failures after take-off. Use of NDB or VDF for training by arrangement with ATC and subject to IFR and scheduled movements. Parking for Customs: ACFT for Customs clearance should park within the area bounded by yellow lines on the E side in front of the terminal building, or as instructed by ATC. After heavy rain, standing water may persist on grass areas.

Helicopter Operations: Extensive helicopter training takes place in area W of Rwy03/21 ('W') alongside E perimeter fence ('E') and N of VDF aerial ('X'). An additional area ('N') is used for sloping GND training adjacent to N windsock on NW side of AD. Helicopter circuits will vary in direction. Helicopter arrivals and departures should follow ATC instructions closely and will be subject to specific ATC authorisation to cross Rwys, more than one of which may be in use at any one time. Helicopters should avoid over-flying built up areas that are adjacent to the arrival and departure routes.

Radio failure procedures: By day ACFT should join overhead the AD, fit into the traffic pattern and overfly the Rwy required to be used at 500ft before positioning for landing. By night ACFT should join overhead the AD and position to overfly the TWR at 500ft before positioning for landing. Standard light signals should be followed. Visual aids to location: Ibn SH Green.

Warnings

Caution soft GND either side of Twy K. Enter/exit using marked points only.

Operating Hrs
Mon-Sat 0700-1900 Sun 0800-1900
Mon-Sat 0700-0800 strictly PPR (Summer)
Mon 0800-1800 Tue-Sat 0800-1900 Sun 0900-1800
Mon-Sat 0800-0900 strictly PPR (Winter)
and by arrangement

Circuits
All LH 1100ft QFE Helis 600ft QFE. Also see remarks

Landing fee   500kgs-1.5MT £13.50 inc.VAT
                     1.5MT-2.5MT £27 inc.VAT
£5 reduction for PFA members on official business

Maintenance
AS Engineering   **Tel:** 01273 464791
Jade Air   **Tel:** 01273 464013
KB Air   **Tel:** 01273 453333
Sern Air   **Tel:** 01273 461665
Tyrell Aviation   **Tel:** 01273 461310
Fuel   AVGAS 100LL AVTUR JET A1

Operator
Brighton Hove & Worthing Joint Municipal Airport Committee
Shoreham Airport, Shoreham-by-Sea, West Sussex BN4 5FJ
Tel: 01273 296900/296888(ATC)
Fax: 01273 296899

Restaurants
Restaurant, refreshments and Club facilities available
                   Tel: 01273 452300

Taxis
at Terminal   **Tel:** 01273 461655
Car Hire
Europcar   **Tel:** 01273 329332
Avis   **Tel:** 01273 673738
Hertz   **Tel:** 01273 738227

Weather Info   M T9 Fax 422 A BNMC

Visual Reference Points (VRPs)
Brighton Marina
N5048.65 W00006.05
Henfield
N5055.80 W00016.60
Littlehampton
N5048.77 W00032.78

SHOTTESWELL (Church Farm Banbury)

ELEVATION	LOCATION				
530ft 17mb	3nm N of Banbury N5206.25.W00122.80	DTY 116.40	250	11	– •• / – / – • – –
		HON 113.65	150	18.5	• • • • / – – – / – •

Footpath to Shotteswell

400m x 18m

853m x 18m

Rough ground

Crops

10ft hedge

5ft hedge

Hanwell 3/4 mile
DO NOT overfly

N

60 · 15 · 27 · 33 · A41

S

RWY	SURFACE	TORA	LDA	LIGHTING
15/33	Grass	853x18	U/L	Nil
09/27	Grass	400x18	U/L	Nil

	Non-radio
APP	Birmingham 118.05

Remarks
PPR not required, considerate visitors welcome at own risk. Rwy15/33 smooth slightly undulating surface. Rwy09/27 use only when crosswind precludes use of 15/33. Orange & white windsock on N boundary. Rwy surface maintenance excellent. Fishing lake available.

Warnings
Trees along E edge of strip may cause windshear even in light wind conditions. 4ft hedge rows up to Thr all Rwys. Crops E edge 15/33 & S edge 09/27. Rwy09/27 only recommended for use by microlights, STOL ACFT & experienced pilots due to parked ACFT & hangars Thr 27. Also upslope from 27 Thr. Avoid overflying local villages particularly Hanwell on 33 APP.

Operator	Mr F Spencer DFC & Bar
	Church Farm, Shotteswell
	Tel: 01295 730275
	Fax: 01295 738557

Restaurants
The Wobbly Wheel Motel 0.75 mile from AD

Taxis	**Tel:** 01295 270011
	Tel: 01295 264774
Car Hire	
Weather Info	AirCen BNMC

Operating Hrs	SR-SS
Circuits	1000ft QFE
Landing fee	Nil
Maintenance	Nil
Fuel	Nil

ELEVATION	LOCATION		
110ft 4mb	6nm ESE of Bedford N5205.33.W00019.09 **Diversion AD**	BKY 116.25 298 15.2	— • • • / — • — / — • — —
PPR		BNN 113.75 026 23.4	— • • • / — • / — •

DO NOT overfly Home Farm

613m

04

22

C

N

RWY	SURFACE	TORA	LDA	LIGHTING
04/22	Grass	613	U/L	Nil

	Shuttleworth
A/G	123.05 Display days only

Remarks

PPR by telephone essential. AD closed some days for public events, consult NOTAMs. On flying days and flying evenings parking is limited. PPR should be made well in advance. Last landing 1300 (days), 1730 (evenings). Special admission charges apply. Use of Rwy12/30 will not normally be authorised. Vacate Rwy04/22 to the NW after landing. Dep will not be authorised until after the display. Dep do not back track Rwys. Lookout for non-radio ACFT and ACFT on display practice.

Warnings

Parts of the AD are prone to waterlogging after heavy rain. Pilots should enquire about these when telephoning for PPR. Manoeuvring should be confined to the Rwy in the effected areas. Sheep may be present on movement area in the winter. Local habitation, particularly within 1nm should not be overflown below 1500ft. Beware of trees on APP to Rwy12. ACFT must be parked well clear of the end or sides of Rwy12/30 at the NW end where manoeuvring space is restricted. Helicopters must land airside of spectator fence line and not in the museum car park.

Operating Hrs 0900-1700

Circuits	LH 800 ft
Landing fee	No PPR £25

£6.00 per person inc admission OAP £4 per person inc admission Child £3.00 inc admission to museum

Maintenance	Available in emergency only
Fuel	AVGAS 100LL Flying days only

Operator The Shuttleworth Trust
Old Warden/Biggleswade Aerodrome, Northill, Biggleswade Beds SG18 9EP.
Tel: 01767 627288
Fax: 01767 626229

Restaurants
Full facilities available until 1700 (1600 Nov-Mar)

Taxis
Tel: 01767 316438
Maurice   **Tel:** 01234 262222
Car Hire   On request or
Biggleswade Mtr Co **Tel:** 01767 313788

Weather Info   AirCen BNMC

SITTLES FARM (Lichfield)

ELEVATION	LOCATION				
170ft 5mb **PPR**	3nm E of Lichfield N5242.30 W00144.50	**TNT 115.70** **HON 113.65**	192 357	21 21	– / – • / – • • • • / – – – / – •

Roddige Airfield

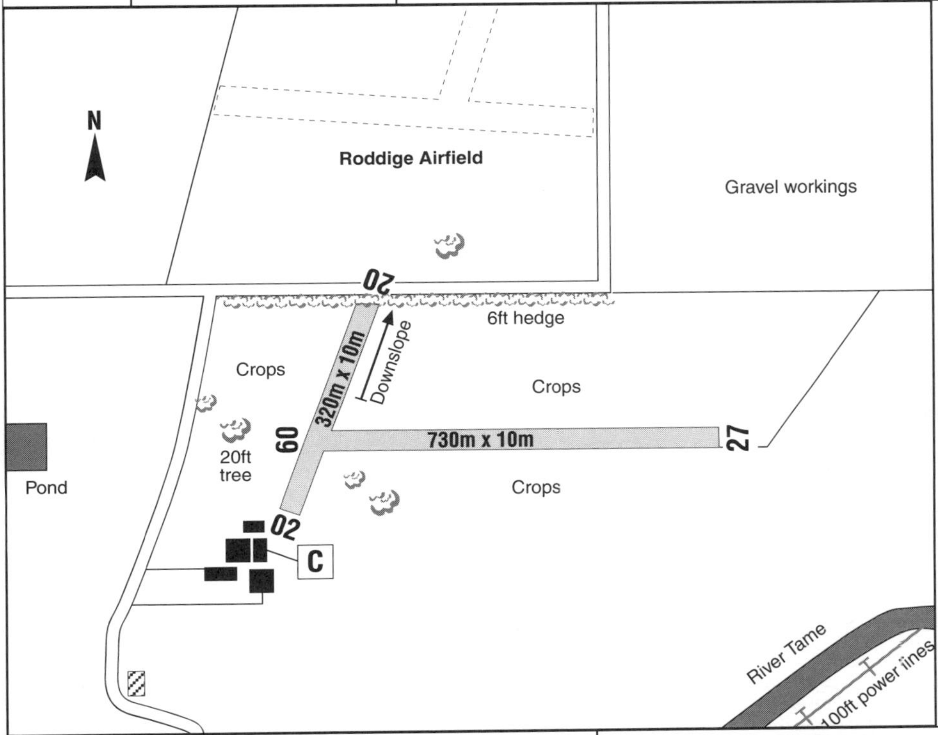

Gravel workings

N

6ft hedge

Crops

Crops

320m x 10m

Downslope

60

730m x 10m

27

20ft tree

Crops

Pond

02

C

River Tame

100ft power lines

Effective date: 30/11/99

S

RWY	SURFACE	TORA	LDA	LIGHTING
09/27	Grass	730x10	U/L	Nil
02*/20	Grass	320x10	U/L	Nil

*Rwy02 has downslope in last 150m

Non Radio

APP (Birmingham)   118.05
Roddige AD is close to the N & operates A/G on 129.825

Remarks
PPR by telephone. Visiting ACFT welcome at pilots own risk. Rwys well maintained.

Warnings
Roddige AD is close to N AD boundary with daily Microlight activity. Powerlines 100ft agl run along River Tame and cross Rwy27 approach 1000m from Thr. Crops grown up to edge of strip. Caution downslope last half Rwy02. Noise: Avoid overflight of local villages. See circuit details.

Operator   Mr Tony Birch The Cottage
Bennets Lane, Pattingham, Wolverhampton WV6 7AY
Tel: 01902 700790
Tel: 07973 686645 (Mobile)

Restaurant   Tea & Coffee available farm can provide group catering on open days for 200-300 people

Taxi/Car Hire

Weather Info   AirCen MWC

Operating Hrs	SR-SS
Circuits	Join overhead & descend on live side fly circuits around farm not across Rwys 09 RH, 27.LH, 800ft QFE
Landing Fee	Nil
Maintenance **Fuel**	Nil Nil MOGAS available from garage 0.5nm

ELEVATION	LOCATION	SKEGNESS (Water Leisure Park)		
10ft 0mb	1.5nm N of Skegness (town Ctr 4nm) N5310.40.E00020.00			
PPR		OTR 113.9	157	35	– – – / – / • – •
		GAM 112.80	102	45.5	– – • / • – / – –

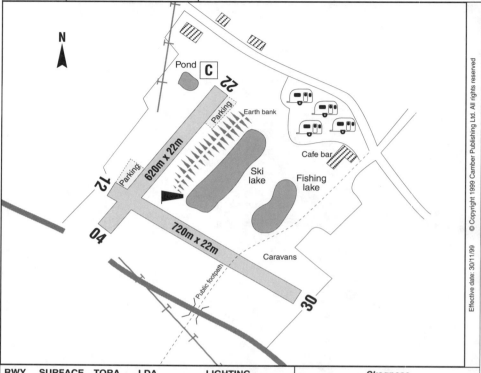

N

Pond

C

22

Parking

Earth bank

Parking

12

Parking

620m x 22m

04

720m x 22m

Ski lake

Fishing lake

Cafe bar

Caravans

Public footpath

30

Effective date: 30/11/99

RWY	SURFACE	TORA	LDA	LIGHTING
12/30	Grass	720x22	U/L	Nil
04/22	Grass	620x22	U/L	Nil

Skegness	
A/G	132.425
APP	Conningsby 120.80

Remarks

Skegness Aero club, AD situated within Water Leisure Park complex 0.5nm from Butlins Fun Coast World (day tickets available).

Warnings

AD close to N boundary of the Wash AIAA. ACFT arriving from S must contact Coningsby 120.80 during their ops Hrs, other times Waddington 127.35.

Noise: Rwy12 departs; make early left turn on track 100° & climb over coast before turning left. Rwy22; make crosswind turn keep church on left. Do not turn downwind until over coast. Rwy04; Do not turn downwind until over coast. ensure base leg turn is made before built up area of Skegness, turn final after passing church on right.

Operator   Mr M C Burnett (Skegness Aero Club)
Water Leisure Park, Walls Lane, Skegness
Mobile: 07741 014808
Tel: 01754 610315 (home)
Tel: 01754 769019 (office)
Fax: 01754 610847

Restaurants
Availble in Water Leisure Park during summer season

Taxis
Freds   **Tel:** 01754 765040
Car Hire   Availble by arrangement

Weather Info   AirCen MWC

Operating Hrs	Available on request
Circuits	04 RH 12/22/30 LH 800ft QFE
Landing fee	Club membership
Maintenance M3 Fuel	**Tel:** 01754 611127 Nil

ELEVATION	LOCATION	EGCV				SLEAP
275ft 9mb	10nm N of Shrewsbury N5250.03.W00246.30 **Diversion AD**	WAL 114.10	165	35.9	• — — / • — / • — • •	
		MCT 113.55	217	36.4	— — / • — • / —	
PPR		SWB 116.8	310	4.5	• • • / • — — / — • • •	

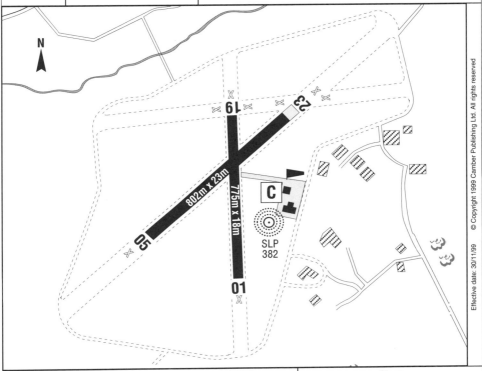

RWY	SURFACE	TORA	LDA	LIGHTING			
05/23*	Asphalt	802	802	Thr Rwy LITAS 3.5°			
01/19	Asphalt	775	775	Nil			

*Additional 50nm starter extension available for Rwy23 by daylight only

	Sleap
APP	**Shawbury MATZ 120.775**
A/G	**122.45**
NDB	**SLP 382** **on A/D range 10nm**

Remarks

PPR by telephone. AD not available for public transport passenger flights. Inbound ACFT are to contact Shawbury on 120.77 weekdays. Visual aid to location: Ibn Green SP. ACFT not to be parked on the grass parallel to the Twy or opposite to fuel pumps. Used for helicopter training Mon-Fri visiting ACFT must obtain a telephone briefing.

Warnings

Glider launching takes place on the AD. The Twy from the apron near ATC to the Rwy intersection is the only Twy available for use. Pilots are warned that deviation from the marked movement area can be hazardous.

Operator	Shropshire Aero Club Ltd Sleap Aerodrome, Myddle, Shropshire SY4 3HE **Tel:** 01939 232882 **Fax:** 01939 235058
Restaurants	Hot & cold food/drinks available Sat/Sun
Taxis	
	Tel: 01939 234562(Day) **Tel:** 01948 880594(Eves)
Car Hire	
Weather Info	AirCen MWC

Operating Hrs

Sat-Wed 0800-1600 Thu-Fri 0800-2015 (Summer)
+1Hr Winter

Circuits	Variable
Landing fee	Single £5.00 Twin £10.00 inc.VAT
Maintenance	Shropshire Light Aviation **Tel:** 01939 290861
Fuel	AVGAS 100LL

Sleap Circuit Traffic Zone Operation

Effective date: 30/11/99

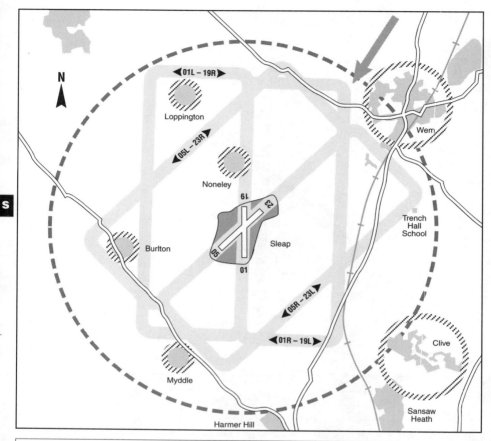

Circuit Height 1000ft QFE

Circuits generally left hand except when RAF Shawbury is active, when circuits will be to W of AD.

Circuits should be contained within the ATZ (large broken circle). Circuit patterns shown are required maxima.

Avoid overflying Wem, Clive, Myddle, Loppington, Noneley & Burlton.

Arriving ACFT should carry out standard 2000ft overhead joining procedure.

ACFT approaching Rwy23 on a straight-in or long final should keep to the W of Wem (approximate track 220°).

ACFT, especially high-powered singles or twins, departing from Rwy01 should make a 10° right turn after take-off to avoid Noneley.

Blank page

Effective date: 30/11/99

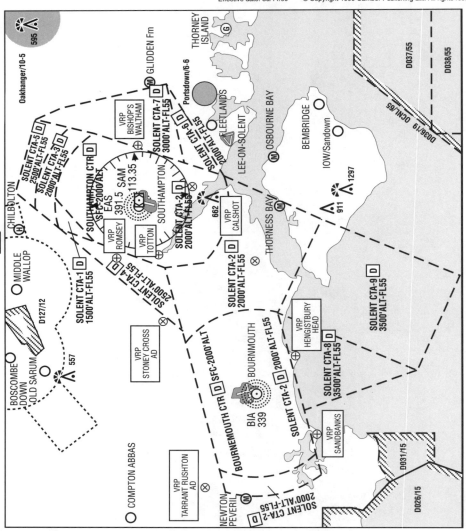

CTA/CTR Class D Airspace

Normal CTA/CTR Class D Airspace rules apply.

These rules do not apply to non-radio ACFT by day provided they have obtained permission and maintain 5km visibility, 1500m horizontally and 1000ft vertically away from cloud, or for gliders provided they maintain 8km visibility, 1500m horizontally and 1000ft vertically away from cloud.

VFR Transit Traffic

VFR traffic wishing to transit the Southampton CTR from the E or W should plan to route via ROMSEY-SAM Bishops Waltham or vice versa.

Visual Reference Points (VRPs)

VRP	VOR/NDB	VOR/DME
Bishops Waltham N5057.28 W00112.58	SAM R095°/EAS 095°M	SAM 095°/5nm
Calshot N5049.07 W00119.75	SAM R180°/BIA 088°M	SAM 180°/8nm
Romsey N5059.45 W00129.75	SAM R295°/EAS 296°M	SAM 295°/6nm
Totton N5055.20 W00129.33	SAM R253°/EAS 252°M	SAM 253°/6nm

ELEVATION	LOCATION		
44ft 2mb	3.5nm NNE of Southampton N5057.02.W00121.41 **Diversion AD**	SAM 113.35 On A/D MID 114.00 263 28.3	• • • / • – / – – – – / • • / – • •

Effective date: 30/11/99

S

RWY	SURFACE	TORA	LDA	LIGHTING
02	Asphalt	1723	1650	Ap Thr Rwy PAPI 3°
20	Asphalt	1650	1605	Ap Thr Rwy PAPI 3°

Rwy02 Thr displaced by 73m. Rwy20 Thr displaced by 45m

Southampton

ATIS	113.35 (SAM VOR)
ZONE	Solent APP
	120.225
APP	128.85
RAD	128.85 120.225
TWR	118.20
FIRE	121.60
VOR/DME	SAM 113.35
ILS/DME	I-SN 110.75 Rwy20
NDB	EAS 391.50
	on A/D range 15nm

Remarks

Non-radio ACFT not accepted. Class D Airspace. Landing and taxiing in grass areas prohibited. Use of AD by training flights is subject to approval from the AD operator. Requests for approval to be made to the ATC briefing unit Tel: 02380 627102.

Noise Preferential Routes & Procedures: After take-off on Rwy20 ACFT should, not below 500ft agl, turn right to make good track of 218°M maintaining this track to 2000ft (Southampton Airport QNH) or until reaching Southampton Water. The above routing is compatible with ATC requirements; in individual cases it may be varied by ATC. GA ACFT parking stands 6-11, S or N Ga aprons (except resident flying schools) are required to use AD GND transport. ACFT commanders are responsible for the safety of themselves, pax, or crew when airside. When GND transport is not provided all pax and crew are to be escorted by the ACFT commander, Circuit training by helicopters is not permitted.

Warnings

Circuits	Day 1000ft QNH Night 1500ft QNH
Landing fee	On application

Maintenance
Osprey Aviation	**Tel:** 02380 620727
Fuel	AVGAS 100LL AVTUR JET A1

Operator   Southampton International Airport Ltd
Southampton-Eleigh Airport, Southampton SO18 2NL
Tel: 02380 629600 (APT switchboard)
Tel: 02380 627113 (Airport Duty Manager)
Tel: 02380 627102 (FBU)
Fax: 02380 629300 **Fax:** 02380 629210 (Duty Ops Mgr)

Restaurants	Cafe bar at AD

Taxis
Beeline   **Tel:** 02380 617517
Car Hire
Budget (at terminal) **Tel:** 02380 650537

Weather Info	M T9 A Fax 424 VS BNMC

Operating Hrs   Mon-Thu 0545-2000, PPR 2000-2030, Fri 0545-2115, Sat 0630-1915, Sun 0800-200 (Summer). Mon-Fri 0645-2100, Sat 0730-2000, Sun 0900-2100 (Winter). And by arrangement

ELEVATION	LOCATION	EGMC				SOUTHEND
48ft 2mb	1.5nm N of Southend-on-Sea N5134.28 E00041.73	DET 117.30	017	16.5	– •• / • / –	
		LAM 115.60	106	20.8	• – •• / • – / – –	
PPR		CLN 114.55	229	23.7	– • – • / • – •• / – •	

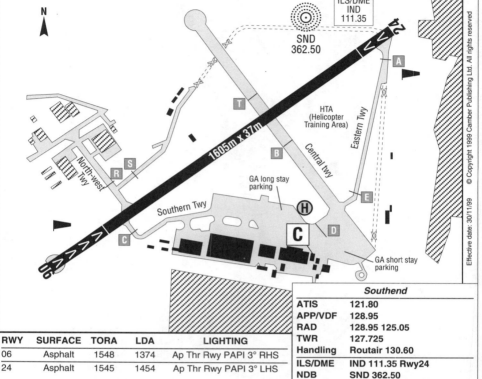

ILS/DME IND 111.35
SND 362.50
HTA (Helicopter Training Area)
GA long stay parking
GA short stay parking

RWY	SURFACE	TORA	LDA	LIGHTING
06	Asphalt	1548	1374	Ap Thr Rwy PAPI 3° RHS
24	Asphalt	1545	1454	Ap Thr Rwy PAPI 3° LHS

	Southend
ATIS	121.80
APP/VDF	128.95
RAD	128.95 125.05
TWR	127.725
Handling	Routair 130.60
ILS/DME	IND 111.35 Rwy24
NDB	SND 362.50 on A/D range 20nm

Remarks

PPR non-radio ACFT. On departure all propeller driven ACFT must climb straight ahead at least 600ft aal before turning. Departure Rwy24 propeller driven ACFT requiring a left turn shall, pass 600ft aal, maintain track 190° to N bank River Thames, or until Detling DME 13nm or less, before setting course. A busy public road crosses extended Rwy centreline at SW end Rwy06/24. approaching Rwy06/24 in VMC intercept Rwy extended centreline min. range 2nm from touchdown not below PAPI APP slope 3°. All training flights, including qualifying cross-countries, PPR ATC & may be curtailed/refused at short notice due traffic & airspace limitations. Helicopter training takes place in grass areas Rwy06/24, E of disused Rwy15/33 near NW end disused Rwy15/33. Helicopter circuits normally parallel to fixed wing Rwy in use at 500ft/1000ft as advised by ATC. Visual aids to location: Abn White flashing. Handling provided by Southend Handling Tel: 01702 391700 Routair Tel: 01702 544594.

Warnings

AD control & vehicular GND movement control radio frequencies combined. Pilots will hear controller transmissions to both vehicles & ACFT on 127.725 but will not hear vehicle responses. Not all taxiways are available for use. Deviation from marked movement area hazardous.

Operating Hrs	H24 PPR 2100-0700 (Summer) 2200-0800 (Winter)

Circuits	Variable at the discretion of ATC
Landing fee	£12 per 1000kgs +VAT £12 minimum
Maintenance	Available (major)
Fuel	AVGAS 100LL AVTUR JET A1

Operator	Regional Airports Ltd

London Southend Airport, Southend-on-Sea, Essex SS2 6YF
Tel: 01702 340201 (Switchboard)
Tel: 01702 608120 (ATC)
Fax: 01702 608128 (ATC)

Restaurant	Restaurant buffet and bar in Terminal

Also Aviators & Thames Estuary clubs

Taxis	
At terminal	**Tel:** 01702 334455
Car Hire	
Budget	**Tel:** 01268 772774
Hertz	**Tel:** 01702 546666

Weather Info	M T9 A Fax 426 VS BNMC

Visual Reference Points (VRPs)

Billericay	N5138.00 E00025.00
Maldon	N5143.70 E00041.00
Sheerness	N5126.50 E00044.90
S Woodham Ferrers	N5139.00 E00037.00
St Marys Marsh	N5128.50 E00036.00

ELEVATION	LOCATION	**EGSG**		**STAPLEFORD**
185ft 6mb	4.5nm N of Romford N5139.15.E00009.35			
	Diversion AD			
PPR				

LAM 115.60	010	0.8	• — • • / • — / — —
BPK 117.50	126	11.3	— • • • / • — — • / — • —
BKY 116.25	174	20.4	— • • • / — • — / — • — —

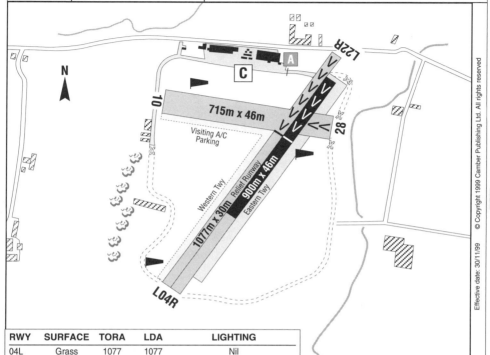

RWY	SURFACE	TORA	LDA	LIGHTING
04L	Grass	1077	1077	Nil
04R	Grass/Asphalt	900	900	Ap Thr Rwy LITAS 4.5° RHS
22L*	Grass/Asphalt	1077	900	Ap Thr Rwy APAPI 4.25° LHS
22R*	Grass	900	900	Nil
10	Grass	500	698	Nil
28	Grass	715	500	Nil

*600mx18m asphalt insert starts 17m after beginning of TORA

Stapleford	
A/G/AFIS	122.80
VOR/DME	LAM 115.60 450m S of Thr04

Remarks

Outside published Hrs of operation two Hrs PPR. Noise Abatement Procedures: Rwy28 Dep; ACFT should maintain the Rwy heading until passing 1000ft agl. Rwy22 Dep: No right turn below 1000ft agl. Avoid over-flying villages of Abridge and Lambourne below 1000ft agl. A licensed relief Rwy has been established to the W, parallel to and adjoining Rwy04/22. The Rwy is marked with white corners and white painted edge markers. Pilots may be asked to use this Rwy at certain times.

Warnings

Radio mast 295ft aal SW of the AD and 1.2nm from 04 Thr in line with Rwy04/22. Do not land short of displaced Thr Rwy22L/22R. Power cables 210ft agl running NW/SE 1nm NE of Rwy22 Thr.

Maintenance	
Stapleford Maint.	**Tel:** 01708 688449
Fuel	AVGAS 100LL JET A1 with PPR **Tel:** 0181 500 3030

Operator	The Herts and Essex Aero Club Ltd

Stapleford Aerodrome, Stapleford, Romford, Essex RM4 1SJ
Tel: 01708 688380
Fax: 01708 688421

Restaurants	Cafe & bar at the AD

Taxis	
Theydon Bois	**Tel:** 01992 814 335
Car Hire	
Hertz	**Tel:** 01708 721882

Weather Info	AirSE BNMC

Operating Hrs	0730-SS (Summer) 0830-SS (Winter) and by arrangement
Circuits	LH 1200ft QNH
Landing fee	Single £5.00 Twin £10 plus £2.30 per night parking inc.VAT

STOKE AIRFIELD

ELEVATION	LOCATION
10ft 0mb	4nm W of Sheerness N5126.64 E00037.96

DET 117.30   012   7.5   – • • / • / –

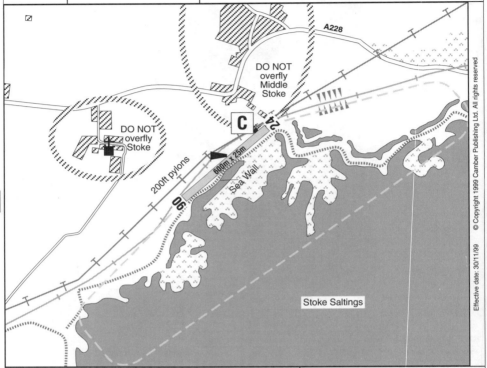

RWY	SURFACE	TORA	LDA	LIGHTING		Stoke	
06/24	Grass	600x25	U/L	Nil		A/G	129.825

Remarks
PPR not required, visiting ACFT & microlights welcome. Microlight training site please keep a good lookout & make blind calls on 129.825 if no reply. The strip has a very slight curve over its entire length. Please taxy on the seawall side of the Rwy & park with propellor close to the bushes by the caravan. Visitors book in at club hut.

Warnings
National grid transmission lines 200ft high parallel to Rwy and final APP on landward side. A railway passes along this side of the AD between the Rwy & pylons. The seaward marsh is SSSI do not overfly below 500ft QFE.

Operating Hrs SR-SS Last permitted take-off 2000 local

Circuits
Join overhead at 1500ft QFE circuit seaward at 500ft QFE (Slightly offset final APP to avoid transmission lines)

Landing fee £2

Maintenance Medway Microlight Factory
200yds from AD Mon-Fri 0900-1700 sales service & maintenace
Fuel MOGAS
at local village 0800-2000 (local) 7-days
(transport available with notice)
Hangarage for de-rigged microlights

Operator Keith Reynolds, Medway Microlights
Stoke Airfield, Stoke, Rochester, Kent ME3 9RN
Tel: 01634 270236 (No PPR required)
Mobile: 07775 742582

Restaurants/Accomodation Hot & cold drinks & hot food available accomodation can be arranged

Taxis
Hoo Cabs **Tel:** 01634 251234
Car Hire Nil

Weather Info AirSE BNMC

ELEVATION	LOCATION	**EGPO**	**STORNOWAY**

ELEVATION	LOCATION
25ft	2nm E of Stornoway
1mb	N5812.82.W00619.73
PPR	

STN 115.10	284	5.0	••• / – / – •
BEN 114.40	047	55.2	– ••• / • / – •

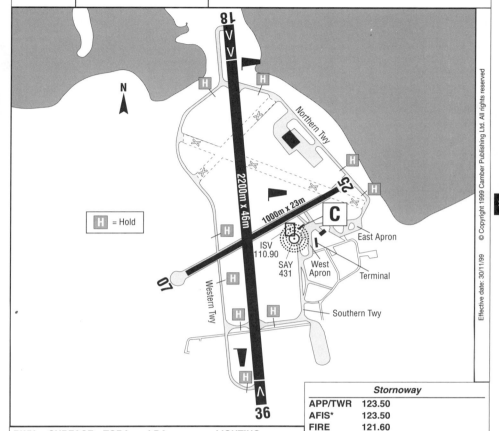

H = Hold

RWY	SURFACE	TORA	LDA	LIGHTING
18	Asphalt	2200	2080	Ap Thr Rwy PAPI 3°
36	Asphalt	2080	2080	Ap Thr Rwy PAPI 3°
07	Asphalt	1000	1000	Thr Rwy APAPI 4° LHS
25	Asphalt	1000	1000	Thr Rwy APAPI 3.5° LHS

Stornoway	
APP/TWR	**123.50**
AFIS*	**123.50**
FIRE	**121.60**
VOR/DME	**STN 115.10 284/5nm to A/D**
DME	**ISV 110.90**
NDB	**SAY 431**
	on A/D range 60nm
* Available outside Hrs of ATC	

Remarks
PPR essential 3hrs before arrival. Rwy36 app. lights terminate 150m short of Thr. Take-offs by ACFT required to use a licensed AD in visibility's of 600m or less not permitted, except Emergency Air Ambulance Flights, when arrangements will be made to inspect and protect the Rwy in use. Rwy07/25 not available for night landings. Visual Aid to Location: Abn White/Green flashing. Limited customs available.

Warnings
Grass areas are soft and unsafe. No GND signals except light signals. The N and S Twys on E side of AD are 15m wide. Only marked Twys to be used. The Thr of Rwy36 is displaced as a public road crosses the app. Use minimum app. angles of 3° as indicated by PAPI. The 120m of asphalt Rwy extending beyond Rwy36 Thr. is not available for ACFT manoeuvring or as a starter extension. A SK61 Coastguard helicopter operates & will be given priority over other traffic when on SAR duties.

Operating Hrs
Mon-Fri 0730-1600 Sat 0730-1400 (3 Apr-8 May 2 Oct-30 Oct) Sat 0730-1445 (15 May-25 Sep) Mon-Fri 0830-1700 (Winter)

Circuits	18/25 LH 07/36 RH
Landing fee	£10.65 inc.VAT ACFT up to 3MT VFR cash or cheque on day
Maintenance	Nil
Fuel	AVGAS 100LL AVTUR JET A1 (limited) **Tel:** 01851 703026
Operator	HIAL Stornoway Aerodrome
Isle of Lewis HS2 0BN	
Tel: 01851 702256 **Tel:** 01851 702282 (MET)	
Fax: 01851 703115 **Telex:** 75495	
Restaurants	Refreshments only at the AD Pubs and restaurants in Stornoway
Taxis	
Central	**Tel:** 01851 706900
Car Hire	
Stornoway Car Hire	**Tel:** 01851 702658
Weather Info	M T9 T18 Fax 428 VSc GWC

ELEVATION	LOCATION			
120ft	4nm SE of Crieff			
4mb	N5619.50.W00344.91			
PPR				

GOW 115.40   047   35.9   – – • / – – – / • – –

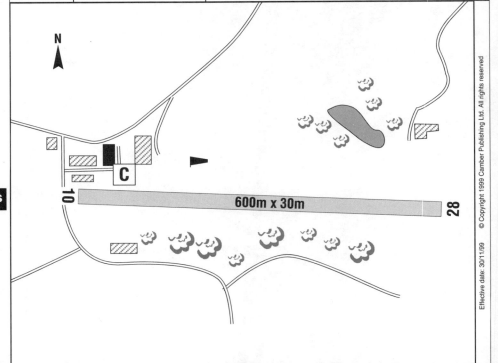

600m x 30m

10   28

RWY	SURFACE	TORA	LDA	LIGHTING		*Strathallan*	
10/28	Grass	600x30	U/L	Nil		A/G	129.90

Remarks
PPR by telephone. Call Strathallan on 129.90, if no response, assume no parachuting. Para-dropping ACFT will advise. Before starting engines, obtain permission on 129.90. Non-radio ACFT must provide accurate ETA.

Warnings
Intensive free-fall parachuting takes place up to FL120. ACFT must not overfly the AD. High GND 1225ft aal (1345ft amsl) 4nm SE of the AD. Sheep may graze on AD.

Operator	Scottish Parachute Club
	Strathallan Aerodrome, Auchterarder
	Tayside Region PH3 1LA
	Tel: 01764 662572 (weekends)
	Tel: 01764 832462 (weekdays)
Restaurants	Cafe at weekends 0900-2100 (local)
Taxis/Car Hire	Arranged on request
Weather Info	AirSc GWC

Operating Hrs	Fri-Sun 0900-2100 or SS (local)

Circuits
10 RH 28 LH 1000ft QFE no overhead joins

Landing fee	Nil
Maintenance	Nil
Fuel	Nil

ELEVATION	LOCATION	EGER	STRONSAY
39ft 1mb	15nm NE by N of Kirkwall Airport N5909.48.W00238.48	KWL 108.60 041 14.2 — • — / • — — / • — • •	
PPR		SUM 117.35 231 59.8 • • • / • • — / — —	

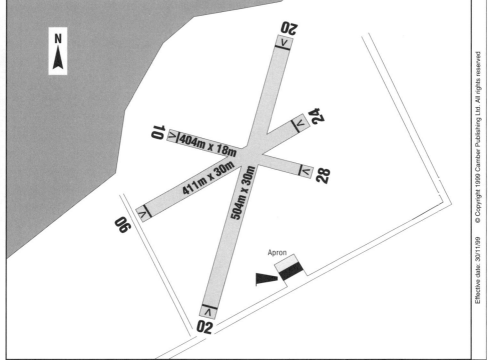

RWY	SURFACE	TORA	LDA	LIGHTING
02	Grass	504	464	Nil
20	Grass	484	464	Nil
06/24	Grass	411	391	Nil
10	Grass	360	340	Nil
28	Grass	384	340	Nil

Non-Radio		
APP	Kirkwall 118.30	

Remarks
Licensed AD (day use only). Visiting ACFT accepted at pilot's own risk. Scheduled Air Services daily Monday to Saturday.

Warnings

Operator — Orkney Islands Council
Stronsay Aerodrome, Kirkwall, Orkney KW15 1Nᵛ
Tel: 01856 873535
Fax: 01856 876094

Restaurants — Woodlea Restaurant & Takeaway
(Wed & W/E's) **Tel:** 01857 616337

Taxis
Peace **Tel:** 01857 616335
Williamson **Tel:** 01857 616255
Car Hire
Peace **Tel:** 01857 616335

Weather Info — AirSc GWC

Operating Hrs	SR-SS
Circuits	
Landing fee	Nil
Maintenance Fuel	Nil Nil

ELEVATION	LOCATION				STRUBBY
47ft 1mb **PPR**	4nm SW of Mablethorpe N5318.28 E00010.20	GAM 112.80	092	40.5	— — • / • — / — —

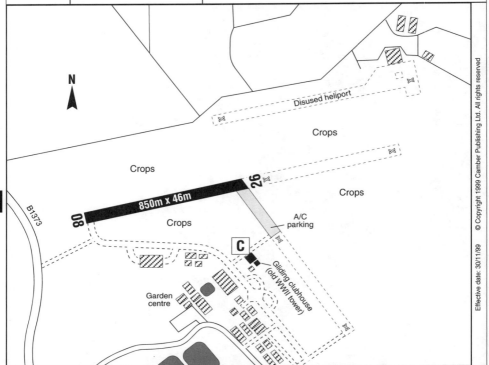

RWY	SURFACE	TORA	LDA	LIGHTING	Strubby Base
08/26	Tarmac/Concrete	850x46	U/L	Nil	A/G 130.10*

* Glider ops. Rarely manned

Remarks
PPR by telephone. Visiting powered ACFT welcome at pilots own risk. Gliders using Winch and Aerotow. Heliport in NE corner of WWII AD now disused.

Warnings
Grass section Rwy08/26 NOT suitable powered ACFT. Keep good lookout for gliders and cables. Radio rarely manned please make blind circuit calls. Small manouvering area marked, all other hard surfaces not available for ACFT use.

Operator	Lincolnshire Gliding Club Ltd
	Strubby Airfield, Alford, Lincolnshire LN13 1AA
	Tel: 01507 450294/450698
Restaurant	Café at nearby Garden Centre
Taxi/Car Hire	
Weather Info	AirN MWC

Operating Hours	SR-SS
Circuits	
Landing Fee	£5
Maintenance	Nil
Fuel	Nil

ELEVATION	LOCATION		STUBTON PARK
72ft 2mb **PPR**	3nm SE of Newark N5302.15 W00041.11	**GAM 112.80** 152 17 $--\bullet/\bullet-/--$	

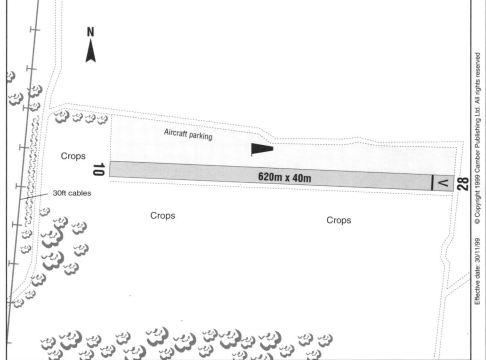

RWY	SURFACE	TORA	LDA	LIGHTING
10/28	Grass	620x40	U/L	Nil

Rwy10 Thr displaced by 180m

	Stubton
APP	**(Waddington) 127.35**
APP	**(Cranwell) 119.375**
A/G	**119.425***
*Not always manned	

Remarks
PPR by telephone. Visiting ACFT welcome at pilots own risk. AD close to boundaries of Waddington/Cranwell/Barkston Heath CMATZ. ACFT approaching from N contact Waddington, 127.35. ACFT approaching from S contact Cranwell, 119.375. Departing- contact appropriate ATC unit for departure direction. Noise: Avoid overflight of local habitation.

Warnings
Displaced Thr on Rwy10 to avoid 30ft power cables and hedge. Public track crosses Rwy28 Thr. Hougham Microlight airfield 1.5nm S. D305, Small arms danger area up to 1500ft, 2nm N. Gliding activity at Winthorpe, 4nm NW.

Operator	Mr J Jeckells, B+D Burtt Ltd
	Brandon, Grantham, Lincolnshire NG32 2AY
Tel:	01636 626223
Fax:	01636 626639

Restaurant	

Taxi/Car Hire	

Weather Info	AirCen MWC

Operating Hrs	SR-SS
Circuits	10 LH 28 RH 1000ft QFE
Landing Fee	On application
Maintenance **Fuel**	Nil Nil

ELEVATION	LOCATION		
58ft 2mb	4nm SE of Gainsborough N5322.87 W00041.12	GAM 112.80 062 11.1	– – • / • – / – –
PPR		OTR 113.90 233 28.2	– – – / – / • – •

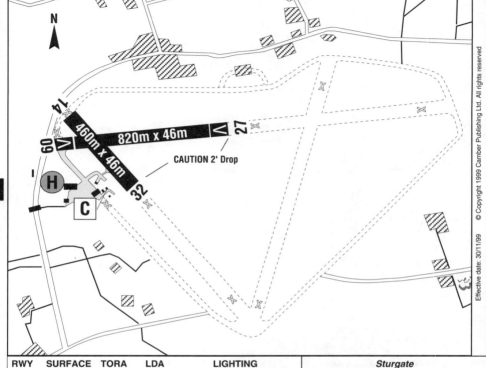

CAUTION 2' Drop

RWY	SURFACE	TORA	LDA	LIGHTING
09	Asphalt	805	705	Thr Rwy PAPI 3° RHS
27	Asphalt	790*	790	Thr Rwy AVASIS 3°
14/32	Asphalt	460	U/L	Nil

*An additional 30m is available during daylight Hrs

	Sturgate
APP	Waddington MATZ 127.35
A/G	130.30

Remarks
AD is not available at weekends for public transport passenger flights required to use a licensed AD. Rwy14/32 is not available for ACFT required to use a licensed AD. Non-radio ACFT should remain well clear of the MATZ. Flight within Sturgate AD Traffic Zone is limited to 1500ft aal unless prior arrangement has been made with Waddington. When within 10nm of Sturgate, pilots should use the MATZ altimeter setting. Visual aids to location: Ibn SG Green. At certain times during weekdays pilots will be subject to military ATC.

Warnings
The SE end of Rwy14/32 ends abruptly in a 2ft drop indicated by a white line and a row of crosses. A road crosses the approach short of the threshold of Rwy09.

Operator	Eastern-Air Executive Ltd, Sturgate Aerodrome, Gainsborough, Lincolnshire DN21 5PA Tel: 01427 838280 (Mon-Fri) Tel: 01427 838305 (W/E) Fax: 01427 838416 Telex: 56387 EEX G
Restaurants	Local pub meals available, ask for recommendations
Taxis/Car Hire	Arrangement can be made through Eastern Executive Ops on request by R/T
Weather Info	AirN MWC

Operating Hrs	Mon-Fri 0800-1600 (Summer) Mon-Fri 0900-1600 (Winter) and by arrangement
Circuits	Variable
Landing fee	Single £5.00 Twin £15.00
Maintenance Fuel	Eastern Air Tel: 01427 838280 AVGAS 100LL

ELEVATION	LOCATION	**EGPB**			**SUMBURGH**
19ft 1mb	17nm S of Lerwick N5952.73.W00117.73	SUM 117.35	On A/D	••• / •• – / – –	
		KWL 108.60	049 73.7	– • – / • – – / • – ••	

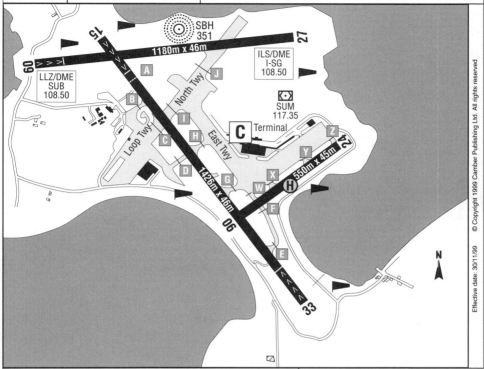

RWY	SURFACE	TORA	LDA	LIGHTING
09	Asphalt	1090	1083	Ap Thr Rwy PAPI 3° LHS
27	Asphalt	1123	1093	Ap Thr Rwy PAPI 3° LHS
15	Asphalt	1426	1239	Thr Rwy APAPI 4° LHS
33	Asphalt	1426	1239	Thr Rwy
06	Asphalt Heli Rwy		550x45m	Thr Rwy
24	Asphalt Heli Rwy		550x45m	Ap Thr Rwy

	Sumburgh
ATIS	125.85
APP	123.15
RAD	131.30 119.25 (if dir)
	121.50
TWR	118.25
FIRE	121.60
VOR/DME	SUM 117.35 on A/D
ILS/DME	I-SG 108.50 Rwy27
LLZ/DME	SUB 108.50 Rwy09
NDB	SBH 351 on A/D
	range 25nm

Remarks
SAR Bristow Helicopters (HMCG). A coastguard SK61 helicopter operates from Sumburgh & will be given priority over all other traffic when operating on SAR duties. These operations may take place 24Hrs using the callsign "RESCUE 117". Use of Rwys: Except helicopters, night landings are not permitted on Rwy15/33 except in an emergency. Night take-offs from Rwy15/33 are restricted to operators with procedures accepted by the CAA. The helicopter Rwy06/24 is not to be used by fixed wing ACFT. Pilots not using a resident handling agent must ensure that all relevant airport documentation is completed upon initial arrival. Such documentation may be obtained from the Airport security staff in the Wilsness terminal. Start-up must be requested on Twr frequency. Grass areas soft and unsafe only marked Twys to be used.

Warnings
During strong wind conditions turbulence may be expected on APP to, or climb out from, any Rwy. Bird colonies are active throughout the year. No GND signals except light signals. Pilots using the N taxiway are reminded to adhere to the marked centreline. A separate vehicle route is marked on the north side of part of this taxiway. Thr Rwy09/27 are positioned 98 and 90m respectively from concrete sea defences and the open sea.

Operating Hrs
Mon-Fri 0630-1930 Sat-Sun 0800-1630 (Summer)
Mon-Fri 0730-2030 Sat-Sun 0900-1730 (Winter)
and by arrangement

Circuits

| Landing fee | £10.40 inc.VAT ACFT under 3MT |
| | VFR cash/cheque on day |

Maintenance	Nil
Fuel	AVGAS 100LL AVTUR JET A1
Northair	**Tel: 01950 460367 Fax: 01950 460182**

Operator   HIAL Sumburgh Airport
Virkie, Shetland ZE3 9JP
Tel: 01950 460654 (HIAL)
Tel: 01950 460173 (ATC)
Tel: 01244 727199 (Sumburgh APP)
Fax: 01950 460218 (HIAL)
Fax: 01950 460718 (ATC)

| **Restaurant** | At Terminal |

GND floor Buffet 1st floor Self-Service Restaurant

Taxis	Available at Terminal
Car Hire	Europcar &Avis agents:
Bolts Car Hire	**Tel:** 01950 460777

| **Weather Info** | M T9 Fax 432 A VSc GWC |

CTA/CTR-Class D Airspace
Normal CTA/CTR Class D Airspace rules apply.
When Danger Area D901 is active ATC will not issue any
clearance that takes the ACFT through that part of the
CTR/CTA that overlaps the Danger Area.
Helicopter operating VFR, or at night SVFR, may be routed
via a VRP.

Helicopter Operations
Helicopter operations in support of N Sea oil rigs may take
place outside the published Hrs of AD availability. Helicopters
are treated as fixed wing traffic and should normally GND taxi,
unless skid equipped, between the Rwys and parking areas.
In adverse weather conditions and during snow-clearing
operations, hover taxiing of wheeled helicopters may be
permitted by ATC. 'Rotors running' refuelling of helicopters
with passengers on board is only permitted during
exceptionally severe wind conditions and with the permission
of ATC. Helicopter parking spots 1-9 are designated quick
turnround spots and should not be occupied for more than 15
minutes. Long term parking spots 10-19.

Fixed wing parking
a) stands 20,21 and 22; for ACFT requiring customs
clearance.
b) stands 22, 23; for schedule services.
c) stands 25-28; fast turnround, oil related ACFT on a first
come, first served basis
d) stands 29 and 30; all other fixed-wing ACFT.

Visual Reference Points (VRPs)

VRP	VOR/DME
Bodam	SUM 019/2.4nm
N5955.10 W00116.10	
Mousa	SUM 034/8.3nm
N6000.00 W00109.60	

ELEVATION	LOCATION					SUTTON MEADOWS
8ft 0mb	5nm W of Ely N.5223.12.E00003.84	BKY 116.25	002	24	– • • / – • – / – • – –	
		DTY 116.40	077	45	– • • / – / – • – –	
PPR						

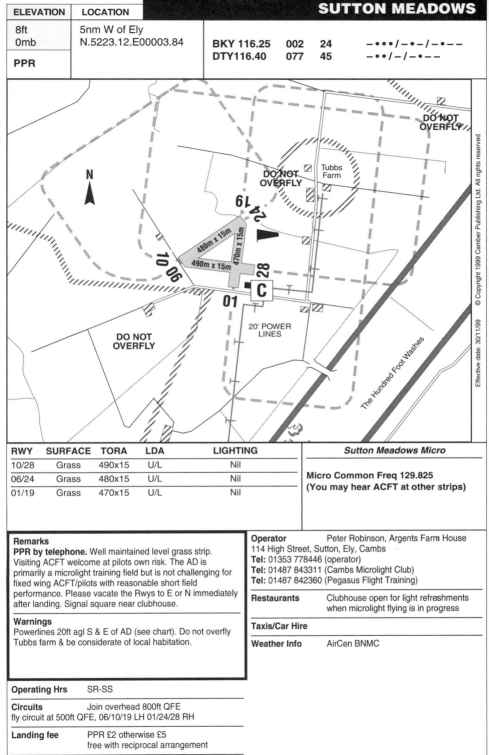

RWY	SURFACE	TORA	LDA	LIGHTING
10/28	Grass	490x15	U/L	Nil
06/24	Grass	480x15	U/L	Nil
01/19	Grass	470x15	U/L	Nil

Sutton Meadows Micro

Micro Common Freq 129.825
(You may hear ACFT at other strips)

Remarks

PPR by telephone. Well maintained level grass strip. Visiting ACFT welcome at pilots own risk. The AD is primarily a microlight training field but is not challenging for fixed wing ACFT/pilots with reasonable short field performance. Please vacate the Rwys to E or N immediately after landing. Signal square near clubhouse.

Warnings

Powerlines 20ft agl S & E of AD (see chart). Do not overfly Tubbs farm & be considerate of local habitation.

Operator	Peter Robinson, Argents Farm House
114 High Street, Sutton, Ely, Cambs	
Tel: 01353 778446 (operator)	
Tel: 01487 843311 (Cambs Microlight Club)	
Tel: 01487 842360 (Pegasus Flight Training)	
Restaurants	Clubhouse open for light refreshments when microlight flying is in progress
Taxis/Car Hire	
Weather Info	AirCen BNMC

Operating Hrs	SR-SS
Circuits	Join overhead 800ft QFE
fly circuit at 500ft QFE, 06/10/19 LH 01/24/28 RH	
Landing fee	PPR £2 otherwise £5 free with reciprocal arrangement
Maintenance	Nil
Fuel	MOGAS limited quantities by arrangement

ELEVATION	LOCATION	**EGFH**					**SWANSEA**

299ft 10mb	5nm WSW of Swansea N5136.32.W00404.07 **Diversion AD**	**BCN 117.45**	**265**	**30.5**	– • • • / – • – • / – •
		STU 113.10	**129**	**43.0**	• • • / – / • • –

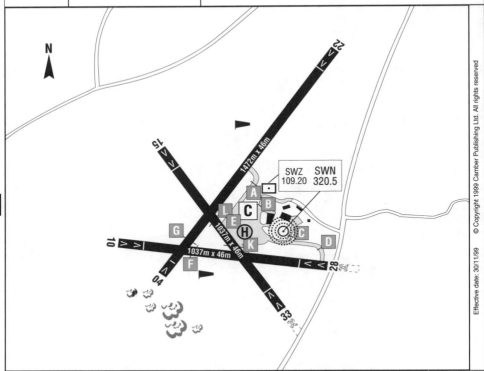

RWY	SURFACE	TORA	LDA	LIGHTING
04	Concrete	1351	1351	Ap Thr Rwy APAPI 3° LHS
22	Concrete	1352	1261	Ap Thr Rwy APAPI 3.25° LHS
10*	Asphalt	896	896	Nil
28*	Asphalt	940	827	Nil
15*	Asphalt	904	904	Thr Rwy
33*	Asphalt	909	849	Thr Rwy

*not available to ACFT exceeding 5700kgs MTWA except in emergency

Swansea

APP/TWR*/	
VDF*	119.70
A/G	119.70
* Operating Hrs by arrangement	
NDB	SWN 320.5 on A/D range 15nm
DME	SWZ 109.20 Zero range at Thr 04 & 22

Remarks
Non-radio ACFT not accepted. Light ACFT experiencing radio failure in VMC are to carry out the standard overhead join for the Rwy in use as notified by either previous departure clearance or joining instructions passed by ATC. Rwy15/33 is not available for ACFT required to use a licensed AD.

Warnings
Unserviceable portions of the Rwys short of THrs to Rwy10 & 28 are marked by white crosses. A road crosses near the thresholds of Rwy28 & 33 and is marked by orange triangular markers outside the AD and orange/white circular markers on the AD side. Not all taxiways are usable. Deviation from marked manoeuvring area can be hazardous.

Operating Hrs   0800-1700 (Summer) 0900-1700 (Winter)
Frequently open outside these Hrs – check by telephone

Circuits

Landing fee   Private singles £5
Free with fuel uplift of 20ltrs or more

Maintenance
Swansea Aviation   **Tel:** 01792 204063
Fuel   AVGAS 100LL AVTUR JET A1

Operator   Swansea Aviation Ltd
Swansea Aerodrome, Fairwood Common, Swansea SA2 7JU
Tel: 01792 204063 (Airport) **Tel:** 01792 207550 (ATC)
Fax: 01792 297923

Restaurants
Licensed Restaurant on A/D during airport Hrs

Taxis
Airport Taxis   **Tel:** 01792 298703
Car Hire
Europcar   **Tel:** 01792 650526
Hertz   **Tel:** 01792 586117

Weather Info   M T9 Fax 434 BNMC

ELEVATION	LOCATION		**SWANTON MORLEY**		
155ft 5mb PPR	13nm WNW of Norwich N5243.72.E00057.65	**CLN 114.55**	**357**	**53.2**	— • — • / • — • • / — •

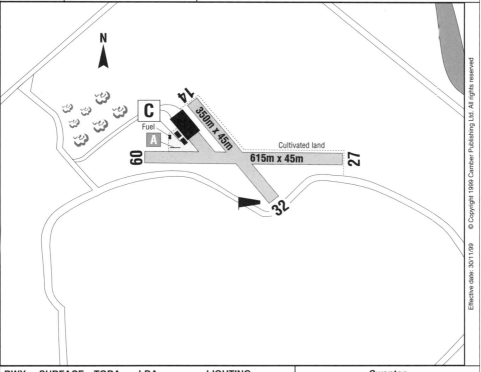

RWY	SURFACE	TORA	LDA	LIGHTING
09/27	Grass	615x45	U/L	Nil
14/32	Grass	350x45	U/L	Nil

	Swanton
APP	**Marham MATZ 124.15**
A/G	**123.50**

Remarks
On APP call RAF Marham initially. If no reply on Swanton frequency, transmit intentions blind.

Warnings
Avoid overflying neighbouring villages particularly the chicken farm 1nm N of AD. Military helicopters may operate from the barracks on the old RAF technical site.

Maintenance
Eastern Stearman **Tel:** 01362 638193
Roger Burrows **Tel:** 01362 638033 (AD)
Tel: 01953 882276 (home)
(Wood & Fabric ACFT repa r & rebuilds)
Fuel AVGAS 100LL

Operator Mr JK Avis
Tel: 01362 638193
Fax: 01362 638113
Tel: 01362 638088 (Tyrell Aviation PPL Hire)

Restaurants Visitors centre with cafeteria & shop

Taxis/Car Hire Arranged at AD

Weather Info AirS BNMC

Operating Hrs Available on request

Circuits To S 800ft QFE

Landing fee £5.00 no charge with fuel uplift

ELEVATION	LOCATION	**EGBM**				**TATENHILL**

ELEVATION	LOCATION				
450ft 15mb	4nm W of Burton-on-Trent N5248.85 W00145.67	TNT 115.70	199	14.8	– / – • / –
PPR	**Diversion AD**	HON 113.65	358	27.6	• • • • / – – – / – •

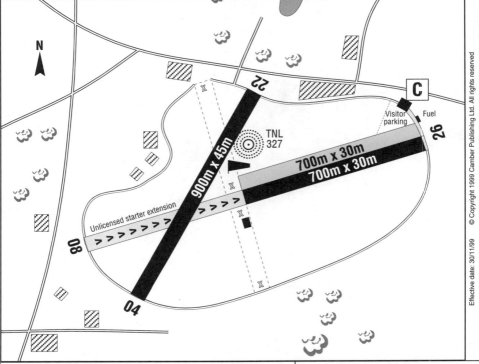

RWY	SURFACE	TORA	LDA	LIGHTING
08/26	Asphalt	700	700	by special arrangement
08/26	Grass	700x30	U/L	Nil
04/22	Asphalt	900x46	U/L	Nil

U/L 500m starter ext Rwy08

	Tatenhill
APP	E Mids 119.65
A/G	124.075
NDB	TNL 327 Range 10nm

Remarks
PPR non-radio ACFT not accepted. Pilots should note the proximity of the Birmingham and E Midlands CTA and are advised to call Birmingham or E Midlands for traffic information before calling Tatenhill. Join circuits overhead. Night flying by arrangement.

Warnings
Fences adjacent to some Rwys. Pilots are advised to keep a good lookout for military traffic. Gliding may take place at Cross Hayes (N5247.40 W00149.14)

Operator	Tatenhill Aviation, Tatenhill Airfield Newborough Road, Needwood Burton-on-Trent Staffs DE13 9PD **Tel:** 01283 575283 **Fax:** 01283 575650
Restaurants	Tea & coffee available
Taxis/Car Hire	By arrangement
Weather Info	AirCen MWC

Operating Hrs	0800-1600 (Summer) + 1Hr Winter
Circuits	08/22/26 LH 04 RH 1000ft QFE
Landing fee	Single £5.00 Twin £10.00

Maintenance
Tatenhill Aviation **Tel:** 01283 575283
Fuel AVGAS 100LL

ELEVATION	LOCATION	**EGNV**		**TEESSIDE**
120ft 4mb	4.7nm SE of Darlington N5430.55 W00125.76	**NEW 114.25** **POL 112.10**	169 33.2 033 51.7	– • / • / • – – • – – • / – – – / • – • •

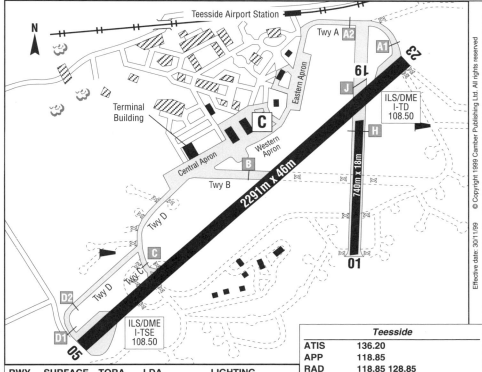

RWY	SURFACE	TORA	LDA	LIGHTING
05/23	Asphalt	2291	2291	Ap Thr Rwy PAPI 3° LHS
01/19*	Asphalt	740	740	Nil

*01/09 only available daytime to locally based ACFT up to 5700kg MTOW, withdrawn in poor visibility

Teesside	
ATIS	136.20
APP	118.85
RAD	118.85 128.85
VDF	118.85 119.80 128.85
TWR	119.80
ILS/DME	I-TD 108.50 Rwy23
ILS/DME	I-TSE 108.50 Rwy05
NDB*	TD 347.5 range 25nm
	*TD 233/3.9 to Thr 23

Remarks

Not available to non-radio ACFT. Class D Airspace. Third Party Insurance Cover of at least £500,000 required. Aerobatics and other unusual flight manoeuvres are prohibited within the ATZ except with prior written permission from the Airport Managing Director. Twy10/28 is available for GND movement only. Access to Rwy05/23 via Holding Points A, D, E & F only. Hold E is 280m from Rwy05 Thr. Training flights require prior arrangement with the Managing Director. A helicopter training area for use by locally based helicopters is located in the S W corner of the AD. Unless otherwise instructed by ATC, ACFT using the ILS in IMC or VMC shall not descend below 1800ft aal before intercepting the glidepath, nor thereafter fly below it. ACFT approaching without assistance from RADAR or ILS must not fly lower than the ILS glidepath or RADAR APP procedure. Booking-out details will not be accepted on RTF.

Warning

At both ends of Rwy05/23 its width is twice that of the associated edge lights. Rwy centreline lighting is not installed, so take care to line up correctly, especially at night or in poor visibility. Deer hazard, please report sightings to ATC.

Circuits	Variable Light ACFT 1000ft QFE Large ACFT minimum 1500ft QFE
Landing fee	£13.10 per metric tonne +VAT
	Singles up to 2MT 25% discount if paid at the time
Maintenance	Available (minor) Teesside General Aviation **Tel:** 01325 333115
Fuel	AVGAS 100LL AVTUR JET A1
Operator	Teesside Int Airport Ltd Darlington, Co. Durham DL2 1LU **Tel:** 01325 332811 **Fax:** 01325 332810 **Telex:** 587635
Restaurant	Restaurant and buffet at Terminal
St George Hotel	**Tel:** 01325 332631 (on AD)

Taxis
Teesside Airport Taxis **Tel:** 01325 332177
Buses available at Terminal to Darlington

Car Hire
Avis	**Tel:** 01325 332091
Hertz	**Tel:** 01325 332600
Europcar	**Tel:** 01325 333329

Weather Info
M T9 Fax 436 VN MWC

Operating Hrs   H24 PPR 2100-0500

Visual Reference Points (VRPs)

VRP	VOR/NDB	VOR/DME
Hartlepool N5441.00 W00112.83	NEW R148°/TD 036°M	NEW 148°/27nm
Motorway Jctn A1(M)&A66(M) N5430.00 W00137.60	NEW R182°/TD 257°M	NEW 182°/32nm
Nallerton N5420.33 W00125.92		NEW 174°/43nm
Redcar Racecourse N5436.43 W00103.85	NEW R146°/TD 079°M	NEW 146°/34nm
Sedgefield Racecourse N5438.75 W00128.10		NEW 168°/25nm
Stokesley N5428.18 W00111.68		NEW 159°/38nm

T

ELEVATION	LOCATION	**EGCP**			**THORNE (Doncaster)**	
10ft 0mb	10nm WNW of Scunthorpe N5337.20 W00055.41	GAM 112.80	008	20.5	– – • / • – / – –	
PPR		OTR 113.90	265	30	– – – / – / • – •	

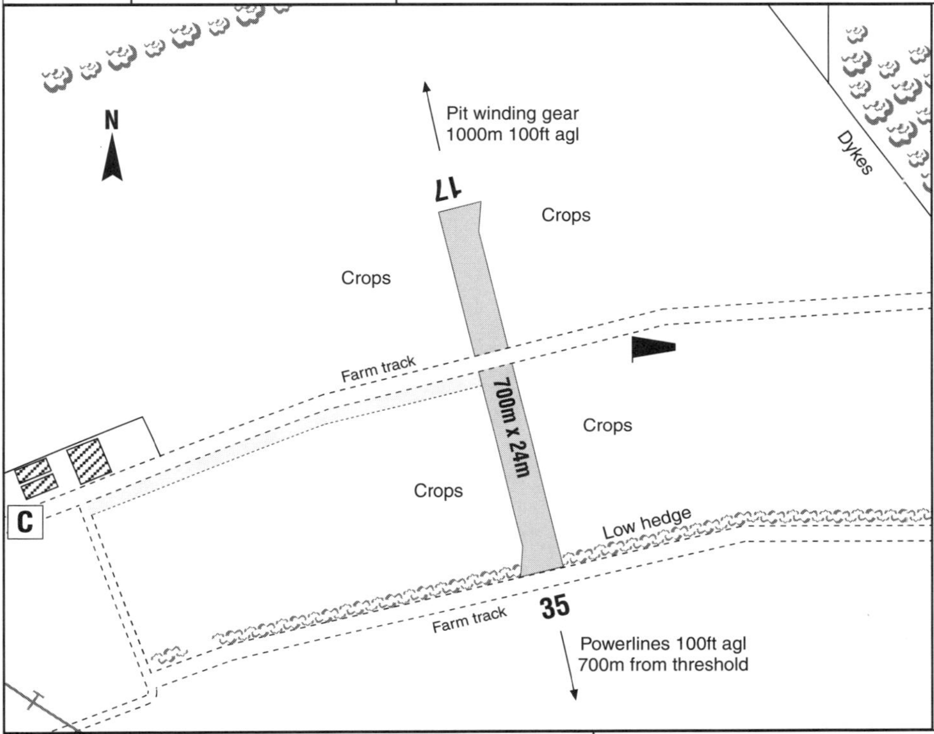

N

Pit winding gear 1000m 100ft agl

17

Crops

Crops

Dykes

700m x 24m

Farm track

Crops

Crops

Crops

Low hedge

Farm track

35

C

Powerlines 100ft agl 700m from threshold

T

RWY	SURFACE	TORA	LDA	LIGHTING		*Non Radio*
17/35	Grass	700x24	U/L	Nil		LARS (Waddington) 127.35

Remarks
PPR by telephone. No microlights. Business use only. Aid to location: Pit head winding gear 1000m from Thr of Rwy17. Good flat strip, farm track crosses Rwy at midpoint but level with surface, does not constitute a hazard. Windsock displayed to E of AD.

Warnings
AD be subject to waterlogging in winter months. National Grid powerlines/pylons to S. Keep good lookout for low flying military ACFT in local area. Noise. Circuits flown to E to avoid overflight of local habitation.

Operator	Paul Burtwistle, Dairy Farm, Thorne Doncaster, South Yorkshire **Tel**: 01405 812260 **Tel**: 07836 693943 (mobile)
Restaurant	
Taxi/Car Hire	
Weather Info	AirN MCW

Operating Hrs	SR-SS
Circuits	Standard overhead join circuits to E 1000ft QFE
Landing Fee	Advised with PPR
Maintenance Fuel	Nil Nil

ELEVATION	LOCATION	EGHO				THRUXTON
330ft 11mb	4.5nm W of Andover N5112.62 W00135.90	SAM 113.35	333	18.1		•••/•–/––
PPR		CPT 114.35	225	21.1		–•–•/•–––•/–

RWY	SURFACE	TORA	LDA	LIGHTING
07*	Asphalt	770	760	Thr Rwy APAPI 4° LHS
25	Asphalt	770	770	Thr Rwy APAPI 4° LHS
13/31	Grass	750	750	Nil

* Rwy07 U/L starter extension 220m

	Thruxton
APP	Boscombe MATZ 126.70
A/G	130.45

Remarks

Inbound ACFT should call Boscombe Down before entering the CMATZ, controllers will ensure that the ACFT is level at 1500ft Regional QNH before calling Thruxton. Outbound Dept ACFT should call Boscombe Down before climbing through 800ft Thruxton QFE or climb once clear of the CMATZ. W Deps should obtain onward clearance from Boscombe Down before leaving Thruxton ATZ. Non-radio ACFT may route to/from Thruxton via Chilbolton at 1000ft agl on a track of 310°/130° M. When Rwy07/25 is in use landing ACFT should clear the Rwy to the S on to the Twy when safe. Visual aid to location: Ibn Green TX.

Warnings

APP Thruxton avoid Danger Areas D123, D125, D125A, D126 and D127. Caution is also necessary due to the proximity of Middle Wallop AD 4nm S of Thruxton where there is intensive flying training in fixed and rotary wing ACFT. An instrument APP service operates within 070° to 080° up to 8nm from Middle Wallop and may be used for practice in VMC conditions. The perimeter track is permanently obstructed and is not available for ACFT. Power cables cross final APP Rwy25 200m from Thr.

Operating Hrs & by arrangement	0800-1600 (Summer) + 1Hr Winter
Circuits	07/31 LH 13/25 RH 800ft QFE
Landing Fee	Single £8.00 Twin £15.00 inc VAT discount for fuel uplift of 65ltrs or more

Maintenance
Earthline **Tel:**01264 771327
Fuel AVGAS 100LL AVTUR JET A1

Operator Western Air Training Ltd
Thruxton Aerodrome, Andover, Hampshire SP11 8PW
Tel: 01264 772352/772171
Fax: 01264 773913

Restaurants
Refreshments and Club facilities available at the AD

Taxis	**Tel:** 01264 353536
Car Hire	
Europcar	**Tel:** 01264 355137
National	**Tel:** 01264 338181
Weather Info	AirSW BNMC

© Copyright 1999 Camber Publishing Ltd. All rights reserved
Effective date: 30/11/99

ELEVATION	LOCATION				
25ft 0mb	5nm SW of Basildon N5132.17 E00022.00				
		LAM 115.60	133	10.5	• — • • / • — / — —
PPR		BIG 115.10	050	17.5	— • • • / • • / — — •

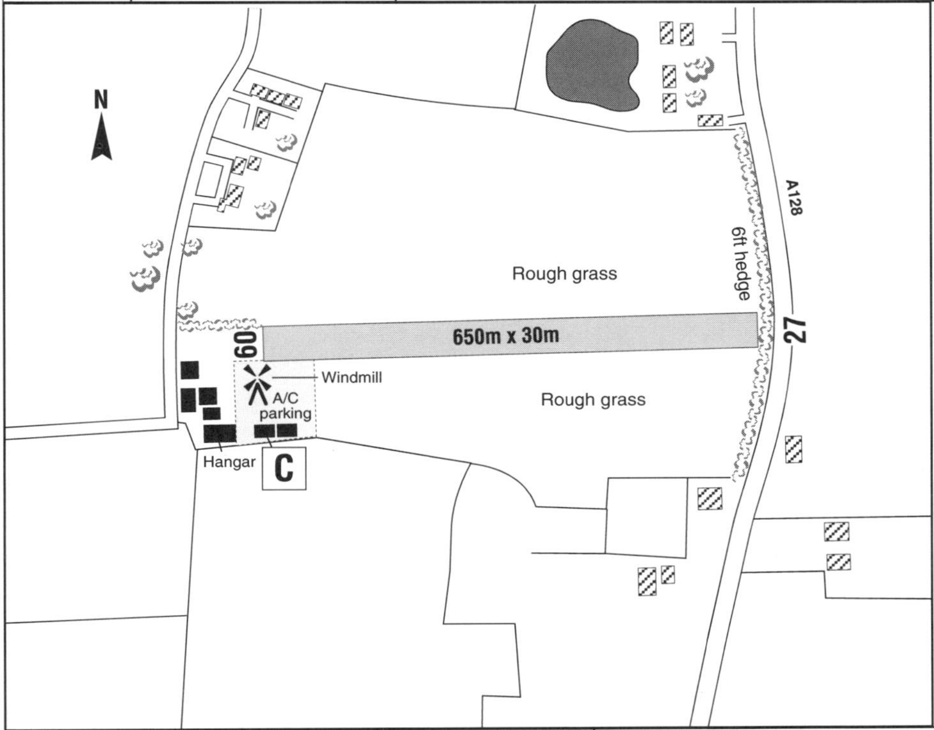

THURROCK

N

A128

6ft hedge

Rough grass

650m x 30m

09

27

← Windmill

A/C parking

Rough grass

Hangar

C

T

RWY	SURFACE	TORA	LDA	LIGHTING
09/27	Grass	650x30	U/L	Nil

Rwy is part of large field which allows run-off to S &N of strip

Non-Radio

APP   (Thames Radar) 132.7

Remarks
PPR by telephone. Visitors welcome at pilots own risk. Light ACFT parked on the AD aids location. Noise:Avoid overflight of local habitation. No training

Warnings
Caution, high sided vehicles on A128 crosses 27 Thr. There is a 6ft hedge between road and Thr. Trees and hedge adjacent 09 Thr.

Operator   Thurrock Leisure, Thurrock Airfield
Tilbury Rd, Orsett Essex
Tel: 01375 891165

Restaurant

Taxis
Abbey Cars   **Tel:** 01277 812812
Car Hire

Weather Info   AirSE BNMC

Operating Hrs	SR-SS
Circuits	LH 1000ft QFE. No training
Landing Fee	Nil
Maintenance **Fuel**	Hangarage and parking by arrangement AVGAS 100LL

ELEVATION	LOCATION				TIBENHAM (Priory Farm)

ELEVATION	LOCATION
186ft 6mb	1nm W of Tibenham AD N5227.00 E00107.00
PPR	

BKY 116.25	058	47.5	− • • • / − • − / − • − −
CLN 114.55	001	36	− • − • / • − • • / − •

Effective date: 30/11/99

N

19

Ditch

V

Crops

Ditch

Crops

660m x 30m

Λ

01

Aircraft parking

Priory Farm

To Tibbenham village

T

RWY	SURFACE	TORA	LDA	LIGHTING
01/19	Grass	650	500	Nil

	Non-radio
LARS	Lakenheath 128.90 Priory Microlight 129.825 Make blind calls

Remarks
PPR by telephone. U/L AD. Visiting ACFT welcome at own risk. Hangarage for visitors available by prior arrangement. Annual fly-in please check aviation press for details.

Warnings
Keep a good lookout for glider activity from Tibenham AD 1nm to E. APP to Rwy01 is over farm buildings with group of trees to left of Thr. A low hedge extends across Rwy01 Thr from right. Use Rwy19 for landing when conditions permit. A ditch runs along full length of Rwy19 crossing Thr. Crops grow up to edge of strip on E side. **Noise:** Do not overfly Tibenham village NNE of AD.

Operator	Bob Sage, Priory Farm, Tibenham Norfolk, Norwich NR1 6NY **Tel/Fax:** 01379 677334
Restaurants	By arrangement
Taxis Diss **Car Hire**	**Tel:** 01362 696161 Nil
Weather Info	AirS BNMC

Operating Hrs	1000-2000 (local)
Circuits	Overhead joins 01 LH 19 RH at 500ft QFE
Landing fee	Nil
Maintenance Fuel	Nil AVGAS 100LL by arrangement

ELEVATION	LOCATION				
301ft 10mb	2nm SE of Whitchurch N5255.93 W00238.83	WAL 114.10	154	32.5	• – – / • – / • – • •
PPR		MCT 113.55	212	29.5	– – / – • – • / –
		SWB 116.8	005	8.5	• • • / • – – / – • • •

N

15

Manure heaps

792m x 30m

Parachute drop zone

Entrance

Parking

C

A41

33

RWY	SURFACE	TORA	LDA	LIGHTING
15/33	Tarmac	792x30	U/L	Nil

	Tilstock
LARS	Shawbury 120.775
A/G	122.075

Remarks
PPR by telephone, closed Sunday. Intensive parachute activity up to FL150. Visiting light ACFT welcome at owner's risk. The AD is situated under the N portion of Shawbury MATZ & the following procedures apply: **Arrivals** contact Shawbury 120.775 when 20nm from Tilstock. **Departures** ring Shawbury ATC 01939 250351 Ext 7232, at least 10 mins before departure stating "Tilstock departure" with flight details. Then: **1** Maintain VMC & climb not above 1000ft Tilstock QFE until in contact Shawbury or well clear extended centreline Shawbury Rwy18/36. **2** After initial (or if no) contact turn heading 050°M, remain VMC continue climb. After Shawbury contact turn onto agreed track, otherwise turn onto desired track after passing AUDLEM 050/6.5nm Tilstock.
3 W/E PH & evenings when Shawbury limited activity/LARS unavailable, call Shawbury TWR 120.775 when airborne for info on Shawbury & Ternhill activity.

Warnings
No overhead joins or circuits. Narrow Twy between parking area & Rwy with no passing places. AD sometimes used for other activities that makes PPR essential. Manure piles up to 15ft high are often present on the N end of Rwy.

Operating Hrs	Available on request
Circuits	Join downwind at 1000ft QFE
Landing fee	£10 cash
Maintenance	Nil
Fuel	AVGAS 100LL available by prior arrangement
Operator	The Parachute Centre Tilstock Aerodrome, Whitchurch, Shropshire SY13 2HA **Tel:** 01948 841111 (Parachute Centre) **Tel:** 01948 663239 (Landowner Mr RT Matson for PPR)
Restaurants	Snacks tea & coffee available at AD
Taxis Halls	**Tel:** 01948 662222
Car Hire	Nil
Weather Info	AirCen MWC

ELEVATION	LOCATION	**EGPU**		**TIRE**
38ft 1mb	2.5nm NNE of Balemartin N5629.93 W00652.20	**TIR 117.70**	**On AD**	– / • • / • – •
PPR		**BEN 114.40**	**173 60.8**	– • • • / • / – •

17 600m x 18m
11
35 820m x 19m
23
29 1472 x 30m
05
93'amsl
(H)
100' amsl
TIR 117.70

RWY	SURFACE	TORA	LDA	LIGHTING
05	Asphalt	1402	1402	Thr Rwy APAPI 3° LHS
23	Asphalt	1402	1350	Thr Rwy APAPI 3° LHS
11/29	Asphalt	820	820	Nil
17/35	Asphalt	600	600	Nil

	Tiree
FIS	**Scottish 127.275**
AFIS	**122.70**
VOR/DME	**TIR 117.70 on AD**

Remarks
Visual aid to location: Abn White flashing. Grass areas soft and unsafe use marked Twys only

Warnings
All Twys are closed except between the control TWR and the Thr of Rwy11. Unserviceable sections of Rwy are fenced off and marked with crosses. No GND signals except light signals. The useable portion of Rwy17/35 is marked with white sidelines.

Operator	HIAL Tiree Aerodrome Isle of Tiree, Argyll PA77 6UW **Tel:** 018792 20456 **Fax:** 018792 20714
Restaurants Lodge Hotel	**Tel:** 018792 20684 (Bar lunches)
Taxis J Kennedy **Car Hire** Tiree Motor Co A MacLennan Mtrs	**Tel:** 018792 20419 **Tel:** 018792 20469 **Tel:** 018792 20555
Weather Info	M T9 Fax 438 GWC

Operating Hrs   Mon-Fri 1100-1500 Sat 1030-1200
and by arrangement.
Times are subject to variation due to tides at Barra

Circuits

Landing fee   £10.65 inc.VAT under 3MT
VFR cash/cheque

Maintenance   Nil
Fuel   Nil

ELEVATION	LOCATION				TOP FARM
200ft 6mb	7nm NW of Royston N5207.45 W00007.20 **Diversion AD**	BPK 117.50 BKY 116.25	002 323	22.5 10.5	– • • • / • – – • / – • – – • • • / – • – / – • – –
PPR					

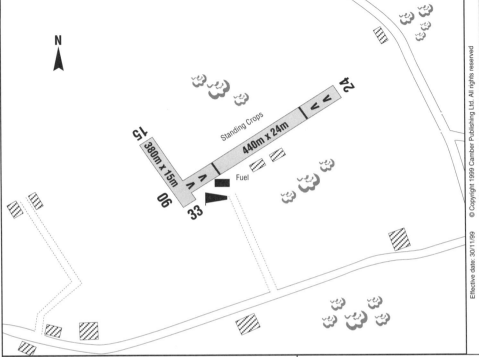

Standing Crops
440m x 24m
380m x 15m
Fuel

N

Effective date: 30/11/99

T

RWY	SURFACE	TORA	LDA	LIGHTING		Non-radio
06/24*	Grass	900x24	U/L	Nil		
15/33	Grass	380x15	U/L	Nil		

Rwy06/24 has 230m overruns at either end.
Rwy15/33 only for use in strong winds Rwy15 has marked upslope

Remarks
PPR by telephone. Visitors welcome at owners own risk. Excellently prepared strip, Rwy06/24 level and smooth. Please avoid overflying local habitation. Do not overfly house on 1nm final for Rwy06. Windsock displayed on S side of Rwy06/24 by hangars. No take-offs after 1400 local on Sundays.

Warnings
There is intense gliding activity at Gransden Lodge 2.5nm to N. The Little Gransden ATZ boundary is 1nm to the N and NW of Top Farm. Sandy TV mast (972ft amsl) is 3nm WNW.

Operator	David Morris, Barmoor House
	Top Farm, Croydon, Royston, Herts SG8 0EQ
	Tel: 01767 631377
	Mobile: 0411 197738

Restaurants
Randall's	**Tel:** 01223 207229 (B&B)
Queen Adelaide	**Tel:** 01223 208278

Taxis
Mayalls	**Tel:** 01763 243225
Car Hire	

Weather Info — AirCen BNMC

Operating Hrs	Available on request No take-offs after 1400hrs Sundays
Circuits	06 RH 24 LH 1100ft QFE
Landing fee	£5.00

Maintenance
Barmoor Aviation	**Tel:** 01767 631377
Fuel	AVGAS 100LL

ELEVATION	LOCATION	**EGXZ**					**TOPCLIFFE**
92ft 3mb	2.5nm SW of Thirsk N5412.33 W00122.93		POL 112.10	047	37.8	• – – •/ – – –/ • – • •	
PPR **MILITARY**			NEW 114.25	173	51.2	– • / • / • – –	

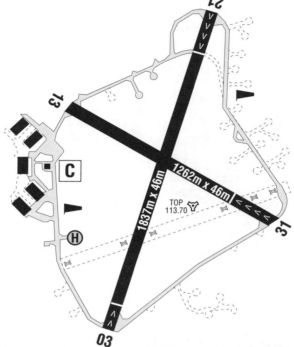

RWY	SURFACE	TORA	LDA	LIGHTING
03	Asphalt	1814	1434	Ap Thr Rwy PAPI 3°
21	Asphalt	1814	1544	Ap Thr Rwy PAPI 3°
13	Asphalt	1242	1242	Thr Rwy PAPI 3°
31	Asphalt	1242	946	Thr Rwy PAPI 3°

	Topcliffe
MATZ	
/LARS	**Leeming 127.75**
APP	**125.00 122.10**
TWR	**122.10**
A/G	**129.90***
	* see Warnings
TACAN	**TOP 113.70 on AD**

Remarks
PPR 24 Hrs notice required. Satellite to Linton-on-Ouse.
IBn TP Red

Warnings
Free-fall parachuting up to FL150 W/E and PH contact A/G
frequency (129.9).

Operator	RAF Topcliffe **Tel:** 01748 875376 (Ops) **Tel:** 01748 875388 (ATC) **Tel:** 01347 848261 Ext.7491 (PPR)
Restaurants	
Taxis/Car Hire	
Weather Info	AirN MWC

Operating Hrs Linton-on-Ouse	0900-1615 Mon-Fri & as required **Tel:** 01347 848261 Ext.7491
Circuits	13/31 RH 03/21 LH
Landing fee	£7.56 +VAT per 500kgs & £8.50 insurance
Maintenance **Fuel**	Nil AVTUR Jet A1

ELEVATION	LOCATION	**EGHY**	**TRURO**
400ft 13mb	3nm WNW of Truro N5016.72 W00508.53 **Diversion AD**	**LND 114.20** 072 20.6	• — • • / — • / — • •
PPR			

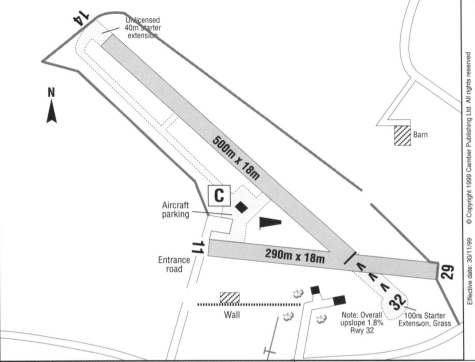

RWY	SURFACE	TORA	LDA	LIGHTING
14/32*	Grass	500x18	U/L	Nil
11/29	Grass	280x18	U/L	Nil

Secondary Rwy only usable after consultation with AD owner
*A 100m starter extension is available prior to Rwy32 Thr (upslope 5.5%)

	Truro
APP	Culdrose 134.05
APP	St Mawgan 126.50
A/G	129.80 by arrangement

Remarks
PPR by telephone. Inbound and outbound ACFT to and from the NE are requested to call St Mawgan on 126.50. AD situated below Culdrose AAIA for info contact Culdrose (134.05).

Warnings
The AD is located under the RNAS Culdrose AIAA. Rwy32 has an upslope of 1.8%. Climb straight ahead for 0.75nm after take-off before turning on-route. Do not deviate to the left. Windshear likely Rwy32 with wind from S.

Operator	Philip Irish Truro Aerodrome Truro Cornwall TR4 9EX **Tel:** 01872 560488
Restaurants	AD owner will advise
Taxis City Taxis	**Tel:** 01872 273053 **Freephone:** 0800 318708
Car Hire Hertz Car Rental	**Tel:** 01872 223638 **Tel:** 01872 676797
Weather Info	AirSW BNMC

Operating Hrs
0800-1900 or SS whichever earliest (Summer) + 1Hr Winter

Circuits	LH 800ft QFE
Landing fee	Single £10.00 Twin £20.00 + VAT (discounts for homebuilt ACFT)
Maintenance Fuel	Corsair **Tel:** 01872 561161 AVGAS 100LL W80 W100

ELEVATION	LOCATION	**EGBT**			**TURWESTON**

ELEVATION	LOCATION				
448ft 15mb	2nm E of Brackley N5202.42 W00105.65 **Diversion AD**	DTY 116.40	182	8.4	– •• / – / – • – –
PPR		BNN 113.75	317	27.7	– ••• / – • / – •

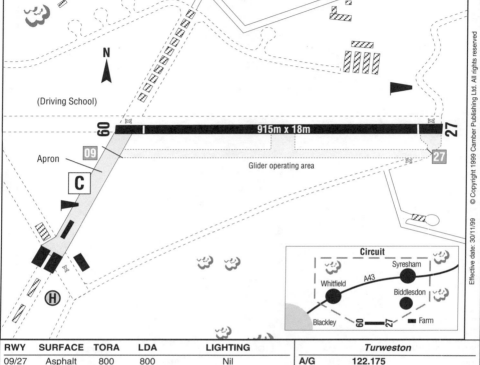

RWY	SURFACE	TORA	LDA	LIGHTING		Turweston
09/27	Asphalt	800	800	Nil	A/G	122.175

Remarks

PPR by telephone to all users, not all ACFT types accepted. This is essential due to restrictions in the number and type of movements. AD is not available for use at night by flights required to use a licensed AD. Noise abatement. Dep Rwy27: after take-off turn right 20° to climb between Brackley and Whitfield. Dep Rwy09: after take-off turn left 20° to avoid over-flying farmhouse on extended centreline. Avoid over-flying local habitation and maintain circuit position on downwind legs to the N of A43. Rwy27: FLY OFFSET final track 250° to Thr. Tailwheel ACFT may with prior permission land & take-off on the grass Twy. Winch launched gliding W/E and PH. Glider circuit to S of AD. No deadside.

Warnings

Radio Masts 232° aal/680ft amsl 220°/3.5nm. Power cables run NW/SE 1nm W of AD. Not all Twys are available for use. Deviation from the marked manoeuvring area can be hazardous. Caution EG D129 Weston on the Green Active H24.

Operating Hrs   Mon-Fri 0700-1900 Sat 0800-1700
Sun & PH 0900-1700 (Summer)
Mon-Fri 0800-2000 or SS Sat 0900-1800 or SS
Sun & PH 1000-1800 or SS (Winter)

Circuits   To the N, 09LH, 27RH, 1000ft QFE

Landing Fee   Single £6.00 Twin £9.00
Touch and goes half price Free with fuel uplift of +60ltrs

Maintenance   Available
Fuel   AVGAS 100LL

Operator   Turweston Flight Centre Ltd
Turweston Aerodrome, Brackley, Northants NN13 5YD
Tel: 01280 701167 (Ops) **Fax:** 01280 704647
Tel: 0121 782 9704 (Customs)

Restaurants/accomodation
Arlene's Cafe on AD (Closed Monday)
Mrs Owen   **Tel:** 01280 704843
Mrs Harris   **Tel:** 01869 811365

Taxis
TJ Cabs   **Tel:** 01280 704330
Premier Cabs   **Tel:** 01280 700608
Car Hire
Target will pick up at AD contact ATC for details

Weather Info   AirCen BNMC

ELEVATION	LOCATION	EGPW				UNST

ELEVATION	LOCATION				
62ft 2mb	On the Isle of Unst (Shetland Islands) N6044.83.W00051.23	SUM 117.35	021	53.6	••• / •• – / – –
PPR					

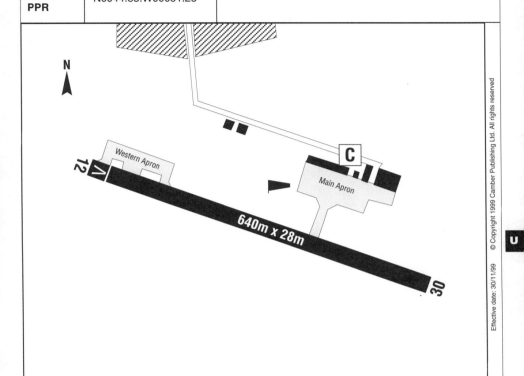

RWY	SURFACE	TORA	LDA	LIGHTING
12*	Asphalt	640	610	Thr Rwy PAPI 4.5° LHS
30	Asphalt	610	610	Ap Thr Rwy PAPI 4.5° LHS

*Green wing bars for displaced landing Thr Rwy12

	Unst
APP	Sumburgh Radar 123.15
A/G/AFIS	130.35
NDB*	UT 325 range 20nm *UT 299/1.0 to Thr30

Remarks
All ACFT operators are reminded to check with ATC re. the availability of services before nominating this AD as a diversion AD. Visual aid to location: Ibn Green UT.

Warnings
Rising ground exists in the take-off path of Rwy30. Frequent helicopter activity outside AD Hrs. No ground signals except light signals.

Operator	Serco Aviation Services
	Unst Aerodrome, Baltasound, Shetland ZE2 9DT
Tel: 01957 711887 (AD)	
Tel/Fax: 01957 711541	

Restaurants	Nil

Taxis	
PT Coaches	**Tel:** 01957 711666
Car Hire	

Weather Info	M T9 Fax 442 GWC

Operating Hrs	Mon-Fri 1000-1400 (Summer) +1Hr Winter and by arrangement
Circuits	30 RH 12 LH. 1000ft QFE
Landing fee	On application
Maintenance Fuel	Nil Nil

ELEVATION	LOCATION	EGOV	VALLEY

ELEVATION	LOCATION
37ft 1mb	5nm SE of Holyhead N5314.89.W00432.12
PPR MILITARY	

WAL 114.10	268	50.8	• – – / • – / • – • •
IOM 112.20	178	50.0	• • / – – – / – –

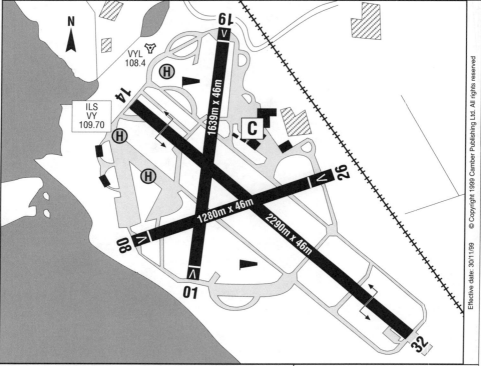

RWY	SURFACE	TORA	LDA	LIGHTING
14/32	Asphalt	2290	2290	Ap Thr Rwy PAPI 3°
01	Asphalt	1572	1572	Thr Rwy PAPI 3°
19	Asphalt	1571	1571	Ap Thr Rwy PAPI 3°
08	Asphalt	1280	1066	Nil
26	Asphalt	1280	1158	Nil

Valley	
APP/MATZ/	
LARS	134.35
RAD	123.30
TWR	122.10
TACAN	VYL 108.40 on A/D
ILS	VY 109.70 Rwy14

Remarks
This AD is PPR to all ACFT other than emergency. Inbound civil ACFT are to make contact with ATC at a min. range of 30nm. Variable circuits and two Rwys may be in use at once. Rwys32 &19 permanently RH circuits. Flying training takes place between 0830-1730. Valley can only accept 1 visiting ACFT movement during any 30 minute period. Limited radar service at a range exceeding 12nm in the sector SE of the AD. Special procedures apply for fixed wing ACFT and helicopters. Visual aid to location: Ibn VY Red.

Warnings
Intensive visual circuit flying at Mona (094°/6nm). Avoid over-flying Rhosneigr (SSE of the AD) below 2000ft agl. Arrester gear 390m from Thr 14/32.

Maintenance	Nil
Fuel	AVGAS 100LL (limited) JET A1
Operator	RAF Valley Holyhead, Gwynedd LL65 3NY **Tel:** 01407 762241 Ext.7299/7582
Restaurants	
Taxis/Car Hire	
Weather Info	M T Fax 444 MWC

Operating Hrs	Mon-Thu 0700-2259 Fri 0700-1700 +1Hr Winter
Circuits	See Remarks
Landing fee	£7.56 +VAT per 500kgs & £8.50 insurance

ELEVATION	LOCATION	**EGXW**	**WADDINGTON**

231ft 8mb	3.5nm S of Lincoln N5309.97 W00031.43
PPR MILITARY	

GAM 112.80	120	16.8	− − • / • − / − −
OTR 113.90	211	35.4	− − − / − / • − •

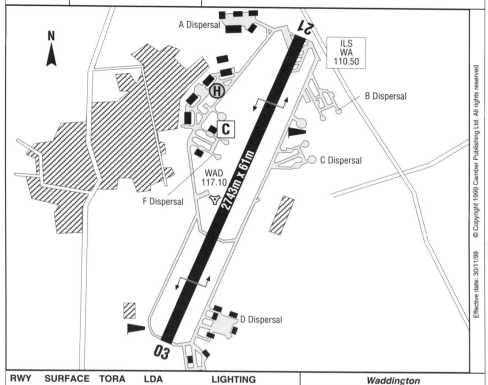

A Dispersal

ILS WA 110.50

B Dispersal

(H)

C

C Dispersal

WAD 117.10

F Dispersal

2743m x 61m

D Dispersal

03

RWY	SURFACE	TORA	LDA	LIGHTING
03/21	Asphalt	2743	2743	Ap Thr Rwy PAPI 3°

Waddington	
APP/MATZ	
/LARS	127.35
RAD	125.35 123.30
TWR	**Use alloted freq**
TACAN	**WAD 117.10 on A/D**
ILS	**WA 110.50 Rwy21**

Remarks
PPR 24 Hrs notice required. IBn WA Red. ATZ active H24

Warnings
Caution arrester gear 610m from Thr03/21. Due to high usage slot times must be ashered to. Dep into sector 130-220 will not normally be approved due to Cranwell operations, plan to avoid this sector. Strong W Winds can produce marked turbulence on final for Rwy21.

Operator	RAF Waddington
Tel: 01522 720271 Ext.7451 (ATC) Ext. 7301 (Ops)	
Restaurants	
Taxis/Car Hire	
Weather Info	M T Fax 446 MWC

Operating Hrs	H24
Circuits	03 RH 21LH Light ACFT 800ft QFE
Landing fee	£7.56 +VAT per 500kgs & £8.50 insurance
Maintenance	Nil
Fuel	AVGAS 100LL AVTUR Jet A1

ELEVATION	LOCATION
180ft 6mb	4.5nm S of Pontefract N5337.77 W00115.55
PPR	**Diversion AD**

WALTON WOOD

GAM 112.80	336	23.3	– – • / • – / – –
POL 112.10	108	31.0	• – – • / – – – / • – • •

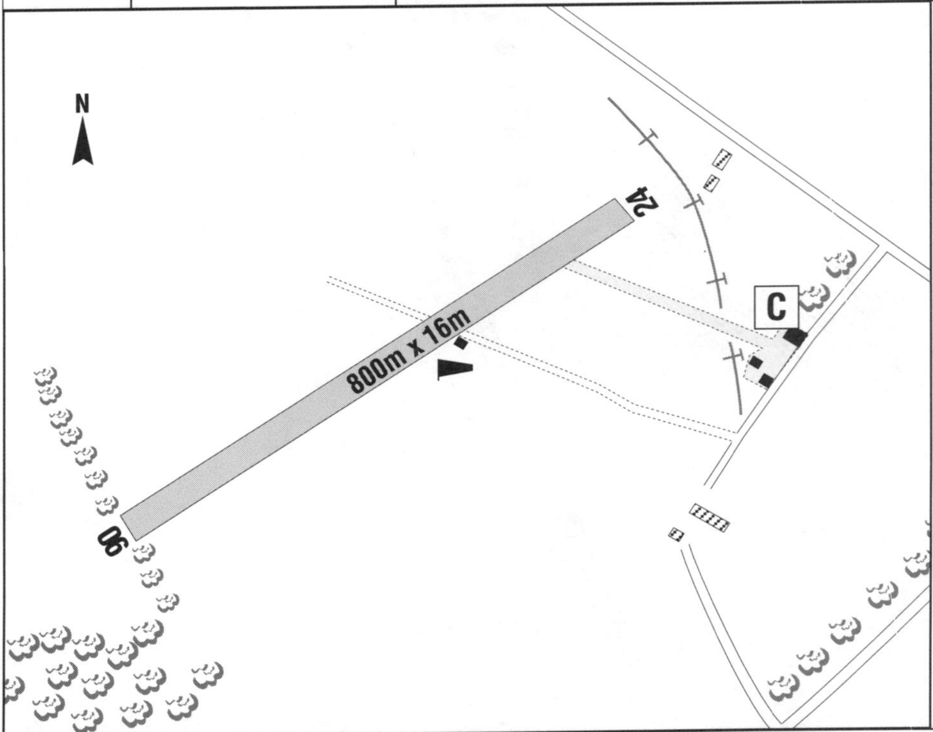

N ↑

24

800m x 16m

06

C

W

RWY	SURFACE	TORA	LDA	LIGHTING
06/24	Grass	800x18	U/L	Nil

	Walton Wood
A/G	123.625

Remarks
PPR by telephone. Rwy can become water logged in Winter.

Warnings
Power lines cross Rwy24 APP 30m from Thr.

Operator	Heliscott Ltd Walton Wood Airfield Thorpe, Audlin, Pontefract, West Yorkshire WF8 3HQ
Tel: 01977 621378	
Fax: 01977 620868	

Restaurants	
Taxis/Car Hire	
Weather Info	AirCen MWC

Operating Hrs	Available on request
Circuits	24 LH 06 RH 1000ft
Landing fee	Single £10.00 Twin £20.00
Maintenance	Nil
Fuel	AVGAS 100LL AVTUR Jet A 1

ELEVATION	LOCATION	EGNO				WARTON

ELEVATION	LOCATION
54ft 2mb	6nm W of Preston Docks N5344.69.W00253.03
PPR	**Diversion AD**

WAL 114.10	030	23.0	• – – / • – / • – ••
POL 112.10	276	27.7	• – – • / – – – / • – ••
MCT 113.55	323	32.1	– – / – • – • / –

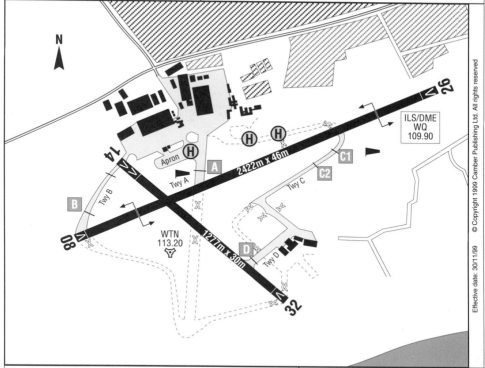

RWY	SURFACE	TORA	LDA	LIGHTING
08	Asphalt	2422	2359	Ap Thr Rwy PAPI 2.83°
26	Asphalt	2407	2407	Ap Thr Rwy PAPI 2.75°
14	Asphalt	1051	891	Thr Rwy APAPI 3° LHS
32	Asphalt	969	861	Thr Rwy APAPI 3° LHS

	Warton
APP/RAD/	
MATZ	129.525
RAD	129.725
TWR	130.80
TACAN	WTN 113.20
ILS/DME	WQ 109.90 Rwy26
NDB*	WTN 337 range 15nm *WTN 258/0.54 to Thr26

Remarks
PPR non-radio ACFT not accepted. Hi-vis. Visiting ACFT on business with Bae only. Red & white marker boards positioned 35m S Rwy08/26 for its full length, 1000m apart. To assist identification of Thr when visually manoeuvring (circling) four sodium lights are visible on base leg & final APP (day only). Visual aids to location: Ibn Green WQ. Abn Green flashing. A marshaller must be present for engine starts.

Warnings
Arrester gear on Rwy08/26. Arrester cable housing located 395m after the start of the full width pavement flush with Rwy. Pilots of light ACFT are advised to touchdown after the cable housing. Beware close proximity of Springfields Restricted Area and Blackpool Airport.

Operator
British Aerospace Defence (Military ACFT Division)
Warton Aerodrome, Preston, Lancs PR4 1AX
Tel: 01772 633333 (AD)
Tel: 01772 852374 (ATC)
Fax: 01772 634706

Restaurants Birley Arms	Pub and Motel rr AD **Tel:** 01772 632201
Taxis/Car Hire	Can be arranged on site
Weather Info	M* AirCen MWC

Operating Hrs	0630-1730 (Summer) +1Hr Winter and by arrangement
Circuits	All circuits to S
Landing fee	On application
Maintenance Fuel	Limited AVTUR JET A1 (Limited)

Visual Reference Points (VRPs)
Blackburn	N5344.85 W00228.78
Formby Point	N5333.12 W00306.32
Garstang	N5354.38 W00246.55
M6/M58 Junction	N5332.07 W00241.87

ELEVATION	LOCATION	**EGUW**			**WATTISHAM**

ELEVATION	LOCATION				
284ft 9mb	8.5nm NW of Ipswich N5207.64 00057.36	CLN 114.55	342	18.1	– • – • / • – • • / – •
PPR MILITARY		BKY 116.25	081	33.9	– • • • / – • – / – • – –

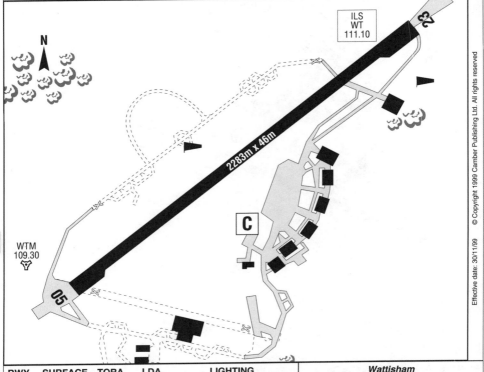

ILS
WT
111.10

2283m x 46m

C

WTM
109.30

W

N

Effective date: 30/11/99 © Copyright 1999 Camber Publishing Ltd. All rights reserved

RWY	SURFACE	TORA	LDA	LIGHTING
05	Asphalt	2424	2284	Ap Thr Rwy PAPI 2.5°
23	Asphalt	2424	2422	Ap Thr Rwy PAPI 2.5°

Wattisham	
APP/MATZ	125.8
RAD	123.30
TWR	122.10
A/G	Anglia Base/ Wattisham Radio 125.8
TACAN	WTM 109.30 on A/D
ILS	WT 111.1 Rwy23

Remarks

Visual aid to location: Ibn WT Red.

Warnings

Intense helicopter flying at all times. Glider flying diaily SR-SS. Aeromodel flying takes place on the AD on Friday evenings and at weekends and Public holidays. Outside normal operating Hrs if no answer on APP/TWR frequency call A/G frequency and request gliders to cease launching prior to arrival and departure. TV mast 933ft aal/1217ft amsl 9nm NE of AD. Caution: Deer on AD. Fixed wing movements restricted to daylight only. 3m fence Rwy23 undershoot. No bird control unit on AD.

Operator	Army Tel: 01449 728234/5
Restaurants	
Taxis/Car Hire	
Weather Info	M T Fax 448 MWC

Operating Hrs	Mon-Fri 0700-1600 (Summer) +1Hr Winter
Circuits	Variable up to 1000ft QFE No deadside
Landing fee	£7.56 +VAT per 500kgs & £8.50 insurance
Maintenance	Nil
Fuel	AVTUR FS 11

ELEVATION	LOCATION	EGBW	WELLESBOURNE MOUNTFORD

ELEVATION	LOCATION		
158ft 5mb	3.3nm E of Stratford-upon-Avon N5211.53 W00136.87	HON 113.65 177 10.1	••••/ – – –/– •
PPR	**Diversion AD**	DTY 116.40 278 18.4	– •• / – / – • – –
		SWB 116.8 115	••• / • – – / – •••

Aerodrome layout: Runways 18/36 (912m x 23m), 05/23 (589m x 18m). Parking, C, Fuel. Wellesbourne village. N arrow.

RWY	SURFACE	TORA	LDA	LIGHTING
05/23	Asphalt	589	589	Nil
18	Asphalt	912	912	Thr Rwy APAPI 3° LHS
36	Asphalt	912	912	Thr Rwy APAPI 4.25° LHS

	Wellesbourne
APP	Birmingham 118.05
AFIS	124.025
	AFIS by arrangement

Remarks
PPR non-radio ACFT not accepted. Pilots are requested to contact Wellesbourne at least 10 minutes before ETA Wellesbourne. Avoid over-flying Wellesbourne village and other built up areas whilst in the circuit. Visual aids to location: Abn green flashing. Certain customs facilities available. Rwy 36 departures immediate turn to track 030° and climb to 1000ft QFE before turning. During the summer 1630-1900 the AD is U/L.

Warnings
The AD is situated 3nm from the southern boundary of the Birmingham CTA (base 1500ft) and below the CTA base 3500 ft. Not all Twys are available for use. Deviation from the marked manoeuvring area can be hazardous.

Operating Hrs
Mon-Fri 0800-1630 Sat-Sun & PH 0800-1900 (Summer)
Mon-Fri 0900-1730 or SS Sat-Sun & PH 0900-1800 (Winter)
and by arrangement NB AD U/L on summer Sat-Sun & PH

Circuits	Variable 1000ft QFE
Landing fee	Single £8.00 Twin £15.00 inc.VAT

Maintenance	Wellesbourne Aircraft Maintenance Tel: 01789 470978
Fuel	AVGAS 100LL AVTUR JET A1 0900-1715 or SS (local Winter) 0800-1900 (local Summer)

Operator	Radmoor Ltd
	Wellesbourne Mountford Aerodrome Stratford-upon-Avon, Warwickshire CV35 9EU **Tel:** 01789 842007 (operator) **Fax:** 01789 470465

Restaurants	AD cafeteria 0900-1900

Taxis	
007	**Tel:** 01789 414007
Main	**Tel:** 01789 414514
Car Hire	
Ford	**Tel:** 01789 267446
Lister	**Tel:** 01789 294477

Weather Info	AirCen BNMC

W

ELEVATION	LOCATION				
233ft 8mb	2nm S of Welshpool N5237.75 W00309.18	WAL 114.10	190	47.0	• – – / • – / • – ••
		HON 113.65	290	58.0	•••• / – – – / – •
PPR		SWB 116.8	250	20.5	••• / • – – / – •••

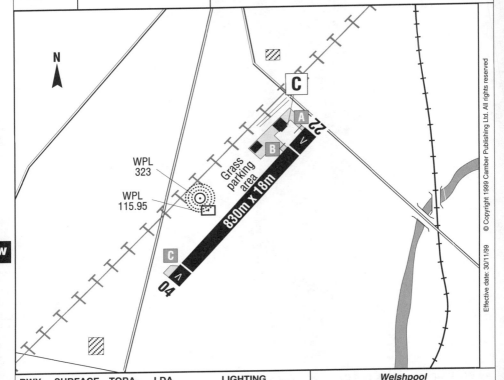

WPL 323

WPL 115.95

Grass parking area

830m x 18m

N

W

RWY	SURFACE	TORA	LDA	LIGHTING
04	Asphalt	812	722	Rwy*
22	Asphalt	820	709	Rwy*

* Available only to based operators

	Welshpool
A/G	123.25
NDB	WPL 323 on A/D range 10nm
DME	WPL 115.95 on A/D

Remarks
PPR non-radio ACFT not accepted. Not available at night to ACFT required to use a licensed AD. AD lighting only available to certain home based operators. ACFT required to use a licensed AD may not operate when the visibility is less than 5.5km or cloudbase is less than 2000ft QFE. No solo flying for the grant of a licence shall take place when the visibility at the AD is less than 8kms or the cloud base is less than 2500ft aal.

Warnings
The AD is situated in the Severn Valley with high GND on both sides. Pilots should not descend below safety height until the Rwy has been positively identified.

Operator	Pool Aviation Ltd
	Montgomeryshire/Welshpool Aerodrome Welshpool, Powys SY21 8SG **Tel:** 01938 555062 **Fax:** 01938 555487
Restaurants	Cafe at airport
Taxis/Car Hire	By arrangement
Weather Info	AirN MWC

Operating Hrs	0800-1600 (Summer) 0900-1700 (Winter)
Circuits	All circuits LH 1500ft QFE
Landing fee	Single £7.00 Twin 12.00 inc VAT
Maintenance	Pool Aviation
Fuel	AVGAS 100LL JET A1 Hrs as AD Hrs

ELEVATION	LOCATION		
57ft 2mb	4nm SE of Stranraer N5451.07 W00456.87	TRN 117.50 200 28.3	– / • – • / – •
PPR MILITARY	**Diversion AD**	BEL 117.20 084 45.8	– • • • / • / • – • •

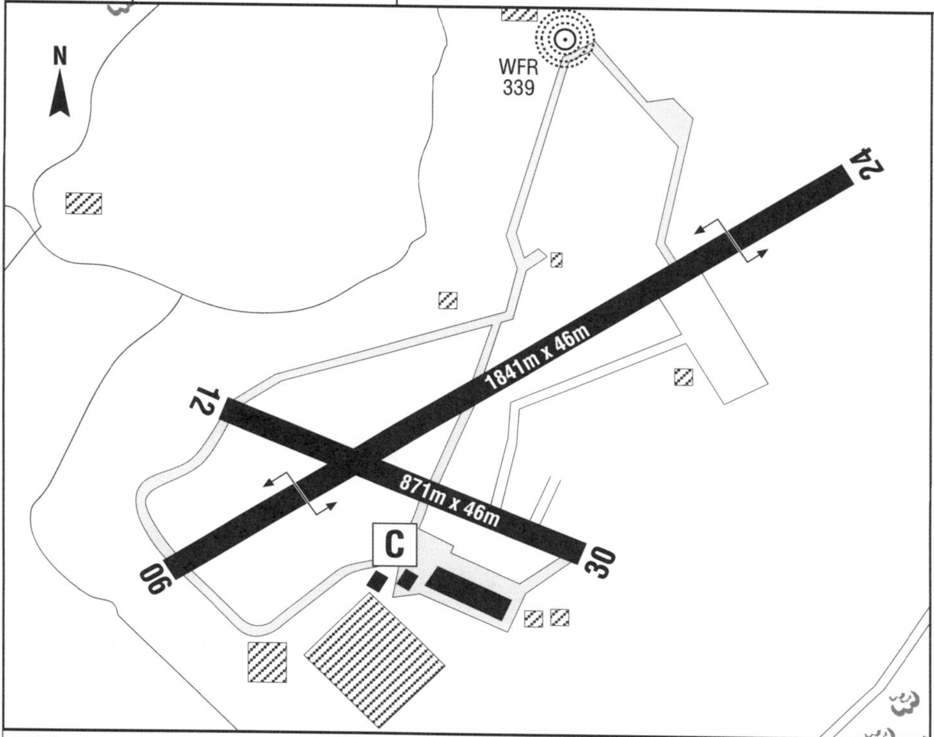

N

WFR 339

24

1841m x 46m

12

871m x 46m

C

30

06

Effective date: 30/11/99

W

RWY	SURFACE	TORA	LDA	LIGHTING
06/24	Asphalt	1841	1841	Ap Thr PAPI 3.5°
12/30	Asphalt	871	871	Nil

Arrester gear 396m from Thr Rwy06/24

West Freugh	
APP/MATZ	130.05
RAD	130.725
TWR	122.55
NDB	WFR 339 range 25nm

Remarks
PPR minimum 24 Hrs required. No night flying facilities. ACFT are to contact West Freugh at 25nm range. ACFT are to avoid over-flying Stranraer below 2000 ft agl. Met forecaster available on Ext.8800.

Warnings
Danger Areas D402/3 which are used by high speed and low flying ACFT overlap the circuit. These Danger Areas are under the control of W Freugh. Risk of bird strikes. AD Hrs may be changed or ATC services reduced at short notice.

Operator MOD (PE) West Freugh Aerodrome
Stranraer, Wigtownshire DG9 9DN
Tel: 01776 888765 (PPR)
Tel: 01776 888791 (ATC)
Fax: 01776 888794 (ATC)

Restaurants

Taxis/Car Hire

Weather Info AirSc GWC

Operating Hrs Mon-Thur 0745-1100 1200-1515 or SS
Fri 0745-1100 1200-1445 (Summer) + 1Hr Winter

Circuits

Landing fee £7.56 +VAT per 500kgs & £8.50 insurance

Maintenance Nil
Fuel AVGAS 100LL AVTUR FS11

WESTBURY-SUB-MENDIP

ELEVATION	LOCATION	
90ft 3mb	3nm WNW of Wells N5113.83 W00243.42	BCN 117.45 152 36.0 –•••/–•–•/–•
PPR		

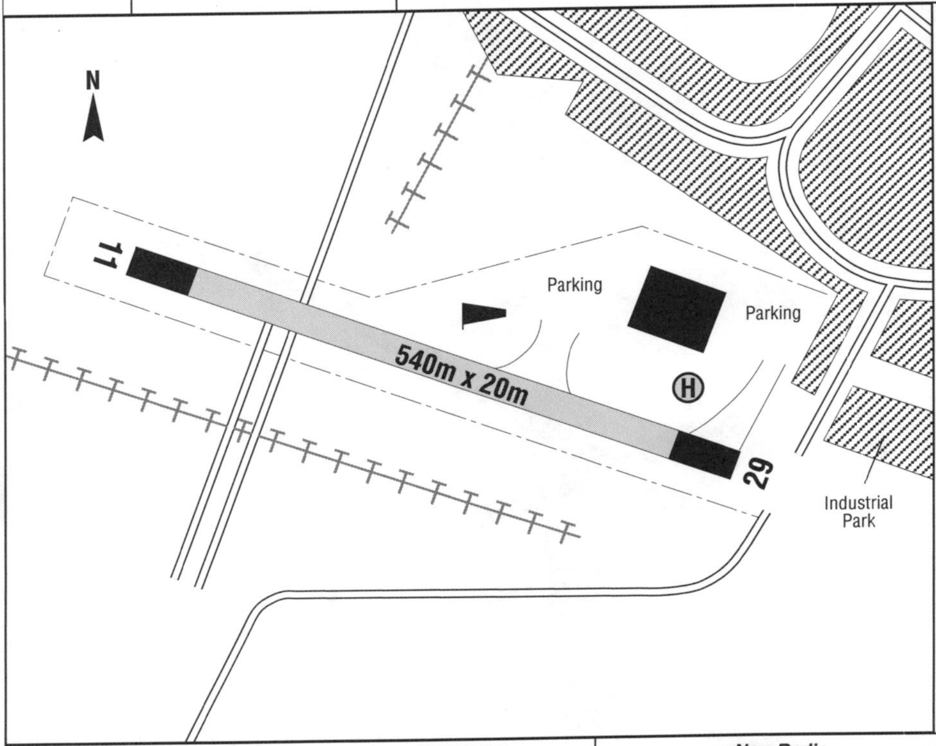

N
11
29
540m x 20m
Parking
Parking
H
Industrial Park

Effective date: 30/11/99

RWY	SURFACE	TORA	LDA	LIGHTING
11/29	Grass/Asph	540x20	U/L	Nil

Non-Radio

APP	Bristol LARS 128.55
APP	Yeovilton LARS 127.35

Remarks
Light ACFT and helicopters welcome at pilot's own risk. Windsock displayed on N side near hangar. Strip is on an old railway embankment & GND slopes away steeply at sides & Rwy29 stop end. **Noise:** Do not overfly Westbury-sub-Mendip.

Warnings
Power cables on S side. Landing strip is located on site of disused railway and is slightly curved.

Operator	John Lloyd & Son Westbury-Sub-Mendip, Somerset **Tel:** 01749 870713 (office Hrs) **Tel:** 01749 870647 (other times)
Restaurants	Railway Inn Westbury-sub-Mendip
Taxis/Car Hire	Available on request
Weather Info	AirSW BNMC

Operating Hrs	0900-2000 daily (local)
Circuits	11 RH 29 LH
Landing Fee	On application
Maintenance	Nil
Fuel	Nil

ELEVATION	LOCATION	EGEW				WESTRAY

ELEVATION	LOCATION
29ft 1mb **PPR**	22nm N of Kirkwall Airport N5921.07 W00257.00

KWL 108.60	004	23.5	– • – / • – – / • – ••
SUM 117.35	246	59.6	••• / •• – / – –

291m x 18m

421m x 18m

535m x 18m

Apron

RWY	SURFACE	TORA	LDA	LIGHTING
09*	Grass	485	505	Nil
27*	Grass	535	485	Nil
13*	Grass	394	359	Nil
31*	Grass	421	359	Nil
01*	Grass	261	235	Nil
19*	Grass	291	218	Nil

* 15m starter extension on all Rwys.
30m starter extension on Rwys01 & 31

	Non-radio	
APP	**Kirkwall 118.30**	

Remarks
Scheduled service operates Monday to Saturday.

Warnings
Rock sub-strata prevents natural drainage of water. After any period of heavy or continuous rainfall pilots intending to land or take off at this AD should establish the location of any significant standing water or mud patches by contacting the AD Manager Tel: 01857 677271.

Operator	Orkney Islands Council Kirkwall, Orkney **Tel:** 01856 873535 **Fax:** 01856 876094

Restaurants
Pierowall Hotel	**Tel:** 01857 677472
Cleaton House	**Tel:** 01857 677508

Taxis/Car Hire
Logies	**Tel:** 01857 677218
Harcus	**Tel:** 01857 677450

Bike Hire
Mrs Bain	**Tel:** 01857 677319 (Rapness)
Mrs Groat	**Tel:** 01857 677374 (Sand O'Gill)

Weather Info	AirSc GWC

Operating Hrs	SR-SS
Circuits	
Landing fee	Nil
Maintenance **Fuel**	Nil Nil

WEYBOURNE (Muckleburgh)

ELEVATION	LOCATION
30ft 1mb	3nm W of Sheringham N5256.81 E00107.32
PPR	

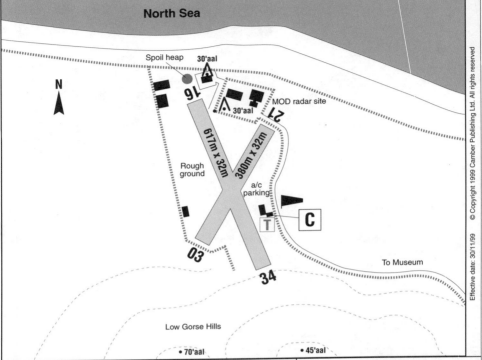

North Sea

Spoil heap · 30'aal · A · MOD radar site · 16 · 30'aal · 21 · 617m x 32m · 380m x 32m · Rough ground · a/c parking · T · C · 03 · 34 · To Museum · Low Gorse Hills · 70'aal · 45'aal

RWY	SURFACE	TORA	LDA	LIGHTING
16/34	Grass	617x32	U/L	Nil
03/21	Grass	380x32	U/L	Nil

Rwy21 slight upslope
Rwy16 slight upslope first half

	Non-radio
LARS	Coltishall 125.90

Remarks
Smallest RAF AD of WW2, Housing the Muckleburgh collection of military vehicles (open Feb-Nov). Strips very well prepared and cut. PPR not required but third party insurance essential. Please book-in at caravan (toilet facilities) key at side. Museum is short walk. Fly-ins welcome, special facilities can be arranged (ie. tank demonstrations). For personal tours or party arrangements at restaurant contact Jenny Billings, Collection manager.

Warnings
Avoid overflying Weybourne & Kelling villages & MOD RAD site close to Thr Rwy21. RAD site also has a number of other antennae (see AD chart). Rwy suface may suffer from rabbit scrapes, please exercise caution. Low gorse hills to S of strip. White post at corner of MOD perimeter fence, encroaches to edge Rwy16 Thr. Model ACFT may operate, one circuit before landing will GND aeromodellers.

Maintenance	Nil
Fuel	Nil

Operator	Muckleburgh Estates Weybourne, Norfolk NR25 7EG
Tel: 01263 588210/588608 (Museum office)	
Fax: 01263 588425	

Restaurants	Licensed restaurant in museum complex

Taxis Car Hire	**Tel:** 01263 822228

Weather Info	AirS BNMC

Operating Hrs	SR-SS
Circuits	1000ft QFE
Landing fee	£4 (donation if not going to museum) (Museum admission £4)

ELEVATION	LOCATION	EGEH			WHALSAY
100ft 3mb	Shetland Islands N6022.62 W00055.33	SUM 117.35	027	32	••• / •• – / – –
PPR					

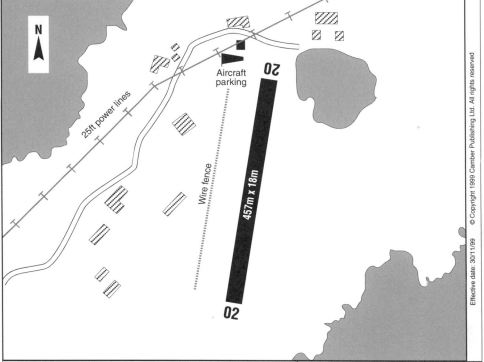

Aircraft parking

N

25ft power lines

Wire fence

457m x 18m

20

02

W

RWY	SURFACE	TORA	LDA	LIGHTING
02/20	Asphalt	457x18	U/L	Nil

Heavily weathered surface with many loose stones

	Non-radio
APP	Sumburgh 123.15

Remarks
PPR by telephone.
Main function is Air Ambulance operations.

Warnings
Rwy surface poor with loose stones. Hill 390ft amsl 222°
3.4nm. AD may be used during daylight Hrs only. Sheep
may be present. The fence to the W of the Rwy has been
known to blow across the strip after high winds.

Operator	Whalsay Development Commitee
	Whalsay Aerodrome, Skaw, Whalsay, Shetland Islands
	Tel: 01806 566449 (PPR thru agent Mr Williamson)
Restaurants	Nil
Taxis	Transport can be provided by
Angus Irvine	**Tel:** 01806 566208
Car Hire	Nil
Weather Info	AirSc GWC

Operating Hrs	SR-SS
Circuits	Suggest standard overhead join with LH circuit 1000ft QFE
Landing fee	£4
Maintenance	Nil
Fuel	Nil

WHARF FARM

ELEVATION	LOCATION				
295ft 9mb	0.25nm W of Market Bosworth N5237.40 W00124.59	TNT 115.70	165	27	– / – • / –
PPR		HON 113.65	034	18.5	• • • • / – – – / – •

W

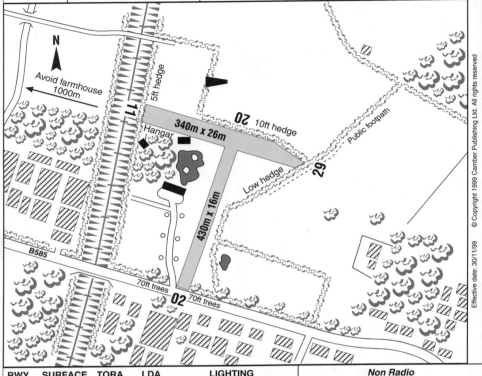

RWY	SURFACE	TORA	LDA	LIGHTING
02/20	Grass	430x16	U/L	Nil
11/29	Grass	340x26	U/L	Nil

Non Radio

APP	(East Mids) 119.65
ATIS	(East Mids) 128.225

Remarks
PPR by telephone. Suitable STOL ACFT welcome at pilots own risk. Windsock occasionally displayed N AD boundary.

Warnings
There are two mature trees either side of short final for Rwy02 and industrial buildings on opposite side of B585 from Rwy. Public footpath crosses short final Rwy29. Railway cutting crosses short final Rwy11, operated by Battlefield line preserved steam railway, operates at weekends only. Please note position of low hedges adjacent to Rwy Thr. Noise: Avoid Market Bosworth E of AD and farmhouse 1000m out on Rwy29 climbout. Electric fences at the side of Rwy.

Operator	Mr L James, Wharf Farm
	Station Road, Market Bosworth, Leicestershire CV3 0PG
	Tel: 01455 290258

Restaurants	
Taxis/Car hire	
Weather info	AirCen MWC

Operating Hrs	SR-SS
Circuits	02/20W, 11/29N 800ft QFE
Landing fee	Nil
Maintenance	Nil
Fuel	Nil

ELEVATION	LOCATION					WHITERASHES
360ft 12mb	7nm N of Aberdeen Airport N5719.40 W00214.30	**ADN 114.30**	050	0.8	• — / — • • / — •	
PPR						

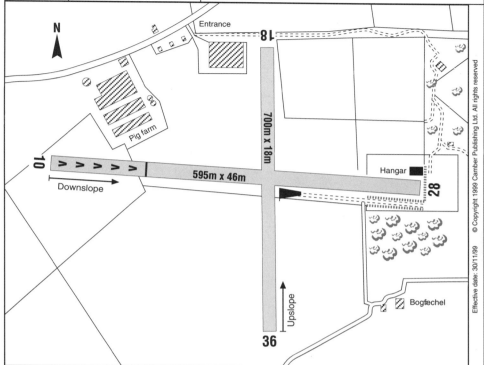

RWY	SURFACE	TORA	LDA	LIGHTING		
10*/28	Grass	595x46	U/L	Nil	**APP**	**(Aberdeen) 120.40**
18/36**	Grass	700x18	U/L	Nil	**A/G**	**129.825**

Whiterashes

*Rwy10 has 275m starter extension and downslope over first 300m
**Rwy36 has upslope on initial portion

Remarks
PPR by telephone. AD siuated within Aberdeen CTR Class D Airspace. All flights must obtain PPR from AD operator. Hangarage available by arrangement.

Warnings
Exercise caution taxying to the hangar due to the close proximity of parked ACFT at Rwy edge. Agricultural work takes place on the grass up to Rwy edges.
Caution: There are 30ft trees at Thr Rwy28 and along S egde of Rwy for the first 150m. Grass cutting may be in progress periodically. There is a hill 678ft amsl 1.5nm SE. Windmill generator 0.8nm S. TV masts (Meldrum VRP) 1245ft amsl 5.5nm WNW. **Note:** There are specific restrictions applied to Inbound and Deptarting ACFT by Aberdeen ATC please see specific VFR/SVFR routeings.

Operating Hrs   Mon-Fri 0630-SS Sat-Sun 0730-SS

Circuits
Circuit patterns must be strictly followed to avoid conflict with Aberdeen APP traffic. Circuits should be kept within 1nm laterally from the field and maximum of 1.5nm final.
10LH 28RH 800ft but not above 600ft on base leg, 36LH 18 RH 800ft. All altitudes QNH

Landing Fee   Nil

Maintenance   Available by arrangement

Fuel   AVGAS 100LL available by arrangement from the AD operator. Outside normal working Hrs a surcharge will be payable. Contact operator for information

Operator   R Ross, 1 Hawthorn Place, Ballater, Grampian, AB35 5H
Tel: 013397 55196
Tel: 07836 375357 (M)
Tel: 01256 704324
Tel/Fax: 01542 882754
E-mail: robert.ross@elfexp.co.uk (will change during 2000 see amendments for details)

Restaurant

Taxi/Car Hire   Nil

Weather Info   AirSc GWC

Effective date: 30/11/99

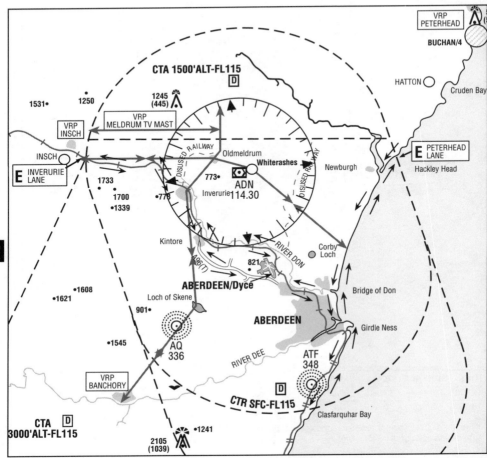

ACFT intending to operate on a regular basis to and from Whiterashes shall adhere *strictly* to the requirements in the AD Operations Manual and mandatory Aberdeen ATC instruction SI 12/96-1 which states the agreed procedures for VFR or SVFR operations.

Visiting ACFT
Visiting ACFT are welcome however any pilot wishing to visit for the first time **MUST** contact the AD OPERATOR via the published telephone numbers REQUESTING a copy of the AD OPERATIONS MANUAL (FLIGHT SECTION) before making the flight. The summary APP and departure routes are to be published. Pilots should avail themselves of the latest revision. The AD Operations Manual contains a page, a copy of which should be requested on initial contact The procedures must be read and understood by the pilot(s) and the acknowledgement page signed and returned to the operator either by fax or by post if time allows.

Mandatory Actions
All flights from the field are required to be Booked Out **BY TELEPHONE (01224 727169)** to Aberdeen ATC flight Clearance not less than 10 minutes prior to the intended departure time PILOTS ARE REMINDED THAT THIS ACTION DOES NOT CONSTITUTE PERMISSION TO ENTER CONTROLLED AIRSPACE Aberdeen flight clearance will record the intended flight details and issue an SSR Transponder code to be used for the flight

Pre-takeoff actions.
When ready for departure and prior to take Off In accordance with SI 12/96-1 a VHF radio call is to be attempted from the ground on 120.40MHz to Aberdeen APP requesting PERMISSION TO ENTER CONTROLLED AIRSPACE and advising ATC of the departure Rwy intended to be used. Pilots should note that there are several areas on the AD proven to be suitable to achieve two way communication with Aberdeen ATC. REMEMBER ALL FLIGHTS whether departing the circuit area or not are conducted IN CONTROLLED AIRSPACE, FOR WHICH PERMISSION IS REQUIRED

ELEVATION	LOCATION	**EGLM**				**WHITE WALTHAM**
130ft 5mb	2nm SW of Maidenhead N5130.05 W00046.42 **Diversion AD**	**LON 113.60**	278	11.8	•—••/———/—•	
PPR		**BNN 113.75**	216	16.0	—•••/—•/—•	
		CPT 114.35	094	16.7	—•—•/•——•/—	

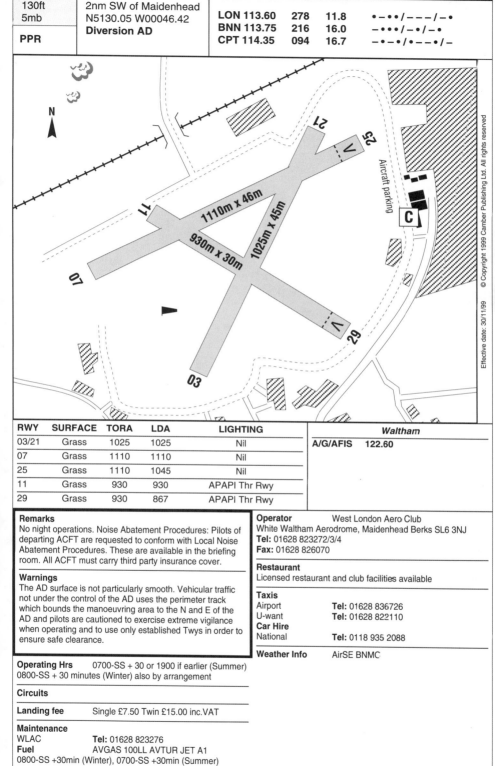

RWY	SURFACE	TORA	LDA	LIGHTING
03/21	Grass	1025	1025	Nil
07	Grass	1110	1110	Nil
25	Grass	1110	1045	Nil
11	Grass	930	930	APAPI Thr Rwy
29	Grass	930	867	APAPI Thr Rwy

Waltham

A/G/AFIS	122.60

Remarks
No night operations. Noise Abatement Procedures: Pilots of departing ACFT are requested to conform with Local Noise Abatement Procedures. These are available in the briefing room. All ACFT must carry third party insurance cover.

Warnings
The AD surface is not particularly smooth. Vehicular traffic not under the control of the AD uses the perimeter track which bounds the manoeuvring area to the N and E of the AD and pilots are cautioned to exercise extreme vigilance when operating and to use only established Twys in order to ensure safe clearance.

Operator West London Aero Club
White Waltham Aerodrome, Maidenhead Berks SL6 3NJ
Tel: 01628 823272/3/4
Fax: 01628 826070

Restaurant
Licensed restaurant and club facilities available

Taxis
Airport **Tel:** 01628 836726
U-want **Tel:** 01628 822110
Car Hire
National **Tel:** 0118 935 2088

Weather Info AirSE BNMC

Operating Hrs 0700-SS + 30 or 1900 if earlier (Summer)
0800-SS + 30 minutes (Winter) also by arrangement

Circuits

Landing fee Single £7.50 Twin £15.00 inc.VAT

Maintenance
WLAC **Tel:** 01628 823276
Fuel AVGAS 100LL AVTUR JET A1
0800-SS +30min (Winter), 0700-SS +30min (Summer)

White Whaltham Circuit

Effective date: 30/11/99

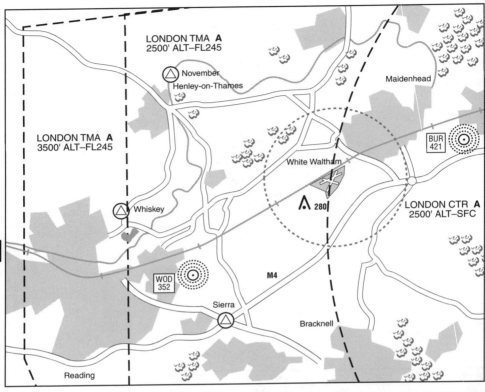

W

Map labels:
- LONDON TMA **A** 2500' ALT–FL245
- November — Henley-on-Thames
- Maidenhead
- LONDON TMA **A** 3500' ALT–FL245
- White Waltham
- BUR 421
- Whiskey
- 280
- LONDON CTR **A** 2500' ALT–SFC
- WOD 352
- M4
- Sierra
- Bracknell
- Reading

Although the E portion of the ATZ is within the London CTZ, flights within the ATZ may take place without compliance with IFR requirements provided that:

1 ACFT must remain clear of cloud & in sight of the surface.

2 ACFT must fly **not above 1500ft QNH** provided that the ACFT can remain at least **500ft below cloud...otherwise 1000ft QNH.**

3 Minimum flight visibility **3km.**

Pilots operating in the local flying area are responsible for their own separation from other air traffic.

VRP's for joining traffic

From the N:	**November**	Bend in the Thames N of Henley-on-Thames
From the W:	**Whiskey**	N of gravel pits by Reading gasometers
From the S:	**Sierra**	M4/A329M jct N of Wokingham

ELEVATION	LOCATION	**EGPC**				**WICK**

ELEVATION	LOCATION		
125ft 4mb	1nm N of Wick N5827.40 W00305.85	**WIK** 113.60 **On A/D** **KWL** 108.60 200 30.9	•– –/••/–•– –•–/•– –/•–••
PPR			

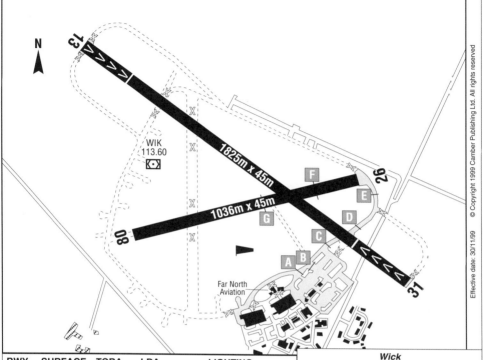

W

RWY	SURFACE	TORA	LDA	LIGHTING
08/26	Asphalt	1036	1036	Thr Rwy, PAPI 4° LHS
13	Asphalt	1740	1283	Ap Thr Rwy PAPI 3° LHS
31	Asphalt	1708	1398	Ap Thr Rwy PAPI 3° LHS

Wick

APP/TWR	**119.70**
FIRE	**121.60**
	Farnor Ops 130.375
VOR/DME	**WIK 113.60 on A/D**
NDB*	**WIK 344 range 30nm**
	*WIK 314/0.85 to Thr31

Remarks
Rwy08/26 not available at night for ACFT required to use a licensed AD. GA handling available from Far North Aviation Tel: 01955 602201, free service with fuel uplift. Far North can provide accommodation & other useful advice. Grass areas soft sand unsafe, only marked Twys to be used.

Warnings
No GND signals except light signals. AD has deer hazard, particularly during dawn/dusk. Pilots are requested to report any animals on the AD to ATC. Agricultural work takes place on the grass areas throughout the year.

Operating Hrs
Mon-Fri 0645-1730 Sat 0800-0945, 1015-1400 (Summer)

Circuits

Landing fee
£10.40 inc.VAT ACFT under 3MT
VFR cash/cheque on day

Maintenance	Nil
Fuel	AVGAS 100LL AVTUR JET A1

Refuelling Hrs during AD Hrs with Far North, outside AD Hrs by arrangement. Tel: 01955 602201 (H24) Radio on 130.375, call "Farnor"

Operator	HIAL Wick Aerodrome

Wick, Caithness KW1 4QP
Tel: 01955 602215 **Fax:** 01955 604447
Tel: 01955 602201 **Fax:** 01955 602203 (Far North H24)

Restaurant	Buffet facilities available at AD

Taxis		Thru Far North or
Miller's Taxis		**Tel:** 01955 603192
Car Hire		Thru Far North or
Practical Car Hire		**Tel:** 01955 604125

Weather Info	M T9 Fax 452 GWC

Visual Reference Points (VRPs)

Duncansby Head Lighthouse	N5838.60 W00301.50
Keiss Village	N5332.00 W00307.40
Loch Watten	N5829.00 W00320.10
Lybster	N5818.00 W00317.10
Thrumster Masts	N5823.58 W00307.43

ELEVATION	LOCATION	**EGNW**		**WICKENBY (Lincoln)**	

ELEVATION	LOCATION				
63ft 2mb	8nm NE of Lincoln N5319.00 W00020.98	GAM 112.80	089	21.5	– – • / • – / – –
PPR		OTR 113.90	206	24.6	– – – / – / • – •

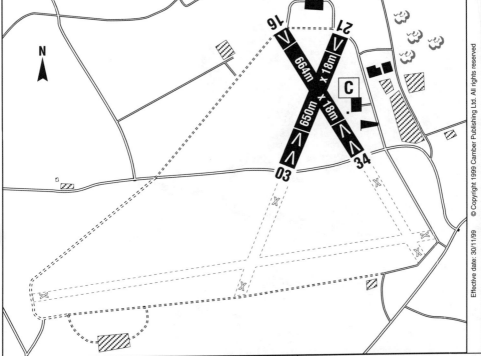

RWY	SURFACE	TORA	LDA	LIGHTING
03	Concrete	635	530	Nil
21	Concrete	635	620	Thr Rwy LITAS 3.5°
16	Concrete	642	630	Nil
34	Concrete	649	500	Nil

	Wickenby
APP	**Waddington MATZ** 127.35
A/G	**122.45**

Remarks
PPR by telephone. Inbound ACFT are requested to contact RAF Waddington. Visual aids to location: Ibn WN Green.

Warnings
The AD is divided by a public road and only the Rwys to the N of the road can be used. A third Rwy09/27 is closed. All ACFT flying in the ATZ should contact Waddington before climbing above 1500ft QFE.

Operator	Lincoln Aviation Ltd Wickenby Aerodrome, Langworth, Lincolnshire LN3 5AX Tel/Fax: 01673 885886
Restaurant	Club facilities available at AD
Taxis/Car Hire	Arranged on request
Weather Info	AirN MWC

Operating Hrs	0900-1900 (local Summer) 0900-SS (local Winter) and by arrangement
Circuits	LH 1000ft QFE
Landing fee	Single £5.00 Twin £10.00 +VAT
Maintenance Air-Tech	**Tel:** 01673 885886 **Tel:** 07957 595835 (mobile)
Fuel	AVGAS 100LL

ELEVATION	LOCATION	**EGXT**	**WITTERING**

ELEVATION	LOCATION		
273ft 9mb	3nm S of Stamford Lincolnshire	HON 113.65 075 46	•••• / – – – / – •
PPR Military	N5236.75 W00028.60	TNT 115.70 126 50.5	– / – • / –

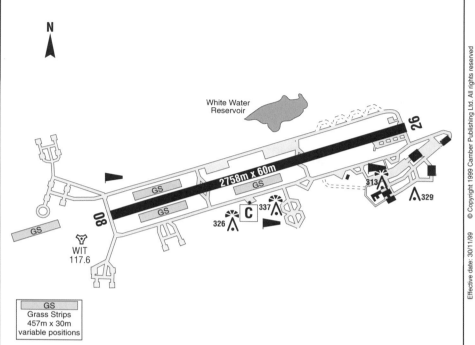

RWY	SURFACE	TORA	LDA	LIGHTING
08/26	Asphalt	2718	2718	Ap Thr Rwy PAPI 2.5 LH

Cottesmore/Wittering

APP	(Cottesmore) 130.20
PAR	(Cottesmore) 123.30
TWR	(Wittering) 118.15
TACAN	WIT 117.60 (On A/D)

Remarks
PPR by telephone essential. RAF AD with based high performance ACFT. AD Situated within CMATZ with Cottesmore who are the controlling authority.

Warnings
AD has various areas of the Twy and dispersals marked as non standard Rwys. There are also numerous cut grass strips within the AD boundary. All such areas are for the use of based AD ONLY. Overflight of the domestic site to the SE and fenced compounds to the SW is forbidden to fixed wing ACFT below 1000ft QFE.

Operator	RAF Wittering Stamford Lincs **Tel:** 01780 783838 Ext 7090/1
Taxi/Car Hire	Nil
Weather Info	M T Fax454 BNMC

Operational Hrs	Mon-Fri 0700-1630 (Summer) Mon-Fri 0800-1700 (Winter)
Circuits	26 LH 08 RH 1000ft QFE
Landing Fee insurance	£7.56 per 500kgs + VAT & £8.50
Maintenance **Fuel**	Not normally available to visiting ACFT JET A1 strictly by prior arrangement only

WOMBLETON (Pickering)

ELEVATION	LOCATION				
120ft 4mb **PPR**	8nm W of Pickering N5414.02 W00058.13 **Diversion AD**	OTR 113.90 POL 112.10	315 054	45 50	– – – / – / • – • • – – • / – – – / • – • •

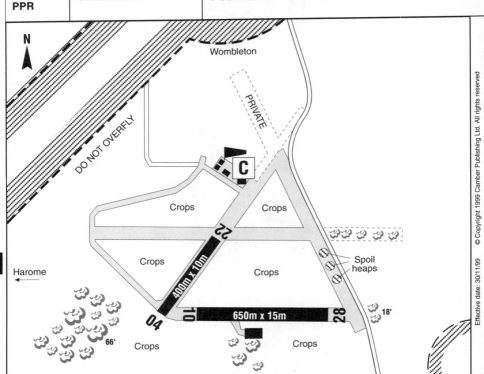

RWY	SURFACE	TORA	LDA	LIGHTING
10/28	Concrete	650	650	Nil
04/22	Asphalt	400	400	Nil
Rwy10/28 prefered				

Wombleton

LARS	**Leeming 127.75**
A/G	**123.225**

Remarks
PPR by telephone. U/L AD. Visitors welcome. Park ACFT near old TWR & enter flight details in AD log. Microlight activity.

Warnings
Farm vehicles, pedestrians, animals & model ACFT may be encountered on AD, please be alert to Rwy incursion at any time. Some AD surfaces rough with loose stones & grass growth at joints. 66ft trees 200m Thr Rwy10. Public road bounded by 18ft trees 150m Thr Rwy28. Two private strips in N portion of AD not to be used by visitors. Kirkbymoorside AD 1.5nm NE of Wombleton. DO NOT OVERFLY the villages of Wombleton & Harome to the W & N of AD. Please modify APP to avoid local houses & obstructions.

Maintenance	Nil
Fuel	Nil
Operator	Windsports Centre Ltd Wombleton Airfield, North Yorkshire **Tel/Fax:** 01751 432356 (PPR)
Restaurant	Tea & coffee available
Taxis/Car Hire	Can be arranged on arrival
Weather Info	AirN MWC

Operating Hrs   Available on request

Circuits
04/10RH, 22/28LH, 1000ft QFE (Light ACFT)
04/28RH, 10/22LH, 500ft QFE (Microlights)

Landing fee   Private Nil
Commercial may be charged a small fee

W

ELEVATION	LOCATION
37ft 1mb	4.5nm SSW of Southport N5334.89 W00303.33
PPR MILITARY	

WAL 114.10	021	11.7	• – – / • – / • – ••
MCT 113.55	303	31.4	– – / – • – • / –

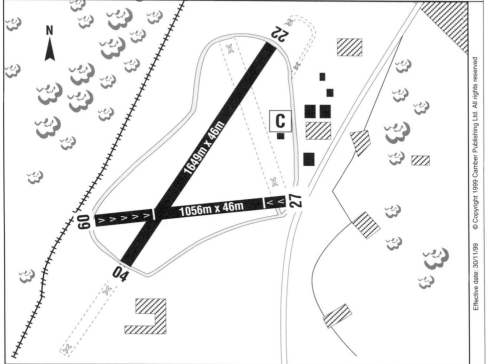

RWY	SURFACE	TORA	LDA	LIGHTING
04/22	Asphalt	1649	1644	Nil
09	Asphalt	1056	710	Nil
27	Asphalt	1056	918	Nil

Woodvale	
APP	121.00
TWR	119.75

Remarks
PPR to private and charter ACFT. Light ACFT activity SR-SS + 30 outside AD Hrs. Circuit can be very busy with University Air Squadron ACFT, which communicate on UHF.

Warnings
Full obstacle clearance criteria not met on APP to all Rwys. Considerable risk of bird strike.

Operator	RAF Woodvale Formby, Liverpool L37 7AD **Tel:** 01704 872287/8 Ext7243 **Fax:** 01704 834805 (Flight plans)
Restaurants	Numerous in Southport
Taxis White Yellow **Car Hire** Dewerdens	 **Tel:** 01704 527777 **Tel:** 01704 531000 **Tel:** 01704 533066
Weather Info	AirCen MWC

Operating Hrs
Wed-Sun 0700-1600 or SS if earlier (Summer) +1Hr Winter
Sometimes 7 days a week notified by Notam

Circuits	Variable 800ft QFE
Landing fee	£7.56 +VAT per 500kgs & £8.50 insurance
Maintenance **Fuel**	Nil AVGAS 100LL (limited)

W

ELEVATION	LOCATION	**EGTB**	**WYCOMBE AIR PARK (Booker)**
520ft 17mb	2.4nm SW of High Wycombe N5136.70 W00048.48	**BNN 113.75** 239 11.8	– • • • / – • / – •
PPR	**Diversion AD**	**LON 113.60** 304 14.5	• – • • / – – – / – •

(Aerodrome diagram showing runways:)
- 17/35 — 695m x 30m (grass)
- 07/25 — 735m x 23m (asphalt)
- 07/25 — 610m x 23m (grass)
- Aircraft parking area, Helihold Z, Heliholds X, R, HTA N, HTA E
- Helipads/markers: B, A, C, S (Heli aiming point), M40 motorway to NE

RWY	SURFACE	TORA	LDA	LIGHTING
07/25	Asphalt	735	735	Thr Rwy LITAS 4°
07/25	Grass	610	610	Nil
17/35	Grass	695	695	Nil

Wycombe	
TWR	**126.55**
GND	**121.775**

Remarks

Gliders fly a circuit opposite to that in use by powered ACFT. Joining ACFT are to position to overfly the AD at 1200ft QFE on the Rwy QDM. When overhead the midpoint of the Rwy turn left or right (depending on the circuit direction) to level at circuit height 1000ft QFE on the crosswind leg prior to turning downwind. Helicopter circuit height 750ft QFE.
Strict Noise Abatement Procedures are enforced - pilots must acquaint themselves with details. Visiting ACFT will not be accepted without prior permission including a briefing. All arriving and departing helicopters must obtain ATC clearance. Maximum care is to be exercised when manoeuvring to/from the helipad, 100m S of ATC TWR. To avoid the effect of downwash on fixed-wing ACFT and gliders, always maintain a minimum distance of 30m from any structure. There will be no helicopter hover movements to the S or W of the SW corner of the helipad. Helicopters are to avoid at all times flying directly over or within 25m of parked ACFT and gliders at low level. Visual aids to location: Ibn WP Green.

Warnings

The AD is close to the London Control Zone and situated below the London Terminal Control Area. The AD is liable to water logging. Intense gliding takes place on and around the AD. Helicopters operate inside fixed-wing circuits. Helicopters must remain well clear of the housing area E of Rwy17/35.

Operating Hrs	0800-1630 (Summer) 0900-1730 (Winter) and by arrangement
Circuits	Variable 1000ft QFE
Landing fee	£12.00 up to 1.5MT
Maintenance **Fuel**	Available AVGAS 100LL AVTUR JET A1
Operator	Airways Association Ltd Wycombe Air Park, Booker, Marlow, Buckinghamshire SL7 3OR **Tel:** 01494 529261 (Admin) **Tel:** 01494 438657 (ATC) **Fax:** 01494 461237 (Admin)
Restaurants	Restaurant and refreshments available
Taxis Neales **Car Hire** National	**Tel:** 01494 463399 **Tel:** 01494 527853
Weather Info	AirSE BNMC

Effective date: 30/11/99

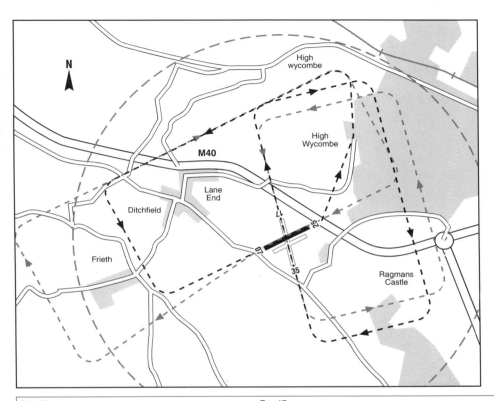

W

Rwy07
Fly **left hand circuit**
1 As soon as safely possible, **but not before the windsock** turn left, Track 020M. At 600ft QFE Track 360M and maintain to circuit height. (Beware close proximity of helicopters during initial climb).
2 Join base leg using corridor between Freith & Lane End.
3 Practice engine failures after take-off are forbidden.
4 After landing vacate right ASAP & taxy between the grass & the hard Rwys as for Rwy25 procedures. Do not roll to the end of 07 without permission.

Rwy25
Fly **right hand circuit**
1 Climbout on track 242°M to avoid Freith.
2 Do not turn crosswind until past Freith.
3 After landing vacate left ASAP & taxy between the grass and hard Rwys unless otherwise directed. Stop short of hard Twy at Bravo & request permission to cross both active 25 & glider landing area.

Rwy17
Fly **left hand circuit**
1 Turn crosswind at 400ft QFE
2 Maintain good lookout for helicopter activity on climbout.
3 After landing vacate left ASAP & taxy parallel to Rwy35 to intersection with 07 grass then taxy down 07 grass to join the hard Twy to the apron, (unless instructed otherwise).

Rwy35
Fly **right hand circuit**
1 Turn crosswind at 600ft QFE
2 After landing vacate right ASAP & taxy parallel to Rwy35 to intersection with 07 grass then taxy down 07 grass to join the hard Twy to the apron, (unless instructed otherwise).

ELEVATION	LOCATION	EGUY				WYTON
135ft 4mb	3nm NE of Huntingdon N5221.40 W00006.37		**BKY 116.25**	350	23	– • • • / – • – / – • – –
PPR			**CFD 116.50**	051	25.5	– • – • / • • – • / – • •

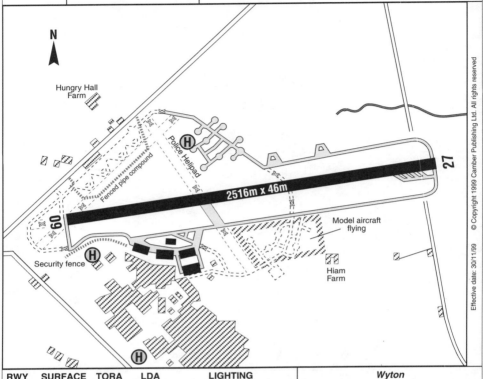

RWY	SURFACE	TORA	LDA	LIGHTING
09/27	Asphalt/Concrete	2516	2516	Nil

	Wyton
APP*	134.05
TWR	122.10

*Outside normal Ops Hrs becomes A/G not always manned

Remarks
PPR strictly by telephone. RAF AD, intensive ab-initio flying training by University Air Squadron ACFT. Noise: Avoid village of Woodhurst 1.5nm N of Rwy27 Thr and Raptor foundation 2.75nm Rwy27 final APP.

Warnings
Turbulence may be encountered over Rwy when wind from S and greater than 15kts. Twy clearance reduced to 17.5 m from centreline to fence S of Rwy09 holding point, Twy available to light aircraft only. No Approach or Runway lighting available. Locally based ACFT and Microlights operate outside normal AD Hrs. Model ACFT operate outside AD Hrs within designated area.

Operator	Bombardier Defence Services RAF Wyton, Huntingdon, Cambridgeshire **Tel:** 01480 52451 Ext 6412
Restaurant	Nil
Taxi/Car Hire	Nil
Weather Info	AirCen BNMC

Operating Hrs	0800-1900 and by arrangement
Circuits	09 LH 27 RH 800ft QFE
Landing Fee	£7.56+VAT per 500kgs & £8.50 insurance
Maintenance	Nil
Fuel	AVGAS 100LL by prior arrangement

ELEVATION	LOCATION		
30ft 1mb	2nm S of Redcar N5435.01 W00103.93	NEW 114.25 147 35 – • / • / • – –	
PPR			

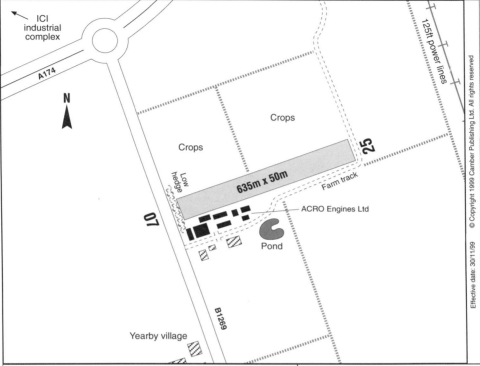

RWY	SURFACE	TORA	LDA	LIGHTING			*Non-radio*
07/25	Grass	635x50	U/L	Nil		APP	Teeside 118.85

Remarks
PPR by telephone essential animals grazing on AD.
Home of Acro Engines Ltd. Windsock displayed with PPR.
AD situated close to the boundary of the Teeside
CTR/CTA. Please contact Teeside APP on
arrival/departure. **Noise:** Avoid overflying village of Yearby,
ICI chemical plant to NW & Redcar.

Warnings
Sheep graze on the strip when flying is not in progress.
Powerlines 125ft agl cross Rwy25 final APP approx 600m
from Thr with a pylon on the centreline.

Operator   J A Towers, Turners Arms
Yearby, Redcar, Teeside TS11 8HH
Tel: 01642 485419 (Operator for PPR)
Tel: 01642 470322 (Acro-PPR if no reply above)
Tel: 01642 484340 (Farm Office)

Restaurants   Nil

Taxis
John   **Tel:** 01642 478583
    Mobile: 0410 102843
Car Hire   Nil

Weather Info   AirN MWC

Operating Hrs	SR-SS
Circuits	07 RH 25 LH 800ft QFE
Landing fee	Nil private Commercial rates with PPR
Maintenance	Acro Engines Ltd

Volkswagen engine conversion & rebuild specialists
    Tel: 01642 470322 (Barry Smith)

Fuel	Nil

ELEVATION	LOCATION	EGHG	YEOVIL (Westland)

ELEVATION	LOCATION
207ft 7mb	1nm W by S of Yeovil N5056.40 W00239.55 **Diversion AD**
PPR	

BHD 112.05	050	45.4	– • • • / • • • • / – • •
SAM 113.35	274	49.7	• • • / • – / – –

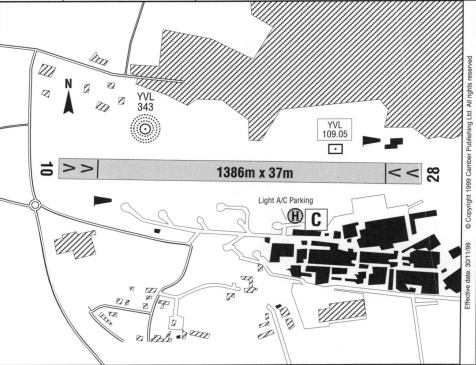

YVL 343

YVL 109.05

10 > > 1386m x 37m < < 28

Light A/C Parking

(H) C

RWY	SURFACE	TORA	LDA	LIGHTING
10	Grass	1376	1224	Ap Rwy
28	Grass	1321	1124	Ap Rwy

	Judwin
APP	Yeovilton LARS 127.35
APP/RAD	130.80
TWR	125.40
A/G*	125.40
	* When ATC not available
NDB	YVL 343 on A/D range 20nm
DME	YVL 109.05 on AD

Remarks
Licensed for night operations by helicopters only. Circuits S of Rwy due to proximity of Yeovilton. Visiting ACFT may be delayed due to helicopter test flying. Visual aids to location: AD name displayed.

Warnings
Noticeable windshear on Rwy28 APP. Displaced landing Thr. The AD surface is convex with a pronounced gradient to the S at the Thr of Rwy10. Caution required after heavy rain. Model ACFT, light ACFT & helicopter flying takes place outside normal Hrs. Beware of bird concentrations. Houses adjacent to the N & E boundaries. High GND rising to 442ft amsl 2.5nm to SW with radio mast 520ft amsl. Trees on high GND rising to 420ft amsl 1nm to E.

Operating Hrs
Mon-Thu 0730-1545 Fri 0700-1515 except PH (Summer) +1Hr Winter
Avail H24 for ambulance medical and Police ACFT not requred to use a licensed AD

Circuits
To the S See Remarks

Landing fee	From £10 + VAT
(homebuilts classics & ACFT uplifting fuel free)	

Maintenance	Limited
Fuel	AVTUR JET A1
During AD Hrs but H24 to ambulance & medical flights	

Operator	Westland Helicopters Ltd
Yeovil Aerodrome, Yeovil, Somerset BA20 2YB	
Tel: 01935 475222 ask for ATC	
Fax: 01935 703055	

Restaurant	Light refreshments available

Taxis/Car Hire	On request to ATC before or after landing
(Booked via ATC to comply with security restrictions)	

Weather Info	M* T9 BNMC

ELEVATION	LOCATION	**EGDY**				**YEOVILTON**
75ft 3mb	4nm N of Yeovil N5100.56 W00238.33	**BCN 117.45**	157	48.5	– • • • / – • – • / – •
PPR MILITARY		**BHD 112.05**	047	49.0	– • • • / • • • • / – • •
		SAM 113.35	280	49.0	• • • / • – / – –

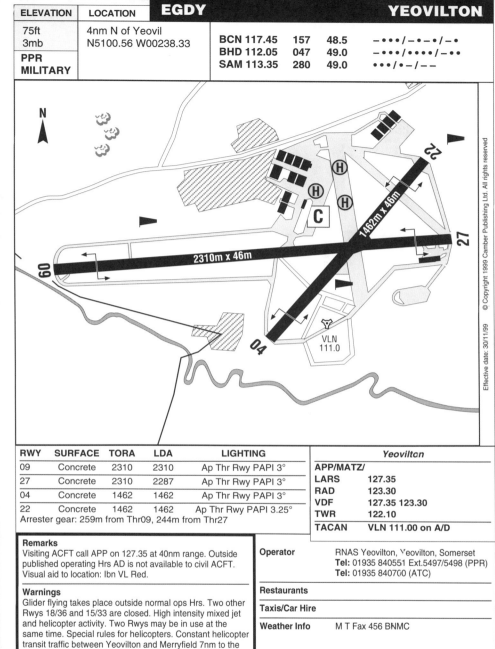

Y

RWY	SURFACE	TORA	LDA	LIGHTING
09	Concrete	2310	2310	Ap Thr Rwy PAPI 3°
27	Concrete	2310	2287	Ap Thr Rwy PAPI 3°
04	Concrete	1462	1462	Ap Thr Rwy PAPI 3°
22	Concrete	1462	1462	Ap Thr Rwy PAPI 3.25°

Arrester gear: 259m from Thr09, 244m from Thr27

Yeovilton	
APP/MATZ/	
LARS	127.35
RAD	123.30
VDF	127.35 123.30
TWR	122.10
TACAN	VLN 111.00 on A/D

Remarks
Visiting ACFT call APP on 127.35 at 40nm range. Outside published operating Hrs AD is not available to civil ACFT. Visual aid to location: Ibn VL Red.

Warnings
Glider flying takes place outside normal ops Hrs. Two other Rwys 18/36 and 15/33 are closed. High intensity mixed jet and helicopter activity. Two Rwys may be in use at the same time. Special rules for helicopters. Constant helicopter transit traffic between Yeovilton and Merryfield 7nm to the WSW. Turbulence and windshear may be experienced on short final to Rwy27.

Operator RNAS Yeovilton, Yeovilton, Somerset
Tel: 01935 840551 Ext.5497/5498 (PPR)
Tel: 01935 840700 (ATC)

Restaurants

Taxis/Car Hire

Weather Info M T Fax 456 BNMC

Operating Hrs
Mon-Thur 0730-1600 Fri 0730-1500 (Summer) + 1Hr Winter

Circuits	04/09 RH 22/27 LH 1000ft QFE
Landing fee	£7.56 +VAT per 500kgs & £8.50 insurance
Maintenance	Nil
Fuel	AVGAS 100LL JET A1

YORK (Rufforth)

ELEVATION	LOCATION				
65ft 2mb	3nm W of York N5356.83 W00110.24 **Diversion AD**	POL 112.10	075	34.9	•––•/–––/•–••
PPR		GAM 112.80	354	40.9	––•/•–/––
		OTR 113.90	298	41.0	–––/–/•–•

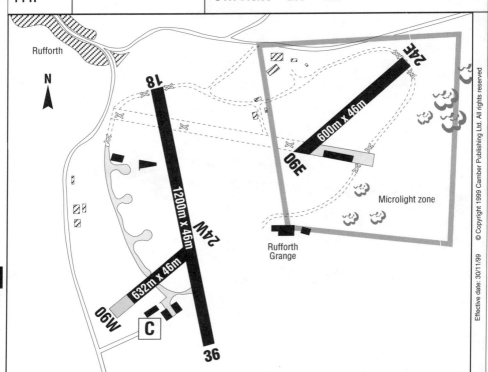

Rufforth

N

18

24E

600m x 46m

06E

Microlight zone

1200m x 46m

24W

632m x 46m

06W

C

36

Rufforth Grange

Effective date: 30/11/99

Y

RWY	SURFACE	TORA	LDA	LIGHTING
18/36*	Asphalt	1200x46	U/L	Nil
06/24W	Asphalt/Grass	632x46	U/L	Nil
06/24E**	Asphalt	600x46	U/L	Nil

* Ignore displaced Thr markings
** Microlight ACFT only See Warnings

	Rufforth
A/G	129.975

Remarks
ACFT landing 24W must avoid microlight circuits on 24E/06E. Avoid over-flying the local farms and villages. Beware gliders and powered ACFT on same circuit. Tug ACFT operate variable circuits.

Warnings
The AD is located on part of a disused AD. The disused parts of the AD are obstructed by farm buildings and equipment. AD is between Church Fenton and Linton-on-Ouse MATZs. Intense gliding activity. Rwys18/36 have displaced Thr marks which should be ignored. Microlights operating from the disused Rwy at the NE side of the AD which is now re-activated as 06E/24E, 600m. Microlight circuits at 500ft aal, LH on Rwy24E, RH on Rwy06E. No overhead joins due cables up to 2000ft agl. No deadside, join downwind.

Maintenance
McClean   **Tel:** 01904 738653
Fuel   AVGAS 100LL (Rufforth W)

Operator   York Gliding Centre
Rufforth Aerodrome, York YO23 3NA
Tel: 01904 738694 (W)
Tel: 01904 738877 (M/lights E)

Restaurants   Vending machine in clubhouse
Pub lunches The Tankard Rufforth 1m

Taxis   **Tel:** 01423 359000
Car Hire
National   **Tel:** 01904 612141

Weather Info   AirN MWC

Operating Hrs   SR-SS

Circuits   18LH, 36RH, 06WLH,
24W normally RH but may vary, not below 800ft QFE

Landing fee   Rufforth E Nil
Rufford W £6.00-£50.00 depending on size

ELEVATION	LOCATION	**LFAC**	**CALAIS-DUNKIRK**

ELEVATION	LOCATION
10ft 0mb	3.5nm ENE of Calais N5057.70 E00157.17
PPR	

DVR 114.95	122	25	– • • / • • • – / • – •
BNE 113.80	009	20	– • • • / – • / •

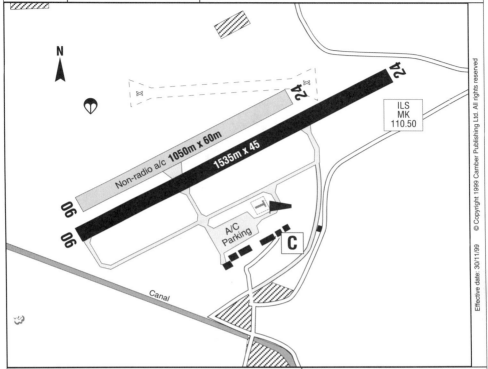

Non-radio a/c 1050m x 60m

1535m x 45

ILS MK 110.50

A/C Parking

C

Canal

RWY	SURFACE	TORA	LDA	LIGHTING
06	Asphalt	1535	1535	Thr Rwy
24	Asphalt	1535	1535	Ap Thr Rwy
06/24	Grass	1050	1050	Nil

	Calais
APP	**Lille 120.375**
TWR	**118.10***
NDB	**MK 418****
ILS	**MK 110.50 Rwy24**

* ouside ops Hrs in French only
** 244/3.9nm to Thr Rwy24

Remarks
PPR for ops at certain times see operating Hrs. Situated within Calais TMA (Class E airspace). SVFR flights requested to contact Lille APP if above 2000ft QNH, if operating below this altitude, call Calais direct. Non-radio ACFT MUST use the grass Rwy. Parachuting takes place at Calais, DZ is to NW Rwy06/24 grass. Customs available 0800-1900 daily Tel: 321 97 90 66.

Warnings
AD surface unusable outside marked or asphalt areas. Danger area 1.5nm NNW AD 0.5nm rtadius, up to 1650ft agl/ Coastal location gives high risk of sea fog.

Maintenance	Nil Hangarage by arrangement
Fuel	AVGAS 100LL Jet A1

Operator
Tel: 00 33 321 82 7059 (ATC)
Tel: 00 33 321 82 7102 (AD)
Fax: 00 33 321 36 7540

Restaurants	On AD
Taxis/Car Hire	Arranged locally
Weather Info	MT **Fax:** 552

Operating Hrs
0800-1900 (1900-2300 PPR for IFR or training flights only)
PPR requests must be made before 1700 same day
PPR for flights wishing to operate 0600-0800 must be obtained previous day

Circuits	Asphalt 06 RH 24 LH Grass 06 LH 24 RH 1000ft QFE
Landing fee	On application

ELEVATION	LOCATION	LFRD	DINARD (Pleurtuit St Malo)

ELEVATION	LOCATION
217ft 7mb	3nm S of Dinard N4835.19 W00204.42
PPR	

DIN 114.30 on A/D — •• / •• / — •

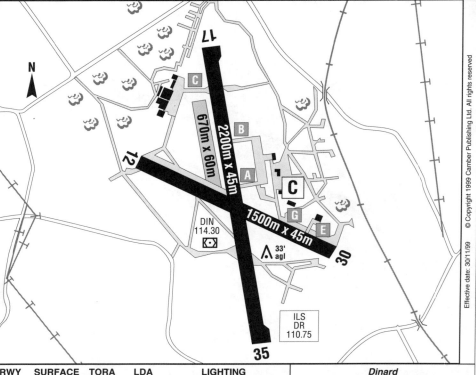

FOR

RWY	SURFACE	TORA	LDA	LIGHTING
35	Asphalt	2200	2200	Ap Thr Rwy PAPI 3°
17	Asphalt	2200	2200	Thr Rwy PAPI 3°
30/12	Asphalt	1500	1500	Nil
35/17*	Grass	670	670	Nil

Local club ACFT use only

Dinard	
FIS	(Brest) 122.80
ATIS	124.575
APP/AFIS	120.15
TWR	121.10
VOR/DME	DIN 114.30 on A/D
ILS	DR 110.75 Rwy35
NDB	DR 390 355° 5.9nm
	Thr35

Remarks
PPR non-radio and SVFR. SVFR weather minima 5000m/1000ft ceiling. Rwy35/17 grass usually available only to locally based ACFT. SVFR flight PPR by telephone. Customs normally available 0730-2030 (local)

Warnings
Mandatory SVFR routing, please check with SVFR request.

Operator
Tel: 00 33 299 46 1681 (AD)
Tel: 00 33 299 46 1846 (Operator)

Restaurants	In the terminal
Taxis	At the terminal
Car Hire	Available in Dinard

Weather Info	M T Fax 544 A. Tel: 99461046

Visual Reference Points (VRPs)
Echo / Pont du Port St Hubert	DIN 131°/5nm
November / Ile de Cezembre	DIN 010°/6nm
November Bravo/ Barrage de la Rance	DIN 057°/3nm
November Echo / Pointe du Grouin	DIN 057°/12nm
November Whisky / Cap Frehel	DIN 307°/11nm
Sierra Whisky / Ploancoet	DIN 241°/7nm
Whisky Juliet / Le Guildo	DIN 265°/5nm

Operating Hrs	H24

Circuits
30 RH 12/17/35 LH Grass 17 RH 35 LH 1000ft QFE

Landing fee	On application

Maintenance	Available
Fuel	AVGAS 100LL AVTUR Jet A1

DUB 114.90   164   4.9   − • • / • • − / − • • •

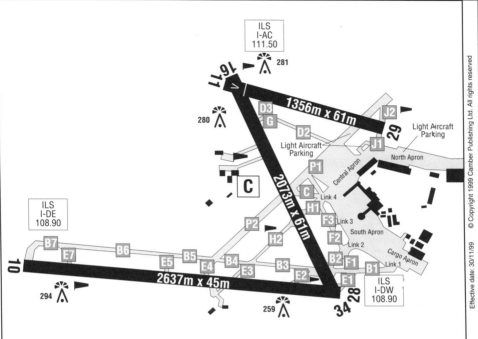

RWY	SURFACE	TORA	LDA	LIGHTING
10/28	Concrete	2637	2637	Ap Thr Rwy PAPI 3°
16/34	Asphalt	2073	2073	Ap Thr Rwy PAPI 3°
11	Asphalt	1356	1254	Ap Thr Rwy PAPI 3.5
29	Asphalt	1356	1356	Ap Thr Rwy PAPI 3

	Dublin
ATIS	124.525
APP	121.10 119.55 118.50
RAD	124.65 129.175 136.05 136.15
TWR	118.60
GND	121.80
DEL	121.875
VOR/DME	DUB 114.90
NDB	GAR 407
NDB	KLY 378
NDB	RSH 326
ILS/DME	I-DE 108.90 Rwy10
ILS/DME	I-DW 108.90 Rwy28
ILS/DME	I-AC 111.50 Rwy16

Remarks
PPR. Flight plans must be filed by ACFT wishing to use Dublin. AVGAS is available 0700-2230 daily; Avtur available H24. Visual aid to location: ABn White/Green. Contact delivery at least 15min proir to start-up.

Warnings
Obstacle 700ft amsl 5nm SE of Rwy34Thr.

Operator
Aer Rianta   **Tel:** 00 3531 8141111
            Fax: 00 3531 8406635

Operating Hrs	H24
Circuits	As instructed by ATC
Landing fee	On application
Maintenance	Available
Fuel	AVGAS 100LL (with Shell) AVTUR Jet A1

Restaurants	In the terminal
Taxis/Car Hire	At the terminal
Weather Info	M. T9 T18 Fax 546 A Vm

ELEVATION	LOCATION	LFBH				LA ROCHELLE (Laleu)
72ft 3mb	1.4nm NW of La Rochelle N4610.80 W00111.15	CGC 116.20 POI 113.30	314 253	48.0 66.2	– • – • / – – • / – • – • • – – • / – – – / • •	

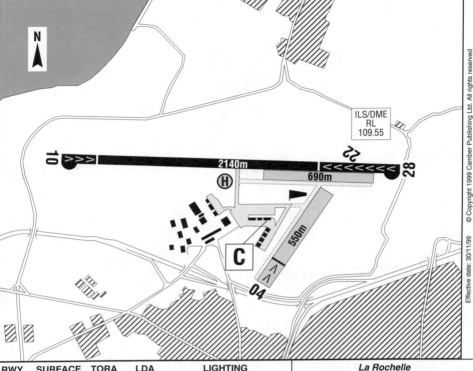

RWY	SURFACE	TORA	LDA	LIGHTING
28	Asphalt	2140	1605	Thr Rwy PAPI* 3.2° LHS
10	Asphalt	2140	1940	Thr Rwy PAPI 3° LHS
28*/10*	Grass	690		
22/04	Grass	550		

*Available only to local ACFT

La Rochelle

FIS	125.30 (Bordeaux Information)
APP/AFIS	119.65
VDF	119.65 118.00
TWR	118.00 118.70
ILS/DME	RL 109.55 Rwy28
NDB	RL* 322 range 25nm *RL 276/4.0 to Thr28

Remarks
Microlight ACFT not accepted. In the visual circuit avoid overflying built-up areas. SVFR minima 1500m, ceiling 700ft. Use of Rwy 28 preferred in winds of less than 4 knots.

Warnings
Only Rwys and marked Twys available for the movement of ACFT.

Operator	CCI La Rochelle 14 Rue du Palais, 17000 La Rochelle
Tel: 00 33 46 42 3026 (AD) **Fax:** 00 33 46 43 1254 (AD)	
Restaurants	In the terminal
Taxis/Car Hire	
Weather Info	M T

Visual Reporting Points (VRPs)
Charron Usseau Nieul-s-Mer & St Vivien

Operating Hrs
Mon-Fri 0400-2100. Sat/Sun & PH 0600-2000 (Summer)
Mon-Fri 0500-2200. Sat/Sun & PH 0800-1800 (Winter)
and by arrangement

Circuits	28/22 RH Min 700ft QFE
Landing fee	On application
Maintenance Fuel	Available plus hangerage AVTUR JET A1 AVGAS 100LL

FOR

ELEVATION	LOCATION	LFAT	LE TOUQUET (Paris Plage)

ELEVATION	LOCATION		
36ft 1mb	1nm E of Le Touquet N5030.90 00137.70	LYD 114.05 140 41.5 • – •• / – • – – / – ••	
PPR		BNE 113.80 245 (12) – ••• / – • / •	

LLZ
LT
110.15

14

190

1850m x 40m

Twy 4

Twy 2

24

C

Twy 1

Twy 3

32

1200m x 40m

06

Effective date: 30/11/99

F O R

RWY	SURFACE	TORA	LDA	LIGHTING
14	Asphalt	1850	1850	Ap Thr Rwy
32	Asphalt	1850	1700	Thr Rwy VASI 3°
24	Asphalt	1200	900	Nil
06	Asphalt	1200	1200	Nil

	Le Touquet	
FIS	(Paris N)	125.70
ATIS		129.125
APP		125.30 118.45
APP Lille		120.375
TWR		118.45 125.30
GND		125.30
NDB	LT 358 138° 1.08nm Rwy14 Thr	
LLZ	LT 110.15 Rwy14	

Remarks
PPR non-radio ACFT.Call TWR 118.45 before starting engine(s) for Dep. SVFR weather minima 3000m/820ft ceiling (arrivals); 1500m / 660ft ceiling (Depts) fixed wing. In winds of less than 4 knots use of Rwy14 is preferred.

Warnings
Rwy06/24 daytime use only. Due to the ADs location is it susceptible to sea fog which can arrive without warning, have an in-land diversion planned. Mandatory SVFR routing, please check with SVFR request.

Operator
Tel: 00 33 321 05 0066

Restaurants	In the terminal
Taxis	At the terminal
Car Hire	Available in Le Touquet

Weather Info	M T Fax 552 A
	Tel: (33) 21 05 13 55

Operating Hrs	0800-2000 (Summer) 0900-1900 (Winter)
Circuits	06/32 RH 24/14 LH 1000ft QFE
Landing fee	On application
Maintenance	Available
Fuel	AVGAS 100LL AVTUR Jet A1

Visual Reference Points (VRPs)

Echo / Neuville		N5028 50 E00146.70
November / Hardelot Plage		N5038 00 E00168.00
November Echo/ Samer		N5038 10 E00144.80
November Mike / Wimereux		N5045 90 E00138.00
Sierra / Rang du Fliers		N5025.00 E00138.60

ELEVATION	LOCATION	**EBOS**	**OSTEND**
13ft 1mb	3nm S of Ostend N5111.98 E00251.82	KOK 114.50 056 10.6 — • — / — — — / — • —	
PPR			

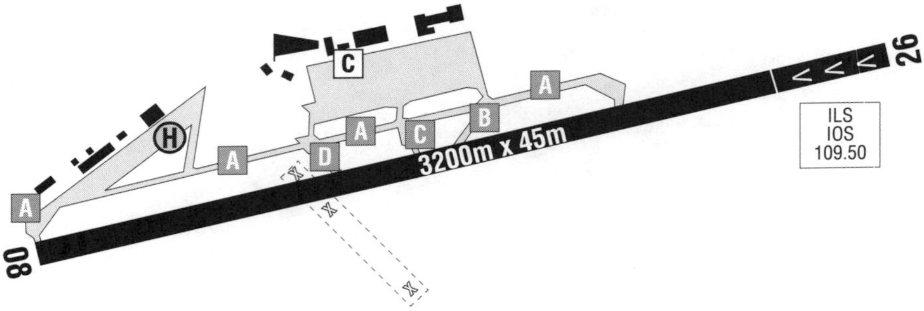

FOR

ILS
IOS
109.50

3200m x 45m

26

08

RWY	SURFACE	TORA	LDA	LIGHTING
26	Asphalt	3200	2785	Ap Thr Rwy PAPI 3°
08	Asphalt	2400	3200	Ap Thr Rwy PAPI 3°

	Ostend
FIS	(Brussels) 126.90
APP	120.60
TWR	118.175
GND	121.90
ILS	IOS 109.50 Rwy26
NDB	ONO 399.5 262° 4.37nm Rwy26
NDB	DD 352 082° 0.7nm Rwy08
NDB	OO 375 262° 0.62nm Rwy26

Remarks
PPR non-radio ACFT (may be subject to prohibition).
AD situated within Class C airspace.

Warnings
ACFT approaching visually should not descend below 1500ft amsl before intercepting the PAPI glideslope, nor fly below this slope once established.

Operator
Tel: 00 (32) 559 551411 (switchboard)
Tel: 00 (32) 559 551464 (self briefing)
Tel: 00 (32) 559 551452 (Met)
Fax: 00 (32) 559 513251 (ATC)

Restaurants	In the terminal
Taxis/Car Hire	At the terminal
Weather Info	M T **Fax:** 562 A **Tel:** (32) 059 551452

Operating Hrs	H24
Circuits	
Landing fee	On application
Maintenance	Available
Fuel	AVGAS 100LL AVTUR Jet A1

Visual Referenc Points (VRPs)
Aalter	N5105.12 E00327.00
Breskens	N5125.00 E00333.00
Dunkerque	N5102.00 E00222.30
Torhout	N5104.10 E00306.11

Private Airfields

Effective date: 30/11/99   © Copyright 1999 Camber Publishing Ltd. All rights reserved

Unless specifically stated otherwise, all the following ADs are **strictly Prior Permission Required**, either in writing or by telephone before departure.

As well as the safety hazards of arriving unannounced and without permission or a proper briefing, such an arrival could well be in breach of aviation legislation, and additionally an act of trespass. Additional hazards may exist at sites used for other activities (such as winch-launched gliders etc.). The possible consequences of making an uninvited arrival at a military AD are quite obvious.

The surface and surrounds of a private airstrip will not be inspected or maintained to the same standards as a licensed AD. Certain airstrips are only safe for use by experienced STOL (Short Take-off & Landing) pilots flying ACFT with good STOL performance.

Please note: Government ADs which have not been upgraded to full page entries this year are now in their own section at the end of this list.

Private Airfields DELETED this year

All the ADs below have been deleted from this guide for various reasons. Often because of inconsiderate visitor use that has caused annoyance to neighbours and put the strip at risk. The owners therefore have requested that we no longer publish details. The fact that an AD is listed below **does not necessarily mean that the AD no longer exists.**

Clough Farm (Skegness)

Fakenham (Manor Farm)

Hull (Hill Farm)

Montrose

Rhos-y-Gilwen

Private Airfields ADDED for 2000

The AD below have agreed to let us publish details for the first time this year. **Please remember that should you use them – and they are all strictly PPR – consideration and good airmanship will ensure they are still available in future years.**

Castle Bytham

Caunton

Cuckoo Tye Farm

Felixkirk

Garforth

Halwell

Hardwicke

Hatton

Ince Blundell

Jubilee Farm (Wisbech)

Lark Engine Farmhouse

Peplow

Plaistows Farm

Roserrow (Polzeath)

Rothwell

Sheepwash

Stalbridge

Stoodleigh Barton

Tarn Farm

Tower Farm

Truleigh Farm

Upfield Farm

Whaley Farm

Woonton

Effective date: 30/11/99 © Copyright 1999 Camber Publishing Ltd. All rights reserved

ABOYNE

N5704.50 W0025.08 1.1nm W of Aboyne (N of River Dee). 460ft amsl.
09L/27R Tarmac 520x 5.5m, 09R/27L Tarmac 540x7m (RH for take-off, LH for landing). Gliding or maintenance related ACFT only. Gliders launch by Aerotow, keep a good lookout at all times. Field grazed by cattle at times. Windsock N of Rwy. Light ACFT & Glider maintenance available. Landing Fee: Gliding Club business or Maintenance £6. Non Gliding Club buisness £15. Motor Gliders £4. Deeside Gliding Club, Waterside, Dinnet. Tel: 01339 885339 (Club Office), 01339 885236 (Alan Middleton, Aboyne ACFT maintenance).

ALLENSMORE

N5200.02 W00250.07 4nm SW of Hereford. 300ft amsl.
N/S Grass 550x50m. Caution: Animals grazing. Large letter A on white background on hangar roof at N end of strip. Landing fee: Subscription to Mission Aviation Fellowship. Fuel:Nil. Mr Powell, Locks Garage, Allensmore, Hereford HR2 9HS. Tel: 01981 570206/3

BOONES FARM (High Garrett)

N5154.28 E00035.00 3nm SW of Halstead & 2nm NE of Braintree. 270ft amsl.
04/22 Grass 738x46m. Rwy has a gentle dip in centre. Beware occasional wild deer on Rwy from surrounding open farmland and overhead power lines 450m from Thr22. Strip is U/L and visitors must have insurance. There is a paved helipad area. Two yellow windsocks are displayed on W side of strip. Circuits 1000ft to SE. Never circuit to NW due to radio mast 305ft agl. Do not overfly village to NW and avoid houses adjacent to Rwy APP. John M. Wicks, Boones Farm, High Garrett, Braintree, Essex CM7 5PB. Tel: 01376 348882 or 07850 312740

BRIDGNORTH (Ditton Priors)

N5230.02 W00234.12 6nm WSW of Bridgnorth, 2nm NE of spot height 1771ft amsl. 690ft amsl.
07/25 Grass 530x16m. Care must be taken as surface may become boggy in winter months and has a 40ft slope up to half distance from E end. APP are preferred from E as W APP overflys the village centre which should be avoided at all times. Strip is surrounded by farmland. Care should also be taken as there are trees close to S side of Rwy. All circuits to the S at 1000ft QFE. Due to Rwy slope it is recommended that take-off be made downhill and landings uphill in light winds. Field is located approximately half a mile E of Ditton Priors village. Landing Fee:Nil. W.E. Lowe, The Wheatlands, Ditton Priors, Bridgenorth, Shropshire. Tel: 01746 712240/712368

BROMSGROVE (Stoney Lane)

N5220 W00159 2nm NW of Redditch. 485ft amsl.
04/22 Grass 350x45m. Strip is only suitable for experienced STOL pilots due to windshear and turbulence. Care must be taken to avoid trees on APP, power cables to SE and high ground to NE. There is a 1:80 Rwy slope to SW. PPR is vital as cattle may be grazing. Join overhead at 1500ft QFE circuits to SE at 800ft QFE. A windsock may be shown on the NW corner of the strip. Please do not overfly built-up areas. Landing fee: £5 for business use. £2 for recreational flyers. Fuel: MOGAS 3nm away 0700-2200. Pilots please note. This strip is occassionally moved within a three field area to suit the demands of agriculture be sure you have identified the correct location! P. Whittaker, 'Longlands', Stoney Lane, Bromsgrove, Worcs B60 1LZ. Tel: 01527 875228

BROOKLANDS

N5121.05 W00028.20 1nm S of Weybridge. 50ft amsl.
01/19 Asphalt 503x30m (displaced Thr). This is the useable portion of a larger tarmac Rwy, the Thrs being displaced by obstructions on either APP. This AD is only available on an invitation basis in conJct with museum activities. Brooklands AD is situated within the London CTR. Flights within a local flying area of 1nm radius, centred on the mid-point of the Rwy, but excluding that part to the E of the B374 road and a line bearing 180° True from the A245/B374 road Jct and excluding the area S of the S boundary of the London CTR, flights without compliance with IFR requirements may take place subject to the following conditions.
1.ACFT to remain below cloud and in sight of the ground.
2.Maximum Alt. 800ft QNH when Heathrow Rwy23 is in use, otherwise 1000ft QNH. (Brooklands ATC will advise).
3.Minimum flight visibility 3km.
4.Prior permission **must** be obtained from the Brooklands museum Trust Ltd.
Note: Pilots of ACFT flying within the local flying area are responsible for providing their own seperation from other ACFT and that they remain within the confines of the local flying area.
Brooklands will advise Heathrow ATC prior to the commencement of flying and acertain the Heathrow Rwy in use.
A/G radio operates on occassions when AD is active. Frequency advised with PPR. Julian Temple Brooklands Museum Trust, Weybridge, Surrey. Tel: 01932 857381 Fax: 01932 855465

BUCKINGHAM (Thornborough Grounds)

N5201 W00058. 2nm ENE of Buckingham. 250ft amsl.
05/23 Grass 460m. Pylons and electric power lines on Rwy APP. Field floods in winter. PPR vital as livestock may be grazing on strip. There is a covered ditch on APP to Rwy05, suitable for taxiing only. Windsock located 275m S of strip. Avoid overflying local Farm houses. C. M. Moore, Thornborough Grounds, Buckingham MK18 2AB. Tel: 01280 812170/814675 Email:MooreCorp1@aol.com

CAMPHILL

N5318.28 W0143.80. 12nm WSW of Sheffield. 1350ft amsl.
02/20 Grass 1400x50m. Gliding Site, Strictly PPR. No powered ACFT except motorgliders permitted. Surface is undulating, APP can be hazardous in poor weather. Accommodation available in the club house. John McKenzie, Derbyshire and Lancashire Gliding Club, Camphill, Great Hucklow, Tideswell, Buxton, SK17 8RQ. Tel: 01298 871270/871207

Effective date: 30/11/99

CASTLE BYTHAM

N5247.57 W00032.54. 5.5nm NE of RAF Cottesmore. 280ft amsl.
15/33 Grass 500x20m. Sheep regularly graze the strip so PPR essential. The strip has a level surface and is just E of the E Coast Mainline between Grantham & Peterborough. (4 track with overhead power cables). The strip is situated beneath the Cottesmore MATZ panhandle and close to it's NE boundary. Arriving and Departing ACFT are requested to contact Cottesmore APP, (130.2, Cottesmore is usually closed at Weekends). Operating Hrs: Daily SR-SS. Landing Fee: Negotiable. Fuel: Nil. Circuits: LH at 800ft QFE. Noise: Please avoid local villages. Restaurants: The Royal Oak at Swaysfield. (just N of the strip). The operator specialises in ACFT restoration & PFA permit issues & renewals. John Seed, Blackspring Farm, Castle Bytham, Grantham, Lincs, NG33 4RR. Tel: 01780 410516

CASTLETOWN

N5835.08 W00320.55 4.5nm E of Thurso 100ft amsl
25/07 Asphalt 1097x45m. 29/11 Asphalt 1028x45m. 34/16 Asphalt 992x45m.
WW II AD. Rwy surfaces are of similar vintage and are rough with loose stones. Twys are useable. There are fences along the Rwy edges.The grass areas are used for agriculture and occasionally cattle may be present. Fuel: Nil.(But AVGAS 100LL & JET A1 and advice available from Far North Aviation at Wick). Hangarage: Nil. Landing Fee: Nil. Visitors are advised to contact Wick TWR/APP, 119.70 as Castletown is on the centreline of Rwy13 at 11nm final. Owner. Mr.George Campbell, Lochside Cottage, Thurdistoft, Castletown, Caithness, KW14 8SX. Tel/Fax: 01847 821575. Tel: 07885 285105

CAUNTON

N5307.05 W00053.50 3.5NM NW of Newark 160ft amsl
This AD is restricted to Microlights only. At the time of going to press the AD was being 'moved' to a neighbouring field and orientation and measured lengths of proposed Rwys are not available. The operator advises that they are likely to be in the region of 450m in length. Visiting Microlights are welcome but obviously must obtain PPR for a full breifing on the new location and specifications. It is planned that MOGAS will be available by arrangement also Tea & Coffee. There is considerable Gliding activity to the S of the strip (at Syerston & Winfield.) Operator: Andy Buchan, Mill House, Muskham Lane, Bathley, Newark, Notts. NE23 6DD. Tel: 01636 708505

CHALLOCK (EGKE)

N5112.50 E00049.75. 4nm NNW of Ashford. 600ft amsl.
NE/SW Grass 800m, N/S Grass 800m. PPR by telephone essential. Glider towing by winch and aerotow takes place here. There are unmarked electric lines along the NE side of the AD. All APP are over tall trees. The surface is undulating and the SW corner is not useable. Operating Hrs by arrangement. DO NOT join overhead. Fuel: Nil. Landing Fee: Nil. Kent Gliding Club, Challock Arodrome, Squids Gate, Challock, Nr Ashford, Kent TN25 4DR.
Tel 01233 740274, 01233 740307. Fax: 01233 740811

CHESSINGTON see RUSHETT FARM

CHILTERN PARK

N5133.36 W00106.59 7nm W of Henley-on-Thames. 180ft amsl.
04/22 Grass 500x25m. Located within the Benson MATZ (120.90). Benson has intensive helicopter activity. Circuits to the W. Keep right of the A4074. Rwy04 Arr/Dept via SSW please avoid local habitation.Intensive Microlight activity, they may be listening out on 129.825. Ensure you clear left after landing. Landing fee £3.00. Dennis Pearson, Chiltern Park Microlight Club, Icknield Farm, Ipsden, Wallingford, Oxon, OX10 6AS.
Tel: 01491 872163, (AD),682874, (evenings).
07958 991586 (Mobile)

CLIPGATE (Barham)

N5111.18 E00109.25. 2nm SW of Aylesham & 5nm SE of Canterbury. 400ft amsl.
03/21 Grass 460x30m. Strip has trees at each end and a slight slope N to S. PPR essential. Windy conditions can cause turbulence. Landmarks to aid location are two motocross tracks on hillside 0.5nm NNW. Windsock displayed to NW side of Rwy. Circuits not below 800ft QFE. No overflying of local villages or to the SE of strip. Visitors are requested to complete AD log before departing and not to engage in local flying or circuits. Mr R. G. Akehurst, Clip Gate Farm, Lodge Leeds, Barham, Nr. Canterbury CT4 6NS.
Email:BobAkehurst@bigfoot.com
Tel: 01227 831327 or 07973 176879 (Mobile)

COLL (Ballard)

N5635.92 W00637.17. Island of Coll, Inner Hebrides. 41ft amsl
11/29 Grass 434x18m. ACFT APP or Dept Coll are to call Tiree 122.70 as the Tiree APP procedure passes close to the Coll circuit. The field N of the Rwy is subject to flooding, manoeuvring is restricted to the marked Rwy and area adjacent to the hut S of the Rwy. The owner has no objection to the strip being used but takes no responsibility for its operation.
Mr A C Brodie, Coll/Ballard Aerodrome, Inner Hebrides, Argyll & Bute Region, Scotland. Tel: 01879 230033

CUCKOO TYE FARM

N5204.50 E00045.50 2nm N of Sudbury town 240ft amsl
09/27 Grass 660x24m. Crops are grown close to the Rwy edge. Windsock displayed a third of the way along Rwy09. Caution there is a radio mast on the workshop close to the S side of the strip. The A134 crosses short final for Rwy09. Strip is close to the N edge of the Wattisham MATZ SW panhandle. Wattisham is busy with mainly Helicopter traffic during weekdays and the operator requests that visitors contact Wattisham APP 125.80. Operating Hrs:PPR SR-SS. Fuel: Nil, Landing Fee:Nil. Maintenance: Nil. Circuits:LH at 1000ft QFE. Mr.P.J.Miller, Cuckoo Tye Farm, Acton, Sudbury, Suffolk, CO10 0AE. Tel: 01787 377233. Fax: 01787 881706

Private Airfields

DONEMANA

N5453.42 W00717.55 10nm S of Londonderry 340ft amsl. 06/24 Asphalt 300x30m. STOL visitors welcome with PPR and at pilots own risk. Due to the difficult nature of this strip a telephone briefing for first time visitors is mandatory. This AD is not notified as a designated point of entry/exit for Northern Ireland under the terms of the prevention of terrorism act but this can be arranged by telephoning the RUC on 01232 650222. TV mast 1931ft amsl, (1031ft agl), 3nm SSW of the AD. Fuel:MOGAS, limited supplies available by prior arrangement. Landing Fee: Nil. Operator. Mr Alfie Danton, Raspberry Hill Farm, 29 Bond's Glen Road, Londonderry, BT47 3ST. Tel/Fax: 02871 398000

DRAYCOTT FARM (Swindon)

N5129.75 W00144.62 5nm S of Swindon, CPT 114.35 R275/19nm. 525ft amsl. 18/36 Grass 600x30m, 08/26 Grass 350m, (LDA 08/26 320) AD situated within Lyneham CTR, contact Lyneham APP 123.40. AD restricted to radio equipped ACFT with MTWA less than 5000 lbs. Circuits at 600ft Lyneham QFE to the W and S. Landing fee: £5. Fuel: Nil. Draycott Flight Centre, Chiseldon, Swindon, Wilts. Tel: 01672 841389/841333. Mobile:07831 237955

DUNSTABLE DOWNS

N5151.98 W00032.90. 1nm SW of Dunstable. 500ft amsl. 04/22 Grass 900x50m, 15/33 Grass 750x50m, 18/36 Grass 500x50m. Circuits variable to NW of the Downs, powered ACFT circuit is outside glider circuit. Permission for use normally restricted to pilots with at least a Silver Gliding Badge and on gliding business. Inbound ACFT contact Luton App,(129.55). AD is located within the Luton CTR. ACFT to taxi behind glider launch points. Intensive gliding activity including winch launching takes place. There are no AD markings. The Downs up to 817ft amsl are located to the E and S of the AD. Rwys have undulating surfaces. For landing information please telephone. Intensive hang gliding takes place along the ridge. Operating Hrs by arrangement. Fuel:AVGAS 100LL available by arrangement. Maintenance; London light ACFT. (Tel: 01582 663419). London Gliding Club, Dunstable Downs, Dunstable, Bedfordshire. Tel: 01582 663419 (PPR). Fax: 01582 665744

EASTBACH (Spence Aerodrome)

N5150.13 W00235.98 6nm S of Ross on Wye, Monmouth.550ft amsl. 01/19 Grass 350m. 06/24 Grass 250m AD situated on sloping ground and only suitable for ACFT with STOL performance. Sheep frequently on landing area. Windsock displayed on bank behind the hangar.Avoid overflying large house to the S of the AD. Fuel: MOGAS (on request). Landing Fee: Nil.Operated by Bruce Morgan & Wendy Durrad, Acorn Cottage, Hangerberry, Lydbrook, Gloucs, GL17 9QG. Tel: 01594 860988 Fax: 01594 861533

EASTON MAUDIT

N5212.80 W00042.10. 7nm ESE of Northampton. 300ft amsl. 16/34 Grass 604x23m. PPR essential. Use of Rwy16 is recommended in light winds due to a pronounced downhill slope at the N end of field. Windsock displayed to W of strip. Power cables running N/S to the W of the strip. Do not overfly farmhouse on APP16 and avoid over-flying village. Landing fee: Nil. Tim Allebone, The Limes, Easton Maudit, Wellingborough, Northants. Tel: 01933 663225 Email:tim.allebone@virgin.net

EAST WINCH

N5243.33 E00031.90. 4nm SE of Kings Lynn. 49ft amsl. 10/28 Grass 850x16m. Situated on the edge of the Marham MATZ. Pilots arriving and departing should contact Marham APP on 124.15 or by telephone 01760 337261. Visiting ACFT not normally accepted unless a customer of Scanrho aviation. Avoid over-flying E Winch village. Crop spraying ACFT operate from this AD. Circuits 10 LH 28 RH at 800ft QFE. Scanrho Aviation, Three Ways, East Winch, Kings Lynn, Norfolk. Tel: 01553 840396, 01553 840262 (Mr Burman) Fax 01485 600413

EATON BRAY see PARK FARM

EDGEHILL see SHENINGTON

EGGESFORD

N5052.13 W00352.13. 4nm E of Winkleigh disused AD. 516ft amsl. 11/29 Grass 630m. Visiting ACFT welcome at pilot's own risk. Strip slopes up at either end. APPes are good with low hedge at 29 Thr and track at 11 Thr. Caution windshear on 29 APP in Serly winds. Windsock displayed to N of 29 Thr. Circuits LH. Avoid village 1nm to S. Sheep graze on AD. N. Skinner, Trenchard Farm, Eggesford, Chumleigh, Devon, EX18 7QY. Tel: 01363 83746. Fax: 01363 83972.

ERROL

N5624.30 W00310.92. 6nm SW of Dundee Airport. 31ft amsl. 05/23 Asphalt 630x46m (Northern part of disused AD). Operating SR-SS, closed Mondays and Thursdays. Contact Leuchars App and Dundee App. Before entering the circuit call DZ Control Errol (usually 123.45). Free-fall parachuting up to FL150. Circuits 23 LH, 05 RH, at 900ft aal. On APP and climb-out maintain Rwy heading for at IE 1nm to avoid houses. Visiting pilots should report to either Fife Parachuting Centre, Muirhouses Farm or Harbour Sawmills Ltd. (on disused Rwy 11). Landing fee: £5.00 single, £10.00 twin. Tel: 01821 642454 (parachute club). Operated by Mr. L. Doe, Muirhouses Farm, Errol. Tel: 01821 642555 (operator-work), 642333 (operator-home), 642355 (Harbour Sawmills, AD). Fax (Mr. Doe): 01821 642825

FEARN

N5745.48 W00356.58 1nm S of Fearn. 25ft amsl. 11/29 Asphalt 1097x46m. (other Rwys are obstructed by fences). AD is situated in D703. An entry/exit sector is established from ground level to 1000ft agl in the segment S of a line joining N5745.00 W00400.42 and N5745.00 W00353.25. Maximum height S of this line is 1000ft agl. DAAIS Tain Range 122.75. Mrs D Sutherland, Tullich Farm, Fearn, Ross-Shire, Highland Region, IV18 0PE. Tel 01862 832278

Effective date: 30/11/99

FELIXKIRK

N5415.11 W00117.93 2nm NE of Thirsk 226ft amsl
01/19 Grass 500x40m. Strictly PPR. Rwy can be soft after prolonged precipitation. National Grid transmission pylons 120ft agl run N-S close to the W of the AD. This AD is the home of Sport Air UK and is situated within the Topcliffe MATZ. (controlling authority Leeming APP 127.75, however ACFT may be transferred to Topcliffe APP 125.00. ACFT departing Felixkirk are advised to call Topcliffe APP initially, it may be possible to get two-way communication on the ground). Operating Hrs: Mon-Fri 0830-1700 local. Closed Weekends. Fuel:Nil. Landing Fee:Nil. Maintenance: Sport Air UK, Rans ACFT specialists. Noise: Please avoid local habitation and particularly Felixkirk village close to the SE of the AD. Circuits: LH. Restaurants: Carpenters Arms, Felixkirk. Mr.John Whiting, Sport Air UK Ltd, The Aerodrome, Felixkirk, Thirsk, Yorkshire, YO7 2DR.
Tel: 01845 537465, Fax: 01845 537791

FLOTTA

N5849.58 W00308.53. 9.5nm SE of Stromness, Orkney. 70ft amsl
16/34 Asphalt 759x18m. Heliport operated by Elf Exploration UK Plc. Fixed wing ACFT accepted when operating Ambulance flights or in emergency only. Visual aid to location is a flare stack, 1.4nm from AD. There is a significant longitudinal slope on the Rwy. No facilities.
Tel. 01856 884000.

FOLKESTONE (Lyminge)

N5109 E00104. 7nm S of Canterbury. 600ft amsl.
06/24 Grass 440x10m. Strip is surrounded to W, E and N by Lyminge Forest - a large wooded area. Caution: trees to 50ft are a hazard at N end of strip. PPR is imperative as there may be farm machinery or people working in soft fruit fields in close proximity. Circuits 800ft QFE 24 LH, 06 RH. Visiting ACFT are requested to avoid all houses. Mr G G Boot. Tel: 01303 227222
Email:Geoffreyboot@compuserve.com

GARFORTH

N5347.30 W00121.50. 6.9nm W of Sherburn-in-Elmet 200ft amsl
10/28 Grass 750x40m. Microlights not accepted. Other visitors welcome with PPR at pilots own risk. The A656 crosses 28 APP on short final. There are National Grid transmission lines and pylons 175ft agl close to the AD which cross the 28 APP between the A656 and Micklefield village, exercise extreme caution. Windsock displayed at Rwy midpoint. The AD is close to the W edge of the Church Fenton MATZ, controlling authority Fenton APP 126.5, (usually closed weekends). Noise: Tight circuits on 10 to avoid overflight of Garforth. Operating Hrs: SR-SS. Fuel: Nil. Maintenance: Nil. Landing Fee: Advised with PPR. Restaurants: The Swan, Aberford, (3nm to N of AD). Chris Makin, Sturton Grange Farm, Garforth, Leeds, LS25 2HB.
Tel: 0113 2862631 Fax: 0113 2873747.

GLENORMISTON ESTATE (Innerleithen)

N5537 W00305. 1nm W of Innerleithen alongside River Tweed, TLA 113.8 R058/11.3nm. 500ft amsl.
13/31 Grass 515x15m. Rwy is level but care must be taken as surface may become boggy at W end. Be aware of power lines and a farm road W of Rwy. APP also need care due to high ground to N and S, Rwy is not aligned with valley at E end. Windsock will be displayed to visiting ACFT after PPR, which is essential. Do not overfly Innerleithen town. J.G. Hogg (owner), Permission from George Askew, Glenormiston, Innerleithen, Peebleshire. Tel: 01896 830940. 07798 574245. Email:glenormistonairstrip@Lineone.net **Note:A second, longer Rwy will be ready during 2000. Details available on request.**

GREEN FARM

N5209 W00133. 3nm SE of Wellesbourne Mountford AD. 360ft amsl.
04/22 Grass 613x30. Displaced Thr on 04 marked by red cones to avoid hedge close to 04 Thr and rough ground which reduces takeoff run on 04 also. Rough area is suitable as overun for 22. Windsocks displayed circuits LH 22 RH 04. Do not overfly Butlers Marston village which is to the E of strip. Call Wellsbourne Radio on 124.025 due to close proximity of ATZ. Caution! Ettington strip is 1.5nm to WSW. Strip is regularly overflown by low level fast jets. Landing Fee:Nil. Terry Cooper, Green Farm, Combrook, Warwickshire. CV35 9HP.
Tel: 01926 640162

GUNTON PARK (Hanworth)

N5250.30 E000119.16. 2nm N of Suffield and 3nm W of Antingham. 100ft amsl.
N/S Grass 800x30m. Rwy undulating with mown dry grass. Caution: Electric power line goes underground in centre of Rwy. PPR imperative due to location of Rwy in middle of a deer park. There is a line of trees S of Rwy and also trees at N end. Visiting ACFT are requested not to overfly Observatory TWR 1nm N and Hall 1nm W of strip. Windsock is displayed on E side. Sally Martin, Gunton Park, Hanworth, Norwich, Norfolk NR11 7HJ.
Tel: 01263 761202. 01263 768667 (Office).
Fax: 01263 761253

HALWELL

N5021.55 W00342.35 5nm WNW of Dartmouth 625ft amsl
09/27 Grass 421x110m. Rwy09 has upslope. The AD is a large grass area which is regularly grazed by sheep. Mainly used by Microlights but suitable light ACFT are welcome with PPR and at pilots own risk. Operating Hrs: 0800-SS, (local). Landing Fee:£2. Fuel:MOGAS available by prior arrangement. Noise: All ACFT approaching the AD are to do so from the NW circuits should be to the N and kept very tight. Do not overfly houses to the W of the AD). Restaurant/Accomodation. The Old Inn, Halwell, (a short walk from the strip).
Tel: 01803 712329. Operator. Mr. Keith Wingate, South Hams Flying Club, 10 hillside Drive, Kingsbridge, Devon, TQ7 1JT. Tel: 01548 857513. Fax: 01548 853556

Effective date: 30/11/99 © Copyright 1999 Camber Publishing Ltd. All rights reserved

HARDWICKE

N5205.30 W00304.20 3NM ENE of Hay on Wye 450ft amsl
09/27 Grass 500x30m. PPR essential as wire fencing may be placed across strip. Sheep graze the AD. The strip is situated within the Wye valley with high ground to the NW & S. Highest point is 4nm due S up to 2306ft amsl. High ground up to 1044ft amsl 1.5nm to the E. Circuits: To the N at 1000ft QFE. Landing Fee: Nil. Fuel: MOGAS available by prior arrangement. Restaurant: Royal Oak, Hardwicke, Tel: 01497 831248. Operators: Graham & Judy Pritchard, New House Farm, Hay on Wye, Worcs. Tel: 01497 831259

HATTON

N5724.45 W00154.93 1nm S of Hatton, Grampian 265ft amsl.
08/26 Grass 650x24m. Visiting ACFT welcome with PPR at owners own risk. Slight upslope on Rwy08. A 30ft agl domestic power line crosses the 26 APP on short final. Strip may be waterlogged after prolonged precipitation. The strip is close to the boundary of the Aberdeen CTA/CTR Aberdeen APP 120.40, and is beneath HMR Whiskey, a published helicopter route for offshore traffic. Heavy commercial helicopters can be expected entering/leaving the Aberdeen zone. Useful weather information can be obtained from Aberdeen ATIS 121.85. Fuel: MOGAS by prior arrangement. Landing Fee: Donations to upkeep welcomed. Circuits: 26 LH 08 RH at 800ft QFE. Noise: Please avoid overflight of local habitation. Operator: James Anderson, Ardiffery Mains, Hatton, Peterhead, Aberdeenshire. AB42 0SD. Tel: 01779 841207

HOOK

N5116.50 W00056.53. 5nm E of Basingstoke. 225ft amsl.
08/26 Grass 609x20m. Slight upslope on 08, grass can become waterlogged in winter. Caution sheep and cattle on strip, power lines and trees on both APP. Preferred landing Rwy26, takeoff 08. Do not overfly Hook village. Windsock by 08 Thr. Audrey Hill, Scotland Farm, Holt Lane, Hook, Hampshire RG27 9EJ Tel: 01256 762423.

HITCHIN see RUSH GREEN

HOUGHAM

N5300.35 W00041.35. 5nm SE of Newark 100ft amsl.
18/36 Grass 402x20m. 09/27 120x20m. (Microlights only). AD is U/L and welcomes light ACFT and microlights at pilot's own risk and on PPR. W boundary of Cranwell MATZ is 2nm E of AD. Circuits to E at 800ft aal; 36 RH 18 LH. There is a short strip across Rwy for microlights (in E or W crosswinds). Windsock E of Rwy. Care should be taken due to a railway embankment with overhead electrification 400m N of 18 Thr and power cables 400m S of 36 Thr (departures from 36 are usually to the left). Please avoid over-flying farms and houses in the vicinity. Microlights may be using 129.825, (common frequency). Landing fee: Donation appreciated. Operated by Hougham Flying Group.
Tel: (PPR) 01400 250293 Mike Barnatt Millns. The Old Coach House, Coach Road, Hougham, Nr Grantham, Lincs, NG32 2JF.

HUNTINGDON see KIMBOLTON

INCE

N5332.30 W00302.25 3nm SSE of RAF Woodvale 10ft amsl
07/25 Grass 410x20m 12/30 Grass 335x20m 18/36 Grass 380x20m Mainly used for Microlight ACFT but Light ACFT are welcome with PPR at pilots own risk. Please be considerate of ab-initio trainees. Caution, there are power cables crossing the 18 APP on short final on the N bank of the river. The AD is close to RAF Woodvale ATZ boundary, 1nm to NNW, Woodvale APP 121.0, TWR 119.75 and University Air Squadron ACFT carry out general handling exercises in the local area. The Liverpool CTR is 3.5nm to the S. Liverpool APP 119.85.Radio:Ince Radio 129.825. Fuel: MOGAS available by arrangement. Landing Fee: £2, Operating Hrs: SR-SS daily. Restaurants/B&B: The Well, Ince Blundell. Noise: Avoid overflying Ince-Blundell village, (close to the S) and local habitation within the circuit. Circuits: Obtain details with PPR, usually an overhead join with descent on dead side to 500ft QFE, (usual Microlight circuit height). Operator: John N, W Lancashire Microlight Club, Ince Blundell, Formby, Merseyside, L38 6JJ. Tel: 0151 929 3319/ 07850 882309 (Mobile)

INNERLEITHEN see GLENORMISTON ESTATE

JUBILEE FARM (Wisbech)

N5238.00 W00003.89 4.5nm SW of Wisbech 5ft amsl
01/19 Grass 565x20m Flat strip with farm buildings very close to the 19 Thr. These not only constitute a hazard but may generate turbulence. There are telegraph poles close to the 01 Thr on either side of the APP but the wires are run underground as they cross the APP. R212, (up to 2000ft) is 1nm S of the strip but this is applicable to helicopters only. Keep a good lookout for low flying military ACFT in the vicinity, particularly during the week. Fuel: Nil, Landing Fee: Nil, Circuits 01 LH 19 RH at 1000ft QFE. Noise: Avoid overflight of local habitation, particularly to the E of AD. Operator: Frank Ball, Jubilee Farm, Tholomas Drove, Wisbech St. Mary, Cambs, PE13 4SP. Tel: 01945 410261

KIMBOLTON (Huntingdon) (Stow Longa).

N5218.98 W00022.75 8nm W of Huntingdon. 1nm W of Grafham Water (reservoir). 246ft amsl.
10/28 Grass 600x12m 13/31 Grass 500x18m 13/31 is not available on kart racing days (2nd Sat. and Sun. of month). Light ACFT welcome at pilot's own risk. Visiting pilots should overfly hangar. If no-one is there, circle over Stow Longa to attract attention. Windsock displayed. Gas Booster Station and tall mast on APP to Rwy31. Transport on request. Landing fee: Nil. R.C. Convine, Yendis, Stow Longa, Hunts.
Tel: 01480 860300

KING'S LYNN (Tilney St. Lawrence)

N5243 E00019. 4.5nm SW of Kings Lynn, 2nm W of River Great Ouse. 10ft amsl.
16/34 Grass 400x32m. Operated for private use, however visiting ACFT welcome at pilot's own risk and strictly PPR. Pylons 200ft high 0.5nm to the N. Orange Windsock displayed. Landing fee: Nil. J. Goodley & Sons, Hirdling House, Tilney St. Lawrence
Tel: 01945 880237

Effective date: 30/11/99 © Copyright 1999 Camber Publishing Ltd. All rights reserved

KIRKCUDBRIGHT (Plunton)

N5451.00 W00409.05 5nm W of Kirkcudbright. 250ft amsl.
02/20 Grass 459m. Light ACFT at pilot's own risk and strictly PPR. It is essential to adhere to the boundary markings which are different grass lengths. Windsock E side of strip. Power cables 400m S of strip. Livestock movements and sheep grazing take place on strip. Picketing facilities. William S. Sproat Esq., Lennox Plunton Farm, Borgue, Kirkcudbright.
Tel: 01557 870210

LAINDON

N5135.67 E00026.76 1.25nm NNW of Basildon. 90ft amsl.
08/26 Grass 475x18m. Upslope on 26, 20ft power lines on APP to 08 on short final. Crops may be grown right up to strip edge. There is a public road at 26 Thr, keep a good lookout for vehicles and pedestrians. Powerlines, 80ft agl parallel the strip to the S.Circuits 1000ft to the N. Do not overfly built up area to the S of the strip. Preferred landing Rwy in light winds 26. George French, High View, 16 Wash Road, Basildon, Essex SS15 4ER.
Tel: 01268 411464

LANE FARM

N5207 W00312. 4nm NW of Hay-on-Wye. 830ft amsl.
06/24 Grass 730x30m (strip width narrows to a minimum of 30m). Strip situated in a valley with high ground all around up to 1671ft amsl, (to W), and 1361ft amsl, (to SW). Caution there are 50ft trees on the N side of the strip and close to both Thrs. Cables run close down the NW side of the strip and cross the 06 APP on very short final, (30ft agl). No windsock. Circuits are to be flown to avoid local villages, the area is very rural! Lane farm is on the NW side of the strip. Landing fee:Nil. This strip is ONLY available to pilots visiting the locality or using Lane farm for B&B or their holiday properties. No casual visitors or strip training please. John Bally, Lane Farm, Paincastle, Hay-on-Wye, Radnorshire. LD2 3JS.
Tel: 01497 851605

LANGHAM

N5256.30 E00057.38. 9nm W of Sheringham. 120ft amsl.
10/28 Concrete 700x15m (former Twy), 02/20 Grass 550x18m. (SW end of disused AD). No circuits. Mast 98ft aal, 250m N of Rwy25 Thr. Trees and huts on APP Rwy28. Due to obstructions exercise extreme caution. M3 maintenance available. Fuel: AVGAS 100LL by arrangement. Landing fee: £20.00. H. Labouchere Esq.
Tel: 01328 830003 Fax: 01328 830232

LARK ENGINE FARMHOUSE

N5224.96 E00022.18 4.5NM ENE of Ely 0ft amsl.
06/24 Grass 600x9m. Flat strip situated within the Mildenhall/Lakenheath CMATZ. Please call Lakenheath APP 128.90. There are trees very close to the APP for 24 on very short final which, as well as constituting an obstruction may also generate rotor in Southerly winds. Farm equipment may be parked close to the Rwy edge. Windsock displayed. Circuits: Join directly downwind, (LH), for both Rwys at 1000ft QFE. Noise: Do not overfly the village of Prickwillow which is 1nm NW of the strip. Landing Fee: Nil. Fuel: Nil. Operating Hrs:SR-SS daily. Mr.Clinton Judd, Lark Engine Farmhouse, Lark Bank, Prickwillow, Ely, Cambridgeshire. CB7 4SW.
Tel/Fax: 01353 688428

LEE-ON-SOLENT (EGHF)

N5048.91 W00112.42 2NM NW of Gosport. 32ft amsl.
05/23 Tarmac 1309x46m.(lighting available). Displaced Thr on 05 by 154m.10/28 Tarmac 1000x46m. Marked as disused but surface useable with caution. 17/35 Tarmac 890x46m. Marked as disused but useable with caution. Operational Hrs strictly with PPR, and is normally only available to civil ACFT in connection with Police operations or having business with Bristow Helicopters Ltd. Operators are to provide evidence of a minimum of £7.5m crown indemnity insurance before landing at this AD. Specific operating procedures apply at this AD. Visiting pilots are required to obtain a comprehensive briefing either in writing or by telephone before departing for Lee. Part of this AD lies within the Fleetlands ATZ all inbound and outbound ACFT should call Fleetlands TWR,(135.70). Police Fixed wing ACFT and SAR helicopters operate H24. Helicopter test flying takes place. Glider flying takes place during daylight hrs. Radio:Nil. Hampshire police air support unit, Lee-on-Solent Airfield, Argus gate, Broom Way, Lee-on-Solent, Hampshire, PO14 9YA.
Tel: 023 92551714 Fax: 023 92899013

LYMM DAM

N5322.00 W00228.00 1nm S of Lymm Cheshire 150ft amsl.
09/27 Grass 500x10m. Visiting PFA type ACFT welcome with PPR and at pilots own risk. AD is within Manchester CTR and prior notice of operation must be obtained by notifying Manchester ATC, (0161 499 5320). Contact should also be made on Manchester RAD frequency 119.4. Normally pilots should plan to route along the Manchester low-level route not above 1250ft QNH then route directly E to Lymm Dam. Outbounds should reverse this course into the low-level route. The Rwy is flat with a pond adjacent and S of the Rwy midpoint. There is a 4ft hedge and minor road close to the 27 Thr with a single telegraph pole in the hedge on the opposite side of the road. A wire fence is close to the 09 Thr. Windsock displayed by the pond. Fuel:Nil. Landing fee:Nil. Taxi: Jolly's, Tel: 01925 755631. Operator. Mr.P.Moore, Beech Tree Farm, High Legh, Knutsford, Cheshire. WA16 6NR. Tel: 01925 753569

MELBOURNE (Melrose Farm)

N5352.03 W00050.27 6nm SSW of Pocklington. 25ft amsl.
06/24 Tarmac 1624x46m. Only active Rwy on disused AD. Caution: power line, (120ft high), crosses APP to 06, farm tractors may be on AD. Drag racers, microlights and autogyros all operate here. Avoid overflying local habitation. Windsock displayed to N of 24 Thr. J Rowbottom, Melrose Farm, Melbourne, York, YO4 4SS.Tel: 01759 318392, Fax: 01759 318948

MOORLANDS (Hull)

N5347.59 W00010.49 7nm ENE of Hull centre. OTR 113.9 R355/6.5nm. 50ft amsl.
08/26 Grass 610x14m Visiting light ACFT welcome at pilot's own risk. Windsock on hangar. Rwy can be soft in winter. Circuits LH at 800ft QFE. D306 1nm to NE. Landing fee: Nil. R. Knapton Moorlands, Humbleton Hall HU11 4ND Tel: 01964 670242

Effective date: 30/11/99

NEWARK (Beeches Farm)

N5309 W00044. 2nm W of Swinderby AD and 5nm NE of Newark. 50ft amsl.

10/28 Grass 517x18m. Rwy is level with good surface. Windsock displayed on hangar roof. Newark - Lincoln railway runs at 90° close to 28 Thr. On N side of strip there is a ditch running from hangar to railway. Visiting ACFT are welcome PPR. Avoid over-flying local villages. Circuits at 800ft aal. Contact Waddington MATZ when in the area. P. L. Clements, Beeches Farm, S Scarle, Nr. Newark, Notts NG23 7JH. Tel: 01636 892273

NEWTON PEVERIL FARM

N5047.38 W00206.03 4nm SE of Blandford Forum 120ft amsl.

27/09 Grass 461x9m. Primarily a Microlight AD. Strip has slight undulation at the 09 Thr. Power cables 25ft agl cross the 27 APP on very short final. There is a stream bounded by trees close to the S of the strip which may cause turbulence with the wind in the SW-SE sector. Cattle may be grazing so PPR even more essential! When APP the field, follow the power cables toward the strip and keep your final turn tight to avoid overflying Sturminster Marshall and other habitation to the E, (if landing 27). When landing 09 follow same procedure but turn inside Charborough Park, ideally do not go W of the A31. All circuits to the S at 500ft QFE. Be aware that the strip is located under the Wern edge of the Solent CTA, (base 2000ft QNH). Bournemouth ATIS can provide useful weather info on 121.95. Landing Fee: Nil. Tim Trenchard, Newton Peveril Farm, Sturminster Marshall, Wimborne, Dorset. Tel: 01258 857205

NUTHAMPSTEAD (Royston)

N5159.40 E00004.07. 4nm SE of Royston. BKY VOR 116.25 on AD. 460ft amsl.

05/23 Grass 700x35m. Grass Rwy located where former Rwy was removed, using the 23 end. PPR at pilot's own risk. Strip clearly marked and it is essential to land only within the markers. The 23 Thr has a steep upslope after which the strip runs level. Cars and tractors may be using the 6m wide concrete strips. Caution! there is a 120ft mast by the office block W of the 05 Thr. Windsock displayed. Circuits 05 RH 23 LH at 800ft. Nuthampstead Airfield Associates Ltd. Keffords, Barley, Royston, Herts SG8 8LB. Tel: 01763 848287 Fax: 01763 849616

NYMPSFIELD (Stroud)

N5142.51 W00217.01. 4nm SW of Stroud. 700ft amsl.

E/W Grass 1120m. The field is undulating, areas N and S side of AD very boggy. Gliding site, Caution cables! - light ACFT accepted strictly PPR by telephone on the day for gliding business only. Trees close to AD boundary and hilly situation of site generate turbulence and wind gradients in crosswinds. NW wind is to be avoided. Landing fee £5.00. Maintenance available. Bristol and Gloucestershire Gliding Club.
Tel: 01453 860342/860060.
01453 860861 (Maintenance, Roger Targett sailplanes).

OAKLANDS (Oxford)

N5150.51 W00126.44 0.5nm N of the Oxford/Worcester railway and 1.5nm NE of the Oxford outer marker. 370ft amsl. 12/30 Grass 400x12m. Visiting ACFT strictly PPR and at pilots own risk.Caution: power lines on APP to 12, 150m from Thr. Windsock displayed to S of strip. Circuits to the S at 600ft, QFE. Do not overfly local villages. Robert J. Stobo, Oaklands Farm, Stonesfield, Oxford OX8 8DW. Tel: 01993 891226

PARK FARM (Eaton Bray)

N5152.50 W00036.50 1.5nm WNW of Dunstable Gliding Site 295ft amsl

28/10 Grass 500x30m. Visiting light ACFT welcome with PPR and owners own risk. Circuits prohibited. Caution! Intense gliding activity at Dunstable. AD is situated inside Luton CTR. Inbound and outbound ACFT must call Luton RAD 129.55. Useful met info can be obtained from Luton ATIS 120.575. There are power cables, (30ft agl), on short final for 28. A fence, (Wire, 5ft high), runs along the S side of the Rwy. There is a small hangar abeam and to the N of the 28 Thr. Windsock displayed on the N AD boundary at the midpoint. Fuel:Nil, Landing fee:Nil. Noise: Avoid overflight of local villages. Particularly Eaton Bray, (short final 28), and Billington, (1.5nm on 10 APP). Operator: Mr.E.French, Brookside, Park Farm, Eaton Bray, Dunstable, Bedfordshire. LU6 2DQ.
Tel: 01525 222368

PEPLOW

N5248.36 W00229.52 5nm S of Market Drayton 222ft amsl

18/36 Asphalt 800x15m. 06/24 Asphalt 600x15m. Visiting light ACFT welcome with PPR at pilots own risk. The Rwys are part of the perimeter track of the wartime AD. All other parts of the AD are unavailable for ACFT use. The perimeter track is used by agricultural machinery pilots are advised to keep a good lookout and be aware of the possibility of debris on Rwys. The AD is situated within the Shawbury/Ternhill CMATZ, controlling authority Shawbury APP 120.775. Visiting ACFT should call Shawbury when Inbound and ASAP after departure. During weekdays there is considerable military helicopter training, often at low level, within the vicinity. Fuel:Nil. Landing Fee:Nil. Maintenance:Nil. Circuits: 18/36 RH 06/24 LH 1000ft QFE. Noise: Please avoid overflight of local habitation. Operator: Mr.D.R.Williams, Standford Service Station, Standford Bridge, Newport, Shropshire. TF10 8BA. Tel: 01952 550261 Fax: 01952 541340

PLAISTOWS

N5143.70 W00022.71 2nm SE of Hemel VRP. Herts 395ft amsl

16/34 Grass 357x20m 12/30 Grass 329x20m Primarily a Microlight AD but suitable STOL ACFT welcome with PPR at pilots own risk. AD is close to the S boundary of the Luton CTR, Luton APP 129.55. Useful weather information can be obtained from Luton ATIS 120.575. Noise: Please avoid local habitation. All circuits LH. Radio: Call downwind and final on 129.825, (Microlight common frequency). Operating Hrs: SR-SS but Dep restricted to between 0800-1900 local. Landing Fee: Donations to the Royal Marsden Hospital. Fuel: MOGAS. Maintenance:Nil Restaurants:The Three Hammers, Chiswell Green, (1nm E of AD). Mr.D.Brunt, Plaistows Farm, Chiswell Green Lane, St.Albans, Herts, AL2 3NT. Tel: 01727 851642

Effective date: 30/11/99 © Copyright 1999 Camber Publishing Ltd. All rights reserved

PORTMOAK (Kinross)

N5611.21 W00319.45. 0.5nm E of Loch Leven, 4nm ESE of Kinross. 360ft amsl.
09/27 Grass 700x15m, 10/28 Grass 900x15m. Powered ACFT only to use 10/28 (N field). Light ACFT accepted at pilot's own risk and strictly PPR. Caution! Winch cables. Pilots of nosewheel ACFT should exercise extreme caution. Do not overfly the site or the nearby villages of Scotlandwell, Kinnesswood or the Vane RSPB Centre on the S side of Loch Leven. Beware of large flocks of birds around the area at all times of the year. Winch and aerotow launching seven days a week. Pilots intending to land at Portmoak should contact Leuchars APP and advise inbound to Portmoak. When within 5nm of Portmoak make all calls blind on 129.975. Do not expect a reply. Keep a good lookout for gliders which regularly fly between ground level and 20000ft. Windsock displayed. Landing fee £5.00. Fuel:AVGAS 100LL by prior arrangement. Scottish Gliding Centre. Tel: 01592 840543 (office) or 01592 840243 (club).

REDLANDS (Swindon)

N5133.30 W00141.33. 1nm E of Swindon, CPT 114.35 R288/18.5nm. 322ft amsl.
06/24 Grass 407x11m 17/35 Grass 274x13m Microlight ACFT only accepted due to planning constraints. PPR SR-SS, Sundays 1000-2000 or SS, (whichever is the earlier), all times local. Visitors welcome with PPR at pilot's own risk 3RD party liability insurance required. APP/Dep via N corridor, fly between the two barns between the AD and the railway line which is 1nm distant. Inbound ACFT at 1500ft QFE. Outbound ACFT climb out over the barns to railway before turning on course. Overhead join at 1500ft QFE. Circuits at 500ft aal. 06/35 LH 24/17 RH. Observe signals square and windsocks, Electric fence on N SIDE OF 06/24 AND W side of 17/35. After landing vacate the Rwys to the Twys ASAP. Avoid over-flying Wanborough and local habitation. Redlands Radio 129.825. Fuel:Nil. Landing fee:£3.50. Help yourself to Tea, Coffee & Biscuits. Toilets on site. Operated by Joe & Sarah Smith Redlands Aerodrome & Microlight Club, Redlands Farm, Wanborough, Swindon, Wilts, SN4 0AA. Tel: 01793 791014

RHIGOS

N5144.34 W00335.05. 8nm W of Merthyr Tydfil. 780ft amsl.
09/27 Grass 550m. Circuits: 09 RH, 27 LH. Avoid over-flying Rhigos village. Hill top site, primarily for gliding. Surface is rough. Caution! cables. Field slopes down from E to W. Caution: after rain due to soft surface. Not suitable for light ACFT in strong S and N winds. Beware of launch cables. Vale of Neath Gliding Club, Rhigos Airfield, Nr Aberdare, Glamorgan, S. Wales. Tel: 01685 811023

ROSEMARKET

N5144.32 W00458.59 4nm S of Haverford W. 160ft amsl.
08/26 Grass 600x15m. upslope on 08. Can be unusable after heavy rain. There is a public road close to the 08 Thr look out for vehicles and pedestrians. Also close to the 08 Thr is a car park. Circuits at 800ft QFE, avoid overflying riding school on N edge of woods to NE of strip. Windsock displayed at E end of strip. MOGAS available by arrangement. This strip is part of a leisure complex and is situated within a 9 hole Golf course. Because of the Rwy siteing prior telephone contact would be appreciated. Golfers are particularly welcomed. Bill & Bridie Young, Dawn till Dusk Golf course, Rosemarket, Milford Haven, Pembs. SA73 1JY Tel: 01437 890231

ROSERROW

N5033.72 W00454.02 1NM SE of Polzeath Cornwall 130ft amsl
09/27 Grass 900x60m. The AD is part of a large Golf course 7 sports complex. PPR is essential, However, light ACFT are very welcome at all times at the pilots own risk. There is also a marked 'H' for helicopter visitors. Overnight parking for fixed wing and rotary visitors is available. No radio but visitors are advised to contact St.Mawgan APP 126.50. Fuel:Nil. Landing Fee:Nil when using club facilities. Restaurants: Available in the Golf club and also in the complex itself. Accommodation available on site. Circuits:Overhead join then circuit at 1000ft QFE. Operating Hrs:SR-SS daily. Operator: Roserrow Golf & Country Club, Roserrow, St.Minver, Wadebridge, Cornwall, PL27 6QT. Tel: 01208 863000 Fax: 01208 863002

ROTHWELL

N5224.70 W00047.40 2NM W of Kettering 400ft amsl.
02/20 Grass 500x14m. Winch launch gliding activity up to 2000ft agl. Caution cables. (Gliders normally operate only at weekends and on public holidays. Strip is situated between the A14 and Thorpe Malsor reservoir. There are 25ft agl street lights on the A14 on short final for Rwy20. Farm vehicles use the Rwy strip as access. Caution low flying military ACFT mainly during the week. Noise: Avoid overflight of Rothwell, close to the NW. And Loddington, close to the SW. Windsock E of Rwy02 Thr. Limited parking available. Radio: A/G 129.90 Rothwell traffic, please make blind calls. Landing Fee:Nil. Fuel:Nil. Circuits:LH at 1000ft QFE. (No overhead joins when gliding in progress). Operating Hrs: SR-SS daily. Mr.G.A.Pentelow, Orton Lodge, Orton Lane, Loddington, Kettering, NN14 1LQ. Tel: 01536 711750

RUSHETT FARM

N5120 W00019. 2nm W of Epsom 160ft amsl.
02/20 Grass 350x15m. Caution: STOL only. Visitors only accepted in connection with Light ACFT Services. B. Woodall, Rushett Farm, Chessington, Surrey KT9 2NH. Tel: 01372 722702 (Owner). Tel: 01372 741976 (Light ACFT Services).

Effective date: 30/11/99 © Copyright 1999 Camber Publishing Ltd. All rights reserved

RUSH GREEN (Hitchin)

N5154.11 W00014.51. 3nm S of Hitchin. 350ft amsl.
34/16 Grass 550x10m. 31/13 Grass 550x10m. Light ACFT welcome during normal working hrs. All circuits to E at 500ft QFE. Strips may be boggy after heavy rain. Visitors requested to book in at caravan. Servicing and repairs available. Located inside Luton CTR, contact Luton APP 129.55. This does not preclude non-radio ACFT, there is a standard entry procedure agreed with Luton obtainable by telephone from Bowker air services. Landing fee Nil for recreational visitors. Commercial: Landing Fee on application. A/G 122.35 on request. Fuel: AVGAS 100LL. W.S. Bowker, Rush Green, Hitchin, Herts. Tel: 01438 355051 or 01462 452295

ST NEOTS (Honeydon)

N5213 W00021. 7nm NNE of Bedford, 1nm SE of Little Staughton AD. 170ft amsl.
E/W Grass 640m, NE/SW Grass 678m, NW/SW Grass 678m. Visitors accepted only with PPR. Caution rough surface, sheep grazing. No Windsock. Mrs.B.Spencer Thomas, Honeydon Farm, Colmworth, Beds. MK44 2LR. Tel: 01234 376393

SANDHILL FARM

N5136.14 W0140.30. 4nm NE of Swindon. 350ft amsl.
06/24 Grass 850m. Primarily a gliding site with winch launches. Beware! cables. Upslope on 06, field may become waterlogged in winter. Circuits 06 LH 24 RH, avoid overflying local villages, But particularly the two farms either side of the B4000 approximately half a mile N of AD, these should not be overflown below 1000ft agl. Windsock at midpoint on Southside. Tea and Coffee available when Gliding in progress. AD open at weekends only. Vale of White Horse Gliding Centre, Sandhill farm, Shrivenham, Wilts. Tel: 01793 783685

SEIGHFORD

N5249.40 W00212.12. 3nm NW of Stafford. 321ft amsl.
13/31 Concrete 500x50m. Available for business use only. Third party insurance must be carried. Call Seighford Glider base Radio 129.90 as there may be glider launching on APP to 13. PPR is essential as vehicles may be on Rwy, area is also liable to frequent crosswinds. 31 has a 5ft fence at end. Windsock displayed. Circuits 1500ft aal, 31 LH, 13 RH. Do not overfly stud farm 0.5nm to left of APP to 31. W. O. Brown, Clanford Hall, Seighford, Staffs. Tel: 01785 282237; Staffordshire Gliding Club Tel: 01785 282575

SHEEPWASH

N5050.10 W00409.50 15NM E of Bude.310ft amsl.
17/35 Grass 700x35m. PPR essential. The strip is sharply undulating and prone to windshear and turbulence. ALL landings on 35 (uphill). Take-off 17 (Downhill). It is extremely important to ascertain wind conditions are suitable before departure for this AD. Visiting ACFT are required to carry third party insurance cover, details of minimum should be obtained with PPR. Windsock displayed. Noise: Avoid Sheepwash village 0.5nm SE of AD. Circuits: Standard overhead join. Fuel: Nil Landing Fee: Donation to upkeep appreciated. Operating Hrs:SR-SS daily. Roger Appleton, Westover, Sheepwash, EX21 5HQ. Tel: 01409 231619

SHENINGTON (Edgehill)

N5205.10 W00128.38. 5nm NW of Banbury. 642ft amsl.
16/34 Concrete 1000m; 05/23 Concrete 700m; 11/29 Grass 1025m. Gliding Site with winch launching. Please avoid overflying local villages – 'fine' for noisy visitors. Caution there is a Kart track on the 05 Thr. Refreshments and toilets available on site.Shenington Radio 129.90, (glider ops). Fuel: Nil. Landing Fee: Nil. Edgehill AD, Shenington, Oxfordshire. Shenington Gliding Club. Tel: 01295 688121 (AD).

SHEPTON MALLET (Lower Withial Farm)

N5108 W00235. 6nm E of Glastonbury, 8nm NNE of Yeovilton AD. 180ft amsl.
05/23 Grass 500x40m. Strictly PPR. Surface can be boggy in winter months. Strip has a slight E upslope and at silage times narrows it to 3.5m. AD is occasionally overgrown with crops or used for grazing livestock. Windsock displayed. Circuits LH 800ft aal. Avoid all local villages and houses. David Stokes, Lower Withial Farm, East Pennard, Shepton Mallet, Somerset BA4 6UE. Tel: 01749 860203

SOLLAS

N5739.51 W00719.33 Beach, 1nm NE of Sollas Village. Nth Uist SL.
NE/SW Sand approx 1 mile in length parallel to shoreline. Firm Sand public beach strip, U/L. No facilities. The useable portion is situated below the High water mark. Pilots should exercise caution during flare and hold-off as height judgement may be difficult over the featureless surface. Preferred landing technique is to use power down to touchdown. S end of strip is sometimes subject to ridgeing and standing water which will be clearly seen by carrying out an inspection overflight. To calculate Tide times subtract 35 mins from the times published for Stornoway or 30 mins from those for Ullapool. A public telephone is situated on the main road 0.5 miles from the end of the landing area. **Note:** A general rule for beach operations. Carry out engine run-up on a suitable area of firm sand around the high-water mark. If ACFT stops on the beach before commencing take-off run for run-up there is a danger of the wheels settling into the sand. This particularly applies to nosewheel ACFT. Information can be obtained from Mr J.A.Macleod(who is a local PPL based in Stornoway). 17 Balallen, Isle of Lewis, H52 9PN. Tel: 01851 830366. Tel: 07778 673513 (Mobile).

SPANHOE

N5233.95 W00036.34. 6nm SW of RAF Wittering. 340ft amsl.
09/27 Concrete/Grass 640x13m. (Grass portion is at stop end of 09). PPR by telephone essential. Normal Operating Hrs 0800-1900, (local time), Monday to Saturday,Closed Sunday. AD situated under the Cottesmore/Wittering CMATZ stub, establish contact with Cottesmore 130.20 before entering the CMATZ. Avoid overflying local villages. Circuits variable at 800ft QFE.Hangarage and maintenance available. Landing fee: on application. Windmill Aviation, Spanhoe Airfield, Laxton, Nr. Corby, Nants.Tel/Fax: 01780 450205 Tel: 01780 450485

Private Airfields

Effective date: 30/11/99 © Copyright 1999 Camber Publishing Ltd. All rights reserved

STALBRIDGE
N5057.26 W00222.22 1.5NM SSW of Henstridge AD. 250ft amsl.
18/36 Grass 600x20m. PPR is essential as strip obstructed by wire cattle fencing which must be removed before use. Rwy slopes down towards the centre from both directions and may become boggy and unuseable after heavy precipitation. AD is close to the Yeovilton MATZ. Military fixed wing and helicopter traffic may be encountered operating at low level. LARS service available from Yeovilton APP 127.35. Noise: Please avoid overflight of local habitation and particularly Stalbridge which is close to the N. Circuits: To the E at 1000ft agl. Landing Fee:Nil. Fuel: Nil. Operating Hrs:SR-SS daily. Barry Mogg, Bibbern Farm, Stalbridge, Dorset, DT10 2SW. Tel: 01963 362277 Fax: 01963 362526.

STONES FARM
N5158.49 E00041.58 3.5nm SSW of Sudbury 207ft amsl.
09/27 Grass 700x20m. Pylons and cables 200m to N of strip. Road close to 09 Thr, caution vehicles. Crops are grown close to the strip edges on both sides. Windsock displayed to the S of the 27 Thr. Circuits at 1000ft QFE either direction but please be considerate of local residents, particularly avoid the white house S of the Thr of Rwy09 at all costs. Transport can be arranged. This strip is close to the Stansted CTA, Wattisham MATZ, and Earls Colne ATZ be aware of airspace restrictions. Martin Gosling, Stones Farm, Wickham St. Paul, Halstead, Essex. CO9 2PS.
Tel: 01787 269369.(Fax: 01787 269029).

STOODLEIGH BARTON
N5057.50 W00332.00 4NM NW of Tiverton 830ft amsl
09/27 Grass 800x75m. Rwy27 has upslope and also a lateral slope down to the S. There is a building on short final to 09 and also powerlines approx 30ft agl running along the E side of the road to Stoodleigh village. Noise: Avoid Stoodleigh village. Circuits: To the S at 1000ft QFE. Operating Hrs:SR-SS daily. Fuel:MOGAS available by prior arrangement. Landing Fee: A donation to the RNLI would be most welcome. Restaurants: Royal Oak, Oakford (1.5m). Tel: 01398 351219. Operator:Mr.W.Knowles, Little Gratton, Stoodleigh, Tiverton, Devon. Tel: 01398 351568 or 07850 384000 (Mobile).

STRATHAVEN
N5540.80 W00406.25. 1.3nm W of Strathaven. 847ft amsl.
08/26 Grass 730x90m. (Marked by white flush slabs). Parts of the grass strips are very bumpy. Light ACFT accepted PPR at pilot's own risk. Glider flying at weekends and Wednesday evenings during summer. Beware! Cables, also intensive Microlight activity. "Strathaven" in white letters is displayed on red hangar roof. Caution: livestock grazing when no gliding in progress. HT wires and trees 35ft high approximately 90m obliquely from E boundary fence.There are trees on RH side - do not touchdown before the end of the trees. Windsock displayed. Strathaven Radio 130.10.(Glider ops).Microlights use 129.825. Landing fee:Nil. Strathclyde Gliding Club. Tel: 01357 520235 (AD)

STRETTON
N5320.70 W00231.50. 3nm SE of Warrington. 270ft amsl.
09/27 parallel Concrete/Grass 400x20m. Rwy is N of disused 09/27 Rwy on Stretton disused AD. Caution 6ft high hedge and public road close to 27 Thr. APP from the S directly to base leg. When landing 09 make offset APP to avoid M56. This will also provide clearance from a cellular telephone mast 130ft agl, 700m out and to the N of 09 APP. Do not overfly house to E of AD. Located within the Manchester Low Level Route - intensive light ACFT traffic up to 1250ft amsl, also VRP for Liverpool/Manchester VFR traffic. PFA or Vintage type ACFT only accepted. J Sykes, Invergordon Nurseries, Swineyard Lane, High Leigh, Knutsford, Cheshire.
Tel: 01925 754027

SUDBURY see WAITS FARM

SUTTON BANK (Thirsk)
N5413.62 W00112.72. 5nm E of Thirsk, 18nm N of York. 920ft amsl.
E/W Grass 549m, NE/SW Grass 732m. PPR. Surface may be soft in places. There are trees to the N & E. Do not APP over steep S and W cliffs with insufficient speed to overcome local downdraughts. Windsock displayed. Radio:Sutton Bank, (glider common frequency) 130.40. Landing fee: nil. Cafe available in clubhouse. Yorkshire Gliding Club (PTY) Ltd, Sutton Bank, Thirsk, North Yorkshire, YO7 2EY. Tel: 01845 597237

SWINDON see DRAYCOTT

TARN FARM
N5356.30 W00250.50 7nm SSW of Lancaster 30ft amsl
18/36 Grass 400x10m. 09/27 Grass 300x10m. Microlight training AD but suitable STOL ACFT accepted with PPR. Sheep graze the AD when Microlights are not active. AD is used by The Ribble Valley Microlight Club & West Coast Microlight school, be considerate of ab-initio pilots in the circuit. Parachuting takes place at Cockerham, 1.5nm NE mainly at weekends. Circuits are variable and will be advised with PPR. Noise: Avoid local habitation, particularly to the W of the AD. Operating Hrs: Mon-Sat:0800-2100 or SS. Sun/PH:1000-2100 or SS. All times local. Landing Fee:£3. Fuel:MOGAS avaiable on request. Maintenance: Keith Worthington, Tel: 01257 453430. Restaurants: The Manor, Cockerham. Barry Kirkland, Apartment H, 23 Oakwood Close, Blackpool, FY4 5FD. Tel: 01253 790538 (AD). 01253 692129 (Home). 07831 841271 (Mobile)

THIRSK see SUTTON BANK

THORPE-LE-SOKEN
N5152.00 E00109.00 1.5nm N of CLN VOR/DME 130ft amsl
18/36 Grass 430x15m Visiting ACFT welcome with PPR at pilots own risk. No circuits please. Flat strip with trees adjacent to hangar which is close to the Rwy on the E side. No wind sock. The 36 APP crosses the B1033 on very short final, keep a good lookout for vehicles and pedestrians. 18 APP has a 4ft hedge at the Thr. Circuits to the W and please avoid overflying local villages. Particularly Thorpe-le-Soken, (1nm to SE of the AD). Fuel:Nil, Landing Fee:Nil. Operated by Mr.C.Neilson, Comarques Farmhouse, Colchester Road, Thorpe-le-Soken. CO16 0LA. Tel: 01255 861687

Effective date: 30/11/99

TIBENHAM

N5227.40 E00109.25. 12nm SW of Norwich. 186ft amsl. 08/26 Tarmac 700x46m, 03/21 Tarmac 914x46m, 15/33 Tarmac 914x46m. Gliding Site, light ACFT accepted on PPR. AD operates 7 days a week in summer; Wednesday, Thursday and weekends in winter. Exercise caution due to rope dragging circuits by tug ACFT, winch launching and aerotows. Tibenham radio 129.975 (powered ACFT), 130.10 (gliders). Fuel: Avgas 100LL. Club facilities available.Landing fee:Nil but visitors are requested to take out day membership (£7). Norfolk Gliding Club. Tel: 01379 677207

TOWER FARM

N5215.44 W00039.55 2NM SSE of Wellingborough 370ft amsl
10/28 Grass 640x24m. Rwy28 has upslope which increases in severity at midpoint then becomes less severe from midpoint on. This aids landing but could constitute a significant hazard on departure. Aid to location: White concrete water twr at W end of strip. Owner recommends that visitors call or listen out with Sywell 122.70 for local traffic information. The strip is situated 2nm NW of Podington disused, (Santa Pod Raceway) where large numbers of spectators congregate for drag racing events spring to autumn mainly PH weekends. Noise: Avoid Woolaston, (close to the W). Circuits: To the N. Operating Hrs: SR-SS daily. Fuel:Nil. Landing Fees:Nil. Operator. Mr.Peter Sumner, Tower Farm, Woolaston, Wellingborough, Nants, NN29 7PJ. Tel: 01933 664225

TRULEIGH FARM

N5053.85 W00015.30 3NM SSE of Henfield VRP (Shoreham). 132ft amsl
10/28 Grass 500x15m. Sheep may be grazing so PPR essential. Strip slopes upward from the E until midpoint. The Rwy is situated between two groups of trees which may cause rotor/windshear. AD can be very wet after prolonged precipitation. Power lines to the E of the strip crossing the 28 APP 900m from Rwy Thr. Radio masts on hill 1nm S of the strip. There are numerous Hang gliding and Paracending sites in the area around the AD and Shoreham ATZ is close to the S. Arr/Dept ACFT are advised to contact Shoreham APP 123.15. Useful weather information can be obtained from Shoreham ATIS 132.40. Windsock displayed to S of Rwy. Noise: Avoid all local habitation but especially the houses 0.5nm to the NE. Circuits: LH at 1000ft QFE. Landing Fee:Nil. Fuel:Nil. Operating Hrs:SR-SS daily. Robin Windus, Truleigh Manor, Edburton, Henfield, Sussex. BN5 9LL. Tel: 01903 813186

UPFIELD FARM

N5133.50 W00253.00 4NM SE of Newport Gwent. 10ft amsl.
04/22 Grass 650x9m. AD strictly PPR as sheep may be grazing. AD may be boggy after prolonged precipitation. The Rwy is very bumpy and is indicated by paving slabs 50ft apart on N side. All ACFT movements should be confined to the Rwy only. Other areas are very soft all year round. There are small trees on the 22 APP on short final. Noise:Please operate considerately and avoid local houses. Circuits: LH. Fuel:MOGAS available on request. Landing Fee: Nil. Operating Hrs: SR-SS daily. K.M.Bowen, Upfield Farm, Whiston, Newport, Gwent, NP18 2PG. Tel: 01633 279222. Fax: 01633 279922

VALLANCE BY-WAYS GATWICK

N5109.17 W00011.40 Adjacent to NW corner of Gatwick airport 202ft amsl.
08/26 Grass 553x9m. Due to the close proximity of Gatwick airport only ACFT with transponder and able to communicate with Gatwick can be accepted Permission from Gatwick must be obtained. There are 60ft trees on the 26 APP and deer may encroach on the strip. Windsock displayed. All circuits must be to the N away from Gatwick but avoiding Charlwood which is to the NW of the strip. There is an ACFT museum on the strip. **Open day 24th-25th June 99 PPR strictly required please**. P.G.Vallance Ltd, Lowfield, Heath Road, Charlwood, Surrey. RH6 0BT Tel/Fax: 01293 862915.or mobile:07836 666817 Email:pgvallance@aol.com Website. http://home.aol.com/pgvallance

WADSWICK STRIP

N5124 W00212. 2nm SE of Colerne AD. 400ft amsl.
28/10 Grass 800x25m. Strip is slightly convex in configuration. Caution! B3109 crosses the undershoot of 10. An access road crosses the strip at the midpoint. Traffic is controlled by traffic lights which are activated by freq 123.1. Ensure you use this facility before landing and takeoff. Although wires at either end of the strip are buried the poles are still in position close to both Thrs on the S side of the Rwy.Windsock displayed. Circuits to S. Avoid overflying the village to the N of the strip on initial APP. Please particularly avoid Hazelbury Manor which is close to the W of strip. Roger Barton, Manor Farm, Wadswick, Corsham, Wiltshire. SN14 9JB. Tel: 01225 811557/810700 Fax: 01225 810307

WAITS FARM (Sudbury)

N5202.05 E00038.07. 4nm W of Sudbury. 200ft amsl.
07/25 Grass 520x20m. Rwy 07 has 1° uphill slope. Footpath crosses Rwy. Windsock displayed. Circuits LH 800ft aal. Avoid overflying local built up areas and traffic and horses on road adjacent to 07 APP. Caution: Ridgewell gliding site (with winch launching) 3nm W. Richard Teverson, Waits Farm, Belchamp Walter, Sudbury, Suffolk CO10 7AR.Tel: 01787 373975

WESTON-ON-THE-GREEN (Oxford)

N5152.80 W00113.10. 7nm N of Oxford, 4nm NE of Oxford AD. 282ft amsl.
01/19 Grass 690m, 06/24 Grass 830m, 10/28 Grass 910m. D129, radius 2nm centred on the AD is RAF parachute drop zone up to FL120, including free-fall parachuting. Caution military ACFT may fly preset range patterns. DAAIS is available through Brize RAD 134.30. The area should be avoided at all times unless PPR to use the AD has been obtained. A/G RAF Weston-on-the-Green 133.65. No landing fee. Owned by MOD and leased by Oxford Gliding Club and RAFSPA (Sport Parachute Association). Cafe at weekends Tel: 01869 343246 (AD), 01869 343265 (gliding Club) or 773210 (launch point), 01993 842551 Ext. 7555/7551 (Brize Norton).

Effective date: 30/11/99

WESTON ZOYLAND

N5106.27 W00254.28. 4nm ESE of Bridgwater. 33ft amsl.
16/34 Asphalt 550x25m numbered, also parallel grass strip 650x15m. Contact Yeovilton RAD on 127.35. Microlight activity. Avoid over-flying Weston Zoyland village. Circle the AD to advise arrival and turn on landing lights on APP and take-off. Weston Zoyland Radio 129.825. Landing fee: £5.00. Mr W Knowles, Little Gratton, Stoodleigh, Tiverton, Devon EX16 9PQ. Tel: 01398 351568 or 07850 384000

WHALEY FARM

N5304.03 W00009.16.1.5NM S of RAF Coningsby 9ft amsl.
09/27 Grass 575x15m. Visiting ACFT welcome with PPR and at pilots own risk. Visitors must have third party insurance cover. There are domestic powerlines 200m from the 27 Thr and 400m from the 09 Thr. Drainage ditch in the undershoot of Rwy09. In extreme wind conditions a wide Twy orientated 18/36 may be available for ACFT operations, please consult owner before any planned use. The AD is situated within the Coningsby ATZ which is active 24hrs. Arriving/Departing ACFT MUST contact Coningsby APP 120.80. If no contact try Coningsby TWR 119.975. There are many based high performance jet ACFT whose circuits will take them overhead this strip. Noise: Please avoid houses to the W. Circuits: Make early turn to the S and leave the Coningsby ATZ NOT ABOVE 500ft QFE. Arriving ACFT should position directly onto final for the appropriate Rwy. Hangarage available. Fuel: Nil. Landing Fee: Donations to upkeep welcomed. Tea & Coffee available for visiting pilots. Mr.W.Shaw, Whaley Farm, New York, Lincolnshire.
Tel: 01205 280329 or 07860 386340 (Mobile)

WHITBY (Egton)

N5427 W00045. 4nm W of Whitby, 3nm NE of Grosmont. 650ft amsl.
E/W Grass 450x100m. Level, but surface may be bumpy and strip is surrounded by trees. During summer sheep graze on Rwy. Situated beside the main Whitby to Guisborough road. Windsock Southside at midpoint. PA Jackson, Finkle House, Great Fryup, Whitby, North Yorkshire. Tel: 01947 897367 (home)

WIGTOWN

N5450.93 W00426.95 1nm S of Wigtown. 20ft amsl.
06/24* Concrete 446x18m. (*30m starter extensions available at both ends of the Rwy). Rwy surface rough.Operating Hrs: PPR by arrangement. Circuits: Rwy06 & 24 LH 800ft. Baldoon Hill - 129ft amsl /109ft aal - is located 300m NW of Rwy06 Thr, care should be taken when aproaching/departing from this direction. Landing Fee: Nil. Mr.A.H.Sprout. Tel 01988 402215

WINFIELD (Berwick on Tweed)

N5544.95 W00209.73. 6nm W of Berwick. 170ft amsl.
13/31 Tarmac 900x46m; 06/24 Tarmac 900x46m. PPR essential, if you obtain PPR then decide not to visit please advise so operator does not need to turn out. A public road runs through the middle of the AD. Windsock displayed. All Rwy thresholds are displaced. Wire fence crosses Thr 24. Landing fee: A charge of £5 is made, the money being used to keep the weeds down on the Rwys. M. Fleming & Sons, Winfield, Berwick-on-Tweed. Tel: 01890 870225 or 870247

WING FARM (Warminster)

N5110 W00212. 1nm S of Shear Water Lake, 2nm SSW of Warminster. 420ft amsl.
09/27 Grass 500x26m. (max take-off run limited to 350m). PPR at pilot's own risk. Visitors and their ACFT must be capable of STOL operations. Thrs are marked with white T markers. All visiting ACFT must carry third party insurance cover. Beware electric power cables 500m from 09 Thr. Uphill slope, (2.2%), on 27. Surface may be soft January to April. All movements are confined to the strip and parking area. Circuits at 500ft aal, avoid low flying over houses in the vicinity. There is a wind indicator T at the W end. Landing fee £4 for private ACFT. £2 for Microlights. Please have correct money as no change is available. Operator: E W B Trollope, Wing Farm, Longbridge Deverill, Warminster, Wilts. BA12 7DD.Tel/Fax: 01985 840401. Maintenance by Airbourne Composites,specialist in Glider and motorglider repairs). Tel: 01985 840981

WOONTON

N5210.33 W0257.58 5nm SSW of Shobdon AD 400ft amsl
16/34 Grass 500x15m. Rwy 34 has a marked upslope. Land 34, depart 16 only. Surface can be soft after prolonged precipitation. Sheep graze the strip so PPR essential. A public footpath crosses the Rwy at 34 touchdown point. Windsock displayed. Caution, low flying military ACFT transit the area during weekdays. Noise: Please avoid local habitation and particularly the village of Woonton which is close to the N of the strip. Fuel: Available by arrangement. Landing Fee: Nil. Operating Hrs: PPR SR-SS daily. The operator can sometimes provide transport if arranged in advance. Operator: Mike Hayes, Chapel Stile Cottage, Woonton Nr Aimeley, Herefordshire. HR3 6QN.
Tel: 01432 277277 Ext 3130, (during office hrs). 01544 340635 (Evenings). Fax: 01432 355988

WROUGHTON (EGDT).

N5130.52 W00147.90 3nm SW of Swindon. 678ft amsl.
04/22 Asphalt 1523x50m. 09/27 Asphalt 1189x50m. Lighting Nil. U/L AD which is open only on declared days to visitors who have obtained PPR. (At time of going to press the AD was not planned to be available to visitors during 2000). Avoid overflying hospital to the E of the AD. Circuits LH not above 800ft QFE. Landing fee advised with PPR. On declared open days Wroughton Radio operates on 125.525. Operator: National Museum of Science and Industry, D4 Admin office, Science Museum, Wroughton Airfield, Swindon, Wilts. SN4 9NS. Tel: 01793 814466

Effective date: 30/11/99

RAF USAF & RN operated AD

BALLYKELLY (EGQB)

N5503.69 W00700.89. 2nm W of Limavady. 18ft amsl.
08/26 Tarmac 1676x46m; 02/20 Tarmac 1835x46m.
Active army AD. Beware of mast 305ft amsl between 20
and 26 Thrs. Note that City of Derry, Eglinton, (5nm W)
has same Rwy directions. ACFT carrying out instrument
APP to Rwy26 at Eglinton pass through the overhead at
1200ft. TACAN. BKL 109.1 on AD. Call Eglinton APP
123.625. Tel. 028 77763221

BARKSTON HEATH (EGYE)

N5257.74 W00033.70. 4.5nm SW of Cranwell. 367ft
amsl.
06/24 Tarmac 1831m (Rwy06 TORA 1831. LDA 1677
Rwy24 TORA 1831. LDA 1829); 11/29 1282m (Rwy11
TORA 1282. LDA 1280. Rwy29 TORA 1282. LDA 1125).
Active RAF AD, controlled by Cranwell. ATZ active 0730-
1730 (local) Mon-Fri, but light ACFT activity outside these
hrs, including aerobatic practice overhead AD. Rwy06/24
operate Right hand circuit. CMATZ 119.375 Cranwell
APP. Barkston TWR 120.425. Tel: 01400 261201 ext.
5200. DATIS available on Ext 5023

COTTESMORE (EGXJ)

N5244.14 W00038.93. 8.5nm E of Melton Mowbray.
461ft amsl.
05/23 Concrete 2744x46m. Arrester gear 390m from
both Thrs. Cables are normally in down position. Active
RAF AD, Operating Hrs 0800-1700 Mon-Fri; ATZ active
H24. CMATZ with Wittering, Cottesmore is controlling
authority,(APP 130.20). Avoid overflying villages in the
vicinity of the AD. Local bird hazard. Rwy23 Right hand
circuit. No visiting ACFT before 0830 local. JET A1
limited quantities available strictly by arrangement. TWR
122.1. TACAN (on AD) CTM 112.3. ILS.23.CM.110.3
Tel: 01572 812241 ext. 7270 PPR (Must be obtained
24hrs in advance).

FAIRFORD (EGVA)

N5141.01 W00147.41. 7nm N of Swindon. 286ft amsl.
09/27 Asphalt 3047m. Military AD activated by NOTAM.
MATZ actvated by NOTAM. Rwy27 is preferred Rwy,
pilots may be required to accept a tailwind. TWR approval
is needed for start up clearance. Initial inbound call to
Brize RAD on 134.30, APP Brize 119.00. Fairford Twr
119.15. TACAN (on AD) FFA 113.40. ILS/DME.27.IFFA
111.1, 09.IFFD.111.1. There are mandatory noise
abatement procedures. Avoid overflying local villages and
built-up areas in the circuit.VFR traffic pattern involves an
overhead join at 2000ft QNH then circuit at 700ft QFE.
This may be varied by ATC. JET A1 available strictly by
arrangement only. Tel: 01285 714805. Advice on
activation thru Mildenhall. Tel: 01638 542125/2627. Fax:
01638 543389 (For PPR through local Duty Officer.
Please state who, where from and why).

LAKENHEATH (EGUL)

N5224.56 E00033.66. 10.5nm E of Ely. 32ft amsl.
06/24 Asphalt 2743x45m. Active USAF AD. ATZ H24
Ops Hrs 0600-2200 Mon-Thu.0600-2000 Fri 0800-2000
Sat-Sun/UK &US PH. (All times local). CMATZ 128.90,
APP (Dep control) 123.3/ 137.20. TWR 122.10. TACAN
(on AD) LKH 110.20 ILS 24 I-LKH 109.9 06 I-LAK 109.9.
JET A1 available strictly by prior arrangement.
Tel: 01638 524186/522439.(Base Ops)PPR 24hrs notice
required

MERRYFIELD

N5057.75 W00256.14. 8nm SE of Taunton. 146ft amsl.
09/27 Asphalt 1831x45m; 03/21 Asphalt 1294x45m;
16/34 Asphalt 1129x45m. ATZ 0700-1700 Mon-Fri,
(Local time). Royal Navy AD, satellite for Yeovilton.
MATZ Yeovilton 127.35; TWR 122.10. Intense helicopter
activity, glider flying outside AD Operating Hrs.
Tel: 01460 52018 (for PPR Yeovilton)
Tel: 01935 840551 Ext 5497/5498

MILDENHALL (EGUN)

N5221.65 E00029.30. 12nm NW of Bury St Edmunds.
33ft amsl.
11/29 Asphalt 2812x45m. Active USAF AD. ATZ H24.
CMATZ Lakenheath 128.90, TWR 122.55. GND:142.275.
DEP RAD:137.20. TACAN (on AD) MLD 115.90 ILS 29 I-
MLD 108.1 11 I-MIL 108.1. JET A1 available strictly by
prior arrangement. All movements under IFR. Departing
ACFT must call TWR for engine start.
Tel: 01638 542251/542253 (PPR 24hrs prior notice
required)

PREDANNACK

N5000.07 W00513.85. 7nm S of Helston. 295ft amsl.
05/23 Asphalt 1814x46m; 01/19 Asphalt 1396x46m;
10/28 Asphalt 1305x46m. 13/31 Asphalt 914x46m. Active
Royal Navy AD, Operating Hrs Mon-Fri as required.
Rwys, other than 05/23 may have loose stones. Satellite
for Culdrose, ATZ active H24. Caution! Rwys have non-
standard markings. Intense helicopter activity, with model
ACFT and gliding outside ops hrs. APP 134.05
(Culdrose) TWR 122.10 (Predannack). When gliding in
progress call 'Predannack Alpha Charlie Base' on
129.975. Tel: 01326 574121 ext.2417 (PPR)

TERNHILL (EGOE)

N5252.27 W00233.01. 2.5nm SW of Market Drayton.
272ft amsl.
05/23 Asphalt 980x45m;(Rwy 05 TORA/LDA 980m.
Rwy23 TORA 980m LDA 791m). 10/28 Asphalt
948x45m.(Rwy 10 TORA/LDA 948m. Rwy 28 TORA 948m
LDA 756m). Active RAF AD - intensive helicopter activity
and motorgliders outside hrs. Variable circuits in operation.
Rwys and Thrs have non standard markings. ATZ active
H24. ACFT are not to cross the road adjacent to Thrs of
Rwys23 & 28 below 50ft. Fixed wing visitors not normally
accepted. APP (Shawbury)120.775. TWR 122.1.
Tel: 01939 250351 ext. 7227 (PPR)

UPAVON

N5117.17 W00146.92. 5nm NW of Tidworth. 575ft amsl.
05/23 Grass 1066m; 08/26 Grass 975m. Active Army AD,
helicopter and fixed wing activity H24, glider flying during
daylight hrs. Situated within Danger Areas D126/D128.
Inbound ACFT to call Salisbury Ops 122.75. All APP to
be made from the N in sector 290-040 degrees (T).
Advisory information may be provided by non-ATC
qualified personnel. No VHF TWR frequency. Landing &
take-off at pilots discretion. There is a mast, (Unlit), 52ft
agl 65ft W of the twr. The southern Twy is closed for
ACFT use. Tel: 01980 615238/615066. Additional AD
information available before departure from Salisbury
Operations Tel: 01980 674710/674730